HERE IS THE NEWS

A CHRONICLE OF THE
20th CENTURY
Volume I: 1901-1950

The Manx Experience

HERE IS THE NEWS

A CHRONICLE OF THE 20th CENTURY

Volume I: 1901-1950

As reported by
TERRY CRINGLE

with additional features by

ROBERT KELLY   **ROBERT E. FORSTER**, *B.A.*
GORDON N. KNIVETON   **FRANK COWIN**, *F.R.I.C.S.*

Edited and designed by
GORDON N. KNIVETON

MERCURY
ASSET MANAGEMENT

The Manx Experience
45 Slieau Dhoo : Tromode Park
Douglas : Isle of Man : IM2 5LG : British Isles

ISBN 1 873120 42 7

**Based upon concept broadcasts by
Manx Radio**

The Publishers are indebted to

for their financial assistance in the
publication of this book

Typeset and originated by The Manx Experience
Printed by
Alden Press

INTRODUCTION

by

**The Hon. Sir Charles Kerruish,
O.B.E., LL.D.(hc), C.P.,
President of Tynwald.**

Charting the historic progress of the Isle of Man towards its current standing in the modern world is an enduring process and one which is to be encouraged whenever possible.

We Manx are a proud race. Equally as proud of our heritage as we are of our present Island nation. That pride is evident in this book.

Some years ago, I was delighted to see the first volume in this series - "Here is the News" - published by The Manx Experience. It covered the period of Manx history up to the end of the 19th Century.

This volume carries on that theme detailing the progress of the Island through the first half of the 20th Century.

The novel method of presentation of the items of news and feature articles as if they were presented on Manx Radio adds greatly to the overall interest of the content.

There will be much interest in this volume and, undoubtedly its companion volume to be published next year, as many of the events recorded here will be well-known to a multitude of readers.

The loss of the *Ellan Vannin,* the opening of Noble's Hospital, internment at Knockaloe, the great fire at Laxey Glen Mills, the closure of Laxey Mines, the tourist boom, the 1930 floods, Royal visits . . . all are recorded here in great detail.

In the arts, the influence of John Millar Nicholson, Hall Caine, and Archibald Knox amongst others, are seen through examples of their work.

The literary and political efforts of Samuel Norris, including his period in gaol, and the editorial influence of George Brown are covered in detail.

The political sector is given particular attention and the parts played by Samuel Harris, A. W. Moore, the MacDonnell Commission, the Manx Labour Party, the Manx Reform Association are all included. The extended fight for constitutional reform and the parts played by the various Governors of the Island make especially interesting reading.

The many triumphs and tragedies involving Manx families have not been omitted and the involvement of the Island, the impact of the conflict and the substantial contribution of Manx service personnel in the 1914-18 War is recorded.

More recently, those of us who recall the events which led up to, and those during, the Second World War will read with interest the graphic accounts of the involvement of our servicemen and women during that period.

All in all, this book provides a record of 20th Century Isle of Man which thoroughly deserves a place on the bookshelves of Manx people everywhere.

The editorial group responsible for the compilation of the contents are to be congratulated on their efforts. Similarly, the publishers, The Manx Experience, along with their sponsors Mercury Asset Management, should rest in the knowledge that they have published a book worthy of record.

Read on, dear reader, and enjoy . . . and when you have finished look forward to Volume II next year.

Tynwald Day 1921. At St John's, the Lieutenant-Governor Sir William Fry follows the sword bearer at the head of the procession to Tynwald Hill for the promulgation of the Acts.

TRAMWAYS COMPANY ASSETS FOR SALE

The echoes of last year's collapse of Dumbell's Bank and the imprisonment of five of its principals on fraud charges, continue to be heard on the Island. High Court lists are long with debt suits and bankruptcies arising from the effect of the collapse on the finances of Manx companies and others such as tradesmen, farmers and boarding-house keepers. We have this report:

It will be recalled that the statements issued by the bank, the largest on the Island, hid the extent to which bank chairman, the late Mr Alexander Bruce, and his cohort, Mr John Shimmon, had permitted the finances of the bank to be stretched to breaking point. They, and bank directors, became involved in many enterprises connected with the burgeoning visiting industry. Mr Bruce was also chairman of the Isle of Man Tramways and Electric Power Company which alone was indebted to the bank to the extent of £150,000. Then the bank was heavily involved in the Brewery Syndicate which aimed to dominate the local licensing trade through ownership of breweries and hotels. On a smaller scale tradesmen were encouraged to borrow heavily to play their part in the tourist industry. It was revealed that the bank was over £500,000 in debt, while directors were paying themselves dividends of 15%.

The liquidation of the Tramways and Electric Power Company is now in the hands of Douglas accountant W. H. Walker, who is also liquidator of the Dumbell Banking Company. The tramway company's assets, which include the profitable Douglas Bay horse trams and the Upper Douglas cable cars, are to be put up for sale by tender beginning in July. Early indications are that Douglas Corporation is prepared to make an offer for the horse tramway and the cable cars. Meanwhile, Ramsey advocate Charles Nelson, one of the bank directors, who has been given five years penal servitude, has been debarred by the Isle of Man Law

One of the Upper Douglas cable cars operated by the Isle of Man Tramways and Electric Power Company passes the portals of the ill-fated Dumbell's Bank. Both the tramways and banking companies are now in liquidation. (Keig Collection)

Society. Also, Mr Walker has successfully obtained judgement for £21,000 in the Chancery Court against the bank's former assistant manager, John Shimmon, who is also serving five years. The money, belonging to a trust fund in the

1901 CENSUS

The Census revealed that the Island's population has decreased by 905 since 1891 to 54,613. Of these, 25,343 are females and 29,270 are males. A breakdown of the statistics into towns and villages is shown below (A comparison with the 1891 figures is shown in italics) :

TOWNS:			
Douglas	-	19,149	*-376*
Ramsey	-	4,672	*-194*
Peel	-	3,306	*-325*
Castletown	-	1,963	*-215*
PARISHES:			
Onchan	-	3,942	*+2,052*
Lonan	-	2,513	*-457*
Braddan	-	2,177	*+136*
Marown	-	973	*+12*
Maughold	-	887	*-95*
Lezayre	-	1,389	*-23*
Andreas	-	1,144	*-95*
Bride	-	539	*-101*
Jurby	-	504	*-39*
German	-	1,230	*-177*
Patrick	-	1,925	*-303*
Michael	-	928	*-77*
Ballaugh	-	712	*-118*
Malew	-	2,113	*-162*
Santon	-	468	*-42*
Arbory	-	802	*-198*
Rushen	-	3,277	*-138*

bank, was lost through the highly speculative Brewery Syndicate.

OVER 4,000 MANX GAELIC SPEAKERS

The 1901 population census published in May shows that the number of people in Manx residence has fallen slightly. The total number recorded was 54,613, a decrease of just under a thousand on the 1891 census. A separate census of the number of Manx Gaelic speakers on the Island has been carried out by Mr A.W. Moore, Speaker of the House of Keys, and Manx historian. It shows that 4,419 people, 8.1% of the population, claim knowledge of their native tongue. They are mostly from country areas, with Bride parish top of the league with 23% (123) of its people conversant with Manx; Douglas (708) and Onchan parish (114) are lowest with 3.7% and 2.9% respectively.

PRESS DEMANDS

Reporting of the proceedings of Tynwald Court resumed in July, following a six-month-long confrontation between the Island's newspapers and the Lieutenant-Governor, Lord Henniker, over accommodation in the Press Gallery. Publishers decided to withdraw their reporters because of cramped and insanitary accommodation. The reporters also complained that their seats were not in a good position in which to hear speakers properly. Now the Lieutenant-Governor has backed down over his refusal to provide improved facilities.

HALL CAINE ELECTED TO KEYS

The distinguished Manx novelist Mr. Hall Caine of Greeba Castle, has won his way into the House of Keys. He was successful in the October bye-election in Ramsey where he defeated Mr. Philip Kermode in a straight fight. He had 458 votes compared with 191 for Mr. Kermode. It has been an eventful year for Mr. Caine with the publication of his new novel "The Eternal City" which has been given a mixed reception by the critics of both Britain and Europe. This year has also seen another local publishing event - the appearance of the book "Manx Worthies" by A. W. Moore, S.H.K.

STORM HAVOC

Following the flood damage of October, which halted train services and swept bridges away, the winter of 1901 has started with the most severe weather in living memory. Winds reached hurricane force and actually blew down a house in Alexander Drive, Douglas. There was also extensive flooding throughout the length of Douglas seafront and into Strand Street and Victoria Street as huge waves were driven by inshore gales. In spite of the conditions, the Steam Packet Company kept services running - and the *S.S. Fenella*, under Captain Roberts, res-

Foxdale. I. O. M.

The fine public clock erected at Foxdale by the Isle of Man Mining Company as a Queen Victoria Memorial. To the right is the Miners' Institute. (R. and L. Kelly Collection)

cued the crew of three of a Cumberland fishing boat being pounded by heavy seas just outside Douglas. It was a feat of remarkable seamanship - after which *Fenella* continued her passage to Liverpool. The *Fenella*, this time under Captain Hodgson, was involved in an earlier incident in which she went aground at Dromore near the Mull of Galloway, in dense fog while on passage from Douglas to Glasgow with 300 passengers, many of them returning holidaymakers. She was floated free at high tide and had to go into dock for repairs. The passengers continued their journey in the steamer *Snaefell II*. The Packet has had an eventful year. In the Mersey there were two incidents. First, the *Ben my Chree II* collided with and

sank a small coaster in August and then the *Tynwald III* collided with and sank a tugboat. In both cases there was no loss of life.

POSSIBLE ROYAL VISIT

Finally, King Edward VII has been proclaimed King of Great Britain and Ireland and Emperor of India from Tynwald Hill, following the much lamented death of Queen Victoria at the beginning of the year. It is hoped that King Edward and Queen Alexandra will take an early opportunity to visit their loyal subjects in the Isle of Man. A spokesman at Government House says it could happen at any time, even next year. It all depends on where His Majesty chooses to turn up in his realm without prior notice.

1901 NEWS IN BRIEF

JANUARY
13 - Civic recognition of New Century at Douglas. Religious service in the Palace.
29 - Death of Queen Victoria
30 - Tynwald Hill ceremony of proclaiming Edward VII King of Great Britain and Ireland, and Emperor of India.

FEBRUARY
2 - National Day of Mourning for funeral of Queen Victoria. Memorial Service at St. George's. Shops and hotels closed all day throughout the Island.

MARCH
31 - Roman Catholic consecration of portion of Borough Cemetery.

APRIL
1 - Population census taken.

MAY
5 - Formation of Manx District of Institute of Journalists.
15 - Inaugural ceremony for public clock erected at Foxdale as Queen Victoria Memorial.

JULY
3 - The Isle of Man Tramways offered for sale by tender.
10 - Consecration of Nave of St. Matthew's new Church.
12 - Tynwald approves scheme to build Fish Hatchery at Port Erin.

AUGUST
3 - Opening of Douglas Fish, Fruit and Vegetable Market by High Bailiff Harris.
20 - 'The Eternal City' by Hall Caine published.

SEPTEMBER
7 - Publication of 'Manx Worthies' by A.W. Moore, S.H.K.

OCTOBER
3 - Opening of new Wesleyan Sunday School at Barregarrow.
9 - Douglas Town Council overwhelmingly approves to make offer of £50,000 for the purchase of horse trams and cable cars.
25 - Hall Caine triumphant at election for Keys.
29 - Peel promenade in danger. Application for relief.

NOVEMBER
3 - Unveiling of Tablet in Lonan Church in memory of Colour-Sergeant Wallace who was killed in the Transvaal War.
12 - Worst Hollantide day weather on record. Terrific hurricane causes great damage.

DECEMBER
4 - Isle of Man Industrial and Fine Arts Exhibition opened by Samuel Webb, Mayor of Douglas.
4 - Publication of Manx Grammar by E. Goodwin, of Peel.

The loyal people of the Isle of Man have been honoured with a visit by our newly-crowned King Edward the Seventh and his consort, Queen Alexandra. And it came as just as much of a surprise as the visit Queen Victoria and Prince Albert paid in the royal yacht 55 years ago. We have this report:

The appearance of the self-same royal yacht, Victoria and Albert, as she steamed into Douglas Bay on 24th August caused a great sensation. And everyone knew the King was on board - the entire country knows he has been on a cruise to aid his recovery from the operation in June which forced postponement of the Coronation. A civic party led by the Mayor, Alderman Samuel Webb, hastened to Victoria Pier - only to see the royal yacht moving on, in a northerly direction. She anchored eventually in Ramsey Bay - as Queen Victoria had done. The Deputy Governor and Clerk of the Rolls Sir James Gell went on board as the new Lieutenant-Governor, Lord Raglan, had not yet taken up his duties. The following day thousands of cheering Manx people had the gratification of seeing the King and Queen come ashore.

First, the Royal Party travelled to Bishopscourt, where they met Bishop Straton, and then proceeded to the grounds of Peel Castle for an *al fresco* lunch. They next visited Cronkbourne House, the residence of Mrs W. F. Moore, mother of the Speaker of the House of Keys. In Douglas, huge crowds lined Prospect Hill and the promenades to catch a glimpse of Their Majesties as they made their way to the terminus of the coastal electric railway. Using the royal coach, they returned to Ramsey and rejoined the royal yacht.

END OF THE BOER WAR

The announcement on 1st June that the opposing sides in the Boer War had agreed peace terms was greeted with great rejoicing and thanksgiving in the Island. Thousands of people celebrated the peace in the streets of Douglas and rockets were fired from Victoria Pier. There were flags and

Crowds gather at Queen's Pier, Ramsey to greet the arrival of King Edward VII and Queen Alexandra. (A Midwood photograph)

bunting everywhere, the schools were closed for the day, and workmen were given a half-day off. The two Manx Volunteer battalions of the King's Liverpool Regiment who left the Island to serve in the war are expected to return home in the near future.

At the Battle of Colenso on 15th December, 1899, 15 year old Bugler John Dunne, from Port St Mary, was involved in a heroic deed when his regiment, the Royal Dublin Fusiliers, attacked Boer positions. Bugler Dunne was sounding the charge and continued to do so after being wounded by shrapnel in the arm.

Later he was received by the Queen who presented him with a medal and a new bugle. On returning to the Island he was given a hero's welcome and was entertained to tea by the Lieutenant-Governor, Lord Henniker.

It will be remembered that last year a tablet was unveiled in Lonan Parish Church in memory of Colour-Sergeant Wallace of the Seaforth Highlanders, who was killed at the Battle of Paaderberg in February, 1900. He was one of 2,200 British soldiers killed when the Boers were attacked across open country in what was the worst battle of the war.

King Edward VII joins his Queen in the royal carriage as they depart Cronkbourne House.

ANGRY SCENES AT THE STRANG

There were angry scenes among the crowds at the latest of this summer's horse racing meetings at The Strang, Braddan. A thousand people paid for admission - only to be told that there was no racing because only two horses had turned up. The races are promoted by Douglas merchant Mr. John Wilson and he was involved in uproar when the crowds did not get their money back. Mr. Wilson's son had taken it to Douglas with him - and was rumoured to have caught the afternoon steamer to Liverpool. Mr. Wilson senior had to be rescued from the crowds by police and taken into protective custody.

NEW LIEUTENANT-GOVERNOR

At a ceremony in Castle Rushen on

The Spencer Balloon prepares to make the first untethered flight in Manx skies.
(Manx National Heritage)

21st October, Lord Raglan was sworn in as the next Lieutenant-Governor of the Isle of Man. His appointment, following the death of his predecessor, Lord Henniker, at Government House on June 27th,

was announced just over a week before the royal visit. Before his Manx appointment Lord Raglan was Britain's Secretary of State for War. The 1st Lord Raglan, his grandfather, was the commander-in-chief of the British Army in the Crimean War.

ASCENT OF BALLOON

The miracle of manned flight has been seen in the Isle of Man for the first time. Large crowds gathered in Peveril Square, Douglas on a cold November morning to see two renowned English aeronauts, the Reverend J. M. Bacona and Mr. Percival Spencer, take off in their 60 foot high balloon. Its canopy was filled with 45,000 cubic feet of gas from the Douglas Gas Light Company's mains and the two men took off in great style to excited cheers. The prevailing winds carried

---

1902 NEWS IN BRIEF

JANUARY
1 - Douglas Corporation take over horse trams and cable cars.
15 - Local Government Board inquires into Laxey drainage and water supply.

FEBRUARY
1 - Sale of electric tramways announced. New company to take over at end of season.
12 - C.B. Nelson, one of Dumbell's Bank convicts, appeals for release and his five year sentence for fraud is quashed; the three year sentence for issuing a false balance sheet, however, remains in force.
25 - A.G.M. of Steam Packet Company sees attempt to provide Sunday sailings for summer passengers defeated. Director resigns.

MARCH
1 - Sad occurrence in Malew. A man dies from starvation.
4 - Keys pass the Commons Tree Planting Bill.
18 - Annual Licensing Court in Douglas sees large number of boarding house licences granted again.
26 - The High Court (Chancery Division) approves Mr W.H. Walker's fee of £8,000 for liquidation of Isle of Man Tramways and Electric Power Company.

APRIL
1 - Second contingent of Manx Volunteers leaves for South Africa.
3 - Opening of new Science buildings at King William's College.
9 - £250 granted for Coronation Celebrations by Douglas Town Council.
9 - Half-yearly meeting of Great Laxey Mining Co. The mines are flooded. Proposed amalgamation of North and Great Laxey Mines. More capital to be raised.

MAY
17 - Release of Mr J.D. Rodgers who was sentenced to 18 months hard labour for being concerned in the issue of false balance-sheets of Dumbell's Banking Company.

JUNE
1 - Official declaration of peace between Britons and Boers.
9 - Opening of Isle of Man Banking Company's magnificent new premises, corner of Prospect Hill and Athol Street.
24 - King's serious illness announced, Coronation postponed.
25 - Douglas celebrates what was to have been the Coronation.
27 - Death of His Excellency Lord Henniker, the Lieutenant-Governor.

JULY
9 - Manx Volunteers return from South Africa and receive enthusiastic reception.

AUGUST
9 - King remits sentence of five years passed on John Shimmon, one of Dumbell's Bank defaulters. Three years' sentence for issuing false balance sheets remains in force.
9 - Coronation of King Edward V11 and Queen Alexandra.
14 - Announcement of Lord Raglan to Governorship - Isle of Man.
21 - Mr Hall Caine opens Ramsey's new baths.
24/25 Visit of King and Queen.

SEPTEMBER
9 - Manx choir competes in Welsh Eisteddfod, and takes fourth position among the nine competing choirs.
13 - Fire at the Palace, Douglas.
20 - Sir James Gell and Mr A.W. Moore appointed to the Royal Victorian Order.
24 - Opening ceremony in connection with Thomas Street new Sunday School.
25 - Extraordinary Meeting of Great Laxey Mining Company. Severe criticism of management. Winding-up and reconstruction of the Company decided upon.

OCTOBER
13 - Election of 15 members of Douglas School Board.
21 - Lord Raglan inaugurated as new Lieutenant-Governor.
22 - Extraordinary Meeting of Great Laxey Mining Company. Vigorous reply of Capt. Radcliffe who resigns after 30 years' connection with the mine.
31 - Further outrages reported at Dalby.

NOVEMBER
1 - Manx Electric Railway Company takes over. To be run as a family business. Company registered with a capital of £250,000.
10 - Great excitement in Douglas as Spencer balloon is first to take to Manx skies.
20 - Lord Raglan seriously ill. Sir James Gell C.V.O. is Acting Governor.

DECEMBER
1 - Dividend of 2s. in the £ paid by Liquidator of Dumbell Banking Company. Total dividends to date 7s. 4d.

---

them 77 miles to Dumfrieshire in Scotland after a 4½ hour journey. Interesting signalling experiments were conducted between the balloon and *H.M.S. Renard* which escorted the balloonists.

DALBY OUTRAGE

The so-called outrage and reign of terror at Dalby has now been debated in the House of Keys. This follows failure of all attempts by the police to stop a campaign of persecution against farmer Mr. Charles Hutchin of Creg Lea, Dalby. Cattle and sheep have been killed in his fields and his farm implements damaged by persons unknown in a terror campaign lasting months. M.H.K.s say it is a reproach to the law-abiding reputation of the Manx people. A farmer neighbour of Mr. Hutchin's, Thomas Teare, of Ballacooil, Dalby, was arraigned before the Court of General Gaol in April charged with stealing one of his sheep. But he was acquitted for lack of evidence.

August 21st was another great day for Ramsey. Here crowds gather to watch the incoming tide fill the new open-air baths on North Shore. This was followed by Mr Hall Caine, Ramsey's M.H.K., officially declaring the baths to be open for public use.

(Manx National Heritage)

THE BALLAKILPHERIC TAY FIGHT

Dear Mr Editer,

I thought I would drop a few lines about our tay fight in our chapel the other day. I don't know thee personol, but I know thee good owl newspapare well. Well, man, I thought thou're seemin' interested in tay fights, and that thou'd lek to know a li'l abour our one at Ballakilpheric, down in the south here. Well, man, the night was fine and I sed to me owl woman thar I'd hev a sight on the tay fight for the sake of owl times. So I got me white shirt on and off I set; but, bhoy veen, when I got to the door I was shaken in my shoes to see the toffs that was theer and the fine gels - if I warn wishing I was young again. Well, man, the smell began to coax me inside, and I begun feeling me pockets for a shillen. Soon's I gor one and in I went and man alive, who do you think I met fus but Big Ned the Boar, and he looked mortal gannel. He was seemen proud cus he had a fine billet taken the money, si gev him me shillen and in for me tay I went. But, bless me, man, I diden know whuch table to go to, for theer was such nice gels smilen on me all roiun', lek if they all wanted me to come to their table. So I met Ned the Gaffer, and he ses to me, "Peradvice, what fine gals thar's at the top table, and they've come all the road from Bradder to wait on us, so we'd batther go the theer table and have a lark with them." So we sat down, but before long, I cud see me bowl Gaffer was in love wis one of the waitresses, for he was haven a mortal fine cooish wis her, and bhoy veen, she was a ginger too. I was thinken if I cud hav gor me own owl woman ourrer the way 'I'd like to hev tried it meself; bur me thar's pullen up to 75 years and non of the bes' looking chaps ether, heden much slent for that part of the business.

However, the time came for the consert and there was the lil schoolmasther in the pulpit, and I axed the joiner - for he was a sort of a boss, to know if it was prachin thar was goin' to be; but to my surprise it was addressen the Mayor of Ronnag he was, and some fella was talken Manx lek mad. Well, bless me, man, up gor a lil feller - they said he was the preacher from Portle-Murrer - and he towl us abour men makin' big forchons. It seemed terble sutable for a Sunday-school consert. I was thinken he was readen newspapers sometimes anyway. Three fellers then was singen so lowe as they call them now, and they was purty oura massey, and there was clappen ov hans mortal altogether. Theer was some feller theer then given a speech - Alf the Mason they said he was - and he towl the gels not to marrie fellers thar was taken a drop, else they'd repent of it; but ther was terble noise, and meself not bein any ov the bess at heeren cudn grip much ov what he was sayen. The lil schoolmasther was in the cheer, but I doan beleev he'd anything to sit on meself, or he wuden hev been so cross. He got cross aglough and he cut the consert short and went home. I was wonderin meself thar they diden thank the nice gels for given out the tay before finishen for all, 'caus I thought meself the tay was the bess par ov it. So I went home to Nan and towl her all the yarn, and was dreamen all night about the fine gels I'd seen. So I'm thinken thar I'll lave thee goodbye now, Mr Editer. Maybe I'll write to thee again when I go to the next tay fight.

Yours truly,

JUAN BLEBB, ESQ.

HERE IS THE NEWS : 1903
THE RELUCTANT LIEUTENANT-GOVERNOR

The Island's new Lieutenant-Governor, Lord Raglan, has finally taken up his duties. He has done so only after conflict with the House of Keys over his apparent reluctance to come to the Island. Since his arrival there have been further problems over his refusal to take up residence in Government House. We have this report:

Lord Raglan was sworn in at Castle Rushen in October last year. A few days later he returned to England - and did not come back. The Manx authorities were told he had contracted influenza and needed a long period of recuperation. This resulted in the Keys passing a resolution expressing dissatisfaction with this state of affairs. Now His Lordship - seven months after his swearing-in - has arrived in Douglas by steamer - to a cool welcome. A small reception party was led by Deputy Governor Sir James Gell. But no M.H.K.'s or members of Douglas Town Council were there. Lord Raglan and his family immediately repaired to the Peveril Hotel. He refused to live in Government House after inspecting it shortly after his swearing-in. He said it was not a fit residence, having no bathroom and smelly drains. The house is rented and it is now proposed in Tynwald Court that the Government should take it into public ownership for £12,000 and carry out suitable repairs and renovations.

DAMAGE TO ST GERMAN'S CHURCH
At the end of February widespread damage was caused by one of the worst storms ever experienced. The worst was to St. German's Church at Peel where the stained glass window in the west end was blown in. The fierce wind then lifted off almost the entire roof. All Saints and St. George's Churches in Douglas also suffered exten-

sive roof damage, local telephone services were disrupted, telegraphic communication with England was broken and fishing boats sank at their moorings. There has also been damage to a large number of houses.

DEATH OF HENRY BLOOM NOBLE
The death has been announced of the Isle of Man's wealthiest resident, Mr. Henry Bloom Noble, of Villa Marina, Douglas where he died on 2nd May. His will has revealed personal estate of £180,000 and there are many bequests to good causes including Noble's Hospital, which was opened at the top of Crellin's Hill, Douglas, in 1888 with funds provided by Mr. Noble. Now trustees have been appointed to administer his estate for the good of the community. Mr. Noble was born in Cumbria and came to the Island in 1835, when he was 25 years old. He

The severe storm damage at St. German's Church, Peel.
(R. and L. Kelly Collection)

built up his fortune in the wine and spirit trade and the timber business - and as a moneylender. During the rapid expansion of Douglas he has also been a shrewd property speculator.

The Executors and Trustees are headed by Mr Noble's close friend and adviser for many years, the Rev William Lefroy, Dean of Norwich. He is to be assisted by Mr Alexander Hill, Manager of the Isle of Man Banking Company Ltd; Mr Robert Clucas M.H.K.; Mr Llewellyn Stanley Kneale, advocate, and Mr Samuel Harris, High Bailiff of Douglas.

SPECTACLE OF WALKING RACE
A walking race has been one of the great summer spectacles in Douglas. There were 30 competitors, all young men staying at the holiday encampment at Howstrake run by Mr. Cunningham. The course took them along the promenades, round the harbour and on to the Marine Drive. The race was started by the Mayor, Alderman Proctor, watched by large crowds. The winner, Mr Smith, from Liverpool, received a gold medal presented by Mr Cunningham.

MANX NATIONAL REFORM LEAGUE
A Manx National Reform League has been set up this autumn with the objective of preserving and extending Manx Home Rule. In particular the League will seek to have taxes in the Island levied by Tynwald rather than the UK authorities. It also wants changes in the Island's administration and judicature. And it has called for what it describes as unnecessary and obsolete public offices like that of Vicar-General, Receiver-General and High Bailiffs in towns outside Douglas to be abolished in order to reduce the cost of the Civil List.

NEW HOUSE OF KEYS
The Island has a new House of Keys following the November General Election.

After a 10-day voting period 13 members have been re-elected unopposed including the Speaker, Mr A. W. Moore, who is one of the M.H.K.s for Middle. Six other members, including Mr Hall Caine, the novelist, were returned after election contests and there are five new members. The old House had been in office for seven years, longer than any previous House in modern times.

The nucleus of Bemahague House was built by Robert Heywood at the end of the 18th century. The house was the preferred residence of Lieutenant-Governor Henry Brougham Loch upon his arrival in 1863. Since then the property has been extended but Lord Raglan has condemned it as being unfit for a Government House. Tynwald has now agreed to purchase and modernise the property. (James Fenton)

COLLISION IN MERSEY

The Steam Packet company steamer, *Douglas,* has been involved in a collision in thick fog in the River Mersey. Under the command of Captain Cannell she rammed and sank the Irish-owned cargo ship *City of Lisbon* near the Pier Head on 6th November. The crew of *City of Lisbon* was taken off by the *Douglas* which was carrying the mails and 50 passengers. She suffered slight damage. The Steam Packet's, *Empress Queen,* had a busy summer on the Liverpool route making full use of her 2,000 passenger capacity. Built at Govan in 1897, she is the largest and fastest paddle steamer ever built for cross-channel service. It takes 32 men to work her furnaces and she holds the record for the Mersey Light to Douglas crossing in under three hours. This summer she was the first Packet ship to be equipped with the new wireless telegraphy equipment by Marconi. However, she is likely to be the last paddle steamer built for the Packet Company, now that screw propellers are finding favour.

1903 NEWS IN BRIEF

JANUARY
6 - Reconstruction of Great Laxey Mines. Startling allegations by Mr Clucas M.H.K., and Mr E. Rydings of the St George's Woollen Mill. Mr Clucas loses his seat on the board.
21 - Conference of the Local Government Bodies. A Municipal Association to be formed.

FEBRUARY
14 - Release of Messrs C.B. Nelson (director) and John Shimmon (secretary) who had been sentenced to three year's penal servitude for publishing false balance-sheets in connection with Dumbell's Bank.
20 - Douglas Boundaries Extension. The Tynwald Committee decide against the the inclusion of Onchan Village.
27 - Great storm. St German's Church, Peel, unroofed.

MARCH
16 - Douglas Town Council levy general rate of 2s 9d in the pound.

APRIL
14 - Douglas Board of Guardians increase Poor Rate from 6¹/₂d to 9d in the pound.
25 - Parish Commissioners meet in Conference, and vote in favour of all elections being by ballot.

MAY
2 - Death of Mr H.B. Noble of Villa Marina, Douglas. Large bequests to the Church, charities etc.
29 - Deputy Governor makes his Financial Statement to the Tynwald Court and his proposal to increase the duty on sugar is approved.
30 - House of Keys carry motion "that the Vicar-General and Archdeacon should not be members of the Legislative Council".

JUNE
3 - Death of Alderman Webb J.P., three times Mayor of Douglas. Arrival of Lord and Lady Raglan after an absence from the Island of seven months.
25 - Opening of New Primitive Church at Port Erin.

JULY
21 - Speaker informs Keys that the Secretary of State declines to take action as to the position of the Vicar-General and Archdeacon as members of the Council.
22 - Final Winding-up Meeting of the Great Laxey Mining Company at Manchester. The liquidator shows that from the date of liquidation (October 22nd, 1902) to the present the Company had made a profit of £1,325 5s 11d.

AUGUST
5 - Opening of the Port St Mary Primitive Methodist New Church.

SEPTEMBER
29 - Tynwald decide that £12,000 from General Funds be applied for the purchase of Government House and lands adjoining. Also, £2,433 for alterations, and that £750 be given to the farmer for surrender of lease.
16 - Mr Hall Caine addresses a public meeting in Ramsey. A scheme for the reform of the Manx Constitution is submitted.
21 - An enthusiastic meeting held in Douglas for the purpose of forming a Manx National Reform League.

NOVEMBER
7 - Deemster Moore gives judgement in the case of Crown v Highway Board. The Crown is entitled to charge royalty upon all stone procured on the Island by the Highway Board and other public bodies for use as road metal.
11-20 General Election of the House of Keys.
25 - Douglas Boot and Clothing Fund annual meeting.

DECEMBER
1-3 - Thirteenth Exhibition promoted by Isle of Man Fine Arts and Industrial Guild in the Palace.
2 - Mr A.W. Moore, C.V.O. re-appointed Speaker of the House of Keys.

MANX NATIONAL REFORM LEAGUE

Towards the end of the year, on 12th November, the Central Hall of Murray's Road Board School was packed to overflowing for what was billed as 'The First National Meeting' of the Manx National Reform League. About 400 people were present, some no doubt attracted by the news that late trains and trams had been organised to get them home. At this meeting the objectives of this new organisation were thoroughly explained and the most dynamic and colourful figure of Manx politics, Mr Hall Caine, was elected President.

Careful enquiries have elicited the fact that this new League is of very recent origin. Indeed, it began just one month before, in Roseberry Buildings at the top of Victoria Street. It was here that six men met in a small room and hammered out what amounted to a programme of Constitutional Reform. One of them, Mr Sam Norris, appears to have been the driving force behind this meeting and its impetus was maintained just over a fortnight later, on 31st October, when a public meeting was held at Hanover Street School, chaired by the Mayor of Douglas, Alderman Proctor, which was attended by 50 or so people. It was agreed that a Manx National Reform League be established, and that the draft programme be confirmed by an elected committee. It is interesting to note that on this Programme Committee were the editors of the *Isle of Man Examiner, Isle of Man Times* and the *Manx Sun* - a fair guarantee that the League's activities would be sympathetically and adequately reported.

To a visitor to our shores, the rapidity with which this new organisation has established itself might seem amazing. However, if such a visitor were to glance at its programme then, apart from a natural astonishment at the political and constitutional situation here, such speed might seem understandable. The main objectives of the League are straightforward. These are: the preservation and extension of Manx Home Rule so that the Manx can regulate their own internal affairs; the election of two thirds of the Legislative Council, either directly or indirectly by the people; no taxation without representation; all taxes to be levied annually and the retrenchment of the Civil List and so on. There are suggested social reforms such as an Employers Liability Act; a demand that no more taxes on food should be imposed until death duties and other methods of direct taxation have been introduced, and there are even hints that voting in elections should be by ballot rather than a show of hands!

The truth of the matter, however, is that far from being of such recent origin, the desire for some form of Constitutional Reform is of very long standing indeed. Almost half a century ago a major step forward occurred when the House of Keys was changed from a self-elected to a popularly elected body. Today, advocates of reform in all probability find the position of the Legislative Council the most powerful and persuasive weapon in their armoury.

The Legislative Council, our second chamber, numbers nine, all of whom are paid officials appointed either by the Crown or the Lord Bishop. They are the Lieutenant-Governor, the two Deemsters, the Clerk of the Rolls, the Bishop, the Vicar-General, the Archdeacon, the Receiver-General and the Attorney-General. It forms, in fact, the Executive Government of the Island and it can pass, reject, amend or initiate legislation. It only needs three to make a quorum. This body effectively ensures that the popularly elected House of Keys remain in a completely inferior and subordinate position in the effective government of the Island. It seems scarcely believable that as long ago as 1821 the members of the House of Keys even then, admittedly not from what would today be considered democratic motives, were calling for the reform of the Council!

Ever since, the House has persistently sought reform. Shortly, the Island will be having a General Election. It is reported that the Manx National Reform League are circulating all potential members of the new House with its programme asking for their support both at the public meetings and, should they be elected, in the new House itself.

The reformers will undoubtedly be hoping that this new House will lose no time in implementing some, if not all, of their proposed reforms. Their opponents will view the possibility of such changes with dismay and a threat to the stability of the Island. It would be unfair that a recent intemperate remark about the supporters of reform as "mushrooms that spring up under our feet but they will have to remain under our feet" is typical of this group as a whole, but it most certainly does little to calm tempers as the Election draws near. One thing seems certain. Whatever happens in the Election the position and composition of the Legislative Council will be seriously considered at last. It would appear inconceivable that the demands for changes in its composition to reflect the democratic pressures extant today, will not be accepted, even in part. It will surely not figure still as a topic in Manx political life in another 80 or a hundred years time!

Roseberry Building, Douglas. It was in a room here that the inaugural meeting of the Manx National Reform League took place in October.

HERE IS THE NEWS : 1904
ROADS CLOSED FOR CAR TRIALS

During May thousands of people in the Isle of Man had their first experience of seeing high speed motor cars in action when the Automobile Club of Great Britain held trials in the Island to decide which drivers and makes of cars should make up the British team for this year's Gordon Bennett Challenge Cup Race in Germany. We have this report:

The Automobile Club decided earlier this year that the Island was the ideal place for the trials because Tynwald, unlike the authorities in the UK, was willing to pass a law under which public roads can be closed for racing. This was promulgated on Tynwald Hill in May at a special ceremony - to which some members of Tynwald were taken by motor car. Since then a course measuring 51 miles has been laid out - from Quarter Bridge in Douglas to Castletown, Foxdale, Kirk Michael, Jurby, Ramsey and back to Quarter Bridge by way of the new Snaefell Mountain Road. The best performers over five laps, in a Hill Climb at Port-e-Vullen and a speed test on Douglas Promenade were chosen to represent Britain. They were Edge in a Napier, Girling in a Wolseley and Jarrott in a Wolseley. The brothers Clifford and Walter Earp would have been in the team, but in speed tests on Douglas promenade they were badly hurt when they crashed into the wall of the Villa Marina. A spectator, William Kerruish, formerly of Douglas, now living in Liverpool, was knocked down and also injured.

MANX NORTHERN RAILWAY TAKEN OVER
Earlier in the year, at the annual general meeting of the Isle of Man Railway Company, shareholders agreed to a takeover of the Manx Northern Railway and the Foxdale Line which has been suffering heavy losses now that lead ore production from the Foxdale mines is declining. This brings all the steam railway operations in the Island under one control. The cost of the takeover will be £67,000 but the company accounts show a healthy position. This

Dressed for the occasion, spectators line the road for their first experience of the noise and thrill of high-speed racing cars. (R. and L. Kelly Collection)

year has been a record one with revenues increased to more than £30,000. Modernisation of the railways is also proceeding. Oil lamps in the trains have been replaced with electric lighting.

DAWSEY KEWLEY DIES
Huge crowds attended the funeral of Douglas boatman David Kewley, known as Dawsey, who was famous for saving at least 20 people from drowning in and around the harbour. He lived at Shaw's Brow and was acknowledged to be a superb oarsman and swimmer - but also a modest man who rarely spoke of his exploits. He died in March aged 54 after a chill developed into pneumonia. The funeral procession was led by Douglas Town Band and the Mayor, Councillor Cubbon, and also directors of the Steam Packet Company. There are plans to erect a granite monument to Dawsey Kewley at Victoria Pier next year.

BID TO CONTROL LIQUOR TRADE
Proposals for the retail liquor trade in the Isle of Man to be placed under the control of a state monopoly have been put forward by Colonel George Moore M.H.K. His intention is to remove the profit motive from publicans and others involved in the liquor trade. Lack of competitive trading, he says, will lead to a reduction in alcohol abuse, which has been shown to lead to murder and other terrible

crimes. Colonel Moore is to hold a series of public meetings in the Island to test public reaction to his scheme.

INDECENT PICTURE POSTCARDS
Two German Jews who own a shop in Walpole Avenue, Douglas, have been convicted by Douglas magistrates on charges of selling indecent picture postcards. Arthur Aaron Applebaum and John Neumann pleaded not guilty and were fined £2 and £1 respectively. Police officers gave evidence of purchasing cards which showed young ladies in their undergarments. The two defendants pleaded that the cards would not have been considered indecent in Germany or France. The magistrates ruled, however, that there were different standards in the Isle of Man.

MINERS KILLED
The end of the year has been saddened by the death of four miners in an underground accident at the Great Laxey mine. They drowned when a wooden platform they were working on collapsed, plunging them into nearly 50 feet of water. The men, aged between 19 and 43, had been working on the installation of new equipment designed to pump water from the mine workings. The accident happened 190 fathoms below the surface. The inquest established that the timbers of the platform were rotten.

Start of the Gordon Bennett Trials at Quarter Bridge.

One of the Wolseleys sets off for Castletown.

One of the Napiers passes the Ballasalla control.

Crowds on Bray Hill watch the rapid descent of a Napier.

Official cars outside the Mitre Hotel, Ramsey.

Start of the Hill Climb staged at Port-e-Vullen.

PHOTOGRAPHS FROM THE R. AND L. KELLY COLLECTION

1904 NEWS IN BRIEF

JANUARY
4 -New premises of Isle of Man Bank Ltd at Port Erin opened.
6 -The loss-making Isle of Man Breweries taken over by Boddington's (I.O.M.) Ltd.
7 -Union Mills Memorial Hall opened.
15 -Douglas Branch of the Manx Reform League demand improvements to pier landing accommodation at Douglas.

FEBRUARY
27 -Annual meeting of the Isle of Man Railway Co. Purchase of Manx Northern and Foxdale lines approved.

MAY
5 -Special ceremony at Tynwald Hill to pass Road Closure Act to enable Motor Trials to be held in Isle of Man.
10 -Motor festival begins. Speed Test over five laps of 51 mile course.
11 -Motor Hill Climbing Tests at Ramsey.
12 -Motor Speed Tests on Douglas Promenade.
18 -First annual meeting of Great Laxey Ltd.
20 -Resignation of Major Spittall as chairman of Great Laxey Ltd.

JULY
13 -Formation of The Baume (Manx) Music Scholarship. The

eccentric Mr Baume was a Frenchman who lived on the South Quay and lived mainly on snails. Though known as a miser, he left considerable sums of money for charitable purposes.

AUGUST
13 -It is feared that the steamer *Juverna*, with a crew of ten, including three Port St Mary men, which left Greenock on Saturday, 13th, has foundered.

SEPTEMBER
6 -Douglas School Board decides on design of new school building in Demesne Road.
8 -At the National Eisteddfod held at Rhyl, Miss Cannell's Ladies Choir is placed joint first. Male Choir came third.

OCTOBER
17-19 -Meetings held at Castletown, Ramsey and Douglas to advo cate the Nationalisation of the Drink Traffic.

DECEMBER
6 -Foundering of the vessel *Wild Rose*, at Liverpool. Capt. Carine and his son, Tom, of Ballafesson, drowned. Three other Manxmen in the crew survived.
10 -Disaster at Great Laxey Mine. Four miners drowned owing to collapse of a platform.

HERE IS THE NEWS : **1905**
DEMAND FOR SHELTERS ON VICTORIA PIER

Demands are increasing for improving the sheltered accommodation and other facilities at Victoria Pier in Douglas for arriving and departing passengers. It has now become clear that unless there are improvements the continuing expansion of the highly lucrative visiting industry will be hit. We have this report:

Matters came to a head on the last Saturday in August when passengers, mostly holidaymakers, suffered dreadfully from lack of shelter in wet and stormy conditions. Many expressed their displeasure. Now a protest meeting has been called in Douglas by the Town Council, under a requisition by the ratepayers. And a deputation from Tynwald Court is to meet the Lieutenant-Governor, Lord Raglan. The 1905 holiday season has been a record one with more than 395,000 passengers landing, of which 17,400 arrived at Ramsey. In 1890 the fine Victoria Pier Building, with its imposing clock tower, was built on the triangular piece of reclaimed land fronting the Peveril Hotel. While the building provides many services for passengers, it affords little shelter for the many thousands who use the Victoria Pier at busy weekends. One suggestion is that a verandah should be added to the three sides of the building. Earlier this year a Tynwald Court committee considered the matter of shelters on the Victoria Pier. It was told that the lack of facilities at busy times often creates a risk to life and limb. But the committee reported that while improvements were necessary, Government did not have the finance to carry them out, without increasing taxation.

SIX DROWNED IN RAMSEY BAY
The year was ushered in with cold and stormy weather which caused several appalling disasters to shipping off the coasts of the British Isles. In the second week of January, the Isle of Man was visited by a terrific gale, accompanied by a heavy fall of snow, which resulted in the wreck of the tug *Conqueror* in Ramsey Bay and the loss of six lives. The tug, having burst her boiler off Castletown, came to anchor in Ramsey Bay, but the fury of the gale was so great that her cables parted, and she was blown towards the North Shore where she grounded opposite Ramsey Hydro. She was 300 yards off shore in the shallow water and was pounded by waves with the Ramsey Lifeboat, *Mary Isabella 2,* powerless to reach her. After five hours of torment the crew decided to jump and take their chances in the sea. But only five of the crew of eleven made it to safety.

GOVERNMENT HOUSE MODERNISATION
In March, Tynwald voted a further £3,500 for the completion of the modernisation scheme of Government House (formerly Bemahague House) to meet the needs of Lord Raglan. The architects have righted matters by pulling down the front of the house and extending it in such a way that the reception room and study have been enlarged, while at the same time a new hall, porch and main staircase have been included. Outside the offending farm buildings have been re-positioned, though the farmhouse has been converted into two staff cottages and the remaining cowhouse into a stable and coach-house. The total cost of the work is nearly £20,000, which is much higher than expected. In the debate, Mr T. H. Cormode, M.H.K. observed that the grounds were to be surrounded by seven foot fencing and trees. He declared, "It's too bad that after the public has paid so sweetly for this that they should be prevented from having a peep at it."

DEATHS OF TWO EMINENT MANXMEN
The year has seen the deaths of two of the Island's most distinguished officials. In March Sir James Gell, Clerk of the Rolls, while at Sunday service in St Mary's Church, Castletown. He was 82. His death occasioned widespread regret, for undoubtedly he was the foremost Manxman of his age. He had, during his career, filled the offices of High-Bailiff of Castletown, Attorney General, First Deemster, and Clerk of the Rolls. For two periods he had

With calls being made to provide shelter for passengers using the Victoria Pier, one suggestion is that a verandah be constructed around the three-sided building of 1890. In front is the new memorial to Dawsey Kewley, life-saving hero of Douglas harbour. (Frank Cowin Library)

THE 20th CENTURY

In September, during the first Car T.T., single-line operations resulted in three of the Snaefell trams being in collision. Some passengers were injured.

acted as Deputy-Governor. His knowledge of Manx history and law was marvellously complete.

Three months later another man who rendered great service died in the person of Mr Samuel Harris who was nearly 90 years old. In the course of his career he had been High-Bailiff of Douglas, Registrar of Deeds, Diocesan Registrar and Vicar-General. It was only failing health that induced him to relinquish these positions only recently. Douglas never had a more respected citizen and it was Samuel Harris who led the way in persuading Tynwald that the town should have control of its affairs through elected Town Commissioners. This was achieved in 1860 and Mr Harris became its first Chairman. He will be remembered by future generations as the instigator of the promenade built for the benefit of locals and visitors alike and now named after him.

PREACHERS GAOLED

Prosecutions have been brought before Douglas magistrates against preachers alleged to have been causing a nuisance on the foreshore in the summer months. The cases were brought by Douglas Corporation and alleged that the byelaws banning preaching within 20 yards of the promenades had been broken. The preachers included Douglas Town and Seamen's Missioner Mr William Kneen and the Reverend Somerset S. McTaggart. They and the others were fined - but on refusing to pay were committed to prison for four days.

BALDWIN RESERVOIR OFFICIALLY OPENED

The new Baldwin Reservoir has been officially opened by the Mayor, Alderman Joseph Kaye. Ironically heavy rain forced postponement by 24 hours of the ceremony planned for 6th September. High winds flattened the refreshment marquee that had been erected. But the celebrations eventually went on as planned. Work on the reservoir, designed to meet the growing need for water in Douglas caused by increasing numbers of summer visitors, has taken nearly five years. The reservoir holds 300 million gallons and has cost £90,000 - but there will be no increase in the town rates.

ACCIDENT ON SNAEFELL SUMMIT RAILWAY

A serious accident occurred on the Snaefell Summit Railway on 14th September when single line operations were in use to take spectators as far as the Bungalow to see the newly-introduced Tourist Trophy Car Race. Apparently an ascending car stalled at Lhergy Veg from either a motor fault or loss of wire contact. The third of a convoy of three cars descending on the same track failed to stop resulting in the three cars crashing into each other. There was a certain amount of panic as passengers jumped out but injuries were none too serious. Nevertheless, compensation paid by the Manx Electric Railway Company is likely to be considerable.

1905 NEWS IN BRIEF

JANUARY
31 - At a Tynwald Court presided over by Lord Raglan petitions for the extensions of the boundaries of Port St Mary and Port Erin were granted.

MARCH
12 - Sir James Gell, Clerk of the Rolls, died.

APRIL
20 - Trial visit of the new Midland Railways' turbine steamer *Manxman* from Heysham to the Island.

MAY
30 - British Eliminating Trials for the Gordon Bennett Cup resulted in Messrs Clifford Earp, Hon.C.S. Rolls and C. Bianchi being chosen.

JUNE
8 - Memorial to the late Dawson ('Dawsey') Kewley erected at the foot of Victoria Pier.
9 - Mr Samuel Harris, late High-Bailiff of Douglas, dies.
26 - Great interest in first visit of the Isle of Man Steam Packet's new turbine steamer *Viking*. The crossing from the mouth of the Mersey to Douglas Head was made in 2 hrs 53 mins.

JULY
21 - Deputation to lay before the Home Office the question of Constitutional Reform was to no avail. The negative response was regarded as a snub to the House of Keys.

AUGUST
17 - First action of Douglas Corporation against the nuisance of preachers on the foreshore. Accused elect to take imprisonment.
18 - Douglas School Board adopted the Fair Wage principle in respect of future contracts.
25 - Wet and very stormy conditions lead to call to provide shelters on Victoria Pier.
  - Concern about accident on Groudle Glen miniature railway. None of the occupants of the carriages were, however, injured.

SEPTEMBER
6 - Official inauguration of the Baldwin Reservoir.
14 - With doubts about the future of the Gordon Bennett Cup international event, the Automobile Club of Great Britain decided to stage an event of its own - the Tourist Trophy Race - where weight, fuel consumption and reliability were of more importance than speed. The race was over four laps of the 51-mile Trials course and was won by J.S. Napier in his Arol-Johnson car.
14 - Accident on Snaefell Summit Railway involving three cars.

NOVEMBER
20 - Douglas Town Council hold special meeting to discuss the serious condition of those unemployed during the winter. It was decided to call a public meeting to urge harbour improvements.

DECEMBER
6 - Douglas Town Council accepts offer of the H.B. Noble Trust to provide the town with Public Baths.
31 - S.S. Argos became a total wreck after running aground at Santon in a severe blizzard.

MR SAMUEL HARRIS : AN OBITUARY

(Manx National Heritage)

The peaceful death of Mr Samuel Harris, at his Marathon home, means that the Island in general, and Douglas in particular, has lost one of its most prominent and influential figures. In March this year, and in his 90th year, he reluctantly laid down the reins of office as High-Bailiff of Douglas. Only two years ago he resigned as Vicar-General. His mind and memory retained practically all their vigour until the close of his public career.

Born in 1815, the late Mr Harris was the son of a Douglas merchant, who carried on business in the neighbourhood of the Market-place in the early years of last century. He received his education at various private schools in Douglas. After serving his articles in the legal profession with Mr James Quirk (then High-Bailiff of Douglas), Mr Harris was called to the Manx Bar in March, 1842. Later, he went into partnership with Mr Albert W. Adams and they were the forerunners of today's firm of Dickinson, Cruickshank and Co. Samuel Harris soon distinguished himself in the courts, and in 1864 he was appointed High-Bailiff. He continued in this office for a remarkable 40 years. In the same year he was made Registrar of Deeds and Vicar-General, a position he occupied for 20 years. In this office he was a judge of the Ecclesiastical Courts. This appointment followed him serving since 1861 as Diocesan Registrar and Secretary to the Lord Bishop.

Mr Harris was a founder and director of the Isle of Man Banking Company Limited, serving as Chairman from 1872 to 1894. He was also a Trustee of the Isle of Man Bank for Savings. Amongst his many other duties, he was Chairman of the Hospital Committee, and of the Committee of the House of Industry; Chairman of the Central Relief Board, the Ladies' Soup Dispensary and the Douglas Coal Fund. Lately he was a Trustee under the will of the late Mr Henry Bloom Noble. In all these positions he showed his profound interest in all work of a charitable or philanthropic nature, but he also had a remarkable capacity for business, being shrewd and cautious to a degree. He was, however, essentially a public-spirited man, with an unusually broad outlook on general affairs.

Whereas the High-Bailiffs of the towns were responsible for the governance and conduct of the towns, there was little they could do to improve the appalling conditions of the streets and houses. Samuel Harris was one of the leading protagonists who persuaded Tynwald that it should divest powers to the townspeople so they could elect Commissioners, levy a rate, have power to introduce their own bye-laws and pursue plans for town improvements. Many public meetings were held and in 1858 the Douglas Town Act was accepted as a way forward. Later, town status would be afforded to Ramsey, Castletown and Peel. In recognition of the part High-Bailiff Harris had played on behalf of the people of Douglas, he was elected as one of the nine new Town Commissioners; topping the poll, and made their first Chairman at the end of July, 1860. This meeting took place in the Old Seneschal's House which Mr Harris made available as their first meeting place.

In an astute move, he leased the Villa Marina mansion to the newly-appointed Lieutenant-Governor Francis Pigott in 1861. Ill-health was to overtake the new Lieutenant-Governor and in 1863 he was succeeded by Henry Brougham Loch. Soon after the latter's arrival, he received a deputation of Douglas Town Commissioners who pressed their case to make their town the centre of government. This is believed to have included an offer of Mr Harris's latest home in Douglas as Government House. Governor Loch was diplomatic in his reply, but when he made Bemahague his residence on the outskirts of Douglas, it was a move which would anticipate the demise of Castletown as the Island's capital. Mr Harris sold the prestigious Villa Marina in 1862 to Mr Henry Bloom Noble, who resided there until his death. Since 1852 Mr Harris had resided at Marathon, formerly Woodville. Mr Harris was a seasoned traveller and after a visit to Greece he changed the name of his residence to Marathon.

Perceiving the future which lay in store for the ill-built, ill-drained little town of Douglas, Samuel Harris set about improving the sea frontage. He acquired a portion of the central foreshore on long lease from the Woods and Forest Commissioners with a view to forming the first of our promenades. In due course it was appropriately named the Harris Promenade, and remains today as a permanent monument to the memory of its originator.

Despite his many commitments, Samuel Harris continued to display a keen and enlightened interest in the corporate life of Douglas and he welcomed the town's incorporation as a borough in 1896. Though not a member of the Corporation, it was felt he should be honoured for what he had achieved. Councillors and Aldermen were unanimous in inviting Mr Harris to become the borough's first Mayor. He had to decline this honour, as he felt he couldn't give sufficient time to this onerous postition. He is to be admired for his true-hearted devotion to the welfare of his fellows. Douglas has lost one of its most virile servants, one who took it from the abyss of squalour and led it to becoming the modern town it is today.

One of the Island's oldest established industries, the Tromode Sailcloth Mills, is to close down with the loss of more than 80 jobs. The company, which was founded in 1790, has been hit by falling orders as demand for sail cloth diminishes in the face of the continuing conversion to steamship operation world-wide. We have this report.

The closure announced in May, is a bitter blow for the closely-knit community of the model village at Cronkbourne where most of the workers and their families live. But the company's owners, W. F. Moore and Son, have made generous provision for those most likely to suffer. There are pensions for long service employees and their widows - and paid passage for those who must now leave the Island to seek work elsewhere. For the last 11 years the sole proprietor of the company has been Mr Arthur W. Moore, better known as Speaker of the House of Keys and a leading Manx historian. He is said to be deeply distressed at having to close a family concern started by his great-great-grandfather and handed down from father to son. He had fought to keep it going. But orders from customers like the Admiralty and leading British and foreign shipping companies have fallen off as steam replaces sail.

FISHERMEN SUFFOCATED
Earlier in the year three fishermen died on board the steam trawler *Rose Anne* as it was moored at the Tongue in Douglas harbour. They suffocated while they were asleep in the fo'c's'le of the vessel - with the stove lit and the doors and portholes closed. They died in their sleep from inhaling the poisonous fumes. The men were all from Peel - William Clucas, John Watterson and John Hughes. The inquest found that their deaths had been caused largely by their own neglect.

HORSE TRAM VICTIM
A six-year-old boy has been run over and killed by a horse tram on Douglas seafront. George Moore, of Hatfield Grove, Douglas, had been standing in the road on the fringe of a large crowd listening to a Salvation

Cronkbourne village, showing some of the 42 tenements provided by the Moore family for their Tromode factory workers. The steps lead to those on the upper level while entrance to the lower level is from the other side of the row. *(Manx National Heritage)*

Army band performing on Harris Promenade. The noise of the band caused the tram horse to bolt and George went under its hooves and under the tram wheels. He was killed instantly. The driver, Thomas Edward Crellin, said the horse went wild at the sound of the band and he was unable to hold it.

T. S. *VIKING* BREAKS RECORDS
The Isle of Man Steam Packet Company's new turbine steamer *Viking*, which went into service last year, is claimed to be the fastest ship in the world. She has established a world record of more than 24 knots and has set new record passage times between Douglas and Liverpool and Fleetwood taking 2 hours 22 minutes on the latter crossing. Meanwhile, summer arrivals in the Island continue to reach new record levels - just under 400,000 in the 1906 season. And Tynwald has finally agreed to improve passenger facilities at Victoria Pier at a cost of more than £2,000.

CAR T.T. WON BY HON. C. S. ROLLS
The 1906 motor car T.T. Race was won by the Honourable C. S. Rolls in

The Hon. Charles Rolls with his Rolls-Royce which won this year's T.T. He completed the four laps of over 40 miles in 4 hours 6 secs. averaging 39.6 m.p.h. *(R. and L. Kelly*

a Rolls-Royce. The races are now held annually in the Island by the Automobile Club of Great Britain. And, since last year, motor cycle trials have been held as an additional speed spectacle. In recognition of the Highway Board's efforts in providing good roads for the races the Automobile Club offered the Board the free gift of a steamroller. But it was refused. A Board spokesman said the gesture was deeply appreciated - but they already had two steamrollers and could not afford the upkeep of a third.

ALEX GILL LOSES LAWSUIT

Mr Alexander Gill, the builder and developer responsible for the new boarding houses along Palace Terrace, Douglas, has lost his lawsuit against the Reverend Frances Westlake. This arose out of a landslide which allegedly caused subsidence below Mr Gill's residence at Little Switzerland. Mr Westlake bought and demolished a cottage on Queen's Promenade in order to build his private hotel, Sea Level. Mr Gill claimed that this caused the landslip below Little Switzerland. But after a 14-day High Court hearing a jury dismissed his claim for damages.

HALL CAINE'S NEW DRAMA

Mr Hall Caine's new play "The Bondman" opened with great success at the Drury Lane Theatre in London. It was given an enthusiastic reception by the full house first night audience and is tipped to be the dramatic success of the season - although some newspaper critics have been less than enthusiastic about its artistic merits. The star part of Greeba is being played by Mrs. Patrick Campbell.

The Steam Packet's record-breaking turbine steamer 'Viking', seen here at Liverpool landing stage. (R. and L. Kelly Collection)

The 'Viking's' dining saloon, worthy of a trans-atlantic liner. (R. and L. Kelly Collection)

1906 NEWS IN BRIEF

JANUARY

4 - New Wesleyan Chapel at Lonan opened.

22 - Establishment of District Nurses throughout the Island in connection with H.B. Noble Trust.

FEBRUARY

8 - The Lieut-Governor and Executive Council consider plan by Church Commissioners to form a new parish in Douglas with a new church to be provided from money made available in will of the late Mr H. B. Noble. Considerable opposition from the Douglas parishes before the scheme was approved.

MARCH

7 - Meeting of the Trades and Labour Council protests against the employment as painters, in the winter months, of the Douglas pier police.

9 - Douglas branch of the R.N.L.I. accept with regret the resignation of Mr T. Bawden, who for 33 years had acted as secretary.

27-29 Guild Music Festival, founded in 1892, continues to be successfully held in the Palace.

APRIL

30 - House of Keys deputation waits on the Governor to discuss Constitutional Reform. Lord Raglan is generally unfavourable to any change.

JUNE

5 - During a dense fog which prevailed off the coast of the Island the Belfast Steamship Company's vessel *Graphic* collided with the three-masted steamer *Empress* near the Calf of Man. As a result the Empress foundered. No lives were lost.

6 - Douglas Town Council agrees to abolish the tolls at the Swing Bridge in the winter months.

28 - The foundation stone of a Cottage Hospital for Ramsey (provided largely by the Noble Trustees) was laid with Masonic ceremonies by the Hon. Arthur Stanley, M.P. for Ormskirk, Provincial Grand Master of the Isle of Man.

JULY

4 - Meeting of the Grand Lodge of the Loyal Orange Institution in Douglas.

10 - Moves in the Town Council to allow the cable cars to run on Sundays outside the hours of Divine services. It was decided to let the matter stand until after the November elections.

AUGUST

2 - Henry Bloom Noble Baths opened in Victoria Street.

31 - During the season the popularity of Laxey Glen and Gardens (recently acquired by the Manx Electric Railway Co.) greatly increased by special engagement of first-class military bands.

- Rushen Abbey also grew in prominence for tourists this summer, and more especially as a rendezvous for picnics for Sunday Schools and similar institutions.

SEPTEMBER

6 - Foundation stone of the 'Ward' Library in Peel laid by the Clerk of the Rolls.

20 - Hall Caine's "Bondman" produced in Drury Lane with great success.

27 - Car T.T. held on revised course of 40 miles which omitted southern section but took the cars through Peel and then on to Ramsey etc. Race was won by the Hon. C.S. Rolls (Rolls-Royce). He completed the four laps in 4 hrs 6 mins averaging 39.6 m.p.h.

OCTOBER

16 - Tynwald approves the construction of a verandah at the Victoria Pier Buildings at a cost of £2,100. Also it was agreed that a fog signal should be placed on Douglas Head at a cost of £2,400.

27 - *The Manx Sun*, founded in 1821, finally ceases publication. It is to be amalgamated with the *Isle of Man Times* in November.

NOVEMBER

1 - The Belvedere Hotel, Loch Promenade, sold at auction for £6,000.

26 - Lord Raglan opens a new Public Hall in Princes Street, Douglas, principally for the purpose of providing free dinners to school children. The hall was built at a cost of £3,000 which was provided by the H.B. Noble Trustees. Mr R.F. Douglas was the builder.

DECEMBER

3 - Meeting of the Governors of Noble's Isle of Man Hospital to discuss offer of £40,000 from the H.B. Noble Trustees to build a new hospital to be erected on the Hills Estate, or to provide for improvements and extension of the present hospital above Crellin's Hill. Meeting found in favour of the latter with the addition of a children's ward.

Following the example of the Automobile Club of Great Britain, its off-shoot, the Auto-Cycle Club, has launched races of its own. They are designed to develop motor-cycles as a means of cheap transport for the ordinary man. Weight of the machine and fuel efficiency are considered more important than speed. Motor-cycle trials were held at the same time as the Gordon Bennett Trials in 1905. A team was selected for the International Cup event held in France, but that event also fell into disrepute and was abandoned. Judging from the interest shown by manufacturers it seems these new races are assured of a great future. We have this report:

The scene at St. John's for the start of the first Tourist Trophy Race organised by the Auto-Cycle Club of Great Britain.   *(R. and L. Kelly Collection)*

The normally peaceful village of St John's was transformed on Thursday, 28th May by the arrival of the entourages of the 25 competing machines. They were divided into two classes with 18 single-cylinder machines in one class and the rest in the twin-cylinder class. The course was over 15 miles taking in Ballacraine, Kirk Michael and Peel. Pedalling was allowed and it was necessary for some machines to negotiate Creg Willy's Sill (The Hill of Willy Sylvester). Practising has shown the road to be extremely dusty and riders have complained about the ruts on the Glen Helen section, caused by the Car T.T. Ten laps needed to be completed, a total distance of 158 miles. Hundreds of spectators took up position at the various vantage points and the first rider was despatched at 10 o'clock, followed by the remainder of the field at one minute intervals, a massed start not finding favour in the conditions. The arrival of each machine from Peel was followed by a flurry of activity as machines were refuelled and times posted on the scoreboard. Great cheers went up as Mr C. R. Collier on a Matchless came home the winner of the single-cylinder class by a clear 11 minutes and averaging 38.22 m.p.h. He was also well ahead of the twin-cylinder class winner who was Mr Rem Fowler riding a Peugeot-engined Norton. To Mr

Collier goes the magnificent Tourist Trophy in the form of a silver statuette of Mercury poised on a winged wheel. It was presented by the Marquis de Mouzilly St Mars who, although he has a French title, is an Englishman and a wealthy patron of motor-cycle sport.

END OF DALBY FEUD?
Earlier in the year the long-running feud between neighbouring Dalby farmers Charles Hutchin and Thomas Teare resulted in Teare being found guilty at the Court of General Gaol of unlawfully wounding Mr Hutchin. Teare, of Ballacooil, was sentenced to three months hard labour. He was alleged to have attacked Mr Hutchin, of Creg Lea, with a spade inflicting serious head injuries. The so-called Dalby outrages started five years ago and resulted in Mr Hutchin's cattle and sheep being killed in clandestine night raids by marauders. The court was told that Teare had been pursuing a blood feud against Mr Hutchin, sparked off by a right of way dispute.

DREADNOUGHTS IN DOUGLAS BAY
The First Division of the Channel Fleet - comprising six mighty battleships and two cruisers - made a brave spectacle when they paid an official visit to Douglas in August. In bright sunshine and calm seas the dread-noughts steamed majestically into the bay and anchored near Onchan Head. The ships are under the command of Admiral Lord Charles Beresford, whose flagship is *HMS King Edward the Seventh*. The ships' companies were given shore leave during their stay and also took part in the Douglas Regatta.

The Rev Thomas Wortley Drury, D.D., who has been appointed Bishop of the Island.

(Frank Cowin Library)

MANXMAN TO BE BISHOP

It has been announced that King Edward V11 has approved the appointment of the Rev. Thomas Wortley Drury D.D. to succeed Bishop Straton as Bishop of Sodor and Man. This is the first time since the 13th century that a Manx-born man has been appointed to this high office. The new bishop is the son of the late Rev. William Drury, the famous and respected Vicar of Braddan. Our new bishop was educated at King William's College and Christ College, Cambridge. After ordination he was curate at Braddan for a short period before becoming a mathematical master at King William's College. He then left the Island and rose through various appointments until becoming Principal of Ridley Hall, Cambridge. He will be consecrated at York in November and will be enthroned in St George's, Douglas, next year.

Old Kirk Braddan is the scene for the popular open-air services for visitors who swarm over the graves and memorials. But is this a desecration of the churchyard?

(Frank Cowin Library)

CHOIR SUCCESS AT BLACKPOOL

This century has seen Manx choirs participating in various major music festivals on the 'mainland'. They have won high honours on more than one occasion but in October this year the greatest ever success was achieved when Mr J.D. Looney's Isle of Man Choir won the Challenge Shield at the Blackpool Music Festival, regarded as the country's top award for choral singing. Earlier in the year the Isle of Man Choir also won the Challenge Shield at the Morecambe Music Festival, while Mr Poulter's choir came first in the Mixed Voice Contest (35 voices). The Isle of Man Choir went to Blackpool as the favourites to win - as they did by a wide points margin to the delight of a large Manx contingent in the audience.

LITTLE SUPPORT FOR LIQUOR CONTROL

Lieutenant Colonel George Moore M.H.K. is to introduce a Bill into the House of Keys next year to nationalise the Island's retail liquor trade. Under its proposals public houses and other liquor outlets would come under the control of a Board of Tynwald. Colonel Moore has been seeking support for this at a series of public meetings in the Island. But the Bill is virtually certain to fail. Only one M.H.K., Mr Ambrose Qualtrough of Rushen, has expressed himself in favour.

MONKEY ESCAPES

Finally, there was great excitement round about Summer Hill, Douglas, following the escape of a large monkey which had been on exhibition at the Camera Obscura at Strathallan. The animal escaped from its cage and began a series of raids on nearby houses in search of food, frightening women and children. Because of its size, armed men were brought in to hunt it down. It was shot and wounded when seen on the roof of a house in Fort William. It took refuge in the scullery of the house where it was finally shot dead.

1907 NEWS IN BRIEF

JANUARY
7 - Opening of Demesne Road New Board School, Douglas.

FEBRUARY
14 - Centenary of Primitive Methodism celebrated throughout the Island.

MARCH
5 - Committee formed to provide Memorial to the late Rev. T.E. Brown.

APRIL
1 - Braddan Vestry decided that Poor Relief in the parish should be met by a poor rate. Arising out of the meeting there was an expression of strong public feeling against the holding of outdoor services in the old churchyard at Braddan.
4 - Great success for Manx choirs at Morecambe Music Festival.

MAY
17-25 Douglas hosts the 17th British National Christian Endeavour Convention. Various denominations throughout the Island involved.
28 - First Tourist Trophy Race for motor cycles held on the St John's 'Short' Course.
29 - Car T.T. won by E. Courtis driving a 20 h.p. Rover averaging 28.8 m.p.h. Heavy Touring Car Race won by G.P. Mills in a 30 h.p. Beeston Humber averaging 28.7 m.p.h.

JULY
23 - Opening of the Ramsey Cottage Hospital, provided by the generosity of the Noble Trust.
25 - Foundation stone of St Matthew's Church Chancel laid by Bishop Straton.

AUGUST
1 - Arrival in Douglas Bay of the First Division of the Channel Fleet, including six battleships and two cruisers.
7 - King approves appointment of Rev. Thomas Drury D.D. as Bishop of Sodor and Man.

SEPTEMBER
9 - Labour dispute at Laxey mines; a threatened strike averted.
26 - Ward Public Library at Peel officially opened.
 - End of month has seen much rain and wind which has seriously damaged corn, potato and other crops.

OCTOBER
5 - Isle of Man Choir victors at Blackpool Music Festival.

DECEMBER
7 - Meeting in Noble's Hall to consider scheme of weekly contributions from workpeople towards the funds of the hospital.
10 - Tynwald inquiry at Laxey as to schemes of water supply.

INTRODUCING THE MANX NATIONAL ANTHEM

The Isle of Man now has its own National Anthem. Beginning 'O Land of Our Birth', the anthem was sung for the first time at the Thursday evening concert of this year's Manx Music Festival. The Palace Ballroom Orchestra, led by Harry Wood, provided the accompaniment and the competing choirs united in a stirring performance. It was noticed that both the Lieutenant-Governor, Lord Raglan, and Lady Raglan remained seated as though they did not consider the words applied to them. But all 3,000 Manx present stood and joined in enthusiastically. Afterwards the tune could be heard being whistled in the streets and sung by housewives in their kitchens. "It's on everyone's lips," says one observer.

The anthem has been composed by Mr W. H. Gill who was born in Sicily, but is proud of his Manx ancestry which can be traced back over a thousand years. In 1848, at the age of nine, William Gill came to the Isle of Man and resided with his uncle, the vicar of Malew. He was educated at King William's College but pursued his career in London. He kept in close contact with the Island, however, and assisted Deemster J. F. Gill and his friend, Dr John Clague of Castletown, in collecting traditional Manx music. The songs were arranged for voice with piano accompaniment by Mr Gill and published in 'The Manx Song Book' over ten years ago. Included is everyone's favourite - 'Ellan Vannin' - which many believe should be adopted as the Island's anthem. The words were written by Eliza Craven Green who was born in Richmond and was an amateur theatrical. She first came to the Island as a performer in 1835 and lived at Ballaughton, Braddan. The words of 'Ellan Vannin' were published in the *Manx Sun* in 1854 and were set to music by J. Townsend of Manchester. Soon, everyone came to love it. However, because of its sentimental character, it has not been deemed appropriate as an anthem.

Mr Gill has adapted one of the most popular, though rather mournful, traditional Manx ballads - 'Mylecharane'. It has been used as a hymn tune and a dance. It is purely Manx in character but the tune has been twisted and distorted over the centuries so that no one can say what the original was like. Thus Mr Gill has felt free to make changes to the music in order to make it fit his words. His aim has been to write what he hopes will be a solid and stately choral hymn. "I have ventured with a boldness akin to presumption," he says, "to do for our nation now what far abler hands ought to have done long ago." Mr Gill has written eight verses with the idea that certain ones can be used as an anthem, and others as a hymn for general public worship.

Those who are not Manx-born may well consider that adoption of the Manx National Anthem, and the possible abandonment of "God Save the King", to be an act of disloyalty. Mr Gill certainly does not propose this, however. He believes that his anthem should stand "side by side" with the British anthem. Lady Raglan, though unable to stand for its first performance, has said that she is "pleased" with the new anthem and is prepared to encourage it. Whilst "God Save the King" must be played in the presence of Lord Raglan, as the Crown representative, she says, she sees no reason why it should not be followed by Mr Gill's anthem. Thus, in a shrewd move which is likely to appease Manx nationalism and the current demands for Constitutional Reform, she has intimated that she would like to adopt the anthem as her own, and whenever she attends a public function alone the Manx National Anthem should be played. Thus the Isle of Man seems set to be a community of two anthems - the Manx one usually secondary to "God Save the King."

The scene at the opening of Ramsey Cottage Hospital on 23rd July. The hospital has been provided by the Henry Bloom Noble Trustees.

(Manx National Heritage)

Easter Monday. Lady Raglan lays the foundation stone of the Lych Gate at the entrance to Kirk Michael Church. It is to be built to the design of Armitage Rigby.

October 16th. Lady Raglan officially opens the Lych Gate. Its purpose is to house the fine collection of ancient crosses including one by Gaut, the notable Scandinavian sculptor.

Recent years have seen the arrival of thousands of Territorials attached to various regiments of the British Army. Summer training camps are set up at Ramsey and, shown here, at Knockaloe, near Peel.

STRONG OPPOSITION TO SUNDAY SAILINGS

The year started with a great public debate which has arisen over the idea of Sunday ferry sailings being introduced by the Steam Packet Company during the summer season. Church leaders have spearheaded strong opposition to this disturbance of the Sabbath - although holidaymakers want more week-end services. We have this report:

The matter remains unresolved at the present time. The Packet Company's articles of association forbid Sunday services and the company held a poll of its shareholders which produced a narrow majority against change. There has also been opposition by the Lieutenant-Governor, Lord Raglan, and the idea has been condemned in a motion passed by the House of Keys. But supporters of the move say most of the Island's growing number of summer visitors can travel only at the week-ends and Sunday sailings would lead to even greater growth. The shareholders have decided that a final decision must be left to the directors - but they themselves are split on the issue. Meanwhile, the company's new turbine steamer *Ben-my-Chree*, which went into service this summer, has been withdrawn after being run into by an Irish steamship while at anchor in the Mersey. *Ben-my-Chree* has taken over from the *Viking* - which went into service last summer - as the world's fastest cross-channel steamer, capable of nearly 25$^1/_2$ knots. Only the great Transatlantic liners are faster.

PRESENTATION TO JOHN RONEY

Earlier this year a lugsail boat paid for by public subscription has been presented to Douglas boatman John Roney, better known as Ganja, who in the last 40 years has been credited with rescuing 40 people from drowning in Douglas Bay and Harbour. Most rescues occurred during his 15 years as attendant at the

The Steam Packet's latest passenger vessel 'Ben my Chree' arrived in Douglas for the first time in July. Capable of over 25 knots she is claimed to be the fastest cross-channel steamer in service.

(Manx National Heritage)

Port Skillion baths at Douglas Head. The Mayor, Councillor Joseph Sharp, made the presentation and the 18 foot vessel, which cost £18, was launched near the Victoria Pier. The Mayor said it would give Ganja a living now that constant immersions in the sea have left him suffering badly from rheumatism.

Miss Maria Louisa Wood - doyen of Manx music and founder of 'The Guild'. See News in Brief.

(Manx National Heritage)

MEETING WITH HOME SECRETARY

A House of Keys deputation sent in February to present the Home Secretary with a petition for Constitutional Reform for the Island, has reported having a favourable reception. It is hoped that this will lead to the Legislative Council being more representative of the Manx people when advising the Lieutenant-Governor on financial and other political affairs. The Legislative Council continues to be made up of the Lieutenant-Governor, the Bishop and their appointed officials, and the House of Keys have little say in the way the Island is administered.

Meanwhile, Mr Hall Caine, President of the Manx National Reform League, has announced he will not be seeking re-election as M.H.K. for Ramsey in the November General Election. He says his writing of novels and plays gives him little spare time.

DALBY FEUD CONTINUES

The reign of terror against Dalby farmer Mr Charles Hutchin continues. The work of incendiaries has destroyed outbuildings and killed a horse and a cow at his farm, Creg Lea. Police say it was arson - but nobody has been brought to justice. There has been a feud for some years between Mr Hutchin and neighbouring farmer Thomas Teare of Ballacooil over a right of way dispute. Since 1902 there have been night raids on Mr Hutchin's farm and cattle have been killed. Then last year Teare was given three months hard labour at General Gaol for unlawfully wounding Mr Hutchin in an attack with a spade which caused serious head injuries. In May Mr Hutchin was awarded £200 damages for the personal injuries he sustained.

BID TO BAN TOUTING

Court action is being taken against people in the Island who cause a nuisance by touting in the street for the custom of holidaymakers. In what is regarded as a test case, High Bailiff Gell imposed a ten shilling fine on boarding house keeper Caroline Goodman, of Oban House, Loch Promenade. She was alleged to have called out the name of her establish-

The Sir William Hillary memorial. See News in Brief

ment to visitors coming from the boat in Douglas Harbour. Prosecutions are also being brought for alleged touting by pleasure boat owners, car hire men and photographers.

ACCIDENT AT RAMSEY

A woman has died following a collision between a Manx Electric Railway car and a horse-drawn carriage full of holidaymakers on a day out. Eight other people were injured in the collision on the railway crossing at Ramsey. And two men have been lost in a fishing lugger disaster off Port Erin. They were the 30-year-old boatman, Joseph Shimmin, and a visitor from Manchester, 19-year-old Mr Henry Nordlinger. They left on a fishing trip at six o'clock in the morning and did not return. After a widespread search they were presumed to have drowned. A fund set up for the fisherman's family has raised £120.

SNAEFELL MINE TO CLOSE

Snaefell Mine has had to close down. A heavy fall of rock in the main shaft in September has sealed off the lower levels of the mine workings and efforts to shift it have failed. Nearly 50 jobs have been lost. Mine officials say a rich vein of ore is still there but now out of reach. There is more hopeful news in the Island's mining industry, however. New lead mines have been opened at Glen Rushen.

1908 NEWS IN BRIEF

JANUARY
2 - Opening of extension to Onchan School.
9 - Bishop Drury enthroned at St George's Church.

MARCH
16 - Public meeting of protest against Sunday sailings, at the Grand Theatre, Douglas.
23 - Launch of new turbine steamer *Ben-my-Chree* at Barrow.

APRIL
30 - Presentation to Miss M.L. Wood, founder of the Guild, of 200 guineas on the completion of 50 years' connection with musical affairs in the Isle of Man.

JUNE
1 - Territorials at Peel. Arrival of first contingent.
5 - Death of fisherman Edward Fargher of Cregneash, poet in both Manx and English, and collector of Manx folklore

JULY
1 - Henry Bloom Noble Baths, Victoria Street, formally opened.
15 - Arrival of the *Ben-my-Chree* after a record trip of 2h. 18min. from the Mersey to Douglas Head.
18 - Weekly service of steamship sailings between Peel and Belfast inaugurated for the summer months.

AUGUST
12 - Memorial Tablet to commemorate Sir William Hillary, founder of the Royal National Lifeboat Institution, presented by Mr Samuel Norris and associates to Douglas Corporation. The Tablet has been affixed to the Shelter on the Harris Promenade.
23 - Death of Dr John Clague of Crofton, Castletown, collector of old Manx tunes and songs. He was assisted by Deemster F. Gill and W.H. Gill, resulting in the publishing of the 'Manx National Song Book' in 1896.

24 - Steamer *Ben-my-Chree* in collision in Mersey. She will be out of action for rest of season.
26 - Bazaar in aid of Peel Church Spire Fund opened by Lord Raglan.
29-31 Visit of section of the Atlantic Fleet to Douglas Bay. Visit marred by severe storm conditions.

SEPTEMBER
1 - Closing of Snaefell Mine.
21 - Consecration of new chancel in St Matthew's Church, Douglas.
22 - Auto-Cycle Races held at St John's. 1, Marshall (Triumph) 2, C.R. Collier (Matchless).
24 - Royal Automobile Club's 'Four-inch' Race. 1. Watson (Hutton) 2, Guinness (Darracq) 3, George (Darracq).

OCTOBER
17 - Mr Noah Moore's Choir came second at the Blackpool Music Festival. Mr Looney's Isle of Man Choir was placed fifth.

NOVEMBER
3 - Opening of Glen Rushen Lead Mines.
17 - H.B. Noble Trustees wipe out long-standing debt of £18,000 of Noble's Isle of Man Hospital.
19 - Opening of grand new organ in Victoria Street Church, Douglas. The instrument cost £1,200.
24 - First meeting of newly-elected House of Keys. Mr A.W. Moore C.V.O. re-instated as Speaker.

DECEMBER
26 and
28 - Douglas Choral Union perform the comic opera 'Pepita'.

MOTOR RACING : REVIEWING THE SITUATION

National newspapers which branded the Isle of Man the "Isle of Manslaughter" have been proved scaremongers. The most controversial autocar race ever, preceded by dire warnings of impending disaster, has been held without catastrophic disaster. There have been some nasty accidents but, fortunately, without serious injury. Afterwards, Prince Francis of Teck, told race fans at the prize presentations that they should be singing the hymn "Now thank we all our God."

The campaign against September's Autocar T.T. was led by the *Times* of London. Ever since the Royal Automobile Club introduced trials to the Island in 1904, and then the Autocar T.T. in 1905, there have been vast technological strides as a result of the engineering challenges posed by the races. It was argued earlier this year that the cars had become so powerful that they could wreak havoc among spectators if there were accidents. The campaign's intention was to stop autocar racing over the 37 mile Snaefell Mountain Course. The Manx authorities dismissed the fears as scaremongering and the R.A.C. decided to press ahead. However, it seems now that the R.A.C. will withdraw from organising the event for a while to allow all this scaremongering to die down. This has the support of the motor manufacturers.

Within the Manx tourist industry this will be a sad blow though it must be said that the number of spectators arriving here has not matched the predictions which encouraged Tynwald to authorise road closing for the first time in 1904. Autocycle racing, meanwhile, has started to develop a greater appeal. When the Auto-Cycle Union introduced their own trials in 1905 there was only a very limited response, but since the launch of the Auto-Cycle T.T. in 1907 there has been a greater interest in the two-wheeled sport.

Farmers and church leaders, in particular, will welcome a reduction in racing. In return for compensation, farmers have tolerated the widespread slaughter by speeding autocars of poultry accustomed to roaming country highways without being molested. What has antagonised farmers has been the organising of racing in late September which has clashed with harvest time. Disruptions then, including the use of farm horses for the movement of course equipment when they are needed for harvesting, led to farmers getting racing transferred

An exciting chase at Cronk ny Mona in this year's T.T.
(R. and L. Kelly Collection)

to May-June in 1907. But this year the Autocar T.T. was held again in September.

Church opposition stems from the noisy practising and wild and dangerous driving by race supporters on Sundays. This has disrupted church services and affected attendance. From the outset, race officials of both the R.A.C and A-C.U. have been under pressure to prevent the peace of the Sabbath being broken. One famous autocar driver was actually banned from the 1906 race because his mechanician took a car out for a test drive early one Sunday morning. This has had some effect, but restraining over-enthusiastic race fans is proving more difficult. Locals refer to their activities as "scorching" and such behaviour is alienating the support of those who do not gain a direct benefit from tourism. It is happening even in the busy centre of Douglas. Horses are being startled by the noise and women say their Sunday dresses are being ruined.

Woodlands, 14th September, 1905. Two of the Napier entries on the start line for the first Car T.T.
(R. and L. Kelly Collection)

A competitor speeds safely over Sulby Bridge in the 1906 T.T.
(R. and L. Kelly Collection)

Not so lucky at Sulby is this Rover which came to grief a year later. *(R. and L. Kelly Collection)*

"Scorching" by enthusiasts on four or two wheels over dry earthen roads tends to throw up huge clouds of dust. On race days a special milky-white acidic compound is poured on difficult sections. This tends to stop the dust rising temporarily, albeit at the price of irritating eyes and burning clothes if it does get airborne. The ultimate solution, of course, is the provision of better road surfaces, either through covering the roads with compacted loose stones or laying tarmacadam. This is being done gradually, partly financed by the R.A.C., and suggests that racing will stimulate widespread improvements for all road users eventually. Meanwhile, hard racing on wet roads tends to rut them badly. Highway staff have to rake them manually to break down the mounds of mud. So deep can the ruts become that autocyclists say that if they get their wheels trapped in them they find it difficult to escape.

The Auto-Cycle T.T. causes less inconvenience because it is run over a shorter course with a start in the centre of St John's. Even this, however, has its critics. Some people believe that public roads should not be shut for any reason. The result is that roads are not closed for practising and riders have to accept the risk of encountering private traffic. Carters of fresh fish from Peel to Douglas in the early mornings insist they

have a right of movement. The Autocycle T.T. is becoming so popular that the course is becoming overcrowded and, with speeds increasing year by year, the A-C.U. may move the race to the more challenging Snaefell Course. It would have been used already but for the inability of belt-drive machines to complete the mountain climb from Ramsey. Even on the short course, there used to be problems in ascending Creg Willey's. Many riders had to jump off their machines and run alongside them or give them pedal assistance. Now the latter is forbidden and the more powerful machines that have been developed can make the ascent without assistance.

Since the R.A.C. have decided to abandon racing on the Isle of Man, at least for the foreseeable future, a greater interest in the two-wheeled sport has become apparent. Autocycle manufacturers are showing increasing interest in entering their machines and displaying to the ordinary man in the street this cheaper form of transport. It is also apparent that the Manx people seem to have a greater affinity with the budget-racers than the millionaires and socialites who dominate autocar racing. Certainly, all the indications are that the Auto-Cycle T.T. will attract crowds in greater numbers each year - and that is what all the noise and dust is about!

Two cars speeding on the Mountain road during the 1906 T.T.

(R. and L. Kelly Collection)

TYNWALD MATTERS : THE WASTED YEARS

The wasted years! Is that how future generations of Manx men and women will view the five years that have elapsed since the so-called reforming Keys assembled in 1903? Over those years petitions advocating various aspects of constitutional reform have been submitted by the Keys to both the Governor and the Home Office; indeed deputations have visited both. Yet there seems to be no progress at all, perhaps some say because of the intransigence of Lord Raglan, while others attach more importance to the alleged timidity and lack of courage on the part of Keys' members.

However, all has not been lost - or has it? A year ago the Higher Education Bill at long last was passed. That this is a necessary measure, few would deny. The English Education Act of 1902 had established there is a substantial degree of rationalisation in the old administrative system and it seemed sensible for us to follow, if not slavishly, then perhaps selectively. Here we have first a Board, then a Council of Education with local School Boards, 21 in number, providing free education in every parish and town. The problem became how to marry a form of Higher Education to this existing provision. Was public money to be used to provide new Higher Schools; would the old battle lines between Denominational and Board Schools be withdrawn; would the confusion over names - Higher Grade, Higher Elementary, Grammar, Secondary - be sorted out? And perhaps above all, would the interests on the country districts be subordinated to Douglas?

These concerns guaranteed that when in 1905 a Higher Education Bill was introduced into the Legislative Council the Keys, confronted by what was described as a confused tangle, threw it out unanimously. However, what might be termed the 'educational party' persisted and, undaunted, introduced once more a Higher Education Bill into Council and Keys. It is true to say that this was a revised Bill, that the Draconian approach of the first bill was ameliorated, that issues may have been fudged, but this time there was enough common ground to gain the necessary support. The main provision is that there are to be four authorities, elected by members of the current School Boards, loosely under the authority of the Council of Education. It means that there are now 25 local Boards for a pupil population of about 6,000, an over-indulgence in administrators, perhaps!

But will this bill be effective? The Keys threw out the one attempt to give it some teeth, the clause making the provision of Higher Education compulsory. The powers to establish, maintain and keep efficient a secondary school or schools have been left purely voluntary, and it requires little perception to forecast that little will be done to put into effect the hopes of the originators of the Bill. No doubt the pressure groups that argued 30 years ago against the provision of elementary education will deploy the same, or similar arguments with the financial responsibilities for any ventures being once more the most powerful and emotive issue.

Still, it breaks the log-jam. Education has once again been brought to the fore in Manx politics as people are aware that elsewhere opportunities are being made available through schools for children from all classes. It may well be that the on-going attempts to revise the constitutional structures of the Island, with inevitable attention focussed on the financial arrangements, might be seen as providing an alternative route to tackling the issue which concerns those seeking the advancement of the Manx people.

Two of the competitors in the Car T.T. receive attention and refuel at the Ramsey depots. In the background can be seen Albert Road School, opened in 1905 by the Ramsey School Board.

(R. and L. Kelly Collection)

ELLAN VANNIN SUNK IN THE MERSEY - 35 LOST

The Steam Packet Company steamer *Ellan Vannin* has sunk at the mouth of the River Mersey with the loss of all on board - 35 passengers and crew. In one of the Island's worst maritime tragedies she is believed to have foundered in a matter of minutes in fierce tidal seas whipped up by hurricane force winds. We have this report:

Ellan Vannin, one of the Packet's smallest and oldest ships - she was launched 60 years ago - left Ramsey shortly after one o'clock in the morning for Liverpool. The weather was fine but then a powerful December gale blew up and she became overdue arriving at the Prince's Landing Stage. After 16 hours without news it became clear that there had been a disaster of some kind. Then lifebelts and other flotsam were reported in the sea by the crew of the Formby Lightship. It now appears that Ellan Vannin sank in 30 feet of water a mile Liverpool side of the Mersey Bar, apparently having been caught suddenly in fierce tides and 80 mile an hour winds which overwhelmed her. It is believed that it happened so suddenly nearly everybody went down with her. Only a few bodies have been washed up. Divers have located her on the bottom but she is silting up quickly with sand, and visibility is limited. There is to be a Board of Trade Inquiry and a Disaster Fund has been launched for the many families in the Island who have been bereaved.

DIAMOND KING'S SON KILLED

Earlier in the year Mr Thomas Moore Mylchreest, 25-year-old son of the late Mr Joseph Mylchreest, better known as the Diamond King, of the White House, Kirk Michael, was killed in a motor cycle accident. His Triumph machine was in collision with a farmer's cart on the Poortown Road as he rode home after playing football for Peel. He was one of the best-liked young men in the west of the Island, where he managed the large estate left by his father. Joseph Mylchreest emigrated to South Africa more than 30 years ago and made his fortune in the diamond fields, before settling back in the Island in 1888.

The 'Ellan Vannin' in happier times, seen here leaving the Red Pier, Douglas.
(R. and L. Kelly Collection)

NEW FIRE ENGINE FOR DOUGLAS

Douglas Corporation's new steam fire engine, named "The Raglan", has successfully completed its trials by dealing with a mock fire at the Villiers Hotel. The engine, pulled by three horses, galloped to the scene from the fire station in John Street by way of Prospect Hill, Finch Road, Church Road and Loch Promenade. But it nearly failed to arrive. It collided with a cart, skidded and three firemen were thrown off. They were slightly injured and the fire under the boiler went out. But steam was raised again in nine minutes and large crowds at the Jubilee Clock saw "Raglan's" hoses firing jets of water 150 feet in the air.

FISHERMAN PRESUMED DROWNED

Mystery surrounds the disappearance of a 21-year-old Douglas fisherman, Robert Swindlehurst, while sailing his cutter home from a trip to Port St Mary. He had set sail about 9 pm on a clear summer evening with a crewman, Nathan Jones, after spending

Douglas Corporation's new fire engine named 'The Raglan'.
(R. and L. Kelly Collection)

The funeral cortege of the late Mr A. W. Moore, C.V.O., S.H.K., passes Woodlands on its way to the new Braddan Cemetery. See News in Brief.

(Manx National Heritage)

GAOL FOR SHOOTING POLICEMAN

A German shoemaker working in Douglas has been sentenced to 10 years' penal servitude at the November Court of General Gaol for the attempted murder by shooting of a Manx policeman. It was alleged that 31-year-old Alfred Andersen fired two pistol shots at P.C. Stanley Cain on Central Promenade after being challenged by the officer who was enquiring about an injury to a dog. Andersen pulled the gun from his coat pocket and shot P.C. Cain twice in the head. Later, after being cornered by a crowd near the Peveril Hotel, he was disarmed and arrested by Constables W. Charles Cain and Henry Watterson. P.C. Charles Cain escaped injury when Andersen shot at him. The gun misfired. P.C. Stanley Cain is recovering well from his head wounds.

some time in a public house. Jones fell asleep leaving Swindlehurst at the tiller - and awoke in blazing sunshine next morning with the cutter aground near Santon Head - and no sign of Swindlehurst. He is presumed to have fallen overboard and drowned.

SUFFRAGISTS CAMPAIGN ON ISLAND

Suffragists who have been causing disruption in England with their fierce campaigning for votes for women, have been visiting the Isle of Man - and causing more trouble. During the summer they have held public meetings in Douglas, Ramsey and Port Erin - where rowdy audiences of young men on holiday gave them a hot reception. At the Ramsey meeting fighting broke out and the suffragists were roughly handled. Among the leaders of the Movement in Britain is Mrs Emmeline Pankhurst and her daughters. Mrs Pankhurst is of Manx descent, her mother being born in Lonan. She was married in Braddan.

GOOD HERRING SEASON

Both Peel and Port St Mary have reported heavy catches of herring being landed during the summer. At Port St Mary some thirty boats have been engaged in the fishing and the herring have been fetching good prices. From sixty to eighty persons - mostly Irish lassies - have been busy cleaning and curing the heaps of fish landed and preparing them for export. Visitors to the port looked on the hive of activity with great interest from day to day.

CONTROVERSY OVER OLD AGE PENSIONS

Throughout the year there have been stormy debates in Tynwald over proposals that elderly people in the Isle of Man should be paid old age pensions by the Government, as they are in Britain. There have been strong demands for the pensions at public meetings throughout the Island. But in Tynwald the Lieutenant-Governor, Lord Raglan said there would have to be new taxation to raise the necessary revenue. Members were told an income tax might have to be introduced. The latest news is that a House of Keys Committee, which was deputed to interview the Governor, has reported that His Excellency could not see his way to introducing a pension scheme in the Isle of Man.

1909 NEWS IN BRIEF

JANUARY
12 - At a meeting of the House of Keys, a motion reaffirming the proposal for Reform of the Constitution, as contained in the petition to the Home Secretary, was carried by 18 votes to 6.

APRIL
22 - Several actions against the Manx Electric Railway for damages caused to passengers (visitors) injured in an accident at Ramsey last September were heard, and successfully sustained.

23 - Villa Marina house and grounds offered to Douglas by Noble's Trustees for £60,000 in Corporation Bonds at 3½ per cent; the Trustees to spend £20,000 on buildings, and £40,000 of the money to be ear-marked by the Trustees for educational and charitable purposes. Offer provisionally accepted by the Finance Committee of the Council.

30 - Deadlock between the Keys and Council on the Lieutenant-Governor's taxation proposals, owing to the refusal of the Lieutenant-Governor to indicate the direction in which the additional revenue from the imposition of spirit and tobacco duties would be devoted. Next day the Keys gave way on the understanding that the Lieutenant-Governor should waive his objections to an Estate Duties Bill, and agree to submit an Old Age Pensions Scheme.

JULY
15 - Foundation stone of St Andrew's (Presbyterian) new School laid in Finch Road.

AUGUST
3 - Conductor on Manx Elecric Railway killed when he fell from the footboard on to the metals between the car and trailer.

25 - Foundation stones of Port Erin New Wesleyan Church laid.

SEPTEMBER
23 - International Auto-Cycle Race won by H.A. Collier on a Matchless.

OCTOBER
16 - Douglas Male Choristers secured First Prize at Blackpool Music Festival.

21 - Visit of Rechabite High Officers. Meetings held throughout the Island.

NOVEMBER
12 - Death of Mr A.W. Moore, C.V.O., Speaker of the House of Keys, at the age of 56 years.

24 - Election of Mr Dalrymple Maitland, J.P., C.P., to the Speakership of the House of Keys.

DECEMBER
27 - Opera 'H.M.S. Pinafore' performed by Douglas Choral Union at the Gaiety Theatre.

MR ARTHUR WILLIAM MOORE, M.A., C.V.O., S.H.K.

The untimely death of Mr Arthur William Moore, Speaker of the House of Keys, on 12th November was not entirely unexpected. Aged 56 years, he had not enjoyed good health for some time. When the House of Keys re-assembled after the summer recess the Speaker, though obviously very ill, felt it his duty to be in his place. He conducted the business before the House in his usual clear fashion; but this was to be his last public appearance.

Arthur William Moore was the surviving son of the late Mr William Fine Moore, of Cronkbourne, near Douglas. Mr W.F. Moore inherited the famous sailcloth factory which had been established by his father, the late Mr James Moore. Begun in Duke Street about 1790, it moved to Wellington Street, then known as Factory Lane. The manufactory then moved to larger premises at Tromode where 150 workers were employed in the spinning and weaving of flax. Sailcloth was a speciality and lucrative orders were received from the Admiralty and the Mercantile Marine; one contract was to supply sails for Brunel's Great Britain. Cronkbourne Village, with its 42 dwellings, was created for the workers which is the largest example of industrial housing in the Isle of Man.

(Manx National Heritage)

Born at Cronkbourne House in 1853, Arthur William had a privileged upbringing and was educated at Rugby School and Trinity College, Cambridge, where he specialised in history and gained his M.A. degree. At university he joined in sporting activities, excelling in rowing and rugby football, being awarded a 'blue' for the latter. During vacations he travelled widely both in Britain and Europe; on a visit to Rome a friend gained him an audience with the Pope. At home he was a frequent visitor to Andreas rectory where his uncle the Ven. Joseph Christian Moore, Archdeacon of Man, resided.

On returning to the Isle of Man he joined his father in the management of the Tromode manufactory, taking over completely in the 1880s, following the death of his father. He formed the Cronkbourne Cricket Club for his workpeople and the club was soon able to hold its own throughout the Island. However, by the end of the century the competition from steamships was playing havoc with the future of sailing craft and Mr Moore very reluctantly decided to close the Tromode works. He made generous arrangements to secure a livelihood for his employees.

For the 1883 General Election, Mr Moore offered himself as a candidate for Middle Sheading and was successfully returned. He was then aged 30, and retained the confidence of the electors in subsequent elections. He was most conscientious in his duties and, while caring for the interests of his constituents, was more national than parochial in his outlook. Certainly he was on the side of national progress and the uplifting of the people. While not noted as an orator, he was an effective speaker respected for his sound common-sense.

Mr Moore was exceedingly jealous of the rights and privileges of the House of Keys. When it came into conflict with the Lieutenant-Governor and Council, he tenaciously championed the House. But he was a tactful man and his wise counsel frequently avoided friction and deadlock. He was an ardent educationalist and was a strong advocate of secondary education and the centralisation of the Manx educational system. On the vexed question of Constitutional Reform he generally supported the agitation, but it was well-known that he was not a 'whole-hogger' in the matter - he hoped, as it were, that by pressing for all the points in the reform petition, the House would secure just and reasonable concessions. Great as Mr Moore's services were to the Legislature, his principal claim to distinction is in regard to his publications dealing with the Isle of Man. His interest in the Manx language, folk lore, and country traditions resulted in three volumes of the 'Manx Note Book' being published between 1885 and 1887. Prior to this he had published 'Place Names and Surnames of the Isle of Man' having gone through all the parish registers. In 1889 he published his 'Climate of the Isle of Man' based on his own observations at Cronkbourne. His meticulous researches involved consulting the Journals of the self-elected House of Keys and visiting Knowsley Hall to consult the Derby papers relating to the Isle of Man. This resulted in the publication in 1900 of 'The History of the Isle of Man' in two volumes, now accepted as the standard history of the Island. This was followed by a school version for the benefit of Manx children. In 1903 his 'Manx Worthies' was published which is also a valuable source of reference.

A devout Anglican, Mr Moore married Louisa Elizabeth, daughter of the Ven. J. Hughes-Games, Archdeacon of Man. At his home, Woodbourne House, he entertained many eminent vistors to the Island. A frequent visitor was T.E. Brown, following his retirement to Ramsey. Mr Moore's mother continues to live at Cronkbourne House and it was here that King Edward V11 and his entourage were entertained during their visit in 1902. Mr Speaker was foremost in the arrangements, and following the royal visit the Commandership of the Victorian Order was conferred upon him by the Sovereign, much to the delight of all Manxmen.

HERE IS THE NEWS: 1910

THE *ELLAN VANNIN* : RESULT OF INQUIRY

The Board of Trade inquiry held on the 8th, 9th and 10th March, into the loss of the Steam Packet Company passenger steamer *Ellan Vannin* has decided that she sank after being swamped by huge seas. Theories that she might have sunk after collision with another vessel have been discounted. We have this report:

Ellan Vannin sank with the loss of all 35 on board early on a dark December morning last year just after passing the Mersey bar on her way into Liverpool. Witnesses at the three-day inquiry, which was held in Liverpool, said the weather was the worst ever seen in the Mersey channel and the 60-year-old vessel, although seaworthy, succumbed to giant waves breaking over her stern. She sank quickly, stern first, and her bows broke off. The collision theory started when a bottle was washed up with a message in it purporting to be from a member of the crew, saying that they were sinking after being hit by another ship. But this has now been discounted as a hoax. The bodies of 18 of the 35 passengers and crew were washed up after the disaster. No others have been found. The wreck is now to be blown up to prevent it becoming a navigational hazard.

The Disaster Fund has raised over £13,000 with contributions received from all parts of the world and including £1,000 from the Steam Packet Company. A Conference of members of the Liverpool and Douglas committees, that had a hand in the collection of subscriptions, has already met in Liverpool and approved a scheme of helping the many dependents of those lost in the tragedy.

HOUSES FOR THE PEOPLE

Earlier in the year, Douglas Corporation was given permission by Tynwald to borrow £3,000 for the construction of artisans' dwellings in Lord Street. There will be seven double tenement buildings in the first phase of the work, which is being carried out following the extensive demolition of the centre of old Douglas. The tenements are intended largely for people whose homes were

An artist's impression of the 'Ellan Vannin' battling her way into the River Mersey.
(R. and L. Kelly Collection)

pulled down and the rents, of between six shillings and seven shillings and sixpence a week, are for those on low earnings.

KING GEORGE V PROCLAIMED

On 6th May the Island, and indeed the whole of the British Empire, was shocked to hear of the sudden death of King Edward V11. Doctors announced that His Majesty had died of pneumonia. The following day, his son George V took the oath as King in London. At home this was followed by King George being proclaimed monarch in traditional fashion from the top of Tynwald Hill. The Governor, Lord Raglan, drove to the ceremony in an open coach, in fine weather, all the way from Douglas to St John's. He and the other Island officials then took their oaths of allegiance to the new king. The official memorial service to King Edward V11 was held in St George's Church on 20th May, Similar services were held throughout the Island.

T.T. RACE OBJECTOR

The start of the 1910 T.T. Motor Cycle Race on the St John's course was delayed because of a one-man protest against road closures and noise by local farmer Mr Arthur Matthews. He drove his dogcart into the road near the start, partially blocking the road, and refused to move. There was trouble immediate-

Some of the contingent of 4,000 Territorials arriving at Ramsey for their summer camp at Milntown. *(Midwood/Simkiss Philatelic)*

ly as enraged spectators took the law into their own hands and tried to force him to move. They surrounded the dogcart while he tried to fight them off with his horsewhip. But the crowd manhandled him and his vehicle off the road and the races were able to proceed.

TERRITORIAL ARMY UNITS ON ISLAND

The biggest contingents of Britain's citizen soldiers, the Territorial Army, ever seen in the Isle of Man have been at their annual training camps at Peel and Ramsey. There were more than 12,000 officers and men from the T.A. battalions of a number of Yorkshire infantry regiments. 8,000 men were in camp at Knockaloe in July and 4,000 at Milntown, along with more than 100 horses and many tons of baggage and equipment. The annual camps are now a major boost for the Island's economy.

DOUBLE SHOOTING IN RAMSEY

Two people have died in a double shooting at the Crown Hotel in Ramsey. Police say the landlord, Mr John Pearson, a former British Army cavalryman from Yorkshire, killed 18-year-old barmaid Ellen Loughran with a shotgun while his wife was at Sunday service. The body was found in the hotel yard. Police later found Pearson upstairs suffering from serious gunshot wounds to the head, having turned the gun on himself. He died later in hospital.

Charlie Collier (Matchless) negotiating the streets of Peel. Averaging over 50 m.p.h. this year, Collier is the first rider to win two T.T. Races. Next year the races are being transferred to the more challenging Mountain Course.

(Mannin Collections)

THREE DROWN IN HARBOUR

Mystery surrounds the death by drowning of three people in Douglas Harbour. An inquest jury has returned an open verdict. The dead were 18-year-old Douglas shop assistant Amy Cain and 19-year-old ship's steward Lewis Matthews, who were keeping company, and William McCulloch, an iron fitter, of Llandudno, North Wales. The bodies were found at intervals over three days but no evidence has been found as to how they came to fall into the harbour

August ended with severe weather terminating in a great storm which interfered with shipping, and resulted in the total wreck of the Peel nickey *Fear Not* in Port Erin Bay, with the loss of two lives viz. William Radcliffe and John Crellin. The Peel lifeboat effected a fine rescue of a boating party off Michael on the same day. The Castletown, Douglas, Port St Mary and Port Erin lifeboats were also called out to render assistance to vessels in distress.

1910 NEWS IN BRIEF

JANUARY
30 - Douglas Town Council agree to purchase Villa Marina estate.

FEBRUARY
23 - At the annual meeting of Noble's (Isle of Man) Hospital, it was stated that the New Hospital, on the Hills Estate, was in course of erection. and would be completed within two years.

MARCH
3 - Cardle Wesleyan Methodist Chapel opened.
8 - Board of Trade Inquiry into the loss of the *Ellan Vannin* opened in Liverpool.
12 - Consignment of 50 carcases of Chinese pork arrived in Douglas to be cured and exported. Cargoes arrive almost weekly after being refused admission into England on technical grounds. Considerable opposition to this activity both locally and in the House of Commons.
18 - Scheme to widen base of Victoria Pier turned down by the Governor on financial grounds.

APRIL
5 - Old Age Pension Bill 'hung up' by Legislative Council at 1st Reading.

MAY
5 - The renovated St George's Church was opened by the Archbishop of York.
6 - Death of King Edward V11
11 - George V proclaimed King from the summit of Tynwald Hill.

JUNE
1 - Manx butchers decline to purchase cattle that are not insured or guaranteed by the farmers.
10 - Mr B.E. Sargeaunt appointed Treasurer of the Isle of Man, Clerk to the Council, Secretary to the Lieutenant-Governor, Registrar General and Superintendent of Public Buildings.
18 - Farmers' Club decide to form a company to carry on retail meat business as a result of butchers refusing to accept cattle that are not guaranteed.

JULY
25 - The *Snaefell*, built at Birkenhead, taken over by the Steam Packet Company. She is designed for the winter service between Douglas and Liverpool.

AUGUST
14 - Double shooting tragedy at Ramsey.

OCTOBER
2 - Death of the Hon. J.K. Ward, of Montreal, Canada. A native of Peel, he was a great benefactor to the Island. His will provides annuities to Manx charities and a perpetual subscription of £10 a year to the poor of Peel and Patrick.

NOVEMBER
8 - House of Keys pass by a unanimous vote that the Committee set up to look into Constitutional Reform should consider what further steps should be taken to advance the matter.
23 - Douglas Town Council reject a proposal for the Sunday delivery of letters during the winter months.
29 - Christmas Fair held at The Palace to raise funds for New Church Room at Kirk Braddan.

ELLAN VANNIN DISASTER : FULL DETAILS

Now that the Board of Trade has published the result of its inquiry into the loss of the *Ellan Vannin,* further details have come to light. It was shortly after 1 a.m. on Friday, 3rd December last year, that the steamer left Ramsey bound for Liverpool carrying passengers, mails and cargo. There was a strong breeze blowing from the north-west but nothing to deter the *Ellan Vannin* from sailing. But after about an hour and a half the wind very suddenly increased to almost hurricane force with gusts very rarely experienced in the Irish Sea. The sea ran in a fearful fashion, but as it was aft of the *Ellan Vannin*, no anxiety was felt at the headquarters of the Steam Packet Company. The ship had survived many such ordeals in the past. When, however, telegrams arrived later on the day announcing that the *Ellan Vannin* had not reached her destination, anxiety was expressed, though the officials at Douglas hoped that nothing worse had happened to the steamer than a compulsory run for shelter. But by five o'clock it was realised that a serious situation had arisen and company manager Mr W. M. Corkill summoned the directors to a meeting.

At about seven o'clock a further telegram was received at the office which caused serious concern. It reported that during the day the crew of the Formby Lightship had seen floating in the Mersey Channel lifebuoys inscribed *"Ellan Vannin"*, together with several dead sheep and a quantity of turnips. More disquieting still was the picking up by the lightship crew of a mail basket which was sent to the Birkenhead Post Office and was found to contain letters despatched from Ramsey. The news spread quickly throughout the Island by word of mouth and by telephone. This caused general consternation and mourning though friends and relatives clung to the hope that the vessel was still afloat somewhere in a derelict condition. The steamer carried no deck cargo, so that the flotsam in question must have been dislodged from the holds and saloons of the vessel. Nevertheless, it was not until Saturday afternoon that all hope was abandoned.

Boats of the Mersey Docks Board located the wreck in 30 feet of water about a mile or more on the Liverpool side of the Mersey Bar. The *Ellan Vannin*, it would seem, rode into the Mersey Channel before an 80 mile an hour gale. She probably passed the Bar Lightship at 6.45 a.m. and then met the outgoing tide. At the enquiry it was stated that the sea was of a height of 24 feet with the weather the worst ever experienced in that vicinity. The ship was swept by these mountainous seas which washed away her aft companionway and filled the rear of the vessel. This caused her to sink by the stern, leaving her bows out of the water. While in this position, the pounding of the sea would account for the bows being broken off as described by the divers. The exceptional circumstances does not imply there was any structural weakness. The catastrophe was so sudden that there was probably no time for those on board even to put on lifebelts, which accounts for all 35 on board being lost.

The *Ellan Vannin* began life in 1860 as an iron paddle-steamer built for the Steam Packet in Glasgow and named *Mona's Isle II*. In 1883 she was converted to a twin-screw vessel of 399 tons and became the main mail carrier from Ramsey to Whitehaven, Liverpool and Scotland. She could carry 299 passengers plus cargo and was considered an exceptionally fine ship in bad weather, carrying out the daily mail contract when many other vessels remained in harbour. A Steam Packet spokesman has said that the name '*Ellan Vannin*' will never be used again by the Company.

The 14 passengers who lost their lives were as follows:

Mr MARK H. JOUGHIN, of Ballwhannel, Bride, unmarried. A successful northside farmer and popular local preacher, he was on his way to America to administer a valuable estate in Minnesota which belonged to his late uncle.

Mr W. E. HIGGINBOTHAM, Trafalgar Hotel, Ramsey. He was on his way to Manchester for medical treatment and leaves a widow and two children.

Mr and Mrs HEATON JOHNSON, Beaconsfield Tower, Ramsey. They were returning to Madras where Mr Johnson held an important post in the Civil Service. They leave three children.

Mr R. NEWELL, a stonemason from Surrey working on the new Roman Catholic Church in Ramsey.

Mr W. WILLIAMS, from London. Also a stonemason working on the new church

Mrs W. CRIX and child. Wife of a Ramsey fisherman.

Miss NELLIE FISHER, servant, Queen's Hotel, Ramsey. Leaving to take up new position in England.

Mr E. J. BLEVIN, Little Switzerland, Douglas. An incorporated accountant with offices in Douglas and Liverpool. Ran evening classes for Higher Education Board for the Eastern District.

Mr T. H. QUAYLE of Pear Tree Cottage, Andreas. A steward for the Archdeacon, he was on his way to Liverpool for medical treatment. Leaves a widow and two young children.

Mrs JOHN ALLEN and son. From Hawthorn Cottage, Maughold. Leaves a husband and children.

Miss LOUISE FINDLAY. A domestic servant travelling to Kent to visit her sick mother.

The following are the crew members who left 18 widows and 70 children:

JAMES TEARE, master, who rose from an ordinary seaman and took command of the Ellan Vannin in 1904. He leaves a wife and four children.

JOHN CRAINE, first mate, from Douglas. Joined the Steam Packet Company in 1881 as a galley boy. Leaves a widow and four children.

JOHN KINLEY, second mate, from Surby, Port Erin. Unmarried.

J. CUNNINGHAM, carpenter, who leaves a wife and five children. Settled on the Island after working on the Chicken Rock Lighthouse when it was under construction.

JOHN COOKE, a seaman from Peel. A member of the Peel lifeboat crew who rescued 23 lives when the St George went ashore near Peel Castle some 20 years ago. He leaves a grown-up family.

J. BENSON, a seaman from Ramsey who leaves a wife and five children.

THOMAS CORKISH, a seaman from Ramsey and member of the Ramsey lifeboat crew. He leaves a wife and five children.

WILLIAM KELLY, a seaman from Castletown. Sailed as a second mate in the summer. He leaves a wife and six children.

JAMES CRAWLEY, a seaman from Douglas. Sailed on the Ellan Vannin for many years and as second mate last summer. Leaves a wife and eight children.

ALFRED CLAGUE, a seaman who also held a first officer's certificate. Long-serving crew member who leaves a wife and five children.

EDWARD BELLISS, chief engineer. From Liverpool he leaves a widow and one child.

FRED CRAINE, second engineer, from Douglas. He leaves a widow and one child.

SAMUEL RYDINGS, a donkeyman, from South Quay, Douglas. He leaves a wife and four children.

W. SHIMMIN, a donkeyman from Ramsey who leaves a widow and four children.

WALTER CANNELL, a fireman from Douglas who leaves a widow.

JOHN TAUBMAN, a fireman from Big-Well Street, Douglas, who leaves a wife and two children.

JOSEPH CRELLIN, a fireman from Glenvine. Closely connected with Crosby Methodist Chapel where he was a Sunday School teacher. A staunch Rechabite, he leaves a widow and three young sons.

J. STUBBS, chief steward. From Liverpool he leaves a widow and six children.

BERT HOLLAND, second steward. From Onchan, he leaves a wife and one child.

EDWARD BURKE, a cook, from Douglas, leaving his wife and two children.

MRS CALLISTER, stewardess. A widow, she leaves a young daughter.

A CHRONICLE OF

WRECK OF THE ELLAN VANNIN

MRS HEATON JOHNSON
(Passenger)

J. CUNNINGHAM
(Carpenter)

Captain JAMES TEARE

F. CRAINE
(2nd Engineer)

HEATON JOHNSON
(Passenger)

MARK M. JOUGHIN
(Passenger)

MRS CRIX
(Passenger)

WM. KELLY
(Seaman)

BERT HOLLAND
(Steward)

W. CANNELL
(Fireman)

S. RYDINGS
(Donkeymanr)

J. CRELLIN
(Fireman)

W. SHIMMIN
(Donkeyman)

A. CLAGUE
(Seaman)

THOS. QUAYLE
(Passenger)

J. CRAWLEY
(Seaman)

E. BELLISS
(1st Engineer)

THE ELLAN VANNIN
ENTERING RAMSEY HARBOUR
Built as a paddle steamer by Ted & McGregor, Glasgow, in the year 1860.
Lengthened and converted into a Twin Screw in the year 1883.
FOUNDERED AT THE MERSEY BAR, FRIDAY, DECEMBER 3rd 1909, AND ALL ON BOARD LOST.

J. KINLEY
(2nd Mate)

W. E. HIGGINBOTHAM
(Passenger)

Mrs COLLISTER
(Stewardess)

Miss FISHER
(Passenger)

J. BENSON
(Seaman)

E. J. BLEVIN
(Passenger)

T. CORKISH
(Seaman)

J. COOKE
(Seaman)

J. TAUBMAN
(Fireman)

J. CRAINE
(1st Mate)

From the R. and L. Kelly Collection

HERE IS THE NEWS: 1911

HEAD CONSTABLE: 'NOT GUILTY'

A highly controversial 'not guilty' verdict has been returned by a Court of General Gaol jury on charges of forgery brought against the Island's former Head Constable, 72-year-old Colonel William Freeth. The verdict has been publicly criticised as a travesty of justice. We have this report:

It was only two months after his retirement in July as Head Constable with 23 years service, that Colonel Freeth was sensationally arrested by his successor, Colonel Madoc. Originally he faced charges of embezzlement and forgery involving more than £700 of public funds. The charges related to contracts for the purchase of police uniforms in 1905, 1906 and 1907. After his arrest Colonel Freeth, a Member of the Victorian Order, was committed for trial but at a subsequent court of criminal inquiry set up to decide if there was a case to answer, a jury decided there was not enough evidence on the embezzlement charges. At General Gaol a week later another jury found him not guilty on the forgery charges, again for lack of evidence. Colonel Freeth appeared ill and careworn during the proceedings and there was much sympathy for him - which seemed to sway the jury according to Reverend Wilson Stuart, of Rosemount Wesleyan Church in Douglas. In a forthright sermon Mr. Stuart said the verdict was a condemnation of Manx justice and the Island was eternally disgraced by what was a judicial falsehood in favour of a guilty person held up as a poor old man for whom hearts should be full of pity.

MAN DIES AFTER FIGHT
A man has died following a fist fight over a game of cards at the Mona Social Club in Douglas. He was 38-year-old greengrocer Eugene Charles Agnew, of Albany Street, Douglas, who died from internal injuries after leaving the club, which is below the Walpole Hotel. The man he fought with, 26-year-old wholesale newsagent Benjamin Howarth, was arrested and charged with manslaughter. But the charge was dropped after the inquest decided there was no evidence to show that Agnew's injuries were a direct result of the fight.

T.T. RIDER KILLED
Practising for the T.T. motorcycle races held in June was marred by the death of the first rider in the series which began in 1907. Nineteen-year-old Victor Surridge from Essex, a member of the Rudge-Whitworth team, died instantly from head injuries when he crashed into the rock face at the exit from Glen Helen. Team officials based at the Glen Helen Hotel rushed to give assistance but there was little they could do. As a mark of respect the Rudge-Whitworth team was withdrawn from the races. The tragedy coincides with the motor bikes changing to the Snaefell Mountain Course pioneered by the cars, and although Creg Willey's was part of the St John's Circuit, the jury at the inquest stated they believed the Snaefell Course was too long and had too many bends for riders to learn.

The move to the Snaefell Mountain Course has also seen the introduction of a Junior race for the popular $2^1/2$ h.p. machines. The race was won by a Humber at 42 m.p.h. The Senior Race was a clean sweep for the Indian team from America.

CROWDS DISAPPOINTED BY AVIATOR
The summer season began with a hectic round of attractions organised by Douglas Corporation to celebrate its Jubilee as a municipality and the Coronation of King George V. There were great demonstrations of public boards, Sunday schools etc. to which were added an extensive programme of athletics, motor racing and concerts. At night time the whole extent of the Promenade was lit by electric light fairy lanterns, power being supplied by the Manx Electric Railway Company. One of the highlights, planned for Tynwald Day, was to be an 80 mile race round the Island

Following the move to the Snaefell Mountain Course, Quarterbridge Road was chosen for the start and finish of the motorcycle T.T. Races. Here machines line up for the start of the Senior race. (Mannin Collections)

Famous aviator, Claude Graham-White at the controls of his Farman biplane.
(Keig Collection)

Taking off from the newly-opened Noble's Park, Claude Graham-White achieves the first flight in Manx skies.
(Keig Collection)

between the Steam Packet's *Ben my Chree* and two aeroplanes transported to the Island specially for the occasion. An aerodrome was set up in the newly-opened Noble's Park. Only one of the aeroplanes, a Farman biplane piloted by the famous aviator Claude Graham-White, managed to take off for the race but wind conditions were so treacherous that the pilot had to turn back after reaching Onchan Head. This meant that many thousands occupying vantage points around the Island were to be bitterly disappointed. Nevertheless, Mr Graham-White was back in the air later in the day and was able to escort the *Ben my Chree* back into Douglas. At the Fancy Dress Parade held in the Palace in the evening the pilot was received with thunderous applause.

DOUGLAS TRAMWAYS HIT BY STRIKE

With the celebrations concluded, the Douglas Bay horse trams and the Upper Douglas cable cars were suspended from services for a day. This was the result of drivers and conductors seeking to improve their basic pay of 26s 6d for a week which could be anything up to 114 hours. The Tramways Committee sanctioned new terms which were accepted. The horse tram men gained a 72 hour six day week for 27s, with overtime payment and an extra 4s 6d for Sundays. The cable men also had a reduction in their working week to 72 hours, drivers now being paid 30s and conductors 27s a week; no overtime is available but extra is paid for Sunday working.

The 45 horse trams in operation are highly profitable and carry over 1,750,000 passengers a year, while the 650,000 passengers using the cable cars barely cover the cost of the undertaking. Nevertheless, the combined tramways operation makes a valuable contribution to the relief of the town rate.

RAIL STRIKE HITS VISITOR ARRIVALS

The number of summer visitors arriving in Douglas has been severely hit by the week-long railway strike in the U.K. It also caused a panic exodus by thousands of visitors afraid they would be unable to get home. Saturday, 19th August, saw 16,000 departures while arrivals

1911 CENSUS		
The result of this year's Census shows that the Island's population has fallen during the last ten years from 54,613 to 52,006 - a drop of 2,607 or 4.9%. The number of males recorded is 23,953 compared with 28.071 females. While most districts showed a decrease in population, Douglas increased by 1,952, which was the result of a boundary extension in 1904 when the large Ballaquayle estate was transferred from Onchan. The district figures for 1911 are given below together with changes as a percentage of the 1901 figures.		
DOUGLAS	- 21,183	(+ 10%)
Onchan	- 2,099	(- 46%)
Lonan	- 2,528	(+ 0.6%)
Braddan	- 1,993	(- 8.5%)
Marown	- 835	(- 14.1%)
RAMSEY	- 4,247	(- 9.7%)
Maughold	- 833	(- 6%)
Lezayre	- 1,277	(- 8%)
Andreas	- 1,055	(- 7.8%)
Bride	- 494	(- 8.3%)
Jurby	- 516	(+ 1.9%)
PEEL	- 2,605	(- 21%)
German	- 1,139	(- 7.7%)
Patrick	- 1,521	(- 21%)
Michael	- 843	(- 9%)
Ballaugh	- 647	(- 9%)
CASTLETOWN	- 1,817	(- 7.4%)
Malew	- 1,896	(- 10.1%)
Santon	- 444	(- 5%)
Arbory	- 783	(- 2.2%)
Rushen	- 3,251	(- 1%)
TOTAL	- *52,006*	*(-4.99%)*

were down from 15,000 to 5,000. The British Government sent the Royal Navy cruiser *H.M.S. Warrior* to Douglas in case the strike spread to steamship services. Wireless communications between the *Warrior* and Whitehall were exhibited outside the Government offices and created great interest.

BISHOP CONDEMNS YOUNG VISITORS

The Bishop of Sodor and Man, the Right Reverend Thomas Drury, has made a strong attack on impropriety of behaviour by young visitors to the Island. In a hard-hitting sermon he said young men and women were too familiar with each other. They were to be seen in public places lounging in each other's arms - which was "sickly, unwholesome and fraught with serious peril." This follows criticism by church leaders in the Island of alleged licentious conduct by people attending the free concerts held in public houses in the summer.

REPORT OF MacDONNELL COMMISSION

Finally, the end of the year has seen the long-awaited publication of the details of Constitutional Reform as contained in the report of the MacDonnell Commission. The Commission visited Douglas in May to take evidence after being appointed by Home Secretary Winston Churchill. Chaired by Lord MacDonnell, the Commission agrees that some of the Governor's outright control over Manx Government expenditure should be handed over to Tynwald. However, the report is unlikely to satisfy many reformers who are seeking a greater degree of national autonomy.

Posing for this photograph of 1899 is a group of Foxdale miners together with students of the Mining School. Captain Kitto, principal of the Mining Company, is seen standing on the far right.

(Manx National Heritage)

1911 NEWS IN BRIEF

JANUARY

31 - Deadlock between Keys and Governor and Council over money votes.

FEBRUARY

8 - Tynwald Committee to report on improvement and construction of new roadways and the development of sea fisheries at Peel.

MARCH

1 - Question asked in the House of Commons as to what the Home Office proposes to do over the Manx deadlock. Home Secretary signals approval of the Lieutenant-Governor's action.

2 - Steam Packet Company report 1910 as record year - nearly a million passengers carried. Dividend of 6% approved.

8 - Tynwald Inquiry concerning the development of roadways and fisheries at Port St Mary.

12 - Meeting in Victoria Street Wesleyan Church, Douglas, to protest against free concerts in public houses.

12 - Death of Mr A. N. Laughton, High-Bailiff of Peel and former M.H.K., after a distinguished career.

APRIL

1 - Visit of the Chief Scout, Lieut-General Sir Robert Baden-Powell, the hero of Mafeking in the Boer War. Huge demonstration of nearly 300 Boy Scouts at Glen Helen and entertainment in Gaiety Theatre.

4 - Annual meeting of the IOM Homes for Orphan and Destitute Children. First meeting in new building at Glencrutchery.

6 - Extraordinary meeting of shareholders in the Isle of Man Mining Company (Foxdale Mines), at Liverpool. Resolution passed to wind up the company, which had worked the mines since 1828.

11 - Onchan Village Commissioners apply to Tynwald for powers to construct a separate water supply but meets with strenuous opposition from Douglas.

17 - Scene at St Barnabas Church, Douglas, vestry meeting, upon legality of the presence of ladies at vestry meetings being questioned.

21 - Tynwald agrees to further expenditure on the Douglas water undertaking. Motor speed limit finally abolished.

28 - Primitive Methodist Synod (Liverpool Dist.) begins at Laxey.

MAY

8 - Lieutenant-Governor's financial statement shows increase in revenue; surplus of over £10,000.

9 - Question in House of Commons regarding Old Age Pensions in the Isle of Man. Home Secretary replies that it was a matter for Tynwald but the Commission to visit the Island would consider its financial administration.

JUNE

20 - Public meeting in Town Hall to protest against the perpetuation of alleged illegalities at Cunningham's Holiday Camp. Demands for the Camp to be subject to bye-laws.

22 - Coronation of King George V celebrated throughout Island.

26 - Strike by Steam Packet Company's firemen. Higher wages granted.

28-8th July - Douglas Jubilee Celebrations

JULY

5 - Foundation stone laying for new tower of St German's Church, Peel.

7 - Colonel Madoc appointed Chief Constable of the Isle of Man.

10 - Douglas tramways traffic suspended because of strike.

11 - Tynwald Committee appointed to consider the agricultural industry. New pier sanctioned for Port Erin as a protection for boatmen and fishermen.

17 - Re-union at Ballasalla of home, colonial and foreign Manx residents. Manx National Society formed.

AUGUST

5 - (Saturday) Record arrivals of visitors - 30,000.

5 - Sensational attack by Hall Caine on Manx judges and juries.

7 - (Bank Holiday) Arrival of 17,000 visitors.

10 - Agricultural Society's annual show at the Nunnery.

SEPTEMBER

5 - Tynwald Ceremony at St John's. Belated promulgation of new laws.

12 - Rosemount Church spire completed with suitable ceremony.

13 - Colonel Wm Freeth, ex-Head Constable, arrested on charges of forgery and embezzlement.

OCTOBER

28 - Anti-vaccinators concerning smallpox before High-Bailiff Gell at Castletown. Emphatic protests uttered.

NOVEMBER

13 - MacDonnell Report re Constitutional Reform received.

18 - Ballaugh anti-vaccinator released from prison.

21 - Sale of St George's Woollen Mill, Laxey, the home of 'Ruskin Homespun', to a Leeds man.

DECEMBER

5-7 Industrial Guild Exhibition at the Palace.

FOXDALE MINES IN LIQUIDATION

Tuesday and Wednesday, 3rd and 4th October this year, brought to an end the long and successful mining activities in the Foxdale and Glen Rushen areas. During those two days the mining plant and items of equipment were sold as the result of the Isle of Man Mining Company going into voluntary liquidation. The company was formed in 1828 by a group of Liverpool, Chester and Flintshire businessmen. The rich lead and zinc ores were mined as early as 1740, but it was the newly-formed Mining Company which was to exploit the area to the full by means of a series of shafts in the neighbourhood of Foxdale and reaching westwards to Glen Rushen. An intricate system of water leats provided power for waterwheels, for washing the ore as well for the steam engines. Modern mining methods were introduced and it was the beam engines that provided power for the actual mining operations.

Initially, the ore was carried by horse and cart to Peel for export, the carts returning laden with coal for the steam engines. In 1874 agreement was reached whereby the Isle of Man Railway Company would handle these loads between St John's and Peel. Then the Foxdale Railway Company was formed and permission was given to lay a 2½ mile track from St John's to Foxdale. However, before the line was completed Manx Northern leased the new railway, hoping to benefit from linking with their 19 mile line to Ramsey for transporting the ore and coal. To cope with the gradient up to Foxdale, Manx Northern invested in a new and powerful engine, named 'Caledonia' which began operating in 1886.

The Glen Rushen group of mines consisted of three shafts named Beckwith's, Cross-vein (sometimes known as 'Snuff the Wind' because of its prominent site) and the nearby Dixon's. But the main complex of mines was closer to Foxdale with shafts spread over a wide area. Originally separate units, many in recent years have been inter-connected making for easier working. Closest to Foxdale village are the shafts of Upper Old Foxdale, Lower Old Foxdale, Old Flappy and Maghie's. West of Kionslieu Dam is the group containing the Louisa Mine, named after the wife of Mine's Captain Edward Bawden who came from Cornwall and whose family was prominent in the Mining Company. Further shafts were located east of the Eairy Dam, known as East or Central Foxdale. Two further mines were Townsend's, Cornelly to the north of Eairy and Bell's Hole to the north of Foxdale village.

Lead ore, with a high silver content, was by far the most important product and the combined output of the Foxdale Mines was averaging 4,000 tons a year during the 1880s and 1890s, making Foxdale the leading producer of lead ore in the British Isles. The beginning of the century saw a decline until production ceased altogether earlier this year. The price of lead ore was falling largely due to the influx of cheaper ores from abroad. Hence the present situation. Foxdale as a mining centre, and once the proud supporter of a school of mining, is now no more, whilst the sale tells something of its former glory.

Pumping and winding engines, hauling skips and pit cages, drills, stone breakers and crushers, jiggers and buddles, were all up for sale. No less than 14 waterwheels of varying sizes may well suit other local enterprises and it is said that the proprietor of Silverdale Glen may be interested in one of the smaller ones for the children's roundabout. Perhaps unexpected was the quantity of railway equipment - about 60 tons of rail and some 26 trucks (but no engines!) of some six different gauges varying from 19 inches to 5 feet. The sale was conducted by Geo. W. Dixon and Co. of Liverpool and such was the interest in the sale that special trains were arranged to and from Foxdale, connecting with the Douglas, Peel and Ramsey trains at St. John's.

The complex of the Upper Foxdale Mines looking towards the village from the clock tower.

(Manx National Heritage)

TYNWALD MATTERS : REPORT OF MacDONNELL COMMISSION

The year has seen the publication of perhaps the most important report ever made on the Constitution of the Isle of Man. With commendable speed the MacDonnell Commission has produced its considered views upon the several matters that were put before it. The arrival of the members of the Commission in May will be remembered by everyone. At one and the same time they represented the hopes of what may be termed the reformers and the concerns of those of a more conservative bent. The Commission occupied the Tynwald Court from the 15th to the 22nd of that month. They listened to and took evidence from individuals who ranged from paid officials of the Crown to perhaps self-styled reforming journalists. These sessions were followed by no fewer than three further sittings at the Home Office in London. From start to finish the whole process has taken but four short months - or as the Reform League was founded in 1903 - eight long years!

During those years petitions or reports demanding reform of the Manx Constitution seem to have emanated regularly from the House of Keys. The points being made have apparently now had a sympathetic reception. In both 1909 and 1910 more arguments and debates over subjects such as the Old Age Pension Bill and the attitude of the Legislative Council kept the matter at the forefront of Manx politics. Comments from conservative elements that over the last quarter of a century the calibre of M.H.K.s had steadily declined, did little to cool tempers. But to be honest, until this year the adamant opposition of the Lieutenant-Governor, the Council and the established order seemed easily to quell the desires of the reforming group, despite the existence of a supposedly Liberal Government and Home Secretary in Winston Churchill.

What happened then to precipitate action in this contentious field? Oddly enough, it seems an almost minor dispute about financial provisions for advertising the visiting industry did the trick. In short, the Keys wanted to increase the amount by £1,000 or so. The Lieutenant-Governor deemed that the Keys had no right to make any financial proposals concerning the public revenue without his consent. The Keys responded by refusing to continue with business in Tynwald until the matter was resolved. The deadlock was raised in the House of Commons and in April a Committee of Inquiry was appointed to examine the Keys' petition of 1907. It was to report on whether or not changes in the Manx Constitution and the administrative structures, civil, judicial and financial, were worth considering. Lord MacDonnell was appointed chairman - a man of great experience in every respect, not least perhaps in

The Home Office Manx Reform Commission with its chairman, Lord MacDonnell, seated centre.
(Frank Cowin Library)

the fact that he is an Irishman, well versed in such matters.

During the taking of evidence it rapidly became clear that while the conservative opposition remained solidly united, the aspirations of those seeking reforms were so diverse as to prevent any consensus, let alone unanimity, emerging. Indeed, Lord MacDonnell himself, judging from some of his comments, seems to have been rather taken aback by the lack of desire or resolution in pursuing the objective of responsible government. Many of the witnesses supporting reform were content to leave ultimate political power in the hands of the Lieutenant-Governor. Given this state of affairs, here on the Island there is little wonder that MacDonnell's recommendations have been eagerly awaited.

In brief, it is re-affirmed that the Secretary of State exercises ultimate authority in the Government of the Isle of Man, the Lieutenant-Governor to be appointed for a fixed term of seven to ten years at a salary of £2,000 per annum. It is recommended that the Legislative Council should consist of ten members, excluding the Lieutenant-Governor, of whom four are to be elected by the House of Keys from their own number or from the electorate in general. The remaining six are the Lord Bishop, the two Deemsters, the Attorney-General and two appointees of the Lieutenant-Governor. The Vicar-General and the Archdeacon are to be dropped.

It is also recommended that a Finance and General Purpose Committee should be established to advise the Governor, a recommendation that perhaps Lord MacDonnell sees as a means of persuading reluctant Keys' members to start considering aspects of responsible government. Certain changes are also advocated in the judicial system and some stringent criticism is made of the diverse nature of our educational administration, with a strong recommendation for a far more centralised system.

Many of the Commission's conclusions will be welcomed, many vehemently opposed. For those primarily concerned with constitutional affairs, the introduction of the principle of election, either directly or indirectly, into the Legislative Council and the creation of a Finance and General Purpose body might well turn out to be the most significant points in the report. However, the Commission's work is done, its stature and repute unquestioned and its conclusions now in the public domain. There would seem to be little doubt that despite the sustained opposition of powerful interests on the Island, several, if not all of its recommendations will be implemented without delay.

HERE IS THE NEWS : 1912
NEW NOBLE'S ISLE OF MAN HOSPITAL

The new Noble's Hospital in Westmoreland Road, Douglas, the latest magnificent gift to the town under the will of the late Henry Bloom Noble, has been officially opened by the Lieutenant-Governor, Lord Raglan and Lady Raglan at a great civic celebration. The Hospital has taken three years to build at a cost of more than £20,000. We have this report:

Henry Bloom Noble, businessman, property speculator and money lender, was the Island's richest man when he died leaving £180,000 in 1903. Since then his trustees, under instructions in his will, have given away large sums for the benefit of the town he adopted as his home when he moved to Douglas from Whitehaven as a young man. His other gifts include the Noble's Baths in Victoria Street and the laying out of new playing fields at Glencrutchery to be known as Noble's Park. And next year sees the opening of the new Kursaal concert hall in the Villa Marina public gardens. The original Villa Marina, Mr. Noble's handsome private residence on the seafront, has been demolished to make way for the new development. The new Noble's Hospital, with its 60 patient beds, taken along with other health service improvements, including the building of the new Ramsey Cottage Hospital, reflect Mr Noble's great interest in health care. He built the first Noble's Hospital at the top of Crellin's Hill which was opened in 1888. A new role must now be found for this imposing red brick building.

TELEGRAPH CABLE SEVERED

In January the electric telegraph service between the Isle of Man and England was shut down for a week after a fishing boat ran aground on Cornaa beach in rough weather and cut the submarine cable from St. Bee's Head. The cable comes ashore at Cornaa. The steam trawler *Maud*, from Fleetwood, had 10 men on board. They were brought ashore safely with the aid of the manager and staff of the Barony Farm. Repairs to the cable were eventually carried out by the cable ship *Monarch*.

FIRE AT ST. THOMAS'S

In February a fierce fire gutted the tower of St. Thomas's Church, Douglas, and extensively damaged the rest of the building and the organ. The blaze, which started in the belfry, was discovered as the congregation was leaving after a Sunday evening service. Large crowds gathered as the flames spread rapidly - and there was anger when the steam fire engine did not reach the scene for 45 minutes. Its crew were booed as they fought for three and a half hours to bring the flames under control. The cause of the fire is not known. No-one was hurt.

TITANIC MEMORIAL SERVICE

1912 will be recorded in history as the year of the sinking of the White Star liner *Titanic*. She went down after hitting an iceberg in the North Atlantic. A great memorial service for those lost was held in the Palace Ballroom, Douglas. It was led by the Lord Bishop, Dr. Denton Thompson, and 6,000 people attended. The service followed a civic procession from the Town Hall. The congregation sang a hymn written specially for the occasion by the Manx novelist and playwright Mr. Hall Caine.

The Henry Bloom Noble Trustees who have funded the new hospital. Standing, left to right, are Mr Llewellyn Kneale, Advocate, and Mr Alfred Tyson, secretary. Seated are Mr Alexander Hill, Manager of the Isle of Man Bank, Mr Thomas Kelly, Clerk of the Rolls, and Mr Robert Clucas, M.H.K.

(Manx National Heritage)

The 'unsinkable' liner was on her maiden voyage and was speeding through an ice field hoping to win the 'Blue Riband' for the fastest Atlantic crossing. Over 1,500 lives were lost out of the 2,340 passengers and crew on board.

MIXED BATHING REJECTED

Proposals to allow mixed bathing on the foreshore at Douglas have been rejected by the Town Council. Voting against amendments to the byelaws, Councillors said there had been disgraceful scenes at Port Jack as a result of men and women bathing together there. Meanwhile Douglas Licensing Court has granted a large number of applications for the new singing and dancing licences for public houses, provided for under the 1912 Licensing Act. This was in spite of fierce opposition in court by the Bishop and clergy of the Island who described the move as a moral curse on Douglas.

LAXEY MINER KILLED

A young man has been killed in a horrific underground accident at the Laxey Mines. Twenty-one-year old Matthias Cowley, was badly mutilat-

DOUGLAS. A Scramble over the Rocks at Port Jack.

Such scenes as this at Port Jack have been described as 'disgraceful' by Town Councillors. The ban on mixed bathing on Douglas foreshore is to remain.

(R & L. Kelly Collection)

ed and had his head blown off when he was taking charges out of a dynamite storage box. It happened 185ft below ground in the Dumbell Shaft when a charge went off in his hand. He was due to be married the follow-

ing day. September has seen another tragedy at sea. Two Castletown fishermen, Joseph Clucas and James Quayle, died when their boat foundered in rough seas in Castletown bay.

1912 NEWS IN BRIEF

JANUARY
29 - Annual Meeting of Isle of Man Bank Ltd. A 'record volume of business' reported; 15% dividend approved.

MARCH
10 - Annual session of the Licensing Court for the Douglas District. Rev. Wilson Stuart of Rosemount strenuously opposed the granting of boarding-house licences. The court refused new applications for these licences, but granted renewals.

19-21 Manx Music Festival at the Palace, Douglas. 'Coming of Age' celebrations.

APRIL
1 - Lecture by Professor Annett (formerly of Liverpool University) on Tuberculosis in the Isle of Man. Startling figures are given concerning the proportion of Insular diseased cattle.
8 - Foundation stone laid of Michael New Wesleyan Chapel.
10 - Mr William Cubbon, journalist, appointed Public Librarian by Douglas Town Council.
11 - A decorative scheme of electric lighting of the sea front proposed at meeting of Douglas Town Council was lost by the Mayor's casting vote.
18 - Enthronement of Bishop Denton Thompson at St George's Church.
19 - Correspondence on National Insurance scheme, passed between the Lieut-Governor and Insular Friendly Societies, discussed at the Rechabite District Meeting.
26 - Professor Annett lectured on Consumption and made appeal to Manx people to grapple with the disease.

MAY
26 - Tynwald Court discuss Insular finances. Demand for reduction of taxation. There was straight talk on subject of Old Age Pensions. Governor agrees to set up a Commission.

JUNE
12 - Douglas Town Council agreed to increase the minimum labourer's wage from £1 to £1 1s for 56 hours week.

JULY
3 - New Ramsey - Whitehaven steamer service opened for summer.
10 - Opening of Braddan New Church Hall.
16 - First Licensing Court in Douglas to consider granting of music and dancing licences. Personal opposition by Bishop Thompson and the Revs. Wilson Stuart and Henry Cooper to holding concerts in public-houses.
20 - Tynwald approves loan of £1,000 to Port Erin Commissioners to defray law costs and and expenses in connection with the Brow's purchase.

AUGUST
First prosecution under the Music and Singing Act. High-Bailiff decided that voluntary singing and music in a public-house are allowable.

SEPTEMBER
11 - Official opening of New Hospital in Westmoreland Road.

OCTOBER
21 - Insular Boy Scouts celebrated Trafalgar Day. Wreaths laid on Capt. Quilliam's grave in Arbory Churchyard.

NOVEMBER
1 - Another Dumbell's Bank dividend announced - 6d in the £. Previous dividends amounted to 11s 7d.
20 - In the Legislative Council, on the first reading of the Divorce Bill, the Attorney-General gave expression to his conscientious objections against divorce, and he, with the Vicar-General and the Archdeacon, left the Chamber.
28 - Harbour Commissioners' report on Douglas Harbour recommends extension of Red Pier. Tramway connection with Railway Station deferred.

OPENING OF THE NEW NOBLE'S HOSPITAL

The new 60-bed Noble's Hospital has been opened at Douglas amid great celebrations. In glorious weather, on Wednesday, 11th September, there was a procession through town, an open day at the hospital and fund-raising concerts all day in the Villa Marina grounds. Entertainment was provided by the Imperial Viennese Band and the Douglas Head Entertainers. The Palace Ballroom orchestra, meanwhile, conducted by Harry Wood, played at the hospital.

The hospital has been acclaimed as one of the finest and most up-to-date, for its size, in the British Isles. Yet it has not cost the Manx people a penny. The entire capital cost of £20,000 has been financed from the estate of the late Henry Bloom Noble. On Wednesday it was described as being "greater and of more importance than any other gift that has ever been made." The hospital has been designed by hospital specialist William Henman and built by Douglas contractor, Mark Carine. Equipment includes its own electricity generator and the latest X-ray facilities. These were displayed and explained on Wednesday by X-ray pioneer, Dr. Hall-Edwards.

To attend the opening, government officials, members of local authorities and societies - foremost among them the Freemasons - processed from Douglas Town Hall to the hospital. They did so via Great George Street, Church Street, Upper Church Street and Westmoreland Road. An estimated 4,500 schoolchildren, who had been given a half-day holiday, lined the route. After a short service of dedication, conducted by the Lord Bishop, the hospital was opened by Lieutenant-Governor, Lord Raglan.

For now, at least, recent controversy surrounding the hospital appears to have been forgotten. Many people remain unhappy, however, about its location. They believe the three acre green-field site, on former allotment gardens in the Hills estate, to be too remote from Douglas town centre. Staff, doctors and even hospital governors are worried about the walking that will be entailed in getting to and from the place.

Ever since the hospital was planned the arguments have raged. Opponents wanted the existing hospital, opened in September 1888 at the top of Crellin's Hill, to be expanded. Plans were even prepared to develop adjoining property and the terraced houses on the opposite side of Crellin's Hill but they were abandoned when experts said that remodelling an existing building was never satisfactory. The Noble Trustees bought the green-field site for £2,740 and passed it to the hospital Trustees. They point now to the benefits that compensate for the hospital's remoteness. The site provides maximum sunshine and fresh air, they say, which are the finest doctors of all. The hospital is not shut in by houses either so there is room for expansion and that will surely come as medical services improve. The population of the Island has changed little but demand for hospitalisation, notably because of the growing number of services that can be provided, has vastly outstripped the facilities that were previously available. Surgery, for example, has become less feared because of the development of anaesthesia. Twenty years ago people were still being operated upon in public wards without anaesthetic.

Opening of the hospital follows a period of financial uncertainty. Despite relying on voluntary work by doctors and surgeons, the first Noble's Hospital got into debt. There were fears that its running costs might have to be transferred to the rate fund and cost 6d in the £. Last year a public appeal was launched to clear £800 of debt. When subscriptions reached £600, the Noble Trustees provided the final £200.

Now the finances of the new hospital are reported to be excellent. It has no debt and the Noble Trustees have given it investment capital of £20,000 which is expected to produce an annual income of £600. Hospital administrators are anxious not to lose voluntary support, howev-

The buildings of the new Noble's Isle of Man Hospital.

(R. & L. Kelly Collection)

Medical Staff - Back row standing, left to right: Mr J. J. James (Hon. Dental Surgeon), Dr A. H. Rentoul (House Surgeon) and Dr T. A. Woods (Hon. Surgeon). Sitting, left to right: Dr Cordiner (Hon. Asst. Surgeon), Dr C. S. Pantin (Hon. Surgeon), Dr Lionel Woods (Hon. Asst. Surgeon), Dr T. A. Wood (Hon. Surgeon) and Dr T. Mackenzie (Hon. Physician).

(R. & L. Kelly Collection)

er. Every penny is needed from subscriptions and special efforts, they say, because demand for hospital services is still rising.

Medical attention focusses now on the Island's other needs. A maternity hospital is needed almost as much as the new Noble's Hospital, say doctors. Many of the hovels in old Douglas are unfit for babies to be born in but doctors doubt that the Island can afford what is needed. Pressure is mounting also for a hospital for incurables. At present poor people are being left to die at home.

Meanwhile, there is controversy over what should be done about infectious diseases. Anti-vaccinators are being prosecuted in increasing numbers. Smallpox used to take a terrible toll. Although its prevalence has lessened because of legally-enforced vaccination, it still has not been conquered. Doctors are warning that an outbreak now would destroy the Manx tourist industry. Even so, many parents are refusing to have their children vaccinated because they are afraid of exposing their children to the remote risks associated with it. Many of the "conscientious objectors" who are being prosecuted say they will not pay their fines and will accept the alternative of five or seven days imprisonment. As the threat of

smallpox has receded the House of Keys is expected to change the law to allow conscientious objectors to make their own decisions on vaccination.

Medical attention is expected to focus then on other infectious diseases which are claiming lives every week. Diptheria is one. The most feared, however, is Tuberculosis (otherwise known as Consumption or "the White Plague"). Doctors say that Consumption is preventable but nothing is being done to combat it. Sweeping measures of hygiene are required. The question is: Has the Island the will and the resources to do what is required?

Nursing Staff - Back row, standing, left to right: Nurses Anderson, Shimmin, Rogers, Jackson, Cowell, Joughin, Lay and Cowin. Sitting, left to right: Nurse Lewin, Sister Callister, Matron (Miss Bridson), Sister Stuart and Nurse Quayle. *(R. & L. Kelly Collection)*

HERE IS THE NEWS : 1913
RECORD SUMMER SEASON

The Island has had a record summer for visitors. Nearly 616,000 people were landed at Douglas and Ramsey, an increase of 122,000 over the previous record, set in 1911, when the half-million mark was passed for the first time. Last summer railway strikes and bad weather reduced numbers. But now the future of the visiting industry looks secure. We have this report:

Douglas is now one of the leading holiday resorts of the British Isles - and it is improving its amenities every year. The new Kursaal in the Villa Marina Gardens was opened with civic ceremony on 19th July by Lord and Lady Raglan. The unique building is octagonal in shape and its roof, spanning 100 feet and without lateral support, is the largest of its kind in Britain. His Excellency said the Kursaal would provide for a better class of visitor than those interested only in dancing, variety turns and the cinematograph. Representatives of nearly 60 of Britain's top newspapers and magazines reported the opening ceremony and the Isle of Man is being dubbed as 'the great Island playground of the North'. Highlight of the week is the Sunday night concert and one of the first artistes to appear was the world-renowned opera singer, Madame Melba.

Two days later, and not to be outdone, the Palace and Derby Castle Co. Ltd opened its magnificent Coliseum Theatre capable of seating 3,500 people. All seats were filled for the appearance of one of the country's most famous music hall stars, Vesta Tilley. The Coliseum is linked internally to the huge Palace Ballroom where 3,000 couples can dance to one of the leading orchestras. The Ballroom can quite justifiably claim to be the largest and finest in the world. In August, the first purpose-built cinema opened to cater for this latest form of entertainment. Situated in the main shopping thoroughfare in Douglas it is known as The Strand. With the Steam Packet Company building and bringing into service a new steamer every summer, numbers of visitors are expected to continue to rise. The Island's Board of Advertising says

(Above) The interior of the Villa Marina Kursaal which was officially opened on 19th July. Two days later, the Palace Coliseum (below), with seating for 3,500, was opened.
(R. & L. Kelly Collection)

in its annual report that very soon after next year, 1914, the Isle of Man should be in sight of receiving a million visitors.

VACCINATION OBJECTORS FINED

The year began with fourteen more people being fined at the High-Bailiff's Court for refusing to have their children vaccinated against the scourge of smallpox. Some refused to pay the fines and opted for prison sentences. A number of other parents were similarly dealt with last year. They are people who have a conscientious objection to vaccination. But the law of the Isle of Man, unlike the law in England, does not allow people to refuse vaccination for conscientious reasons - and the Legislature

has refused to change this.

Later in the year the House of Keys agreed to the Act being amended by a conscience clause, but this was rejected by the Legislative Council.

METHODIST MINISTER LIBELLED

One of the Island's most controversial clergymen, the Reverend Wilson Stuart, has won libel damages of £200 against the *Isle of Man Times*. Mr. Stuart, Minister of Rosemount Wesleyan Church in Douglas, has been outspoken in the pulpit about riotous and indecent behaviour at public house concerts. And a letter published in the *Times* attacked him as "a bawling blockhead" and "a bigotted, beerless, beardless, childless master of woman-dodging arts, a tackless, taxless fish-blooded bachelor." Deemster Moore described it as a gross and serious libel. Defendants were ordered to pay costs and publish an ample apology.

DEEMSTER THREATENED

A man who threatened to shoot Deemster Callow has been sentenced to six months hard labour at the Court of General Gaol. Harry Thorpe, a 37-year-old Manchester man living at Ash Cottage, Greeba, sent his death threat to the Deemster by telegram and by postcard. And when police went to arrest him they found a loaded Colt automatic on his person. Thorpe had called Deemster Callow corrupt and a scoundrel after he had refused to deal with a legal dispute for debt involving Thorpe.

DEATH OF JOHN MILLER NICHOLSON

In March the Isle of Man's greatest native born painter, John Miller Nicholson, died at the age of 73. He won international recognition as a water colourist when he came to the notice of John Ruskin who encouraged him to go to Italy to work and study. Nicholson was self-taught, but he never received the full acclaim

Each Sunday thousands of visitors attend morning service at Old Kirk Braddan. As a result of claims that the churchyard is being desecrated, the service is to be held in the grounds of the new church from next season.

(Frank Cowin Library)

he merited because he painted to please himself and refused to exhibit his work in search of public recognition. Critics say he could have been one of Britain's greatest Victorian painters.

SECOND T.T. RIDER KILLED

The T.T. races have suffered their second fatality. Rudge-Whitworth works team rider Frank Bateman, who was 23, crashed to his death at Creg-ny-Baa while trying to overtake other riders at nearly 70 miles an hour. There were new attempts to sabotage the races. Before the start Highway Board men found broken glass and nails strewn at four different places round the T.T. Course. The course was immediately cleared and the races were able to proceed.

The use of the Snaefell

Familiar sight at Peel each year is the arrival of thousands of Territorials for the summer camps at Knockaloe. Here men of the Sherwood Foresters have disembarked from the newly-commissioned 'King Orry'.

(Les Clarke Collection)

Mountain Course has meant that many more residents are being inconvenienced and there have been complaints about noise and the wild behaviour by the growing number of T.T. followers. To make matters worse most of the British manufacturers agreed to boycott the races and there was talk of moving the Races elsewhere. It was due to the diplomacy of A-C.U. Secretary Mr Tom Loughborough that agreement was reached with the Manx authorities to make the Course available again.

POSTCARDS TO BE CENSORED

The Isle of Man is alone in Britain in its new initiative designed to censor seaside postcards and ban those which are indecent. In successive summers there have been prosecutions brought against Douglas shopkeepers who have sold offensive cards. Now the police are co-operating in a scheme under which postcard manufacturers have to submit examples of their products to a

Laxey Glen Gardens. Behind the bandstand and dance floor can be seen the Pavilion which has now been destroyed by fire.
(Frank Cowin Library)

small committee of shopkeepers. The standard of cards is now much improved.

FIRE DESTROYS LAXEY PAVILION

One of the fiercest and most spectacular fires ever seen in the Island has destroyed the wooden tea rooms and pavilion at Laxey Glen Gardens, causing £4000 worth of damage. Only one wall was left standing and the Island has lost a highly popular attraction for visitors. But proprietor Mr. Robert Williamson has kept the business going - in a large hired marquee. He hopes to have a new pavilion built for the 1914 season.

1913 NEWS IN BRIEF

JANUARY
8 - Douglas Town Council decide upon independent electrical installation for the lighting of the Villa Marina. Noble's Trustees gave £3,500 for furnishing of the new Kursaal Hall.
13 - Report of the Insular Commissioners on Old Age Pensions. Estimated cost is £20,000 a year.
18 - Isle of Man Farmers' Club protest at town members harassing farmers by introducing legislation to register dairies and dealing with milk supply.

MARCH
3 - At the annual meeting of the Isle of Man Railway Company an extension of the Foxdale line over Barrule Mountain was suggested.
6 - The Lord Bishop, at a mass Temperance meeting, denounced the Press for its poisonous criticism, and a Resolution is carried to abolish all free concerts in public-houses.
11 - Launch of new geared turbine steamer 'King Orry' at Birkenhead.
21 - Wholesale refusal of singing licences by the Douglas Licensing Board.
24 - Death of artist John Miller Nicholson.
25 - St Ninian's Church, Douglas, dedicated for Divine worship.

APRIL
2 - Heated discussion in House of Keys on the Medical Officer of Health and Dairies Bill. Country members wreck the Bill.
7 - Vicar and Wardens of Braddan convene meeting to discuss alleged desecration of graves by the holding of season open-air services. Decision made to hold the services in 'old fortification' below Kirby Farm and in the grounds of the new church.
21 - Opening of the newly-built picturedrome in Walpole Avenue, under the name of The Pier Pavilion.

MAY
3 - Messrs Holroyd and Son (Laxey) received an order from the King for Manx Ruskin homespun cloth.
28 - Great walking match round Island won by H. Bridson in 18 hours 56 minutes.
29 - Peel to Douglas 'Marathon' won by J.C. Cunningham in 1 hour, 13 minutes, 15 seconds.

JULY
19 - Opening by Lord and Lady Raglan of Villa Marina Kursaal.
21 - Opening of Palace Coliseum variety theatre.

AUGUST
2 - Strand Cinema, Strand Street, opened.
13 - Laxey Pavilion burnt down. Estimated damage £4,000.

SEPTEMBER
3 - Lord and Lady Raglan inaugurate the open access system at the Douglas Free Library. Ordering from catalogue ceases.
16 - Government circular against raffling at bazaars causes crisis. Onchan Church Bazaar Committee in quandary but decide to comply.
28 - Father Vaughan preaches at St Mary's R.C. Church against Hall Caine's book "The Woman Thou Gavest Me."

OCTOBER
7 - Final sitting of the House of Keys. Constitutional Reform commended to the electorate.
9 - The Reform Party open campaign with a meeting in Rushen Sheading.

NOVEMBER
12 - Dramatic performance of T.E. Brown's poem 'Betsy Lee' at the Coliseum.
12-21 General Election of the House of Keys.

DECEMBER
2 - Mr Dalrymple Maitland re-elected Speaker at the first meeting of the newly-elected House of Keys.

JOHN MILLER NICHOLSON: EMINENT MANX ARTIST

Plans to create a Public Art gallery on the Island in which to house some of the finest works of the late John Miller Nicholson have had to be abandoned. Lack of public interest has been blamed but this may not have been due to a lack of appreciation of his many talents. Many Manx people may have believed that 73-year-old Nicholson would not have liked too much fuss. He was such a private man and so disliked talking about his pictures that it was said of him that he "had a large stock of silence at hand'.

The idea of a national memorial to the great Manx artist, self-taught as a child from reading books, was proposed at a meeting in late September 1913 at St Matthew's School, Douglas. The proposer was the Dowager Lady Loch. A memorial was considered fitting for, had it not been for his natural modesty and aversion to publicity, it was reckoned that he would have been ranked as one of Britain's leading Victorian artists. Some of his paintings were popular buys at London and Manchester exhibitions.

John Miller Nicholson (1840-1913)

another great Manx artist, the production of a marble bust, the erection in Douglas of a commemorative tablet or the establishment of a permanent collection of Nicholson's paintings. This was interpreted by his friends as implying some form of gallery. This was possible as many of Nicholson's paintings which he would not sell have been presented to Douglas.

Nicholson painted for the sheer love of it, preferring seclusion to company. When an appreciative audience applauded the scenery he had produced for a play at the Theatre Royal in Douglas and called for him to appear on stage, he beat a hasty retreat. According to a friend, Joseph Douglas, the sale of his work was always a secondary consideration. Hence his reluctance at times to sell a particular painting and his rejection, at the height of his popularity, of an offer of one guinea per square inch for as many paintings as he could supply.

An indication of the standard achieved by him is given in the illustrations shown here. They reveal attention to intricate detail despite the fact that he could complete pencil sketches of his subjects in 30 minutes. Many of Nicholson's paintings have a maritime background, reflecting his family's association with the sea. At one time he used to be a regular figure on Douglas beach just before dawn so that he could study cloud effects at dawn and the changing effects of early light on the sea and the headlands.

Ideas for a lasting memorial to Nicholson varied between the commissioning of a portrait of Nicholson by

Following his death, private owners of some of his best pictures, in oils, water colours and pastels, loaned them for an exhibition in December in association with the Isle of Man Fine Arts and Industrial Guild. The long term hope now is that one day a Manx Museum with an adequate Picture Gallery will be established. Funding, however, is likely to be a problem for some time to come.

In the meantime, at least one viewable and impressive memorial remains. It is in the murals at St Thomas' Church in Douglas which he designed gratuitously and supervised others in painting in 1897 and 1898 in return only for the cost of material and wages.

BALDWIN MILL.

THE OLD FISH MARKET AND HARBOUR, DOUGLAS.

CONCERN FOR OUR MORALS

Within recent weeks observers of the ever-changing Manx holiday scene will have been intrigued by the no doubt well-meaning efforts of the guardians of public morals to sanitise the libidinous character of our postcards. Large under-dressed ladies found in compromising positions with small moustachioed gentlemen will, it appears, no longer be acceptable under the voluntary system of censorship that is being established.

This particular enterprise may well be treated in a jocular fashion but, at the same time, it can more seriously and properly be regarded as a genuine attempt to stem what many here see as a steady deterioration in public standards of behaviour. In recent times the Licensing Act opened the flood gates, it is alleged, for a tide of lewd and immoral behaviour. Indeed, the Bishop has not minced his words in describing it as a moral curse, adding that young men and women are becoming too familiar with each other and lounging in each others arms - conduct which is "sickly, unwholesome and fraught with serious peril." Other church and chapel leaders have fulminated about young men drinking until two o'clock in the morning and complained bitterly about what are described as shebeens springing up all over Douglas. The song books of the concert rooms are held to be full of "vulgar, sordid and indecent songs" that lead apparently to indelicate thoughts.

Gambling, too, appears to be increasing at an alarming rate. Only a short while ago betting premises were raided in Granville Street and the seven men discovered there were taken to the police station by wagonette. Unfortunately, in Victoria Street an axle pin failed and a wheel fell off. The result was that, much to the amusement of onlookers, the villains had to be marched the rest of the way. More serious was the case where a man died recently in a fight over a game of cards. This confirmed the worst fears of not only the most outspoken critics of such activities, but also of the decent people of the Island.

Even the rapidly developing practice of mixed bathing is held to encourage indecent behaviour, in many cases unintentionally. A gentleman who tried, after bathing, to dress in a circumspect manner on Douglas shore put on his overcoat before stooping down to take

off his bathing drawers, but he forgot that his overcoat had a split down the back!

There appears to be a genuine concern amongst our Island's people about these modern manners but such immodesty is not without its Manx supporters. Not too long ago one of the most outspoken critics of what he sees as outrageous moral laxity, the Wesleyan minister the Rev. Wilson Stuart, was attacked as a "bawling blockhead" and a "bigotted fish-blooded bachelor". As these words appeared in the *Isle of Man Times* it is not surprising that the minister was awarded £200 in libel damages.

To attempt to put all these matters into some sort of perspective, there is no doubt that this century will see great changes in all manner of things that will affect our daily lives. Even so, it will behove us all to do our best to see that standards of decency, of tasteful behaviour, and of plain common-sense will prevail, whatever the years may bring.

The postcards shown here have met the approval of the Censoring Committee set up by the local shopkeepers.

(Postcards from the Frank Cowin Library and the R. & L. Kelly Collection)

HERE IS THE NEWS : 1914
WAR BRINGS BLEAK PROSPECT

Life in the Isle of Man has been completely transformed following the outbreak of war between Britain and Germany on August 4th this year. The holiday season has been brought to an abrupt standstill, causing problems for many businesses. Hundreds of young Manxmen are answering Lord Kitchener's call to arms and are enlisting in the Armed Forces. And there have already been casualties. We have this report:

In what was a carefree Isle of Man full of visitors the rumblings of war in the Balkans went almost unnoticed. Then, with the start of hostilities coinciding with the August Bank Holiday, the prospects of a record season were dashed overnight. People left the Island in large numbers - and arrivals fell away amid rumours of food scarcity and steamer cancellations. Meanwhile, men from the Island are in the forefront of the fighting. The two Regular Army officer sons of the Lieutenant-Governor, Lord Raglan, the Honourable Wellesley Somerset and the Honourable Nigel Somerset, have both been wounded in the fighting in France and Belgium. They are recovering in hospital in England. His Excellency received the sad news on 18th September, his 57th birthday. There has been news, too, that a Douglas man, 29-year-old Private Thomas Sayle, serving as a Regular with the Wiltshire Regiment, was killed at Mons. He is thought to be the first Manxman to die. Meanwhile, 18 German and Austrian aliens working in the Island, mostly as waiters, have been rounded up and detained.

CABLE CAR ACCIDENT
On New Year's Day a number of people were injured in the first serious accident on the Douglas cable tramway since it opened 18 years ago. A tram going down Prospect Hill came to an abrupt halt when its braking gripper caught in a loose pulley in the culvert the cable runs through. Conductor James Teare was thrown through a glass panel and sustained serious cuts and driver James Kelly suffered head injuries. A number of passengers were slightly hurt.

Carefree holidaymakers enjoying a night of dancing at Derby Castle. Now the music has stopped and our visitors have departed. But for how long?
(Mannin Collections)

COUNCIL REJECTS REFORMS
The fierce struggle in the Island's Legislature over constitutional reform remains unresolved. Bills which would transfer more control over Island affairs from the Lieutenant-Governor to the House of Keys have been passed by the Keys. But they were thrown out by the Legislative Council - which is itself a target for reform by removal of Crown appointee members like the Vicar-General. There followed a serious confrontation between Keys and Council. Since then, Britain's Home Secretary has stepped in and ordered that the Bills be re-introduced into the Legislature.

MYSTERY UNSOLVED
The mystery of who murdered 55-year-old Douglas widow Mrs Frances Quayle earlier this year now seems certain to go down as the great unsolved Manx crime of 1914. Investigations by the Manx police, assisted by officers from Scotland Yard, have proved fruitless. Mrs. Quayle, who ran a grocery and wines and spirits shop at 40 Bucks Road, Douglas, was found bludgeoned to death in a small garden behind Tynwald Street where she used to keep pet rabbits. She was rumoured to have large sums of money hidden away but there has been no evidence of robbery.

It is thought the murder was committed between 10 and 11 o'clock on the night of Saturday, 25th April, but it was not until Monday morning that her body was found lying in a pool of blood in the garden. The instrument used to perpetrate the crime was found at the southern end of Princes Street and many persons of the vagrant class were questioned. At the inquest on 15th May an open verdict was returned.

THIRD T.T. RIDER KILLED
There has been criticism in the English press of safety standards in the T.T. races following the death of a competitor in the 1914 meeting near the top of Bray Hill. Irish rider Frederick Walker had just finished in third place in the Junior T.T. when he crashed into a spectator barrier across the top of Ballaquayle Road. Witnesses said he obviously had no idea the barrier was there. It consisted of a telegraph pole laid on top of wooden supports. The jury at the inquest recommended that rope barriers be used in future.

FORTUNE FOR CAPTAIN OF THE PARISH
A member of a well-known Manx Family, Mr. Thomas Moore, of Billown, has inherited nearly a million pounds under the will of a relative who has died in New Zealand. It was left to him by his first cousin, Mrs. Annie Townsend, daughter of

Plenty of willing hands help launch the Avro 504 seaplane. Flights around the bay were one of the attractions of the Douglas Carnival. (*Keig Collection*)

George Moore who was born at the family home at Billown but emigrated to New Zealand in 1812, where he made his fortune as a landowner and sheep farmer. Mr. Thomas Moore is a J.P. and Captain of the Parish of Malew.

SHEBEEN OPERATOR IMPRISONED

A man accused of running a shebeen in a stable in Well Road Hill, Douglas, has appeared before the High-Bailiff charged with selling drink without a licence. Police who kept observation on the stable said a stream of people was seen going into the stable on a Sunday morning from as early as 5 a.m. They came out with bottles of rum and whisky. Ryan was fined £15 but refused to pay and was committed to prison. As he was taken from the courthouse a large crowd of

friends and supporters were waiting to cheer him. And he shouted to them: "So long boys. Drink hearty."

DOUGLAS CARNIVAL

The assassination of the Archduke Franz Ferdinand in Sarajevo at the end of June, passed unnoticed as Douglas was gripped in Carnival mood. Widely advertised, the Carnival attracted 15,000 visitors in the quieter part of the season. Features of the Carnival were the frequent parades along the streets and sea front of decorated cars and fancy dress processions. Then there were the battles of flowers and confetti at night, with the Promenade specially illuminated. Other features included fancy dress balls, pyrotechnical exhibitions, gymkhanas, regattas and a great marathon. Adding to the scene were two famous aviators who gave

breathtaking displays over Douglas Bay. Sponsored by the *Daily Mail*, there were also short 'flips' for lucky coupon winners, which all added up to a highly successful Carnival which came to an end on July 6th.

ENEMY ALIENS SHOT

Cunningham's Holiday Camp has been rapidly converted into an Enemy Aliens Internment Camp, surrounded by barbed wire and guarded by armed guards. Here are confined aliens of German and Austrian extraction thought to be a threat to national security. The end of September saw the first batch arrive and the total quickly rose to 2,600. They are accommodated in the bell tents of the campers, and eat in the huge dining hall. Already, there has been considerable unrest within the camp. While wooden chalets are being built, the internees have complained about the cold and crowded accommodation within the tents; the food supplied by the Cunninghams is said to be bad and monotonous. Matters came to a head in the dining room when a serious riot broke out. The heavily outnumbered guards opened fire and five aliens were killed, while several others were wounded. This was followed by two detainees being dealt with by a military court for breaching camp regulations. One was given five years penal servitude for stirring up disaffection within the camp. The other was given two months for writing home to Germany - in invisible ink.

1914 NEWS IN BRIEF

JANUARY
5 - After having been discontinued for a period, the free dinners for poor school children in Douglas were resumed.
6 - Constitutional Reform Bill introduced in the House of Keys.
17 - Board of Advertising puts on record its declared aim for a million summer visitors.

FEBRUARY
3 - Tynwald votes £6,000 for dredging of Peel harbour.
21 - Importation of cattle etc. banned owing to prevalence of foot and mouth disease in Ireland.
26 - Another ward at Noble's Hospital to be opened during year.

MARCH
3 - Third reading of the Constitutional Reform Bill carried by 12 votes in House of Keys.
25 - St Ninian's Church consecrated by Lord Bishop.
31 - Opening of Manx Music Festival. Record entry of 419, representing 3,358 competitors.

APRIL
13 - Opening of Sulby new Methodist Church.
17 - Legislative Council reject Reform Bill.
21 - Keys strongly deprecates the Council's rejection.

MAY
5-7 Anniversary of the birth of T.E. Brown commemorated by unveiling of portraits of the Manx poet in all Insular schools.
19 & 21 - Auto-cycle T.T. Races held. Rider killed at the end of the Junior Race.

JUNE
10 & 11 - R.A.C. Autocar T.T. resumed after gap of six years. The race, over two days, was won by K.L. Guinness (Sunbeam) averaging 56.44 m.p.h.

15 - Memorial tablet unveiled at Windsor Mount, Ramsey, to the late Rev. T. E. Brown.

JULY
18 - Serious damage by caterpillars to turnip crop reported.
29 - Pulrose Estate sold by public auction to Douglas Corporation for £19,000.

AUGUST
1 - Douglas Corporation inaugurate first automobile 'bus service from Peel Road to Victoria Pier.
4 - Great Britain declares war on Germany.
13 - Isle of Man Volunteers mobilised for sentry duty on the Island.
15 - Over 400 Manx residents have responded to Lord Kitchener's appeal for young men to join the British Army.
15 - Large number of horses commandeered for war purposes.
19 - Loyal Manx Association formed for home military service. Legislative Buildings and General Post Office to be guarded.
20 - Lieutenant-Governor addresses public meeting in the Kursaal to form a Needlework Guild for the Eastern District to provide clothes for soldiers and sailors and their dependents.

SEPTEMBER
2 - Cunningham's Holiday Camp converted into Enemy Aliens Internment Camp.
5 - Lieutenant-Governor authorises second company of Isle of Man Volunteers to be formed.
18 - Tynwald votes £10,000 as a contribution from the Island to the Imperial Treasury towards the expenditure on war.

NOVEMBER
17 - First enemy aliens arrive at Knockaloe Internment Camp.

IMPACT OF THE WAR IN EUROPE

The idea that the war would be over by Christmas has long been dispelled. In the past we have viewed with interest the visit of flotillas of the Royal Navy and welcomed the annual visits of thousands of Territorials of the British Army for their summer camps. They seemed to be a safeguard of our safety, security and stability which has allowed the Island to become a major holiday resort. Usually we are on the fringe of great events, but now we are part of them. All of us have watched with dismay the almost inevitable descent into war. The construction of the great alliance systems, Germany and Austro-Hungary opposed by France, Russia and Britain, divided Europe into two armed camps. The competition to build warships, the nationalist demands in the Balkans, the posturing of Kaiser William 11, all led irrevocably to conflict. When Archduke Franz Ferdinand of Austria was assassinated in Sarajevo by a Serbian terrorist, the connections of the Alliance system pulled the whole of Europe inexorably into a state of war.

On 4th August Great Britain entered the war, and on the 17th Japan, Britain's ally, issued an ultimatum to Germany to preserve the peace in the Far East. Since then we have witnessed from afar the scarcely believable advance of the German hordes across neutral Belgium, and the heroic stand of the small British Expeditionary Force at the Battle of Mons. In September, a last-ditch stand was made along the Marne which saved Paris from certain enemy occupation. Now it seems that the frontline trenches stretch from Switzerland to the English Channel and the names of insignificant little towns such as Ypres are becoming household names. Casualty lists already number not just hundreds but thousands, not only in the west but also in the east where the Russian and Austro-German armies are locked in battle.

These terrible events have been brought home to us by the disastrous end to the summer season which saw the exodus of visitors as they rushed homeward to prepare for the conflict. Already boarding-house keepers are finding it difficult, if not impossible, to maintain payments of their rents and, as the conflict seems set to continue, what of the next season? Matters can only get worse and there are bound to be large-scale closures and bankruptcies not just among the boarding-houses but also in the dozens of smaller businesses engaged in supplying the visitors' needs. Major schemes by Government and Douglas Town Council, which provide winter employment, are being abandoned. Hundreds, too, of our young men have answered the call to the colours and the towns and villages are the poorer for their absence. Already there have been the inevitable casualties bringing grief to their families. The recruiting drive continues unabated and even horses are being commandeered for war service. The best horses have already left leaving farms, businesses, and even the Douglas Bay Tramway, with the mimimum number to survive.

Within a month of war being declared, Cunningham's Holiday Camp was commandeered and turned into a detention camp for enemy aliens and was soon filled to capacity by some 2,600 detainees. At night the camp is brightly illuminated and the glow can be seen for miles away. Strange, then, that the gas lamps along Douglas promenades have been extinguished to escape the attention of German surface raiders and U-boats lurking in the Irish Sea.

The tented accommodation at Cunningham's Holiday Camp is now filled with enemy internees. In the background can be seen the huge dining hall in which the recent riot took place.

More and more aliens have poured into the Isle of Man and a huge camp has been constructed hastily at Knockaloe in the west of the Island, the site being formerly used by Territorials for their summer visits. Following a deputation from the Imperial Government at the end of October a series of wooden huts has been constructed for accommodation and on 17th November the first 432 prisoners arrived, followed shortly by a further 450. They arrived on the *Snaefell* which then became the fifth Steam Packet vessel to be commandeered for war duty. At night the little village of Patrick is swept by searchlights and it is said that soon 10,000 prisoners will be held behind the barbed wire at Knockaloe, though this seems barely credible. On the other hand, there is to be a rail link built from Peel to connect with Knockaloe, and the Isle of Man Railway Company is being called upon to provide an engine and wagons to supply the camp with stores and coal. All this is, of course, at the expense of the Imperial Government.

There is no doubt that the internment camps will need to be supplied with huge quantities of foodstuffs of all kinds so that our farmers and fishermen will find a ready market and no doubt there will be rich pickings for contractors. The camps will also have to be maintained so there should be plenty of work for builders and their employees. Far from being utterly distasteful, the provision of the camps for the enemy aliens might prove to be an advantage that will at least do something to offset the disadvantages foretold. It is also hoped that the Manx Government will be mindful of the widespread economic distress of those relying on the visiting industry and will take steps to alleviate their plight. Then it may be that the Island will come through what is described as an Armageddon in a reasonable state.

HERE IS THE NEWS : 1915
ISLAND HEADING FOR DISASTER

The Great War between Britain and Germany has become a national disaster on an unprecedented scale for the Isle of Man. Three thousand men from the Island have joined the Forces - and casualties have been heavy. Meanwhile, the once prosperous holiday industry is in ruins, inflicting severe financial hardship on many people in the Island. We have this report:

The deaths of Manxmen fighting on the Western Front are being reported every week and the toll at sea is also severe. Seventeen men from the Island are dead or missing after the sinking by a German gunboat in the North Sea of the former Steam Packet Company ship *Ramsey*, which had been pressed into war service by the Navy as a patrol vessel. And ten Manxmen are missing presumed killed among the 500 lost in the sinking of the battleship *HMS Goliath* which was torpedoed in the Dardanelles. On the home front, instead of the usual more than 600,000 summer visitors, Douglas has welcomed an estimated 15,000. As a good season puts £1½ million into the Isle of Man economy boarding-house keepers and other traders are in serious difficulties. There was a near riot at the doors of the Tynwald Chamber as 200 protesting women tried to get in to hear a debate on the situation. They struggled with police and order was restored only following the appearance of an armed sentry. Demands are being made for the Westminster Government to give the Island financial assistance. Because it relies on communications by sea it has been hit worse than other British resorts.

VILLA MARINA LOSS
At the beginning of the year the Town Clerk of Douglas reported that the Villa Marina showed a total loss of about £3,000 for 1914. It had been expected that a profit would have been made in the anticipated record season. But the coming of war ruined any hope of this being achieved. Meanwhile, Douglas Town Council has decided that in future only British bands will be engaged for the Villa Marina. When

Design of the medals presented by the Manchester Manx Society to the crew members of the 'Wanderer'.

war started the band employed was Herr Simon Worm's Orchestra, which came under verbal attack-even though most of its members were British. Also, it has been decided that the name 'Kursaal' is to be dropped because of its Austro-German connotations.

ANGRY OUTCRY AT FOOD PRICES
Attempts to increase the price of staple foods in the Isle of Man because of increases in production costs forced by the war have been beaten by angry public opinion. Dairymen tried to raise the price of a quart of milk by a penny to fourpence. But the public outcry forced them to drop the price again within 24 hours. Meanwhile the bakery trade tried to raise the price of bread - from eightpence to ninepence for a four pound loaf. But this was defeated in the same way.

ALIEN CAMP ESCAPEES
There have been a number of escapes by detainees in the Island's two alien camps. Three former German merchant seamen forced their way through barbed wire fencing to get out of the former Cunningham's Holiday Camp in Douglas. They were later caught by police as they walked along the railway line at Crogga, near Port Soderick. At a Military Court they were sentenced to six months imprisonment with hard labour. And a detainee who escaped from the camp at Knockaloe brandished a knife when Police Constable J. E. Lace made to arrest

him near Kirk Michael. He surrendered when an Army patrol arrived.

PEEL FISHING BOAT TO THE RESCUE
The crew of the Peel fishing lugger *Wanderer* saved 140 passengers and crew from the sea after the American liner *Lusitania* was sunk by a German U-boat off the Irish coast on 7th May. Fourteen hundred out of the *Lusitania's* nearly 2000 passengers and crew were lost. *Wanderer*, with a seven-man crew under the skipper William Ball, was working nearby in the Kinsale mackerel fishery when the liner went down. At the Tynwald Ceremony on 5th July, Lord Raglan presented medals to the *Wanderer's* crew. Meanwhile, a U-boat sank the Irish collier *Downshire* nine miles off the Calf of Man. Chief Officer Thomas Turnbull, from Croit-e-Caley, Colby, was among those who were saved by the Port Erin lifeboat.

M.H.K. IN PRISON
Rushen M.H.K. Mr. Ambrose Qualtrough has gone to prison after refusing to pay a £10 fine imposed by the High-Bailiff for spreading a false and alarming report in contravention of the Defence of the Realm Act. Mr Qualtrough was alleged to have spread a rumour in the south of the Island that 4,000 aliens had escaped in Douglas and were looting shops. He later refused, when ordered by His Excellency, Lord Raglan, to say who he had heard the rumour from. Mr. Qualtrough served 12 days in prison in spite of a public

Heroes of the day! The seven-man crew of the 'Wanderer' proudly display their medals presented to them by Lord Raglan during the Tynwald Ceremony. The skipper, William Ball from Jurby, is third from the left with his 20-year-old son Stanley standing next to him. The other crew members are William Gell from Ramsey, and Thomas Woods, Robert Watterson, John Macdonald and Harry Costain, all from Peel.

(The photograph belongs to the Ball family and appears in Marjorie West's book 'Island at War'.)

petition to the Lieutenant-Governor for his release. When he returned home to Port Erin he was cheered by a large crowd of constituents.

FARMER FINED
In another offence against the Defence of the Realm Act, John Corlett, a farmer of The Cronk, Andreas, was fined £10 by the High-Bailiff for publicly using words calculated to prejudice recruiting to H.M. Forces. Corlett was alleged to have spoken loudly about local men who had volunteered for Army service, saying they were "lazy clowns trying to get out of doing honest work at home." It happened following a meeting in Ballakaneen Wesleyan Chapel where Mr. Willie Radcliffe M.H.K., the speaker, was harangued by Corlett - who in court withdrew his remarks and apologised.

1915 NEWS IN BRIEF

JANUARY
30 - Enemy submarines reported off Liverpool; four tramp steamers sunk.

FEBRUARY
3 - Recruiting drive throughout Island to raise a Manx battalion of the Royal Scots, numbering 500.
11 - As a means of economy all streets lights in Douglas to be turned down at 9 p.m. This led to the lighting of most of the gas lamps being discontinued entirely.
14 - Farewell service, St. Thomas's Church, for the three companies of Volunteers about to leave for military duty.

MAY
5 - Intimation received from the Admiralty that none of the Isle of Man steamers could be released for passenger service.
7 - American liner *Lusitania* torpedoed off Irish coast. Peel fishing boat rescues 140 survivors.
13 - Deputation of women waited on the Lieutenant-Governor urging the need of Government assistance for boarding and lodging-house proprietors.

JUNE
1 - Labour Exchange opened to aid those seeking employment in England.
3 - Tynwald deputation to Home Office to urge the need for financial assistance for the Island.
21 - Parishioners decide to proceed with the re-building of the spire of St German's Church, Peel.
26 - Government estimate deficiency of £26,722 for current year.

JULY
1 - The Rev. C. Copeland Smith inaugurated a stocking factory in Douglas, to provide an industry for Manx women during the time of war stress. By November, some 200 were employed in this way.
5 - World Manx Association Gathering at Great Meadow, Castletown.
10 - Lonan Parish Church reopened after extensive renovation to the interior.
12 - It was reported to Douglas Town Council that the sale of 18 horses for war service had realised £1079.

AUGUST
5 - Public meeting in Douglas to support the Municipal Association's scheme asking for Government assistance for payment of rates etc.
12 - Municipal Association's appeal for Government assistance re urban rates turned down by Lord Raglan.
17 - Annexation of Isle of Man to Lancashire as a means of getting assistance from Imperial Government receives little support in House of Keys.
22 - Dedication of new tower added to Arbory Church.

SEPTEMBER
17 - At a recruiting meeting in Douglas, the Lieutenant-Governor gave as an estimate that 3,000 men from the Isle of Man are engaged in military service.

NOVEMBER
2 - Motion that direct taxation should be in the form of Income Tax fails by one vote in the House of Keys. Additional Customs duties imposed but it was decided to exempt Manx manufactured tobacco from the extra imposte, by way of encouraging an insular industry.

An artist's dramatic portrayal of the part the 'Wanderer' played in the rescue of passengers from the stricken 'Lusitania'.

(Isle of Man Post Office)

"We had rather an exciting experience on Friday afternoon, about 2.30 p.m. We were coming in with about 800 mackerel. the wind light and ahead, and we put off to sea again for another shot, rather than lose the night. When we were six or seven miles off the Old Head we saw the 'Lusitania' sink, after being torpedoed by a submarine, about three miles SSW outside of us. We made straight for the scene of the disaster. We picked up the first boats a quarter of a mile inside of where she sunk, and there we got four boat loads put aboard us. We couldn't take any more, as we had two boats in tow, full of passengers. We were the only boat there for two hours. Then the patrol boats came out from Queenstown. We had a busy time making tea for them - and all our milk and tea is gone and a lot of clothes as well, and the bottle of whisky we had leaving home. The people were in a sorry plight, most of them having been in the water. We took them to within two miles of the Old Head, when it fell calm, and there was a little air ahead. The tug boat 'Flying Fish' from Queenstown then came up and took them from us . . . It was an awful sight to see her sinking, and to see the plight of these people."

William Ball,
Skipper.

"We saw the 'Lusitania' going east. We knew it was one of them big liners by her four funnels, so we put the watch on. We were lying in bed when the man on watch shouted that the four-funnelled boat was sinking. I got up out of bed and on deck, and I saw her go down. She went down bow first. We were going off south, and we kept away to the SSW. So we went out to where it took place - to within a quarter of a mile from where she went down, and we picked up four yawls. We took 110 people out of the first two yawls, and about fifty or sixty out of the next two; and we took two yawls in tow. We were at her a good while before any other boat. The first person we took on board was a child of two months. We had four or five children on board and a lot of women. I gave a pair of trousers, a waistcoat, and an oil-coat to some of them. Some of us gave a lot in that way. One of the women had her arm broke, and one had her leg broke, and many of them were very exhausted."

Stanley Ball,
Skipper's son.

EXTRACTS FROM LETTERS TO MR CHARLES MORRISON OF PEEL, OWNER OF THE 'WANDERER'.

THE MENACE OF GERMAN SUBMARINES

The Admiralty has now commandeered eleven of the finest ships of The Isle of Man Steam Packet Company. The ships are being armed and equipped for a variety of duties, such as naval patrol vessels and troop transports across the English Channel. This leaves but four vessels to maintain our lifeline for passengers, cargo and fuel. Nevertheless, it was hoped that some of the pleasure traffic to Douglas and Ramsey would continue and be sufficient to give a viable income for those engaged in the visiting industry. All such hopes were dashed when the German authorities attempted to blockade Great Britain, their submarines meeting at the outset with considerable success. Losses of British merchant ships in home waters quickly mounted and the submarines extended their operations into the Irish Sea. So adventurous were they that they destroyed vessels in the River Mersey while others were sent to the bottom in the stretch of sea between the Island and England. This had an alarming effect on those contemplating a holiday in the Isle of Man and, while the Royal Navy quickly and effectively responded to the situation, it will be a long time before confidence is restored. The sinking of the *Lusitania* with great loss of life has not helped matters. Summer arrivals have been negligible. A few more might have come but the Admiralty stopped the Heysham-Douglas service and forbade a double daily service from Liverpool in August.

The awful failure of the holiday season has been disastrous for all parts of the Island and the crisis is likely to get worse. Very many persons have not been able to pay any portion of their rents, while the rating authorities are at their wits' end to recover rates. Tradesmen cannot get in their debts, and mortgagees are wondering how property-owners will be able to cover interest charges. Already there is considerable agitation, and it is becoming more and more organised, for some sort of financial assistance. There have been near riots on Prospect Hill as people have tried to enter the Tynwald chamber to hear debates on the matter. People are suffering, people are going hungry and some are having to sell household goods to make ends meet. There have been grants to the most distressed from the National Relief (Prince of Wales) Fund, while employment has been found to some extent by the Needlework Guild and the Manx Industries Association, and for men employed at the two alien camps.

A committee of the Tynwald Court has suggested advances to persons financially prejudiced by the war, and application has been made to the Imperial Government for leave to devote £50,000 of Manx Funds for that purpose. The Treasury, however, are adamant that such relief should be paid for out of a local income tax, rather than adding to indirect taxes, such as on food. While income tax has long been established in England there is a strong reluctance on the part of members of Tynwald to apply such a tax in the Isle of Man and so it appears that there is little hope of any sort of national relief for those who are in desperate straits.

TYNWALD MATTERS : WHERE NOW REFORM?

It is now four years since the report of the MacDonnell Commission was received with approbation by many Manx citizens, whether of the reforming lobby or not. But nothing happened, and in May, 1912 two of our M.H.K.s visited the Home Office to enquire about the delay. Again nothing happened. January, 1913 saw a resolution expressing "surprise and disappointment" that the Home Secretary had not dealt with the matter of reform the previous autumn. Finally, in July that year, Lord Raglan announced the Home Secretary's decisions on the MacDonnell recommendations. Most were accepted, but there was to be no Finance and General Purpose Committee involving Keys' members and to act as adviser to the Lieutenant-Governor; and it was clearly confirmed that financial expenditure could only be initiated by the responsible Executive. But Lord Raglan was to see that the Bills to implement these recommendations were prepared for consideration and acceptance, or refusal, by the Manx Legislature.

November, 1913 saw a new House of Keys elected and during the run-up to the election the anti-reformers made such a major effort that in Douglas, for example, every seat but one was taken by those against reform. But despite this, in the new House of Keys there was still a majority, albeit a bare one, for reform. The new House assembled and proceeded with the business of the Island but no Reform Bills came its way. Finally, one Bill prepared by the Attorney-General arrived for consideration. The Keys complained that this was a composite Bill. So without further ado the Keys divided it into seven separate Bills and were willing to pass some and reject others.

The Reform Bills were passed with a comfortable majority but when the first of these Reform Bills was put before the Council it was rejected out of hand. Naturally enough this outraged the Keys who argued that Lord Raglan had been instructed to prepare several Bills, and not one. Consequently stalemate ensued, and one that a conference between Council and Keys failed to resolve. Fortunately, before a major crisis could develop, on the 25th May, 1914 the Home Secretary requested the Lieutenant-Governor to introduce into the Legislative Council the seven Bills that the Keys had devised from the original Bill. In June the seven Bills had their first reading in the Council, these being: the Isle of Man Constitutional Amendment Bill; the Isle of Man Judicature Bill; the Criminal Code Amendment Bill; the Finance Bill; the Education Acts Amendment Bill; the Poor Relief Acts Amendment Bill; the Highway Acts Amendments Bill.

One might be forgiven for thinking that this was such a signal victory for the reforming movement that the battle, after twelve years, was finally won. But in August a far more serious battle was joined. Great campaigns are now being fought in France and other parts of Europe and the Island is deeply involved in playing its part. At the beginning of this year, therefore, the Lieutenant-Governor felt that in the circumstances, and the illness of the Attorney-General also being a useful contributory factor, further consideration of the Bills should be postponed. Few will now disagree that any hopes of political reform in the near future have been dashed, and will have to wait until the war is over and victory is ours.

On 17th November Mr Samuel Norris, journalist, was released from the Victoria Road Prison after serving 28 days for contempt of court. He was set free after apologising to purge his contempt - and he was cheered by a large crowd as he walked free outside the Court-house. He has been hailed as a hero in the fight for justice and assistance for those who continue to suffer great hardship because of the war situation. We have this report:

Mr Norris, a leading reformer, is secretary of the War Rights Union and has taken up the cause of the boarding-house keepers. In many a rousing speech he appealed to the authorities to bring relief by reducing the amount of rates and rent to be paid. Many of the holiday establishments are now empty and proprietors have sold the furniture to help make ends meet. Cargoes of furniture have already left the Island. But matters were brought to a head when members of the War Rights Union objected to the sale of furniture in connection with the enforcement of judgements against ten persons, in respect of unpaid Douglas Borough rates for 1915. As a result of the uproarious proceedings, Mr Norris and eight Douglas householders were prosecuted, at the instance of the Coroner for Middle Sheading. The charge was that they obstructed the coroner in carrying out his duties in the sale of goods seized under the execution of the High Court. Dealing with the charge were Lord Raglan and

The demonstration at Tynwald Hill on 5th July. (Frank Cowin Library)

Deemsters Moore and Callow. While Mr Norris maintained that he had not wilfully caused any obstruction, he was found guilty by the Court and, refusing to apologise, was committed to gaol. The other defendants, also refusing to apologise, were fined £1.

Mr Norris almost immediately petitioned the Home Secretary for his release, and his petition was supported by a memorial signed by 3,000 Manx residents. Home Secretary, Mr Herbert Samuel, declined to interfere with what he declared was the Lieutenant-Governor's prerogative. The Home Secretary further stated that, in regard to the petition for Reform and the removal of the Lieutenant-Governor, no representations had been made to him by the Manx Legislature. Subsequently, Mr Norris came forward and apolo-

gised for, and undertook not to repeat, his contempt, whereupon he was discharged from gaol on 17th November.

GOVERNOR BOOED AT TYNWALD

After being absent through serious illness for nine months, Lord Raglan was able to return to the Island for the ancient ceremony on Tynwald Hill. He returned to unprecedented scenes as placards bearing slogans such as 'WE WANT A NEW GOVERNOR', 'TAXATION ON WEALTH', 'NO FOOD TAXES' and 'RELIEF OF WAR DISTRESS' were supported by loud chanting from many of the 6,000 present. The Lieutenant-Governor and members of Tynwald were booed and catcalled, and as Lord Raglan took the Royal Salute by the Guard of Honour a sod was thrown, hitting him on the hand. A memorial was present-

What a Reynolds Newspaper cartoonist thinks of Lord Raglan and the Manx political situation.

ed to the Lieutenant-Governor on Tynwald Hill against food taxes and the insufficiency of the grants made by Tynwald. Later, a Committee of the Court was appointed to examine the document. They reported it "contained expressions which were not respectful, decorous, nor was it temperate of language." Acceptance of the petition was therefore refused.

MOUNTING CASUALTIES

The number of Manx families grieving the loss of loved ones grows weekly. The casualty lists have included the names of a large number of Manx soldiers and sailors - especially soldiers. It is some consolation that most of these come under the headings 'wounded' or 'missing', or 'prisoners of war', but a considerable number of our gallant young men have died on the battle fields. The dead include Lieutenant John Dalrymple, son of Speaker of the House of Keys, Mr Dalrymple Maitland.

CONSCIENTIOUS OBJECTOR IN CUSTODY

Following the introduction of compulsory military service in Great Britain at the beginning of the year, Tynwald passed a resolution requesting the Imperial Parliament to extend the Military Service Act to the Isle of Man. This came into operation in March and all men between the ages of 19 and 41 are required for military service for the duration of the war. Tribunals were set up for dealing with applications for exemptions.

A conscientious objector had to be carried on board a steamer in Douglas to take him to Liverpool and the custody of the military authorities. Insurance agent Elijah Oliver, of Laxey, who failed to answer his call-up under the Military Service Act, was ordered by High-Bailiff James Gell to be conscripted for non-combatant service. When he refused to walk on the steamer at Victoria Pier, he had to be put on a stretcher and carried on board - while waving to the watching crowds.

MORE ALIEN ESCAPEES

The year began with four former German merchant seamen coming close to getting away from the Island. After escaping from Knockaloe they were caught the same evening setting sail from Peel in a motor-yawl they had stolen. Police commandeered a boat to chase after them and force their surrender. Home-made charts found in their possession showed they planned to sail to a neutral port in Norway. In April there was a disturbance at Knockaloe Camp, and when those involved refused to disperse a sentry opened fire and three prisoners were wounded.

TRACTION ENGINE FATALITIES

Two men were killed when their traction engine went out of control going down Crogga Hill, Santon, with a 14 ton threshing machine in tow. The traction engine smashed into the roadside banking and the mill landed on top of it, crushing the two men to

death, They were on their way to Southampton Farm, Port Soderick when the accident happened.

HALL CAINE'S 'MANXMAN' FILMED

In September there was great excitement in the Island caused by the London Film Company carrying out location shooting for a film based on Hall Caine's novel 'The Manxman'. Major scenes were shot at St John's, where a mock Tynwald ceremony was staged with the aid of hundreds of willing local people who took part in the crowd scenes. There was also filming at Douglas quayside, Niarbyl, Rushen Abbey, the Nunnery and St. Trinian's Church. The Board of Advertising has given the company every help, recognising that the film will give the Island valuable publicity.

STEAM TRAIN DERAILED

Finally, in October a steam train was derailed in the railway cutting through the grounds of the Nunnery when three boys heaped sand on the line. It happened as the locomotive *Mona* was approaching Douglas. The fireman sustained a broken collar bone as the engine hit the embankment. Three boys aged 15 and 16 later admitted the offence at Douglas Children's Court when High-Bailiff Gell warned that they could have caused a major disaster. Under the terms of the Children's Act he imposed fines of £2 and £1 on the boys' parents for failing to supervise them properly.

1916 NEWS IN BRIEF

FEBRUARY
7 - *H.M.S. Peel Castle* damaged by fire in the Straits of Dover when on duty as an auxiliary helping to guard these vital waters. Since refitting at Chatham she is now operating from the Orkneys, equipped with depth charge throwers.

MARCH
10 - Tynwald votes £20,000 for relief of rates for the year.
21 - Tynwald imposes additional tax of sixpence per pound on tea, bringing duty up to elevenpence.

APRIL
4,5,6 - 25th annual Manx Music Festival successfully held in the Villa Marina.
24 - Opening of Michael Primitive Methodist new hall and Sunday School.

MAY
9 - Summer-Time Act, extended to the Isle of Man by an Order in Council, came into force. Clocks were put forward one hour bringing lighter nights and saving fuel.
31 - Great sea fight off the coast of Jutland between British and German fleets. After a prolonged battle, the Germans retreated to their base. Three Manxmen among the fatal casualties.

JUNE
6 - The cruiser *H.M.S. Hampshire*, with Lord Kitchener, Secretary of State for War, and his staff on board, was sunk by a mine off the Orkneys. All hands lost with the exception of seven men who were rescued from a raft. Lord Kitchener was on his way to Russia and the news has been met with dismay.

JULY
3 - Great carnage as the Somme campaign opens. 26 British divisions involved,
5 - Tynwald Ceremony marked by demonstrations against food taxes and deficiency of relief grants for rates.

AUGUST
16 - Estate Duties Bill signed in Tynwald, imposing direct taxation for the first time in the Island. However, Tynwald's condition that they control the revenue raised is not likely to be accepted by the Imperial Government, which has the final say in such matters.

SEPTEMBER
15 - Owing to an attack of swine fever, 200 pigs were slaughtered at Kerro Dhoo, Foxdale, under the Cattle Diseases Prevention Act.
30 - The three remaining Steam Packet vessels brought 36,000 visitors to the Island, compared with 15,000 last year.

NOVEMBER
6 - Rise in price of flour and bread announced by Isle of Man Bakers' Association. Quartern loaf to rise by one penny to tenpence.
25 - Mr J. A. Brown, editor of the *Isle of Man Times*, charged before the High Court with contempt in commenting on the imprisonment of Mr Samuel Norris. The Court accepted his apology and imposed a fine of £50.

DECEMBER
5 - Isle of Man Volunteers disbanded and transferred to Imperial forces, thus saving the Manx Exchequer £30,000 a year.

HERE IS THE NEWS : 1917
BENEFITS FOR ISLAND'S ECONOMY

In spite of the virtual destruction of the Isle of Man visiting industry by the Great War, the Island's economy is gaining benefit overall. This was revealed in Tynwald when Lieutenant-Governor Raglan presented his annual financial statement - which showed a record surplus of £35,000, nearly twice as much as for last year. We have this report:

Government revenue for the financial year 1916-17 soared to over £128,500 of which, it was stated, £60,000 was received from excisable articles consumed at the Alien Camps. Government expenditure was £93,375, less than estimated. The Lieutenant-Governor said an even greater surplus could be expected in 1918, but warned that the revenue from the Camps would vanish when the war is over, and it might be some time before the visiting industry could get back on its feet and restore the economic balance.

While the war has meant great hardship and even ruin for many, farmers have been undoubtedly enriched. Prices of agricultural produce have gone up enormously - oats have sold at 32s 6d per boll and potatoes at £12 per ton, prices which have never been approached hitherto. Cattle, sheep, and pigs, too have yielded the farmers huge profits, and altogether what is now the leading industry of the Island has made tremendous advances, thanks to the war. Work is provided for local men in maintaining the Camps, while those contracted to supply the inmates are making substantial profits. Figures released by the Imperial Government show that the cost of maintaining the two Camps on the Island amounted to £570,000 for the year ending March, 1917.

The demand for food is such that the Government has issued an order prohibiting the export of oats, oatmeal, turnips and potatoes except under licence. Later, similar restrictions applied to milk and eggs. Government officials have calculated that the amount of food and goods imported is sufficient to avoid actual rationing. They estimate that there is sufficient for a daily supply per head of population of 9 oz of bread, 1.75 oz of sugar and 6 oz of potatoes. As the latter is particularly scarce a form of rationing has been formulated by Government Office. The price is fixed at 1d per pound and is proving a boon to large numbers of people. To ease the potato shortage people are encouraged to buy substitutes if they can afford it, and to eat turnips in place of potatoes during April. And those with pleasure boats are urged to use them for catching fish to relieve the demand for meat.

Government subsidies have helped to keep down the price of bread and this November the price of a 4lb loaf has been reduced from a shilling back to nine pence. This has been made possible by Tynwald sanctioning a grant of a further £20,000 from the Accumulated Fund to cover the next six months. The Imperial Government has permitted this use of funds provided that the Isle of Man introduces income tax in the near future as a means of raising the necessary revenue.

LOSS OF BEN MY CHREE

At the beginning of the year the Island was shocked at the news that the Steam Packet flagship had been sunk in the eastern Mediterranean. The Ben my Chree (111) was built at Barrow in Furness in 1908 and her triple-screw turbine made her the fastest cross-channel passenger ship afloat. She could carry over 2,500 passengers and was used on the Liverpool route. Commandeered at the beginning of the war, she was converted at the Cammell Laird Yards in Birkenhead into a seaplane carrier. A large hangar built aft could accommodate four Short 184 seaplanes equipped to carry a torpedo or bombs. Cranes were fitted to hoist the seaplanes in and out of the water.

By the middle of 1915 the Ben had been despatched to the Dardenelles and played her part in the ill-fated Gallipoli campaign. Her 'planes were used as spotters for naval guns against Turkish positions and she was the last to leave the area after the Gallipoli evacuation. Following this, her place in naval history was secured when one of her aircraft torpedoed and sank a Turkish supply ship - the first successful attack of its kind. That was on 12th August, 1915. In 1916, after passing through the Suez Canal into the Red Sea, the Ben was used to bombard Arab camps and railways. She then returned to normal duties and on 17th January was anchored off the island of Castellorizo. The Ben was about two miles off the coast when a Turkish battery opened up causing considerable damage and setting her on fire. She began to sink and the 250 on board were forced to abandon ship, all reaching shore safely by one of the motor lifeboats. After five hours of shelling, the Ben my Chree finally settled in the water as a burnt out wreck.

RISING CASUALTIES

The toll of young Manxmen serving

The Island was shocked to hear of the sinking of the 'Ben my Chree' after being set on fire by Turkish gunfire. Fortunately no lives were lost. The flagship of the Steam Packet fleet was converted into a seaplane carrier in 1915, and saw action in the Dardenelles, playing her part in the ill-fated Gallipoli campaign.   (Manx National Heritage)

with the Armed Forces gets worse. Every week the newspapers have deaths to report and it is now estimated that at least 700 of our men have died. Fighting has been particularly fierce in Flanders around Ypres and Passchendale this summer. With the United States in the war since April, American forces are desparately awaited now that the Bolsheviks have pulled Russia out of the war, thus releasing German troops for the Western Front.

HERDMAN INSTITUTE OPENED

Back at home, the new George Herdman Institute has been officially opened at Port Erin. It has been endowed by marine biologist Professor W. A. Herdman, in memory of his son, Second Lieutenant George Herdman, of the Kings Liverpool Regiment, who was killed on the first day of the Battle of the Somme in July last year, leading his men Over the Top. Professor Herdman intends the institute to be a place of relaxation and improvement for the young men of Port Erin.

BISHOP IN DISPUTE WITH VICAR

There has been a public controversy between the Lord Bishop, Dr. Denton Thompson, and the Vicar of St. Matthews in Douglas, the Reverend H. S. Taggart, over the latter allowing candidates at a confirmation service to wear coloured vestments instead of white. The Bishop refused to take part in the service - and accused Mr. Taggart of going back on a promise to use white vestments only. Mr. Taggart denies this and says

STONEPIER WEYMOUTH.

Last of the Steam Packet paddlers, the 'Mona's Queen' serves as a troop transport across the English Channel. In January she had the rare distinction of sinking a German submarine for which Captain Cain and his crew have been rewarded. The 'Mona's Queen' is seen here at Weymouth in her wartime camouflage.
(R. & L. Kelly Collection)

the confirmation candidates themselves asked for a change. The controversy has provoked a great debate in the local press.

YOUTH CAPTURES ESCAPEE

There continue to be frequent escapes by detainees from the alien camps. Escapees are always recaptured quickly, however - in one case by a 15-year-old boy. The man got away from a working party at Andreas and when young Stanley Quaye, whose father is a police constable in Ramsey, saw him walking along the road at Regaby, he suspected it was the missing man. Stanley stopped him and, single-handed, questioned him and then challenged him. The man admitted he was the escapee - and gave himself up to

Stanley who took him to Ramsey police station in a commandeered milk float.

HOUSEWIFE HARBOURS ALIENS

Meanwhile, a Ramsey housewife has been sent to prison for a month by the High-Bailiff for harbouring two escaped aliens. Forty-year-old Sarah Radcliffe, of Auckland Lane, Ramsey, pleaded not guilty. She said the two aliens asked her for food, saying they would pay for a meal, and she fed them - not realising they were escapees. The High-Bailiff ruled, however, that she must have had her suspicions about them and should have told the authorities immediately. She was also fined £1 for refusing to answer questions by the police.

1917 NEWS IN BRIEF

FEBRUARY
7 - On a moonlit night, and when crossing to France with 1,000 troops on board, the Steam Packet's *Mona's Queen* struck an attacking German U-boat with one of her paddles, sinking the submarine. The *Mona's Queen* carried on to Le Havre and then returned for major repair work at Southampton. Later, Captain Cain and his crew were awarded £300 for sinking the U-boat.
14 - Death of Miss Sophia Morrison of Peel, folk lore collector and author of 'Manx Fairy Tales'.
27 - The Lieutenant-Governor approves a scheme constituting the Laxey district a separate parish.

MARCH
3-10 - Severe spell of cold, stormy weather; snow fell heavily; railways and steamer services disorganised.

APRIL
6-11 - Severe weather marked the Easter holidays; heavy snowfalls.

MAY
30 - Steam Packet Company awarded £40,000 in the King's Bench Division for loss of the *Ramsey* sunk on Government service in the North Sea.

JUNE
4 - While inspecting Knockaloe Detention Camp, the Commandant, Colonel F.W. Panzera, died with tragic suddenness.

26 - In Tynwald, passing an education vote of £13,346, it was stated that twenty years ago 8,064 children were being educated in Manx schools, as against the last return - 5,966.

AUGUST
4 - Third anniversary of the war. Intercession services held in various parts of the Island.
6 - First cinema exhibition on the Isle of Man of successful adaptation of Hall Caine's novel 'The Manxman', at Villa Marina; witnessed by full houses daily and nightly.

SEPTEMBER
30 - Great quantities of rain fell during the month; harvesting of crops more or less a disaster.

NOVEMBER
5 - Highway Board awarded £275 from Corlett and Sons Ltd of Laxey Flour Mill in respect of extraordinary damage to the Laxey-Douglas main road, occasioned by defendant's lorry.
12 - Hollantide Fair held in Douglas Cattle Market.
World Manx Association held their T. E. Brown Festival in Villa Marina.
Meeting of Manx Society. Mona Douglas appointed secretary.
13 - Third reading of Judicature Amendment Bill to abolish the office of Clerk of the Rolls passed by Council.
20 - Keys pass second reading of Income Tax Bill proposing an assessment of 1s. in the £. The five members for Douglas

PRISONERS PLAN MASS BREAK-OUT FROM KNOCKALOE

A planned mass break-out next year from the Prisoner of War Internment Camp at Knockaloe has been uncovered. The audacious plan could have led to considerable fighting on the Island and a naval engagement offshore. Intelligence sources suggest that internees were planning to seize a Manx steamer and sail it to Germany, surrounded by a protective screen of U-boats. Now that the plot has been discovered by British Intelligence, however, security has been tightened sufficiently to make a break-out impossible.

It is believed that the German military prepared plans recently for six U-boats to go to Manx waters between 29th March and 2nd April next year. Their arrival was planned to co-incide with a break-out from Knockaloe. U-boat commanders were told to stop the passage of all vessels in the area, presumably British warships, other than a particular one from the Isle of Man. This, they were advised, would be carrying a large number of Germans who planned to break out from the Knockaloe Camp.

Manx Government Secretary, Bertram Sargeaunt, confirms that a marked naval chart of the Irish Sea has been found by camp guards. It was hidden in a false bottom of a box sent to one of the internees. Its origin has not been disclosed but Archie Knox, the Manx artist who leads a unit responsible for intercepting smuggled messages, has confirmed that messages and German newspapers have been found in tinned foods and sausages sent to internees via agencies in neutral countries. Locally-based enemy agents is another possible source. Several have been caught. One was found operating a lamp on the coast at night, signalling, it is believed, to U-boats.

British authorities have played down the likely risks to the community. Most prisoners are civilian, they say. However, with upwards of 30,000 of them crowded into two internment camps - one at the former Cunningham's Holiday Camp in Victoria Road, Douglas and the other at Knockaloe - the possibility exists that among them there are many potential fighters for the hard-pressed Fatherland. When the *Lusitania*

was sunk by a German U-boat in May 1915, some of them were heard to cheer the news. They have disturbing military tendencies too. The first internees brought to Douglas and Peel by steamer marched to their prisons with a military step and some to their own music. At Knockaloe they even made dummy wooden rifles and used them for drilling until the Home Secretary intervened.

Knockaloe was once a popular site as a camp for visiting Territorial Army regiments. It is now a huge wooden township of 26,000 internees plus 2,500 guards. That makes it the biggest internment camp ever established by Britain. It is so big that a railway line for the delivery of food and coal has been built from Peel. Electricity is fed from a gas-powered generator at the Glenfaba Brick Works. The camp is divided into compounds 100 yards square, usually 1,000 internees to each. A compound consists of five huts, a kitchen, a recreation room, a bath house and latrines. Cinder roads have been strengthened with railway sleepers. Initially the camp was limited to 5,000 but the sinking of the *Lusitania* so increased public hostility to anyone of German extraction that the rounding up in Britain of enemy aliens was intensified. They included entire orchestras so internees are enjoying high quality concerts.

Compounds were built by Manx contractors at the rate of one and a half a week, usually just a week before the latest batch of internees were due.

According to the American press, Knockaloe is an experiment in communal feeding. The average weekly cost for each internee has been put at two dollars. Catering has been contracted out to Douglas cafe proprietor, Arthur Binns Crookall, but doctors are studying the diet and making changes according to experience. The cooking is being undertaken by internees, some of whom are the finest chefs from the biggest hotels and restaurants in Britain. Indeed, at one time the meals for internees were considered so superior to those served at the British Officers' Mess that the officers had their English cook discharged and replaced by one of the internees!

A general view of Knockaloe Camp showing the layout of the compounds, each of which is self-contained and accommodates a thousand prisoners.

(R. & L. Kelly Collection)

(Above) The entrance to the camp showing the engine 'Caledonia' which hauls stores and coal along the 1¹/₂ mile line built from Peel. (Right) The camp bakeries produce thousands of loaves each day. (Manx National Heritage)

Many internees are being put to work. Some are making brushes for supply to a company which used to import German products. Government Secretary, Bertram Sargeaunt, says that gangs of 50 internees are doing quarrying and road work for the Highway Board. Gangs of 100 are helping to reclaim wasteland for agricultural use. Sulby River has been widened and deepened. According to Archie Knox, however, the workers are mainly Austrians and Serbians. "Sons of the Fatherland" do not work.

Many artistic internees are making and selling souvenirs of the camp. These include carved bones and brassware made from shell cases. Officially, internees have been banned from using British currency ever since the discovery on escapees of large amounts of money which would have sustained them whilst at large. Now they are restricted to using camp vouchers for trading. Illicit trading does happen, however, both with the guards and Manx people. A single cigarette can be sold in the compounds for 6d. Every internee is

expected to have a glass of whisky this Christmas, says Mr. Knox, because there is so much stored in the compounds.

Times are getting harder nevertheless. The worsening food situation in the U.K. is expected to lead to a ban in the New Year on aliens receiving food parcels from friends in the U.K. The only parcels which will be accepted then will be those sent from the enemy through agencies in neutral countries.

Mr. Knox says that upwards of 2,500 parcels arrive every day. These rise to 5,000 at Christmas and Whit. At first these contained first-rate quality food, each item tied up in white paper with a coloured ribbon and a flower, mainly a piece of heather. The contents have been reduced now, however, to just bread and potatoes in respect of parcels from home. Red Cross parcels usually contain only a piece of sausage and a bag of meal, packed with shavings in a box made to hold six times the quantity. Accompanying letters say, "Don't grouse. It's the best we can do for you."

Perhaps this is why the internees and the German military decided that it was time to stage a mass breakout. Here was something which would give their hardpressed, war-weary kin in Germany a dramatic boost to their morale.

(Left) Interior of one of the recreation huts, this one being used for playing games such as draughts and chess.
(Manx National Heritage)

(Below) A group of talented musicians who form one of the many camp orchestras. (R. & L. Kelly Collection)

HERE IS THE NEWS : 1918
END OF THE GREAT WAR ORDEAL

The Great War is over at long last. The news of the signing of the Armistice was transmitted to Douglas by wireless and telegraph from the Eiffel Tower in Paris at 11 a.m. precisely on 11th November, ending the greatest ordeal the Isle of Man has ever had to undergo. We have this report:

A total of 8,261 men in the Island answered Britain's call to arms, apart from many women who served in the nursing services. Of all Manxmen of military age 82.3% went to the war - believed to be the highest proportion of any country in the Empire. The losses have also been high - 1,165 have been killed serving with the British and Colonial forces. As many again have been wounded or taken prisoner. Decorations for gallantry won by our men total 260, including two Victoria Crosses. In what has been described as 'the war to end all war' 10,000,000 have been killed on both sides, one million from Britain and the Empire.

The Steam Packet Company have lost a further two ships, making a total of four of the 12 requisitioned by the Admiralty. In June the *Snaefell* was returning from the Dardenelles when she was sunk in the Mediterranean by a torpedo. It has also been revealed that the *Empress Queen* was lost after hitting rocks off the Isle of Wight. She was held in high regard as a reliable paddle-steamer and was ideal for transporting troops across the Channel. It can also be revealed that the paddler *Mona's Isle 111*, which was sold to the Admiralty in 1915, will not be returning to the Steam Packet fleet. Among her varied missions was patrolling the west coast of Ireland and acting as a rescue ship.

The war ended with a notable triumph for the Steam Packet's vessel *King Orry*. On 21st November the German High Fleet sailed into captivity to be met by the British Grand Fleet based at Scapa Flow. They sailed under Sir David Beatty and it was the *King Orry* which led the scores of German warships in the great surrender. She was the sole representative of the little ships of the

The 'King Orry' in line with the British Fleet as they lead the German Grand Fleet into captivity at Scapa Flow.
(Frank Cowin Library)

Mercantile Marine which had also played a gallant part in the war. The *King Orry* is expected back in Douglas next year.

THE 'BREAD' STRIKE BRINGS INCOME TAX

While momentous events were taking place on the battle fields of northern France, the Island was paralysed by a General Strike, the result of the Government's decision to end the flour subsidy which had kept the price of a four-pound loaf to ninepence. Public meetings were held throughout the Island, ending in a massive gathering on the foreshore at Broadway, Douglas. At all the meetings the blame was being put on the Keys for failing to progress the Income Tax Bill without the offending clause which demanded that Tynwald should have sole control of the money raised; it is thought most unlikely that the British Treasury will agree to this. At the same time, Governor Raglan was not prepared to seek further approval for the use of the Accumulated Fund, now in a healthy state. On the 1st July the master bakers announced that the price of a loaf would have to rise to one shilling. Lord Raglan, using his emergency powers, fixed the price at 10½ pence. The bakers promptly replied that they would shut down the bake-houses. The Legislature was unable to agree on the next step

and the 5th July Tynwald Ceremony was abandoned for the first time ever.

The response of the trade union leaders was to call a strike of all organised labour with the demands that the price of bread should be maintained and that there should be no further increased taxation on food. The result was an overwhelming response by the workers. All transport stopped; Douglas gas works closed, shops and workshops came to a halt - and there was no bread. Fears of looting and riots resulted in Lord Raglan closing all public houses. On the afternoon of the Tynwald Day holiday the Governor capitulated and informed the Strike Committee that the flour subsidy would continue as long as it did in England, and there would be no further increase in indirect taxes. On seeking advice from the Home Office he was ordered to bring in income tax within seven days. If this was not done then English rates would be introduced, beginning at 2/- on incomes of £500. After dragging their feet for so long, members of both Houses hastily, though not without hours of wrangling, agreed that the lower rate of Manx tax should begin at 1/6d rising to 2/7½d on incomes of over £1,500. Incomes not exceeding £130 p.a. are exempt. The Income Tax Bill was signed on 18th July, thus beginning the first

A CHRONICLE OF

form of direct taxation in the Isle of Man.

MANX INDUSTRIES ASSOCIATION

Much gratitude is being extended to the Rev. Copeland Smith, minister of Victoria Street Methodist Church, for his outstanding work in finding employment for women and girls. Early in the war he started with six girls working in the vestry of his church with knitting machines. Soon large Government orders were received and big premises occupied. The Manx Industrial Association Ltd was formed though not a penny went for personal gain. Branches were opened in all parts of the Island and many hundreds of women were employed. Over 3,000,000 pairs of socks have been knitted, together with quantities of overcoats and shirts. Mr Smith persuaded the great firm of Vickers, at Barrow, to open an airship factory in Douglas, and the Derby Castle and the Palace became hives of industry. Many others were employed in the making of shells, brushes, gloves, clogs and toys by firms such as Gelling's Foundry and Emett and Son.

NICHOLSON PAINTINGS FOR THE NATION

Fifty-eight paintings by John Miller Nicholson, the great Manx artist who died five years ago, have been bought as the nucleus of a Manx National Art Collection. They are to be exhibited in Douglas Town Hall until a National Gallery is built. The purchase was made under the will of one of the most extraordinary men ever to live in the Island, the French eccentric Pierre Henry Josef Baume, who lived in 'Baume's Castle' on South Quay, Douglas. A miserly man of great wealth he was believed to have fled to the Island, in the middle of the last century, after a career as an international spy.

BACK TO NORMAL?

Hopes are high that the Island's visiting industry will return to prosperity in the summer of 1919. There were encouraging signs this summer when, in spite of the Steam Packet company having only three small vessels in service, and continuing fears of U-boat attacks in the Irish Sea, Douglas had 97,000 visitors. This is only a sixth of the pre-war number when the industry was worth £1¹/₂ million a year to the Manx economy. But a good sign was that many thousands more would have come but for transportation difficulties.

MANX LABOUR PARTY FORMED

A dramatic new political development for the Island, where there are no political parties, has been the for-mation of a Manx Labour Party. It was in the early part of this year that representatives of 12 trade unions in the Island held a meeting in Douglas. It was decided then to form the party, which will be independent of the Labour Party in Britain. This has been followed by the first annual party conference at which a programme of political and social reform was agreed.

THE GOVERNOR RESIGNS

At the conclusion of the December meeting of Tynwald, Lord Raglan announced that he had resigned his appointment as Lieutenant-Governor of the Isle of Man, a post he has held for the past 16 years. Now that the Great War is over and there is much to do in reconstructing the Island's economy, he thinks the time has come to hand over to a younger man. His Excellency thanked the Court for their courtesy and loyal support, but to the members the news came as a 'bombshell'.

Away from his governmental duties, Lord Raglan has shown great interest in preserving the Island's rich wealth of monuments and antiquities. He used his influence to preserve the fabric of Castle Rushen which is now in use as a storehouse for the collection of museum artefacts. Since 1909 he has been a worthy President of the Isle of Man Natural History and Antiquarian Society.

1918 NEWS IN BRIEF

JANUARY
7 - Mr B.E. Sergeaunt, Government Secretary, appointed by the King an Officer of the Order of the British Empire (O.B.E.).

FEBRUARY
2 - Rev G. Tinsley, Superintendent of the Peel Wesleyan Circuit, sentenced to three months imprisonment with hard labour on a charge of having made statements likely to prejudice the recruiting of H.M. Forces. He was released from gaol on 1st March and returned to England.

APRIL
20 - The employees of Great Laxey Mine came out on strike on a refusal of the directors to concede an increase in wages. The Minister of Munitions ordered the men to return to work pending a decision in the matter.
26 - Tynwald agrees increased taxes on tobacco, spirits and beers.

MAY
11 - Military Service age raised to 51. Men of 18 years have already been called up.

JUNE
8 - Mr Thomas Henry Hall Caine awarded a Knighthood of the Most Excellent Order of the British Empire in recognition of the use made by the British Government of his literary skills during the war.
22 - First appointment of a K.C. as a Judge of the Manx Appeal Court. Sir Francis Taylor sat on the Staff of Government for the first time on 1st October.
28 - Financial statement shows surplus of £40,000 for the past year.

JULY
27 - Marked increase in visitors. Remarkable scenes at Douglas Market as prices rise - eggs 6d each, butter 3s 6d a pound.

AUGUST
6 - First cinema exhibition on the Isle of Man of successful adaptation of Hall Caine's novel 'The Manxman', at Villa Marina; witnessed by full houses daily and nightly.

SEPTEMBER
15 - Compulsory Early Closing Order became operative. Shops to close at 6 p.m. on first three days of week, 1 p.m. Thursdays, 7pm on Fridays and 8pm on Saturdays.
15 - Torrential rain fell for 24 hours. Douglas registered 4.68 inches.

OCTOBER
30 - The Onchan Dorcas Society decided that voluntary system of poor relief in the parish be discontinued. Matters to be dealt with through rate of Poor Relief Guardians.

NOVEMBER
1 - Epidemic of influenza throughout the Island. Fortunately there were few fatal cases compared with England and elsewhere.
11 - Armistice signed by Germany, followed by Bulgaria, Turkey and Austria. Thanksgiving Services held, and general manifestation of rejoicing.
17 - Villa Marina packed with 3,500 for Service of Thanksgiving. Addresses given by Lord Raglan, Sir Hall Caine and Bishop Thomas Denton.
26 - Tynwald votes £20,000 to provide out-of-work donations for those returning from war service.

DECEMBER
19 - Manx National Thanksgiving Fete held in the Villa Marina. Over £5,000 raised for war charities to help suitable cases such as war widows and their children.

LORD RAGLAN - THE GREAT DICTATOR

Lord Raglan was the grandson of Raglan of Crimea fame and is distantly related to royalty. At the beginning of the Boer War he was appointed Under-Secretary for War in the Conservative Government. As a result of a serious debacle in the running of the war, he lost this position in February, 1902. Later that year he was appointed Lieutenant-Governor of the Isle of Man, though apparently with little enthusiasm, His long absences, with pay, became something of a scandal and when eventually he settled at Bemahague, it soon became obvious that he regarded the Governorship as his inalienable right. By his training and temperament he was well qualified to resist acceptance of liberal ideals. He paid scant regard to the representatives of the people, thus dashing any hopes that the House of Keys would give a lead in furthering the interests of the Manx people as a whole.

Once in harness, Lord Raglan threw himself into the social life of the Island; no charitable event lacked his presence, and that of Lady Raglan. He had a happy knack of making himself agreeable in any company. This was especially true of those who were 'in his pocket' - those who were his appointees resulting from his great powers of patronage in judicial, civil, military and even ecclesiastical appointments. As head of the Legislature, the Judiciary, and the Police, he had many great admirers and willing supporters in whatever policy he pursued. He made it clear he had contempt for the social legislation being introduced by the British liberal governments and statesmen - the Government which had appointed him!

His chief henchmen have been members of the Legislative Council. Of these, the one who most ardently supported the Lieutenant-Governor was the Attorney-General, Mr G. A. Ring. The son of an Irish doctor, he was known as one of the ablest members of the Manx Bar. He held advanced political ideals, but these soon evaporated upon his official appointment. Through his influence two of his closest friends were given secure posts as Vicar-General and Deemster, both of which carried salaries and votes in the Council. The Attorney-General was thus able to command three votes on any question which came before the Council whose members invariably supported His Excellency in his desire to obstruct any moves for change. The Lord Bishop also supported His Excellency, as did his nominees in the Council - the Archdeacon and Vicar-General. Any member of the House of Keys who spoke up for reforms had not a single supporter in the Council.

Lord Raglan always dismissed any suggestions for political reform with a curt reply, showing his true colours - that of a despotic ruler. On the question of banning children from public houses he commented, "I drank bucketfuls of beer before I was sixteen, and I am none the worse for it!" When a member of the Keys deplored the fact that the Manx people had no old age pensions, as in England, Lord Raglan exclaimed, "There is no question of rights in this matter of old age pensions. People are not born into the world with an old age pension label placard on their backs!" This was from a man who was born into the world with a pension label on his back of £2,000 a year! The suggestion that death duties were a proper way of funding help for the aged was dismissed with the haughty reply, "I look upon death duties as about the most offensive form of taxation that anybody ever devised." This was the man who confronted the Reform Movement led by the secretary of the Reform Committee, Mr Samuel Norris. As a

Lord Raglan, C.B.E., C.B., Lieutenant-Governor, 1902-1919.
(Frank Cowin Library)

journalist and frequent visitor to the Legislature, no one was better placed to let the Manx people know the true position. He has been unflagging in his efforts through his newspaper reporting and articles, by addressing political meetings, organising passive resistance and the demonstration at Tynwald, and writing Petitions to Parliament and to the Home Secretary. He had pointed out that the extraordinary strong financial position of the Manx Government has not all been obtained at the expense of the British taxpayer. The civil population, numbering at the end of the war about 40,000, has been called upon by the Insular Government to bear its part by increased taxation on items of food and drink. Yet there has still been no provision for the old, the sick, and the unemployed. Workmen's compensation for injuries received during employment has just been announced - a step in the right direction; and in recognition of the people's war services, adult suffrage is to be approved for elections to the House of Keys.

Lord Raglan's resignation, after 16 years of Governorship, has come as a thunderbolt and caused consternation to some of his associates in the Legislature; in other quarters it has given much satisfaction and raised hopes of progress that have long smouldered in the political and public life of the Island. Mr Norris has already written to Prime Minister David Lloyd George on behalf of the 'Manx Reform Committee' earnestly seeking the assurance that Lord Raglan's successor should be appointed for a fixed term of years, and that whoever it is should be someone who is sympathetic to the constitutional, judicial and social reforms so long promised to the people of the Island and so long postponed. The announcement as to who will be the next Lieutenant-Governor is eagerly awaited.

HERE IS THE NEWS : 1919
RECEPTION FOR WAR HEROES

A reception has been held at the Villa Marina for more than 100 of the 269 officers and men from the Isle of Man who were decorated for bravery in the Great War, which ended in November last year. They included three women nurses whose courage under fire was recognised. We have this report:

It is an indication of the modesty of the Manx that few of the heroes wore their medals to the reception. Unfortunately the guests did not include the two Manx winners of the V.C. Private Abraham Acton, serving with the Border Regiment, won his V.C. in France in 1914 and was killed the following year. Private Harry Christian, who won his V.C. with the King's Own Royal Lancaster Regiment on the Western Front in 1915, no longer lives in the Island. Meanwhile, the Peace Treaty between the Allies and Germany was officially signed at Versailles in June this year. The announce-

ment caused spontaneous celebrations throughout the Island and church services were held in many parts. At night, Douglas Promenade was electrically lit and flares were lighted. The Island's official peace celebrations were held over, however, until the end of the summer. This was done in order that the visiting industry could work hard at recovering from the slump inflicted on it during the war years.

Strong pleas to the British Government for the release of Steam Packet vessels from naval duties were only partially successful and the Steam Packet Company could only call upon seven ships for the summer season. These included the *King Orry* and the paddler *Mona's Queen*, both of which earned honours with the Mercantile Fleet. With little time to build new ships, the Steam Packet has adopted a policy of buying from other companies. With about half the normal fleet carrying

capacity, 343,000 summer passengers arrived between Easter and the end of the season. It was a very satisfying result, although well short of the record figure of nearly 614,000 in 1913.

INFLUENZA CLAIMS
88 VICTIMS

The year began with a deadly influenza epidemic which saw a Government Order closing all schools, churches and places of entertainment for almost two months. The outbreak was part of the one which hit Britain and Europe soon after the Armistice. The only worship to take place was at a united open-air service at Peel. Eighty-eight deaths were recorded on the Island, including that of Mr Alexander Gill, the far-sighted developer who built many of the terraces of boarding houses along Douglas seafront and in Onchan. He will be remembered for the generous assistance he gave to tenants during the war.

At the end of the season a grand National Reception was held at the Nunnery for the soldiers and sailors who had taken part in the Great War.

(Douglas Corporation)

NEW LIEUTENANT-GOVERNOR SWORN IN

On 1st April Lord Raglan's successor, Major General William Fry, C.B., C.V.O. was sworn in at Castle Rushen as the Island's new Lieutenant-Governor. Born in Dublin, he entered the Army in 1878 and is no stranger to the Isle of Man having been a young subaltern in charge of the company of regular soldiers based at the Castletown barracks. That was 37 years ago. Since then William Fry has risen through the ranks. He saw service in India and South Africa until he was given command of a division on the Western Front for the last two years of the war. Latterly he was in charge of the Irish Command based in Dublin. Taking over the reins of Government in the castle he remembers so well, he says, is "the proudest moment of his life." His appointment is to last for seven years.

The new Lieutenant-Governor is married to a Manx lady whom he met while stationed at Castletown. In 1886 he married Ellen Margaret, eldest daughter of Sir John Goldie-Taubman, former Speaker of the House of Keys. Her uncle was Sir George Goldie of Nigeria fame, and her brother, Mr Leigh Goldie-Taubman presently occupies the Nunnery, their ancestral home. Lady Fry takes a great interest in Manx affairs and socially she has already achieved marked success.

MANX FLYER KILLED

Manx war hero Captain Elgie Jefferson of the RAF was killed when his aeroplane crashed into the Channel when he was flying mails and official despatches from London to the British Embassy in Paris. Twenty-three-year-old Captain Jefferson was the son of Mr and Mrs Thomas Elgie Jefferson of Ballahot, Malew. After leaving King William's College he joined up in 1914, taking part in the air war on the Western Front and winning the

The Island's new Lieutenant-Governor, Major-General William Fry, C.B.

(Frank Cowin Library)

Croix-de-Guerre.

In January this year he flew from Hooton in a Bristol fighter and landed in a field near his parents' home. The flight took 40 minutes. Captain Jefferson made history by being the first Manxman to fly across the Irish Sea to the Isle of Man.

PLEASURE FLYING

The craze for pleasure flying came to the Isle of Man this summer when two Avro 504K aircraft, modified to carry two passengers, crossed from Blackpool. Permission had been obtained from Douglas Corporation to use part of the beach and the grass area on Queen's Promenade as an aerodrome. Lieut Moxon was in charge of the operation and many people took the opportunity of experiencing their first flight, a 'flip' round the bay costing one guinea. First to take to the air were the 70-year old Mayor, Mr John Kelly and the Town Clerk, Mr Alexander Robertson. After landing, Lieut. Moxon hailed the flight as 'the inau-

guration of civil flying' in the Isle of Man. Miss Florrie Ford also went up during a break from her performances at the Derby Castle. Lieut Moxon also secured the right to use North Shore, Ramsey for pleasure flying and members of Ramsey Commissioners were treated to flights over Ramsey.

What can be regarded as the first commercial flight to the Island also occurred during the summer when copies of the *Daily News* were flown from Lake Windermere in the early morning to Douglas Bay. The service lasted for a fortnight and General Fry was presented with the first 'Seaplane Edition'. The aircraft was an Avro seaplane, and its pilot was Captain Howard Pixton who became famous for winning the prestigious Schneider Trophy for England in 1914.

MEN KILLED IN ACCIDENTS

On the same day in August, two men met with fatal accidents. Edward Cringle (21), a brewery carter, was crushed while lowering a cask of whisky into the cellar of The Bowling Green Hotel, Douglas. And Thomas Harold Moore (29) while feeding a bone-crushing mill at his father's manure factory at Baldwin was caught by the arm. He was trapped for two hours before a blacksmith released him but died later in Noble's Hospital.

INCOME TAX CUT

The Manx Budget statement issued in June shows that the Island's financial condition continues to prosper with a record surplus of £88,000 for the previous year. Substantial increases were imposed in time for the season on British beer, Manx-brewed beer and spirits. However, the total assessment for income tax amounted to £66,000, considerably more than was expected. Consequently, Tynwald has reduced the rates which now begin at 10d rising to a maximum of 1s 5d. At the same time the sugar tax was abolished, though duties on tea, coffee, tobacco etc. remain.

FIRST POST-WAR ELECTIONS

The beginning of November saw a week of voting in the General Election and a new House of Keys has taken office with 11 new members. They include four representatives of the Labour Party formed last year. Journalist and printer Mr Samuel Norris topped the poll with 2,469 votes in North Douglas, the largest constituency of all. Because of this he is being officially called the 'Senior Member' of the new House.

At the first meeting of the 24 members, Mr George Frederick Clucas, M.A. was elected Speaker of the House of Keys. He succeeds the highly-respected Mr Dalrymple Maitland who died earlier in the year. Head of a great Manx family, Mr Clucas graduated at Cambridge and is qualified for admission to both the English and Manx Bars. After being on the 'mainland' for some years, Mr Clucas returned to his residence at Cronkbourne and was elected as the

The summer season saw the return of pleasure flying from Douglas beach. Here, two Avro 504 aircraft are parked at their 'aerodrome' on Queen's Promenade.

(Alan Daugherty Collection)

member for Middle to succeed the late Mr Dalrymple Maitland. The new Speaker takes a deep interest in Manx history and is a member of the Manx Society and the World Manx Association.

1919 NEWS IN BRIEF

JANUARY

14 - House of Keys informed by the Imperial Government that it consents to future Governorships being limited to a number of years.

22 - Douglas building trade dispute settled by arbitration. Rate for plumbers, masons and joiners settled at 1s. an hour for a 55 hour week. Labourers to be paid 10$\frac{1}{2}$d per hour.

28 - Lord Raglan agrees to provide money for a Workmen's Insurance scheme.

FEBRUARY

22 - Legislative Council passes Adult Suffrage Bill.

24 - Much inconvenience caused as a result of telegraphic communications being interrupted by broken cable. Wireless telegraphy in temporary use.

25 - At the Annual Meeting of the H. B. Noble Nursing Fund, Rev. W. J. Karran offered Keppel Gate Hotel, which he owned, for the purpose of a sanitorium.

25/26 Historic Steam Packet annual meeting when three of the seven directors were in favour of winding up, or nationalisation, to bring about a division of the Company's large assets - about £1,000,000. Major English shareholder blocks the move. Dividend of 10% with 10% bonus declared.

MARCH

1 - New cattle mart opened in Tynwald Street.

2 - Enemy aliens at the Douglas Detention Camp present illuminated address to the Bishop in recognition of the part he had played in ministering to them.

11 - Government Order prohibiting the slaughter of lambs before 1st May. Lambs of 80 lb. may be slaughtered after 1st April.

22 - Peel Licensing Court refuse Sunday cinema licence.

25 - Mr Dalrymple Maitland, J.P., Speaker of the House of Keys since 1909, died at Brook Mooar, Union Mills, aged 71 years. He was chairman of the Asylums and Assessment Boards and his private interests included being chairman of the Steam Packet Company, the Railway Company and the I.O.M. Banking Company.

25 - Visit of R34, the largest airship, which passed over Douglas whilst on a trial trip round Ireland. In July, the R34 was the first to make a return trip to America.

28 - Douglas Detention Camp evacuated.

APRIL

3 - Installation at Castle Rushen of Major-General Fry as Lieutenant-Governor of the Isle of Man, by Lord Raglan.

8-10 - Great success of Manx Music Festival. Prizes presented by the new Governor.

27 - Fierce blizzard lasting several hours sweeps over Island.

MAY

13 - Legislative Council adopt Constitution Amendment Bill whereby the Vicar-General, Archdeacon and Receiver-General are removed as ex-officio members of the Council.

JUNE

2 - After sinking a submarine, steaming 66,700 miles and carrying about half a million troops between England and France, the Steam Packet Co's last paddle-steamer *Mona's Queen* resumed passenger service on the Liverpool-Douglas station.

26 - Laxey miners informed that their war bonus of 15s. per week is to be discontinued. Miners resolve unanimously they are not prepared to work for pre-war wages owing to impossibility of living decently on the money.

28 - Treaty of Versailles signed. Great rejoicings throughout the Island.

JULY

5 - Tynwald Day sees 19 Acts promulgated, including the Workmen's Compensation Act.

8 - Complaints made to Tynwald regarding the high price of potatoes - 5d. per pound.

16 - Ramsey Town Commissioners informed that it is hoped to resume steamer services in 1920.

25 - Laxey miners appeal to all Trade Unionists for assistance.

SEPTEMBER

10 - Acute crisis in the labour dispute in connection with Laxey mines. Men decide to hold out for rates of pay demanded, aware that such a decision may entail the closing of the mines altogether.

NOVEMBER

11 - Newly-elected House of Keys meet for the first time.

- Armistice Day commemorated at the request of His Majesty, all business being suspended for two minutes from 11 o'clock forenoon.

HERE IS THE NEWS : 1920
VISIT OF KING GEORGE V AND QUEEN MARY

During July, the Island has had its third royal visit in 73 years. King George and Queen Mary spent 9½ hours on shore after landing at Ramsey from the royal yacht - following the example of Edward the Seventh in 1902 and Queen Victoria in 1847. The royal yacht was accompanied by 30 ships of the Royal Navy, including five 'Super Dreadnoughts". We have this report:

The difference with this royal visit is that it was announced and planned well in advance. The first two happened without warning. And because bad weather forced the royal yacht into Ramsey again, instead of Douglas, the Northern capital is being dubbed Royal Ramsey. The royal visitors were driven into Douglas to meet huge crowds, including Great War veterans, near Douglas harbour. Over-excited people broke through barriers and caused some confusion. Later the King and Queen were greeted at Villa Marina by 4000 children, clad all in white, who sang the two National Anthems. In a speech there the King made references to the Island's sacrifice of its young men in the Great War - and the hardship suffered by people at home through the virtual shut-down of the visiting industry. The royal party was given an enthusiastic welcome wherever they went in the Island - although the disruption of the schedules caused by the diversion to Ramsey meant disappointment for some places, expecially Laxey. A highlight of the visit came when the King conferred a knighthood on the Lieutenant-Governor, Major General William Fry, now Sir William. Government Secretary, Mr. B. E. Sargeaunt and Chief Constable Colonel H. W. Madoc were both made Members of the Victorian Order.

VICTORY CARNIVAL
A splendid Victory Carnival was held in Douglas on 14th June to announce to the remainder of the British Isles that the Island is now back in business as a holiday resort. It lasted a week and received widespread newspaper publicity. As a result the Island this year had its second best season ever with more than 555,000 visitors, only 61,000 fewer than in the record 1913 season. A midsummer blow to the visiting industry, however, was the destruction by fire of the Palace Ballroom in Douglas. But the Palace Company is planning to have it re-built for the 1921 season.

Kirk Michael's impressive ceremonial archway through which Their Majesties passed on the royal tour.

(R. & L. Kelly Collection)

END OF PLEASURE FLYING
Pleasure flying returned to Douglas when the International Aviation Company of Liverpool were granted the concession to use the 'aerodrome' on Queen's Promenade, Douglas. But the de Havilland aircraft have been involved in crashes, fortunately without serious injury. One machine came down in the bay but stayed afloat. Its pilot and passengers sat on the wings until a rescue boat arrived. In another crash a machine somersaulted while landing and finished upside down. The pilot was flung clear but the mechanic was trapped underneath for some time.

However, a memorial, signed by 20 occupiers along the front of Queen's Promenade, was presented to Douglas Corporation claiming an infringement of rights whereby the grass area was not available for their guests or for the purpose of drying bed linen. An appeal for an injunction has been upheld in the High Court and the aerodrome facilities are to be withdrawn for next year.

BOY RUN OVER BY CABLE CAR
In a tragic accident a small boy has had a leg amputated after being run over by a cable tram car in Bucks

King George and Queen Mary arriving at the Queen's Pier, Ramsey. His Majesty is inspecting his gloves after touching the railings which had just been painted!

(R. & L. Kelly Collection)

Road, Douglas. Five-year-old Charles Turner, whose parents live in Manchester, was on holiday in Douglas with his grandmother. Doctors at Noble's Hospital managed to save one leg but the other had to be taken off. Meanwhile, tragedy was averted after the Scottish steamer *George L. Munro* foundered in heavy seas off Douglas. Her crew escaped in a lifeboat - which was leaking and began sinking. They were rescued by two Douglas fishermen in a lugger.

SANTON WAR MEMORIAL UNVEILED

The Island's first memorial to the dead of the Great War has been unveiled at Santon, commemorating the deaths of six local men. It is made of red sandstone surmounted by a Celtic cross and stands on the main Douglas - Castletown road near the turning down to Port Grenaugh. Similar memorials are going up in other towns and villages. The one at Santon has been followed by those at St. Mark's and Ramsey. There is to be one on Douglas seafront - and there will be a Manx National War memorial at St. John's.

WORK FOR UNEMPLOYED

After a mass meeting 500 unemployed men, most of them ex-Servicemen, marched on Government Office in Douglas to ask the Lieutenant-Governor to receive a deputation from them. The men, who have been unable to find work at the end of the visiting season, want the Government to set up winter work schemes. Winter unemployment is a traditional problem for the Island, brought back following the end of the Great War. To ease the situation Tynwald is to spend £8000 on new road schemes.

GREAT LAXEY MINES CLOSED

The Great Laxey Mining Company has closed down and the company has gone into liquidation. A five-month long pay strike by the miners is being partly blamed.

A company spokesman said Laxey's lead and blende had found a ready market for years but newly-discovered deposits in Australia brought world prices down. He said Laxey might have been saved, however, if the men had not insisted on pursuing industrial action. He said they had been led like sheep by the Workers Union.

Parliament Square, Ramsey, was thronged with people anxious to gain a glimpse of the new King and Queen.
                                            (R. & L. Kelly Collection)

This triumphal arch greeted visitors arriving for the Douglas Victory Carnival held in June.
                                            (R. & L. Kelly Collection)

Disaster struck in July when the Palace Ballroom was completely gutted by fire. It is planned to have it rebuilt for next season.
                                            (R. & L. Kelly Collection)

In March, the first old age pensions were distributed to men and women of 70 years and over. Here, those living in an old people's institute in Douglas receive their 10 shilling postal orders. Mr Samuel Norris, M.H.K., and Chairman of the Old Age Pensions Commission, can be seen standing next to the postman.

(Frank Cowin Library)

1920 NEWS IN BRIEF

JANUARY

20 - Mr Norris's resolution of protest against the huge increases in official salaries since 1914 without the knowledge of Tynwald is further discussed. Governor replies such matters are restricted by the Home Secretary. The Keys then withdraw in protest and resolve not to meet in Tynwald.

24 - New scales for police show constables are to start on 70s a week plus numerous allowances. Great disquiet results throughout the Island.

26 - Isle of Man Banking Co. Ltd declare dividend of 20% with 5% bonus.

FEBRUARY

2 - At annual meeting of the House of Industry the character of the institution is severely criticised, and a reform committee appointed.

13 - Mr Norris to head Keys' deputation to meet Home Secretary concerning the rights of Tynwald to financial control.

MARCH

4 - Disgraceful termination of a football match at Ramsey, the referee and several players being assaulted.

5 - First Old Age Pensions paid in the Island. Over 1,000 people receive postal orders for 10 shillings.

27 - Steam Packet Company purchases *Viper* from G. and J. Burns of Scotland and is renamed *Snaefell (IV)*. The *Manxman* has been purchased from the Admiralty having been previously owned by the Midland Railway Company who used her on the Heysham-Douglas route. A third vessel, the *Onward*, is to be purchased from the Chatham Railway Company and will be renamed *Mona's Isle (IV)*. In July the *Viking* is to be bought back from the Admiralty after serving as a seaplane carrier named *H.M.S. Vindex*.

APRIL

12 - Price of 4lb. loaf raised to 1/1d.

13 - Legislative Council reject 'the conscientious clause' in the Vaccination Bill.

13-15 Manx Music Festival, 1990 entrants.

MAY

3 - Death of Mr John Holland, a well-known artist.

4 - Keys abandon 'strike' and resume Tynwald business.

17 - Tynwald hears that Home Secretary has decided that both Keys and Council are to be consulted about intended taxation and expenditure. A Keys committee to confer with Governor on preparation of Budget.

18 - Old Age Pensions and National Insurance Bill passed.

31 - T.T. practising starts, after an absence of six years. End of Course altered from Cronk ny Mona to take in Signpost Corner, the Nook and Governor's Bridge.

JUNE

5 - Tynwald overrules Highway Board, and prevents motoring on the Sundays before and after the T.T. Races.

14 - Douglas Victory Carnival Week begins.

17 - Local rider Douggie Brown (Norton) finishes second to T. C. de la Hay (Sunbeam) in the Senior T.T.

22 - Motor ambulance formally presented to Noble's Hospital.

28 - Lieutenant-Governor informs Tynwald of a surplus of £172,800 for the past year. In response to requests from the Imperial Government, Lieutenant-Governor proposes that £150,000 be given as a war-contribution and that £50,000 of the Imperial war debt be taken over.

JULY

6 - Tynwald rejects Lieutenant-Governor's proposal to abolish all taxes on tea, coffee and cocoa. Money raised should be used to increase the bread subsidy in the winter.

14-15 Visit of King George V and Queen Mary.

16 - Palace Ballroom destroyed by fire.

17 - Exhibition in London of paintings of Manx scenery by Mr W. Hoggatt of Port St Mary.

AUGUST

7 - Port St Mary annual regatta revived.

30 - *Daily Mail* carries article which describes the sea-bathing conditions at Douglas the worst that has been seen. Allegation is promptly repudiated by the Chief Constable.

SEPTEMBER

14 - Death of Mr Frederick Buxton, entertainment manager.

OCTOBER

1 - Elementary teachers give notice to cease their employment, as a result of salary dispute.

19 - Election of first directors of Manx National Health Insurance Society created by the Health Insurance Act.

27 - Mass meeting of unemployed, mainly ex-service men, sends deputation to Governor to urge the provision of public works.

NOVEMBER

2 - Shop Hours Bill passed fixing hours for the winter.

9 - Tynwald agrees to pay school teachers according to the English 'Burnham Scale'

9 - Tynwald votes £10,000 for repair of roads to relieve unemployment.

9 - The Great Laxey Mining Company goes into liquidation.

23 - Annual meeting of the Palace and Derby Castle Company. Capital increased to purchase the Grand Theatre, Victoria Street and Buxton's Pierrot Village, Central Promenade.

28 - Footballer awarded £14 damages against another player who assaulted him in the course of a game.

DECEMBER

1 - Peel Town Commissioners receive a letter from the Local Government Board threatening a public inquiry if the proceedings of the Commissioners continue to be of a disorderly character.

3 - Elections completed for the Central Authority created by the newly-passed Education Act.

10 - First meeting of the Isle of Man Education Authority.

TYNWALD MATTERS: KEYS WIN BATTLE

One of the first concerns of our Lieutenant-Governor was to guide the Constitution Amendment Bill on to the Statute Book. It makes sweeping changes to the make-up of the Legislative Council. The Archdeacon, Vicar-General and Receiver-General are no longer ex-officio members of the Council. They have been replaced by two non-official members nominated by the Lieutenant-Governor and four others elected by the Keys, these six to hold office for eight years. The new Legislative Council, therefore, is a body of eleven members - the above six and the Lord Bishop, the two Deemsters and the Attorney-General, with the Lieutenant-Governor presiding, but without a vote. This will, no doubt, come as a relief to everyone, especially those of the Reform Movement who, 17 years ago, foresaw that only changes in the composition of the Council would lead to the wishes of the electorate being implemented.

The Great War changed everything - the breakdown of apparently permanent social barriers, the increased awareness of our young men who served on the fighting fronts, and the raised expectations of the fairer sex - have formed the present political climate. This has been reflected in the new House of Keys which now has a reformist majority, including the doughty Samuel Norris and four members of the Manx Labour Party. There was little delay in passing the Old Age Pensions Bill and arrangements were made quickly for interim payments. More dramatic events ensued as a result of the demand by Keys' members to be consulted on financial matters, including the right to scrutinise salaries of those on the Civil List. Objections from the Council resulted in the Keys withdrawing their co-operation in Tynwald affairs for a period of nearly four months. "To your tents, O Israel" was nothing less than a strike. The Keys made it abundantly clear that, as representatives of those paying taxes, they should have a say in how the money should be spent. A deputation, led by Samuel Norris, visited the Home Secretary and, subsequently, explicit recommendations from the Home Secretary, the Rt Hon. Edward Short, were received. He said that all expenses of government should first be put to the Finance Committee of the Keys and, furthermore, that the Manx budget and its supplementary estimates should be placed in advance before the Keys.

These are major changes. They elevate mightily the position of the Keys and to the most wildly optimistic imaginable it might perhaps be seen as giving some semblance of reality to the notion of Manx Home Rule. Perhaps the recent decision to clothe our Speaker in wig and gown, copying the Speaker of the House of Commons, is a symbol of more independent times to come.

ENTER THE MANX LABOUR PARTY

The election to the House of Keys of four members of the Manx Labour Party must bring great satisfaction and encouragement to those who met for their first Conference in Salisbury Hall, Victoria Street, Douglas in September, 1918. No party emerges from nothing. A socialist group held regular meetings in Douglas in the 1890s. In Rushen the Progressive Association has for some time advanced the banner of Radicalism, while small branches of the Independent Labour Party have emerged in several places. In Douglas the attempts to establish the Workers' Union has also helped to establish a radical climate of opinion. When Mr. W. C. Craine of the I.L.P. stood in Douglas during the 1908 Elections, many thought it was 'a straw in the wind'. He failed, but won the support of 282 voters.

As the Great War drew to a close our particular circumstances were instrumental in the rapid evolution of this new political force. The battle over the introduction of Income Tax, the struggle for Old Age Pensions, but more importantly, the Bread Strike of July, 1918 brought home to the workers the necessity of concerted political action if their standard of living was to be improved. This led to the formation of the Manx Labour Party. The first Conference met in private session and at it an Executive of 15 members was elected - a roll call of prominent supporters such as Christopher Shimmin, Alfred Teare, Richard Kneen, James Corrin and so on. Two are women - Annie Watterson representing class teachers and Nellie Taylor of the Shop Assistants Union. The Conference then went into public session, not too well attended it must be said, and Mr. William P. Clucas of Peel was elected Chairman and the Programme confirmed. Apart from the advocacy of nationalisation, the Party pressed for Unemployment Insurance, Workmen's Compensation, a 48 hour week, a single Education Authority and the re-distribution of seats in the Keys to lessen the dominance of the country areas. A National Health Insurance, a National Sanitorium and Hospital were also advocated. To advance them, meetings are held at a variety of halls in Douglas. The aspirations of the artisan classes are being targeted and open-air meetings have also been held in such places as the Market Place, Shaw's Brow, Back Strand Street, Frederick Street and so on. Indeed, at the Market Place Mr. Alfred Teare used a rickety chair as a rostrum! The rest of the Island is not being neglected. The four present Labour members are Mr Gerald Bridson (Middle), Mr J. R. Corrin (Rushen), Mr Christopher Shimmin (Peel) and Mr Alfred Teare (South Douglas). Other candidates stood in Michael, Garff and Glenfaba.

As to how powerful the Manx Labour Party will become depends on a number of factors. If social conditions worsen and if the Government is unsympathetic to the concerns of the workers, then support will inevitably increase. The quality of the new Labour representatives is undoubtedly high, and should this remain so there will be many citizens tempted to vote for other Labour candidates even though they are not Labour supporters themselves. If the Labour Party is able to organise itself in all constituencies, then even the conservative rural areas might provide surprises. The next few years is likely to prove a fascinating time for students of Manx politics. One thing seems certain, future Houses are unlikely to be described, as was the 1913 Keys, as "a pronounced collection of mediocrities".

HERE IS THE NEWS : 1921
ALARMING DROP IN POPULATION FIGURES

Figures resulting from this year's Census show a further drop in the Island's population. It has sent alarm bells ringing in Government circles. We have this report:

The latest population figure of 49,078 is the lowest since the middle of last century, when the Island recovered from the major emigrations of the 1820s and 1830s. From 1850 onwards the population had grown to about 55,000. It even held reasonably firm at the start of this century, despite further emigration encouraged by newspaper columns full of advice to would-be emigrants. Now, however, it has declined by another 3,000 since the 1911 Census when the population was 52,016. This is a fall of 5.4%. The male population has dropped to 22,127, a drop of 7.7% which can partly be accounted for by the heavy casualties suffered during the last war. The female population stands at 27,106, a fall of 3.5%.

The reasons for decrease in the population are not hard to find. Dramatic falls in the parishes of Patrick and Lonan reflect the savage effects of the decline in the mining industries of those areas. Other calamities have exacerbated the employment situation. During the year nearly 300 jobs have been lost through disastrous fires which destroyed the Laxey Flour Mills and the Manx Industries' factory at Castle Hill, Douglas. Add to these the depressing problem of winter unemployment when the summer demands of the visiting industry leave a surplus of manpower unable to find work at the end of September. Islands in this modern era seem, perhaps inevitably, to export their children and young people. All the more reason they should be properly educated and trained so that they can hold their own when venturing into the world beyond.

THREATS TO THE T.T. RACES
This year's T.T. Races were jeopardised by the coal strike in Britain. This strike forced the Steam Packet Company to reduce sailings at the beginning of the season to one on alternate days. It looked as though the races would have to be cancelled,

The disastrous fire which gutted the building of the Laxey Glen Flour Mills, causing considerable unemployment. The Douglas Fire Brigade can be seen in attendance.   (R. and L. Kelly Collection)

but this was averted by the company using expensively-purchased Continental coal to restore services.

Since then, the Auto-Cycle Union threatened to move the T.T. to Belgium. It said the move would attract more Continental riders and the Belgium Government had offered support. There was discontent also about profiteering and poor facilities on the Island. Many minds were exercised over the matter but it was a deputation from Douglas Town Council, with their spokesman Mr George Brown of the *Isle of Man Times* and local representative of the A-C.U., who solved the crisis.

EIGHT-YEAR-OLD BIRCHED
There has been a great public outcry over the harshness of a sentence of four strokes of the birch imposed by the High-Bailiff on an eight-year-old boy who stole bread from a Douglas bakery. The House of Keys asked Lieutenant-Governor, Major General Sir William Fry, to intervene. But Sir William said he was powerless to act. The punishment had already been meted out anyway. The Keys then asked the Lieutenant-Governor to set up a commission of inquiry into the high cost of bread and other necessities of life in the Island. M.H.K.'s have also decided that they should be paid. They are to get £50 a year and £10 travelling expenses for carrying out their public duties.

WAR HERO RELEASED
Great War hero Captain Thomas William Nelson, M.C., has been released on licence from the Island's prison where he was serving a six month sentence for burglary. His tragic story was revealed in the Court of General Gaol. When war broke out in 1914 he was a humble 17-year-old carter in Douglas. He volun-

THE 1921 CENSUS		
Details for towns and parishes are shown with a percentage comparison with the 1911 Census. The decrease of 2,783 is shared by all towns and parishes except Onchan, Rushen and Castletown		
DOUGLAS	- 20,192	(-4.7%)
Onchan	- 2,336	(+11.3%)
Lonan	- 2,106	(-16.7%)
Braddan	- 1,765	(-11.5%)
Marown	- 814	(-2.6%)
RAMSEY	- 4,121	(-3.0%)
Maughold	- 774	(-16.7%)
Lezayre	- 1,101	(-13.8%)
Andreas	- 996	(-5.5%)
Bride	- 449	(-9.2%)
Jurby	- 447	(-13.8%)
PEEL	- 2,455	(-5.8%)
German	- 1.077	(-5.6%)
Patrick	- 1,138	(-25.2%)
Michael	- 749	(-11.3%)
Ballaugh	- 628	(-3.0%)
CASTLETOWN	- 1,860	(+2.3%)
Malew	- 1,570	(-17.3%)
Santon	- 387	(-12.9%)
Arbory	- 766	(-2.6%)
Rushen	- 3,347	(+2.9%)
TOTAL	*-49,078*	*(-5.4%)*

teered, was commissioned in the field, rose to the rank of captain, and won his Military Cross on the Western Front. But on returning to his native Island he could find no work and he began drinking and then turned to crime. Money has been raised by public subscription to give Captain Nelson a new life in America.

SUNDAY DRINKING BANNED

The day of the *bonafide* traveller, the only person able to get a drink in a Manx public house on a Sunday, is over. A Bill passed by the House of Keys outlaws the practice. Members heard that the drinkers of Douglas would travel just enough of a distance outside the town and then make

a nuisance of themselves in country pubs by claiming their right to drink. The Bill also imposes statutory opening and closing hours on shops in the Island for the first time.

MANX WOMAN MURDERED

A Belgian commercial traveller, 48-year-old Edouard Braehm, has been charged with the murder in Liverpool of a Manx woman, 37-year-old waitress Mary Clarke, formerly of Jurby. Her naked and mutilated body was found in a lodging house bedroom occupied by Braehm who was staying in Liverpool while selling ladies' underwear. Her family still live at Jurby. She left the Island in 1913 after being convicted on charges of immorality and she was said to have

lived a life of depravity in Liverpool. Braehm's trial will take place in Belgium next year.

KING ORRY STRANDED

The Steam Packet Company vessel *King Orry*, famous for leading the German High Seas Fleet into captivity at Scapa Flow in 1918, went aground with 1,300 holidaymakers on board in thick fog in the Mersey. She narrowly avoided a terrible disaster. She missed the rocks and the Perch Rock lighthouse at New Brighton by about 10 yards. The ship was left high and dry by the falling tide enabling many passengers to disembark, by climbing down fire brigade ladders. No one was hurt.

1921 NEWS IN BRIEF

JANUARY
13 - Laxey Glen Flour Mills, which supplied the whole Island during the war, was gutted by fire.
17 - Manx bakers reduce the price of a 4lb. loaf from 1/1d to 1/-
  - Building trades strike ends; wages agreed at 2/-d an hour for 49½-hour week.
21-28 Local Government Board conduct an enquiry into public health administration in Peel. Sensational evidence as to disorderliness at Commissioners' meetings; "every member in turn called a liar".
24 - Annual meeting of I.O.M. Banking Company. Record £2 million held; dividend of 20% declared with 5% bonus.
25 - Keys pass an Income Tax Amendment Bill increasing allowances for wife, children and dependants.

FEBRUARY
1 - Deemster Moore orders liquidation of Dumbell's Bank to be completed by end of summer season.
8 - Rent Restriction Bill signed in Tynwald, continuing protection of tenants until 1923. Landlords permitted to raise house rents no more than 50% of pre-war figure.
15 - Local Government Board censures Peel Commissioners and orders certain works to be completed within prescribed periods.
23 - Tynwald Court accepts the offer of the Noble's Trustees to give the old hospital to the public for purpose of a National Museum.

MARCH
9 - House of Keys agrees to pay members £50 per annum, plus travel allowances and additional salaries for chairmen of Boards.
15 - Shop Hours Bill passed which provides compulsory hours of closing in the winter; summer hours left to wishes of trades involved. All shops to close on Sundays at 10.30 a.m. Strong opposition from public-house and sweetshop proprietors.

APRIL
1 - Serious fire in the factories of the Manx Industries Association at Castle Hill, Douglas.
3 - Following the withdrawal of the Government flour subsidy, the price of a 4lb. loaf is raised to 1/2d.
9 - Negotiations between the liquidators of Great Laxey Mining Company and Mr Robert Williamson for the sale of the mine property fall through.
10 - Agricultural Society's spring show. A number of pedigree bulls purchased by the Board of Agriculture re-sold to local farmers.
10 - Shipping services reduced to alternate days because of coal strike.
12 - After pressure from Imperial Government, Tynwald Court decides to take liability of £250,000 War Loan as a contribution to the Imperial War Debt.
23 - The Noble's Trustees announce gift of £32,000 for the teaching of women and girls in domestic subjects.

JUNE
11 - Wages of plumbers and joiners reduced to 1/8½d an hour.
16 - A number of motorists fined for riding on the Sunday before T.T. racing without the requisite permit from the Chief Constable.

JULY
2 - Asenath Kelly (20) killed after being impaled on a hayfork while working on a farm in Onchan.
9 - Winifred Gawne, a girl cyclist, killed after a collision with a motor charabanc at the Three Roads, Port Erin.
14 - Several Douglas shopkeepers fined for selling on Sundays in defiance of the new Shop Hours Bill.
14 - Oswald Clark (18) killed while riding a horse at the Belle Vue races.
14 - British coal imported after British coal strike ends.
15 - Tynwald Committee recommends various public works, including a covered shelter on the Victoria Pier, at a cost of £122,000
18 - King sends a telegram of congratulations upon the opening of the new Palace Lido which replaces the ballroom destroyed by fire last year.
28 - A decision by the High-Bailff of Douglas virtually permits the sale of fruit on Sundays.

AUGUST
1 - George Quayle (17), a railway employee, killed by falling under a train at Port Erin.
29 - Schooner *Jessie Sinclair* of Port St Mary takes fire off the coast of North Wales and is totally destroyed.

SEPTEMBER
20 - Largely-attended public meeting at Peel requests the Central Education Authority to reconsider its decision not to build a secondary school in Peel.
24 - Negotiations re-opened for sale of Great Laxey Mines.
29 - I.O.M. Employers' Federation and the Douglas branch of the Workers' Union fix standard wage of 26/- a week.

OCTOBER
18 - House of Keys requests Governor to appoint a committee to enquire into price of bread and meat and other necessities of life, with a view to introducing anti-profiteering legislation.

NOVEMBER
8 - Hundreds of unemployed men march to the offices of the Douglas Board of Guardians and to the Tynwald Court to plead for relief work. Tynwald agrees to provide more money throughout the Island, mainly for road works.
8 - Tynwald reverses its decision to ban use of motor vehicles on the Sunday preceding the T.T. races.
23 - Manx Industries' Association closes down its works, causing 250 to become unemployed.
29 - More difficulty over the Shop Hours Act. Various tradesmen exempted from limitation of opening hours.

SAVING THE T.T.: A DASHED NEAR THING!

The T.T. has been saved - for now at least. Threats by the Auto-Cycle Union to take the race meeting to Belgium have been successfully resisted. The battle has been a hard one, however, and those responsible for winning it, notably George Brown, the Island's member of the A-C.U., are warning against complacency. At Mr Brown's instigation, there are plans within the Manx Motor Cycle Club to launch an Amateur T.T. as soon as possible and certainly within the next couple of years. This will be an insurance cover, he suggests, against future threats to remove the T.T. from the Island. The Amateur T. T. will be a September event but will be capable of being switched to June if the Island loses the T.T.

The next threat to the race meeting could come if road racing is permitted in England. Already the Auto-Cycle Union has considered a plan for a short circuit around a golf course. This has been dismissed as not being a viable alternative to the Snaefell Mountain Course but now the A-C.U. is sponsoring through Lord Brabazon, a former Car T.T. driver on the Isle of Man, a Bill to legalise road racing in England on four days a year. This, perhaps, was the plan all along. It is said that the threatened removal of the T.T. to a 31½ mile course based around Spa and Francorchamps in Belgium was intended as a lever to force British authorities to legalise road racing in Britain. Hostility to the idea is such in the House of Commons, however, that it is not likely to get anywhere. The Isle of Man cannot afford to be complacent, though. One can expect the campaigning in London to continue.

Mr George A. Brown of the Isle of Man Weekly Times, and Manx representative on the Auto-Cycle Union. It was his impassioned speech which saved the T.T. Races from being removed from the Island.
(Manx National Heritage)

Belgium, meanwhile, remains keen to attract the T.T. business. It has offered to provide 1,000 soldiers as marshals, Customs concessions and a low fixed-price tariff at hotels for race fans. This alone made the threat to the T.T. a very real one. The A-C.U. argued, meanwhile, that the latest 500 c.c. machines had outgrown the Manx course. The roads were too narrow, it said, and there were too many intricate corners. There were numerous other reasons, however. The trade and competitors were angry about the rising costs of competing on the Island. These included extortionate fees by harbour porters in the removal from steamers of motorcycles and the imposition by the Highway Board of road tax and temporary licence fees for all motorcyclists visiting the Island. The A-C.U. was fed up, too, with having to finance the costly erection and dismantling every year of the wooden grandstand at the start in Glencrutchery Road. The A-C.U. believed the Island was "bleeding motorcyclists". Belgium's Motorcycle Federation, on the other hand, was prepared to subsidise the T.T. Hostility was increased by the many irritations caused by Manx restrictions. These included the ban some years ago of motorcycling on race-week Sunday because of the noise caused during church services. This has given rise to that Sunday being known as "Sad Sunday".

More recently, Douglas Corporation banned the carrying of pillion riders on Douglas promenade. The final irritation came recently when the Highway Board approved an application by the R.A.C. to re-stage the T.T. car races next year at the end of June. This meant practising earlier

The grandstand at the start and finish of the T.T. Course near the lower end of Glencrutchery Road, Douglas. The A-C.U. are objecting to having to pay for the cost of erecting and dismantling the grandstand each year.
(R. and L. Kelly Collection)

(Above) The A-C.U. control box in Parliament Square, Ramsey from where passage of riders is reported to the scoreboard operators at the start and finish. *(Manx National Heritage)*
(Right) Howard Davies with his Junior A.J.S. on which he came second this year. Riding the same machine he won the Senior T.T. - a unique achievement. *(R. and L. Kelly Collection)*

in the month. The rutted state of the roads after car racing meant that motorcycle racing soon afterwards would be impossible and the A-C.U. considered a May event much too early in the year, particularly in respect of light for early morning practices. The Highway Board granted the R.A.C's application on the grounds that it was the first received in respect of road closing for 1922. The A-C.U. believed that as the organisers of a well-established event, they should have been given first choice of race dates.

It was soon after this that the Competitions and Management Committee of the A-C.U. announced that it had accepted the Belgian offer and the T.T. would be transferred to Belgium in 1922. The T.T. was saved for the Isle of Man at a stormy two-day meeting of the A-C.U's full General Committee at Leicester in October when the decision was due to be ratified. The General Committee agreed to meet a delegation from Douglas Town Council with George Brown acting as spokesman. At the outset the delegation was heckled and treated with scorn.

On the second day Mr Brown launched an impas-

sioned plea to committee members on behalf of the Island. He condemned Belgium's course as being less testing and indicated that petty irritations on the Island would be removed. If there was any gratitude in the British motorcycle trade, he added, it should be directed, not to the Belgians for what they promised, but to the Isle of Man for what it had done over the years. The Island merited the benefit of every possible doubt. His speech was so emotional that when he concluded he was greeted by cheers - and a change of mind by sufficient A-C.U. committee members to save the T.T. for the Island - subject to satisfactory Manx guarantees.

These include the provision of a harbour crane to remove motorcycles from Steam Packet vessels, the abandonment of road taxes on visiting race fans, a forward-looking plan for the improvement of the course and a commitment by Douglas Corporation to build a permanent grandstand which the A-C.U. can use. Abandonment of the controversial "Sad Sunday" has also been conceded. Many Manx people reckon now it will be known in future as "Mad".

Destroyed by fire last year, the wooden structure of the original Palace Ballroom has been replaced by this magnificent building which is said to be the largest ballroom in Europe. It is known as the Palace Lido. This artistic impression is to be the subject of one of the popular postcards issued by Valentine and Sons of Dundee. *(Douglas Corporation)*

TYNWALD MATTERS:
NEW CENTRAL EDUCATION AUTHORITY

A new era of public education began on 14th December last year when the Central Education Authority met for the first time in the Town Hall, Douglas. Under the Education Act, 25 members have been elected on a similar basis to the House of Keys. In addition there are four co-opted members, including three ladies. They are joined by Mrs Williamson who was elected for Garff, so making a total of four as required by the Act. With the thorny question of teachers' salaries having already been settled, it seemed there were no big issues left. Nevertheless, there were elections in eight of the eleven constituencies. One major issue which developed was the furious debate about the provision of secondary schools for Ramsey and Peel, and not concentrating that level of education in Douglas.

The new Authority, for long the cherished ambition of educational reformers and advocated firmly by the MacDonnell Commission, resolves the bizarre situation of having 25 separate local boards dealing with school organisation, each with its own approach. The resulting wide variations could only impede progress in this vital component of Manx life for the advancement of our children. It must be said that the new Authority got down to business with commendable speed. Mr J. Philips (Douglas) was elected chairman and Mr T. B. Cowley (Ramsey) as vice-chairman. Chairmen of the various committees were also appointed, and at the next meeting in January of this year such matters as a seal, number of staff and the location of an office in Strand Street, Douglas were determined. The first all-Island education rate was fixed in February at 1/8½d in the £ and the rate of payment for members was set at 10/6d a meeting with a travel allowance of 3d a mile.

In April, Mr F. R. Grundey, B.Sc., headmaster of the Island's only secondary school for the past 18 years, was appointed Director of Education. The school was opened in 1894 in Park Road, Douglas. At first it had less than a hundred pupils, but under Mr Grundey's expertise and authority the school has achieved considerable success and now has 550 boys and girls. Mr Frederick Grundey, still under 50, is a keen sportsman and an ardent Freemason, currently holding the rank of Provincial Grand Senior Warden. His place at Park Road has been taken by Mr A. H. Sykes, M.Sc., from Widnes.

A major concern of the new authority is the establishment of an organised system of secondary education throughout the Island. In regard to this, the status of the endowed Grammar Schools in Douglas, Castletown and Ramsey, and other endowed schools, has occasioned considerable discussion. But it has now been announced that a new secondary school is to be built in Douglas, probably in the area of St. Ninian's Church. It is likely to be some years before this new school is built and negotiations are being conducted to purchase or lease the Douglas Grammar School in Dalton Street. The accommodation provided will act as an 'overflow' for Park Road School. Those in the north will be pleased to learn that the Authority also plans to provide a secondary school in Ramsey. The Trustees of Ramsey Grammar School have agreed that their school should pass to the Central Education Authority while retaining the name Grammar School. This is to come into effect next year and will operate in the old Grammar School in Waterloo Road with additional accommodation found in the Wesleyan School. This is regarded as a temporary measure until the Authority is able to build a new secondary school for the north.

There has been strong dissatisfaction expressed in the west since the Authority has been unable to commit itself to building a secondary school in Peel. It looks as though children from this area will have to join those from the south in travelling to Douglas if they wish to benefit from a secondary education. Nevertheless, the Central Education Authority has made a start in carrying out its weighty responsibilities and we wish it well.

The Eastern District Secondary School in Park Road, Douglas, is the only Higher Grade school on the Island. It opened in 1894 with 100 pupils but now has over 500 boys and girls.

(Frank Cowin Library)

HERE IS THE NEWS : **1922**
MANX INDUSTRIES ASSOCIATION FAILS

The story of one of the Isle of Man's Home Front heroes of the Great War has ended in sad misfortune. The Reverend C. Copeland Smith, who started a factory which gave employment to hundreds of women in Douglas through the war years, has been made bankrupt. We have this report:

Mr. Copeland Smith received public thanks for his efforts at the end of the war by resolution of Tynwald Court. He was a Wesleyan minister in Douglas when the war started and caused widespread local unemployment. He started the non-profit making Manx Industries Association to produce knitted woollen goods. Soon he was employing 500 women at a time when the visiting industry was virtually shut down and his output went to help the war effort. After the war he decided to continue the Manx Industries Association as a full commercial venture with himself as managing director. But last year a disastrous fire caused extensive damage to his factory premises at Castle Hill - and within months Mr. Copeland Smith had to petition for adjudication as a bankrupt. This followed a court claim by the Isle of Man Bank for repayment of a £1,221 9s loan. The High Court was told that it was misfortune that had led to the situation and not speculation or extravagance on his part. Mr. Copeland Smith now intends to emigrate to America.

BANK LIQUIDATION COMPLETED
The liquidation of Dumbell's Bank has been completed - after 22 years. The collapse of the bank in 1900 was the worst financial disaster ever to hit the Isle of Man. Since then Douglas accountants W. H. Walker and Company have been realising the assets and have just made a final dividend payment to creditors of 6s 2d in the pound. This brings the total dividend paid to 12s 7½d.

TERRITORIALS RUN RIOT
In August, Territorial Army soldiers on their annual camp in the Island ran riot in Ramsey and besieged the town's police station for more than an hour. The six officers inside had to draw their staffs when the building was surrounded by drunken men of the 55th West Lancashire Division after the pubs had closed on Saturday night. They were angry over the arrest earlier in the evening of a local civilian. The men dispersed when officers arrived on the scene - but they ignored orders by their C.O. General Sir Charles Nicholson, that they should form up and march back to camp.

MANX P.C. HAILED A HERO
A Manx police officer serving with the Manchester Constabulary has been hailed as a hero after being shot and wounded while chasing a gang of men who robbed a post office. Twenty-three-year-old P.C. Robert Corlett, who left Douglas for Manchester two years ago, was shot as he chased the men down the street armed only with his staff. He has since recovered and three men have been gaoled at Manchester Assizes for their part in the robbery. The man who fired the shot was given ten years. P.C. Corlett was commended by the judge for his courage.

LAXEY MINE CLOSED AGAIN
Seven months after being re-opened, work has stopped at the Laxey Mines

Manx Industries Association's manufactory at Castle Hill, Douglas, which was destroyed by fire last year. The Association has now been declared bankrupt and is having to close down all its other centres with the loss of hundreds of jobs for girls and young women.

(Manx National Heritage)

This Midwood photograph shows the extent of the huge Territorial encampment at Milntown, Lezayre. The arrival of the Territorials is a big event each year and local schools are closed for the day.

(R. and L. Kelly Collection)

in consequence of a serious fire on the washing-floors which destroyed the crushing and washing machinery. Nearly 80 men are affected. The mines closed in 1920 because of financial difficulties but in April this year operations were resumed when the mines were purchased by Mr Robert Williamson, the local merchant and owner of the Laxey Glen Gardens. The Government has agreed to help by providing an interest-free loan of £2,000 which will keep the men employed in breaking ore, while the machinery is being repaired.

TRAGIC ACCIDENTS

The year has not been without some horrific accidents. In April 62-year-old Henry Crellin, who had for several years been a prisoner of war in Germany, was killed by the falling of a gate while he was employed on dismantling the wartime Knockaloe Camp. In May, Robert Kewley (36) was working in Mr Percy Daugherty's sugar-boiling factory in Nelson Street, Douglas when his overalls became entangled in the axle of a flywheel and he was dragged into the machinery. He was killed instantly. In August Mr R. J. Clague of Douglas, seedsman and Government valuer of agricultural land, was killed after being knocked down by a Corporation motor-bus. And in December two other Manxmen,

Douglas garage proprietor Tom Sheard is the first Manxman to win a T.T. race. He is seen here sitting astride the A.J.S. machine on which he won this year's Junior event.

(R. and L. Kelly Collection)

Robert Marsden and James Quirk, met violent deaths when the schooner *Enigma* foundered off the Cumberland coast. All hands were lost. The schooner had formerly been registered at Castletown. She had an interesting history of adventure while engaged in illicit trading in Oriental waters.

MANXMAN WINS T.T.

A T.T. race has been won by a Manxman for the first time. Well-known Tom Sheard, a 33-year old Douglas garage proprietor, who hails originally from Peel, won the 5-lap Junior race on an A.J.S. at a record speed of 54.75 m.p.h. Newcomer to the races, 17-year-old Stanley Woods caused quite a stir when taking on petrol at the pits. His Cotton machine went on fire but, despite burns, the young Irishman was able to continue and finished fifth. Record speeds were also recorded by Alec Bennett (Sunbeam) who won the Senior race at 58.31 m.p.h., and Lightweight winner G. S. Davidson (Levis) at 49.89 m.p.h. The A-C.U. has announced that they intend to include a sidecar race next year. Following the motorcycle races car racing returned later in June, the first since 1914. Shockingly bad weather affected the races and prevented high speeds being recorded.

1922 NEWS IN BRIEF

FEBRUARY

7 - Bill exempting conscientious objectors from the obligation to have their children vaccinated against smallpox passes both branches of the Legislature.

8 - Death of of Mr R.C. Cain, draper, Douglas.

26 - Steam Packet chairman Mr C.T.W. Hughes-Games promises lower fares, but warns Legislature against imposing restrictions to which visitors are unaccustomed at home.

APRIL

6 - Sensation caused in football circles by the refusal of Ramsey to play extra time in a semi-final of the Hospital Cup. Subsequently, the Cup was awarded to Gymnasium, an appeal by Ramsey to the English F.A. proving unsuccessful.

11 - Tynwald considers a scheme to lengthen the Red Pier. Admiralty expert to be consulted.

17 - Laxey Mines bought at public auction by local merchant Mr R. Williamson.

24-27 Annual Music Festival - 2,252 competitors. As usual, guest soloists performed at the Thursday evening concert. A feature of the festival was a performance by children representing all the elementary schools of the Island.

MAY

4 - Douglas District Licensing Authority rejects applications from 58 boarding-house keepers to sell spirits, as well as beer and wines.

13 - H.B. Noble Trustees announce their final benefactions, principal of which is an endowment of £10,000 for the establishment of scholarships to Liverpool University.

JULY

11 - Payment of members of the Manx Legislature comes into operation.

13 - Edouard Braehm sentenced in Antwerp to penal servitude for

life for murdering Mary Sarah Clarke, a native of the Isle of Man. It is almost a year to the day that the murder took place in a boarding-house in Liverpool.

26 - Central Education Authority decides that the marriage of a female teacher is to be considered equivalent to resignation.

26 - Douglas Grammar School to be leased for the next five years and used as an adjunct to the Douglas Secondary School.

SEPTEMBER

4 - New Secondary School opened in Ramsey.

13 - Isle of Man Railway directors accede to request to increase the service to and from Foxdale.

OCTOBER

12 - Opening of the Women's Residential and Day College in Douglas for instruction in domestic subjects.

24 - Tynwald votes £17,896 for public works throughout the Island in relief of unemployment. Douglas Corporation granted £20,000 for road repairs.

31 - Tynwald overwhelmingly accepts recommendation to maintain the number of Insular police, but cuts wages of newly-recruited constables to 50/- a week.

NOVEMBER

2 - Opening of the Manx Museum, in premises formerly used as Noble's Hospital.

10 - Between 300 and 400 unemployed men march to Government Office; deputation sees Governor and Douglas Guardians. Tynwald is criticised for not giving more effective assistance.

21 - Washing-floors at Laxey Mines destroyed by fire.

DECEMBER

6 - Annual meeting of Manx Electric Railway Company in London. Number of passengers carried rose to over 700,000 during the year. Profit shown as rising to £24,457.

TYNWALD MATTERS : A NATIONAL MUSEUM AT LAST!

The Isle of Man has its long-planned National Museum at last. At 3 p.m. on Thursday, 2nd November, a numerous company of ladies and gentlemen saw His Excellency Sir William Fry, accompanied by Lady Fry, welcomed by Deemster Callow to perform the opening ceremony of the Manx Museum. They were the first two to pass through the turnstile. Eventually 416 people entered the building that day. Many of them heard the interesting addresses from His Excellency and the Deemster, delivered in the Art Gallery.

A place where the important artefacts, relics, paintings and antiquities in general that provide the bedrock of what may be seen as the Manx heritage, has long been desired. The move by the five Noble's Trustees to convey by deed of October last year what has been referred to in common parlance as "Noble's Old Hospital", precipitated a decision on the matter. As no other suitable buildings were offered, or were available, Tynwald Court found itself more or less obliged to accept this opportunity. Its agreement, one supposes, was influenced by the offer by the Duke of Atholl, widely reported here last April, that he would be sympathetic to the idea of establishing such an institution and some of his Manx coins might be an interesting feature. It appears that Hall Caine was instrumental in drawing the Duke's attention to the affair.

In the following months the main concern was to ensure that the Museum should attract as wide a

Mr Philip M. C. Kermode, the highly respected Manx scholar who has been appointed Curator of the Manx Museum.

public as possible, by the range of its exhibits and, indeed, that this public should be reflected in the composition of the Trustees. By the middle of the year it had been decided that the new venture should be known as the Manx Museum rather than Noble's Museum, and that the staff should consist of a curator at a salary of £350 a year, a secretary at £250, a caretaker-attendant at £125 and a turnstile attendant at £52 a year. Their appointments, and more especially their salaries, were not achieved without furious and, on occasions, acrimonious debate. However, good sense won the day. Most felt that to guarantee the future reputation of the Museum, such salaries were essential to ensure the high quality of the staff.

A fine start has already been made. Many exhibits and relics previously held in places such as Castle Rushen have already found a new home in the Museum. For the next few months, in order to attract as many of the local population as possible, admission is to be free, and not 6d as originally fixed. The new curator is the studious Mr P. M. C. Kermode and the new secretary and librarian is the lively and enthusiastic Mr William Cubbon - both gentlemen of high academic reputation. They are also members of the Isle of Man Natural History and Antiquarian Society. Mr Kermode was a founder member in 1879. A great deal of credit goes to the Society who have long campaigned for the Museum we have today. With its continued support, we can rest assured that the Museum is in safe hands.

WHAT FUTURE FOR THE LAXEY MINES?

The problems concerning the Laxey mines continue. It does seem, however, that there is the likelihood of a resolution soon. Mr Robert Williamson, proprietor of the Laxey Glen Gardens and various other Island enterprises has purchased the lease of the mines. Since then, however, a serious fire on the washing floors has put the future of the whole operation in jeopardy, although the Government has provided a loan of £2,000 so that the miners can be retained and employed to deal with the ore manually, pending the repair of the machinery.

Mining in Laxey seems to have started tentatively about 140 years ago, but it was not until the 1830s that the efforts met with any real success. At that time the lease was held by the Lonan Mining Association who held all the mining rights in the parishes of Lonan and Maughold. The rest of the Island's mining rights were held by the Isle of Man Mining Company who centred their activities at Foxdale. The Lonan Association was reformed as the Laxey Mining Company in 1848 and as the century progressed, so the Laxey mines expanded and entered a period of considerable prosperity. The mines became a leading producer of zinc ore, though lead (with high silver content) and copper were also mined. There were problems with regard to labour and about 50 years ago a major strike seriously disrupted the whole mining operation. Out-of-work Cornish miners were brought in to help break the strike. Over the years the mining company went through a number of changes of name and organisation. Various subsidiary workings were separated off as independent companies.

The construction of the *Lady Isabella* water wheel in 1854 was to provide additional power to keep the mines clear of water so that the miners were able to open up levels hundreds of feet below ground. This was also the time when the washing floors were constructed to cope with the annual production of thousands of tons of ore. Responsible for this highly successful enterprise were the 'Big Three' who were in charge at the time. Chairman of the Laxey Mining Company was advocate, banker and entrepreneur Mr G.W. Dumbell. He had the foresight to provide the base for the spectacular expansion of the company and its activities. His name has been denigrated in recent years because of the infamous crash of the bank he founded. Mr Dumbell died in 1887, long before the bank failure occurred,

The Mines Captain, or Manager, was Mr Richard Rowe who provided the technical mining expertise. Originating from Cornwall, he came to Laxey from Northern Ireland where he had been employed in mines in which Mr Dumbell had an interest. After settling in Laxey he became involved in many varied activities, some in conjunction with Mr Dumbell, but others on his own account. The latter included the development of harbour facilities and the founding of Laxey Flour Mills. After he ceased to be Mines Captain he retired to Douglas and, like Mr Dumbell, became a Member of the House of Keys. He died in 1888 and is buried in the new burial ground at Lonan. Mr Rowe's superintendent engineer was Mr Robert Casement, a native of Laxey and the son of a wheelwright. He was largely self-taught but was responsible for the design of the great Laxey water wheel and the washing floors. Mr Casement died in 1894 and is also buried at Lonan.

By 1890 the company was beginning to feel the effects of cheap ore being imported from such countries as South Africa. Some of the miners producing this 'foreign' ore had once worked at Laxey but had left as the workforce, once numbering 600, was gradually reduced. Some of the miners intended to stay away permanently but others retained their roots and had families in Laxey to support. These men sent or brought money home, often enough to improve and extend the family dwelling. Many of these houses now have exotic names taken from the mining areas where the money was earned. These house names, and even terrace and road names, are a phenomenon of recent times and are presumably here to stay, just like the centuries-old farm names.

Laxey, of course, was not the only Manx mine to suffer from the overseas competition. By the time of the Great War all the other mines, including those of Foxdale, were closed, leaving Laxey the sole producer. To meet the demands of the war effort miners received a war bonus payment and it was the withdrawal of this inducement after the war which led to strike action. Many of the miners who had served in the army had returned with ideas of militant trade unionism. They also had the backing of the local Workers' Union. It was the deadlock which ensued that led to the closure of the mines and its ultimate sale. It was then that Mr Williamson stepped in and by his purchase has provided some hope for the miners whose livelihood still depends on the success of the mines. It also gives hope for the village community, while Mr Williamson is attempting to provide limited protection to his own commercial interests in the area.

The washing floors at Laxey which suffered a serious fire at the end of November. It is hoped that repairs to the machinery will be completed early in the new year so that production can resume.

(Frank Cowin Library)

HERE IS THE NEWS : 1923
RACE FOR AMATEURS ON THE T.T. COURSE

September saw the first of a new series of motor cycle races on the T.T. Course - the Manx Amateur Motor Cycle Road Race which has already been dubbed as the 'Amateur T.T.' We have this report.

The new race is the result of a determined effort, lasting over two years, by the Manx Motor Cycle Club. Despite early opposition from the Auto-Cycle Union of Great Britain, and concerns in Tynwald about interfering with the harvest, it is now seen not only as a means of extending the season, but also as a replacement should anything happen to the T.T. Races. The race provides a challenge for non-professional riders by defining 'amateur' as a rider using a stock machine with no pecuniary reward from the manufacturers of machines or accessories, even down to boot laces! Mayor of Douglas Alderman A. B. Crookall, M.H.K. has presented the Club with a magnificent trophy, said to be the most handsome in motor-cycling sport. There were 33 entries in the first race and after 5 laps the winner was Welshman Leslie Randles (Sunbeam) at 52.77 m.p.h.

The event was hailed as a great success which augurs well for the future. But the dangers of riding on the famous course were brought home once again by the death of the first Manx rider on the T.T. Course. The victim was 21-year-old Ned Brew, a coach driver. He lived with his parents at Glendhoo Cottage which is on the course between Hillberry and Cronk-ny-Mona. During practising, Ned went into a speed wobble and crashed as he raised a hand to wave to his sister Gertrude, who was watching in the lane outside the family home.

As for this year's T.T. held in June, the Senior was won by Manxman Tom Sheard, winner of last year's Junior race. Riding a Douglas twin in very wet conditions, he averaged 55.55 m.p.h. Victory in the Junior went to the young Irish rider Stanley Woods on a Cotton at a record speed of 55.73 m.p.h.; and the Lightweight race went to J.A. Porter (New Gerrard) at 51.93 m.p.h., another record. Great interest was shown

The magnificent trophy which is to be awarded to the winner of the Amateur T.T. The trophy has been donated by the Mayor of Douglas, Ald. A. B. Crookall, M.H.K.
(R. and L. Kelly Collection)

in the first Sidecar event with Freddie Dixon (Douglas) winning over the three laps at 53.15 m.p.h. The races were marred by the death of 35-year-old James Varney from Barnstaple, Devon who died from injuries after crashing at Greeba Bridge at 60 m.p.h.

SINGING HALLS IN THE CLEAR
Two well-known Douglas showmen, Bert Feldman and Laurence Wright, have been found 'not guilty' by the High-Bailiff of using their community singing halls in Strand Street as concert rooms, without a licence. The court was told the premises were open to the street and could hold up to one hundred people. Led by a small orchestra, they were encouraged to sing popular songs of the day - and to buy the sheet music that was on sale. Mr. Feldman and Mr. Wright argued that they were not putting on entertainment but using their premises only for the sale of music.

ELECTRICITY SUPPLY FOR DOUGLAS
The first public electricity supply has been started in Douglas, by the Corporation. The generator in the newly-built municipal power station on the North Quay was started up at Whitsun. It provides current for

street lighting in many parts of the town, following months of work in laying underground mains. The Borough Electrical Engineer, Mr. Bertram Kelly, said the Corporation was now getting increasing inquiries from boarding houses, private householders and shops, seeking to abandon gas and take electricity.

FOUR YEARS FOR ATTEMPTED MURDER
A man who cut his girl friend's throat after a quarrel was sentenced to four years penal servitude at the Court of General Gaol for attempted murder. The court heard that 22-year-old Albert Shimmin, of 23 St. George's Walk, Douglas, attacked 21-year-old Edna Corkill at her home in Bathurst Street when she returned his engagement ring. Afterwards, still carrying a blood-stained razor, he surrendered to a policeman. Miss Corkill has since recovered from her injuries.

More sensational was another case in the Court of General Gaol Delivery. A 30-year-old visitor from Stalybridge was found not guilty of indecently assaulting a girl of 14. Subsequently, the Speaker of the House of Keys asked in Tynwald for the names of the jurymen who arrived at this verdict. Indignation was expressed in many quarters, at what was considered an attempt to intimidate jurymen by holding them up to public abuse.

TRAGIC DEATHS
A young Manxman serving in the R.A.F., 18-year-old Lieutenant Frederick Harris, has been killed in a plane crash in England. He was the great-grandson of Mr. Samuel Harris, the late High-Bailiff of Douglas. In another local tragedy a woman has been burned to death in a fire which destroyed her home, Tuck Mills Cottage, at Santon. Seventy-three-year-old widow Mrs. Margaret Keggin lived there with her three sons. She is believed to have lit the living room fire when she was there alone and to have fallen asleep sitting beside it, allowing sparks to set her dress alight.

Florence Kinrade, a Manxwoman resident in Liverpool, was killed while a passenger being driven in a motor car late at night from Port Erin to Douglas. The sensational inquiry resulted in a Coroner's jury finding the driver blameless. The cause of the accident was a pile of stones left by Highway Board men in the gutter. This caused the car to collide with a wall.

In another road accident a motor-cyclist was run over and killed by a motor coach. The coach driver was sentenced to six months hard labour.

S.S. DOUGLAS
SUNK IN MERSEY

The Steam Packet Company vessel *S.S. Douglas* has been sunk in collision with another ship in the Mersey. It happened as the *Douglas* left Brunswick Dock for a midnight sailing to the Island with cargo, mails and 15 passengers. The *Douglas*, of only 813 tons, was hit by the 5,700 ton cargo vessel *Artemisia* and almost cut in half. But all passengers and crew were saved. Many climbed up rope ladders to the deck of the *Artemisia*. The *Douglas* sank minutes later.

DEMANDS OF
BRITISH GOVERNMENT

The Manx Government was shocked at the beginning of the year when an unexpected demand was received from the British Government for an increase in the annual contribution to

On a bleak November day, the Island's National Memorial to its 1,170 war dead was unveiled by the Lieutenant-Governor, Major General Sir William Fry, at St John's. (Manx National Heritage)

the Imperial Exchequer from £10,000 to £150,000. The Island has already agreed to take over responsibility for £250,000 of War Loan and is paying £20,000 a year towards this. The money is required to help pay off Britain's enormous national debt arising from the Great War. A committee has been considering the matter throughout the year and now Tynwald has decided to make a one-off payment of £200,000 along with the purchase by the Manx Government of all Crown Rights in the Island. Tynwald is also seeking full control over all the Island's finances. A committee has been appointed to negotiate with the British Government.

MANX NATIONAL
WAR MEMORIAL

The Manx National War Memorial at St. Johns, bearing the names of 1,170 Manxmen killed in the Great War, has been unveiled by the Lieutenant-Governor, Major General Sir William Fry. Fifteen hundred people, mostly relatives of the dead, gathered for the ceremony on a bleak winter day. Many were in tears as the Last Post was sounded. The memorial, built of Scottish granite, is the work of Douglas sculptor Mr. T. H. Royston. Its Celtic carvings were designed by Mr. P. M. C. Kermode, Curator of the Manx Museum and an acclaimed expert on the local Celtic and Scandinavian Crosses.

1923 NEWS IN BRIEF

JANUARY
11 - 100th anniversary of Primitive Methodism on the Island.
13 - Outcry over couple to be gaoled for disobeying a High Court order to quit their house.They said they had nowhere else to go.
19 - Tynwald rejects plans to extend the Red Pier at a cost of £282,000.

FEBRUARY
10 - I.O.M. Agricultural Society reconstituted. Northern and Southern branches amalgamated.
13 - By the Speaker's casting vote, Keys decided not to restore the 'bona fide traveller' facilities for obtaining drink on Sundays.

MARCH
15 - Plans announced to extend Noble's Hospital by the erection of a private wing.
25 - A Manx Girl Guides' Choir under Mr Noah Moore wins the Challenge Banner at the annual London Music Festival.

APRIL
9-12 - Annual Guild Music Festival. Winners of the six special solo classes compete for the Cleveland Gold Medal, presented by the Manx Society of Cleveland, Ohio, U.S.A. The judge was the popular baritone Peter Dawson who awarded the medal to Alan Quirk, winner of the bass class. His is trained by school teacher Miss Effie Fayle.

MAY
7 - Tynwald adopts policy of making loans at low rates of interest available for the construction of private dwelling-houses.
15 - Mr Gerald Bridson, the well-known Labour M.H.K., walks round the Island touching the doors of the 17 parish churches, a distance of approximately 80 miles. This remarkable feat was accomplished in 20 hours 23 mins.
21 - About 6,000 Territorials arrive for fortnight's camp near Ramsey.
30 - Isle of Man Education Authority (formerly the Central Education Authority) adopts a scheme for the medical inspection and treatment of school children.

JUNE
5 - Income Tax fixed at 8d to 1/2d as compared with 5d to 8½d last year.
5 - Threatened strike by Workers' Union averted after Highway Board abandons proposal to lower wages of high-road labourers.
5 - Castletown and Gymnasium football teams suspended for refusing to pay fines of £20 for refusing to play on Whit Monday, as ordered by F.A. Executive. (Fines were eventually paid, under protest, and the suspension removed.)
27-30 Douglas visited by the Fifth Destroyer Flotilla of the Atlantic Fleet.

JULY
1 Jubilee of the Isle of Man Railway Company.
5 - Tynwald Day. Speeches by overseas Manxmen at the World Manx Association's annual gathering at The Nunnery.

SEPTEMBER
15 - P.C. Charles Kissack killed at Ballaugh Bridge while riding a motor cycle.
20 - First 'Amateur T.T.' motor cycle race.
26 - Publication of Sir Hall Caine's novel "The Woman of Knockaloe" which is set in the Isle of Man during the Great War. In May the author celebrated his 70th birthday.
30 - The *Clan McMaster*, an ocean-going steamer of 11,000 to 12,000 tons, wrecked in the Sound of the Calf of Man.

NOVEMBER
8 - National War Memorial unveiled at Tynwald Hill.
12 - Board of Agriculture purchases the estate of Knockaloe for the purpose of an experimental farm.

DECEMBER
1 - Woodbourne House, residence of the late Mr A.W. Moore, S.H.K. for many years, purchased and to be reconstructed as a Masonic temple.
18 - Legislative Council rejects Keys' Bill extending Rent Restriction Act to 1925. Period of control will end in May, 1924.

EXPLORING THE ISLAND BY CHARABANC

Cut-price competition among charabanc operators and haggling by holidaymakers for the best deal is bringing down the price of summer excursions on the Isle of Man. Eddie McCartin, who operates the White Motors Fleet, a name which reflects their white livery and vehicle names such as 'White Rose' and 'White Lady', complains that fare-cutting has reached a suicidal extent. Tours which cost £1 in 1920 are being marketed now at less than half that. Some are being cut further to 7s 6d and there are suggestions in the trade that the bottom has not been reached yet. This implies that although chara operators have established exclusive visiting rights at local hotels and guest houses whereby they can enter dining rooms at breakfast time and tell visitors about their latest tours, many visitors must be declining what is being offered. They must be sacrificing the opportunity of being picked up at their accommodation in favour of going round the many chara stands in lower Douglas and negotiating there with operators who may have empty seats and prefer to fill them at a more competitive price than leave them empty. There are reports of some fares being cut by six shillings. For the Crossley seven seaters and Lancia 15- and 18-seaters this must be uneconomic, but Berliet 23-seaters and A.B.C. and Halley 28-seaters may still be viable at these rates.

Fare-cutting reflects the rising number of charabancs being brought to the Island whilst the number of traditional horse-drawn carriages and wagonettes do not appear to have diminished. Clearly something must give eventually. The smaller charas will be priced out of the market and the longer, superior tours that the bigger charas can provide will bring about the demise of the carriages and wagonettes. One indicator of this has been the introduction this summer by chara operators of 'Round the Island' excursions. The idea of 'doing the Island' in a day has so appealed to visitors that the Steam Packet has been providing five 'Round the Island' sailings a week.

(Frank Cowin Library)

Horse-drawn vehicles have been unable to pack in enough miles in a day for a land-based rival but the chara operators have decided that they can do so. The open-topped charas leave Douglas at between 10 a.m. and 11 a.m. and return in time for tea at 5 p.m., the passengers usually singing the latest hit songs as they do so.

When police studied what the chara men were offering they decided that something was amiss. Although most charabancs, apart from some of the largest ones, are now fitted with pneumatic tyres, they are still limited to a maximum speed on the Island's bumpy, earthen roads of 12 m.p.h. In the six to seven hour excursions, however, it was reckoned that travellers would be taken 70 miles and be given long sight-seeing stops at Ramsey, Peel and a resort in the south.

After doing their sums, police armed with stopwatches hid behind hedges at Ballaugh and timed the charas over a measured mile. It is said they undertook their operation with all the meticulous thoroughness that has become expected of T.T. race timekeepers. The result, after they compared their times, was the prosecution of chara drivers for travelling at between 17 and 24 m.p.h., no doubt churning up large dust clouds behind them.

Undeterred, the charabanc men plan to maintain their speeds, particularly as their vehicles and road conditions are gradually being improved. The police, equally, are determined to pounce again next year - this time with timings over a four mile stretch between the milestone on Richmond Hill and the milestone on Glashen Hill at Ballasalla. No doubt there will be a lot more prosecutions but the chara men are undeterred. This is the future, they believe. Speed limits are bound to be raised.

One casualty of faster traffic will be the spontaneous roadside performances by country children. It has become a tradition for them to run behind wagonettes and the slower charas, shouting and singing in the hope that passengers will throw them halfpennies in return for their

(R. and L. Kelly Collection)

(R. and L. Kelly Collection)

efforts. One salute by passengers is to shout "Hi, Kelly!" to the children. Many young boys sport abrasions of the nose. This is because they respond to the salutation by standing on their noses.

Cheaper fares mean increasing numbers of holiday-makers can afford to get out of Douglas to explore what else the Island has to offer. Some, of course, like many of the yarns the chara drivers tell, are total inventions. That includes the Fairy Bridge on the main road south from Douglas. The correct one is inaccessible to chara traffic but what visitor will know that? Another invention is the supposed oyster bed at Port Soderick. Whatever oysters are landed from there were put there before the season started.

Glens are doing good business, charging between 4d and 6d admission. Glen Helen features a zoo from which a badger escaped recently. For the more daring there is a climb up Ramsey's Albert Tower. Refreshments are available. The Manx Electric Railway has a uniformed guide at the summit of Snaefell to point out the scenery on a clear day from a wooden platform. Small charas operating from The Bungalow, the point where the M.E.R. line crosses the Mountain Road, take people down to Tholt-y-Will to see the waterfall and have refreshments there. They can also go on to Sulby railway station. This was the pioneering service which introduced the first solid-tyred motorised charas to the Island in 1902.

Throughout the Island there are open-air shows by talented concert parties. Onchan's Happy Valley rivals the Douglas Head open-air theatre. Peel has a wooden stand on the beach. One of the annual and popular attractions at Ramsey's Cosy Corner is the Manx Mascots Concert Party led by the comedian Norman Langford, manager of the Cosy Corner for the pierrot-master of Douglas, Fred Buxton. The Mascots have been performing at Ramsey since before the Great War. They are so good that in a few years time they plan to go professional and tour Britain's holiday resorts.

Rushen Abbey is a particularly popular drive for charas. Besides its historic associations and a museum which displays the skeletons of supposed Manx kings dug up on the abbey grounds, visitors love the gardens and the famous strawberry and cream teas. The fruit jams, made and bottled on the premises for many years, are outstanding. Evening concerts and dances, meanwhile, in the glass-covered and open-sided pavilion attract steady attendances.

Churches remain the biggest attractions on Sundays. People call it "doing their Sabbath duty." For many years, however, the churches have been so full at the height of the season that open-air services have been held on Douglas Head and in the grounds of Braddan Church. Upwards of 30,000 and sometimes more make the pilgrimage to Braddan on Sunday mornings, many on foot, others by wagonette, chara and special trains. On warm, fine days many of the congregation make the outing a social occasion and make long detours on foot to walk through the scenic Nunnery Grounds.

Thatched cottage, Crosby village. *(Frank Cowin Library)*

Fishermen's cottages, Niarbyl. *(Frank Cowin Library)*

PROPERTY TENANTS UNDER THREAT OF EVICTION

The expiry of the Rent Restriction Act, which gave tenants of houses protection against excessive rents, has resulted in scores of house possession cases being brought in the High Courts on the Island. In some cases the Deemsters have imposed prison sentences on tenants who have refused to obey notice to quit orders. We have this report:

The Act was alleged to work against the interests of landlords, making them unable to get a profitable rent return on their properties. Its expiry on May 12th exposed tenants to the risk of notice to quit if they could not afford to pay more. In cases where they refused to move, or could not find alternative accommodation, they were committed to prison. This led to threats by the Manx Labour Party of a General Strike. In fact, Labour M.H.Ks Walter Craine and Gerald Bridson went to London to protest to Home Secretary Mr. Arthur Henderson but he said he had no authority to intervene. The first court suits for possession were heard a week after the Act expired. But in making orders the Deemsters La Mothe and Callow gave tenants up to three months to find other accommodation if they could. The situation was a major issue in this year's General Election to the House of Keys, with Labour candidates pledging to bring back rent restriction next year. Meanwhile, to ease the situation, Douglas Corporation and the Government are stepping up the provision of public housing.

CLERGYMAN PAYS FOR HOAX

A clergyman from the Island, the Reverend Walter Karran, of "Marathon", Douglas, has been fined £10 with 25 guineas costs for sending a hoax telegram to the Bishop of Sodor and Man, Dr. Denton Thompson. The telegram, which Karran asked a woman to send for him after she had sailed from Douglas to Liverpool, purported to be from the Prime Minister, Mr. Baldwin. It asked the Bishop to meet Mr. Baldwin at the Adelphi Hotel, Liverpool, the following day and the Bishop, thinking he was to be given a new appointment, made the journey.

Following its success at the London Music Festival, the Manx Ladies' Choir was invited to perform on the wireless for a special programme broadcast on 2LO. The members are seen here in the studio with their conductor, Mr Noah Moore, L.R.A.M., seated centre.

(Manx National Heritage)

Karran was described in court as an inveterate practical joker.

MANX LADIES' CHOIR ON THE 'WIRELESS'

In April the Manx Ladies' Choir, under the direction of Mr. Noah Moore, manager of the Villa Marina, scored a remarkable success in competition in London. It won the principal challenge shield at the London Music Festival, in the presence of Princess Mary, in competition against choirs from all over the south of England. The choir's success attracted considerable press coverage in London. And before coming home they sang on the "wireless", on 2LO, to an estimated audience of three million people.

MANXMAN SHOT IN CLEVELAND, OHIO

A Manxman living in America has been murdered in what appears to be a mistaken gangland killing in Cleveland, Ohio. Thirty-seven-year-old Mr. John Edwin Caine, formerly of Peel, was walking home when a gunman leapt from a large black car and shot him three times. Mr. Caine, married with two children, worked as an automobile machinist - and he is believed to be the victim of mistaken

identity. It's thought the assassin was out to kill a police patrolman who lives in the same street.

MORE TRAGEDIES AT SEA

1924 has been a bad year for the Isle of Man for tragedy at sea. In January thirteen men, including one Manxman, Henry Gill, died when the Fleetwood trawler *Angle* was wrecked on the Bahama Bank, off Ramsey. And three Manxmen were drowned when the Irish Steamer *Lismore* capsized and sank off Waterford in July. They were her skipper, Captain John Sayle, of Castletown, William Gale and Thomas Watterson. There was also an unusual case in June of shipwreck when the Steam Packet vessel *Peel Castle* went aground in thick fog with 600 passengers on board - in the middle of Douglas beach. She re-floated on the rising tide 12 hours later.

CENTENARY OF R.N.L.I.

The centenary of the Royal National Lifeboat Institution has been celebrated in Douglas on May 17th and 18th. The R.N.L.I. was founded in London in 1824 at a meeting convened by Sir William Hillary who lived on Prospect Hill, Douglas and later at the Fort Anne. R.N.L.I. chairman Sir Godfrey Baring, a member of the City banking family, said of his visit to the Island that it was like treading hallowed ground. During the year a new lifeboat house has been built in the Douglas outer harbour. It is designed to accommodate one of the new motor lifeboats now coming into service.

DOUGLAS WAR MEMORIAL UNVEILED

Douglas War Memorial has been unveiled on Harris Promenade by the Earl of Derby. It bears the names of more than 700 men of the town who died in the Great War. Nearly 400 of them were infantrymen who served with famous Lancashire, Cheshire and Liverpool regiments. Lord Derby is the 17th earl. He is a former British Secretary of State for War and former British Ambassador in Paris. During his visit to the Island he became the first ever Freeman of the Borough of Douglas.

ARREST OF TRAWLER IN MANX WATERS

For the first time a fishing trawler from outside the Isle of Man has been arrested by the Royal Navy for fishing illegally inside the Island's three-mile limit. The Fleetwood

A photograph of the 11,500 ton Clan MacMaster taken last year after the vessel was stranded and badly holed on a shelf of rock in the Sound.   *(R. and L. Kelly Collection)*

trawler *Whitby* was two miles off Noggin Head, near Port St. Mary, when she was stopped by the Navy gunboat *H.M.S. Cherwell*. The encounter happened at midnight. *Cherwell,* disguised as a drifter, approached to within a hundred yards of the *Whitby* without navigation lights and then trapped her in a blaze of searchlights. In the High-Bailiff's Court the *Whitby's* skipper, Henry Stanley, was fined £20 and his fishing gear, worth £60, was confiscated.

1924 NEWS IN BRIEF

FEBRUARY

15 - The first Nonconformist (Congregationalist) chaplain to the House of Keys appointed.

17 - Manx Labour Party organises a mass meeting to protest against the loss of the Rent Restrictions Act. General strike suggested.

MARCH

19 - Manx Temperance Federation suggests that country licensees should not serve the drivers of motor hackney carriages.

MAY

1 - End of Manx Music Festival in which 2,913 took part. During the competitions three sisters - Misses Eileen, Lilian and Annie Pickard - obtained first prizes in their respective solo classes.

16 - Publication of "The Manx Manorial Roll of the Isle of Man 1511-1515", translated by Rev. Theophilus Talbot.

17-18 Celebrations of the centenary of the R.N.L.I.

19 - Rent Act crisis begins. First suits brought by landlords for possession of decontrolled houses.

27 - Budget Day. Cocoa duty reduced and Income Tax rates increased ranging from 10d to 1/5^1/2d in the £.

29 - Douglas War Memorial unveiled.

JUNE

10 - Marshall Braid of Castletown, aged 16, unsuccessfully challenges Mr Gerald Bridson M.H.K. in a walk round the 17 parish churches.

12 - The *Manx Maid* introduced into Steam Packet service. Built by Cammel Laird in 1910 she was previously used on the Southampton-Channel Island service. Of 1,500 tons she has been converted to oil burning and can carry 1,470 passengers.

20 - Visit to Douglas of *H.M.S. Malaya*, the world's second largest battleship.

23 - Kenneth Twemlow, an amateur aged only 20, won the Junior T.T. riding a New Imperial. On the first lap Jimmy Simpson was the first rider ever to complete a lap of the course at over 60 m.p.h.

27 - Edwin Twemlow, brother to Kenneth, won the Lightweight T.T., also on a New Imperial. Both had first ridden in last year's 'Amateur T.T.'

JULY

5 - Owing to the illness of Sir William Fry, Deemster La Mothe presides at Tynwald as Deputy-Governor. He refuses to permit the Nonconformist chaplain to the House of Keys to take part in the service at St John's Chapel, although the Bishop had agreed.

21 - Mr Philip Corlett, the Ramsey bellman, imprisoned for failing to give up possession of his house, but released the following day, the Government having compulsorily placed an unoccupied house at his disposal.

AUGUST

13 - The Ramsey Cake Mills, established by Messrs Corlett and Cowley Ltd four years ago, destroyed by fire.

SEPTEMBER

11 - Second Amateur T.T., again won by Leonard Randles.

OCTOBER

1 - Re-opening of the Laxey Glen Mills, reconstructed after the fire of 1921.

7 - Tynwald Court passes a scheme which purports to meet the winter's unemployment problem.

31 - Death of the Lord Bishop of Sodor and Man, Dr Denton Thompson.

NOVEMBER

6 - Election of the new House of Keys completed. Five Labour Party members successful. Mr J.D. Qualtrough returned unopposed at Castletown.

28 - The Rev. Charles L. Thornton-Duesbery, M.A., a native of the Isle of Man appointed bishop.

THE WRECK OF THE *S.S. CLAN MacMASTER*

One of the most amazing marathons in Manx shipwreck history is coming to an end. The *S.S. Clan MacMaster,* which has been stranded on a shelf of rock in the Sound since September last year and attracted thousands of sightseers, is breaking up. It could be years before the entire shell of the vessel totally disappears and a generation or more before the remnants on the seabed disintegrate. But the incredible sight of a stranded ocean-going freighter at what is one of the Island's most scenic areas will soon be gone.

The 11,500 ton member of the celebrated Clan Line of Glasgow went aground at high tide and in thick fog about 1.30 a.m. on Sunday, 30th September, 1923. She was en route from Glasgow to Liverpool at the time, having been partially loaded in Scotland with cargo for the East. The remainder was to be loaded at Liverpool. There was dense fog and while the crew were attempting to get a bearing from the Chicken Rock lighthouse, the *Clan MacMaster* entered the Sound from the west. She was caught by the powerful current and driven onto a reef between the Calf of Man and Thousla Rock. She went aground as far aft as her engine room, was holed near the bow and became firmly fixed there by a rock which speared the double hull.

The 71 Lascars, who composed the majority of the crew, escaped from the vessel by lifeboat and sought sanctuary in a small house, known as Jane's Cottage near the landing jetty on the Calf of Man. Lascars are Indian boatmen, usually from Kathiawar, who serve as deckhands aboard British ocean-going vessels. Also serving on the *Clan MacMaster* were nine white crew but they remained aboard the stricken freighter.

Rescue services were activated only gradually after a distress message by wireless was picked up in Liverpool. The Lloyd's agent on the Island did not hear of the wreck until he received a telegram from Liverpool. He despatched two local launches, the *May* and *White Heather,* to provide whatever assistance was needed. Port Erin lifeboat was launched about noon and Castletown Rocket Brigade went later.

Immediate aid, however, was not required. No one was injured and, as the £100,000 vessel was secured by rock, and the white crewmen were operating pumps to keep the water out, there was no immediate danger of the seven-year-old *Clan MacMaster* slipping into deeper water and going under. Those in charge were content to await the arrival of the Liverpool Salvage Company's steamer, *Ranger.* She reached the Island by Sunday midnight but, because of the fog, was unable to enter the Sound until the following day.

In the next couple of days the *Ranger* provided some assistance despite the sea becoming choppy. Members of the white crew were able to leave the *Clan MacMaster,* visit Port St. Mary and then return. It became apparent very soon, however, that the freighter was past saving. She was too securely fastened on that rock, her stern swinging from side to side as waves hit her. As she settled, her decks became awash at high tides and cracks began to appear in her hull. Everyone knew then that it was only a matter of time before she would start to break up. When some of her cased cargo was washed out of the number 4 hold by the Sound's strong tidal currents, the *Ranger* and the motor launches collected what they could. Thereafter, the emphasis was on rescuing the Lascars from the Calf of Man and salvaging cargo.

The Lascars were removed from the Calf by breeches buoy. This was undertaken with considerable difficulty as it took a lot of persuading to get many of the Lascars to entrust themselves to this form of rescue. They were brought to Douglas on Wednesday night after the sheep aboard the *Clan MacMaster*, which Lascars bring with them on voyages, were slaughtered. By then all shops were closed. Police and the local agent for the Shipwrecked Mariners Association arranged for food to be obtained. The Lascars were transferred to Liverpool aboard the Steam Packet Company's *Mona* which sailed next day. They were made "as comfortable as possible" by the laying of straw on a deck for them to lie upon.

Included in the *Clan MacMaster's* 3,000 ton cargo were motor cars, sewing machines, cotton, silk, coal and whisky. During the winter the *S.S. Trover* removed some of the cargo but not all was salvageable.

When the wreck disintegrates sufficiently to disappear below the surface the tidal currents at the Sound are expected to sweep larger remnants of the vessel and her cargo out to sea and, perhaps, on to the Calf of Man. It is said that large numbers of footpieces for treadle sewing machines which are being beached there are likely to be used for fencing on the Calf, while many households in the south of the Island have acquired brand-new Singer sewing machines which are being put to good family use!

A recent photograph showing the stricken Clan MacMaster slowly sinking in the waters of the Sound as she gradually breaks up.
(R. and L. Kelly Collection)

HERE IS THE NEWS : 1925
WORST YEAR FOR ROAD AND RAIL ACCIDENTS

As the year draws to a close it will be looked upon as the worst ever for road and rail fatalities. Seven people, including two children, have been killed on the roads and three, including one child, have been killed in accidents on the railways. We have this report:

With just two days to go before Christmas, the people of Castletown were saddened by a most tragic accident which occurred when a van driven by 43-year-old William Cowin crashed into the harbour in a blinding snowstorm after missing the entrance to the iron bridge across the harbour. He was drowned, along with a four-year-old girl passenger, Renee Mylchreest, of Bank House, who he was giving a lift home along with her mother. Mrs Annie Mylchreest was saved from the icy waters by Cornelius Hayes, the mate of a schooner moored nearby. Mr Hayes has been given a gold watch by the townsfolk for his bravery in rescuing the mother of the dead child. The Harbour Commissioners are to provide better lighting to the entrance to the bridge.

Two local motor-cyclists were killed in accidents on consecutive days at the end of September. Arthur William Whittaker (21) of Foxdale died after being in collision with a motor-van. And on the following day, William Gilmore Kelly (21) died from injuries sustained after colliding with another motor-cyclist on Broadway, Douglas. During the summer an elderly lady, on holiday from Liverpool, was knocked down and killed by a motor car on Douglas Promenade, while in Ramsey a six-year-old local boy, Sidney Gwilliam, died after being hit by a car on South Promenade.

In August, Douglas Railway Station was the scene of a shocking accident when a train, arriving from Peel, failed to stop in time and overshot the platform, ending up only yards from the booking office. The fireman, 50-year-old William Robinson was thrown out and killed. The inquiry revealed that, while shunting at Union Mills, the deceased mistook a signal given by the guard, started the train too soon and left behind the

The scene at Douglas Railway Station on 22nd August, following the crash of the engine No 3 'Pender' after overshooting the platform. The impact resulted in the fireman William Robinson, being thrown out and killed.

guard and brakesman. The driver, using his own brakes was unable to bring the train to a halt in time. It was said also that had there been telephonic communication between Union Mills and the Douglas signal box, the driver could have been warned to slow down sooner.

Two further deaths occurred in connection with the Manx Electric Railway. At the end of July, 10-year-old Robert Stanley Joughin was knocked down and killed by a tram at Ballagawne crossing as he walked home from school. A month later farmer Thomas Kermode of Dreemskerry, Maughold, was killed by an electric car at the Dreemskerry crossing near his home.

RENT CONTROL RETURNS
After a bitter constitutional struggle with the Legislative Council, the House of Keys has succeeded in getting a new Rent Restriction Bill on to the Statute Book. Controls will last for two years and apply to houses in Douglas rented pre-war at £40 a year and under, and £25 elsewhere in the Island. Government officials hope that by 1928 the housing problems will be eased by the public sector building programme. Last year the expiry of rent controls resulted in orders to quit being imposed on tenants by landlords seeking higher rents.

MANX BISHOP ENTHRONED
The new Lord Bishop, the Rt. Rev. Canon Charles Leonard Thornton-Duesbery, has been enthroned at St. George's in Douglas. He succeeds Dr. Denton Thompson who died last year. The new Bishop was formerly rector of Holy Trinity at Marylebone in London and he is the son of the late Capt. W. Thornton-Duesbery of Ballacosnahan, Patrick. His brother, Hugh, lives at Port Soderick. The Bishop was born at Swiss Cottage, Glen Helen and in his younger days he was noted for his prowess as a rugby player. He is only the second Manx-born Bishop in modern times.

JUNE EFFORT COMMITTEE
Throughout June a programme of fetes, fancy dress parades, illuminations, etc, was staged in Douglas by the June Effort Committee. Its object was to attract more visitors to the Island during the early part of the season. The voluntary committee was set up earlier in the year on the initiative of Councillor A. B. Crookall, M.H.K., who is now in his third term of office as Mayor of Douglas and has been made an Alderman. Along with the attractions it was also hoped to offer reduced

1925

ENTHRONEMENT OF NEW MANX BISHOP

prices for travel, accommodation and goods. However, this was only partially successful as the Steam Packet Company refused to lower its fares, and many traders were reluctant to reduce prices.

CLIFF TRAGEDIES
During the summer two people were killed in cliff falls in the Island. Twelve-year-old Rodney Hartley, a King William's College boy, whose father is a doctor working in West Africa, was killed in a 150 foot fall near the Sugar Loaf Rock while looking for seabirds' eggs. And thirty-two-year-old Frederick Carine, of Four Roads, Port St. Mary, fell 40 feet while out on an evening stroll on Bradda Head. He is believed to have lost his footing on dry grass at the cliff top.

AMATEUR T.T. RIDER KILLED
A rider was killed on the first day of practising for the 1925 Amateur T.T. Races. He was believed to have crashed trying to

The newly-enthroned bishop, the Right Reverend Charles C. Thornton-Duesbery, M.A., a native of the Isle of Man. *(Manx National Heritage)*

avoid a dog which had strayed on to the Course. Twenty-two-year-old James Temple was a student at Cambridge University. He died at Glentramman when he crashed at speed into a telegraph pole - which was almost uprooted in the impact. In another incident Arthur Marsden from Douglas was seriously injured.

WIRELESS AID TO TEACHING
Finally, a novel method of teaching children in the Island has been introduced by Mr. R. P. Hewitt, headmaster of Foxdale elementary school. He has installed a wireless set in the classroom, at his own expense, and selected programmes are being listened to by youngsters as part of the school curriculum. Mr. Hewitt says this will broaden the children's outlook on life - and prevent them growing up with too much of a parochial attitude. Wireless programmes are also used in some schools in London, and France and Germany.

1925 NEWS IN BRIEF

JANUARY
1 - Formal opening of the new Masonic Temple in Douglas.
4 - Death of the Island's 'grand old lady,' Miss M.L. Wood, who was a music teacher for over 60 years and principal founder of the Manx Music Festival.
5 - Inquest at Parville, Arbory, on John Edward Maiden (33), a manservant, who comitted suicide by shooting after attacking his mistress with a hammer.

FEBRUARY
18 - John Edgar Costain, mate of the steamer *Ben Blanche,* drowned in Ramsey harbour.
22/23 Centenary celebrated of the founding of the Presbyterian Church in Douglas.
21 - Death of Mr G.H. Wood, for 50 years secretary, manager of director of the I.O.M. Railway Company.

MAY
1 - New plant installed at Glenfaba brickworks, Peel, capable of producing nearly 10,000 'sand-lime' bricks daily.
8 - Specimen of the Rudolph rorqual whale washed ashore at Langness.
21 - Great Rechabite procession and demonstration (the first for 20 years) held in Douglas.
23 - Home Office suggests that Deemsters be paid £1,200 a year and the Attorney-General £1,400 and, despite protests from the Keys, insists upon the Attorney-General receiving a higher figure than the Deemsters.

JUNE
9 - Keys object to increase in beer duty, but accept it on being informed by the Governor that the proceeds will be used to aid the programme of unemployment schemes.

21 - Christening of the lifeboat *Manchester and Salford* in the Manchester Ship Canal and presented by the R.N.L.I branch of those two cities to the Douglas Committee. The lifeboat is one of the first motor-powered type to enter service.

JULY
6 - The Duke of Atholl, whose ancestors were Lords of Man, attends the Tynwald Ceremony.

SEPTEMBER
5 - Lady visitor from Manchester falls between the ship's side and the wall of the Victoria Pier while attempting to board the *Snaefell* and sustains fatal injuries.

OCTOBER
9 - Passenger figures for the season total 534,460, which is an increase on last year, but 81,000 less than the 1913 record total of 615,726.
10 - Manx Ladies' Choir, conductor Mr Noah Moore, wins Wallasey Music Festival. Mixed Choir placed second.
16 - Douglas Town Council to lay a second water main from the Baldwin reservoir.

NOVEMBER
1 - Unveiling of window in St Mathew's Church, Douglas, in memory of Miss M.L. Wood.
9 - Councillor A. B. Crookall, M.H.K., elected Mayor of Douglas for the fourth time, and also elected as Alderman.
12 - Hollantide Day. Second *Cruinnaght* promoted by the W.M.A. and the Manx Society. Competitions in Manx music, literature, arts and crafts, and confectionery etc.
17 - Elections to the Isle of Man Education Authority completed, at the end of that body's first term of five years.
19-21 Dense fog in Mersey prevents steamer services to and from Liverpool for two days.

THE 20th CENTURY

93

A WHALE OF A JOB

Manx Museum Trustees have taken possession of the huge dead whale that was washed ashore at Langness. Though the remnants of supposed sea serpents have been discovered occasionally, and giant basking sharks have been landed by fishermen, nothing like this has ever been seen before. The whale, when discovered by King William's College pupils in the narrow Horses Gully at Langness, measured 48 feet 6 inches, was seven feet high and weighed an estimated 40 tons.

The plan is to put its skeleton on display in a Whale Room at the Museum, though when that will be is uncertain. There is nowhere in the existing building at the former Noble's Hospital that is suitable. The plan is to suspend the skeleton from a light and airy ceiling so that visitors can see it easily. To make that possible an extension will have to be built and current estimates are that it may be ten years before finance is available for that. Meanwhile, the bones will have to be kept in store.

The whale, a female and still not a fully-grown member of the Rorqual species, which can grow to 60 feet, is believed to have come ashore with the high tide at midday on Friday, 8th May. It is not known whether she was alive. It has been speculated that she was the whale reported to have been struck by the liner *Montrose* off Queenstown some days earlier, but there is insufficient evidence of damage to her carcase to confirm this.

Once her discovery was reported to Castletown Coastguard Station, sightseers arrived at Langness in increasing numbers. Thousands visited the spot in glorious weather on the Saturday and Sunday. Among them were souvenir hunters who removed pieces of whale bone. This was stopped, however, before serious damage was caused. The Manx Museum Trustees intervened with the erection of warning notices to the effect that the

The 40-ton whale after being hauled by a tug on to the beach at Derbyhaven. *(R. and L. Kelly Collection)*

whale had been seized on behalf of the Crown and anyone interfering with it would be prosecuted.

Later, a tug was used to tow the carcase out of the gully and into Derbyhaven. Strong tidal currents swept the monster back into the sea for quarter of a mile before it was finally beached. Two traction engines were then used to haul the carcase on to three linked trailers and tow the latter to Litt's Manure Works at Baldwin. A police escort warned householders on the route to close their windows because of the smell.

Litt's stripped off the flesh and this was used in its manure-making process. The remainder of the whale was buried in sand and left there for some months to allow natural processes to rid the bones of their oil. As it will be many years before a proper display can be arranged, a flipper has now been removed and encased in glass for public exhibition.

After being secured on trailers, the whale is moved away with the help of two traction engines, the destination being Litt's Manure Works at Baldwin.
(Manx National Heritage)

HERE IS THE NEWS : 1926

SIR CLAUDE HILL SWORN IN AS NEW LIEUTENANT-GOVERNOR

After completing his fixed term of office as Lieutenant-Governor of the Isle of Man, Major-General Sir William Fry left the Island at the end of March. Before his departure, presentations of illuminated addresses were made to Sir William from the Tynwald Court and Douglas Town Council. These were made in appreciation of the advancements made during the past seven years, including the difficult post-war years. In May his successor, Sir Claude Hamilton Hill, K.C.S.I, C.I.E., was sworn in at Castle Rushen. We have this report:

The Manx people are congratulating themselves on the appointment of Sir Claude Hill as the new Lieutenant-Governor. He comes with a wide experience in many branches of public life and is an agreeable man of the world. Born in 1866, Sir Claude has had a distinguished career in the Indian Civil Service culminating in being Finance Minister of the Viceroy's Executive Council. He retired from this position in 1921 and has been Director-General of the League of Red Cross Societies until his appointment to the Isle of Man. He and his charming wife, Lady Hill, have a son and two daughters, the youngest of whom resides with her parents at Government House.

His Excellency arrives at a time of crisis with Whitehall which is forcing a decision concerning the long-running controversy over the Island's contribution to the huge Imperial war debt. He will need all his diplomatic skills and knowledge of financial affairs to bring about a satisfactory outcome of this thorny question. Upon his arrival His Excellency set about the task of mastering the intricacies of the Island's finances and finding a compromise solution acceptable to both the Imperial and Manx governments. His proposals are awaited with great interest.

BOOM TIME FOR THE RAILWAYS

At the annual meeting of the Isle of Man Railway Company held in March, shareholders were informed that the number of passengers carried during 1925 had risen to 1,344,620.

His Excellency Sir Claude Hamilton Hill, K.C.S.I., C.I.E. *(Manx National Heritage)*

This is 64,760 more than the previous year and represents a record in the annals of the railway. A dividend of 5% was declared with a bonus of 1%. This year has seen the arrival of the company's latest engine, numbered 16 and named *Mannin*. It was purchased from the Beyer, Peacock Company of Manchester, suppliers of the earlier engines to the Isle of Man Railway, and is capable of hauling longer trains.

The Manx Electric Railway Company held its annual meeting in London at the end of last year, and it, too, showed record passenger returns. During the year 739,967 passengers were carried, an increase of 126,814 on 1924. The company's meticulous records show that 333,755 passenger miles had been covered together with 43,054 goods miles. A dividend of $5^1/2\%$ was declared on preference shares.

THE GENERAL STRIKE

The General Strike throughout Britain, the first of its kind, had a serious effect on the Island's visiting industry even though Manx workers were exempted from the strike. Although the strike crumbled after nine days in May, the miners continued their action throughout the summer with serious consequences for the British economy which was reflected in our own economy. One of the worst effects was the shortage of coal for the Steam Packet vessels. Visitor arrivals plummeted to 384,000, compared with 540,000 last year. Everybody's 'takings' were down and any hope of the railways matching their records of last year were dashed from the beginning of the season. The spectre of winter unemployment arrived sooner than usual. In September hundreds of jobless men demonstrated in the streets of Douglas.

BABY BOY DROWNS AT SILVERDALE

A baby boy drowned in the two-foot deep artificial lake at Silverdale while with his parents, who were on the annual outing of the Mona Tent of Rechabites in May. Eighteen-months-old John James Leneghan wandered away from his parents, Mr. and Mrs. Daniel Leneghan, of Nelson Street, Douglas. He was found lying on the bottom of the lake. In another child tragedy a twelve-year-old Douglas boy, Frank Kennedy, was killed after falling 100 feet down the cliffs behind the boarding houses at Palace Terrace. He was on the cliffs collecting firewood.

T.T. CONTROVERSY

Crowds of T.T. fans rioted when the A-C.U. disqualified an Italian rider after the Lightweight T.T. Pietro Ghersi, on a Moto-Guzzi, finished second after a close and thrilling duel with Irish rider Paddy Johnston. He was then disqualified when it was found that he had used an unspecified spark plug in his machine. At the prize-giving in the Villa Marina his supporters ran on to the seafront, hijacked a bus, went to Ghersi's hotel - and carried him back to the Villa in triumph, raising him onto the stage. The A.C.U. refused to change its decision - but later decided to give him a special award.

PULROSE DEVELOPMENTS

Douglas Town Council has decided that a municipal golf course should be built on the Pulrose Estate on the outskirts of the town. It will be opened next year. The council has also announced plans for building 100 houses at Pulrose. A building firm from outside the Island has undertaken to build the houses at a cost of £54,000 using a new quick-build system. Under this the main construction is carried out using concrete and asbestos.

MORE ROAD FATALITIES

The number of fatal road accidents continues to rise. After seven deaths last year the total this year has risen to ten, including two children. In February John Penrice (10) was killed by a motor car when running out of the Sunday School connected with Cronk-y-Voddy Church; Nancy Wilson, a child of nine, succumbed to injuries caused by an accident in Market Street, Peel between a small pram the deceased was wheeling, and a motor lorry. In neither case were the drivers of the vehicles to blame.

Two were killed in separate incidents involving Highway Board wagons - William Boyde (25) of Ballaleigh, Michael, and Joseph Taylor (36), an employee in the telephone department at the Douglas Post Office. Mr Taylor was riding a motor-cycle at the time of the accident near to Oatlands quarry, Santon.

Motor-cycles were involved in three further fatalities. Roy Morgan (21), a visitor from Liverpool, was killed when riding a motor-cycle belonging to a T.T. competitor. The machine finished fifth in the Senior race the following day. At the end of August, Stanley Birt (22), of Swansea, an intending competitor in the Amateur T.T. was killed while riding his machine in Victoria Road, Douglas, about an hour after his arrival by steamer. Also in August, Thomas Faragher (23) was killed while riding pillion on a motor-cycle

Tynwald has given approval for Port Erin Commissioners to purchase the popular baths at Traie Meanagh. The baths were constructed by Mr H.N. Laughton, who has done much to develop Port Erin as a visitor resort. *(R. and L. Kelly Collection)*

driven by his brother which came into collision with a beast at the gates of the field at Milntown, near Ramsey, where the I.O.M. Agricultural Society's summer show was held. Another pillion rider, George Branney (22) of Douglas was killed at Greeba Bridge in September.

In a bizarre accident Miss L.G. Whitworth, of Greeba, a well-known resident, sustained fatal injuries through being flung from a dog-cart which she was driving near Belle Vue, Douglas. And in November, misfortune befell Allan Fairley (27), assistant engineer to the Harbour Board, when he was killed by the falling of a felled tree upon his

motor-car near 'Ivy Cottage,' Old Castletown Road, Douglas.

PEG-LEG CALEY IN MORE TROUBLE

Finally, the notorious Douglas bad character Peg-Leg Caley is in trouble with the law again. This follows a disturbance at his tenement house in Barrack Street - a vile den of methylated spirits drinkers. Caley has been charged with using foul language while breaking up a fight between his wife and another woman in which they tore off each other's clothes. Police said the denizens of Caley's tenement reach the point of madness under the influence of meths.

1926 NEWS IN BRIEF

JANUARY
1 - Mersey Docks and Harbour Board announce that they are going to build a shelter at the Liverpool landing-stage for the benefit of passengers waiting to embark on Manx steamers.
20-23 Douglas Choral Union, for the third time in its 30 years' history, performs Gilbert and Sullivan's comic opera, 'The Mikado.'
28 - Annual meeting of the Isle of Man Bank Ltd. Deposits remain at over £2,000,000 and a dividend of 25% is declared.

FEBRUARY
27 - Annual meeting of the Steam Packet Company. Dividend declared at 5%. It was announced that a new steamer is to be built, but the Company has been obliged to yield to a claim for English income tax on 55% of its profit.

MARCH
16 - Tynwald grants Port Erin Village Commissioners leave to purchase the baths at Traie Meanagh, constructed by the late Mr A. N. Laughton.

APRIL
29 - Rev. C. A. Cannan, B.A., instituted Vicar of Michael, his native parish.

MAY
1 - Coalminers' strike begins.
3-12 General Strike of various classes of workmen throughout Britain.

JUNE
1 - 'June Effort' campaign begins with the ceremony of 'Crowning the Rose Queen.'
15 - Wong Bin (23), whose father keeps a Chinese laundry in Douglas, hangs himself in a fit of depression apparently caused by a longing to return to China.
22 - Budget Day. New taxes levied on matches, playing cards and opera glasses.

JULY
28 - Douglas Town Council take the sensational course of rescinding their decision of a fortnight ago, to adopt oil-fuel, in preference to steam, as the motive power for the extension to their generating plant on North Quay. This means they have rejected the advice of Mr Dykes, their consultant engineer and brings into question his remuneration. Council prepared to employ a K.C., if necessary.

SEPTEMBER
5 - Miss Norah Moore, a student at the Royal College of Music, and daughter of Mr Noah Moore L.R.A.M., makes a triumphant debut as a soprano soloist at the weekly Sunday evening concert at the Villa Marina.
26 - The Lord Bishop attends Jubilee celebrations of the consecration of the 'new' church at Braddan.

OCTOBER
1 - A continuance of importation of coal direct from the Continent becomes necessary owing to the Ministry of Mines forbidding the shipment of coal from British ports.

NOVEMBER
5 - Tynwald, after a debate extending over four days, accepts Governor's proposals to settle the dispute over the contribution to the Imperial war debt.
9 - Ald. A. B. Crookall, M.H.K., J.P., elected Mayor of Douglas for the fifth year in succession.
13 - The Lieutenant-Governor inaugurates a movement for the establishment of a Manx branch of the British Red Cross Society.

DECEMBER
15 - Formal opening of an extension to Noble's Hospital, consisting of a private ward wing, thus increasing the hospital's accommodation to 72 beds.

TYNWALD MATTERS:

LIEUTENANT-GOVERNOR ENDS WAR DEBT CONTROVERSY

The Great War lasted for four years, but the argument over the Island's financial contribution to the expenses has rumbled on for eight. Now at last a solution has been found to the satisfaction of both the Imperial and Manx governments.

It was in 1918 that a proposal was made by the Home Office that the Isle of Man and the Channel Islands should share in the immense cost of the war. After some debate the Manx government agreed to accept liability for £250,000 War Stock to be paid in 20 annual instalments. This was in addition to the £10,000 contributed annually under the 1866 Statute. However, while the offer was accepted by Whitehall, it was made clear that it was "neither sufficient nor satisfactory" - a remark which presaged future problems.

In 1922 the matter was once again raised in London, it being pointed out that the Island continued to enjoy the full protection given by the forces of the Crown and all diplomatic services abroad. The Manx government was further reminded that there had been a considerable increase in its annual revenues, from £85,000 in 1914 to £369,000 in 1921. The Imperial government consequently proposed that our £10,000 should be increased to £150,000 per annum, with an immediate payment of £100,000 from the Manx Accumulated Fund. This proposal received very short shrift from Tynwald which countered with a proposal of making an *ex gratia* payment of £200,000 plus the transfer of Crown properties to the Island. This received equally short shrift from London. Matters were then put in the hands of a Committee of the Privy Council, ironically but perhaps inevitably, headed by the Duke of Atholl.

This Committee visited the Isle of Man, and also the other islands, and met with Tynwald Committees both here and in London. The deliberations resulted in the Imperial Government being advised to demand from the Island £100,000 a year for 50 years, and £50,000 a year after that in perpetuity. This would replace the £10,000 already in place and the £20,000 being paid in connection with the liability for War Stock. Any feeling on the Island that the Manx should play its part in peace, as it had done in war, was severely damaged by these recommendations. The latest proposals were seen as severe and punitive, and were rejected out of hand.

For long it had seemed impossible to reconcile the Tynwald estimates of what the Island could reasonably afford, and what Whitehall saw as affordable. Repeatedly, the Island advanced its lopsided economy as a major factor - full summer employment followed by severe winter unemployment. The first call upon the increased revenues was to provide work schemes to alleviate this desperate situation. Fear of an increase in Income Tax was another incentive to oppose the British suggestion. And this year the strike of the coalminers, leading to the General Strike, has been seen as a threat to the Island, even if it only meant that there was no coal for the Steam Packet boats to bring the visitors here!

The Treasury retaliated by pointing out starkly that whereas the United Kingdom was paying £11 per head to defray war costs, Australia and New Zealand £5, the Isle of Man was only contributing £2 a head, and was not even paying the war pensions for Manx servicemen and their dependants. British newspapers were making stringent criticism of the Manx stance and were scathing about those who escaped to the Isle of Man to take advantage of the more relaxed tax regime. Then there was the famous cartoon showing Winston Churchill wielding a pair of shears as he chased fat and well-fleeced sheep through a door marked 'Isle of Man and Channel Islands.' The demands of the Committee's report made no mention of improving the Island's constitutional position, dear to the hearts of many Manxmen and women. The subject was dismissed in the report with the statement: "The power of the Imperial Parliament in the matter is thought to be unquestioned."

By May of this year the Home Office was pressing hard for a decision on the Privy Council Committee's recommendations. Tynwald had prevaricated with the coal strike and the impending appointment of a new Lieutenant-Governor being given as reasons. The Home Office would have to wait, but the arrival of Sir Claude Hill in that month brought some necessary focus into the discussions. Generally speaking, people were becoming tired of the seemingly incessant arguments. Many felt that at least the Island should accept responsibility for Manx war pensions. All in all, Lieutenant-Governor Hill found a climate of opinion that would favour a settlement without further delay. By the autumn, the Lieutenant-Governor had clarified his ideas and on 12th October he made his statement to Tynwald. In it he proposed that £500,000 War Stock should be taken over, £100,000 paid now, and £30,000 paid over 25 years, and that the Island should pay the local war pensions. This, His Excellency said, could be achieved without any fresh taxation except for a small increase in the higher rates of Income Tax.

These were dramatic proposals and several members of the House of Keys said they should go to the electorate before such a decision was made. This was rejected, but numerous public meetings were held to inform people. Then, on 5th November, Tynwald witnessed the conclusion of the saga as the debate unfolded on the Lieutenant-Governor's proposals. Many powerful and persuasive speeches were made, but the most impressive was that of Sir Claude himself. When summing up he displayed a mixture of cool reason, an astute financial analysis, and an appeal to our patriotism and innate sense of fair play. It was what political observers described as the most moving speech ever made in Tynwald, and it won the day. The Legislative Council supported the Lieutenant-Governor unanimously while the Keys voted 15 to 9 in favour. In December the Imperial government accepted Tynwald's offer. The story had run its course and as a final word on the subject one English newspaper commented : "The Island plays up and pays up."

EDUCATION WEEK - A CELEBRATION

Five years of dramatic achievement in the field of education have been celebrated in a series of events held during May this year. It is five years since the Central Education Authority was given responsibility for providing a standardised education for all Island children. Since 1923 the authority has been known as the Isle of Man Education Authority and its members are proud of the progress they have made. By prudent management the schools are now better maintained and staffed than ever before. Many schools were neglected during the Great War but during the last five years these have been repaired, re-decorated, equipped with new heating and sanitary facilities, and with modern desks and other equipment. This has included pianos and even sewing machines in the larger schools. Four of the older and smaller schools in the south are to be replaced by a new school at Four Roads while another four will be replaced by a new school at Laxey.

The thorny problem of religious education has been resolved by the introduction of syllabi in both elementary and secondary schools. The first half hour of each school day is given over to a religious service and instruction of a non-denominational nature. The temperance movement has been pleased to note that monthly lessons are being provided on the misuse and abuse of food and alcohol.

Higher education is being pursued vigorously. Construction of a new secondary school for boys at St. Ninian's, Douglas, has been underway since 1924 and will be ready for occupation next year. Park Road School will then be given over to girls only. New premises for Ramsey Grammar School are also planned. Since being established in 1922, it has operated in temporary premises. Scholarships for the more able pupils are available throughout the Island while those who pass the entrance examination at eleven years can pay a small fee of five guineas a year, parents being able to pay in three term instalments. It is realised, however, that many poor families are not in a position to cover this fee, especially when one considers the cost represents two weeks' wages for the average labourer. Then there is the scourge of winter unemployment. To meet the needs of these children, and those who don't wish to enter secondary schools, classes in advanced education are now available in elementary schools. Pupils who live more than three miles from a secondary school are entitled to free travel if facilities are available. Usually this is by rail but in some cases motor charabancs are being used.

Tables, crockery and cutlery have been introduced for children who bring packed meals with them at lunchtime. Arrangements have been made for them to be served tea, coffee or cocoa. Another development is the introduction of a rural library service for youngsters. This has been financed in part by a grant from the Carnegie Trust. Schools are being used as distribution centres and the head teachers are acting as honorary librarians.

Another responsibility of the Education Authority is the provision of a School Medical Service. This was established three years ago despite claims that, because of its health-giving air and lack of an industrial community, the Island did not need it. Now all children receive medical inspections on school premises, in the presence of parents if they so wish, on starting school, at eight years, at 13 and (in the case of secondary schools) at 15.

Introduction of the service has demonstrated that a substantially higher percentage of Manx children are suffering from health problems compared with children in England and Wales, where the benefits of a school health service have been available for many years. Three times

Citizens in the making.

Gardening.

Needlework in central hall.

Boys' woodwork.

Physical exercises.

Handwork in a rural school.

(Illustrations from the R. and L. Kelly Collection)

as many Manx children have been found to have Tuberculosis; twice as many have been found to have defective vision; five times as many suffer from squint; and more than twice as many have been found to have problems associated with their tonsils and ears. About 19 times as many have enlarged cervical glands. It is hoped that the School Medical Service will lead parents into a greater awareness of their children's ailments and that they will be more ready to seek medical advice and treatment, whether they can afford to do so or not.

Cases noted for treatment are re-inspected every six months and, where necessary, the parents are visited by the school nurses. "Sometimes," says an Authority member, "a great deal of perseverance and tact on the part of the nurses is required to obtain consent to the necessary treatment, but an increasing number of parents are now welcoming the opportunities for treatment offered by the Authority."

All cases are referred initially to a child's family doctor, but in respect of certain categories if the parent is unable to pay the doctor's private fees, or if the latter is unwilling to undertake the treatment, the School Medical Service assumes responsibility. These concern defective

The School Dental Clinic.

vision, enlarged tonsils and adenoids, minor ailments such as discharging ears, sore eyes, skin diseases and X-ray treatment at Noble's Hospital for ringworm. Minor ailments are treated at school clinics at Douglas, Ramsey, Castletown, Peel and Laxey.

The condition of children's teeth has also been revealed as a cause for concern. The school dental officer reports that 85% of children in 1924, and 75.2% last year, were found to have tooth decay. Where possible they were referred to their family dentist but in the majority of cases they did not have one. In cases such as these the school dentist now undertakes to give the treatment and a "decided improvement" has been noted.

The object of 'Education Week' has been to publicise the achievements of the Island's education service. During the week public meetings were held and 'Open' Days gave parents a chance to see their children engaged in their normal studies and to look round the schools. There were athletic festivals in the four districts and examples of school work were placed on public exhibition. Displays were provided in the Villa Marina Reading Room, the Centenary Hall, Peel, St. Mary's Church School, Castletown, St. Mary's Hall, Port St. Mary and Queen's Hall, Ramsey.

Physics laboratory.

Chemistry laboratory.

Gymnasium.

Technical College for women.

School of Art.

School clinic.

(Illustrations from the R. and L. Kelly Collection)

HERE IS THE NEWS : 1927
MOTOR BUSES UPSET RAILWAYS' MONOPOLY

The railway transport services in the Isle of Man have been thrown into turmoil by the introduction of motor omnibuses for the first time. To many, they are seen as offering a quicker and more convenient means of transport compared with the steam and electric railways. But the railway companies are fighting back with lower fares and improved timetables. We have this report:

Two 'bus companies began operating early in the summer, after being given permission to operate a network of services to most places on the Island. Manxland Bus Services Ltd is an off-shoot of Cumberland Motor Services Ltd and has a fleet of red 'buses. As if not to be outdone, three local companies operating charabanc services have combined and operate 'buses under the general title of Manx Motors Ltd. Their buses appear in either white or blue. After a disastrous season last year, the railway companies have been quick to respond to this unwelcome competition. First, the I.O.M. Railway Company, under their new manager, Mr A. M. Sheard, issued its summer timetable. It provided for a sensational 100 trains daily, and at pre-war fares, reducing the Douglas to Ramsey return to 2s 6d. Trains were timed to link with midnight boats and there were late trains nightly. A motor van delivery service for goods has also been introduced. And the Manx Electric Railway has announced that for the winter their fares are to be drastically reduced with a Douglas to Ramsey return at 1s.6d. Douglas Corporation are adding to their fleet of 'buses annually with the total now approaching 20. The Tramways Committee have announced that Douglas Bay horse tramway is to close for the winter and will be replaced by 'buses. However, the Council is virtually unanimous in agreeing that the horse trams, a famous symbol of Douglas, will continue to operate in the summers.

RAMSEY ROCKET BRIGADE AND LIFEBOAT IN ACTION
Terrific gales at the end of January

Concert party formed by pupils of Park Road School. The year has seen them separate and become founder members of the Douglas High School for Boys and the Douglas High School for Girls. The photograph is taken in the playing field of the new Boys High School whose headmaster, Mr A. H. Sykes, is seated in the centre. Staff member, Mr George Shaw, is standing on the far left and his colleague, Mr Bob Callow, is on the far right. *(Manx National Heritage)*

saw the call out of the Ramsey, Peel and Port Erin lifeboats. Especial gallantry was shown by the Ramsey lifeboat crew and the Ramsey rocket brigade. They saved the lives of nine men on board a Russian barqentine driven ashore on the Ayres, near

After taking three years to build at the top of Somerset Road, the new Douglas High School for Boys was officially opened on 17th May. Here boys transferring from Park Road line up in front of the main entrance for the ceremony. *(Frank Cowin Library)*

Knock-e-Dhooney. Afterwards two men were fined ten shillings each for looting a compass and a ship's clock from the wreck. In June, the Ramsey lifeboat was back in action and rescued six crewmen from a Fleetwood fishing trawler driven on the rocks at Ballure. Lifeboatman Harry Christian narrowly escaped death when he was washed off the launching carriage as the lifeboat was being launched.

NEW SECONDARY SCHOOL
On 17th May, the new secondary school was officially opened at the top of Somerset Road, opposite St Ninian's Church. It has cost £50,000 to build and is regarded as one of the finest of its kind in the British Isles. But it has come under criticism because of its high cost and its position. Its critics say children leaving the school find themselves on some of the busiest roads in Douglas. The school is to be called Douglas High School for Boys and will provide places for about 300 boys at present attending the Eastern District Secondary School and Douglas Grammar School. Mr W. H. Sykes is the school's headmaster, after transferring from the school on Park Road which will become the Douglas High School for Girls.

Saturday night at the Guild is Children's Festival night. Begun in 1922, children from all the Island's elementary schools combine for the occasion. As for the Cleveland Medal night and the Choirs night, special late night trains and trams are laid on for those coming from country areas.

TWO T.T. RIDERS KILLED

Two riders were killed in this year's T.T. event. Popular rider Charles Birkin was killed when he crashed his Norton into a stone wall on a fast corner at Rhencullen, Kirk Michael. The accident occurred during early morning practice, when the roads are not officially closed. Birkins was forced to swerve when confronted with a fish delivery cart. In the Lightweight Race John Cooke, from Birkenhead, died in a crash on the Mountain Road, three miles north of the Bungalow. This is one of the more remote parts of the Course and no one saw the crash. It was some hours before a doctor was able to reach him.

YEAR'S TOLL OF FATALITIES

The year has been another exceptionally bad year for other fatal accidents. Seven people have been killed in road accidents. Two died in house fires; a 14-year-old boy died under the wheels of a train at Port St Mary station; a Manchester visitor drowned in the pool below Glen Maye waterfall; a ten-year-old girl died in a cliff fall on Douglas Head. In a tragic house accident in Ramsey, a three-year-old was scalded to death after falling into a bath of boiling water. There have also been a remarkable number of five people killed after falling from windows in various parts of the Island, including boarding houses. And the coxswain of Port St Mary lifeboat died in the premature explosion of a maroon being set off to announce Lifeboat Day.

GOVERNOR SEEKS MORE KEYS' INVOLVEMENT

The Lieutenant-Governor, Sir Claude Hill has personally initiated a momentous change in Manx consitutional policy by inviting the House of Keys to elect an Executive Council of four, together with the Speaker, to consult with him on matters relating to Insular government. He told Tynwald he believed the elected representatives of the people were not closely enough involved in running the Island's affairs. The new body is seen as the first step towards the formation of a Manx cabinet.

LAXEY MINES TO CLOSE FOR GOOD

Finally, the Great Laxey Mines seem to have come to the end of the road. Notices have been posted saying all the men have been laid off because of the fall in the world price of lead. The mines closed and went into liquidation in 1920 but they were re-opened two years later when they were bought by Laxey businessman Mr. Robert Williamson. Since then mining operations have continued with varying degrees of success. Since Mr. Williamson's death in March, the future has been in serious doubt.

1927 NEWS IN BRIEF

FEBRUARY
21 - I.O.M. Steam Packet's annual meeting hears that owing to the General Strike and prolonged coal strike of last year, 289,556 fewer passengers were carried than in 1925.
16 - Isle of Man Red Cross Society formed. Active anti-tuberculosis campaign urged as first task for the Society.

MARCH
11 - Death of Mr Robert Williamson, an outstanding figure in the public and commercial life of Laxey, and senior ex-member of the Manx Legislature.
29 - Tynwald considers report from the chief inspector of the Electricity Commissioners which condemns the Douglas Corporation's proposals to extend its generating plant on the North Quay. Consideration deferred for the appointment of another expert.

APRIL
1 - Death of Mr Philip Kneale, town crier, Ramsey.
2 - Mr Noah Moore's Manx Ladies' Choir wins the Dawnay Shield at the London Music Festival for the third time.
6 - Launch at Birkenhead of the I.O.M. Steam Packet's *Ben my Chree*, the fourth of that name.
6 - After approaches from I.O.M. Advertising Board, the L.M.S. Railway agree to continue steamer service from Heysham.
14 - Formal opening of the new school at the Four Roads, Rushen, which replaces the four existing schools in various parts of the parish.
21 - I.O.M. Antiquarian Society informed by its President, Mr W.C. Cubbon, of important discoveries at Rushen Abbey.
27 - Alderman A. B. Crookall, M.H.K. and Mayor of Douglas, presents to the town a fully furnished and equipped maternity home, named after his late wife, Mrs Jane Crookall. It is in Demesne Road and is run by Trustees and honorary surgeon Dr Dorothy Pantin.

24 - Budget Day. Deficit shown on Customs revenue and Accumulated Fund down to £446. New duties on wines, foreign motorcar tyres, tobacco, matches and foreign-made pottery. Income Tax rates remain at 1s. to 3s.6d in the £.

JUNE
3 - Speaker of the House of Keys, Mr G. F. Clucas, made C.B.E.
5 - Opening of the Royalty Cinema by the Palace and Derby Castle Company on the site of the old Pier Pavilion in Walpole Avenue, Douglas.
11 - Arrival of Manx Homecoming Party. Great emotional scenes.
30 - Gift to Noble's Hospital by the family of the late Mr Joseph Cunningham, M.L.C., of a new wing equipped for X-ray treatment and for 'ultra-violet' and electro-medical treatment generally.

JULY
4 - Opening of *Palais de Danse* by the Strand Cinema Company.
29 - Directors of the Manx National Health Insurance Society, set up five years ago, decide to increase the sickness benefits to 17s. weekly for men and 13s for women, and to arrange for free dental treatment.

AUGUST
8 - Official opening of Pulrose Golf Course.

OCTOBER
3 - 'Ramsey Cushag' Choir conducted by Mrs Black, L.R.A.M., wins the ladies' class at the Wallasey Music Festival.
18 - Wanderer's A.F.C. Male Voice Choir, under Mr R. E. Cubbon, gained first prize at the Blackpool Music Festival. Mr Alan Quirk was placed second in the bass solo class.

DECEMBER
15 - Members of the I.O.M. Natural History and Antiquarian Society learn of discoveries made by Mr P. M. C. Kermode at Knock-e-Dhooney, Andreas, which indicate the very rare relic in the British Isles of a Norse 'ship burial.'

THE PILGRIMAGE OF THE HOMECOMERS

There hasn't been a dry eye. Emotions have run high. Such are the verdicts of the Island's first great Homecoming. Over 300 came from North America; some Manx-born, others of Manx descent who had never seen the Island before. The sense of belonging remained, however, and the welcome they received was no less warm. Everyone agrees that the 1927 Homecoming should not be the last. Many of those who came are descendants of those who emigrated in past centuries to seek a new life as pioneers in the new territories of America and Canada. It is said that there are as many people of Manx descent living in these parts as are on the Isle of Man today. Now greater prosperity and better means of travel mean that they can make pilgrimages to seek out their origins. One such is Cleveland-born Hannah Brew, aged 82 years, who has at last visited the birthplace of her parents.

There are many Manx Societies throughout the world, including Australia and New Zealand. In 1911 Mr Richard Cain of Braddan formed the World Manx Association to liaise with Manx Societies. Every year a growing number of those who are Manx at heart arrive for the Tynwald Ceremony and the Association's gathering at the Nunnery. This has led to this year's Homecoming. To help organise the event about 20, including Mr Cain and the Mayor of Douglas, travelled to Canada to act as an escort party. They visited Toronto and Cleveland, Ohio where there are large concentrations of Manx people. The Homecomers set sail in the White Star liner *Albertica* which arrived in Douglas Bay precisely on time on the morning of 11th June. The liner was flying the Manx flag and fired a rocket to announce her arrival. It was the *Peel Castle*, dressed overall, which acted as a tender to bring everyone ashore. A massed choir welcomed them with strains of 'Ellan Vannin', 'Ramsey Town' and the Manx National Anthem.

The Homecoming coincided with the T.T. Races and there were many receptions in different parts of the Island. Highlight of the visit was attendance at the Tynwald Fair, followed by a great gathering at the Nunnery. Rain did not dampen anyone's enthusiasm. At one reception in the Villa Marina grounds, local children gave a demonstration which ended by them forming a large and colourful Three Legs of Man. On another occasion His Excellency hosted a conference in the Legislative Council chamber. This led to the formation of a body which, with Government support, will help young Manx people to emigrate and get established in North America and Australia.

Another result is a strengthening of the bond between

Acting as a tender, the Peel Castle transfers the Homecomers to Victoria Pier where thousands await to give them a rousing reception.
(Manx National Heritage)

Manx people in North America. They have agreed to hold an annual Convention. The first will be held next year in Cleveland where there are more people of Manx descent than anywhere else. The Cleveland-based Mona's Relief Society was probably formed in 1855, one of its founders being Thomas Quayle, who pioneered ship building on the Great Lakes. The Friendly Society has done much to help those who have met misfortune far from home. The Society organised other activities such as a debating society and annual Manx Suppers. It even had its own burial lot and monument in Cleveland's Woodland Cemetery. The Society donated money to assist widows and orphans following the loss of the *Ellan Vannin,* and also during the last war. In 1866 the Cleveland Manx started 'The Mona's Vocal Society' to teach young Manx-Americans traditional Manx songs. This led to a unique bond with the homeland and in 1923 the Cleveland Manx Societies combined resources to present every year a gold medal as the premier award for soloists at the Manx Music Festival. Since then it has become the 'blue riband' of the 'Guild.'

Now that the Homecomers have gone after such a memorable visit, the World Manx Association will be encouraged to organise further Homecomings. Certainly there is a strong desire to bind together Manx people across the thousands of miles of oceans, something which is hoped will continue for many generations to come.

At a reception for the Homecomers in the Villa Marina Gardens, hundreds of school children assemble to form a colourful display of the Three Legs.
(R. and L. Kelly Collection)

HERE IS THE NEWS : 1928
PROSPECT OF REGULAR AIR SERVICES

Hopes that regular air services to and from the Isle of Man can start soon have been raised by a visit to the Island by an airliner of Britain's Imperial Airways. Her pilot says there is already an excellent site for an aerodrome in the Island, near Castletown. We have this report:

Imperial Airways' Handley Page Hampstead airliner which landed at Ronaldsway loaded with 'Motor Cycle' magazines. Its pilot, Captain G. P. Olley, foresees Ronaldsway as being used for regular air services. (Alan Daugherty Collection)

The three-engined Handley Page Hampstead aircraft, capable of carrying 14 passengers in great comfort, took off from Croydon at 1.00 p.m. After a refuelling stop in Manchester it landed in a farm field at Ronaldsway 4¹/₂ hours later. The aircraft is capable of 120 miles an hour which makes it the fastest machine in commercial service in the world. It usually flies on Imperial Airways' routes across Europe. On this occasion the aircraft was carrying a ton of *The Motor Cycle* magazines for T.T. fans. During a short stay on the Island it has been taking local people on pleasure flights. The pilot is Captain G. P. Olley, one of the senior pilots with Imperial Airways. He says there is no reason why the Isle of Man should not be linked into the existing network of air services in the British Isles. The fields at Ronaldsway are "a natural aerodrome, as good as Croydon." The other big advance in modern communications is a plan to link up the Island to the rest of the British Isles by telephone for the first time. The necessary seabed cable is expected to be laid from the coast of Lancashire next year.

NEW BISHOP APPOINTED
The untimely death occurred in March of the Lord Bishop Dr. Charles L. Thornton-Duesbery, a Manxman by birth. He had only been three years in office. He has been succeeded by the Rt. Rev. W. Stanton Jones, D.D. He is already closely involved in the on-going battle by church leaders to preserve the traditional Manx Sunday. A victory for the campaign has been two successive decisions by Douglas Town Council not to allow golf to be played on the new municipal course at Pulrose on Sundays.

ROADS CLOSED FOR T.T. PRACTICES
Roads are to be closed for practising as well as racing on the T.T. Course in future. This follows the death in T.T. practice last year of Charles Birkin. He crashed at Rhencullen when trying to avoid a fish cart on the road. The necessary Bill has gone through the Legislative Council - in spite of protests that early morning road closing will inconvenience traders and farmers taking goods into the town markets. The new rule applies to the Amateur T.T. in September as well as the T.T.

SERIOUS M.E.R. ACCIDENT
The excellent safety record of the

The Lord Bishop, the Rt. Rev. W. Stanton Jones, D.D., after his enthronement at St. George's Church, Douglas. (R. and L. Kelly Collection)

Manx Electric Railway was marred on 8th August when a car and trailer full of passengers stopped at Fairy Cottage to pick up two permanent way men returning to Laxey. It was then that another fully-laden car and trailer appeared rounding the bend but the motorman was unable to bring his car to a stop. Some managed to jump before the collision, but 32 casualties were taken to Noble's Hospital with injuries, including fractures. A young lady from Birmingham had to have a foot amputated. The official inquiry found the accident was caused by failure to observe company safety rules. Manager Mr Edmundson stated that over 60 million passengers had been carried by the railway without a mishap of this kind. Relatives were unable to get information that night because the Post Office telegraph service had shut down. This has led to renewed demands for the Post Office to provide telephonic links with the Island.

The steam railway has not been free from accidents, either. September saw an incident at Port Soderick station when an engine overturned and two coaches derailed. No one was hurt. In November, a more spectacular accident occurred when the engine *Tynwald* was on its way to Douglas with a Market Day Special from Port Erin. In the cutting below Oakhill Bridge, it collided with the *G. H. Wood* which was being steam tested after a major overhaul. The impact resulted in both engines being locked together and badly damaged. Both crews were injured, though not seriously and the Locomotive Superintendent, testing the *G. H. Wood*, was trapped on the footplate. The lone passenger on the train was a young lady who, frightened but unhurt, took to her heels and reached home sooner than expected. It is still the proud boast of the Railway Company that, after 50 years' service, no passenger lives have been lost in a railway accident.

CHARABANC IN HORRIFIC CRASH

In a horrific accident in October, at Cross Four Ways, Malew, 14 passengers were trapped beneath a charabanc which overturned after being struck by a four-seater motorcar. One of the passengers, Miss Florence Piercy (32) of Leigh Terrace, Douglas died 12 days later in Noble's Hospital. At the official inquiry, the driver of the motorcar was found to be at fault but was not guilty of culpable negli-

gence. Earlier in the year a child of four was knocked down and killed by a motorbus, the first fatality of its kind. A young man on holiday was knocked down and killed on Douglas promenade by the Douglas fire-engine speeding to a blaze in Onchan. There were three deaths also from drowning as a result of falling overboard from steamers.

RAINSTORMS BRING FLOODS

The closing months of 1928 have seen some of the worst weather in the Island in living memory. Heavy rainstorms caused extensive flooding in and around Douglas. One and a quarter inches of rain fell in an hour and a half. Houses had to be evacuated and cattle and sheep were marooned on high ground in the fields. Clucas' Laundry at Tromode also had to be evacuated and Belle Vue Racecourse was under five feet of water. Train and bus services were temporarily dislocated. This was followed by gales so fierce that they blew down

the 28 foot high stone Celtic cross on Douglas Head erected by the Goldie-Taubman family of the Nunnery in memory of the Manxmen who died in the Great War. Repair work will start shortly. And the gable of the 1st Douglas Scouts new headquarters in Demesne Road was blown in and many houses damaged.

LUXURY STEAM YACHT REGISTERED

Finally, a magnificent new luxury steam yacht has been registered in Douglas. It belongs to 26-year-old Mr. Colby Cubbin, of Strathallan Road, Onchan, who designed the £20,000 vessel himself and named it *Glen Strathallan*. She is a well-appointed craft with five state rooms, a dining saloon seating 18 - and there is even a deck garage for a motor car. Mr. Cubbin is a wealthy man who has inherited a fortune from his late father, property owner, Mr. Robert Cubbon. The yacht's upkeep will cost £3,000 a year.

1928 NEWS IN BRIEF

JANUARY
13 - As a result of the Unemployment Commissioners' report, the Lieutenant-Governor announces he is prepared to fund 75% of the wages bill of a local authority incurred in approved development schemes; and 50% of moneys paid by the Board of Guardians to men on the unemployed register unable to obtain work.
17 - Keys accept Lieutenant-Governor's proposal to set up an Advisory Committee to confer with him on legislation/administration.

FEBRUARY
1 - Castletown Town Commissioners initiate proposals to extend the town's water supply to parishes of Arbory and Malew.
27 - I.O.M. Red Cross Society gives addresses and lantern lectures on public health throughout the Island.
28 - At the Annual meeting of the I.O.M. Steam Packet Company, it is announced that it is intended to take over the Heysham route.

MARCH
8 - Gift Sale raises £1,300 for the Red Cross Society, one of its objects being to create child welfare centres.
30 - Tynwald votes £4,000 as a loan to Messrs Williamson if a development scheme for the Great Laxey Mines is approved.

APRIL
4 - After a dispute between Ramsey Commissioners and the local butchers, provisional agreement is reached for the erection of a public abattoir at Ramsey.
11 - Sunday golf on the Douglas municipal links vetoed by the casting vote of the Mayor.

MAY
5 - Manx Ladies' Choir wins at Morecambe Music Festival.
8 - Port Erin Commissioners again decide that their public baths should not be open on Sundays; prohibition on the hiring of deck-chairs is removed.
22 - Betting Bill passed by both Council and Keys prohibiting the use of lands for the purpose of betting, its object being to prevent greyhound racing. After a heated debate, betting at horse racing as at Belle Vue is allowed to continue.

JUNE
7 - Manxland Bus Services Ltd report a million passengers carried since the company started business in May last year.
11 - Budget Day. Tynwald follows the Imperial Government by introducing a petrol tax, the proceeds of which are to remit rates upon agricultural lands, railways and productive industries.
13 - Controversy caused by Ramsey Town Commissioners refusing to have flags flown from the promenades on Sundays, and refusing to permit Sunday displays of swimming from the Queen's Pier, where a toll is charged for admission.
30 - Filming begins on the Island of a version of Sir Hall Caine's 'Bondman.'

JULY
3 - Enthronement in St George's Church of the Rev W. Stanton Jones, D.D., as Lord Bishop of Sodor and Man.
16 - First Highland Gathering organised at the Nunnery. Competitions for pipe bands, solo piping, juvenile dancing, throwing the caber etc. It being 'Scotch Week,' over 14,000 attended making it the largest crowd ever seen in the Isle of Man, except for the Kirk Braddan services.
21 - Opening of the handsome new premises erected for the Isle of Man Bank's branch at Ramsey.
31 - After months of impasse, the Legislative Council agrees with Keys that the subsidy of £200 per house built by local authorities should continue for one year only.

AUGUST
4 - August 'Bank Holiday Saturday.' New record of arrivals set up - 31,920 persons being landed at Douglas.
7 - Douglas Corporation succeeds in bringing injunctions under the Singing Rooms Act against Mr Bert Feldman and Mr Lawrence Wright. They promise remedies for the nuisances alleged.
25 - Serious fire at Laxey Flour Mills

SEPTEMBER
4-6 - Amateur T.T. Senior race won for the second time by Percy Hunt. On the last lap he set up an absolute course record of 71.05 m.p.h. (31mins 52s.). Fastest lap in the June races is held by Jimmy Simpson who lapped at 70.43 m.p.h. (32mins. 9s.) in the 1926 Senior T.T.
5 - Mr George Howie takes up his duties as the first Agricultural Adviser for the Island.
12 - Douglas Town Council decide to build 100 new houses at Pulrose Park.

OCTOBER
16 - Tynwald approves £24,500 for the purpose of widening and strengthening portion of Victoria Pier.
19 - Tynwald approves £78,000 scheme for widening of Douglas Promenade from base of Victoria Pier to Regent Street.
24 - Lieutenant-Governor appoints Mr J.R. Corrin M.H.K. (Rushen) to the Legislative Council. He is the first Labour Party member of the Council.

NOVEMBER
20 - Gaming and Betting Bill introduced by the Lieutenant-Governor. It prohibits credit betting, and football coupon betting, making it an offence to send bets to bookmakers by letter, telegrams or 'phone. Bill will not apply to Island racecourses.

DECEMBER
27 - Mr James Kelly (82), Port St Mary, dies with his hands on the helm while steering the relief boat on a journey to the Chickens Rock Lighthouse.

THE NUISANCE OF THE SINGING HALLS

Curbs on public singing look like making Douglas a quieter place. Ever since the late Victorian boom in tourism the Isle of Man has been a popular summer location for music publishers to promote their latest songs. Singers have been employed at booths on Douglas promenade and in Strand Street. The sale of sheet music has been the main objective. Hence the establishment at law five years ago that the singing rooms were not places of entertainment and, therefore, did not require music licences. The small singing booths have disappeared but have been replaced by large singing halls which attract hundreds of visitors, especially during wet weather. The rooms open shortly after 10 a.m. until 10 p.m., six days a week. A professional singer, accompanied by a pianist, leads the singing and everyone is encouraged to join in the choruses. The hits of the day are decided by the number of music sheets sold. The operators of the singing rooms are rival music publishers Bert Feldman and Lawrence Wright. It was Mr Feldman who brought popular music hall artiste Florrie Forde to the Island. The singing rooms are in Strand Street with their frontages open to attract the maximum attention. The result is considerable congestion in the shopping thoroughfare, and the noise which can be unbearable.

For years shopkeepers have complained about the effect the singing rooms are having on their businesses. If they can't stand the noise, people pass on quickly. Mr Feldman has responded by building a small shop an either side of his room to reduce the noise level on the street. But this has failed to please everyone. This year matters were made worse by the arrival of the 'Tommy Talkers' which are like a child's toy trumpet. They are available everywhere and when blown produce a raucous sound. High-spirited holidaymakers have always loved to sing and dance in the streets until late at night. The 'Tommy Talkers' add to the din and while few want to dampen holiday spirits, it can be the last straw for householders with young children.

While nothing could be done about the 'Tommy Talkers,' shopkeepers petitioned Douglas Corporation to restrain the use of the singing rooms. In August Mr Feldman and Mr Wright were both brought to court. There were plenty of witnesses to testify as to the nuisance caused by the singing rooms. Both proprietors promised to provide sound proofing, possibly by the use of plate glass screens or folding doors. In the meantime, Mr Wright told his demonstrators to be less vocal but further complaints led to them appearing before a Deemster to show why they should not be committed for contempt of court. Apologies and assurances were soon forthcoming. By next summer they know they must cut the noise or face the prospect of imprisonment.

Possible closure of the the halls has been mentioned but public support for the halls is such that there is no immediate risk of that. The business to be done makes sound proofing worthwhile. Whilst the growing popularity of the gramophone and wireless may lead to a reduction, eventually, in the use of the piano at home the demand for sheet music is not likely to diminish for at least another generation. Meanwhile, there is a tendency for shopkeepers to get private homes well away from the heart of the town. If this continues there will be fewer complaints about singing. The halls should then be able to function as in the past, without shutting themselves off from passing trade.

(Below) Another busy week-end scene as thousands of visitors depart for their home towns. They look well-satisfied and, no doubt, have enjoyed a happy (and noisy!) holiday. Queuing for steamers in wet weather causes many complaints. (Douglas Corporation)

HERE IS THE NEWS : 1929
G. P. O. PROVIDES FIRST TELEPHONE LINKS

The Isle of Man is now in direct telephone contact with the rest of the British Isles and other parts of the world. This follows the laying of a telephone cable on the seabed from the Lancashire coast at Norbreck to Port Grenaugh. We have this report:

The historic first telephone call between the Isle of Man and England was made by the Lieutenant-Governor on 26th June. Sir Claude used a telephone in the Tynwald Chamber. He interrupted the debate in progress and, after a slight hitch, was put through to the Postmaster-General in London. Shortly after this courtesy call there was an exchange of greetings between the Mayor of Douglas, Alderman W. Quirk, and the Lord Mayor of Liverpool. It is through Liverpool that 'trunk calls' will be processed. During the conversation the Lord Mayor requested a Manx cat. A fine specimen is now domiciled in Liverpool Town Hall.

Until now the Island has been regarded as existing in isolation from the rest of the British Isles because of the absence of verbal communication. It has had to rely on a telegraph cable with England and, in emergencies, wireless communication by Morse Code. The new telephone service comes at a time when the telegraph cable for telegrams is reaching the end of its life. The cable comes in at Cornaa and has been subject to repeated breakdowns, sometimes for more than a week. One of the latest happened when a picnic party lit a fire over an exposed part of the cable where it came ashore.

The cable-laying operation from Norbreck to Port Grenaugh was completed on 5th June, the 63 miles of 2.3 inch cable weighing 1,355 tons. The specialised work was carried out by the crew of the cable-laying ship *Faraday* which followed a route marked by buoys which were illuminated by gas at night. Extensive testing followed while another cable was laid between Port Erin and Belfast. Port Erin is the site of a repeater station to amplify voice transmissions to Ireland.

Meanwhile, the former Douglas Grammar School in Dalton Street

The Isle of Man Railway Company's determination to compete with the emerging bus operators resulted in no fewer than 22 Thorneycroft buses being purchased last year, operating under the name of Isle of Man Road Services. Above is an example of the 20-seater A2 type, and below one of the 28-seater BC type. The purchase of the rival companies means that Isle of Man Road Services now has a fleet of 82 buses made up of various sorts. *(Manx National Heritage)*

has been acquired and the site is to be used for a new telephone exchange. The Post Office believes this to be necessary because the link with the U.K. is expected to encourage the installation of more telephones on the Island. This will be a boon to local businesses, and to hoteliers and boarding-house keepers who can be put in quick contact with any part of the British Isles. The telephones were put to good use during the September races when reporters sent 20,000 words of copy to English newspapers. Another exciting development is the ability for the Island to be featured on the wireless. At the moment mobile transmitters are unable to reach the B.B.C.'s main transmitters, but programmes can

now be sent by telephone. On the evening of 12th September, an eye-witness account of the Senior Amateur T.T. Race that day was broadcast by the B.B.C. It is planned to follow this first broadcast from the Isle of Man with coverage of next year's T.T. Races and the Tynwald Ceremony.

WORST SNOWSTORM THIS CENTURY

Monday, 11th February, brought severe snowstorms which brought rail and road traffic to a standstill. At sea, the *Peel Castle* was held up at the Mersey Bar through her steering gear being frozen. She reached Liverpool eleven hours late. The *Mona* spent the night at sea arriving at Douglas 26 hours after leaving

A CHRONICLE OF

The De Havilland DH 61 'Giant Moth' which was flown to the Island by the famous aviator Sir Alan Cobham.

Young Manx air enthusiasts with Sir Alan Cobham between 'flying experience' flights from Ronaldsway.

Liverpool. School children returning home were stranded at Ballasalla and Michael and had to be found accommodation in houses and cottages overnight. Snow-drifts in places were 15 feet high - funerals and weddings had to be postponed. The following day the sitting of the House of Keys was adjourned, as was a Court meeting at Douglas when only three of the ten summoned jurors appeared. The snow was followed by eight degrees of frost and farmers suffered heavy losses of sheep and lambs.

RAILWAY COMPANY WINS WAR OF THE BUSES

In March last year, at the Annual Meeting of the I.O.M. Railway Company, the Chairman, Mr A. H. Teare M.H.K., remarked, "We shall not lower the flag one inch." He was alluding to the increasing competition being provided by the two main motorbus companies operating throughout the Island. These companies, Manxland Bus Services and Manx Motors, were themselves locked in fierce competition. The Railway Company was already a partner in the consortium behind Manx Motors, but in April of last year the Railway Company withdrew their interest and invested in a fleet of 22 Thornycroft buses which operated in competition with the other two services under the name of Isle of Man Road Services. Manxland Bus Services had carried over a million passengers in its first year, but the situation was somewhat farcical and the aggressive I.O.M. Railway Company purchased both of its competitors in February of this year.

The company now operates 82 buses in all, a motley collection of Thornycrofts, ADCs and Leylands appearing in a variety of colours. The red of the former Manxland

Motor Services Limited has been adopted as the standard colour. Isle of Man Road Services. will be run as a separate company, with accountant Mr A. M. Sheard becoming secretary and manager of both the railway and bus companies. With trains and buses working in conjunction, it would appear the future of Manx transport is secure for many years to come.

UNUSUAL T.T. VISITORS

T.T. fans were amazed at the arrival of two Germans who had flown from Stuttgart via Croydon to witness the Junior T.T. After landing on Douglas Head the machine was dismantled and garaged behind the Esplanade as though it were a Baby Austin. The intrepid flyers were well looked after at the Peveril Hotel, headquarters of the A-C.U. On the Tuesday after the race they took off from the beach and returned safely to Germany.

Run in glorious weather, the Senior Race was won by Charlie

Dodson (Sunbeam) who set up a new lap record of 73.55 m.p.h. During the race, Douglas Lamb was involved in a multiple crash at Greeba Bridge and died later in Noble's Hospital. Also involved in the accident were Walter Handley and Jimmy Simpson. Earlier in the week Cecil Ashby died after being hurled from his machine at Ballacraine during the Junior Race which was won by Freddy Hicks on a Velocette. The Italian rider Ghersi was leading the Lightweight on a Moto Guzzi until hit by mechanical trouble. This let Syd Crabtree (Excelsior) through to win.

WARNING BY SIR HALL CAINE

On 23rd July, Sir Hall Caine was admitted to the Honorary Freedom of the Borough of Douglas. Thus the words of T. E. Brown, written 40 years ago, have come true: "But the little Island will do justice to its author yet." In his address to the Council, the playwright and novelist warned that

Members of Ramsey Fire Brigade with their newly-acquired second-hand fire engine - a 1914 Hadfield. The recent photograph was taken outside the fire-engine house adjacent to the Town Hall in Parliament Square.

(R. and L. Kelly Collection)

the Island will face serious competition from Continental resorts soon. He said that more and more people were going to places like the Riviera, because it was cheaper to go there than to the Isle of Man. Meanwhile, church leaders have accused Douglas of becoming too Continental. This follows a decision to allow Sunday golf at Pulrose, a move which was rejected twice last year.

VISIT OF SIR ALAN COBHAM

August Bank Holiday saw the visit of the famous aviator Sir Alan Cobham, when he landed at Ronaldsway in his DH 61 Giant Moth 'Spirit of Britain'. His visit was part of his 'Circuit of Britain' which Sir Alan had undertaken to popularise flying and encourage the provison of aerodromes. He was met by the Mayor and other civic dignitaries of Douglas who were give a flight in the 14-seat aircraft. The following day children chosen by 'Uncle Jack' of the *Isle of Man Examiner* enjoyed their first experience of flying. The programme, however, was interrupted when the DH 61 hit a rut when taxiing and tackle from Qualtrough's timber yard was used to help effect repairs. On the Monday Sir Alan departed for Stanley Park, Blackpool. On board were journalist Mr R. C. Stephen and T.T. winner Tom Sheard. They can both claim to

be the first Manxmen to cross the Irish Sea as passengers.

SEAMAN LOST IN MERSEY

A 31-year-old seaman on the *Ben-my-Chree* was swept overboard and drowned as the steamer, on her last voyage of the season, passed the Mersey Bar Lightship in a fierce gale. Horace Cain of Port St Mary was one of a number of men hit by a huge wave as they worked on the fo'c's'le deck. Earlier in the year, the crew of four men and a cat were rescued by Ramsey lifeboat *Matthew Simpson* from the Manx schooner *Venus* as it was being driven on to the rocks at Maughold Head in heavy seas. She was on her way from Douglas to Ardrossan with a cargo of scrap metal.

ELECTION SHOCKS

The General Election in November brought shocks to long standing members. In Ramsey, Mr A. H. Teare, the town's member for 11 years and chairman of the I.O.M. Railway Company, was ousted by comparative stranger Mr W .H. Alcock. In Rushen, Mr Ambrose Qualtrough, who had served as a member for 21 years, ended up bottom of the poll. In North Douglas Alderman A. B. Crookall gained a record 4,004 votes but Mr Samuel Norris failed to be re-elected, losing

The November General Election saw the shock defeat of Mr Samuel Norris, the Island's leading political reformer, who first entered the House of Keys in 1919. He was narrowly defeated, but plans to stand again at the next opportunity. (Frank Cowin Library)

his seat to Mr John Kelly (Labour) by four votes. The Manx Labour Party now has seven members including Messrs A. H. Teare and W. C. Craine, both of whom were returned unopposed for South Douglas. The Election also saw the first woman to enter the lists. Miss Louisa Nelson of Ramsey, came bottom of the poll with 48 votes. Afterwards she joked that she got one vote for every year of her age!

1929 NEWS IN BRIEF

JANUARY
10 - New school opened in Laxey by the Lieutenant-Governor. It replaces the National School, the Infants School and those at Ballagawne and South Cape. The new school is the first to have electricity, having its own generator.

FEBRUARY
19 - Keys reject Agricultural Holdings Bill which was to have given farmers security of tenure. The Bill would have been passed had three supporters not been absent because of illness.
27 - Education Authority decides to raise the school leaving age to 15 as from 1st April, 1932.
27 - Steam Packet announce that a new steamer capable of carrying 2,500 passengers is to be built for the Fleetwood route.
28 - Fishery Board reports decline of the Manx herring fishing.

MARCH
15 - Despite strong opposition from the Manx Temperance Federation, Douglas Licensing Authority permits intoxicants to be served to guests of lodgers with a meal.
16 - Ramsey Ladies' Choir wins Dawny Shield at London Music Festival - fourth time the trophy has been won by a Manx choir.

APRIL
25 - Launch of the *Peveril* at Birkenhead - the first cargo vessel built for the Steam Packet Company. Will enter service in June.
30 - Installation in the Picture House cinema of Western Electric sound system has brought 'talkies' to the Isle of Man.

JUNE
6 - Budget Day. Duty on tea abolished at a cost of £10,000. Basic income tax rate reduced from 1s to 10d. Accumulated Fund now stands at £50,000.
7 - Keys win battle with Council to abolish 4d tax on gallon of petrol.
27 - Push Bike T.T. won by S.R. Taggart (Douglas) in 1 hr 57 mins 36 sec - a record for the course.
28 - Government Commission recommends an £85,000 electricity scheme for the Island.
28 - Tynwald approves extension to the Red Pier at cost of £262,000.

JULY
8 - Widows', Orphans and Old Age Contributory Pensions Act of 1929 comes into force. Two-thirds of Island's population came within its scope.
8 - Castle Rushen, Peel Castle and Tynwald Fair ground returned to the ownership of the Manx Government.
9 - Water Supply Bill passed by the Legislature. Local Government Board charged with seeing that public water supply is provided for villages and hamlets as well as the towns outside Douglas.
15 - Second Highland Gathering held at the Nunnery.

AUGUST
3 - Bank Holiday Saturday. Immense crowds landed at Douglas despite atrocious sea conditions. Over 54,000 passengers arrived and departed.
17 - Ramsey Lifeboat Committee celebrate the centenary of the lifeboat station. Since records were kept in 1868, 426 lives have been saved by the Ramsey lifeboats.
26 - Telephone service extended to include America.
30 - The film of Sir Hall Caine's novel 'The Manxman' banned by the Irish Free State, the censor having taken objection to the story as a whole.

SEPTEMBER
3-6 - I.O.M. Natural History and Antiquarian Society celebrates its 50th anniversary. Excursions arranged to various parts of the Island.
12 - Foundation stone laid for new Wesleyan Sunday School at Hillberry.

OCTOBER
4 - Steam Packet's *Mona's Queen* and *Fenella* sold by private treaty.
4 - Purchase of Port Erin Brows by Commissioners approved at a cost of £4,000.
27 - Two R.A.F. flying boats visited the Island in the course of an aerial survey of the British Isles. Landings effected in Douglas and Castletown Bays.

NOVEMBER
7-15 House of Keys General Election.

'NO HERRING, NO WEDDING'

This proverb of old is a reminder that the Fishing has been an essential part of Manx life for many centuries. The fisherman/crofter formed the greater part of the Manx population and this close, daily contact with Nature, both on land and at sea, did much to mould our distinctive characteristics and temperament. Our Deemsters still take the oath to administer justice as impartially and "as indifferently as the herring backbone doth lie in the midst of the fish." Our great 18th century Bishop, Thomas Wilson, even inserted into the Litany a prayer that the Manx might continue to enjoy "the blessings of the seas."

Today, however, there is not much enjoyment left and the reports and statistics they contain make very dismal reading indeed. Last season in the herring fleet there were only 13 Manx Nobbies commissioned compared with 129 boats from non-Manx ports. And the last of the Nickies which had been operating from Port St Mary was not fitted out for last season. Of the 1,470 men engaged in the fishing, only 65 were Manxmen. This is a far cry from the situation in 1883, less than fifty years ago, when out of the Island's population of 52,000 about 13,000 men and women were engaged one way or another in the great herring enterprise. Peel alone had 240 boats employing 1,680 men. And, of course, with the development of the Kinsale fishing and then the Scottish grounds, the season, if so it can be called, lasted a good proportion of the year.

The financial value of the catches was, of course, considerable. Fifty years ago it was worth over £42,000 with catches landed at Peel alone accounting for about £23,000. The impact of such financial success was immense and the industry was rightly seen as the bedrock upon which our prosperity depended. That rock, however, proved fault-ridden. If Peel is taken as the yardstick, the 240 boats of 1883 had dwindled to 55 in 1897, and the 1,680 men to 265. By 1914, if all the Manx ports are taken together, the Manx fleet only totalled 57 vessels.

Needless to say, the reasons for this rapid decline have been the subject for furious debate over the years. Steps to reverse the trend have provoked even more hot-tempered argument. The steam trawlers have been blamed because they are alleged to have damaged the spawning grounds. There now exist large-scale fisheries elsewhere, and in many cases they are more commercially advanced. Furthermore, as fishing techniques develop more expensive equipment is needed in order to compete effectively, but the Manx crews simply did not possess the resources to buy it. Perhaps, too, the collapse of the Dumbell's Bank in 1900 made capital investment in the industry a greater risk than it had seemed before. There might, though, be an easier explanation. A fisherman's life is a hard one, and insecurity and uncertainty are an inevitable part of it. Today, with the rapid expansion of our visiting industry, there are more congenial ways of earning a living, even though the season may only last for a few months. Holiday-makers are providing excellent employment opportunities. These are helping to compensate for those lost in both the traditional fishing and mining industries, both now evidently in terminal decline.

That famous Manxman, Sir Hall Caine, has sounded a cautionary note. He points out that as the annual holiday habit becomes more widespread, resorts on Continental Europe could become our rivals. This seems most unlikely, however. The traditional British seaside holiday in our bracing weather seems set fair to retain its popularity for many more decades to come.

Gone are the Nickies and Nobbies of the last century. They have been replaced by the steam trawlers, seen here at Peel, which are being accused of damaging the spawning grounds. Only a few local men can now afford the expensive equipment necessary to be competitive.

(Manx National Heritage)

HERE IS THE NEWS : 1930
INSANE MURDERER SENT TO BROADMOOR

The murderer of 62-year-old Mr Percy William Brooke, a retired farmer and shepherd of Churchtown, Lezayre, has been sent for detention at Broadmoor Criminal Lunatic Asylum, after being found 'guilty but insane' by a General Gaol jury. We have this report:

Mr Brooke was shot dead on 13th October as he was about to mount the stairs in an isolated cottage which he owned at Lhergyrhenny on the slopes of Snaefell, above Tholt-y-Will. Suspicion immediately fell on Thomas Edward Kissack who had escaped from the Mental Hospital at Ballamona two days previously. He was known to have an obsession with guns. The discovery of Mr Brooke's body led to the biggest manhunt the Island has ever seen. Kissack had escaped from Mr Brooke's cottage with a shotgun, and armed policemen were joined by civilians who scoured the surrounding mountain areas in wet and misty conditions. After 28 hours of searching, Kissack was confronted by Sergt Philip Henry Watterson as he was hiding among the derelict buildings of The Close, a long-deserted farmstead on the slopes of Beinn-y-Phott, above Druidale. Armed with a revolver, Sergt Watterson shouted, "Hands up, Kissack. Drop that gun!" Kissack did so, screaming in sudden terror at being discovered. He was weak and exhausted, and offered no resistance when taken to Douglas Police Station.

Kissack appeared on a charge of murder at a Court of General Gaol Delivery, presided over by Deemster Farrant, at the end of November. The Attorney-General, Mr R. B. Moore, and his son, Mr George E. Moore, appeared for the Crown, and Mr J. H. L. Cowin and Mr Howard D. Lay, for the prisoner. The defence's main argument was that the gun went off accidentally when the accused was taken by surprise by Mr Brooke. Four doctors testified that Kissack was of unsound mind. It took the jury three hours before it reached the unanimous verdict that Kissack was guilty of murder, but that he was insane at the time he committed the murder and, therefore, not responsible for his action.

The derelict buildings of the The Close where murderer Edward Kissack gave himself up to the police. In the distance is the deserted farmstead of Crammag and the slopes of Snaefell

Kissack was born in a farm labourer's cottage in Lonan and had been a mental patient for some years. He is the first Manxman to be tried for murder for 40 years.

AGATHA CHRISTIE'S TREASURE HUNT
The famous author Agatha Christie was enlisted by the June Effort Committee to help it bring more early season visitors to the Island. She wrote a mystery story called "Manx Gold" which was serialised in the *Daily Dispatch*. The tale gave clues to the location of four gold snuff boxes, each containing a £100 token, which had been buried at different places in the Island. Three of the snuff boxes were unearthed on Fort Island, on Peel Hill and near the Mull Circle above Port Erin. The fourth snuff box was undetected in the Mooragh Park, Ramsey.

CLAIM BY MISTRESS DISMISSED
The Chancery Court in Douglas was told the late Colonel George Moore of Great Meadow, and Castletown M.H.K. from 1903 to 1918, used to have a mistress. She is Miss Emma Ross of Brighton who brought a claim for £57 which she alleged she was owed by the colonel's family. This was in connection with an agreement between her and Mrs Moore whereby Mrs Moore agreed to pay her £1 per week on condition she did not come to the Isle of Man or write to any member of the family. The payments ceased in 1928. After a long deliberation the case was dismissed by Deemster La Mothe, on the grounds that the payments had been made quite voluntarily and without a written agreement.

REPRESENTATIVES AT ALTHING CELEBRATIONS
In July Deemster Farrant and Speaker of the House of Keys Mr. G. F. Clucas, M.A. went to Iceland to represent Tynwald at the one thousandth anniversary celebrations of the Icelandic parliament, the Althing. Like Tynwald the Althing has its roots in Viking times. Meanwhile M.H.K.'s are speculating on whether Tynwald itself is a thousand years old, and whether a similar celebration should be held in the Island.

NEW NAME FOR 'AMATEUR T.T.'
In January a sensation was caused in the motor-cycling world when the Auto-Cycle Union refused to permit the Manx Motor Cycle Club to hold the Amateur T.T. in September. This followed protests from the Motor Cycle Manufacturer's Association that certain riders had been in receipt of bonuses of various kinds contrary to the rules. The stewards were aware

110

General view of the Douglas piers showing, on the left, the Imperial Buildings, head office of the Steam Packet Company. The distinctive beacon on the Red Pier has now been demolished as work begins on constructing a new pier. *(Frank Cowin Library)*

The S. S. Mona, when attempting to reach harbour in thick fog, went aground on Conister Rock on 2nd July. She was refloated the next day. The outer face of Victoria Pier has now been painted white to give extra guidance. *(Manx National Heritage)*

of this and had suspended a number of riders, including last year's Senior winner. To the A-C.U. the term 'amateur' was far too ambiguous and something had to be done. His Excellency Sir Claude Hill brought both bodies together and the situation was resolved cordially. The race was renamed the Manx Grand Prix. In future only competitors domiciled in the British Isles will be accepted, provided they have not previously taken part in an international race. There is no definition of amateur to worry about.

Since 1928, separate races have been provided for Junior machines (350 c.c.) and Senior machines (500 c.c.). Entries this year topped 100 for the first time. Local rider Wilfred Harding came second in the Junior race on a Velocette.

WORST FLOODS
FOR A CENTURY
The worst floods for a century occurred in the early hours of the morning of 18th September. Abnormal damage was done at Laxey, Glen Auldyn, Sulby and

Rushen Abbey. Houses were flooded leaving people homeless, rivers burst their banks and bridges collapsed. Two boats were torn from their moorings in Castletown by the force of the swollen Silverburn river. There were heavy losses of crops and livestock on farms, but no person was injured. It is estimated that over £100,000 of damage was caused. A Relief Fund was set up by the Mayor of Douglas with the Lieutenant-Governor asking for Tynwald support. The Red Cross Society is administering the Fund so

On 22nd June, homecomers from America and Canada arrived at Douglas and were given a tumultuous reception. The Second Homecoming was marked by visits to out-towns during the week and the Third Annual Convention of the North American Manx Association was held in the Villa Marina. *(Manx National Heritage)*

that those in distress can be helped.

The worst area to be affected was Glen Road, Laxey, as a result of thousands of tons of debris being jammed behind the wier used to supply the Manx Electric Railway's hydro-electric plant. The water overflowed on to Glen Road and flooded houses as far down as the harbour. Many families had their possessions ruined. The railway company has been brought to court by the Highway Board. An injunction has been placed upon it to remove the debris and keep the bed of the Laxey river clear in future. The Manx Electric Railway is also having to pay the Highway Board £3,472 for road repairs and other expenses.

The scene in Glen Road, Laxey on 18th September showing how the blocked weir above the Electric Railway's turbine generating plant caused the river to overflow and demolish part of the roadway.   *(Frank Cowin Library)*

1930 NEWS IN BRIEF

JANUARY

2 - Tragic start to year. Three die of heart disease and a fourth shot himself during a fit of insanity.

4 - A carter employed by the Steam Packet Company is run over and killed by a loaded horse-drawn lorry on Gas Works Hill, Douglas.

7 - An elderly couple are found dead in their home in Hill Street, Douglas. Both were found to have died from heart disease.

FEBRUARY

13 - Bonniest Baby competition held in Villa Marina before a 2,000 audience. 240 babies were entered and the youngest, 5½ month-old Peter Leece of Fistard, Port St Mary, was adjudged the winner.

16 - Government Fishery patrol boat *Liffey* arrests three trawlers off Bulgham Head for fishing within the three mile limit. Two of the skippers were fined £30, and the third was fined £50 for trying to escape.

MARCH

4 - Launch of the *Lady of Mann* from the yards of Messrs Vickers-Armstrongs, Barrow-in-Furness, as part of the centenary celebrations of the Isle of Man Steam Packet Company Ltd.

28 - After passing all its stages through the Legislature, the Gaming and Betting Bill which aimed to restrict methods of betting, failed as a result of only 12 Keys' members signing, instead of the requisite 13.

APRIL

1 - Sydney Mercer, a Liverpool-Manxman, reached Ramsey Harbour after a voyage from Liverpool in an open boat. The journey took 40 hours.

5 - In the early hours a fire at the Laxey depot of the M.E.R. destroyed the building and 11 cars. A cigarette-end is thought to have ignited accumulated dust. The building and the trailer cars are to be replaced.

5 - Ramsey Cushag Choir win 'Dawnay Shield' for a second time at the London Music Festival.

8 - Legislative Council pass Bill to supply electric light, heat and power throughout the Island.

28 - 39th Manx Music Festival begins. Later in the week Mr Alan Quirk wins Cleveland Medal for the second time.

MAY

2 - Manx Labour Party Annual Conference held at Laxey. Sweeping proposals adopted, including death duties and a pension of £1 a week for those reaching the age of 65.

5 - 100th anniversary of the birth of Manx poet T.E. Brown celebrated by huge demonstration in Villa Marina. All schools visited and presented with a framed portrait of the national poet. The B.B.C. makes special broadcasts from its Manchester and Daventry stations.

6 - House of Keys vote to increase their salaries from £50 to £100 a year

13 - Keys change their mind over salary increase, refusing the third reading of the Bill by 11 votes to 10.

JUNE

10 - Miss Mercedes Gleitze, the English Channel swimmer, completed 37 hours' continuous swimming at Noble's Baths, Douglas, thus creating a new British record for endurance swimming.

13 - Miss Cleitze leaves Douglas to swim round the Island. She completed this amazing feat of swimming 100 miles in 56 hours 45 mins.

22 - Homecomers from America and Canada receive tumultuous welcome by large crowds as they arrive at Douglas.

23-27 Third Annual Convention of the North American Association held at Villa Marina.

27 - Isle of Man Road Services Ltd registered as a private company to effect the amalgamation of former bus companies.

29 - Broadcast of service from St George's Church followed, by an appeal by Lady Hill on behalf of Noble's Hospital.

JULY

2 - The *Mona* in command of Captain G. Woods stranded on Conister Rock at 4.40 a.m. while trying to enter Douglas Harbour in thick fog. The vessel was refloated 25 hours later.

4 - Douglas Festival Choir, under Mr Noah Moore, broadcasts concert from Groudle Glen.

5 - Broadcast by the B.B.C. of Tynwald Ceremony.

8 - Tynwald votes £8,000 to provide cash prizes for T.T., and to assist overseas competitors.

13-17 M.C.C. team played matches on Island. They beat Ramsey and drew with King William's College and an Island Eleven.

21 - Third Annual Highland Gathering held at the Nunnery.

29 - Airship *R100* passes over Douglas on its flight from Cardington to Montreal.

AUGUST

12 - Port St Mary Regatta marred by the drowning of Mr William Halsall of Lime Street, Port St Mary, when his yacht 'Puffin' foundered.

30 - Three R.A.F. seaplanes land in Ramsey Bay through fog while flying from Calshot to Stranraer.

SEPTEMBER

2 - Two baboons escape from show cages on Onchan Head. One was shot on the pleasure ground and the other in a bedroom in the Douglas Bay Hotel.

18 - Severe flooding in many parts of Island.

OCTOBER

20-25 Blackpool Music Festival. The Victoria Quartette, composed of Messrs C. Cowell and E. Kelly of Onchan, and H. Kelly and G. Peters of Douglas, acclaimed winners in the Male Voice Quartet class. Castletown Ladies', Peel Castle Ladies' and Peel Wesleyan Church Choirs all highly placed in their classes.

NOVEMBER

1 - Unemployment relief schemes begin, 300 men found work. Many employed on the second stage of widening the Loch Promenade, Douglas.

20 - Conference at Government Office relative to the possible construction of a Manx aerodrome.

MORE ABOUT THE FLOOD DAMAGE

The Isle of Man is counting the cost of the worst flooding in living memory. People in low-lying districts near to rivers lost almost all their household and personal possessions after "walls of water" thundered down from the hillsides. Stone walls and bridges were swept away and Laxey breakwater was split to its foundations. It happened during hurricane force winds and a cloudburst of tropical storm intensity.

Victims recall being awakened in the early hours of the morning by the sound of a distant roar as the avalanche of water approached. Some slept through it only to be awakened afterwards to discover that their homes had been flooded to a depth of four feet. At Tromode the alarm was raised by someone firing a rifle into the air. At Glen Vine a woman who lives in a house on the main road was awakened by the sound of her pet cat scratching at the door of her bedroom. On getting up to investigate she found three feet of water downstairs and the cat's kittens desperately swimming in it.

Most of the flood water dispersed quickly once the torrential rain eased off but it left masses of rubble and mud which will take ages to remove from homes. The damage this will have caused to factories such as the Tynwald Mill at St. John's, the Sulby Mill, the Ruskin Mill at Laxey and Clucas's Laundry at Tromode can scarcely be imagined.

The force of the water was such in some cases, notably at Glen Auldyn and Glen Road, Laxey, which have suffered flash floods before, that it smashed down cottage doors, swept through properties and, in so doing, broke the crockery and removed the furnishings. The discovery on the shore at Maughold of a wooden garden gate is evidence of the horror that engulfed the Island. At Injebreck an acre of young trees was swept away.

The quantity of rain varied from district to district. At Douglas only 2.75 inches of rain fell. A rainfall gauge at King William's College, Castletown however, recorded 3.12 inches. The worst was recorded by Ramsey Town Commissioners. It measured an incredible 4.35 inches.

The run-off from the hills soon turned into a raging and unstoppable torrent. It caused landslides, ripped up the roadway at Glen Auldyn and blocked the steam railway track with debris - so severely on the stretch between Sulby and Ramsey that it was several days before normal services could be resumed.

The walled garden at Rushen Abbey was flooded to a depth of four feet and the Abbey's popular jam factory was inundated. Pulrose estate was practically marooned when the concrete pillars and carriageway of the bridge into Pulrose Park from Peel Road, Douglas, were swept away.

A: *The force of the flood waters in Glen Mooar caused considerable damage to the arched viaduct connecting the Laxey Wheel with the engine shaft.*

B *and* C.: *Scenes of devastation in Glen Road, Laxey, where the Ruskin Mill and neighbouring properties have suffered severe flood damage.*

D: *A view of the catastrophic damage caused to the roadway and bridge in Glen Auldyn*

(Illustrations from the R. and L. Kelly Collection)

RAMSEY CHILDREN'S HOME CELEBRATES

Sixty years of caring at Ramsey for orphaned and homeless children has just been celebrated with a commemorative concert in the hall of the Grammar School in Waterloo Road.

It is reckoned that many hundreds of destitute children owe a new start in life to the Ramsey Children's Home - so many, in fact, that during the Great War it was calculated that approximately 1,000 old boys served in Britain's armed forces. It is the Home's proud boast that no needy Manx child or soldier's child has ever been precluded from admission.

According to its records, the Home was established by a Miss Gibson and several other women, principally to meet the needs of the north and west of the Island, though children from England were accepted occasionally. Ramsey Town Commissioners exempted it from paying rates and Peel's church wardens paid one shilling a week towards its operating costs. Miss Gibson managed the Home for 20 years, with the assistance of Ramsey's most prominent businessmen, and arranged that on her death it should pass to the National Children's Home and Orphanage. This is what happened and the Home is now one of 30 branches administered by the national institution.

Members of the Crennell family have provided considerable help. The late William Crennell M.H.K., was secretary for many years and married the Home's superintendent, Miss Hurley. Mr. Crennell's sister, Kate, is the current superintendent.

The Ramsey Home currently has 70 children in residence. The Home is divided between two buildings - Ballacloan, with its large open playing fields in front, and the 20-roomed Dalmeny. Built in 1906 at a cost of £5,000, it was known then as The Dalmeny Hydro.

The latter was acquired in 1917, two years after an unsuccessful attempt to obtain funds from the H. B. Noble Trustees who were dispensing money for charitable purposes throughout the Island. Dalmeny's purchase in the darkest days of the Great War was made possible by a collapse in property values which resulted in it being placed on the market at only half its original worth. The National Children's Home took out an option on it following a visit to Ramsey by the N.C.H.'s principal, the Reverend Hodson Smith, and then local supporters embarked on extensive fund-raising by volunteers. The purchase and furnishing of Dalmeny at a total cost of £3,000 was included in a £100,000 national plan to celebrate the golden jubilee of the National Children's Home.

Flag Days, the selling of patriotic badges and public subscriptions helped raise part of the cost of the Ramsey project. The rest came through a donation of £1,000 from a Mr. Mason who joined the committee. Lady Raglan performed the opening ceremony in 1918.

A: *The Children's Home and Orphanage at Ballacloan, Ramsey, overlooking the extensive playing field.*

B: *Some of the little ones in care at Ballacloan.*

C: *Another view of Ballacloan. Additional accommodation is provided at Dalmeny.*

(Illustrations from the R. and L. Kelly Collection)

LADY OF MANN - PRIDE OF THE FLEET

The Isle of Man Steam Packet Company Limited is celebrating its centenary with a magnificent addition to its fleet. It was a proud moment for the directors under chairman Mr C. T. W. Hughes-Games, when the steamer was launched on 4th March at the Barrow-in-Furness yards of Vickers Armstrong. Guests included His Excellency Sir Claude Hill and Lady Hill, Mayor of Douglas, Councillor W. Quirk, Captain W. Cain (Commodore of the Steam Packet fleet), Captain W. Gawne (designated to command the new vessel) and representatives of the staffs of the Steam Packet Company and Vickers-Armstrong. But all eyes were on Her Grace the Duchess of Atholl as she broke the ceremonial bottle upon the ship's side and pronounced, "Good luck to the *Lady of Mann*, and to all who sail in her, for all time to come." The name of the ship is in honour of the Duchess whose husband's ancestors were former rulers of the Isle of Man under the British Crown, and bore the title of Lord of Mann.

Launched by a duchess, and fit for a duchess! The vessel has been fitted out to the highest standards by skilled craftsmen, retained by Vickers-Armstrongs after many have been laid off because of a slump in orders following the Wall Street crash of last year. Her keel was laid on 26th October and in the amazingly short time of just over four months the ship was ready for launching. With a gross tonnage of 3,104, the *Lady of Mann* is the largest vessel ever to see service with the Steam Packet Company. She is 500 tons heavier than the *Ben my Chree* to which she bears a close resemblance. On 13th June she paid her first visit to Douglas after completing her speed trials in Scottish waters, when her design speed of 22 knots was easily achieved. Her twin screws are powered by two sets of geared turbines, the boilers being oil-fired.

With a crew of 81 the *Lady of Mann* is certified to carry 2,873 passengers. First class accommodation consists of sumptuously appointed lounges and cabins, a tea room, dining room with the finest silverware, a smoke room and spacious sleeping accommodation. A most elegant feature is the main staircase which is made of mahogany. Steerage accommodation is also of a high standard with lounges provided with upholstered seating and comfortable bunks. Already affectionately known as 'The Lady,' she made her maiden voyage from Fleetwood on 28th June. A month later she travelled from the

This dramatic painting of the approaching 'Lady of Mann' is by the famous marine artist, Norman Wilkinson. The painting has been commissioned by the Steam Packet Company and the artwork is to be incorporated in a series of advertising posters displayed in railway stations throughout Britain.

Lune Buoy to Douglas in 2 hours 6 minutes, averaging 23.33 knots. Her time was just three minutes short of the record held by the *Viking* since 1907. The *Lady of Mann* gives her passengers the experience of voyaging on a mini-Cunarder, being as fast and as luxurious.

The Steam Packet fleet now consists of 17 vessels, three of which are used for cargo only. Names of the ships are given below, together with the year in which they entered service with the company.

LADY OF MANN (new 1930); RUSHEN CASTLE (1928); RAMSEY TOWN (1928); VICTORIA (1928); BEN MY CHREE 1V (new 1927); MANX MAID (1924); SNAEFELL 1V (1920); MONA'S ISLE 1V (1920); MANXMAN (1920); MONA 1V (1919); KING ORRY 111 (new 1913); PEEL CASTLE (1912); VIKING (new 1905) and TYNWALD 111 (new 1891). Cargo: PEVERIL 11 (new 1929); CUSHAG (1920) and TYRCONNEL (1911).

The 'Lady of Mann's' First Class Lounge

The elegant First Class Tea Room.

HERE IS THE NEWS : 1931
ATTEMPTED MURDER ON MARINE DRIVE

A man who shot and seriously injured a young holiday couple on the Marine Drive, Douglas Head, has been brought to trial at a Court of General Gaol Delivery. John William Collister, aged 37, has been sentenced to seven years' penal servitude for attemped murder. He lived at Oak Hill Cottages, Braddan, and was employed as an inspector by the Marine Drive Company. We have this report.

Sweethearts Irene Livesey (21) from Rochdale and Duncan Fleming (22) from Glasgow were sitting on the grass on the evening of 23rd July near the electric tram sheds at Little Ness. It was then that they were approached from behind by Collister who fired his shotgun at them. In spite of his wounds Mr Fleming grappled with Collister but was shot twice more and collapsed after being stabbed with a knife. Collister then attacked Miss Livesey and tried to throw her over the cliffs. But she was able to escape and succeeded in reaching the toll-gate and summoning assistance. Collister made off but was arrested the following day. At his fourth appearance in court, on 10th August, Miss Livesey had sufficiently recovered from her ordeal to be able to relate her version of what had happened, and Collister was committed for trial on a charge of attempting to murder Mr Fleming.

The trial took place on 27th and 28th October and the court heard that Collister's duty was to keep poachers and trespassers off the Marine Drive. He pleaded not guilty and claimed that his gun had gone off by accident. The defence case was based on the fact there was no apparent motive. But the prosecution said Collister was a scheming liar and Miss Livesey said during his attack the defendant had a wild cynical expression on his face. As he tried to push her over the cliff she shouted at him, "You are a darned rotter." Collister was found guilty and Deemster Farrant passed sentence of seven years' penal servitude for the attemped murder of Mr Fleming. He was also found guilty of shooting at Miss Livesey with intent to cause grievous bodily harm for which he was sentenced

View of the Marine Drive showing the viaducts of the Douglas Southern Electric Tramway at Wall berry and Horse Leap, beyond which is Little Ness where the crime was committed.

(Frank Cowin Library)

to five years' penal servitude, both sentences to run concurrently. In his closing remarks the Deemster said there should be greater control over the possession of shotguns. Collister has now left the Island to serve out his sentence.

ISLAND FOG-BOUND
In the New Year the Island was largely cut off from the outside world for four days when unprecedented fog shrouded Merseyside. There were

---

THE 1931 CENSUS
It should be noted that the village districts of Port St Mary and Port Erin have been separated from Rushen parish, Laxey from Lonan and Michael from Michael parish. In order to ascertain the true comparison in these districts with the population of 1921, the village figures of 1931 should be added to the respective parishes.

DOUGLAS	-	19,329	*(- 4.9%)*
RAMSEY	-	4,198	*(+ 1.2%)*
PEEL	-	2,476	*(+ 0.3%)*
CASTLETOWN		1,713	*(- 8.8%)*
Port Erin	-	1,123	
Port St Mary	-	1,166	
Laxey	-	1,296	
Onchan Village		1,715	
Michael Village		333	
Andreas Parish		981	*(- 1.7%)*
Arbory	-	766	*(- 1.0%)*
Ballaugh	-	562	*(-10.5%)*
Braddan	-	3,170	*(+80.0%)*
Bride	-	451	*(+ 0.0%)*
German	-	993	*(- 7.8%)*
Jurby	-	386	*(-13.8%)*
Lezayre	-	1,141	*(+ 3.6%)*
Lonan	-	848	*(+ 1.9%)*
Malew	-	1,472	*(- 1.2%)*
Marown	-	816	*(+ 0.0%)*
Maughold	-	784	*(- 1.1%)*
Michael	-	329	*(-11.0%)*
Onchan	-	847	*(+10.0%)*
Patrick	-	1,076	*(- 5.5%)*
Rushen	-	978	*(- 2.5%)*
Santon	-	396	*(+ 2.3%)*
TOTAL	-	*49,338*	*(+ 0.5%)*

---

only three Steam Packet sailings possible Both the *Mona* and *Rushen Castle* were fog-bound in the Mersey and there were no deliveries of English mail or newspapers.

TEN PERISH ON ROCKS
During March the Glasgow steamer *Citrine* of 582 tons struck rocks near Bradda Head in thick fog and sank almost immediately. Ten crew were lost. Two survivors spent the night on the rocks and reached Port Erin early next morning and gave the first news of the tragedy. They said only a few crewmen could swim and the ship went down so fast there was no time to launch a lifeboat. One body was recovered during the day and at the subsequent inquest it was recommended that the Board of Trade should provide coastguards for the coastline between the Sound and Fleshwick. At a meeting of the Port Erin branch of the R.N.L.I. it was suggested that a light and sound signal should be placed at Niarbyl Point.

LATEST POPULATION DETAILS
The result of the Census taken on the night of 24th April shows the Island's population stood at 49,338, a slight increase compared with the 1921 figure of 49,078. However, when the number of those who are not permanent residents is removed from the overall figure, the total of Manx residents falls to 48,352, the lowest since 1841. Douglas has the largest concentration of people at just over 19,300, - 39% of the total population. Ramsey, with over 4,000 is the second most populous. The Census reveals that nearly 10% of the male population

were unemployed and that there are over 4,000 more women than men.

NORTONS BEAT FOREIGN CHALLENGE

This year's T.T. Races were the most international ever. Riders came from Germany, Italy, Belgium and Sweden to take part. But they failed to break the domination of British riders and machines. Percy Hunt achieved a remarkable 'double' for the Norton factory by winning the Junior race at 73.94 m.p.h. and Senior at 77.90 m.p.h. Again it was Jimmy Simpson,

yet to win a race, who set the fastest lap - the first to break the 80 m.p.h. barrier. The dominance of Rudge machines was broken but Graham Walker won the Lightweight 250 c.c. event for them, completing the seven laps at a record 68.98 m.p.h. The Senior was marred by the death of A.J.S. rider Fred Hicks from Birmingham who was killed on the 4th lap crashing into Central Stores at Union Mills.

DEATH OF SIR HALL CAINE

On 31st August the great Manx nov-

elist and playwright Sir Hall Caine died at his home, Greeba Castle. He was 78. He left a huge fortune of more than a quarter-of-a-million pounds but there were no charitable bequests. His two sons were the main beneficiaries. Sir Hall Caine was born in Liverpool into a family of crofters from Ballaugh and, after going to London, his first novel was published in 1883. For 30 years he was the highest-paid writer in Britain and his works were filmed. But critics have questioned whether or not his books have lasting literary merit.

1931 NEWS IN BRIEF

JANUARY
30 - Publication of report of Industrial Commission dealing with the subject of milk for public consumption. Recommendations include provision of a better water supply to farms; improvements of cowsheds and registration of dairymen; inspection of herds of cattle on discovery of a case of bovine tuberculosis, and the regular veterinary inspection of all cattle. The Commissioners also declared themselves not satisfied with the purity of milk sold and suggested steps should be taken to provide for the processing of milk before sale.

MARCH
17 - Spirited debate in House of Keys on Divorce Bill, which was given a third reading by 19 votes to 5.
18 - Education Authority decided to include the teaching of Manx history in insular schools.
21 - After 2½ years' deliberation Housing Commission recommends that large areas of Douglas should be demolished to make room for more sanitary dwellings.
30 - By a majority, a Tynwald Committee fails to recommend the appointment of a veterinary surgeon "having regard to the existing and impending financial position of the Insular Revenue."

APRIL
1 - Castletown A.F.C. suspended for a year for alleged insubordination to the Disciplinary Committee of the Isle of Man Football Association.
14 - House of Keys request the Lieutenant-Governor to have prepared a Bill setting up a public Board for the distribution and sale of electricity.
21 - Official returns issued by the Harbour Board showed that the number of passengers landed at Douglas between May and September, 1930, was 487,404½ compared with 555,211 in the corresponding months of 1929.
27-30 40th Manx Music Festival held in the Palace, Douglas. Surprise was created by the defeat in the bass class of Mr Alan Quirk, twice winner of the Cleveland Medal, by Mr Sydney Quayle of Castletown. The 'Cleveland' was won by Mrs J. Cowley of Foxdale, this being the first time that an out-town vocalist had secured the coveted honour.
28 - House of Keys rose in revolt on receipt of a letter from Sir Claude Hill which stated that he regretted he could not comply with their request to introduce a Bill for a public supply of electricity. A constitutional crisis was narrowly averted, and it was decided that His Excellency should be invited to receive the Keys' Consultative Committee in audience.

MAY
9 - Manx Labour Party Conference rejected 'vote of censure' on Party members in House of Keys. A resolution in favour of a maximum working week of 44 hours was carried.
14 - While the *Rushen Castle* was on its way from Liverpool to Douglas a man leaped overboard and was drowned. Later a suicide note, signed 'R.L. Beausire,' was found in a private cabin.
14 - John James Skillicorn, an old offender, was sent to prison for two months for stealing a doormat from the house of Deemster Farrant. On being arrested Skillicorn was alleged to have said "it was better to steal from a rich man than a poor man."
19 - Legislative Council rejected Bill to allow licensed premises in Onchan to remain open until 11 p.m. during the season, as in Douglas.
19 - Dispute with Lieutenant-Governor settled by His Excellency's intimation that a Bill to set up a public Board to supply electricity is to be introduced next session.

JUNE
7 - Earthquake shocks felt in all parts of the Island, this being the first local record of a tremor for over 100 years.
9 - Manx Budget showed a surplus of £13,000 during the year. Expected deficit of £70,000 in the coming year is to be met by continuation of petrol duty; levying of income tax on English shops and companies trading in the Island, and raising of starting rate of income tax from 10d. to 1s. in the pound.
16 - After agreeing to allow Sunday boating in the bay, Port Erin Commissioners took another step towards freedom by allowing the Traie Maenagh baths to be open on Sundays!
20 - First theatrical show broadcast from the Island, being transmitted by the submarine cable. The show was 'Gay Dogs' being performed at the Palace Coliseum.
29 - Wealthy Yorkshireman Mr J. A. Popplewell buys the Calf of Man, after Tynwald Committee rejects proposal that it should be purchased for the Manx nation.

JULY
6 - Broadcast of Tynwald Ceremony.
16 - Ramsey's new motor lifeboat *Lady Harrison* christened by Lady Hill in the presence of Col. Preston-Hillary, great-grandson of Sir William Hillary, founder of the R.N.L.I. The new lifeboat replaces the pulling and sailing *Matthew Simpson*.

AUGUST
7 - High-Bailiff Cowley judges that the taking of photographs on Sunday was a contravention of the Shop Hours Act.

SEPTEMBER
3 - Work commenced on the erection of a new telephone exchange on the site of the old Grammar School, Dalton Street, Douglas.
4 - Funeral of Sir Thomas Hall Caine, the interment being in Maughold churchyard.
18 - Weekes report issued dealing with the state of Island's rivers.
30 - Sir Alan Cobham arrived in the Island to make a survey of possible aerodrome sites on behalf of the Manx Government.

OCTOBER
16 - Tynwald levied additional taxes to balance the Budget, consequent upon the decline in revenue following a further fall in visitor arrivals during the past season. Tobacco and petrol duties to be raised to English levels and the duty on imported beers to be increased.
19 - Pulrose bridge opened.
20 - Castletown Ladies' Choir secured first prize by ten marks at the Blackpool Music Festival. This was followed by the Ramsey Male Voice Choir winning their class.

NOVEMBER
3 - House of Keys gave second reading to the Isle of Man Electric Light and Power Bill.
23 - Heavy rain caused more flooding, damage being done at Glen Auldyn, Laxey and Glen Helen.

DECEMBER
5 - Tynwald endorses decision of Highways Board for restoration at Glen Auldyn despite objections from the local inhabitants.
8 - Tynwald vote £900 to enable the Board of Agriculture to introduce a scheme for the cultivation of flax.
13 - Education Authority reverse their decision of a month earlier to reduce salaries of teachers by 10%.
21 - Comprehensive report issued detailing unemployment insurance scheme.
21 - Conference at Government Office relative to the possible construction of a Manx aerodrome.

SIR HALL CAINE : AUTHOR EXTRAORDINAIRE

The most famous Manxman of all time, the author, journalist and politician, Sir Hall Caine, has been laid to rest at Kirk Maughold. He died, aged 78, on 31st August. Prior to his funeral there were proposals for him to be buried in the grounds of Peel Castle and Cathedral. Some thought it would be appropriate for a Manx national shrine to be the final resting place of such a national figure, especially one who had lived for sometime in Peel. The idea was discarded, however, without apparent explanation. It may be significant, though, that there is speculation within his family that his body may be exhumed eventually and transferred to a private grave in the grounds of his beloved Greeba Castle. They said this would be appropriate as he loved the castle "beyond anything." It was in a small literary studio in the grounds that he wrote some of his greatest novels. It was there that he had been working on his unfinished epic, *The Life of Christ*, now reported to be so long that substantial editing will have to be undertaken if it is to be published.

From a portrait of Sir Hall Caine.
(Frank Cowin Library)

for several months. Several days earlier he had developed a temperature and had become delirious.

The entire Isle of Man was plunged into mourning. He may have angered some Manxmen by the way he had characterised them in his books, notably *The Manxman* (published 1894). He may have irritated others with his sense of self-importance and his modelling of his physical appearance on William Shakespeare. He may have earned a reputation also for stinginess, a trait developed during the poverty of his youth. Yet his death left everyone with a deep sense of loss. Blinds were drawn on most properties on the day of his funeral. The cortege, flanked by police motorcycle outriders, went to Maughold via Douglas, the mountain road and Ramsey, the town which he represented as M.H.K. from 1901 to 1908.

Members of Tynwald are expected to consider the legal position of the author's reburial this autumn. Once the emotion of the moment has passed, however, the chances are that the idea of exhumation will be abandoned. Sir Hall Caine chose his grave in Maughold churchyard, after all, only two weeks prior to his death, whilst on a visit there with his doctor. It was his alternative to a previously preferred burial site on Maughold Head. He abandoned this location because of its inaccessibility.

Maughold had a particular significance for the author. Although a small thatched cottage at Ballaugh was his paternal ancestral home and Liverpool was the home of his parents when he was a child, it was at Maughold that he started his writing career. He served there as an assistant to an uncle who was schoolmaster and then replaced him totally for a year when the uncle died. At a time when few people could read or write, Sir Hall Caine wrote many wills and letters for the local people. His first published work, meanwhile, consisted of articles and letters on religious and political issues written gratuitously for the *Mona's Herald*. He always remembered his uncle as being the one who predicted that he might earn his living one day from the pen.

Tributes have been flowing in from all over the world. Messages of sympathy include ones from the King and Queen and Prime Minister Ramsay MacDonald. Sir Hall Caine died at Greeba Castle with his family at his bedside after being in indifferent health

Sir Hall Caine rose from humble beginnings, raised partly in Liverpool and the rest of the time with his grandmother and uncles in the Isle of Man. "Hommybeg," as he was known to his grandmother at Ballaugh, had a predisposition to write from an early age. His early training in England was for a career as an architect but his natural inclination to write led him into freelance journalism. This helped to launch him as a novelist. His first book, set in Peel, failed to achieve anything of consequence. Success came with *The Shadow of a Crime* which was published in 1885. Subsequent books included *The Deemster* (1887) and *The Master of Man* (1921). More than 10 million copies of his books were sold. *Barbed Wire - The Woman of Knockaloe*, the first novel to be produced about the Great War and set in the Knockaloe Internment Camp, sold more than half a million copies alone. Most of his principal novels were dramatised and some turned into films.

Knighted in 1918, following his propaganda work for the British Government during the Great War, he was referred to on the Island at first as Sir Thomas. Tom was a childhood name. People stopped referring to him as such when he said that he preferred to be known as Sir Hall Caine. The Freedom of Douglas was bestowed on him in 1929.

Sir Hall Caine was intensely patriotic. A story is told of him getting into a fury whilst dining at the London's Savoy Hotel with some leading publishers and representatives of the Irish republican movement. He was offered a blank cheque to go to Ireland with a "safe conduct badge" to write a book which showed the republican movement there in a good light. He dismissed the offer.

HERE IS THE NEWS : 1932
FIGHT TO REMOVE SUNDAY RESTRICTIONS

A huge public protest meeting in Douglas over continuing restrictions imposed on the Island's holidaymakers - in particular the Sunday closure of pubs and restrictions on Sunday shop hours - has led to a major social and political clash in the Island. We have this report.

Three thousand people attended the meeting at the Villa Marina and it led to the formation of the **Manx Reform Association. This body says the visiting industry is being strangled by puritanical and Sabbatarian principles. It says reactionary legislation is restricting people's pleasures on Sundays and has led to closure of the popular Belle Vue racecourse in Douglas. The Association says the root cause of the problem is the predominance of country representation in the House of Keys compared with town representation and it intends to seek electoral reform which will restore the balance and give Douglas, in particular, more say in what happens. The Association and its meetings have been bitterly opposed by supporters of the temperance movement in the Island. Also, the Bishop, Dr William Stanton Jones, has directed severe criticism against it. He says demanding more freedom from Sunday restrictions is an unworthy reflection on the character of the Island's visitors. Dr Stanton Jones says the Church has a duty to maintain moral and spiritual values and to protect the character of the Manx Sunday**

MEDAL FOR POLICE SERGEANT

On New Year's Day it was announced that Police Sergeant Philip Watterson had been awarded the King's Police Medal for gallantry. He was the officer who, in October, 1930 confronted and arrested the armed lunatic Thomas Kissack at the lonely farmstead of The Close, near Druidale. It followed the murder of Mr Percy Brooke, and Kissack is now confined in Broadmoor. Sgt. Watterson travelled to Buckingham Palace in February and received the medal from the hand of His Majesty.

ATTACK ON BISHOP

A printed document which made an anonymous personal attack on Lord Bishop Stanton Jones was circulated to members of the Legislature early in March. The letter alleged that the Bill to amend the Bishop's Temporalities Act will divert Diocesan revenue to the income of the bishop instead of that of the clergy. The bishop already receives £2,000 per annum, plus his residence at Bishopscourt. At the Diocesan Conference a week later the Rev. Canon Quine, M.A., Vicar of Lonan, made the sensational admission that he was the author of the letter. The Conference considered it was an unwarranted attack on the bishop. For printing the letter without an imprint, Henry C. Clarke of Peel was fined £5 by Deemster La Mothe.

DHOON GLEN HOTEL DESTROYED

Before the season started one of the most picturesque country pubs in the Island, the Dhoon Glen Hotel, was destroyed by fire. The mainly timber structure was reduced to ashes in an hour, causing £4,300 worth of damage. Licensee Reginald Cain and his wife were out at the time visiting relatives in Douglas. The cause of the blaze is unknown.

TOWER OF REFUGE CENTENARY

Centenary celebrations in connection with the Tower of Refuge took place in May. Sir Godfrey Baring, chairman of the Royal National Lifeboat Institution, attended the celebrations to pay tribute to the memory of Sir

The popular Dhoon Glen Hotel and Refreshment Rooms belonging to the Manx Electric Railway Company were completely destroyed by fire on 3rd April. The cause of the fire is unknown. *(Frank Cowin Library)*

The Island's five lifeboats gather in Douglas harbour to play their part in the Centenary Celebrations of the Tower of Refuge, built by Sir William Hillary. *(Manx National Heritage)*

William Hillary, founder of the R.N.L.I. and responsible for the erection of the Tower of Refuge. Sir Godfrey unveiled plaques on the tower and at Fort Anne. The occasion was marked also by the Island's five lifeboats assembling at the Lifeboat House. The Douglas motor lifeboat *Manchester and Salford* was joined by the pull and sail lifeboats *Henry Kirk* from Peel, the *Matthew Simpson* from Ramsey, the *Ethel Day Cardwell* from Port Erin and the *Marianne* from Port St Mary.

FIRST ISLAND AIR SERVICE

The year has seen the first scheduled air service to and from the Island. It is the brainchild of Flight-Lieutenant R. H. C. Monk who is the pilot of a Saro *Cutty Sark* which is the first passenger-carrying flying boat to be built. It can carry four passengers and the twin-engined amphibian machine makes the crossing from Blackpool in 40 minutes. The service is twice daily, weather permitting, and the flying boat lands in Douglas Bay or, if the sea is rough, in the calmer waters of Derbyhaven. The large field at Ronaldsway Farm, where petrol supplies are available, can also be used. The service began at Easter and continued throughout the summer from June to September. Return fare is £3 and during the summer 348 passengers were carried. Before leaving Blackpool Flt-Lt Monk telephones the Island's travel agency, run by Mr W. H. Chapman, to let it be known where he intends to land. One of the agency's staff, Mr Jack Cretney is then despatched to arrange for a row-ing-boat to meet the passengers. Flt-Lt Monk plans to return next season.

An attempt to start a regular service from Liverpool was made by Captain Campbell Shaw and the famous racing pilot Tommy Rose. Using a similar Saro amphibian flying boat, the service was advertised but met with little success. Tommy Rose spent most of the time giving pleasure flights, but in August a mishap occurred when attempting to take off from Douglas with four passengers. About a quarter of a mile out to sea the flying boat was seen to submerge suddenly and sank until only the wings were above water. A speedboat went to the rescue and took the passengers back to Victoria Pier. It is believed that the machine hit a submerged object which penetrated the hull.

AIR RACE MEETING

Sponsored by the June Effort and Season Extension Committee, an exciting air race was held on Saturday, 18th June. The idea originated from the Lancashire Aero Club, members of which are Kenneth Twemlow, 1924 Junior T.T. winner, and Mr Howard Pixton, winner of the Schneider Trophy in 1914 and who is now resident on the Island. Entry was limited by the Air Ministry to ten aircraft which were to fly from Blackpool escorted by a flying boat. The entrants, including leading British sporting aviators, duly arrived on the Friday but the escorting flying boat, Flt.-Lt. Monk's *Cutty Sark,* was forced to return to Blackpool after developing engine trouble.

The course from Ronaldsway headed northwards over Douglas Bay to Maughold Head with turning points at Bride Church, Peel Castle and Tynwald Hill. The two-lap race of 108 miles was a handicap event with starting times decided by the expected performance of each individual aircraft. The race was very much a hedge-hopping event and huge crowds gathered at vantage points to watch the exciting spectacle. Winner was Ashley Hall in a Cirrus Moth at 102 m.p.h. who was being chased by second-place pilot Geoffrey Clapham in a Pobjoy Swift at 126 m.p.h.

After the race the crowd of over a thousand at Ronaldsway was entertained by a display of flour bomb dropping, aerobatics and balloon bursting. It was after the latter that the meeting was marred when King's Cup winner Miss Winifred Brown, flying an Avro Sports Avian, came in too low to land and hit a lady spectator sitting on a hedge. The lady, Mrs Ennett from Castletown, suffered a fractured thigh. Just before the accident Mrs Ennett had thrown her two-year-old son Derek down to her husband who had jumped off the hedge at the approach of the Avian. Apart from this unfortunate incident it had been a successful meeting held in perfect weather. It is hoped that similar meetings will be held in the future.

ISLAND HIT BY RAINSTORM

The greatest rainstorm in living memory swept the whole Island in August. It was accompanied by heavy peals of thunder and vivid flashes of lightning. The Douglas promenade was flooded and thousands of visitors heading for an evening's pleasure were soaked. Women and children were carried to safety and the six-hour storm flooded boarding house basements and shops in Strand Street. Peel also suffered flooding and at Dalby a house was severely damaged by lightning. A cottage in Patrick was also struck and its chimney stack shattered. In Douglas the fall of rain was registered at 3.29 inches.

FIRST TRAFFIC LIGHTS

The Island now has its first set of automatic traffic lights. They were erected in December at the junction of Avondale Road and Woodbourne Road in Douglas, a traffic accident blackspot. The lights normally change every 25 seconds and they operate daily from 7 a.m. to midnight.

The Saro 'Cutty Sark' with which Flight-Lieutenant R.H.C. Monk inaugurated the first scheduled passenger service to the Isle of Man.

The Avro Avian, flown by Miss Winifred Brown at the Air Race Meeting, comes to grief on landing, injuring Mrs Ennett of Castletown.

1932 NEWS IN BRIEF

JANUARY

7 - Mr William Cunningham of Douglas Holiday Camp, having obtained his pilot's licence, flew to the Island from Chester. He is the first Manxman to privately own an aeroplane and fly to the Island. The Avro Sports Avian, costing £825, is based at Ronaldsway.

FEBRUARY

18 and 20 - The Manx Legion Players produced the greatest of all anti-war plays - *Journey's End* - in the Gaiety Theatre.

MARCH

28 - Resignation of the Rev. R. H. Reid, M.A., from the living as Vicar of Malew in order to take over the headmastership of the Douglas Collegiate School in succession to his father, the late Mr Robert I. Reid.

31 - Mr T. C. Corris, former headmaster of Hanover Street School, takes over as head of Murray's Road School from Mr F. B. Bunting who has resigned.

APRIL

27 - Mr Allan Quirk wins the Cleveland Medal at the Manx Music Festival for the third time.

MAY

4 - Following the public protest meeting against Sunday restrictions, a deputation from the House of Keys waits upon His Excellency against their continuance.

5 - Great Rechabite Demonstration in the Villa Marina with all out-town districts taking part.

7 - Sensation caused when it became known that the Ramsey premises of Mr W. K. Callow, greengrocer and sub-postmaster, had been forcibly entered and a safe containing stamps and postal orders valued at £100 were missing.

13 - The new bridge and road at Glen Auldyn formally declared open. The Glen suffered severe damage in the floods of 1930.

24 - House of Keys pass the Pure Milk Bill by 16 votes to 5.

31 - Manx Budget shows a surplus in hand. Duty on imported beer to be reduced. £10,000 to be transferred from general revenue to the Income Tax Fund to obviate any change in Income Tax for the current year.

JUNE

9 - Arrival of H.R.H. Prince George for three-day visit.

16 - Bicycle T.T. Race won by A.H. Tasker of Onchan in record time of 1 hour 57 mins 30 secs. 18 cyclists started and 14 finished.

17 - Broadcast by the Attorney-General (Mr R.B. Moore) from the B.B.C. North Regional Station on 'Manx Folk Songs' with vocal illustrations by local artistes.

23 - 125th Anniversary of Sulby Wesleyan Methodist Sunday School commemorated by a big demonstration in the village.

26 - Man jumped overboard from the *Mona's Isle* during crossing from Liverpool and was drowned.

JULY

1 - Farm labourer from Derbyhaven sentenced to eight months imprisonment with hard labour at the Court of General Gaol for having carnal knowledge of a girl of 13 years of age, and under the age of 16 years.

3 - Broadcast of Evensong from St. George's Church, the service being conducted by the vicar, the Rev. C. V. Stockwood, M.A.

5 - Running commentary of Tynwald Ceremony broadcast on the North Regional programme.

14 - Opening of the new Salvation Army Citadel in Lord Street by General Edward J. Higgins, the head of the Salvation Army.

15 - Councillor T. C. Cowin of Douglas fined 5 shillings by High-Bailiff Lay for selling two chocolate eclairs and a cream crisp on the previous Sunday in his cafe, contrary to the Shop Hours Act.

18 - Record crowd of 13,000 attended the Manx Highland Gathering at the Nunnery. Present was Sir Harry Lauder who sang to the Gathering.

27 - Figures released from Government Office show that there were 313 street accidents in the Island during 1931. There were 226 injuries caused, six of which were fatal.

AUGUST

1 - Mr J. Graham Oates, a Manx motorcyclist, left St John's on a motorcycle combination - 'Miss Manxland' - on a journey of 16,000 miles through Great Britain and Canada and back.

SEPTEMBER

23 - Following the laying of a cable across the Sound to the Calf of Man, Mr J. A. Popplewell, the owner, made the first telephone call.

OCTOBER

5 - At a public meeting of the unemployed of Laxey, a resolution was passed protesting against the decision of the Harbour Commissioners failing to comply to a petition asking for a safe path to be constructed to the Laxey breakwater.

25 - First members of the Isle of Man Electricity Board appointed, with Mr A. B. Crookall, M.H.K., J.P., as chairman. Subsequently, Mr Crookall resigned from the Douglas Town Council on which he has served for a period of 21 years.

26 - Outstanding triumphs for Manx choirs at the Blackpool Music Festival. Ramsey Male Voice Choir and the Wanderers' Male Voice Choir were placed first and second respectively in their classes. Peel Castle Ladies' Choir, and Peel Athol Street Methodist Choir were placed second and third in their respective classes.

28 - Harbour Board figures issued show that the number of passenger arrivals and departures at Douglas during the year ending September, 1932 was 1,027,474½, which compares with the 1931 total of 957,259.

NOVEMBER

3 - Sgt. W. H. Quine, police sergeant at Laxey, seriously assaulted in the course of his duties at the Lonan Root Show Dance in the Laxey Glen Gardens.

5 - Mr William Cubbon, F.R.S.A.I., appointed Curator of the Manx Museum in succession to Mr P. M. C. Kermode, F.S.A., M.A., who died in September, aged 77 years.

8 - Tynwald imposes heavy duties on all animals, and meat and poultry of all kinds, except bacon, exported from the Irish Free State into the Island. This is in response to the excessive importation of fat and store cattle from the Free State.

17 - Proposal to run car races round the streets of Douglas in 1933 approved by the Society of Motor Manufacturers and Traders.

29 - Mr J. Hardy, assistant secretary of the I.O.M. Referees' Association, suspended from refereeing following an incident in a dressing room where, allegedly, he offered to fight a player.

30 - Education Committee announce 'cut' in teachers' salaries.

TYNWALD MATTERS:
AIMS OF THE MANX REFORM ASSOCIATION

Those of us who believed, perhaps foolishly, that the chill winds of the world-wide economic depression might somehow miss striking the Isle of Man are becoming increasingly worried about our visiting industry and the Island's dependence on it. It seems unlikely that the tens, indeed hundreds of thousands of visitors from the great industrial areas of the United Kingdom will still flock here undiminished.

The first straw in the wind might be the failure of the Villa Marina with a huge deficit last year, and the closure of the ever-popular race course at Belle Vue. Certainly the Boarding House and Apartment Keepers Association is worried enough to start mobilising support and going into battle against the 'Restrictionists' - a powerful body of opinion determinedly opposed to such measures as the opening of cinemas on Sundays, an extension of shop hours, the provision of alcohol with meals on Sundays, and so on.

By the end of spring those dependent on the visiting industry were aroused enough to organise a public meeting in the Villa Marina, held on 14th March. Chaired by the Mayor of Douglas, Alderman E. C. Hudson, and attended by some 3,000 people the success of the meeting must have delighted the organisers. At this meeting it became clear that far from simply resisting the attacks of the 'Restrictionists,' there were strong feelings that a more offensive stance should be developed. In quick time a new political body, the Manx Reform Association, sprang into being and, on 8th April, its programme was endorsed at a public meeting attended by over 2,000 in the Grand Theatre in Victoria Street, Douglas. At this meeting it rapidly transpired that a very clear Town versus Country division existed, with a strong feeling that the Country districts, with powerful temperance and conservative pressures, were dominating insular life. Four main points were developed by the Reformers and of these the first was Redistribution. Douglas, Peel and Ramsey account for 19,000 voters and have seven Keys' representatives, whilst the rural areas have 18,000 voters but are represented by 17 in the House of Keys. The case for some kind of redistribution is, therefore, very strong indeed. The remaining three points, the abolition of shop hours restrictions, the provision of reasonable facilities for Sunday refreshment and entertainment and the restoration of horse racing while of more immediate application, do not carry the same potential for significant change.

That these proposals were gladly supported by other parts of the Island dependent on the Visiting Industry is hardly surprising. Public meetings at Ramsey, Peel and Port Erin demonstrated overwhelming support, despite alleged attempts by Temperance supporters to pack the meetings. In May the Lord Bishop openly criticised the policy of the Manx Reform Association at the annual Convocation at Bishopscourt. His pronouncement has done little but exacerbate the situation.

The general unease here about our economic prospects were put into focus by the report of the Manx Economic Committee issued at the end of November. Its swingeing proposals include the abolition of the post of Chief Constable at the next vacancy; the addition of five years to the police retiring age, and the Medical Insurance pay to be cut. These proposals, at this stage, have been adopted by the House of Keys, but a proposal that the office of Second Deemster should be abolished was defeated by the Speaker's casting vote. At the November meeting of the Education Authority it was announced that there was to be a 10% 'cut' in teachers' salaries. But has all this been some sort of illusion, a spectre glimpsed and misunderstood? It might well be, yet in June we had an absolutely splendid Budget. We found a surplus of £16,000, an Accumulated Fund of £48,000, the funding of War Loan approved and the best news of all, no fresh taxation.

The Reform Association remains in being, but its continuation will depend, quite simply, on disaster. A bad season next year and the year after will without doubt mean that the General Election in 1934 will see the Reform Association candidates sweep the board in the towns. Without wishing the Association ill, we hope and pray that if ever a political party were to wither on the vine, let it be this one.

His Royal Highness Prince George turns on a brew at the Castletown Brewery at the beginning of his three-day visit.

(R. and L. Kelly Collection)

Crowds gather outside the Town Hall, Douglas, where Prince George received an official welcome to the capital.

(R. and L. Kelly Collection)

PRINCE GEORGE PAYS 'FLYING' VISIT

Prince George, the fourth and youngest son of King George V and Queen Mary, made history on Thursday, 8th June, by flying to the Island in an open two-seater monoplane. He did so virtually unprotected, wearing only an ordinary grey lounge suit and, in doing so, he became the first member of the Royal Family to fly to the Island. The de Havilland Puss Moth he used was one owned by his brother, the Prince of Wales. Prince George had been using it to make an aerial tour of the north of England. The prince made the one-hour flight to Ronaldsway from Liverpool's Speke Airport accompanied by a Gipsy Moth which carried his equerry. Two large R.A.F. flying boats acted as escorts in case of problems but there were none.

By flying without special uniform or leather helmet, Prince George was able to alight from his aircraft and be greeted immediately by the Lieutenant-Governor, Sir Claude Hill, without having to divest himself of flying kit in front of the public. His three-day visit began at Castletown where he turned on a brew of Manx ale at Castletown Brewery. He was presented with a black rumpy Manx kitten "for luck" by nine-year-old Ella Bridson of Ballabeg. After cradling the kitten in his arms, the prince passed it to his equerry for transfer to Government House. This was followed by an official welcome to the Island's ancient capital in the Market Place and a tour of Castle Rushen. The prince then had time for a game of golf at the Fort Island Links, and in the evening attended a dinner party and reception at Government House.

On Friday Prince George was at the T.T. Grandstand as guest of honour for the Senior Race which was celebrating its 21st meeting on the Snaefell Mountain Course. The prince witnessed the race from the Grandstand and Creg-ny-Baa. He saw Stanley Woods complete the second successive 'double' for the Norton factory. Second was Jimmy Guthrie and third was Jimmy Simpson, both on Nortons. At night Prince George presented the awards in the Palace Ballroom. Normally this takes place in the Villa Marina Gardens and is attended by some 6,000 race fans, but the prince requested that the ceremony be moved indoors in view of the possibility of bad weather. This caused some ill-feeling on the Island because the capacity of the Villa Marina is no more that 2,500. Instead, a hasty move was made to the Palace Ballroom, and a record 10,000 people saw the prince make the presentations to the heroes of the day.

In the afternoon, after the Senior Race, the prince

Prince George being greeted at Ronaldsway by His Excellency, Sir Claude Hill, after flying by de Havilland Puss Moth from Speke, Liverpool. (R. and L. Kelly Collection)

was accompanied by Deemster Farrant to Peel Castle where, amid the ruins, he received the address of welcome. A visit was then made to Tynwald Hill where His Royal Highness laid a wreath on the National War Memorial. The prince then journeyed to Tynwald Woollen Mills and inspected the premises. After partaking of tea at Cronkbourne, Prince George proceeded to Noble's Hospital where he declared the new orthopaedic wing open.

On Saturday the prince was conducted round the T.T. Course and it proved to be an eventful experience. Two accompanying cars broke down, one at Ramsey (where the prince was presented with an address of welcome) and one on the mountain climb. Then the prince's own car sustained a puncture at Cronk-ny-Mona. Whilst the wheel was being changed he was regaled by an old woman who lived nearby and sang the National Anthem to him! She was rather out of tune, it is claimed, but her gesture seems to have amused the prince!

Back in Douglas, the prince paid a visit to the Town Hall where he received an official welcome to the capital. His Royal Highness was then entertained as guest of the Douglas Rotary Club at a luncheon in Castle Mona Hotel. Prince George then returned to Ronaldsway where he bade farewell after a memorable visit. Still without protective helmet or flying suit, the prince took off in the Puss Moth for the return to Speke as the two flying boats flew overhead. At the time of writing, what happened to the Manx kitten is unknown.

Prince George chats with Stanley Woods who won the Senior T.T. following his success in the Junior Race.

(Frank Cowin Library)

After partaking of afternoon tea at Cronkbourne House, the Prince (centre) departs to open the new orthopaedic wing at Noble's Hospital.

(R. and L. Kelly Collection)

ROYAL VISIT TO MOORE'S WOOLLEN MILLS, ST. JOHN'S

The inclusion of Moore's Woollen Mills in the busy schedule of visits by Prince George is a tribute to the enterprise of Mr T. C. Moore, J.P. While his family have operated a woollen mill on the site since 1856, it was Mr Moore who had the foresight to expand the operation and provide a modern and spacious building to accommodate the latest machinery. Use is made of local wool and employment is provided for over 100 workers, many of whom would otherwise be unemployed. The success of the mill is a result of Manx Tweed earning a world-wide reputation for quality. Large consignments are exported to countries as far away as America and China. While Mr T. C. Moore remains as governing director, Mr T. R. Moore is the managing director and is as progressive as his father.

Mill workers in happy mood as they wait to greet Prince George.

Decorated for the occasion, the front of the new buildings.

Sorting the fleeces in preparation for steam cleaning.

View showing the extent of the spinning section.

Worker attending one of the looms.

Checking the final product for faults.

The sorting room where consignments are made up.

HERE IS THE NEWS : 1933
WIDENING OF LOCH PROMENADE MAKES PROGRESS

One of the greatest public works schemes ever undertaken in the Island - the widening of Loch Promenade in Douglas from Victoria Pier to the War Memorial - is progressing well. Work is scheduled to end next year and the Home Secretary, Sir John Gilmour, has been invited to carry out the opening ceremony in June. We have this report:

The building of the original **Loch Promenade on land reclaimed from the sea was completed in 1875. It was 80 feet wide - and now, after six years' work, it has been widened by a further 100 feet. The roadway is now a much broader highway and the scheme will be completed by sunken marine gardens, with a boating pool and illuminated fountains, lying between it and a new 50 foot wide walkway on the sea side. The cost, £173,000, has been shared by Douglas Corporation and the Government. Design and supervision has been carried out by Borough Engineer and Surveyor Mr. H. A. Bridge and his deputy, Mr. J. C. Bregazzi. All the work, apart from specialised projects, is being carried out by Manx companies. It is being undertaken in the winter months only, taking men off the dole to join a workforce of up to 160. Materials include 50,000 tons of concrete, over 200,000 tons of rubble for infill - and 3,400 huge two-ton blocks which form the face of the sea wall. The scheme makes Douglas one of the most spectacular resorts in Britain. A feature of the south end of the gardens will be a sundial made originally for the Duke of Orleans, Pretender to the French throne, when he fled to Britain to escape the French Revolution in the late 18th century.**

GAS EXPLOSION SHAKES CHURCH

In January, Loch Promenade was shaken by a huge gas main explosion which damaged Loch Parade Church and three adjoining boarding houses. No one was hurt but damage was extensive. People had been reporting a smell of gas for several days before the underground explosion blew out a manhole cover and sent flames shooting up in the air.

Begun in 1929, the widening of the Loch Promenade is progressing well and is due to be completed for next year's season. The winter-work scheme is jointly funded by Douglas Corporation and the Government. *(Frank Cowin Library)*

CUT IN TEACHERS' PAY

The Education Authority has cut the salaries of elementary and secondary school teachers in the Island by 10 per cent, in spite of strong union protests. The cuts, from 1st April, are in line with those made in the U.K. where the Depression has forced cost-cutting throughout public services. The Manx teachers argue the situation in the Island is not the same. They say they'll continue working - but under protest.

VISIT OF FAMOUS FLYERS

On Thursday, 14th April Amy Johnson and her husband Jim Mollison flew from London to spend a few days on the Island. Mr Mollison arrived at Ronaldsway in the DH 80A Puss Moth *Desert Cloud* in which Miss Johnson had broken her husband's London-Cape Town record. Flying in her DH 60G Moth named *Jason 4* Miss Johnson missed Ronaldsway and landed in a field at the Vollan Farm, near Ramsey. That night they stayed at the Derbyhaven Hotel and the following day were feted wherever they went, including lunch at Government House. They were also guests at the Peveril Motorcycle Club's Dinner at Glen Helen. President Mr Charles Gill, M.H.K., gave a toast to the Mollisons and complimented Jim on his recent crossing of the North and South Atlantic. A Douglas Fir Tree was planted in the grounds to mark the visit.

NORTONS UNAPPROACHABLE

Stanley Woods was very much the hero of this year's T.T. For the second year running he won the Junior and Senior Races. Riding Nortons, he set race and lap records in both events with the Senior lap record now standing at 27 mins 22 secs - a speed of over 82 m.p.h. He was supported by Jimmy Guthrie, Tim Hunt and Jimmy Simpson who between them made a clean sweep of the top places in both events. Woods has now won six T.T. victories, one more than Alec Bennett, the leading rider of the 'twenties. The Dublin rider has come a long way since driving motorcycles to help with deliveries in his father's wholesale confectionery business. He is now in big demand from rival manufacturers. The Lightweight Race was a much more open affair with a variety of machines competing for honours. The race was won by Syd Gleaves riding an experimental Excelsior at record speed. His teammate, Frank Longman, who won the 1928 event, unfortunately was killed after crashing at Glentramman, Lezayre, on the second lap.

'ROUND THE HOUSES' CAR RACES

July saw car racing return to the Isle of Man in the form of Monte Carlo style 'round the houses' events staged in Douglas. A tricky five-mile course started opposite the Villa Marina and included many of the streets and roads of the town. Two races of 50 laps were staged - the Mannin Beg for the smaller cars, and Mannin Moar for the more powerful ones. A combination of noise and speed made for spectacular viewing by the huge crowds. Freddie Dixon, in a Riley, came home the winner of the Mannin Beg, averaging 54.41 m.p.h. The Hon. Brian Lewis, driving an Alfa Romeo, won the Mannin Moar at 63.05 m.p.h. There were several crashes during the second race and a woman spectator suffered serious injury when a car broke through a barrier at the end of Castle Street.

POSTCARD CENSORSHIP

Since 1913 a committee of shopkeepers of the Island have been responsible for ensuring that the more salacious comic postcards are not made available for the general public. This year Tynwald made censorship official. A Postcard Censoring Committee was set up with powers to ban all cards which are deemed to be an affront to public decency. The Lieutenant-Governor is responsible for nominating three members, one of whom represents the retailers. Hundreds of thousands of postcards leave the Island each year as a cheap way of visitors sending messages home to their relations and friends. Many of the postcards are in colour and are a useful way of advertising the Island. Comic postcards are also popular. Now, publishers must get Censorship Committee approval before marketing a new card.

EXTENSION OF ELECTRICITY SUPPLY

The Board of Electricity's scheme to gradually provide electricity to areas of the Island outside Douglas and Onchan came to fruition in August. Supplies are being purchased from the Corporation's power station at Pulrose. Lady Hill, wife of the Lieut-Governor, switched on electric current to Peel, Port Erin, Port St Mary and places en route, by the pressing of

Jim Mollison and Amy Johnson at Ronaldsway, with the Puss Moth 'Desert Cloud' in which Miss Johnson broke the London-Capetown record. (Frank Cowin Library)

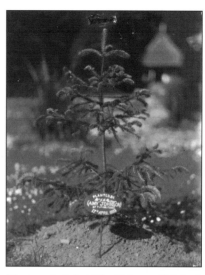

The tree planted at Glen Helen on 12th April by Miss Johnson to commemorate her visit to the Island.

a button at Pulrose. Ramsey received its first supply in September and Kirk Michael the following month. In December, despite local protests, the Board acquired the undertaking carried on for several years by the Laxey Electric Light and Power Co., which supplied Laxey, Lonan and Maughold areas with current.

MENACE OF THE PICKPOCKETS

Pickpockets continued to be a major criminal nuisance on the Island this summer. The High-Bailiff was quick to hand out some hefty prison sentences. A famous Continental pickpocket, 36-year-old Henry Ankel was accused of trying to pick a pocket of a passenger on board a steamer arriving in Douglas. The passenger turned out to be a retired Liverpool policeman who detained Ankel. He was found to have 15 previous convictions against him on the Continent and had served sentences from six days to two years. At Douglas Police Court he was sentenced to three months' imprisonment without hard

labour. Later, three men were sentenced to six months hard labour after stealing considerable sums of money from a Manchester visitor by picking pockets. All three had previous convictions in England.

SUCCESS FOR NEW AIR SERVICE

While British Amphibious returned with curtailed flights from Blackpool, this year has seen a more ambitious service provided by Blackpool and West Coast Air Services Ltd. with flights into Ronaldsway. It is the brainchild of Captain John C. Higgins who obtained financial backing to form this new company. At first, 4-seater de Havilland Fox Moths were used but in June one of the new 8-seater de Havilland Dragons was acquired. This aircraft maintained a daily schedule from Liverpool and Blackpool, with another from Liverpool via Blackpool. The service proved both convenient and popular and by the end of September, when the service stopped, 1,863 passengers had been carried.

A Riley in the Mannin Beg race roars up Buck's Road at the junction with Tynwald Street.
(R. and L. Kelly Collection)

The brand new DH 84 Dragon used by Blackpool and West Coast Air Services Ltd., on scheduled flights from Liverpool and Blackpool.
(Terry Faragher Collection)

1933

NEW LIEUTENANT-GOVERNOR During October Sir Claude Hill left the Island at the conclusion of his seven-year term as Lieutenant-Governor. Prior to his departure many official farewell tributes were paid to him. On 8th November his successor, Sir Montagu Sherard Dawes Butler, K.C.S.I., C.I.E., C.V.O., M.A., arrived. He was welcomed by a large number of Insular officials and thousands of people at the Victoria Pier. Before coming to the Island Sir Montagu was Governor of the Central Province of India.

He was installed as Lieutenant-Governor and Captain-General according to ancient ritual at Castle Rushen, the ceremony being broadcast by several Regional transmitters. Sir Montagu presided at the December meeting of Tynwald. Replying to speeches of welcome His Excellency said, "I come to the Island with a desire to work with wise colleagues and in harmony with the Legislature on a basis of mutual trust and understanding."

(Right) His Excellency Sir Montagu Butler.
(Manx National Heritage)

1933 NEWS IN BRIEF

FEBRUARY

8 - Mrs Marion Shimmin, widow of Mr C.R. Shimmin, former M.H.K. for Peel who died recently, returned unopposed in the by-election. Mrs Shimmin thus became the first woman member in the House of Keys.

22 - Death of Mr Archibald Knox, the famous Manx artist and designer.

MARCH

18 - The proprietor of the Raglan Cafe, Peel, was granted a licence to serve beer and wines with meals during the day - this being the first such licence to be granted by the Licensing Bench. Subsequently, the licence was withdrawn by the Appeal Court on the application of the Temperance Federation.

APRIL

11 - Mrs Mary Ann Gelling (80) of Quine's Hill, Braddan burned to death following the overturning of an oil stove in her bedroom, resulting in her clothes catching fire. In his efforts to smother the flames, her husband was severely burned and died next day. Verdicts of 'Accidental Death' recorded in each case.

15/16 - Visit of Mr and Mrs Jim Mollison, famous aviators.

24 - Drama contest introduced into the Manx Music Festival. Six local societies competed in one-act plays of their own choice. Miss Mona Clucas of Peel won the Cleveland Medal test.

MAY

9 - House of Keys and Legislative Council fail to agree on important changes in National Health and Compulsory Pensions Bill.

9 - The Cosy Cinema, Castletown, refused licence to open on Sundays.

13 - Attempt to revive the Sidecar T.T., last held in 1925, fails through lack of entries.

27 - Douglas Town Council decide to construct 150 houses at Pulrose, in addition to the 250 already occupied..

JUNE

6 - Budget shows increased surpluses in the Accumulated Fund and in Customs revenue. The funding of the Island's War Contribution resulted in considerable relief to the Insular revenue by extending the period of repayment. Effect was to reduce Income Tax from 1s. to 10d. and the limit from 3/6 to 2/11. Small increase on the duty on matches and wines imposed.

7 - New promenade at Peel, constructed at a cost of £8,000, opened by the Lieut-Governor.

12 - Mr William Lay appointed first full-time High-Bailiff for the whole Island.

17 - 'Manxie,' - a pure-bred jet black Manx cat from Braddan - left Liverpool on the Cunard liner *Franconia* for New York en route to Hollywood, to be received by Mickey Mouse cartoonist Walt Disney.

JULY

13 - Total number of accidents reported to the police in 1932 rose to 395. Injured totalled 297 but there were only four fatalities, a decrease of two.

28 - Visit of the Most Rev. William Temple, Archbishop of York, principally in connection with the centenary celebrations of King William's College. On the Sunday after his arrival he preached to a congregation of 15,000 people at the open-air service at Kirk Braddan.

AUGUST

3 - All-Island Electricity Scheme inaugurated.

28 - Miss Rhoda Kelly (19), a waitress at Rushen Abbey, died as a result of an accident between a pedestrian and a bicycle which she was riding.

SEPTEMBER

5 - Junior M.G.P. won by Austin Munks (Velocette) ahead of F.L. Frith (Norton). J.H. White (Velocette) from Cambridge University made the fastest lap at 75.64 m.p.h. and is the first to complete a lap in under 30 minutes. Trophy for the fastest 250 c.c. machine was won by R. Harris on a New Imperial.

7 - Senior M.G.P. won by H.L. Daniell from London at record speed, with a new lap record of 29 mins 5 secs - 77.86 m.p.h. There has been a record entry of 118 for this year's races. A. Pilling from Huddersfield died during the practices following a crash at Hillberry.

11 - New Ramsey Grammar School situated on the Milntown estate, adjoining Lezayre Road, opened.

12 - Ballaugh parishioners request Local Government Board to prepare a water supply scheme following the recent water shortage.

17 - Great parade of 600 ex-servicemen at St John's as gesture of gratitude to Lieutenant-Governor Sir Claude Hill whose term of office ends this year.

26 - Steam Packet's oldest vessel, the *Tynwald* built in 1891, sold for breaking-up purposes.

OCTOBER

3 - Meeting of the Boards of Poor Relief Guardians decide overwhelmingly that unemployment relief should be a national charge, and not dependent on a local rate.

5 - Inauguration of St John's Water Undertaking, when new reservoir was opened at Ballaspet.

6 - Centenary of Crosby Methodist Chapel.

23 - Woodside Ladies' Choir and Peel Castle Choir gained first and second prizes in their class at Blackpool Music Festival.

24 - Sir Claude Hill leaves Island after being Lieutenant-Governor for 7½ years.

25 - Education Authority decides to erect an infants' school at Pulrose for 240 children at a cost of £8,100.

NOVEMBER

9 - Sir Montagu Butler installed at Castle Rushen as Lieutenant-Governor of the Isle of Man.

16 - New telephone exchange opened in Dalton Street, Douglas.

18 - Mr John Henry Lockart Cowin, a 34 year-old Douglas advocate, wins by-election in Middle, heavily defeating Mr Gerald Bridson, the Labour Party candidate.

23 - Official passenger returns reveal that from May to September, 1932 a total of 478,947 arrived at Douglas, compared with 451,078 for the same period in 1931. The approximate figure for the 1933 period is 505,000.

28 - Agricultural Holdings Bill, a measure establishing a Rent Court, giving security of tenure and providing for compensation for disturbance, passed the third reading in the House of Keys.

29 - Education Authority decides that a supply of milk should be given to children attending the elementary schools in the Island.

30 - The corn threshing machine at Glen Darragh, Marown suffers disastrous fire. Douglas Fire Brigade in attendance for four hours.

DECEMBER

17 - *Ben Blanche* coastal steamer of the Ramsey Shipping Company ran ashore at Port Eynon, ten miles from Swansea. The seven Manx crewmen were rescued by the Mumbles Head lifeboat, but the vessel was a total wreck.

ARCHIBALD KNOX : ARTIST OF WORLD RENOWN

The artist Archibald Knox died in February this year aged 69. Archie, as he was known to everyone, was buried in the new cemetery at Braddan. He was born nearby at Tromode in 1865. It was here that his parents from Scotland settled and his father, Robert Knox, was a successful engineer specialising in marine and fishing machinery, his work complementing the sailcloth factory at Tromode. Knox began his education at St Barnabas Church of England School before progressing to Douglas Grammar School. There, his headmaster was the noted Manx and Celtic scholar, Rev. John Quine who is now Canon Quine, Vicar of Lonan.

In 1878 Knox returned to his old school at St Barnabas as a pupil teacher while, at the same time, attending the recently opened Douglas School of Art. Here he completed a six year course and qualified as a teacher, having gained his Art Master's Certificate. In 1892 he gained a silver medal for historic ornamentation, having specialised in Celtic interlace design. From that time until 1896 he is thought to have worked part time in the offices of Hugh Mackay Baillie Scott, the architect and designer, examples of whose houses are so much a feature of the Little Switzerland area. Scott was also responsible for the parish hall in Onchan and the police station in Castletown.

In 1897, at the age of 33, Knox left the Island to take up a teaching post at Redhill in Surrey, where he joined another Manx artist - Alfred James Collister, who had also been a pupil at the Douglas School of Art. They were to be life-long friends and painting companions, often working together and producing paintings of the same scene. It is strange that Knox rarely signed, or sold his paintings. Collister eventually became head of the Redhill Art School and later moved to the Art Schools of Wimbledon and Kingston-on-Thames. At different times, Knox was to follow his friend as a member of his teaching staff and when Collister married, Knox was his best man. Collister now has a house in Littlehampton, Surrey so it is unlikely that he will return to the Island, apart from the occasional painting trip.

In 1899 the notable jewellery firm of Liberty and Co. of London started to produce their Cymric range of silverware, followed the next year by a range of Tudric pewter. From this time Knox, with his special style of Celtic revival, became inextricably linked with these Liberty products and he established himself as one of the foremost designers in the English Art Nouveau movement. Whilst certain of his designs are clearly estab-

lished, many others can be attributed to him and his influence permeates the whole range of Liberty's products.

He returned to the Island for a short spell when he lived at Sulby, but then returned to London and moved on to America. By 1912 he was back in the Isle of Man and during the years of the Great War was employed as chief censor at the Alien's Internment Camp at Knockaloe. The return of peace saw him continue his design work but now based on the Island, though making occasional visits to London and farther afield. He also found time to teach part time at the Douglas High Schools. There will be many who recall vividly his taking over their work if it attracted his attention!

Increasingly, Knox's designs appeared on war memorials and tombstones. At the time of his death he was working on the designs of the memorial tomb at Maughold of that other notable Manxman, Sir Hall Caine. It is said that these last designs are to be completed by two of his London-based former students, the Misses Tuckfield.

In 1911, the Knox Guild of Design and Craft was founded in Kingston by his former students as a tribute to their teacher. Here on the Island it is these tombstone designs, such as those found at Onchan, Lonan, Braddan and St Runius, plus the war memorials at Onchan and Michael, that are a constant reminder of his skill. One which perhaps gave him a saddened pride, is the tombstone of fellow artist John Miller Nicholson, in Douglas Borough Cemetery. It is so pierced to evoke thoughts of an artist's palette with its symbolising not only of Nicholson's own considerable talent, but also his involvement with the Douglas School of Art which had nurtured Knox and his friend Collister.

Archie Knox will also be remembered for his puzzling and intriguing illustrations included in Sophia Morrison's *Manx Fairy Tales*. Then there is the Roll of Honour of the Douglas High School for Boys at St Ninian's. Its carpet pages of intricate design and its immaculate and unique style of lettering, record the names of former pupils of the Eastern Secondary School who served in the Great War, with those who died especially marked. Beyond our shores it is said that many important Museums and Art Galleries have acquired some of the more special examples of his metalwork designs. Perhaps one day, because of his genius, those items produced for normal trade by Liberty's will become collectors' items in their own right, and will no doubt ensure that the name, and fame, of Archibald Knox is not forgotten.

EXAMPLES OF THE WORK OF ARCHIBALD KNOX

1. *'God's shield to protect me.'*

2. *'Tudric' pewter clock with enamelled face for Liberty, c 1903.*

3. **'**God's way to lie before me.'*

4. *Silver tea service and tray for Liberty.*

5. *Title page for the Manx Music Festival programme, first used in 1927.*

1, 3 *and* **6:** *Illuminated lettering from 'Deer's Cry' and 'St. Patrick's Hymn'.*

6. *'To the virtue of His resurrection.'*

(Manx National Heritage)

HERE IS THE NEWS : 1934
FAMOUS RACING DRIVER GAOLED

One of Britain's most famous racing drivers, Kaye Don, has been gaoled for four months by the Court of General Gaol for manslaughter. His driving was blamed for the death of his mechanic, 27-year-old Francis Tayler, who was with him when he crashed at the top of the Whitebridge Hill while on an unofficial test run in his MG in readiness for this year's Mannin Beg round-the-houses racing in Douglas. We have this report:

The MG collided with a hackney car owned by Mr. W. R. Caine of Laxey. Evidence was given that the MG had no lights on in near darkness and appeared to be driven by a madman. Tayler was thrown out and died later. Don was trapped in the cockpit and spent 17 days in Noble's Hospital. His trial, held in the Tynwald Court Chamber, under Deemster Farrant, lasted four days with large crowds of spectators and reporters and photographers from the English press. Don's defence was that the crash was caused by a steering failure. The case caused widespread newspaper comment with the Island's firm stand being praised. But in the prison in Victoria Road, Douglas, Don appeared to lead a privileged life. He was allowed to wear his own clothes, have his meals sent in and sleep in his own bed. It was denied that influence in high places was brought to bear. But there were renewed accusations when, after completing 10 weeks of his sentence, he was released on the orders of the Lieutenant-Governor, Sir Montagu Butler. The official reason was that he was on the brink of a nervous breakdown and was released on health grounds. English press reports, however, revealed that on arrival in Liverpool he drove all the way home to Weybridge in Surrey in thick fog with no apparent ill-effects, and went straight back to work in his business - before going on holiday to Florida.

CAR RACES
A ROARING SUCCESS

The races themselves were a great success. The start was on Douglas Promenade and the five mile course went up Broadway and Bray Hill, along Glencrutchery Road and down

A section of the crowd gathered outside Government Buildings, Douglas, in the hope of gaining admission to Kaye Don's trial for manslaughter. *(Frank Cowin Library)*

Summer Hill. Norman Black driving an MG Magnette won the Mannin Beg race at 70.99 m.p.h. The winner of the big race, the Mannin Moar, was the Honourable Brian Lewis in an Alfa Romeo at 75 m.p.h. A Lancashire woman spectator, badly injured in last year's races when a Bugatti crashed into a barrier, has been awarded £1,190 damages against the Highway and Transport Board which was responsible for course safety.

'DOUBLE' FOR GUTHRIE

In this year's T.T. works' rider Jimmy Guthrie completed another brilliant double for Nortons with victory in the Junior and Senior races. A strong foreign challenge was once again beaten by British machines. Rudges dominated the Lightweight event with Jimmy Simpson, Ernie Nott and Graham Walker taking the first three places. So lady luck at last smiled on Jimmy Simpson, famous for setting lap records, and great were the rejoicings for his first T.T. win. In the process he lifted the Lightweight lap record to 73.64 m.p.h. But the race was marred by the death of Syd Crabtree, a former Lightweight T.T. winner who crashed into a gate on the Mountain Road in thick fog.

WAR INCIDENT REVEALED

The sensational story of a Great War incident in the Island that was not made public at the time on security grounds has emerged with the retirement of Peel policeman Constable Albert Bell. Single-handed he disarmed the drunken captain of a Royal Navy minesweeper that put into Ramsey. The captain ran amok on the quayside armed with two loaded revolvers. Constable Bell, who was later awarded the King's Police Medal, disarmed him and also one of his crew who was armed with a rifle.

FREE MILK FOR
POOR CHILDREN

Poor children in the Island are to be entitled to free milk at school. The Education Authority has decided that a third of a pint a day will be given to all youngsters who need it on health grounds. It is expected that about 800 children will claim it. Those whose parents can afford it, must pay.

FATAL CLIFF FALL
AT PORT JACK

Heavy drinking by visitors has been blamed for a fatal cliff fall at Port Jack, Onchan. A young Manchester man, George Emsall, fell 64 feet after he had been out drinking with a young lady visitor from Preston. They had been at Derby Castle then went to Port Jack where he fell from the top of the cliff, pulling her with him. She survived because she landed on him. And at Bradda Head five fishermen risked their lives in gale force winds and blinding rain to recover the body of a young visitor who had fallen 300 feet down the cliffs, coming to rest on a narrow ledge.

TWO DIE IN EXPLOSIONS

Two men have been killed in explosions in the Island. Onchan builder's labourer Wilfred Cowell, who was 30, died in the premature detonation of explosives being used in the sinking of a well at Dreemlang Farm. And sixty-eight-year-old Thomas Kaighin was killed during blasting operations at the Douglas Corporation stone quarry at South Quay.

CHILDREN IN TRAGIC ACCIDENTS

It has been a particularly sad year for children involved in accidents. A four-year-old girl died after being knocked down by a train at Bishopscourt. Peggy Crellin, who lived nearby at Orrisdale Farm, had strayed on to the line. She suffered horrific injuries and died in Ramsey Cottage Hospital. In Douglas a boy of 2½ years died from injuries sustained after being knocked down by a motor car in Tynwald Street. Another boy died from injuries after being knocked down by a car in Athol Street.

ANOTHER BUMPER SEASON

The Island has enjoyed another highly successful visiting season and August Bank Holiday was an all-time record with over 40,000 people pouring into Douglas. The Steam Packet operated two dozen sailings in 24 hours. After the depressed years of the beginning of this decade, it is confidently predicted that the all-important summer arrival figures will show that once again over half a million visitors have come to our shores. All places of entertainment have done excellent business with full houses for Florrie Forde at Derby Castle. There were also record crowds of 30,000 at the Sunday morning open-air service at Kirk Braddan.

The Children's Pool being 'raided' after the official opening of Loch Promenade Marine Gardens by Home Secretary, Sir John Gilmour, M.P. on 23rd June. (Frank Cowin Library)

The new 20 h.p. Commer ambulance presented to Noble's Hospital by Mrs Ellen Cubbin of Strathallan, Onchan, and her son, Mr R. Colby Cubbin.

Nortons, for the third successive year, won the Junior and Senior Races. This year, the 'double' was achieved by Jimmy Guthrie, seen here in the paddock after the Senior Race. (R. and L. Kelly Collection)

Holder of many lap records, a smiling Jimmy Simpson is congratulated by his wife after winning his first T.T., riding for Rudge in this year's Lightweight Race. (Frank Cowin Library)

The Mona's Queen approaching the Victoria Pier, Douglas, at the conclusion of her maiden voyage from Liverpool on 27th June.

(Frank Cowin Library)

Douglas fire-engine at the scene of the fire at Mr A. E. Taylor's barn at Kewaigue, shortly after the collapse of the roof.

(Frank Cowin Library)

1934 NEWS IN BRIEF

FEBRUARY

15 - By-election in North Douglas caused by the elevation of Alderman A. B. Crookall to the Legislative Council to replace the late Mr J. D. Qualtrough, Receiver-General. Late nomination was Mr Samuel Norris who had been narrowly defeated in the 1929 General Election. Mr Norris regained his seat with 3,043 votes. The other candidate was Mr T. C. Cowin.

15 - Peel A.F.C. struck out of the I.O.M. Football Association Cup competition, and five players suspended by the Disciplinary Committee of the F.A., as a result of incidents which arose in a match between Ramsey and Peel in that competition.

16 - Large public meeting in Douglas agrees that the Mannin car races should again be held this year.

MARCH

10 - Protests against the continued 'cut' in teachers' salaries voiced by Mr J. P. Qualtrough, president of the local branch of the National Association of Schoolmasters.

13 - Authority for dealing with rivers and watercourses designated to Highway Board instead of Harbour Commissioners, in Land Drainage Bill, given a third reading by the Legislative Council.

16 - Centenary of the I.O.M. Bank for Savings, founded in 1834 under the presidency of Sir William Hillary.

APRIL

9 - Railway Air Services introduce scheduled flights linking the Isle of Man with Manchester and Belfast.

25 - Cleveland Medal won for the third time by Mrs L. M. R. Bull (mezzo-soprano).

MAY

30 - Education Authority adopt recommendations for partial restoration of deduction made in teachers' salaries.

JUNE

7 - Sir Montagu Butler introduces his first Budget. There was a surplus of £64,418 on the financial year. Reduction of 2d (from 10d to 8d) in unit rate of income tax proposed. Also that grants to local authorities in aid of work schemes should be raised from 50% to 75%; that relief pay grants to Boards of Guardians also be raised to 75%; that debts due to Douglas Corporation and Braddan Commissioners on account of housing be paid out of Accumulated Fund and that water and drainage schemes should be financed from the same source. Total government expenditure for year estimated at £386,378.

7 - Filtration plant in connection with Douglas water-undertaking, costing £82,000, opened by Mayor of Douglas, Alderman J. H. Skillicorn J.P.

12 - Agricultural Marketing Bill, proposing the establishment of marketing schemes by co-operative effort by farmers, carried in the Legislative Council with amendments, which were accepted by the House of Keys.

23 - New Loch Promenade and Marine Gardens formally declared open by Sir John Gilmour, M.P., Secretary of State for the Home Department. The entire six year scheme cost £173,000.

27 - Maiden voyage of *Mona's Queen III* making the crossing from Liverpool Landing Stage to Douglas Head in 3 hrs 20mins, an average speed of 21.8 knots.

JULY

3 - Level and Croit-e-Caley (Rushen) drainage scheme completed at a cost of £3,000.

23 - Announcement made in Chancery Division that settlement had been reached in long-running dispute in connection with the estate of the late Sir Hall Caine who died in 1931.

26 - Three stained-glass windows in honour of the national poet, T. E. Brown, unveiled in Manx Museum.

AUGUST

15 - Thrilling rescue by a Douglas boat owner, Mr John Clague, of two young men whose rowing boat was caught in a tidal race off Douglas Head and overturned.

20 - First Air Mail service inaugurated at Head Post Office in Regent Street, Douglas, when His Excellency Sir Montagu Butler posted a letter addressed to the Postmaster-General in London. The letter was one of 797 which was flown by a Dragon aircraft of Railway Air Services to Manchester. Flying conditions were extremely turbulent and it was necessary to carry the in-coming mail by sea. (The air mail contract lasted until 29th September).

SEPTEMBER

13 - Senior Grand Prix won by D. J. Pirie on a Norton. The Junior race was won by J. H. White, also on a Norton. During the early morning practices two riders were killed, one hitting a stone wall at Kirk Michael, and the other at Sulby Bridge after being dazzled by the early morning sun.

22 - Manx football team defeated Liverpool Collegiate Old Boys 7-3 at Liverpool.

OCTOBER

15 - New ambulance presented to Noble's Hospital by Mrs Ellen Cubbin, of Strathallan, and her son, Mr R. Colby Cubbin.

26 - Manx football season opened with "unofficial" referees, the Referees' Association having withdrawn their services owing to a dispute with I.O.M. Football Association.

NOVEMBER

16 - Arrangements completed between Manx Electric Railway Co, and I.O.M. Electricity Board for bulk supply of current for running of railway.

22 - Retirement, through ill-health, of Deemster F. M. La Mothe, from First Deemstership and Clerkship of Rolls. His successor, Deemster R. D. Farrant, and new Second Deemster, Mr W. Percy Cowley, J.P., sworn in.

23/29 General Election of House of Keys.

DECEMBER

3 - Inaugural meeting of the I.O.M. Development Board.

5 - Mr H. L. Fletcher, B.A. (Oxon.) appointed Director of Education in succession to Mr F. R. Grundey, B.Sc., F.C.S., resigned.

11 - First meeting of new House of Keys. Mr G. F. Clucas re-elected Speaker.

26 - Easterly gale prevented *Peel Castle* leaving Douglas harbour. The *Rushen Castle*, which was sheltering in Port Erin, proceeded to Peel, from which port she sailed to Liverpool.

THE WATER WE DRINK

Yellow water looks like being a thing of the past - at least in Douglas and its immediate neighbourhood. So, too, the arrival with it of tiny strangers known as cyclops - otherwise the freshwater shrimp - and daphne. According to the experts neither are harmful to human health but the 24,300 consumers in the Douglas area have not found their presence particularly pleasant. The revolution in drinking water is down to the introduction for the first time of filtration. The first filtered water started to reach consumers as from 23rd April. Officialy, however, the Glencrutchery Filter Plant, which makes it possible, was opened by the Mayor of Douglas, Alderman J.H. Skillicorn, on Thursday, 7th June. The date was significant because that day was the 100th anniversary of Tynwald granting legal powers to the original Douglas Water Company to supply piped water to the town.

Until now water came direct from the reservoirs. It was stained yellow by peat from the gathering ground; it was contaminated by particles of vegetable matter; it was acidic enough to attack lead and copper piping, and it hosted the cyclops and daphne. The new filter plant makes the water free from bacteria, colour and foreign matter (whether alive or dead). It also makes it alkaline so that it will not attack piping. A further benefit is that it gains a bright and sparkling appearance.

Provision of a filtration and sterilisation plant just off Glencrutchery Road was recommended to Douglas Corporation by a consulting analyst in January last year. The Corporation Water Engineer, Mr T.C. Greenfield, whose name has been adopted for the narrow road which runs alongside the plant, designed an appropriate scheme and work started on it immediately after Tynwald grant-

ed it approval in June last year. It proved to be an invaluable aid to reducing unemployment, especially during the winter. Apart from the provision of technical equipment, the work was undertaken by direct labour under Mr Greenwood's personal supervision and upwards of 300 men were engaged on it. The final cost is put at £82,000 of which £10,000 has been given as a grant from Tynwald.

Filtration is undertaken through two rows of filter drums. Chalk and sulphate of alumina are added to the water as it arrives from the reservoirs and are thoroughly mixed. The water then passes to the filter drums which are mostly filled with specially graded Leighton Buzzard sand. As the water passes through the sand it leaves a gelatinous, sticky coating of insoluble hydrate of alumina on the sand and it is this, being impervious to dirt, colour and micro-organisms, which purifies the water. The sand, of course, has to be cleaned regularly. Impurities are washed out by mechanical stirring of the sand and the simultaneous injection of compressed air. After filtration, the water has lump lime from Billown kilns added to it to control acidity. It is then sterilised by the addition of liquid ammonia and chlorine gases and is then transferred to concrete service reservoirs prior to being distributed to customers.

Beyond the neighbourhood of Douglas the Local Government Board is still carrying out its scheme to distribute water from its own reservoirs to towns and villages throughout the Island, though farms and outlying areas will have to continue to rely on their own pumped water for many years to come. Filtration is also a long way off for those living beyond Douglas, but no doubt this will be achieved one day.

The Filter House, alongside the road to be named after the Douglas Borough Water Engineer, Mr T. C. Greenfield, B.Sc.

The pressure filters which purify the water which is then passed to the service reservoirs before entering the public supply.
(R. and L. Kelly Collection)

APPROVED BY THE CENSOR COMMITTEE!

From the Manx National Heritage Collection

NEW LOOK FOR THE MOUNTAIN ROAD

The mountain road is clear of gates for the first time in generations. It means an end to the irritating practice for motorists of having to stop several times to open and close the gates. It also means an end for the enterprising youngsters who could earn a few pennies by being unofficial gatekeepers during the summer. Years ago a mentally-handicapped individual provided a similar service for carriage and charabanc parties in respect of a gate across an access road at Sulby. In the early days of car and motorcycle racing, especially during early morning practice on unclosed roads, shepherds or race officials served as voluntary gate attendants to ensure the gates were open for competitors, but there were occasions when volunteers failed to attend to this and there were several crashes, fortunately without serious consequences.

The gates were part of a fencing system which divided the common lands into various tenanted holdings for sheep farmers. Now the roadsides have been sealed off with fencing to prevent sheep straying. This consists of miles of ferro-concrete posts linked by strands of wire with netting on the lower part. The iron double gates known as the Second Mountain Gate, had a central upright pillar which was considered to be particularly dangerous. The last two gates to be removed in mid-May, in time for this year's T.T. practices, were one at Beinn-y-Phott and one of the most famous of all, Keppel Gate. This was a narrow gate which sealed off the mountain road immediately before its descent to Creg-ny-Baa.

The removal of the gates is the result of a scheme begun two years ago by the Common Lands Board following a decision by the Highway Board to concentrate on improvements to the mountain road. Its route was laid out in the middle of last century long before it came into prominence as part of the Snaefell Mountain Course. In the 1920s the road was macadamised with the top surface finished with a layer of fine granite chippings. This was a great improvement for vehicles but when it came to racing, riders had to contend with the hazards of punctures and a loose surface. This has now been overcome with the application of tarred macadam, though melting tar can still catch out the unwary.

The first step towards getting rid of the gates was taken in 1931. That was when an experimental device was installed on the Cross Vein Road which branches off from the Shoulder Road over the Glen Rushen commons near the Round Table. When the common lands border-

A T.T. rider on the descent through the hazard of Keppel Gate which has now been removed
(R. and L. Kelly Collection)

ing the roadway were fenced for the first time that year, it was discovered that motorists no longer bothered to close the gate across the road. This, of course, made the fencing useless and allowed sheep to wander from one holding to another. The solution to the problem was the introduction of what became known as a 'by-pass.' A pit was dug in the road and some ready-made ladder grating was laid over it. Cars and motorcycles were capable of driving across this, but sheep would not venture on it.

The success of this idea encouraged the start of work on the T.T. Course in May, 1932. By-pass systems were inappropriate for the course but one was introduced on an access road to enable one of the gates on the course to be removed. This was the East Snaefell Gate - claimed to be the most dangerous obstacle across a public road on the Island. A new by-pass with gate, linked to re-aligned fencing, was established on the Tholt-y-Will Road. The by-pass was to a new Manx design. Steel grating and bars made by Gelling's Foundry of Douglas were laid over a pit 3 feet deep, 8 feet wide and 6 feet long. A flock of sheep was brought to the by-pass to test it and not one would try to cross it. The gates on the mountain road at the Manx Electric Railway crossing have also been removed. The Highway Board now says that metal grids may be introduced elsewhere on the Island eventually, such as on the road between Tholt-y-Will and Sulby. Their provision, however, will depend on the availability of cash.

Opening of the by-pass at Beinn-y-Phott on the Mountain Road.
(Frank Cowin Library)

The Sulby by-pass at the Bungalow.
(Frank Cowin Library)

HERE IS THE NEWS : 1935

WORKERS WIN FIGHT FOR HIGHER WAGES

The Island was brought to a standstill in a General Strike called by the Transport and General Workers Union. The stoppage lasted only 40 hours and brought almost complete victory in a fight for higher wages. It was the Island's first General Strike since 1918. We have this report:

The stage was set in February when the Transport Union demanded a big wage increase to 48 shillings for a 48-hour week - only to have it dismissed out of hand by the Isle of Man Employers' Federation. Four months later, after the employers had refused to shift their position, the strike began with dramatic suddenness at 7.30 a.m. on June 3rd - sanctioned in London by the Union's general secretary, Ernest Bevin. Electricity was cut off, except for hospitals; trains and buses were halted; Steam Packet warehouses were closed and no ships could be unloaded, bringing trade and business to a halt. A demonstration by a thousand men blocked Douglas town centre - but it was entirely peaceful. Strike organisers imposed strict discipline. The Government initiated peace talks on the afternoon of the first day and by the evening of the second day, after candlelit talks in Douglas Town Council Chamber, it was over.

The union won a 46 shilling minimum wage for a 48 hour week. But the strain had told on the local branch secretary, Councillor Alfred Teare, M.H.K. He collapsed with a perforated ulcer immediately afterwards. The strike also had repercussions in Tynwald where moves were started to prevent similar stoppages in the future.

MARKETING ASSOCIATIONS TO HELP FARMERS

The passing of the Agricultural Marketing Acts by Tynwald has been hailed as the start of a new era of prosperity for the Island's farming industry. Locally organised produce marketing will give Manx farmers first claim on sales to the Island market. The move has been described as a practical solution to the long depression in Manx farming. However, a strong protest has been made by the Douglas Boarding and Apartment Association on the grounds that the schemes involve restriction of imports and increased milk prices.

HALL CAINE AIRPORT

Ramsey and the north of the Island now have an airport of their own which has been made possible by funds made available by Sir Derwent and Mr Ralph Hall Caine who are both Members of Parliament. The airport is in memory of their father, the famous Manx novelist and former M.H.K. for Ramsey. The airport makes use of a large expanse of land belonging to Close Lake Farm and is found by the Jurby Road, three miles from Ramsey. A wooden terminal building has been provided and a wireless receiver installed. Throughout the summer, United Airways have operated services to and from Blackpool, Liverpool, Carlisle and Glasgow with nearly 2,000 passengers carried on the latter route.

T.T. HONOURS FOR MOTO GUZZI.

In one of the most exciting races in T.T. history, Stanley Woods won the Senior trophy for the Italians riding a twin-cylinder Moto Guzzi. At the start of the seventh and final lap, Woods sped through the start without stopping to refuel, as race leader Jimmy Guthrie had already done. Woods then hauled back the deficit of 26 seconds and then went on to win by just four seconds. He completed the last lap in 26 mins 40 secs, setting up an incredible lap record at 86.53 m.p.h. In the process he had prevented Junior winner Guthrie notching up yet another 'double' for Nortons. The race was held on a Saturday for the first time because of dense fog on the previous day. Stanley Woods had already won the Lightweight event for the Moto Guzzi team, this being the first time that a foreign manufacturer had won a T.T. trophy. In the Junior race a rider was killed after crashing at Union Mills, and the Lightweight race was marred by the death of previous Junior and Senior M.G.P. winner, Gordon Pirie, who crashed into the new concrete posts at the 33rd milestone.

VISIT OF FAMOUS FILM STAR

As soon as the T.T. period was over, the famous film star Florence Desmond, who has Manx connections, arrived on the Island together with a film unit of Associated Talking Pictures Ltd. With a budget of £50,000 the object was to make a film based on a script by Walter Greenwood, author of *Love on the Dole*. The film is a comedy based on the T.T. Florence Desmond co-stars with George Formby Jnr, whose father is also in show business, and has appeared at the Palace Opera House in Douglas.

The film unit was based at the Majestic Hotel in Onchan and members of the Peveril Motor Cycle Club were called upon to stage the many hair-raising stunts. One involved crashing through the front door of the Ballacraine Hotel. The film is a mix of romance and the thrills and spills of T.T. racing. George Formby plays the part of George Shuttleworth who is determined to beat the stars on his 'Shuttleworth Special'. It is the first big movie for the ukulele-playing George Formby, and it is sure to be a great success with T.T. fans.

DEATH OF ALDERMAN CROOKALL, M.L.C.

In June Alderman A. B. Crookall, J.P., M.L.C., died after a brief illness in Harrogate. He was aged 62. He will be remembered as one of the men most responsible for the development of Douglas, and the Isle of Man, as a leading holiday resort. As a Councillor and Alderman of Douglas he served as the mayor of the town for a remarkable five years. He was member for North Douglas in the House of Keys before elevation to the Legislative Council. Mr Crookall was an astute businessman who made his fortune in the Great War when he won the contract to feed 20,000 enemy aliens at the Knockaloe Camp. Amongst his many charitable acts was the recent provision of a maternity home in Demesne Road, Douglas, which was named in memory of his wife. He has left a large fortune said to be nearly £200,000.

BREACH OF PROMISE CASE SETTLED

Damages of £250 have been paid in an out-of-court settlement of a

1935

breach of promise case brought by a local nurse against a well-known Douglas G.P. It was brought by Nurse Marion McLaren against Dr. Harold de Morgan. A joint statement was issued by the parties following the agreement in the High Court. It said: "The parties became engaged to be married in August 1934 and remained friendly up to six weeks prior to the filing of the action."

ONCHAN WINS TAKE-OVER BATTLE

Finally, Douglas has been unsuccessful in a bid to take over the whole of Onchan village as part of a major extension to its boundary. Tynwald set up a public inquiry in March and the Village Commissioners reacted strongly to the suggestion, claiming it was a case of Douglas trying to drag an unwilling bride to the altar. Tynwald's Select Committee have now reported that Douglas Corporation has not established a case for the incorporation of Onchan within the Borough of Douglas. However, a minority report recommends the extension, but this is most unlikely to be accepted when the matter comes before Tynwald at its meeting in the new year.

All eyes are on Irishman Stanley Woods as he sweeps around the 'dip' at Governor's Bridge on the Senior Moto Guzzi. He went on to snatch victory by four seconds from Scotland's hero, Jimmy Guthrie. (Keig Collection)

1935 NEWS IN BRIEF

JANUARY
7 - Regulations issued by the Rolls Office direct that, in future, Deemsters shall wear judicial robes of scarlet hue on all occasions of national ceremony, at Courts of General Gaol Delivery, and in Superior Jurisdiction of High Court.

FEBRUARY
1 - Blackpool and West Coast Air Services Ltd awarded Air Mail contract. First plane left Ronaldsway in 60 m.p.h. gale and inward plane an hour overdue through struggle against storm.
2 - Manx general workers, through the T.G.W.U., present claim for substantial increase in wages.
20 - Mr Wilfed Harding of Douglas, the well-known T.T. rider, sustained severe injuries when his car overturned on approach to Spring Valley. Three days later it was necessary to amputate his right arm in order to save his life.

MARCH
7 - The new Sunday School and Johnson Memorial Hall of St George's Church, Douglas, formally opened by His Excellency, Sir Montagu Butler.

APRIL
3 - The birth of the one thousandth baby born at the Jane Crookall Maternity Home commemorated with presentation to baby Helen Christian of a silver poringer spoon and serviette ring in engraved case.

MAY
1 - Mr Joe Corrin, of Castletown, a former Island golf champion, won the Cleveland Medal at the Manx Music Festival.
1 - The Manx Elecric Railway, after generating its own supply of current for 40 years, commences to run on current supplied by the I.O.M. Electricity Board.
6 - Silver Jubilee of His Majesty King George V celebrated in every town and village with scenes of great rejoicing.
16 - Malew water and drainage schemes, costing over £17,000, officially declared open.
23 - Mr Joe Corrin, of Castletown, wins the Manx Amateur Golf Championship for the sixth time.
20 - Belle Vue fair ground and race course acquired by Douglas Corporation for £6,250 with intention to convert it into park and playing fields.
31 - Hon. Brian Lewis, driving a Bugatti, won the Mannin Mooar Race at an average speed of 75.57 m.p.h. over the 201.75 miles. The Mannin Beg Race was won by the Hon. Brian Lewis in an E.R.A averaging 67.29 m.p.h.

JUNE
3 - General Strike launched throughout the Island by T.G.W.U.

12 - Douglas Town Council decide to rectify the grave deficiencies in fire-fighting equipment by the purchase of a new Merryweather fire engine with a 100 foot turntable ladder.
13 - In his budget the Lieutenant-Governor highlights the heavy expenditure yet to be faced in connection with housing, water and drainage. No new taxation was imposed for this year.
24 - Mr S.E. Wilson, M.A., appointed Principal of King William's College in succession to Rev. G.H. Harris, M.A., retired.

JULY
1 - About 400 delegates attended T.G.W.U. Conference which opened at Villa Marina.
1 - Six passengers and a pilot had a miraculous escape from death at Ronaldsway aerodrome when a machine failed to rise in 'no wind' conditions and crashed on a hedge. The de Havilland Dragon was completely destroyed by fire. The aircraft belonged to United Airways which was operating the flight on behalf of The Manx Airway formed by the L.M.S. Railway and the Steam Packet Companies.
12 - Start of Scottish Week saw record arrivals of over 12,000. The 'invasion' is considered to be worth about £100,000 to the Isle of Man.

AUGUST
4 - Douglas Corporation horse trams and buses carried 82,000 passengers - a one day's record.

SEPTEMBER
2 - Glen Wyllin, near Kirk Michael, purchased on behalf of the I.O.M. Railway Company with plans to make the pleasure grounds into 'the Ostend of the Isle of Man.'
12 - After winning the Junior M.G.P., F. L. Frith comes second to Dr J. K. Swanson in the Senior race, both riding Nortons.
19 - Island swept by fierce hurricane. For the first time in 30 years the steamer for Liverpool was forced back into harbour after short battle with mountainous seas.

OCTOBER
16 - Fort Anne Hotel sold by public auction on instructions from Receiver for Debenture Holders. Purchased by Manx Hotels Limited for £26,500.
26 - On a flight from Liverpool to Blackpool, and on its way to Ronaldsway, a Railway Air Services aircraft crashed at Bleasdale Moor, near Garstang. The only passenger, 24-year old Mr Ronald Swales from Port Erin, and the pilot were both killed.

NOVEMBER
16 - Mr D. W. Kerruish appointed first veterinary inspector to Manx Government.

THE GREAT STOPPAGE: A REVIEW

The Island is still recovering from the shock of enduring the most complete, and still scarcely believable, shut-down in its history. Fortunately, it does not appear to have damaged the summer season and to that extent the divisions and wounds, it is hoped, will soon heal. It is salutary, however, to review the sequence of events that for two full days at the start of June saw the Island firmly under the control of the strikers of the Transport and General Workers' Union, with the Government apparently impotent.

It will be recalled that in February the local branch of the T.G.W.U. put in a claim to the Isle of Man Employers' Federation that a week's pay for a general unskilled worker should rise from 40 shillings for a 49½hour week to 48 shillings for a 48 hour week. The atmosphere was undoubtedly highly charged, 600 men on winter relief schemes guaranteed that. The response of the Employers' Federation was voiced by a spokesman who said, "We know of no grounds to justify an application for an increase." Matters were made worse in March when the Federation flatly refused to take the dispute to arbitration by the Deemsters, as suggested by the Union. The declaration of record dividends by the Steam Packet and Railway Companies also contributed to a hardening of attitudes.

There seemed to be some hope of progress in April when the Federation convened a special meeting to consider the Union's request. However, the counter-offer of a two shilling a week rise was immediately declined. In May, the situation deteriorated rapidly and the Union announced that it would no longer deal with the Federation as a whole, but would embark on sectional agreements. At the end of the month the refusal of Douglas Town Council to discuss any form of settlement was seen as the last straw, and the immediate arrival of Mr Pugh, a T.G.W.U. area organiser armed with plenary powers by Mr Ernest Bevin, the General Secretary of the Union, may be seen as the essential ingredient in the local branch to initiate strike action.

On Saturday, 1st June, a public meeting was called by the Union. It was held in Salisbury Hall at the corner of Fort Street and Victoria Street, Douglas, and it was not only packed but the street outside was jammed also. At the meeting, at 9 p.m., the strike resolution was passed unanimously. The Union members dispersed to their homes, while the Union leaders settled down to work. By Sunday morning a Strike Committee had been formed and 30 pickets selected and given their instructions. To allay public concerns arrangements were made to ensure that electricity supplies to the hospitals and maternity home were maintained, while measures were taken to ensure that the tram horses were fed.

By this time the gravity of the situation was becoming more fully realised than before, and on Monday morning the whole of Douglas was brought to a standstill. The Electricity and Gas undertakings ceased working; the 'buses were kept in their garages; the boats were greeted by hundreds of strikers and the passengers forced to carry their own luggage. Everywhere in Douglas crowds of men picketed firms, closed warehouses, blocked roads and even the swing bridge was put out of action. Charabancs were filled with men and sent to other parts of the Island to ensure the strike was enforced. The Constabulary, acting under strict orders, behaved with great tact and discretion and, as the strikers marched through the streets of Douglas, they ensured that little or no hooliganism happened. The few strikers who were more vocal were hauled off to the Strike Headquarters where they were kept virtual prisoners. At night the cinemas were closed and those who relied on electric lighting had to resort to candles.

With the Island firmly in the grip of the strikers, the Government Secretary, Mr Bertram Sergeaunt, initiated a series of meetings to try and resolve the bitter situation between the two sides. Meetings were held on Monday evening, Tuesday morning and afternoon. It was during the afternoon that the *Mona's Isle* sailed into Douglas bearing Mr George Brown, editor the *Isle of Man Weekly Times*. His paper had criticised the strikers for threatening lives at Noble's Hospital. Because of this, several hundred strikers on Victoria Pier pushed aside the two policemen on duty and advanced on the boat hurling abuse at Mr Brown. Happily, any serious developments were prevented by one of the strike leaders, Mr John Kelly, who persuaded the men to disperse peacefully. Mr Brown very sensibly took police advice, remained on board and returned to Liverpool where, in most people's view, he did little to help the problem by demanding that troops and extra police be sent to restore the authority of the Manx Government. Very fortunately, wiser heads prevailed.

Tuesday evening saw yet another meeting, and this time it was a decisive one. It lasted from 8 to 11 p.m. and as time went on more and more people congregated in Victoria Street and up Prospect Hill as rumours swept the town. Finally, on this dramatic summer evening, Mr Pugh emerged to announce that the strike was over and a settlement agreed. The basic wage was to be raised to 46 shillings for a 48 hour week in summer, and 44 shillings for a 46 hour week in winter. The roar of approval that went up was heard all over the town. The strike leaders were cheered repeatedly, the lights came on again, while torches were produced and thousands marched along the Promenade and back through Strand Street to celebrate the success of those two astonishing days. The Great Stoppage was ended, and clearly the Island's political and industrial pattern had been changed for ever.

The question now being asked is: What can be done to ensure that the Island should never again be left in such a vulnerable state, and brought to a standstill by any section of the community? This is, of course, a matter for Tynwald. Within a month a 'Strike' resolution has been passed which will aim to facilitate the peaceful settlement of trade disputes by setting up conciliation machinery, which will penalise intimidation, and which will confer on the Governor powers to meet any emergency which may arise and threatens essential services. It will be interesting to see how long it takes this resolution to be translated into legislation. Meanwhile, it is a matter of regret to many that Councillor Alfred Teare, M.H.K., the indefatigable secretary of the local branch of the T.G.W.U. has resigned his position as a result of ill-health. No doubt he has been under tremendous strain and his many supporters will wish him well.

THIS HOLIDAY ISLAND

Three years ago a mood of gloom and depression pervaded the Island. Today, pessimism has been replaced by bright optimism. The arrival figures for this season show that for the third successive year well over half a million visitors have landed on our shores. August Bank Holiday week-ends see the Steam Packet boats working non-stop, and it has been necessary to open the Villa Marina at nights for sleeping space. Such is the crush of people in Douglas that they effectively stop all vehicular traffic and a new term - jay walking - has made its appearance. Undoubtedly, it shows that the Island is geared to what the holidaymakers want, many coming back year after year. Our natural beauties are well documented, as are our sandy shores, our bays and headlands, our heather-clad mountains and the fresh and invigorating air. But for many it is the wide variety of places to visit and the entertainment provided to suit all tastes that attract the greatest fascination.

Shops in Douglas keep open as long as they please; the hotels are open until 11 p.m. and only on Sundays are there some irksome restrictions. Sunny days see the beaches crammed with those wishing to sun themselves or have a bracing dip in the sea. Many are those who end up with sun-burn and peeling skin. Others make use of the ample sporting facilities provided for tennis, golf etc. Then it is time to return to the hotels and boarding-houses for the meal awaiting them. In the evenings there is a wide variety of entertainments to look forward to. Fancy an evening at the pictures? There are cinemas throughout the Island with Douglas providing five to choose from, all showing the latest releases and the most up-to-date talkies. Such has been their popularity that the Grand Theatre in Victoria Street has this year been completely modernised and renamed the Regal Cinema. It joins the Strand, Picture House, Royalty and Crescent cinemas - all providing two changes per week with two shows a night. Admission charges range from 6d to 2 shillings.

If live entertainment is preferred, then what a tremendous selection is on offer. Florrie Forde still packs them in at the Derby Castle, and Sandy Powell at the Onchan Head Pavilion. Other favourites are Harry Lauder, Will Hay and Naughton and Gold. Theatre prices are modest ranging from 6d to 4s. 6d., depending on your pocket. Excellent souvenir programmes cost just one penny. Then there are minstrels and variety troupes performing on Douglas Head and the Crescent Pavilion. But it is dancing that draws the biggest crowds with the floors of the Villa Marina, Palace and Derby Castle packed with girating couples. For 1s 6d they can dance to the most famous and popular orchestras and bands in the British Isles. Decorum is maintained by the Master of Ceremonies who, with white gloves, holds sway and the dancers, in obedience to his commands, gracefully circle the floor in the modern dances such as the slow fox trot

and the quickstep. While this is going on the horse trams are gaily trotting along the promenade ready to return those who are weary back to their hotels.

Of course it is not only Douglas which provides the holidaymakers with what they want. All the towns and villages join in the great enterprise and attract their own clientele. Cheap travel on the steam railway means that no fares are more than three shillings return. There is also available two-day tickets for a similar amount giving unlimited travel, while for an extra half a crown you can have the freedom of the buses for the same period. This means that places like Ramsey, Peel, Castletown, Port Erin and Port St Mary have a daily influx of visitors. The Manx Electric Railway offers 5 shilling 'rover' tickets for two days of travel on its 50 miles (i.e. both sides of the track!) of panoramic beauty including a trip on the Snaefell Mountain Railway. They bring visitors to the many glens including Groudle where a ride on the little steam railway to view the sea lions is a great favourite. Then there are the delights of Laxey Glen Gardens where there is dancing and swings and hobby horses free! On to Ramsey for the Mooragh Park, the Pool and Ballroom.

An attractive alternative to travelling by rail is to enjoy a ride on the charabancs whose proprietors are in fierce competition. The modern charabancs now have hard tops in place of the folding roofs. Some now boast of being luxury coaches and, with more seats available, can keep the prices down. The dearest motor-coach trip is the full-day tour of the Island with stays at Ramsey, Peel (usually for a lunch break), Port Erin and Rushen Abbey. The coach drivers ensure that their customers are back in Douglas by 6 o'clock for the evening meal. But the charabancs have much more to offer with shorter trips to such favourites as Glen Helen, Glen Maye, Glen

The Market Place, Ramsey is a convenient stopping place for charabancs making the 'Round the Island' tour. *(Mannin Collections)*

Opened in 1890, the popular Glen Wyllin Pleasure Grounds have been bought by the Isle of Man Railway. It is planned to construct a lake for motor-boats at the seaward end of the glen.

Wyllin and Bradda Glen - all geared to meet the needs of their visitors. Also popular are the trips to the Point of Ayre and The Sound - there are few places the chara-bancs miss out! On Sunday mornings they join in the great trek to Braddan for the open-air service which shows that our visitors are not just concerned with 'the pleasures of the flesh' but have other priorities.

Thus it can be seen that the Island makes the most of its opportunities and half a million visitors a year means that the happy holiday spirit is joined by an air of prosperity. There is talk that what is needed to make our satisfaction complete would be to have our own radio station to publicise our attractions into other people's homes. The idea was advanced some time ago and it is rumoured that a possible M.H.K. candidate, Mr T. H. L. Cowin, intends to raise the matter at the next election. Who knows? It could lead to a million visitors a year! Perhaps a last observation on another successful season arises from a glance at the adverts now appearing in our newspapers. How about a three-week cruise in the Mediterranean on the White Star liner *Homeric* for 32 guineas. Or a more economic 13 days on the Cunarder *Lancastria* for 13 guineas. There could well be more than a few Manx businessmen and women among them. Others will be content for a short trip away, perhaps, or just put their feet up, content that the rents and rates have been paid now 'the summer day is over, and its busy cares have flown.'

TYNWALD SAYS 'NO' TO NATIONAL AERODROME

Despite protracted negotiations concerning the possibility of a government-owned aerodrome, Tynwald has been unable to agree to such a scheme. The matter has now been dropped. A government committee had sought advice from Sir Alan Cobham and a top Air Ministry official about a site, and it had been agreed, as far back as 1933, that the best would be one to the south-west of Castletown between Red Gap and Scarlett. Other sites considered were at the Strang on the outskirts of Douglas, Ballagilley Farm skirting Castletown Bay, and Ronaldsway Farm whose large field, as though by a process of natural selection, is already being used by air services. However, it was felt that the drainage problems of the area were insuperable and that it would be impossible to provide the required minimum take-off distances in various wind directions.

Both branches of Tynwald met on 22nd March to determine the future development of a national aerodrome. Advocate Mr Gordon Bell represented Olley Air Services Ltd., which now controlled Blackpool and West Coast Air Services Ltd., and which had plans to develop Ronaldsway, confident of overcoming the drainage problems. During the debate it was obvious that agreement could not be reached on the site of a national aerodrome; others felt that what was already being planned at Ronaldsway, and also at Close Lake in the north of the Island, was sufficient to meet the Island's needs without involving Government funds; others were content to adopt a 'wait and see' attitude. While the Legislative Council voted in favour of the motion for a national aerodrome, the House of Keys were divided 15 to 9 against the idea. Thus the motion fell.

NEW METHODIST CHURCH FOR PULROSE

On 14th November the new Pulrose Methodist dual-purpose church and hall was opened by Mr. T. Clucas M.H.K. on a site near the proposed shopping area. The building of the church was undertaken by Mr. T. W. Gelling of Crosby and is to the design of Mr. H. E. Teare. A new feature for such buildings is the cinematographic projection room. The opening of the new church comes at a significant time in the history of Methodism. It will be recalled that the Imperial Parliament passed the Methodist Church Union Act in 1929, enabling the three main branches of the Methodist Church - Wesleyan, Primitive and United - to come together.

From the outset Wesleyan Methodism was strong in the Isle of Man spurred on by John Wesley himself who visited the Island in 1777 and 1781. The Primitive Methodists, often referred to as 'The Ranters,' broke away in 1808 and rapidly strengthened, perhaps aided by an influx of miners before 1850. By then the Wesleyans had 55 chapels throughout the Island with 7,400 members, while the Primitives had 24 chapels and 5,600 members. The total membership was higher than that of all other denominations put together. The United Methodist Church was formed by the uniting of smaller breakaway groups including the Methodist New Connection, the only one to have had a presence on the Island with small numbers in Douglas, Ramsey and Laxey. The only premises the Methodist New Connection had built on the Island was the chapel in Derby Road, Douglas, built in 1889. By 1914 it had closed and was taken over by St. Thomas's Church as their church hall. Pulrose church is within the Douglas Victoria Circuit (the former Wesleyan Circuit), but will the Island see changes to churches and circuits arising from Union now beginning to be seen elsewhere?

HERE IS THE NEWS : 1936
NEW PIER NAMED AFTER KING EDWARD VIII

During the past six years Douglas harbour has undergone a major transformation as work progressed on the construction of a new pier. It has seen the disappearance of the Red Pier which has served the port since 1801 but, being tidal, its use has been limited and it has played little part in handling the great summer influx of visitors. We have this report:

On 24th May, Sir John Simon, the Home Secretary, paid a flying visit to the Island for the opening ceremony of the new pier. Following the death of King George V in January, the Harbour Commissioners approached the Home Secretary and sought permission to name the pier after the new King. It was only days before Sir John's visit that His Majesty had graciously consented to the pier being named the King Edward the Eighth Pier. When Sir John made this announcement by loud speakers from the roof of the pier office, a great cheer went up from the thousands who had assembled for the occasion. The cermony concluded with Sir John stepping down on to the pier and cutting the blue ribbon with a pair of silver scissors.

Great tribute was paid to the Harbour Commissioners and their staff, led by Harbour Engineer, Mr J. C. Brown. Often working in difficult conditions during the past six years, the construction was completed ahead of schedule and at a cost of about £212,000, which is considerably less than the original estimate. The new pier is both wider and longer than the old pier and provides two additional deep water berths. This will relieve the pressure on the Victoria Pier where it has often been necessary to berth ships side by side, an inconvenient arrangement.

The new pier, and its viaduct, will ease the handling of 1,250,000 passengers each summer, when peak week-ends see some 65,000 departures and arrivals - more than the entire population of the Isle of Man! Earlier in the year the Isle of Man Steam Packet Company announced that an order has been placed for two oil-fired turbine-driven steamers with a speed of 21 knots and able to carry 1,800 passengers. They are being built by the Vickers Armstrong Shipyards in Barrow at a cost of over £300,000, and are designed for both summer and winter service. They are due to be launched at the end of the year and will enter service next season. The twin vessels are to be named *Fenella* and *Tynwald*.

FIVE LOST IN THE MERSEY

The year began with the tragic news that five Manxmen had lost their lives when the coastal steamer *Bradda*, a 250-ton vessel owned by Messrs J. B. Kee Ltd, of Ramsey, foundered near Formby Point in the River Mersey estuary during a heavy storm when winds reached 90 miles an hour. The vessel carried a crew of six, and the sole survivor was Samuel Edward Ball, able seaman, of 25, South Promenade, Ramsey. It was the Island's worst peace-time sea disaster since the loss of the *Ellan Vannin* in 1909.

STRIKES TO BE OUTLAWED

In February, Tynwald gave approval to three Bills introduced by the Lieutenant-Governor Sir Montagu Butler. Their aim is to outlaw strike action, such as last year's General Strike which paralysed the Island for 40 hours. The Emergency Powers Bill, The Trades Disputes Bill and The Trades Disputes (Regulation) Bill were all strongly resisted by the Labour Party M.H.K.s, but to no avail. The new legislation enables conciliatory machinery to be set up to settle disputes peacefully, to penalise intimidation, and to confer on the Lieutenant-Governor emergency powers to deal with any threat to public services.

An aerial view of Douglas harbour taken last year and showing, on the left, work on constructing the new pier at an advanced stage. The Harbour Board's project will provide berths to relieve congestion on the Victoria Pier.

BEAUTY QUEEN CHOSEN

In April Miss Harriet Hart of Onchan was acclaimed the Island's Beauty Queen by 3,000 people at the Manx Beauty Contest Final held in the Villa Marina, and organised by the *Isle of Man Examiner*. Her prize included a screen test at Ealing Studios. She was chosen from among 175 girls who entered the competition. Contestants had to send in their photographs for publication, giving the *Examiner* a big circulation boost.

DEATH OF MR AMBROSE QUALTROUGH, M.H.K.

In May 'Father of the House of Keys,' Mr Ambrose Qualtrough, died at his home in Strand Street, Port Erin, at the age of 66. During his long service in the Keys, Mr Qualtrough was a leading reformist and showed great force of character. This January he was involved in fisticuffs in the Keys' smokeroom during an altercation with Mr W.C. Craine (Labour, South Douglas). They pummelled away at each other with their fists, and there was actual bloodshed before Detective-Sergeant Kneen intervened and pulled them apart. While Mr Craine said he was only acting in self-defence, Mr Qualtrough made no comment.

INTERNATIONAL BICYCLE T.T.

On Thursday of T.T. Week the first Manx International T.T. Bicycle Race was staged over one lap of the T.T. Course. The race was open to amateurs and was organised by the Manx Viking Wheelers who have for the past few years organised such a race for local riders. The event was won by Charles Holland of the Midland C. and A.C. in the record time of 1hr 42mins 57secs, an average speed of about 22 m.p.h. Of the 80 riders who started there were 48 finishers. The Manx International is expected to become one of Britain's top amateur road races.

Also held on the Thursday was the Lightweight T.T., held over from the previous day because of bad weather. Winner was A. R. Foster (New Imperial) followed by Tyrrell Smith (Excelsior) and A. Geiss (D.K.W.) in third place. Freddie Frith (Norton) won the Junior race and Jimmy Guthrie (Norton) scored a brilliant Senior win ahead of his adversary of last year, Stanley Woods, now riding for Velocette. Frith came in third.

NAZI SYMPATHISERS ON ISLAND.

In July a visit of 920 tourists was made when the 17,000 ton motor liner *Monte Pastoral* of the Hamburg-South America line anchored in Douglas Bay. Among those who came ashore was a party of German storm troopers wearing swastikas on their uniforms. They marched along the sea front and laid a wreath on the War Memorial, after which they gave Nazi salutes. They also visited the graves of German prisoners who died at Knockaloe in the Great War.

AGRICULTURAL SHOW WASHED OUT

The Isle of Man Agricultural Society's Annual Show held in August was a wash-out this year. Torrential rain fell all day, turning the showfield into a quagmire and reducing attendance. Takings were the lowest on record, at only £10, leaving the Society in debt by more than £1,000. But officials say the show will carry on.

KING'S SHOCK ABDICATION

The British constitutional crisis, about which the general public has been kept in the dark because of a black-out of information in the British press, has been finally resolved. His Majesty made the shock announcement on the wireless, that he is unable to carry on as King of Britain and the Empire without the woman he loves by his side. The crisis arose because of the King's desire to marry Mrs Wallis Simpson, a twice-divorced American lady whose remote ancestors, it is claimed, were rulers of the Isle of Man. Only six months ago the new Douglas pier was named after King Edward. This means the Isle of Man is the only place to have a public work project named after the uncrowned King.

His successor is to be his brother Albert ('Bertie'), Duke of York, whose accession has already been proclaimed from Tynwald Hill in accordance with tradition. In atrocious weather, the members of the Legislature and Government officials travelled to St John's for the proclamation and swore allegiance to His Majesty the King and Lord of Mann, George V1. The Coronation of King George and Queen Elizabeth will take place next May on the day already chosen. We wish them well.

An aerial view of Ronaldsway showing the extent of the new airport. Passenger facilities are found behind the row of farm workers' cottages next to The Crescent, Derbyhaven. On the right, the Balthane road can be seen passing between the farm buildings of Ronaldsway Farm.

(Alan Daugherty Collection)

THE SPECTRE OF UNEMPLOYMENT

While the Island has enjoyed another successful summer season, with plenty of work for all, the spectre of winter unemployment still haunts hundreds of young and not so young men, many with families to support. Tynwald's way of relieving the situation is by way of the Winter Works Schemes which have, for example, resulted in many improvements to the Island's road structure. Over a thousand jobs are created which has brought relief to the Boards of Guardians in their charitable work. But for every man found work, another has to suffer the indignity of relying on money doled out to lessen the hardships. Come the winter months, a familar sight in the towns are groups of men congregating on street corners or in doorways. The situation is not helped by the recessionary years of the early 'thirties which beyond our shores, some are calling the Great Depression.

One attempt to solve the situation has been the setting up of committees throughout the Island to encourage the acquisition of new skills such as how to be cooks and waiters. Recreational facilities have also been provided to keep young men off the streets.

Provision of part-time work, sometimes in collaboration with local authorities, includes the making of footpaths. One result of this has been the creation of the delightful Summer Hill Glen from Governor's Bridge to the old Burnt Mill Hill. Such services are being operated by The Young Men's Development Association formed in 1933 as a successor to the Work for the Workless Committee. Tynwald plays its part by providing grants of three quarters of a wage up to nine shillings a week.

A Social Services Club operates in Castle Street, Douglas. It provides facilities for reading, lectures, gymnastics and for the teaching of carpentry, boot repairing and other skills. Appeals are made to businessmen, and people with resources to shop locally and do more work on their homes in the winter rather than wait until the spring. Any odd job is a welcome alternative to abandoning a generation to the streets. If the international situation continues to worsen with the rise of Fascism and Nazism, perhaps Britain's reluctant rearmament might provide the job opportunities the young men need.

1936 NEWS IN BRIEF

JANUARY

14 - Balance sheet of the Isle of Man Bank shows over £3,000,000 held in accounts. Record dividend of 16½ per cent paid.

21 - News of the death of His Majesty King George V broadcast to the world.

22 - Death of Mr Frank Edmundson, manager and engineer to the Manx Electric Railway for 30 years.

26 - Heavy floods in north of Island. Sulby and Glen Auldyn rivers overflowed their banks. Houses and farms in Sulby and Lezayre district were flooded and railway line under water for considerable distance.

FEBRUARY

4 - Rent Restriction Act extended by Tynwald until May, 1938.

21 - Steam Packet Company turn-over exceeds £500,000 for the first time though net profit for the year shows a decrease.

MARCH

2 - Disclosed that the Bishop's income, nominally supposed to be £2,000 a year, has fallen to £1,400. Church assembly empowered to augment his stipend.

27 - Lieutenant-Governor opened new extension to the Manx Museum. The new additions consist of the A. W. Moore Library, and new Art Gallery, together with offices for various officials. The extension is built at the rear of the Museum and links the wings of the original building.

APRIL

24 - Port St Mary took charge of new lifeboat, the *Sir Heath Harrison*

29 - Cleveland Medal won by Mr Harry Comish who is the first tenor to achieve this.

30 - Mr J. D. Qualtrough's Bill for registration and police inspection of clubs where intoxicating liquor is supplied to members and guests, passed by the Keys.

MAY

10 - Howstrake Road, from Harbour Road, Onchan to Baldromma crossing, reconstructed and widened at a cost of £21,000 and renamed King Edward Road.

28 - R.A.C. International Car Race moved from the streets of Douglas to the outskirts of the town, starting at the Grandstand. The 200-mile race was won by R. J. B. Seaman driving a ten-year-old Delage, with Prince Birabongse of Siam in an E.R.A. coming second.

31 - London - Isle of Man Air Race won by 19-year-old Alex Henshaw in a DH 85 Leopard Moth

JUNE

2 - Whit Monday. First Manx Air Derby held using the course set out in 1932. 15 entries were handicapped for three laps covering 156 miles. First away was R.F. Hall in a 40 h.p. Hillson Praga which completed the course without being caught by the faster machines.

3 - Port St Mary Municipal Golf Links opened.

3 - Onchan Village Commissioners win battle to protect their boundaries against Douglas and take possession of large tract of land from the parish, stretching from Governor's Bridge and Signpost Corner and then straight across to Glenbower, Little Mill.

9 - Annual Budget presented showing a small surplus over the year. No changes in taxation proposed, except for increase of 2d a pound on tea, bringing it up to English level.

16 - Ramsey Commissioners approve housing scheme building 38 houses on the Brookhill Estate at a cost of £21,000.

JULY

22 - Police 'drive' to rid Island of games of gambling nature. Several owners of such machines charged with using their premises as common gaming houses and fines ranging from £2 to £25 imposed.

AUGUST

3 - Former Bank Holiday record smashed when nearly 50,000 holiday-makers were landed on the Island by ships and 'planes.

26 - Miss C. M. Griffiths of Cambridge appointed woman organiser of physical education for schools on the Island.

27 - Ballacregga Reservoir, constructed by the Laxey Village Commissioners, officially opened by the Lieut-Governor.

SEPTEMBER

11 - Austin Munks becomes first rider in the Manx Grand Prix to complete 'the double' by winning the Junior and Senior races. Dennis Parkinson won the Lightweight event.

OCTOBER

1 - Major J. W. Young, O.B.E., commenced duty as Chief Constable succeeding Lt Colonel Madoc who retired after 25 years' service.

29 - Douglas Corporation's new extensions and turbo-alternator plant at Pulrose, costing £45,000, opened by Lieut-Governor.

DECEMBER

10 - Vigorous opposition to Church Bill at Diocesan Conference on proposal to remove Archdeaconry from Andreas.

11 - King Edward VIII announces his abdication of the throne.

12 - George VI proclaimed King and Lord of Mann from Tynwald Hill.

CENTENARY OF THE RECHABITES

Centenary celebrations on the Isle of Man by Manx Rechabites raise intriguing questions about the future: Is the era of Tents, Lodges and Temples - such a feature of Friendly Societies like the Rechabites - slowly passing? Is it possible that there will be no need soon for sashed members of Societies with exotic names to parade through Douglas and other urban communities to the music of pipes and fifes?

They have done it for generations to focus public attention on the need to join a society which helps them in times of adversity. Some societies, like the Benevolent Society of Andreas (formed in 1812) are parish-based. Most provide aid in times of sickness and death. Ballaugh's 200-year-old Fire and Cow fund, however, provides aid for parishioners who are financially crippled by fire or the loss of an only cow.

By far the largest memberships during the last 100 years have been recruited by Manx branches of much bigger English societies such as the Rechabites, the Independent Order of OddFellows, the Royal Antedeluvian Order of Buffaloes (otherwise known as "The Buffs") and the Foresters. They became such an integral part of the Manx community last century that some built public halls. The red-bricked Rechabite Hall and the Odd-Fellows Hall (later a theatre and then Douglas Court House) are still important features of Douglas architecture.

The Rechabites pay benefits for sickness and death and help the poor to save for their old age with endowment policies. Since 1920, however, the growing strength of the Government-aided Manx National Insurance Society which provides sickness, disablement and maternity benefits, including free treatment by doctors, suggests that this will gradually take over from the societies. Significantly, the latter are providing expertise for the new society. In 1926, when the Douglas branches of the Friendly Societies jointly nominated one of their members, Robert Corlett, as a director, they said they did so because they were anxious to ensure that Tynwald's Health Insurance Act was worked efficiently.

The centenary of Manx Rechabitism was marked on 21st March by the issue of a commemorative medal and a parade in Douglas by 750 members. Carrying banners and wands, they marched to the Villa Marina grounds to hear celebratory addresses by officials.

The Rechabites were started in Salford in August, 1835 as an offshoot to the newly-emerging teetotal movement which had been launched in Preston. Before being accepted as a Rechabite, a prospective member had to sign a declaration of abstinence. A Manxman, James Teare, was associated with the founders of the teetotal movement. He was an active campaigner for much of his life. It is to him, therefore, that we owe the spreading of the word to the Isle of Man and establishment of a flourishing Manx abstinence movement.

The first local Rechabite Tent, known as "Mona Peaceful", was established in Douglas on 25th July, 1836. Others followed - the "Mona Jonadab Tent" at Michael on 28th February, 1837, the "Mona Joshua Tent" at Peel in March-April, 1837 and the "Mona Daniel Tent" at Castletown on 12th April that year.

Eventually there were a dozen Manx Tents. It was believed that the first all-Juvenile Tent in Britain was Manx and it was possible that the first all-female Tent was a Manx one too. Not all succeeded. Failures included one at Dalby, two at Foxdale and one at Laxey. With a total membership of 1,600, however, the Isle of Man was the biggest single Rechabite District in the British Isles for many years. Gwent and Glamorgan only outstripped it in 1885.

By then Manx Rechabite parades sometimes included three or four bands, including ones from Lancashire and Cheshire. Members wore white sashes suspended from around their necks, and white rosettes. All were obliged, under the threat of a shilling fine, to attend the funeral services of all brethren within two miles of their homes and subsequent interments provided these occurred no more than five miles away.

Many thousands of Manx people still pay small weekly subscriptions to Friendly Societies. There are probably more than 2,600 paid-up Rechabites. As the older generation dies off, however, it seems likely that the Manx National Health Insurance Society will replace the "Friendlies". From its inception in 1920 it has had substantially more contributing members than any Friendly Society, despite the absence of benefits in the first six months and a further six months of reduced benefit rates when reserves were being established. The first annual report in 1921 revealed that 7,880 men and 4,261 women were contributing. Now there are more. This suggests that one day the Health Society will become an integral part of a more ambitious Government welfare service.

(Below) Principal officers of the Isle of Man District of the Independent Order of Rechabites at a recent meeting in the Allan Street Mission Hall, Douglas.

(Frank Cowin Library)

RONALDSWAY WINS AIR MINISTRY APPROVAL

The news at the beginning of the year that developments at Ronaldsway had resulted in the Air Ministry granting an open licence to operate an approved airport must have given Captain Gordon P. Olley great satisfaction. Captain Olley first visited the Island in 1928 and later set up Olley Air Services Ltd, based at Croydon, with the financial support of Sir Hugo Cunliffe-Owen. Charter work resulted in more visits to Ronaldsway and he was so impressed by the progress being made by Blackpool and West Coast Air Services Ltd that he, and Sir Hugo, took steps to take over the company, retaining Captain John Higgins as Chief Pilot. Additional aircraft were provided, making West Coast Air Services stronger and better able to survive in the highly competitive airline business. This was in 1934 and by the end of the year Captain Olley began negotiations to secure the landing rights at Ronaldsway. He set up Isle of Man Air Services Ltd which was to manage the limited facilities at Ronaldsway while controlling the services provided by West Coast Air Services. Captain Olley eagerly awaited Tynwald's decision regarding a national airport, and when it was seen in March, 1935 that there was to be no Government involvement, Isle of Man Air Services was quick to respond.

Almost immediately the much-maligned Ronaldsway became a hive of industry as the great scheme of levelling and draining the 88 acres of two of the sheep-grazing fields got under way. Messrs McKibbin and Kewley of Douglas were awarded the contract and over 50 men were set to work. The stone walls disappeared and the hazard of the mill race across the area was enclosed. The object was to have the work completed for the summer and slight delays were caused by the unearthing of the foundations of ancient dwellings which are believed to belong to a Celtic Iron Age village. Undisturbed burial grounds were also discovered, together with many priceless artefacts such as tools, ornaments and pottery. Manx Museum officials worked closely with the contractors while the finishing touches were put to the area of level green sward.

By the summer, distances from 720 yards to 940 yards in varying directions were available for take-offs and landings, thus meeting the requirements of the Air Ministry. This year has seen the provision of a new and enlarged hangar and workshop of wood and galvanise construction, to which a booking office has been attached. Also a wooden terminal building for passengers has been provided, and Isle of Man Road Services has diverted its Douglas to Castletown route to travel via Derbyhaven with a stop at the new air terminal. For next year the Air Ministry has announced that it is to instal and operate a wireless station for the benefit of aircraft using Ronladsway, Tynwald providing a small contribution towards the cost.

From figures available, it appears that the number of passengers arriving at Ronaldsway during the summer period has grown from 8,000 in 1935 to nearly 12,000 this year. This has been achieved mainly by West Coast and The Manx Airway. The latter is operated by Railway Air Services on behalf of the London Midland and Scottish Railway Company and the Isle of Man Steam Packet Company, which recognises the threat of this new form of transport. Services to the Island are provided from Manchester, Liverpool, Blackpool, Leeds/Bradford, Carlisle, Glasgow and Belfast, while the new Irish airline Aer Lingus Teoranta began a service from Dublin this year. For 1936 West Coast Air Services took delivery of two four-engined DH 86 'Express' airliners capable of carrying 14 passengers. They joined two DH 84 Dragons and one of the new DH 89 Rapides. The latter eight-seater is also used by The Manx Airway. One of these set up a record time of 29 minutes on a flight from Speke to Ronaldsway. However, there is much duplication of services and it is problematical as to how long the situation can be maintained. Prices are highly competitive with the Liverpool return offered at £2.50 by both airlines. This, of course, is much more expensive than travelling by steamer.

Regarding the future, Captain Olley has further secured the interests of Isle of Man Air Services Ltd. Originally he negotiated with Mr A. B. Crookall, M.L.C., the owner of the Ronaldsway estate, and Mr William Faragher, the tenant of Ronaldsway farm. Following the death of Mr Crookall, his interests are now in the hands of trustees headed by accountant Mr J. B. Garside. They have agreed to the extension of the lease of the airfield for another 12 years, fixing the rental to the farmer at £220 per year. There is also an option for increasing the airfield to 150 acres. Landing and passenger fees have also been settled with the proviso that all users of Ronaldsway should be treated the same. It is also stipulated that the grazing rights are retained by the farmer. Sheep are usually put out at night and it has become the custom for traffic and engineering staff to ride out on motor bikes in the morning to round up and move the animals for the day's operations.

It can be seen that the enterprise of Captain Olley has resulted in the Island being provided with a fine modern airport which will play an increasingly important part in the economic life of the Isle of Man. Captain Olley is deserving of much credit.

One of the new de Havilland Rapides seen here at Ronaldsway. It is operated by Railway Air Services on behalf of The Manx Airway, which is jointly funded by the L.M.S. Railway and I.O.M. Steam Packet Companies. (Terry Faragher Collection)

The threat of another Great War looms over Europe. The rise of Adolf Hitler in Nazi Germany is casting a shadow which is reaching out to the Isle of Man. Air raid precautions are being considered and the Government has appointed a National Defence Commission. We have this report.

The five-man Commission led by Deemster Percy Cowley has been to London for talks with the War Office on the Island's role in another war. The Government has also set up an Air Raid Precautions Committee because of concern about bombing raids and the effects of poison gas and incendiary bombs. Hundreds of gas masks are to be stored ready for distribution should the need arise. The police are all trained in dealing with gas attacks and a gas chamber installed at the Drill Hall on Peel Road, Douglas, has been used for training purposes. There are also plans for training air raid wardens. The Government, in an effort to dispel public anxiety, says the Island is unlikely to be a target of military importance. On the other hand, it is believed that negotiations have taken place with the Air Ministry for the establishment of a base on the Island which will form part of the Royal Air Force's great expansion scheme. No details have been made public.

Meanwhile, life on the Island has continued as usual and the vast majority of people have been preoccupied in catering for the 578,000 visitors who arrived during the season. This is the second highest total recorded, only being beaten by the peak summer of 1913. To help cope with the increased traffic, the Steam Packet Company now have in service their two new steamers, the *Tynwald* and *Fenella*.

ISLAND HIT BY BLIZZARDS
The winter weather saw some of the worst on record. In February, a fierce blizzard swept the Island and caused considerable dislocation of transport and communications. Roads in many parts were blocked by drifts up to 15 feet deep, and Ramsey was without electricity for 23 hours. This was followed by severe gales in March and during what was described as a

Occupiers of these houses on the Vollan Crescent, Ramsey, were forced to quit their homes in March after heavy seas had smashed through the promenade wall. (Frank Cowin Library)

'night of terror' the residents on Vollan Crescent, Ramsey were forced to abandon their homes. The households were threatened as huge waves smashed the protective sea wall along the Mooragh Promenade

SHIPS IN DISTRESS
The 9,400 ton cargo liner *Ross* of Newcastle-upon-Tyne went aground on the Calf of Man while bound for Liverpool. She was aground for five hours and women and children were taken off by Port St Mary lifeboat as a precaution. A second steamer to go aground was the *Duke of Lancaster* at the Point of Ayre. She had 400 pas-

The approach to Creg-ny-Baa after the blizzard in February. (Frank Cowin Library)

sengers on board who had to wait for her to be refloated.

SHOCKING ROAD ACCIDENT
In the Island's most shocking road accident ever a mother pushing her pram along the main road at Spring Valley was hit and killed by a car. Mrs Catherine Bridson of The Cooil, Braddan was on her way home after dark. The pram was thrown 30 yards and wrecked, but her 22-month old baby son escaped with minor injuries. The driver of the car, J. K. Clarke of Foxdale, was subsequently sentenced to six month's imprisonment for driving to public danger. In another tragic accident, lifeboatman John Evans, of Port St Mary, was killed, and three others injured, when the boat and carriage ran uncontrolled down the slipway.

EDUCATION REFORMS
Sweeping reforms in the education system of the Island have been announced in a report on the re-organisation of schools adopted by the Education Authority, under its new director, Mr H. L. Fletcher, M.A. The reforms include the raising of the school-leaving age to 15 years without exemption, putting it ahead of England. Two new senior schools are to be built in Douglas and one in Ramsey; and Hanover Street School in Douglas is to be closed. Charges involve a capital expenditure of £80,000 and an annual increase of £7,500 in cost of the education service.

CORONATION DAY

May 12th will be remembered for the enthusiastic celebrations for the Coronation of King George VI and Queen Elizabeth. There was a magnificent display of loyalty throughout the Island and His Excellency the Lieutenant-Governor and Lady Butler made an 80-mile tour and saw displays of pageantry and gay celebrations in the towns and villages. Coronation mugs and medals were presented to all school children, those of Onchan assembling in the grounds of Government House to receive theirs from the hands of Sir Montagu and Lady Butler. At Malew's Coronation Garden Fete a Coronation Baby was chosen. He is the 11-month-old Keith McArd, son of Rushen M.H.K., Mr John McArd.

LAST CAR RACE

The R.A.C. International Car Race this year was won by the popular Prince Birabongse of Siam in his famous yellow and blue E.R.A., named 'Romulus.' During practising Philip Jucker, a company director from Surrey, died when he crashed into a Manx Electric Railway pole at Port Jack, Onchan. Begun in 1933, it has been announced that there are no plans to hold a car racing event next year.

In the T.T., Italian rider Omobono Tenni became the first continental rider to win a T.T. race with his victory in the Lightweight race at record speed riding for Moto Guzzi. Nortons continued their dominance of the bigger classes, though strongly challenged by the Velocettes of Stanley Woods. Junior winner was Jimmy Guthrie who was joined by Freddie Frith in setting up a new record lap of over 85 m.p.h. It was

Sir Montagu and Lady Butler, with German pilots Hans Seidemann and Ernst Gerbrecht, examine the damage done to the wing of Seidemann's Messerschmitt as a result of being hit by a seagull.

Frith who won the Senior race during which he was the first to lap the course at over 90 m.p.h. In August the racing fraternity was saddened to learn of the death of Jimmy Guthrie after crashing on the last bend of the German Grand Prix. This great rider from Scotland won six T.T. Races and upheld Britain's honour with victories in many foreign races.

VICTORY FOR GERMAN PILOT

Great excitement was caused by the entry of two Messershmitt Bf 108s in this year's air races. Flown by Major Seidemann and Ernst Gerbrecht, the sports monoplanes were painted dark blue and bore the German swastika on the tail fins. There were 20 starters for the London - Isle of Man Air Race for which local brewery boss, Mr J. M. Cubbon had donated a magnificent Challenge Cup. As the machines approached Maughold Head for the

turn to the finishing line across Douglas Bay, utter chaos was caused by thick mist. Some pilots turned back to Blackpool while others chose to land in fields in the north of the Island. Alex Henshaw, last year's winner, elected to fly down the west coast of the Island. Only five aircraft were seen to cross Douglas Bay. Amazingly, they didn't include Major Seidemann who was the first to land at Ronaldsway. When informed he had missed the finishing line he immediately took off again and flew to Douglas. As a result, the stewards had to deal with protests, but Major Seidemann was declared the winner as he was the only competitor to have been recorded at Maughold Head! The major declared, "It is better to race in peace than in war."

The Manx Air Derby was held on Whit Monday and huge crowds assembled at Ronaldsway to see if

The International Bicycle T.T., first held last year, is already proving a popular event. Here riders sweep around Quarterbridge, while in the background, the new café and shop are taking shape.

(Frank Cowin Library)

the Germans could claim another victory. In the event they completed the race second and third behind one of the first away, S.T. Lowe in one of the little Comper Swifts. Alex Henshaw in one of the new Percival Mew Gulls was the fastest over the three laps at 213 m.p.h. and finished close behind the Messerschmitts.

POLICE CARS INTRODUCED

The Manx Constabulary has been equipped with two motor cars for the first time. One is stationed in Douglas on standby to deal with emergencies. The second one is being used to maintain patrols around the Island. Up to now Manx policemen have gone about their duties either on foot or by bicycle, or sometimes using public transport. As the number of cars on Manx roads increases so does the number of accidents. Last year 11 people were killed in road accidents and 342 were injured.

AIR SERVICES AMALGAMATE

As the summer progressed, it became obvious at Ronaldsway that the free-for-all provision of air services was providing too many seats for too few passengers. The economic depression is still having its effect and the number of passengers handled by West Coast and the Manx Airway has shown a decrease compared with last year. It has been revealed that the latter was operating at a loss. However, common sense has prevailed and negotiations between the two companies resulted in the announcement at the end of August that all scheduled services will in future be a joint venture under the name of Isle of Man Air Services. The new set-up is to be financed with a total capital of £75,000, provided equally by Olley Air Services Ltd, the Steam Packet Company and the L.M.S. Railway Company. The first chairman is to be Captain Gordon Olley. All services will be maintained as hitherto and there will be a daily I.O.M./Blackpool/Liverpool/Manchester service throughout the coming winter. There will also be an additional mail route to Liverpool. It has also been announced that all services using Hall Caine Airport, in use for the past three years, are to be terminated, though Scottish Airways will continue the Glasgow service to Ronaldsway.

GOVERNOR RESIGNS

The news in March that Sir Montagu Butler had decided to relinquish Governorship of the Island was received with considerable regret. He has proved to be one of the most personally popular Lieutenant-Governors the Island has ever had. With still three years of his term to go, Sir Montagu has accepted an invitation to become Master of Pembroke College, Cambridge.

Sir Montagu's successor is Vice-Admiral the Hon. William Spencer Leveson-Gower, C.B., D.S.O., R.N. (Retd). He is a descendant of the Duke of Sutherland and the Marquises of Stafford. His wife is Lady Margaret Rose Leveson-Gower (nee Bowes-Lyon) who is the younger sister of Her Majesty Queen Elizabeth. The new Lieutenant-Governor arrived on 1st October and was sworn in at Castle Rushen the following day.

DEATH OF MR SPEAKER

Finally, the whole Island has been saddened by the news of the sudden death of Sir Frederick Clucas, C.B.E., J.P., M.A., Speaker of the House of Keys. He passed away in Noble's Hospital on 11th November. Lady Clucas collapsed on receiving the news and died six hours after her husband. The Speaker, who held this high office since 1919, had his knighthood conferred upon him in the Coronation Honours List earlier this year. Sir Frederick brought a quiet dignity to his office and was prominent in business affairs, while he and Lady Clucas played their part in the social life of the Island.

The new Speaker of the House of Keys is to be Mr J. D. Qualtrough who has been the member for Castletown since 1919. He holds strong views on such matters as temperance, betting and the preservation of Sundays.

Sir Frederick Clucas, C.B.E., Speaker of the House of Keys, who died suddenly in December

---

1937 NEWS IN BRIEF

JANUARY

14 - Mrs Catherine Quinney, the Island's only centenarian, died at Castletown. She was born on 24th December, 1836.

FEBRUARY

18 - Benefactor presents the Calf of Man to the National Trust

MARCH

24 - Sir Montagu Butler announces his intention to relinquish Governorship of the Island.

APRIL

22 - Most important road scheme ever carried out by Douglas Town Council - widening and reconstruction of Peel Road from Circular Road to Quarterbridge at a cost of £40,000 - completed and opened by Lieut-Governor.

MAY

9 - Warm-hearted welcome for a party of Homecomers when they landed on Victoria Pier from the liner *Athenia*.

12 - Coronation of King George V1 and Queen Elizabeth.

JUNE

1 - Employers' Federation and the T.G.W.U. reach agreement on summer wages which are to rise from 46s to 50s for men working in Douglas and Onchan for a 48 hour week. Wages rise to 48s a week in other districts. Slightly lower rates will apply to the winter months.

15 - Great effort to revive Manx fishing industry resulted in launching and christening of four boats being put into commission by IOM Fisheries Ltd, built by 75% Government loan.

JULY

8 - Reconstructed bridge over Douglas Harbour, replacing old Stone Bridge, opened by Mayor of Douglas, Alderman T. W. Cain, J.P.

14 - Damages of £11,500 - the highest ever on the Island - awarded to Mr and Mrs W. E. Teare of Ballagarraghyn, German. They were both severely injured when a Manx Airway aircraft crashed on take-off at Ronaldsway two years ago.

24 - Radio beacon inaugurated on Victoria Pier.

24 - Barrovian Hall at King William's College opened by old scholar Sir William Bragg, O.M., K.B.E., D.S.O.

AUGUST

24 - Extensions to Ramsey Cottage Hospital opened by His Excellency.

SEPTEMBER

9 - Maurice Cann completes brilliant 'double' in the Manx Grand Prix. Lightweight race was won by Dennis Parkinson for the second successive year.

OCTOBER

19 - Divorce Bill given second reading in the House of Keys.

31 - Well Road Methodist Church, Douglas, celebrates centenary.

NOVEMBER

1 - General Committee of Jane Crookall Maternity Home decide to build and equip a modern Home.

11 - Death of Sir Frederick Clucas, C.B.E., J.P., M.A., Speaker of the House of Keys.

CORONATION
CELEBRATIONS

Douglas children, too young to attend school, are seen here receiving their Coronation mugs and medals at the Town Hall.
(Frank Cowin Library)

Ramsey also staged a successful carnival, the centre-piece of the procession being the Coronation 'coach' seen here in Parliament Street.
(R. and L. Kelly Collection)

Villages and parishes also joined in the celebrations with children of Malew being given a special treat at Silverdale. Note the boy in the foreground wearing his Coronation medal.
(Frank Cowin Library)

CALF OF MAN PRESENTED TO NATIONAL TRUST

After being in private hands for many years, the Calf of Man has been placed in the care of the National Trust. In 1931 the Calf was purchased by Mr J. A. Popplewell, a wealthy Yorkshireman and head of a firm of multiple grocers in Leeds. He bought it from another Yorkshireman, mill owner Mr Samuel Haig. He had owned it for 20 years and spent nearly eight months a year there. At the time it was reported the population was 49 and it supported a thriving farm with much of the island being grazed by sheep and cattle. In 1930, when the Calf of Man was put up for sale, a group of patriotic Manxmen did their best to persuade Tynwald to buy it for the nation, but a Tynwald committee reported against the proposal. Instead, Mr Popplewell acquired it for £4,000 and an annual rate bill of £15 6s 1d - not bad at all for some 600 acres and a farmhouse and outbuildings still in good repair!.

Earlier this year it was announced that an anonymous benefactor had presented the island to the National Trust for Places of Historic Interest and Natural Beauty. It was subsequently disclosed that the donor was Mr F. J. Dickens of Lancashire - said to be a descendant of Charles Dickens who had Manx connections. Subject to the approval of Tynwald, the Calf is to be administered by a Tynwald body made up of prominent Manxmen, and it has been unequivocally stated that the rights and duties of our own Manx Museum and National Trust are absolutely safeguarded. Indeed, it seems likely that the 'prominent Manxmen' will be found to be already heavily involved in the activities of our own Trust.

To many, even of our own people, the Calf of Man is an unfamiliar piece of land at the end of a long road winding southwards from Port Erin or Port St Mary. Yet it is part and parcel of our history. Many years ago the Calf of Man Crucifixion cross-slab was found making it clear that this remote islet was an important very early Christian site. Romantic stories are told about hermits and those who have sought refuge there from the law. But it is the bird life that has attracted the attention of ornithologists. They are enthralled by the wide range of bird species to be found there, some excedingly rare,

such as the chough. Colonies of puffins have for centuries inhabited the Calf, especially a distinctive variety of puffin which warranted the name of Manx Shearwater. Small in size and looking like a white-breasted pigeon, it nested in rabbit holes and at daybreak they would disappear out to sea, endlessly skimming over the waves. When it was discovered they had commercial value they were mercilessly harvested in late summer and then pickled and salted to be sold as a delicacy. The oil was also valuable and was used to treat wool while the feathers provided soft warm feathers for cushions and bedding. The Manx Shearwater, sadly, disappeared at the beginning of last century, not through over-exploitation, but by falling prey to rats which swam ashore from a wrecked vessel. The trade, however, continued with the larger puffins which are better able to protect themselves with their strong triangular beaks.

During the Napoleonic Wars a proposal to establish a prisoner-of-war camp here was seriously considered. It was considered again in the early days of the Great War, but the idea was abandoned in favour of the Knockaloe Internment Camp because of supply problems. A bridge across the Sound was considered necessary.

The Calf has also played its part in maritime history, and here in 1818 twin lighthouses to the design of Robert Stevenson were built to beam on the treacherous reef known as Chicken Rock. The lighthouse keepers and their families lived here until 1865 when the present Chicken Rock lighthouse was built. Few people have seen these solid old lighthouses but the day will come when the Calf of Man will become more familiar to our people who will be able to experience for themselves its peace and tranquility. Perhaps, if we had our own National Trust to administer them, future Tynwalds might look more sympathetically and with less tardiness on acquiring sites, or buildings, or pockets of land of major historical significance for the Manx people.

The farmhouse and outbuildings which are still in a remarkably good state of repair.
(Manx National Heritage)

HERE IS THE NEWS : 1938
WAR THREAT RECEDES, BUT PREPARATIONS CONTINUE

The threat of another world war that has hung over Britain and Europe throughout this summer has been lifted. Prime Minister Chamberlain has returned from his meeting in Munich with Herr Hitler and Signor Mussolini. While the Sudetenland has been sacrificed, the remainder of Czechoslovakia has been safeguarded from German occupation. At the end of September, Mr Chamberlain returned with the message: "Peace in our time," much to the relief of the world. The crisis may be over, but the defensive preparations already in hand are to continue here, as in Britain. We have this report:

In January, the Manx Government's Central Air Raid Precautions Committee announced its plans to combat the dangers of air raids. They include raising a force of 600 air raid wardens, the provision of bomb shelters and measures to deal with gas attacks. In June it was announced that a Manx Territorial Unit was to be established, consisting of two anti-aircraft gun batteries totalling over 300 men. Recruiting began at the Drill Hall in Peel Road, Douglas, and one of the first to sign on was Thomas Miller of Vicarage Road, Braddan. He had been a battery sergeant major in the Royal Artillery in the 1914-1918 war. Agreement has also been reached with the War Office that the Island is to be involved in the £11 million Expansion Scheme for the Royal Air Force. Work on constructing an airfield in the parish of Jurby has already begun. And His Excellency has announced in Tynwald that the Isle of Man is to make its contribution to the cost of the Imperial Government's re-armament programme, to the extent of £20,000 annually which is to be raised by taxation. As the war clouds hung over Britain during the summer, it is not surprising that the number of visitors arriving by sea and air has dropped by about 50,000.

BUILDING PROJECTS
A number of major building works were started during the year. The biggest is the £65,000 Corporation scheme to widen the promenade at Derby Castle. This will take until 1941 to complete. The Corporation is also spending £3,000 on giving the front of the Villa Marina a new look. The original entrance is to be replaced by a new one at ground level and will be built of brick with cement rendering. It will be in modern *art deco* style and will be embelished with neon strip lighting. The work is to be completed in time for next season. Meanwhile, derelict stone houses at the Brown Bobby on Peel Road have been demolished. A petrol station is to be built on the site.

FIREMAN ELECTROCUTED
A fireman was killed on duty on the Island for the first time. Douglas fire brigade was called to a blaze at Brown's menswear shop on North Quay, next to the Clarendon hotel. Fireman Robert Edward Kenna was electrocuted when he stumbled when removing burning debris from the building and touched a live wire. It was later learned that there was no instruction at Pulrose power station for shutting off the power supply to buildings on fire.

LIFEBOAT COXSWAIN DROWNS IN HARBOUR
In a further tragedy, the cox'n of Ramsey lifeboat, 56-year-old Jack Lord, was drowned in Ramsey harbour. Mr Lord worked as a harbour boatman and he was in a small boat helping with the unroping of a steamer about to leave harbour when it happened. His boat capsized and he was thrown into the water. Mr Lord began swimming but at the inquest it was shown that he drowned when hit by the shock of being immersed in ice cold water.

AIR RACE MEETING
Famous aviator Alex Henshaw regards the Isle of Man Air Race Meeting as the finest of its kind in the world. Now organised by the Royal Aero Club, this year saw 33 aircraft compete in the London - Isle of Man Handicap Race with the finishing line moved to Ronaldsway. Six countries were represented including Germany, Czechoslovakia, Switzerland. Latvia and America. Winner was Stan Lowe in a Comper Swift, formerly owned by the Duke of Windsor. The Manx Air Derby was postponed until the day after Whit Monday because of bad weath-

The new Lieutenant-Governor, Vice-Admiral the Hon. William Spencer Leveson-Gower, C.B., D.S.O., and his wife Lady Rose Leveson-Gower, who is a sister of Her Majesty the Queen. (Frank Cowin Library)

er. It had the usual exciting climax with John Rush first across the line in a Hawker Tomtit. German pilot Ernst Gerbacht was second in a Focke Wolfe biplane, followed by Alex Henshaw in his Percival Mew Gull. Next came three Bf 108s which had played follow-my-leader throughout the race. The Tynwald Air Race for smaller machines was just as dramatic, and a delighted Stan Lowe won the new Olley Cup. He also won the Manx Air Derby last year.

T.T. TROPHY FOR GERMANY
This year the Germans made a determined effort with the B.M.W. and D.K.W. factories entering supercharged machines for the first time. Development had been aided by Government assistance in recognition of the national prestige to be gained from a T.T. victory. The B.M.W challenge faded when their top rider, Karl Gall was seriously injured in practice. But success in the Lightweight went to the D.K.W. rider, Ewald Kluge who completed

the Lightweight race eight minutes ahead of a string of Excelsiors, headed by 'Ginger' Wood. Kluge was also the first to lap in this class at over 80 m.p.h. Observers regard the supercharged D.K.W. as the noisiest ever; at the Grandstand it could be heard as far away as Keppel Gate as it swept down to Creg ny Baa.

Stanley Woods won the Junior for Velocette and went on to gain second place in the Senior. The race was another thriller which resulted in Norton works' rider Harold Daniell notching up his first win. To gain the lead Daniell put in the first sub-25 minute laps and raised the lap record to 91 m.p.h. He beat Woods by 15 seconds who, in turn, finished 1.5 seconds ahead of Freddie Frith riding for Norton.

TRAGIC LOSS AT SEA

In one of the Island's worst sea disasters, the six-man crew of the Ramsey Steamship Company's vessel *Ben Seyr* died when she sank in severe autumn gales. Five were Manxmen and one was from Liverpool. The *Ben Seyr* ('Girl of Liberty') left Ramsey on October 2nd for Cardiff with a cargo of oats. She was last seen three days later sheltering in bad weather off the Irish coast. Nothing more was heard of her, until on October 13th the body of the mate, 33-year-old James Bradford of Church Street, Ramsey, was washed ashore near Heysham. The exact location of the vessel remains a mystery but the most pop-

ular theory is that she lies within a few miles off Langness. The other crew members were Captain W. Crellin of Darragh Road, Port Erin; Engineer William Morrison of Pulrose Park, Douglas; A.B. Dave Lace of Upper Queen's Street, Ramsey; Jerry Thomas of Church Street, Ramsey and A.B. Cecil Horton of Liverpool.

M.H.K.s DOUBLE SALARIES

Members of the House of Keys have voted to double their salaries. In future they will get £100 a year instead of £50. Only three members voted against the move. It was proposed by Mr Eric Faragher, an advocate member of the House. He argued that the low remuneration prevented men of calibre offering themselves because they could not afford to lose wages at their work while giving time to legislative matters.

Throughout the year the question of redistribution of seats in the House of Keys has been under consideration. In May a Committee of enquiry issued a majority report which stated that there was no demand for alteration. This was later countermanded by a proposal for the appointment of a Boundaries Commission to prepare a Bill on redistribution of seats, providing for three more members for Douglas and one for Ramsey. The proposal was rejected by the House which has a clear majority of members from the country districts. At present Douglas has five representatives and Ramsey has one. At a meet-

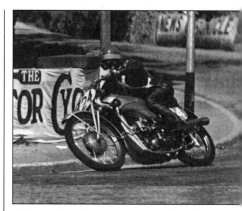

(Above) First German to win a T.T. race, Ewald Kluge rounds Quarterbridge on his Lightweight supercharged D.K.W.

(Below) Senior T.T. winner Harold Daniell on the Norton on which he set up a new lap record of 91 m.p.h.

(R. and L. Kelly Collection)

ing on the subject held in the Villa Marina, Douglas M.H.K. Samuel Norris promised Douglas electors that redistribution would come in two years. A petition is now being circulated for presentation to the Lieutenant-Governor.

1938 NEWS IN BRIEF

JANUARY
3 - Cattle subsidy scheme came into operation, Manx Government paying 5/- per cwt on live weight of approved fat cattle for slaughter in marts.
11 - Bill to raise school leaving age from 14 to 15 passed by Legislative Council.

FEBRUARY
15 - £30,000 scheme to co-ordinate public water supplies of the south of the Island and construction of large reservoir for whole of southern district introduced in Tynwald.
16 - Local Government Board report on provision for fire-fighting in the Isle of Man. Proposed: Central fire station in Douglas; Douglas Corporation to be controlling authority. Increase of personnel of Brigade to 30 men. Subsidiary units at Castletown, Ramsey, Peel, Port Erin, Laxey and Michael.

MARCH
16 - Police Inspector W. Kneen transferred to Douglas from Ramsey as head of new Criminal Investigation Department.

APRIL
1 - Post Office authorities decide to supplement cable service to the Island by using wireless telephony; radio station to be established at Creg-ny-Baa.
5 - Northern Water Board's £100,000 scheme inaugurated.
20 - Radio beacon installed at Cronk-y-Watch, topmost point of Spanish Head, by Northern Lighthouse Board for the guidance of shipping.

JUNE
23 - Third Manx International T.T. Bicycle Race won by Pierre Chauzaud, 'baby' of French team of four crack riders. He completed the two laps of the T.T. Course in 3 hours 31 mins 29.8 secs (average speed 21.41 m.p.h.).

JULY
1 - Rev. C. V. Stockwood, M.A., Vicar of St George's, appointed Archdeacon of Mann in succession to Rev. John Kewley, M.A., Rector of Andreas who has retired after 54 years' service. The Rev H. Maddrell, M.A. has accepted the living at Andreas.
11 - Territorial Association formed for the Isle of Man.
17 - Most Reverend Dr R. Downey, Archbishop of Liverpool, laid foundation stone of Church of the Sacred Heart, at Pulrose.

SEPTEMBER
15 - Junior M.G.P. winner Kenneth Bills completes the 'double' by winning the Senior M.G.P. at 84.72 m.p.h. Dennis Parkinson completes a 'hat-trick' of wins in the Lightweight.

OCTOBER
27 - Miss Lilian Pickard, contralto of Douglas, won coveted Rose Bowl at Blackpool Music Festival.

NOVEMBER
1 - Royal Assent to Island's Divorce Act announced in Tynwald.
20 - Death of Mr J. J. Kneen, M.A., greatest Manx scholar of his day, and author of standard works on Manx subjects. He founded the Manx Language Society and wrote a 'Grammar of the Manx Language' and compiled a 'Manx Dictionary.' Perhaps his greatest work is 'Place Names of the Isle of Man'.

DOUBTFUL FUTURE FOR RAMSEY SALT WORKS

The Isle of Man's 'Mister Salt' is dead. His passing, at the age of 77, robs the Island of the man who exported table salt from Ramsey to millions of homes; supplied salt for the curing of fish for export as far as Russia; and instigated the idea of home-cured bacon - to help use his supply of salt. He will be remembered also as the mining expert who led the first rescue party into the Snaefell mine after the terrible disaster in 1897.

John Todd's death occurred on 1st October at his home, Ecclesall, in Bowring Road, Ramsey where he had been nursed through a long illness by his wife. He was not a Manxman. He originated from Bathgate, West Lothian and then Glasgow, where he was trained as a mining engineer and colliery manager. He had been resident on the Island, however, for 46 years, working as secretary and manager until last year of the Manx Salt and Alkali Company Ltd which he helped establish with Manx and Liverpool investors 37 years ago. His telegraphic business address was 'Sodium, Ramsey, Man.' His business boasted that it could provide every description of salt for domestic, agricultural and manufacturing purposes.

Mr. Todd's association with the Isle of Man dates back to 1891 when a Liverpool firm of engineers started to drill between the Point of Ayre and the Lhen in search of a coalfield which was believed to extend to the Island from England. They found coal but the seams were so thin and so deep that they were not commercially mineable. The project was abandoned but an unexpected discovery led to a change in career for Mr. Todd. Near their second boring at Ballaghenney the coal men discovered evidence of a huge bed of salt, estimated to cover about five square miles mostly under the Irish Sea between the Island and Cumberland. Associated with this was an underground lake or river of brine which was judged to be of the same quality and intensity as used for medicinal purposes at continental brine spas. The brine was approximately 26 per cent salt.

Mr. Todd recognised the commercial possibilities this presented and established, under licence and a long-term lease from the Crown dated 5th July 1895, an extraction operation which was vested in 1902 in the Manx Salt and Alkali Company. The agreement, based on a 'peppercorn' rent and a royalty on every ton of brine extracted, gave him rights to salt over an area of 2,490 acres.

Extraction pipes were drilled at the Point of Ayre to a depth of several hundred feet. A steam-powered pump extracted the brine and a pipeline, five inches in diameter, fed it to a holding tank at Balladoole, Bride. Another pipeline fed the brine from there, and by gravity, to the former Ramsey shipyard on Ramsey quayside. In consequence this became known as 'The Salt Works Site.' In all, there was approximately six miles of pipeline, most of it on the shoreline and subject to repeated damage by erosion and storms. The final stretch was through the Mooragh estate.

Salt was extracted from the brine by evaporation. The brine was put into pans fitted with pipes through which steam was passed from a coal-powered steam engine. This gradually got rid of the water. What remained was an almost pure salt of the highest quality.

Until the Great War the operation successfuly employed 10 or 12 men. But the war brought problems

(Above) A view of the Mooragh Lake, beyond which can be seen the two chimneys of the Ramsey Salt Works. *(Manx National Heritage)*

(Below) Ramsey Harbour showing, on the right, the buildings of the Salt Works occupying the site of the former shipyard.

(Frank Cowin Library)

which led to neglect of buildings, followed by the emergence of cost-cutting rivals. The greatest blow was the loss of the Irish market to German salt. Thereafter the salt works never operated anywhere near capacity. In 1925, for example, 3,500 tons were produced though the capability was 9,000 tons. Recent years have seen the processing of brine dwindle to about 100 tons a week and the buildings are in a dilapidated state.

Mr Todd's death raises a question mark over the future of the Ramsey Salt Works. There needs to be a significant investment in equipment if the works are to remain viable. A complication is that, despite Mr Todd's hostility, extraction of gravel has been permitted on the Ayres. Mr Todd feared that the bore well and the shoreline pumping station could suffer from erosion, as had already been experienced. The original bore well had been washed away and the pipeline broken. An added uncertainty is the possibility that another company may be encouraged by Tynwald to join in the extraction of brine for a spa. According to the experts the brine source is inexhaustible. But the question is: Who is prepared to invest in the salt works whilst uncertainties exist?

HARRY KELLY'S COTTAGE TO BE PRESERVED

The home of the last known person who could speak only Manx Gaelic has proved to be a popular attraction. The Manx Museum opened it to the public for the first time this summer. Now that it is being closed for the winter it is reported that about 3,600 people, many of them Manx, have visited the cottage. The tiny two-roomed 18th century thatched cottage at Cregneash was the home of Harry Kelly who died in 1934. It consists of a kitchen, otherwise known as the Thie Mooar (or Big House), and the bedroom (otherwise known as the Cuillee).

The acquisition of the cottage by the Museum, complete with the original furnishings as used by Mr. Kelly, was suggested last year to Museum Director, William Cubbon, by the Norwegian, Professor Carl Marstrander. The professor, who has the Celtic chair at the University of Oslo, had visited the Island to see Mr. Kelly a number of times, prior to the latter's death, so that he could study Mr. Kelly's use of dialect. When it became known that Mr. Cubbon was anxious to create an open-air folk museum somewhere on the Island

Harry Kelly approaches his cottage which is now to form the centre of the Cregneash Open-Air Folk Museum, the first of its kind. *(Manx National Heritage)*

where the old ways of a traditional fishing community could be preserved, the largely unspoiled Cregneash suggested itself. Now it is being hailed as the first Open-Air Folk Museum in the British Isles.

On hearing of the Manx Museum's interest in it, Harry Kelly's nephew and heir, J. T. Kelly of Port St. Mary, gave the cottage and its contents to the Museum. Another cottage was acquired from him later and one of only two traditional Manx looms known to have survived is to be installed in it.

Since then Harry Kelly's cottage has been restored. Most of the original furniture, meanwhile, has been retained. This includes an old four poster bed which Mr. Kelly brought to Cregneash from a farmhouse on the Calf of Man and cut down to make it fit. The traditional dresser has an excellent display of glistening lustre jugs. One suspects, however, that not all of those belonged to Mr. Kelly. The Museum has been acquiring such things for exhibition ever since an appeal was launched in May to help furnish a Manx Cottage display in the Museum at Douglas.

CENTENARY OF HOUSE OF INDUSTRY

The House of Industry, once the Manx equivalent of an English workhouse for the poor, has celebrated its centenary with the planting by invited V.I.Ps of an avenue of trees. They line the central pathway from Kingswood Grove, Douglas through the large vegetable plot which generations of inmates have cultivated to provide food not only for themselves but for sale to passers-by. Between 28th February and 6th March the House was floodlit at night.

The House of Industry was inspired and largely funded by local churches, notably St. Barnabas' and St. Matthew's of Douglas. Hence the erection of a pulpit from which visiting clergymen could preach to the inmates. Work on building the House started in 1835 and it was ready for occupation by 21st January, 1838. Between 70 and 100 residents became the full-time responsibility of the House but upwards of 130 at any one time were provided with outdoor-relief.

Despite financial problems the House has been constantly upgraded. The quality of resident has also been raised, reflecting a two-class system even among the impoverished. In 1892, when an official Poor Asylum was established, the House of Industry Managers decided that in future only the 'respectable poor' should be admitted to their premises. Since then the number of residents has been reduced significantly. The consequential savings in operational costs has been reflected in a steady improvement in the quality and quantity of food provided for those who remain.

In 1920 the existing building was reconstructed with a flower bed and lawn immediately outside its frontage. This helps to conceal the vegetable garden. Subsequently, electric lighting, central heating and wireless entertainment has been provided.

To mark the centenary the Managers have decided to provide a small extension of the Home, refurbishment of the kitchen and pantries and the provision of more lavatory facilities. Its funding will depend on public subscription but the vice-president of the Managers, Deemster R. D. Farrant, says they are confident that they will not appeal in vain.

The House of Industry showing, on the right, the proposed extension to mark its centenary.
(R. & L. Kelly Collection)

'LADY ISABELLA' RESCUED BY LOCAL MAN

Lady Isabella, the Great Laxey Wheel, reputed to be the largest in the world, has been saved for the nation. Laxey builder and joiner, E. C. Kneale of Baldhoon Road, has commenced a private programme of restoration and already the transformation has been remarkable. She has been repainted with more than a ton of paint and 15 cwt of lime. Her viewing platform, which was the most dilapidated part of her, has been made safe and choking weeds which had been creeping up her arches have been removed.

The appearance of the wheel's surroundings has been improved by the removal of some roofless huts. A derelict café adjoining the wheel has been completely transformed. It was so neglected that two swarms of bees had hived under its floors for 15 years. After driving them out, Mr. Kneale said his men removed over one hundredweight of honey! The ground floor has been opened as a souvenir shop and Mr. Kneale thinks he might create a dance hall on the upper floor. This summer flags have been flying from the wheel and at night she has been floodlit. This has made her an attractive feature of the night sky.

Mr. Kneale acquired a 15 year lease of the wheel in December last year, after fears were expressed that the Great Lady might be in terminal decline. She had not been used to pump water from the old mine workings since the mines were closed by the onset of the Great Depression in 1929. Very occasionally since then an effort had been made to get the wheel turning but this had been only for short demonstrations. By 1937 the popular tourist attraction and landmark had started to show such

The famous Laxey Wheel has received little attention since 1929, but Mr E. C. Kneale of Laxey plans to return it to its former glory and make it once more an attraction for visitors. (Frank Cowin Library)

marked signs of deterioration that her future became the source of concern throughout Britain. It was feared that she might end up being scrapped. An attempt was made to get Tynwald involvement in her rescue but, even as this was underway, Mr. Kneale started negotiations to save the wheel himself and operate her as a commercial tourist attraction. Eventually, he might buy her. His commitment seems so great it would be the logical conclusion.

He opened the restored wheel to the public on Good Friday and plans to produce an 18" x 8" scale model as a souvenir. He made a prototype which he patented and sent to Czechoslovakia for a quotation for production. However, when the Nazis infiltrated the country, nothing was heard until the end of the year when the model was returned in a box covered with swastikas. It now seems unlikely that an alternative manufacturer can be found in time for next season.

RADIO STATION FOR CREG-NY-BAA

Creg-ny-Baa is to be the site for a new telephone radio transmitter and receiving station. It is necessary because of pressure on the undersea cable. Twin towers will support the transmitter wires.

A new access road, meanwhile, continues up to the Mountain Road so that T.T. and M.G.P. race fans can have easier access to viewing positions during race periods. They should be able to walk as far as Windy Corner. Another, but narrower, road is planned to run parallel with the hedge overlooking the T.T. course. The idea is that spectators will be able to park their cars there and obtain meals from a new Roadhouse.

The transmitting station will be provided by the Post Office and the remainder of the development will be undertaken by local businessman and Town Councillor Tom Cowell who owns the surrounding land. His idea is to have his development designated as a T.T. enclosure. He will then charge admission. As a preliminary, a car

and coach enclosure with marquee and a large wooden grandstand, was provided for this year's T.T. It provided views of the fast straight to Brandish Corner.

The land for the transmitter is being acquired for development by the U.K's Office of Works. It follows secret testing by the Post Office of shortwave wireless telephony between the Island and Holyhead in Anglesey. The radio transmitter is being planned by the Post Office to provide extra telephone capacity because there are times when the submarine telephone cable is being used to full capacity. On occasions prospective callers are experiencing long delays in getting their calls put through.

A likely target for completion of the transmitter is July 1939. In view of recent developments on the continent, the remainder of the project will depend then on what the outlook is for peace.

PREPARING FOR THE UNTHINKABLE

The Island plans for war. The politicians say it will not happen. Appeasement of the ruthless Nazi and Fascist dictatorships of Germany and Italy, they believe, has bought 'Peace in our time'. Yet the planning continues. The official policy appears to be to talk-down the fears and yet make preparations. All year sentiment has switched wildly from a sense of imminency of war to there being no prospect of one; from terrible tension to relief. After being dragged to the brink in a confrontation with Germany and Italy, Britain backed away in September. It appeased the dictators but the pessimists are asking: For how long can that satisfy them?

This summer the big fear in Britain and the Isle of Man was the possible indiscriminate dropping of gas bombs on civilian targets. Initially the official line was that the Isle of Man would not be a likely target but that underwent a radical change following the news that an R.A.F. station is to be established at Jurby. Now air raid wardens are being recruited and trained. Every district is providing its own and they include women and children. Eventually, all air raid wardens will receive certificates and badges of office. By the end of the year there will be an estimated 600 of them, many of them ex-servicemen and members of the Loyal Manx Association.

There is still no sign of air raid shelters being built, however. Instead, the emphasis is on educating people on how to make safe places in their homes. Chief Constable J. W. Young says the major threat from the sky will come from high explosives and incendiaries but the public's preoccupation remains with gas. In February plans were prepared by a Central Air Raid Precautions Committee for what were known then as Air Raid Centres. The proposals were that there should be one for every town and village outside Douglas and three for Douglas. The purpose of the four-roomed single storey Air Raid Centres is to provide central stores for gas masks, decontamination materials and other equipment.

Formed in July of this year, the Manx Territorial Army Unit has now been officially named 15th (Isle of Man) Light Anti-Aircraft Brigade R.A. (T.A.). Its Commanding Officer is Lieut-Colonel MacClellan, D.S.O., O.B.E. of Westham Cottage, Castletown, and who is a former officer of the Royal Artillery with a distinguished military record. The War Office has appointed as Adjutant Regular Officer Captain E. L .C. Simson. He and his permanent staff are now based in Belmont Terrace, near to the Drill Hall. Recruiting began in August with a call for 16 officers and 310 other ranks in the age groups 18 to 38 and a limited number of older

men who will not be liable for overseas service. Training, which began in September for the 200 already enlisted, includes an annual camp with weapon training and drills in the evenings. The first commissions gazetted the appointments as Second Lieutenants of Henry Kelly, J. B. Mylchreest, J. D. Clague, J. J. Christian and R. C. Sale, all former King William's College Junior Division O.T.C. Dr H. H. Corrigal has been appointed as Medical Officer.

The Brigade is divided into two Batteries, the 41st and 42nd at Douglas where two Troops of each Battery are based. The Castletown Troop is allocated to 41st Battery and the Ramsey Troop to 42nd Battery. Training is in the ultimate use of the 40mm Bofors gun which is now in production and with which all Light Anti-Aircraft Units will be equipped. The aim is to make the units the finest in the Royal Artillery because they will be the front line of defence against attacks from enemy aircraft. While one of the new guns is eagerly awaited, use is having to be made of antiquated Vickers Mk11 quick-firers. As more men come forward, the end of the year has seen the formation of the 10th (Isle of Man) Company of the Auxiliary Territorial Service with Mrs L. D. Woods as Commanding Officer. The building of a new Drill Hall has been promised. It will contain a large hall with social rooms, gymnasium, showers, Officers and N.C.O.'s messes and canteen, with sports field and parade ground alongside.

Meanwhile new revolvers and ammunition have been issued to police officers in case they have to take enemy airmen into custody after landings on the Island. Police, under the directions of Sergeant T. A. Cringle, the man responsible for conducting the training of air raid wardens, have donned gas masks and, in two by two order, entered a gas chamber at the Drill Hall at Douglas to test their equipment.

The Island's 'Hello Girls' at Douglas telephone exchange have been equipped with special masks which will enable them to stay on station during a gas attack to maintain the Island's vital communications network. Each mask is fitted with microphone and single earphone and plugged in to the switchboard so the wearer can speak to anyone over the phone without difficulty.

Stockpiling of medical dressings has commenced at Noble's Hospital and food stores are being built up by Tynwald. This is because the authorities realise that if the worst does happen and cities such as Liverpool are raided by bombers there could be long periods when supplies will not get through to the Island.

Gas protection instructor Sergeant T. A. Cringle (in mufti) watches a colleague adjust the gas mask which we hope will never be needed.

HERE IS THE NEWS : **1939**
ISLAND AT WAR AGAIN

The dark clouds of war again hang heavy over the Isle of Man, only 21 years after the Armistice ended the Great War. There are fears that the Island could suffer a repeat of the trials and tribulations of that conflict. Manxmen are already dying on the battlefield and at home the visiting industry is under threat. We have this report:

Britain's declaration of war on Germany on Sunday, 3rd September brought an abrupt end to what was left of the 1939 visiting season. Holidaymakers left for home, all places of summer entertainment closed down and steamer and air services were curtailed. And nobody can tell what the future holds. Two anti-aircraft gun batteries of the Island's Territorial Army unit, the Manx Regiment, were mobilised in August and left for service somewhere in England. Recruiting started for a third battery and this went off to war in October. Royal Navy and R.A.F. reservists were called up and local men aged 18 to 41 were made liable for compulsory military service. At home, identity cards and ration cards were issued, as they were throughout Britain. The first Manxman to die on active service, through illness, is believed to be Aircraftsman First Class Frank Corrin, of Port St. Mary, a Regular with an R.A.F. squadron serving in France. But even earlier, within hours of war breaking out, a German U-boat torpedoed and sank the liner *Athenia* off Ireland. The dead included Mrs. Annie Quine, wife of Dr. Thomas Quine, a Manx GP living in Los Angeles.

GAS EXPLOSION IN RAMSEY
A gas explosion devastated the Three C's Cafe in Market Place, Ramsey. Miraculously, no one was killed. A woman who was cleaning the windows was cut by flying glass and a man working on a gas fitting in the cafe was slightly hurt. And a woman working in the butcher's shop next door was hurt when the carcass of a pig hanging from the ceiling fell on her.

SURTAX INTRODUCED
Surtax has been introduced into the Island for the first time when the Lieutenant-Governor, now Earl Granville, presented his 1939 Budget to Tynwald. It will be imposed on incomes of more than £2,000 a year - and fewer than a hundred people in the Island are expected to have to pay it. The maximum rate will be four shillings and sixpence in the pound.

CAUGHT SMUGGLING
A Douglas businessman has been fined £430 for smuggling cigarette lighters into the Island from the Irish Republic. Ernest Gilbert Abels, who runs the Ritz Café at No. 5 Strand Street, smuggled in nearly 800 lighters in order to avoid £60 in Customs duty. He was caught after investigations by Customs officers from London.

AIR RACE CRASH DRAMA
There was drama in this year's air races held in early summer. A Blackburn Bluebird aircraft piloted by 28-year-old Sydney Cummings

NATIONAL REGISTRATION CENSUS
Provisional figures resulting from the Census taken on 29th September show the Island's population now stands at 50,829, an increase of 1,521 compared with the 1931 Census. It should be noted that since the outbreak of war there has been a substantial decrease in the male population, due to men serving in H.M. Forces. Figures below are given with a percentage comparison with 1931:

TOWNS:		
DOUGLAS	- 20.012	(+ 3.5%)
RAMSEY	- 4,240	(+ 1.0%)
PEEL	- 2,523	(+ 1.9%)
CASTLETOWN	- 1,742	(+ 1.7%)
PARISHES:		
Port Erin	- 1,265	(+12.6%)
Port St Mary	- 1,292	(+10.8%)
Laxey	- 1,312	(+ 1.2%)
Onchan	- 2,675	(+56.0%)
Michael	- 343	(+ 3.0%)
Andreas Parish	- 850	(-10.7%)
Arbory	- 709	(- 6.2%)
Ballaugh	- 532	(- 5.1%)
Braddan	- 2.063	(-34.9%)
Bride	- 416	(- 8.0%)
German	- 984	(- 0.9%)
Jurby	- 355	(- 8.0%)
Lezayre	- 1,272	(+11.5%)
Lonan	- 865	(+ 2.0%)
Malew	- 1,751	(+19.0%)
Marown	- 843	(+ 3.3%)
Maughold	- 778	(- 0.9%)
Michael	- 363	(+10.3%)
Onchan	- 1,207	(+30.1%)
Patrick	- 1,013	(- 5.8%)
Rushen	- 1,020	(+ 4.3%)
Santon	- 404	(+ 2.0%)
TOTAL	- 50,829	(+ 3.0%)

from London crashed into the sea off Kirk Michael. He was flying 50 feet up at more than 100 miles an hour when the engine cut out. When the machine hit the sea and sank, Mr. Cummings, who is also a Brooklands racing motorist, struggled out of the cockpit and began swimming to shore. He was picked up by a Peel fishing boat.

Continental competitors in this year's Air Meeting were conspicuous by their absence. There had been a Messerschmitt Bf 108 entered by Air Attache General Lieutenant Wenneger who was anxious to support the races again. It was to have been flown by two of his London staff but the entry was withdrawn when permission from Reichmarshall Goering, commander of the Luftwaffe, had not been forthcoming. Top British racing pilots entered in force and included Tommy Rose, Geoffrey de Havilland, aircraft designer Capt E. W. Percival, Alex Henshaw and his father, Albert Henshaw.

ANOTHER GERMAN T.T. VICTORY
Despite the nervousness of the international situation, 150 entries were received for this year's T.T., the most since 1931. The Germans were back with super-charged B.M.W.s. D.K.W.s and N.S.U.s, while the Italians were represented by the Guzzi and Benelli marques. Hopes of a British victory were ominous after the Norton factory had no official works entries. The reason was that the factory was fully occupied on military contracts. However, Norton's relented and made available last year's machines for Frith and Daniell, though no factory mechanics were available.

British machinery were able to keep their grip on the Junior event with Stanley Woods riding brilliantly to repeat last year's win for Velocette. This means that Woods has now won ten T.T. Taces, more than any other rider. In the Lightweight Race, Woods set up the fastest lap for Moto Guzzi before hitting trouble. It was Ted Mellors who won on the Benelli with last year's winner Ewald Kluge second for D.K.W.

The climax of the week was undoubtedly the Senior Race for which the B.M.W.s had shown their impressive speed during practices,

On the afternoon of Tynwald Day, Norway's Ambassador to London unveiled this fine model of the famous Gokstad longship in the grounds of the Villa Marina. Over a thousand people attended. The model is the first gift to the Museum from the society of the Friends of the Manx Museum.
(Manx National Heritage)

with speeds of 135 m.p.h. on the Sulby Straight, much faster than the Nortons. But the practices had been marred by the death of Karl Gall who suffered a broken skull after crashing his B.M.W. at Ballaugh Bridge. The other two German machines were in the hands of the experienced Georg Meier and British rider Jock West. It was Meier who claimed the Senior Trophy for Germany, winning by two minutes from his teammate and setting up a new race record of 89.38 m.p.h.. He also set up the fastest lap but was unable to beat Daniell's record lap of last year.

JIMMY GUTHRIE MEMORIAL

During the T.T. period race officials and fans gathered for the dedication of the new Jimmy Guthrie Memorial on the mountain climb out of Ramsey. The simple cairn, built of Scarlett limestone, was paid for by public subscription raised by *The Motor Cycle* magazine. It is sited at the location where Guthrie retired on his last T.T. Amongst those present was the German Baron von Falkenhayn. He laid a wreath covered in swastikas, gave the Nazi salute and said "it was in memory of the finest motorcyclist in the world." It was an attempt by the visiting Germans, no doubt, to identify themselves in the public mind as sportsmen and, in so doing, distance themselves from the political arena. Yet, their militaristic salutes said more for what they represented than their words.

PORT ERIN 'THEATRE' DESTROYED

Fire has gutted Port Erin's popular 'theatre' known as Leslie's Pavilion. It was a Tudor-style building which was adapted from one of the internment camp huts from Knockaloe in 1919. The fire happened at the beginning of August when the Blue Dragoons Company was in residence. Early in the afternoon smoke was seen coming from the roof and then flames completely engulfed the building. The heat was so intense that there were fears for the nearby Darnill's Garage. Rushen Fire Brigade arrived with its new fire tender which they had received the day before, but there was little that could be done.

The pavilion, named after its orginator, Harry Leslie, a show business entrepreneur, brought live entertainment to Port Erin which proved popular with visitors and locals alike. Many attended in full evening dress and matinées were put on in wet weather. The pavilion was also used as a dance hall at night and for afternoon tea dances. Winter saw it being used as a picturedrome three nights a week. Electric lighting at one time was provided by Chinese lanterns powered by rechargeable batteries. In latter years, the pavilion was owned by a Manx syndicate which leased the building to concert parties.

PORT ST MARY'S 'TOWN HALL'

An historic Port St. Mary company which helped to enliven the lives of several generations is to be shut down. The Port St Mary Public Hall Company has sold its premises to the Village Commissioners for £1,500. They intend to use it as a municipal building and already it is being dubbed 'The Town Hall'. The company was the inspiration in 1897 of retired Judge Jones from Manchester who had retired to the village. He gained the support of local investors and acquired the site overlooking Chapel Bay. The company then built a main hall with several rooms beneath it. It was soon in regular use for concerts and public meetings. In 1912 it was first used as a cinema, but during the Great War, the Rev. C. Copeland Smith hired the hall as a knitting factory. Thirty local girls were employed in the production of war materials. Since then the hall has been used for 'tay fights', concerts, badminton and even, in 1926, as a skating rink.

1939 NEWS IN BRIEF

FEBRUARY
22 - Steam Packet Company announces intention to introduce Sunday excursions to Island, beginning in June.
24 - Petition for Redistribution of Seats in House of Keys presented to Lieutenant-Governor.

MARCH
1 - Agricultural Commission recommended subsidies, rising from £11.500 to £34,000 in three years, to help agriculture.

APRIL
4 - Shop Hours Bill, permitting limited Sunday trading, introduced and subsequently passed, became law.

JUNE
6 - Surtax on Incomes introduced in Manx Budget.
28 - New Jane Crookall Maternity Home opened.

JULY
5 - Norwegian Minister in London presented Viking Ship model to Manx Museum.
21 - His Excellency the Lieutenant-Governor of Island (the Right Honourable W. Leveson-Gower) succeeded to title of Earl Granville on the death of his elder brother.
30 - Church of the Sacred Heart opened at Pulrose.

AUGUST
4 - Leslie's Pavilion, Port Erin, destroyed by fire.
25 - Two Batteries of Manx Territorials left for service in England.

SEPTEMBER
3 - BRITAIN DECLARED WAR ON GERMANY.
3 - S.S. Athenia torpedoed off Ireland.
15 - Disastrous fire at Isle of Man Examiner Works.

OCTOBER
2 - Third Manx LAA Battery left for service.
10 - TYNWALD APPROVED ADOPTION OF CONSCRIPTION IN THE ISLAND.
31 - Southern Water Board constituted.

NOVEMBER
28 - Manxmen aged 20 and 21 begin registering under National Service (Armed Forces) Act. About 550 men affected.

DECEMBER
11 - Registration of men of 22 years begins. About 200 affected.

NEW JANE CROOKALL MATERNITY HOME

Superstitious women have started closing their eyes or looking the other way when they approach the new Jane Crookall Maternity Home in Douglas. What they are trying to avoid seeing is the figure of a stork. They think that if they once clap eyes on it they are sure to become pregnant. The stork has been placed on a pillar in the centre of an oval rose bed immediately in front of the Maternity Home's Demesne Road entrance. It is regarded as the 'Symbol of Maternity'. No one who arrives by car can fail to miss it without deliberately doing so for the driveway passes round the rose bed. The unexpected reaction by the superstitious might lead to the stork's relocation to a less conspicuous place - perhaps the roof overlooking the entrance. It will still be prominent, of course, but at least women will be able to avoid it more easily by simply not looking up.

The new 'Jane', as it is known, is claimed to be the most up-to-date Maternity Home in the British Isles. One of its most modern features is the provision of light signals instead of bells for patients to summon nurses. When a patient presses a button above her bed, lights will show outside the ward, at the main junction of the corridor, in the matron's office, in the kitchen and in the nurses' room. They will all remain lit until the patient receives attention. This is expected to be a boon to everyone when compared with the incessant ringing of bells in the former Home.

The new Jane Crookall was opened on Wednesday, 28th June, by Lady Rose Leveson-Gower, wife of the Lieutenant-Governor. It is only 12 years since the late philanthropic Alderman A. B. Crookall, five times Mayor of Douglas, purchased, furnished and equipped a Maternity Home elsewhere in Demesne Road in memory of his late wife, Jane. It quickly became evident, however, that it was inadequate to cope with demand.

The new Jane Crookall Maternity Home opened by Lady Rose Leveson-Gower on 28th June. Beware the stork standing in the centre of the rose garden!

(R. and L. Kelly Collection)

Anticipating that this would occur eventually, Mr. Crookall bequeathed £10,000 in his will for improvements. Now his Trustees, with a further £3,000 from his family and £4,500 from the sale of the first Home and the realisation of certain investments which were made possible through public subscriptions and other help, have financed the entire £17,500 cost of building the new two-floor flat-roofed home. Together with donations by friends of the Crookall family, including contributions of material and labour, they have also provided all the furnishings and equipment, including an operating theatre. All maternity wards, including six private ones, are on the ground floor and face south so they will receive the maximum amount of sunshine.

Now that the Trustees have exhausted their investments they are appealing to the public for donations to the Home's Endowment Fund so that the future running of the Home can be guaranteed.

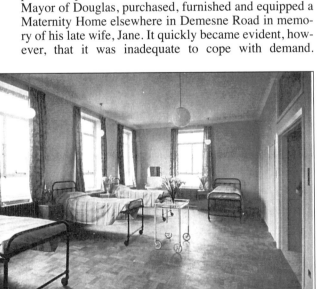

The main ward of the Maternity Home.
(R. and L. Kelly Collection)

One of the private wards.
(R. and L. Kelly Collection)

THE UNTHINKABLE BECOMES THE INEVITABLE

Even to the very end, as Hitler's Nazis invaded Poland, there were some who thought the conflict could be avoided. The Island has enjoyed another successful season with visitors arriving in greater numbers than last year. Despite the unease of the summer, it would appear that many were determined to enjoy their holiday, not knowing what the future would bring. The Manx Motor Cycle Club denied strongly that the September races would be cancelled. Only days later came the reality. On Sunday, 3rd September at 11.15 a.m., whether at home, or in hotels, cafes, churches or chapels, Prime Minister Chamberlain's announcement of war and mobilisation was accepted as inevitable. Almost immediately the Island's centres of live entertainment were closed and contracts with the artistes were deemed void. Phil Richardson's band at the Villa Marina ended a concert with rousing choruses of *Land of Hope and Glory* and the National Anthem, everyone joining in with emotional heartiness. As the great tourist exodus got under way, fearful of U-boat and aircraft attacks, the Manx Grand Prix was finally abandoned. Since then wailing air raid sirens throughout the Island have heightened the sense of expectation. They were sounded four minutes at a time - two minutes with a vibrant tone and two minutes with a continuous note. This is for testing but their eerie, spine-tingling intrusion into everyday life has been a disconcerting reminder of what might happen at any moment.

The declaration of war on Germany brought to a head the tension that had been growing all summer, despite the pre-occupation with a busy season. Public fear turned increasingly to a resolute awareness that the Nazis had to be confronted after they had marched into Czechoslovakia in March. Archdeacon Stockwood summed up many people's feelings when he preached in St George's Church in April, at the first Church Parade of the Manx Territorial Army unit. Hitler was a man drunk with power, he said. There were, indeed, worse things than war. Peace at any price? What price did one put on a nation's soul? Nevertheless, there were many who continued to scoff at the 'jitterbugs' and thought the preparations being made were a waste of time and money. Air attacks were only a remote possibility and would be confined to industrial areas far removed from the Island. Perhaps that view helped the economy-minded in Tynwald when they decided that everyone did not need gas masks. Only 5,000 at most would be needed, sufficient to equip people in essential services.

If one was to seek a defining moment in the change of Manx attitudes towards Hitlerism, the T.T. would be a logical candidate. The Auto-Cycle Union and the Manx Government officials responsible for organising the races were delighted with the strong foreign entry and there was no doubt that most of the foreign riders, if not all, had come for the sport, pure and simple. But there could be no escaping the fact, however, that they had political masters and the latter were interested in building their international prestige through national success at sport. Within the Island there were deep undercurrents of resentment over their presence and these were given expression by the newspapers with unprecedented hostility. To them the unveiling of the Guthrie memorial was marred by the presence of Germans with their swastikas and Nazi salutes. Manx people were urged by the *Isle of Man Examiner* not to hold out the hand of friendship to the foreigners. *The Isle of Man Times* branded the British stars who had agreed to ride for the German and Italian works teams as being disloyal. That led to the B.B.C. radio commentary team dropping from their number Mr George Brown, the Editor of the *Times*. Evidently it was felt that he could not be trusted not to make some insensitive remark on air about Britain's potential enemies.

Like Britain's political appeasers of last year, the A.-C.U., the Lieutenant-Governor and others tried to appease their German and Italian 'guests.' Disassociating themselves from the criticisms, they said that sport and politics should not be allowed to mix. Many race fans appeared to agree. They cheered with enthusiasm when Georg Meier won the Senior race and received the magnificent trophy to take back to Germany. Yet within a month, leaflets would be distributed to every home on the Island about what to do in the event of war.

One morning towards the end of August, early risers in lower Douglas had a disturbing encounter which heightened their sense of foreboding. They met troops armed with fixed bayonets, Bren and Lewis guns. Those who saw them on the quay with stretcher-bearer parties and various military vehicles parked nearby thought that the worst had happened, that war had been declared or the Island had been invaded. In fact, it was a military exercise involving two fully-armed battalions of the Hallamshire Territorial Army Regiment from Sheffield. The men were on a fortnight's camp under canvas at Bibaloe where, throughout the summer, over a thousand Territorials at a time from other units experienced camp life and military training..

That was on Thursday, 24th August and in the afternoon, in the light of the worsening international situation, instant call-up notices were going out to many reservists in the Army, Navy and Air Force. That afternoon also saw messengers and loud speakers summoning the local Territorials. The men abandoned their normal employment, dashed home to change into uniform and then reported to the Drill Hall. Special buses brought men in from Ramsey. That night members of the 41st and 42nd Batteries sailed for Liverpool on board the *Fenella*.

EMERGENCY MEASURES

The War Emergency Committee set up by Tynwald in August has executive powers and already a series of Orders have been issued. Prices of most foodstuffs have been fixed to prevent profiteering and coal has been rationed since the end of September. Catering establishments have to register for supplies of bacon, ham and butter. Closure of all centres of entertainment was considered, because of the risk of bombing, but cinemas have remained open as a help to morale. Restrictions are in force to control the posting of newspapers, books, maps etc. while the taking of certain photographs requires a written permit. The Board of Agriculture now regulates prices in connection with the sale and slaughter of cattle, pigs, sheep and lambs. The export of swedes, turnips and mangolds is forbidden except by permit; farmers are being encouraged to grow more wheat and vegetables. Everyone is being exhorted to 'Dig for Victory', conscious of the U-boat menace of the Great War. Should the need arise, rationing of basic food items will be introduced. Other precautions taken include the storage of precious records and documents in

The unveiling of the Guthrie memorial in June was marred by the presence of Germans bearing swastikas and giving the Nazi salute.
(R. and L. Kelly Collection)

an underground chamber, safe from bombing. There has been a quiet accumulation also of essential items such as water mains pipes so that those blown apart can be replaced quickly. These emergency Orders are being administered by various Divisions of Government Office and cover Food Supplies, Fuel Supplies, Military Service and Censorship.

Now in force are a series of Light Restriction orders which have effectively blacked out the Island from air and sea. Street lamps no longer shine and drapers' shops have done a roaring trade in black-out material for backing curtains. The transformation has been completed in a remarkably short time with Air Raid Wardens, mostly members of the Loyal Manx Association, working closely with the police. Anyone showing the slightest chink of light are warned to "put that light out!" Persistent offenders are liable to a fine of £5 with the added indignity of having their names published in the papers. Bulbs have been removed from little-used rooms while candles and paraffin lamps have come back into their own. Electric torches are now a valued possession for those venturing out in the dark. As with vehicles and cycles, torches are masked by a filter to emit no more than a thin shaft of light. The edge of pavements are being painted black and white as an additional aid. Bonfires have been banned and the Isle of Man Football Association has cancelled all fixtures for the coming season.

Children were given an extra week's holiday in September so that instructions could be given to schools on procedures in the event of air raids. On hearing the sirens all schools are to be evacuated and children who live within eight minutes of the school are to go home. Others are to go to the house of a relative or friend and take shelter, usually under the stairs. Where this is not possible children are to be taken to a safe place away from the school. A practice was held at the end of September, but this was only partially successful because many schools were beyond range of the sirens which could not be heard. More are to be installed as soon as possible.

The nightmare remains of what might happen if the enemy attacks us with gas. Pessimists fear that the Island is woefully equipped in respect of gas masks. There seems to be more official concern, however, about incendiary bombs. Householders are being asked to keep all inflammable materials away from the top floors of their homes, and to have several buckets handy filled with either sand or dry earth. Water must not be used in attempts to extinguish incendiary bombs, say the

experts, as water will make them explode. If gas is used by the enemy it is felt that Liverpool could be targeted and with that in mind all steamer sailings to Liverpool will carry enough gas masks for the protection of passengers arriving at the port. Those who wish to purchase their own can do so at Kennaugh's sports shop in Victoria Street, Douglas.

Meanwhile, every town and village has plans to cope with bombing. Port Erin's scheme, for example, splits the village into three districts, each with its own emergency services depot. A casualty clearance station has been chosen which will be equipped with an ambulance. Equipment of all kinds is in very short supply, but at least it is reassuring to know that plans are already in hand for whatever the future will bring.

STEAM PACKET SHIPS CALLED UP

After completing the hectic summer schedules, there will be no rest for the Steam Packet's fleet of 13 passenger vessels this coming winter. Within a week of the outbreak of war ten of the best ships had been commandeered for war service. First to go before the end of August were three veterans from the Great War - *King Orry, Mona's Isle* and *Manx Maid*. They left to be converted into armed boarding vessels, manned by the Royal Navy and flying the White Ensign. On 2nd September the *Mona's Queen* came under orders, followed quickly by the *Viking, Tynwald, Fenella* and *Manxman*. Within the same week the *Lady of Mann* and *Ben my Chree* had been called up - all to be used as troop carriers in support of the British Expeditionary Force in France. They are not to be armed. Crewed by Company personnel, they will fly the Red Ensign of the Merchant Navy. At home, the *Rushen Castle* will bear the brunt of maintaining services to and from the Island, with support from the *Snaefell* and *Victoria*. Of smaller tonnage, the *Peveril, Conister* and *Cushag* remain to cope with freight.

AIR SERVICES CURTAILED

After the slump of 1937, Isle of Man Air Services have enjoyed two successful seasons, flying some 10,000 passengers into Ronaldsway each summer. The outbreak of war, however, saw the suspension of all civilian flying. The seven aircraft of Isle of Man Air Services (two DH 86s and five DH 89 Rapides) were impressed into service with the Royal Air Force and attached to communications flights. Captain Higgins is now the personal pilot to Air Marshal Barratt who is in command of the R.A.F. component in France. Isle of Man Air Services resumed flying into Ronaldsway at the end of November. Under the control of the Associated Airways Joint Committee, they now provide a daily flight to Liverpool and Belfast, using two of the original Rapides. These aircraft appear in R.A.F. camouflage with yellow undersides. All cabin windows have been blacked out for security reasons. Cameras are not permitted and national identity cards have to be produced before acceptance for a flight.

EVACUEES ARRIVE

Memories of the hardship caused by the Great War for hoteliers and boarding house proprietors have prompted swift action by the Douglas Boarding and Apartment Association. It proposes the filling of hotels and boarding houses with evacuee children. London and Britain's industrial areas are prime targets for Germany's Luftwaffe so youngsters are already being evacuated to places of relative safety. Circulars have been received from the Imperial Government seeking details of accommodation available on the Island. Five hundred hoteliers who met in the Garden Pavilion at the Villa Marina have decided to offer their premises. As yet there has been no official response to the offer, but the first evacuees have already arrived. By mid-September 400 children were housed in various parts of the Island and had been accepted at local schools.

TYNWALD'S WAR COMMITTEE

On 28th November the Lieutenant-Governor, Earl Granville, announced to Tynwald that the A.R.P. and Emergency Committees were to be replaced by a War Committee. In thanking all those involved in the hard work of preparing and introducing the many wartime measures, the Lieutenant-Governor said he proposed to nominate two members of the Council and five Members of the House of Keys with whom he could be in close and regular communication to deal with urgent matters of the day. Both branches of the Legislature confirmed the appointments. The War Committee provides the executive component of the war 'Cabinet' presided over by Earl Granville. The wartime administration of the Island is also subject to the The Isle of Man (War Legislation) Acts of the Imperial Government, whereby legislation concerning the Defence of the Realm can be extended to the Isle of Man. Such matters as the procurement of land and property can be effected by Orders in Council.

CONSCRIPTION BEGINS

The Island quickly showed its loyalty to the Crown and readiness to support the British cause. This was achieved by Tynwald carrying a resolution asking for the extension of the Imperial Parliament's National Service (Armed Forces) Act to the Isle of Man on 5th September, two days after war was declared. The extension was pro-

claimed by Order in Council dated 27th October. The registration of those affected will be undertaken by the Military Service Divison of Government Office which is manned by volunteers under Mr W. D. Moore. By the middle of December all men aged 20, 21 and 22 had registered on separate days according to area, use being made of the Court Houses in Ramsey, Peel and Castletown. In Douglas registration takes place at the headquarters of the Military Service Division in St George's Hall in Hill Street. Every man in the age groups has to register, but those in reserved occupations (based on the list being used in England) are granted deferment. Unclear cases, and those applying for postponement because of family hardship, are dealt with by the Local Tribunal chaired by the High-Bailiff and made up of representatives from various walks of life. The ultimate authority lies in the Appellate Tribunal chaired by Deemster R. D. Farrant, Clerk of the Rolls.

Those required for immediate service are able to express a preference for which of the Armed Forces they wish to join, subject to there being vacancies. The great majority wish to enlist in either the various branches of the Army or trades within the Royal Air Force. The remainder opt for the Royal Navy. The men are given thorough medical examinations by a team of doctors. A room in St George's Hall has been specially heated and equipped with cubicles. Of all the men examined so far almost two thirds have been put in the Grade 1 category. A quarter have been placed in Grades 111 and 1V and are considered unfit for heavy duties. Most men have expressed a cheerful resignation to what lies ahead and are anxious to get started. As yet, no men have received calling up notices, but these are expected to start in the new year. This means the men will be able to enjoy their last Christmas at home, though it will be very different from last Christmas.

The Island's War 'Cabinet' in session and presided over by His Excellency the Lieutenant-Governor, the Right Honourable the Earl Granville, C.B., D.S.O., seated centre. The other members are, from left to right, Messrs W. C. Craine, M.H.K.; A. E. Kitto, M.H.K.; R. G. Johnson, High Bailiff (Secretary of the War Committee); Deemster W. P. Cowley, M.L.C. (Chairman of the War Committee); B. E. Sargeaunt, M.V.O., O.B.E. (Government Secretary and Treasurer); R. B. Moore, M.L.C. (Attorney-General); J. R. Corrin, M.L.C.; S. Norris, M.H.K., D. J. Teare, M.H.K. and A. J. Teare, M.H.K.

(Manx National Heritage)

THE MANX REGIMENT GOES TO WAR

By late afternoon on 24th August, the Drill Hall bustled with men as they responded to the call up. At 7 p.m. the first party marched down Peel Road to Victoria Pier to board the *Fenella* which that night was to make a special trip to Liverpool. The men joked and appeared to make light of what was happening, but the crowds which watched were more sombre. On board the *Fenella* was also the unit's guns. These included a lone Bofors gun which had been delivered in the early spring. It was demonstrated to the public in May on land at Cunningham's Camp where intensive training took place. Camp facilities were used so the men could be billeted at week-ends. Captain John Higgins of Isle of Man Air Services kept the gun layers active with low level flying, diving and swooping over the guns.

The Bofors gun was used as part of an intensive recruitment campaign to bring the unit up to strength. This was achieved in May and there was disappointment for a number of 20 and 21 year-olds. Their names were taken for the possible formation of a third battery. This was authorised on 28th August and the third battery was designated the 129th Battery. Within five days sufficient numbers had signed on to form the battery. This brought the 15th (Isle of Man) Light AA Regiment (The Manx Regiment) up to full strength. The new battery assembled at the Howstrake Holiday Camp before moving to the Majestic Hotel where rifle and marching drill took place, with practice on a dummy Bofors gun comprising poles and bin lids! On 2nd October the 129th, under the command of Captain W. H. Cain, M.C., who had been in command of 41st Battery, left the Island for Liverpool and encamped at the Grand National course at Aintree where they stayed until November.

The 41st and 42nd Batteries on board the *Fenella* arrived in Liverpool on 25th August and soon discovered they were to play their part in the defence of the great port. There were 368 of all ranks in addition to the 31 officers and men attached to Regimental Headquarters which, by 2nd September, was established in the Royal Liver Building. Lieutenant-Colonel MacClellan became the Commanding Officer of the Mersey Docks Light AA Defences under AA Command in the Air Defence of Great Britain. There had been a spate of promotions throughout the year and 41st Battery was in command of Captain W. H. Cain, M.C., to be succeeded later in the month by Captain C. Kniveton, M.C.; the 42nd Battery was in command of Captain S. Molyneux. All have since been promoted Major.

The gun teams of the Batteries were dispersed in the area from Seaforth sands up to the Royal Liver Building and around Birkenhead, manning sites on jetties and the rooftops of warehouses. Equipment should have been 24 of the 40mm quick-firing Bofors guns, but only four were available. Other gun teams had to make do with obsolete Vickers two-pounders and vintage Lewis guns. There was a Church Parade on the morning of Sunday, 3rd September and it was in St. Nicholas' Church that the Prime Minister's broadcast

On the evening of 24th August, members of the 41st and 42nd Batteries left on the 'Fenella' to take up positions on Merseyside.

was heard. At 1.15 p.m. the first anti-aircraft shells fired in the defence of Britain reverberated over the River Mersey. The area was a prohibited flying area; friendly aircraft were instructed to fly with undercarriages down. Two 'planes, with undercarriages up, suddenly appeared flying straight up the Mersey. A challenging round was fired without response, so all guns within range opened up. The 'planes, which turned out to be R.A.F. Hampdens, veered away flashing the signal of the day, but had suffered slight damage. A full-scale inquiry vindicated the gunners. A similar incident followed three days later when two bombers were slightly damaged and landed at Speke. Again the Batteries were complimented, but communications and aircraft recognition were given greater prominence. By the end of the month the 10th (Isle of Man) Company of the A.T.S. arrived in Liverpool and joined the two Batteries for the promised training camp at Cark-in-Cartmel, North Lancashire. Conditions were appalling and life under canvas was dismal.

At the beginning of November, Regimental Headquarters was established at Kemble House, Gloucestershire. Captain W. S. Valentine replaced Captain Simson as Adjutant. Troops from both Batteries were dispersed to various locations in England and were used in the defence of airfields and factories engaged in war production. The first honours for the Regiment came when four gunners from 41st Battery were mentioned in Despatches for braving fierce flames to rescue a pilot whose 'plane crashed near their gun emplacement. They were L/Bombardier G. C. Moore and Gunners J. S. Cubbon, J. S. Harding and L. G. Raineri. The Regimental H.Q. is now at Ashton Keynes and pre-Christmas leave has become possible, Lieutenant Colonel MacClellan added an extra day to the usual seven to allow for travel.

Ten days before Christmas, the 129th Battery moved from Darwen to defend the Gloster Aircraft Factory at Gloucester and the Rotol Airscrew Works at Cheltenham.

ROYAL AIR FORCE STATION JURBY

For the past year or so a favourite outing for those with motor cars has been to visit Jurby where a new airfield has been under construction as part of the Royal Air Force Expansion Scheme. Negotiations between the Air Ministry and the Manx Government began as far back as August, 1937 but it was not until the following April that it became known that an Aircraft Armament Training Camp was to be built in the north of the Island. The Air Ministry delegation chose the flat and low-lying farmlands in the parish of Jurby as being ideal for their purpose. The land was sparsely populated and there was a quiet stretch of sea nearby which was ideal for a bombing range. Weather records for this part of the Island showed it was free of mist for most of the year. Geographically, an airfield here would also fit in with the pattern of defences for the north west of Britain. The land earmarked for the airfield and buildings totalled 307 acres. Over half belonged to Ballamoar. The remainder was taken from the farms of Ballavarran, the Nappins and Ballaworrey. On hearing of the plans, 60 farmers of them signed a petition expressing 'considerable alarm' at the effect the noise of aircraft would have on livestock, the lowering of land values in the area and 'the inevitable risk to life and limb.'

Many Manxmen have been employed in the construction of the airfield at Jurby. Heavy machinery has been used to level the area.

The Lieutenant-Governor gave news of the Air Ministry plans in his Budget Speech in the spring of 1938. They were to be part of the Defence Bill then before Tynwald and in the hands of Mr R. Q. Hampton, M.H.K. When it came to the petition of the Jurby farmers, the Speaker, Mr J. D. Qualtrough, deemed it inadmissible because it appeared as a type-written copy and not the original. However, Mr Hampton was able to allay the fears of the farmers with an assurance from the Air Ministry that they would suffer no ill-effects. Other M.H.Ks pointed out the advantages that the station would bring in the form of winter employment, the supply of farm produce to the camp and the benefits to other Island services. With only one dissenting voice, the Bill was passed in June.

Responsibility for acquiring the land on behalf of the Air Ministry, and ensuring the farmers involved were suitably compensated, was in the hands of the Island's Attorney-General, Mr R. B. Moore. He acted for the Government Property Trustees. A right of access to the coastal stretch as far as the Point of Ayre was also given. This area was required for training purposes and the siting of observation posts for the off-shore bombing ranges. The Air Ministry also required land in Ramsey for a 'speed boat headquarters.' For this purpose Teare's strawberry gardens at the top of the harbour were acquired, together with land next to St Olave's Church Hall for living accommodation.

The contract for the construction of the airfield and its buildings was awarded to the Manchester firm of Messrs Gerrard and Co., and work began in September. Units of heavy machinery never seen on the Island before - caterpillar diggers and huge earth removers - were shipped over. They soon began removing hedges, scattering hundreds of rabbits in the process, and levelling the entire area. Three hundred men were employed, mainly as labourers digging trenches for the electricity cables and the laying of pipes. They travelled by cycle, bus and 'chara and it was this extra time involved that caused a dispute over pay. The skilled tradesmen demanded 1/7½d an hour instead of the northern rate of 1/4d and the Douglas rate of 1/6d. Labourers were on one shilling an hour. Union officials and Gerrard's agreed a compromise so the work was not interrupted. In January, 340 men were making good progress despite the weather. Since then, the buildings have taken shape in the form of two hangars, workshops, wireless and technical rooms, an armoury, sick quarters and classrooms. Heating is from a central coal-fired boiler supplied with water from a towered cistern which is now a landmark in the area. Across the main road from Ramsey is the parade ground surrounded by hutted accommodation and messes for officers, sergeants and other ranks. The huts are made of wood to a Canadian design which uses compressed straw for insulation.

On 18th September, R.A.F. Jurby was officially opened as No 5 Air Observers School and began gearing up to teach navigation, bomb aiming and air to air gunnery. These observer aircrew are required to fly in the new breed of all-metal bombers such as Whitleys, Hampdens and Wellingtons. A change in policy resulted in the dropping of navigation from the curriculum, so Jurby was renamed No 5 Bombing and Gunnery School. One of the first officers to arrive at Jurby was Cyril Radcliffe whose family hails from Douglas. He began his air force career in 1918 as an apprentice at Halton and went on to serve as an observer on the Northwest Frontier, India. He was posted to Jurby as Station Warrant Officer, responsible for the smooth running of the station and the welfare of the students.

HERE IS THE NEWS : 1940
RATIONING BEGINS AND INTERNEES ARRIVE

Just two decades after the end of the Great War the Isle of Man is again feeling the full effect of the conflict in human terms. After a winter of "all quiet on the Western Front," the might of the German army has swept through the Low Countries and into France, encircling British and Allied forces around Dunkirk. We have seen the miracle of the evacuation in which the Steam Packet ships have played a valiant part, but at a cost of three fine vessels and the lives of many Manx seamen. We have followed the aerial battles over southern England as R.A.F. fighters withstood the onslaught of the Luftwaffe, and we have been moved by the inspiring oratory of Prime Minister Winston Churchill. Britain now stands alone, and many of our young men and women have left the Island to prepare for the long conflict ahead. Some of our young men have already been killed in action, while at home the war is already beginning to touch our lives. We have this report.

Everyone recorded in the National Registration Census of last September has been issued with a National Identity Card and a ration book. January saw the War Committee, through the Food Division, introduce the first food rationing with sugar being limited to 12 oz. per person per week. Since then both tea and butter have been rationed. To help make the Island more independent for its food supplies, farmers are to be paid £2 per acre for bringing hitherto uncropped land into cultivation.

It has become clear that the Isle of Man is to become a place of internment for thousands of people with German or Italian connections. There will be no huge internment camps that swelled the Island population in the Great War. Instead, sections of boarding houses in various parts of the Island are being commandeered and fenced off.

The Island has experienced its first air raid alerts, while the threat of invasion by German forces massing across the English Channel has seen the formation of the Local Defence Volunteers, now the Home Guard. These are stirring times, but everyone seems to have adopted a grimly cheerful attitude to the situation and are determined to play

A view of the Ballakermeen High Schools, taken last autumn. Upon completion, the classrooms are being used by H.M.S. St George to instruct young sailors who have chosen the Royal Navy as their career. *(Frank Cowin Library)*

their part, no matter what Adolf Hitler may have in store. In August the *Isle of Man Times* launched an appeal to Manxmen everywhere to donate sufficient money to purchase a Spitfire. The response was overwhelming. Money poured in from many parts; Spitfire parties, dances and swimming galas were held. A total of £10,637 was raised. There was sufficient, with a small Government subsidy, to purchase two of these fine aircraft. Lord Beaverbrook, Minister of Aircraft Production, promised that the Spitfires would be named 'Manxland' and 'North Barrule' and would be in action with front line squadrons of the Royal Air Force.

HOLIDAY CAMPS
TAKEN OVER

It appears that the well-laid plans of the War Office included the take-over of many of the Island's facilities for use as training bases for the long conflict ahead. First to be taken over is Cunningham's Holiday Camp in Douglas for use by the Royal Navy. As early as last September, an advance party of naval officers arrived to make preparations to receive hundreds of seaman boys transferred from training ships elsewhere, and brought together in what has been named *H.M.S. St George*. In fact, so many arrived that Howstrake Holiday Camp in Onchan was used as temporary accommodation. The boys are mostly aged 16 and are making the Royal Navy their career, having signed on for 12 years. At *H.M.S. St*

George they will learn the basic rudiments of seamanship before specialising in such areas as signalling and telegraphy. Already the young men in naval uniform have become a familar sight as they march from their 'ship' to the Ballakermeen High Schools. They are the first pupils of the new schools which were designed for the reorganisation of secondary education on the Island but which has now had to be delayed. The use of Ballakermeen classrooms for instruction purposes means that all the boys can be accommodated at Cunningham's Camp. The Howstrake Camp has become The Royal Marines School of Music, where the young musicians are trained for ceremonial occasions. The bright buildings have been camouflaged with drab paint.

OFFICER CADETS
IN TRAINING

The Villiers Hotel and neighbouring properties on the Loch Promenade are now occupied by officer cadets who have been selected for training as officers in infantry tactics, map-reading and administration. The car park in Lord Street is being used by military transport and Bren-gun carriers. The Island's varied terrain and weather is ideal, and the cadets undertake a rigorous 17-week course designed to develop physical fitness and leadership. The course ends with a Battle Week spent in remote parts of the Island in which the cadets are finally assessed for their suitability. Those who successfully complete the course are then commissioned and posted to regiments within the Army.

The 'Ulster Queen' high and dry on the rocks of Maughold Head. The Ramsey lifeboat 'Lady Harrison' assisted in the rescue of the 146 passengers and crew.　　*(R. and L. Kelly Collection)*

The realistic training results in serious accidents, especially when live ammunition and pyrotechnics are being used. To cope with accidents and other medical cases from the O.C.T.U., the Hotel Majestic in Onchan has been converted into a fully-equipped Military Hospital staffed by the Royal Army Medical Corps and nurses from the Queen Alexandra's Imperial Military Nursing Service. The ballroom is now a surgical ward with 40 beds, while the dining room has been converted into a medical ward with over 80 beds. Cases from other military units on the Island are also admitted.

A YEAR OF SHIPWRECKS

In severe weather which hit the Island in January, a Fleetwood trawler was wrecked at Bulgham Bay with the loss of her entire twelve-man crew. It was the first of a series of shipwrecks on the Island during the year. A Liverpool coaster went aground at Fort Island in a storm and two of her nine-man crew, father and son, were lost. A Northern Ireland coaster was wrecked at Maughold, fortunately without loss of life. One of the most dramatic rescues of modern times took place in February as a result of the passenger vessel *Ulster Queen* running aground to the north of Maughold Head in thick fog. On board were 93 passengers and 53 crew. In the middle of a bitterly cold night three of the ship's lifeboats were lowered and transferred mainly the women and children to the *Duke of Lancaster* which was standing by two miles off shore. By 5.15

a.m. the Ramsey lifeboat *Lady Harrison* arrived and helped to transfer the remainder of the passengers. Nine of the crew were found in lifeboats and were picked up and brought into Ramsey. The rest of the crew were rescued by breeches-buoy by the Ramsey Rocket Brigade. Apart from an Alsatian dog, all lives were saved. Ramsey lifeboat, under Coxswain John Comish, was accredited with the saving of 60 lives. After nearly a month, the *Ulster Queen* was refloated.

HEAVY SNOWFALL

In what has been one of the severest winters for many years, heavy snow fell at the end of January. In some places drifts of 10 feet blocked roads and railway lines. Kirk Michael was marooned for eleven days and flying operations at Jurby were halted for a week because of the snow-covered airfield. In Douglas huge waves destroyed parts of the stone wall protecting the sunken gardens on Loch Promenade. Gales also prevented the Steam Packet vessel *Rushen Castle* from making port in Douglas. She was storm-tossed off the west coast of the Island for 71 hours. Her passengers included the Lieutenant-Governor, Earl Granville, and his daughter.

DISASTROUS FIRES

In February fire gutted a big private residence in Douglas. It was 'Knottfield' in Woodbourne Road, the home of Mr and Mrs Albert Rowell. Mr Rowell led three housemaids

through the smoke to safety from their bedrooms on the upper floors. Albert and his brother Harold own a string of sweet shops in the town and are both keen competitors in the Manx Grand Prix. Riding Nortons, Albert came third in the 1937 Senior race while Harold came seventh. In May another fire badly damaged the premises of men's outfitters Lay and Company in Duke Street, Douglas. The fire occurred early in the morning and the upper floors of the building were gutted and the roof collapsed. The ground floor was flooded but most of the stock was saved.

FIRE BRIGADES REORGANISED

Amongst the many concerns of the War Committee is the state of the Island's fire brigades. In February the Local Government (Fires) Act came into force, creating seven Fire Authority areas. Fire-fighting equipment has been pooled and spread equally throughout the Island. An Auxiliary Fire Service has also been formed. The call for volunteers resulted in 140 men coming forward for training by the Douglas Brigade in the Barrack Street Mission Hall. Equipment is very limited and it is likely to be some time before additional vehicles and trailer-pumps are received.

INCREASE IN AIR SERVICES

From April the skeleton air service introduced last year has been substantially increased with seven daily flights from Liverpool, one of which continues to Belfast. The service is available to local residents but the majority of passengers are officers visiting the Island in connection with the many camps and stations set up on the Island by the War Office.

In March Ronaldsway became the home of the R.A.F.'s Ground Defence School. Men are billeted along Castletown Promenade and within the town itself. Officers taking the course are accommodated in the Fort Island (Golf Links) Hotel which is used also as a school for instruction in the use of Lewis, Browning and Bofors guns. Firing butts have been built on Langness and, near the Lighthouse, machine-gun positions have been built. Ground-to-air firing takes place here, firing at drogues towed by Wallace aircraft out to sea. The course is short and intensive. Airmen are then posted to defend R.A.F. airfields.

BOOMING ECONOMY

Despite the Island's wartime difficulties the Manx economy is booming. Presenting his Budget to Tynwald, the Lieutenant-Governor said that the Manx exchequer had a record surplus of £100,000 for 1939-40 and the economy had performed beyond expectation. His Excellency admitted that the main reason was the boost given to Government revenues by the large number of German and Italian aliens interned on the Island.

In September steps were taken to follow the British Government which has introduced Purchase Tax to help off-set war costs. Inevitably this will lead to higher costs of goods and merchandise in the shops. Cigarettes have gone up 2d a packet to 8¹/₂d. The new tax is estimated to bring in £70,000 to the Government exchequer.

DISMAL VISITING SEASON

The visiting season has become a wartime casualty. In February an optimistic Publicity Board forecast the possibility of up to 50% of the usual visitor numbers arriving in the summer. In fact, there were only 23,000. Nevertheless, the Steam Packet has had packed sailings bringing aliens for the internment camps. A local girl home on leave has reported that one of the crew of a German bomber, killed when it was shot down over the north-east of England, was called Georg Meier. Whether or not he is the winner of last year's Senior T.T. cannot be confirmed, but it does beg the question: "Where is the valuable Senior T.T. Trophy?"

FIRST AIR RAID ALERT

For the purpose of giving air raid warnings the Isle of Man is part of the

---

FIRST WAR CASUALTIES

By the end of the year, notification has been received that 66 men and one woman have been killed by enemy action or are missing, presumed killed.

Totals from the Armed Forces are as follows:

BRITISH ARMY	- 12, including those lost in France and the evacuation
ROYAL AIR FORCE	- 3, in flying operations
ROYAL NAVY	- 11, lost when ships were sunk
MERCHANT NAVY	- 40, including 33 Steam Packet men at Dunkirk
W.R.N.S.	- 1, killed by enemy aircraft

In addition eight have died on active service, including two in accidents not connected with the war.

North-West area which includes Liverpool and Belfast. When an enemy or unidentified aircraft is reported in the area the sirens are sounded so that civilians can take cover and local defence members take up their positions. Practices have been organised by Chief Constable Major J. W. Young who is responsible for the Island's air raid precautions. However, there was considerable confusion when the first real alert was given shortly after noon on Saturday, 31st August. Many thought the sirens were being sounded for another practice and they were not taken seriously. This led to a warning from the Chief Constable who complained about pedestrians walking the streets while cars and buses continued on their journeys. In future all alerts are to be taken seriously and there will be no more practices. Local people in the Dalby area have reported that on the night of 18th September a lone German aircraft dropped four high explosive bombs causing large craters, though without damage or injury. It is thought the crew were lost and jettisoned the bombs before returning to base.

FLEETWOOD TO BE WARTIME PORT

Heavy bombing has caused havoc in the Liverpool dock area which is often heavily congested with convoys of ships waiting to be unloaded. The Royal Navy has mined the Mersey to prevent U-boats approaching the port, and aerial mines have been dropped by the Luftwaffe. Since the outbreak of war a daily service has been maintained by the *Rushen Castle* supported by the *Snaefell* and *Victoria*. But on 27th December, when bound for Douglas with 200 passengers, the *Victoria* was struck by a magnetic mine and holed when nine miles north-west of the Bar Light. A nearby trawler took most of the passengers on to Douglas while the rest returned to Liverpool by a pilot boat. There were no casualties and the *Victoria* was towed back to Liverpool for repairs. This incident, together with the hazards and congestion of Liverpool, has resulted in the Steam Packet announcing that in future Fleetwood will be used for all services to and from the Island. All passengers are subject to strict security at the port.

1940 NEWS IN BRIEF

FEBRUARY

20 - Water scheme for south of Island adopted by Tynwald.

APRIL

5 - Spanish Head has been purchased anonymously for the Manx nation and has been placed in the care of the Society for the Preservation of the Manx Countryside. The mystery benefactor bought the area from Mr J. T. Kelly of Port St Mary, who himself gave Harry Kelly's cottage to the Manx nation in 1937.

9 - Death of Miss Florrie Forde, one of the great ladies of music hall. She was 65, and collapsed and died after singing to an audience of Servicemen in Aberdeen. Appearing mostly at the Derby Castle during the past 36 years, she was a great favourite. She loved the Island and had a holiday cottage at Niarbyl.

9 - GERMANS INVADE DENMARK AND NORWAY

18 - Poor Law Commission recommended Flat Rate for whole Island.

MAY

10 - HOLLAND AND BELGIUM INVADED.

10 - WINSTON CHURCHILL REPLACES NEVILLE CHAMBERLAIN AS PRIME MINISTER.

22 - Local Defence Volunteers formed.

28 - DUNKIRK EVACUATION begins. Three Steam Packet vessels sunk.

JUNE

1 - Norman Lewis Daugherty of Bride, first conscientious objector, had his appeal refused by Tribunal.

11 - MUSSOLINI DECLARES WAR ON FRANCE AND BRITAIN.

14 - GERMANS ENTER PARIS.

16 - Two I.O.M. Air Services DH Rapides abandoned at Bordeaux. Captain Higgins and Captain Greenhalgh escaped to England by fishing boat.

JULY

5 - Honorary degree of M.A. conferred on Mr Wm Cubbon, Curator of the Manx Museum, at Liverpool University.

10 - LUFTWAFFE AND R.A.F. MEET IN FIRST AIR BATTLES OVER CHANNEL

AUGUST

7 - Italians continue to advance into British Somaliland from Abyssinia.

SEPTEMBER

6 - 41st Battery of Manx Regiment credited with shooting down two German Dornier bombers.

7 - War Risks Insurance extended to Isle of Man.

30 - BLITZ OF LONDON BEGINS

NOVEMBER

30 - Blitz of industrial cities begins. Coventry devastated by a night of bombs.

33 MANX CREW AND 3 SHIPS LOST AT DUNKIRK

Three Steam Packet vessels sunk, 33 crew lost, but over 26,000 British and allied troops rescued. These are the grim statistics of recent epic events. With the main part of the British Expeditionary Force trapped in northern France by the rapidly advancing German army, the order was given to commence the evacuation of surviving troops through the port and beaches of Dunkirk. *Operation Dynamo* began on 26th May and hundreds of ships of all shapes and sizes were involved - from large passenger ferries to paddle-steamers and even river boats. Many were lost in the great rescue bid by constant air attacks by the Luftwaffe. The first ship to arrive at Dunkirk was the elderly *Mona's Isle* under Royal Navy command. During an air raid she embarked 1,420 troops and set sail for Dover. She was fired on by shore batteries and machine-gunned from the air. There were casualties among those on her crowded decks but she reached Dover and was greeted as the first ship to complete the round trip. The *Mona's Isle* successfully survived a second trip and brought out a further 1,200 soldiers.

Another of the early arrivals was the *King Orry* which was also flying the White Ensign. She embarked 1,100 troops and left Dunkirk in the early hours of the 27th. She, too, was hit by shore batteries and suffered damage and casualties, but reached Dover by noon. She then returned to Dunkirk and, as she entered the port, came under heavy air attacks resulting in the steering and all bridge instruments being put out of action. It soon became clear the ship was in danger of sinking and, to prevent her being a hazard to other ships, the captain managed to take her out of the harbour. The engine room began to flood and the *King Orry* sank early the following morning. The crew, including four Manx engineers, were rescued.

Since the Blitzkreig of the Low Countries began on 10th May, the *Mona's Queen*, under Captain Radcliffe Duggan and manned by Steam Packet crew, had been on duty virtually non-stop. First, she was ordered to Rotterdam to take on Dutch soldiers but by the time she arrived the port was an inferno and covered in a pall of smoke. On the way back to Dover, Captain Duggan was

diverted to Ostend and the *Mona's Queen* was loaded with soldiers and refugees of many nationalities who were brought safely to Folkestone. The *Mona's Queen* was sent next to Boulogne, this time loaded with 250 tons of explosives accompanied by Irish and Welsh Guards. Their mission was to blow up the port's installations before the arrival of the Germans. Arriving at Boulogne, a chain gang was formed by Chief Officer R. Clucas to man-handle the explosives onto the quayside. While this was happening, retreating troops, many in a sorry state, were scrambling on board. As they were leaving the quayside Stuka dive-bombers attacked the town, but Dover was reached in safety. The *Mona's Queen* was the last ship to leave Boulogne and, on 22nd May, Captain Duggan and his crew received a message from Admiral Ramsay of Dover Command congratulating them on their brave efforts.

On 26th May, the beginning of *Operation Dynamo*, Captain Duggan received orders to proceed to Dunkirk. When within two and a half miles of the port the *Mona's Queen* came under fire from the Calais batteries now in German control. Slight damage was done and after a change in course she was attacked by two dive-bombers, both of which were shot down by R.A.F. Hurricanes. At the pier the *Mona's Queen* took on board 1,200 soldiers and returned to Dover on the night of 27th May. Captain Duggan was then relieved for a well-earned rest. Under the command of the highly-experienced Captain Archibald Holkham, the *Mona's Queen* was ordered back to Dunkirk. At 5.30 a.m. on the 28th, she was hit by an aerial mine which struck her just aft of the funnel. The explosion split the vessel in two and she sank in 90 seconds. Of her 56 crew, the captain and 31 others reached the safety of one of the ship's lifeboats but 24, mostly from the engine room, were either killed or drowned; 20 were Manxmen.

The *Fenella*, under Captain Walter J. Cubbon and crewed by Steam Packet men, arrived in 'Hell's Alley' on 28th May and embarked 650 troops, She then came under a massive air attack during which she was hit by three bombs in quick succession. She was badly damaged and holed below the water-line by flying concrete, resulting in the engine room being flooded. The ship was hastily abandoned and sank soon afterwards. Of the 48 crew, 33 were saved and returned to Dover where one died from severe wounds. Of the 16 who perished, all but three were from the Island. *Fenella's* sister ship, *Tynwald*, evacuated more British and Allied soldiers than any other ship involved in *Operation Dynamo*. First under the command of Captain Wilfred A. Qualtrough, and then Captain John H. Whiteway, the *Tyn-*

(Inset) Hit by an aerial mine as she returned to Dunkirk, the 'Mona's Queen' sank rapidly with the loss of 24 lives. (Main picture) Survivors from the 'Mona's Queen' escaped in one of the ship's lifeboats. (Photographs via Louis Bridson)

168

wald made four perilous trips beginning on 28th May and ending on 4th June when the evacuation was brought to a halt. On that day she was the last to return to England, bringing with her 3,000 French troops. They brought her total which she saved from Dunkirk to 8,953.

The *Manxman* made two trips to Dunkirk and accounted for 2,394 men. Both the *Lady of Mann* and the *Ben My Chree*, the two largest Steam Packet ships played a major role in the Dunkirk evacuation, making good use of their speed and manoeuvrability. Each of these fine vessels evacuated over 4,000 troops. On her first visit to Dunkirk on 31st May, the *Lady*, commanded by Captain Thomas C. Woods, was under fire for six hours while she loaded at the pier, suffering damage from both shore batteries and air attacks. Her gunners claimed one enemy aircraft shot down. The *Lady* was back at Dunkirk on 1st June, and was on her way again the following day when she was ordered to return to Dover because of a lack of waiting troops. Her final visit was made on 4th June when she returned with 1,500 casualties from the devastated port. The *Ben* was also kept busy and completed two round trips under Captain George Woods. It then became necessary to re-crew the ship and Captain Woods was replaced by Captain Thomas E. Cain, D.S.C. He had been Chief Officer on the *Tynwald* and was a veteran of the Great War. Captain Cain was mentioned in despatches on six occasions and was awarded the D.S.C. for the part he played in sinking a U-boat in 1917, when he was captain of the paddler *Mona's Queen*. On the night of 2nd June, and with his new crew on board, Captain Cain set out for a further visit to Dunkirk. However, when crossing the Channel, the *Ben* came into collision with a block ship and had to return to port as a result of the damage caused.

The success of the great evacuation in these dark days gives hope for the future. Already the evacuation is being called a miracle. Over 338,000 British and Allied troops have been saved and are ready to fight again some time in the future. Of these, 26,449, one in every 14, were saved by Steam Packet vessels and their gallant crews. Their normal peace-time duties are far removed from the horrors of being shelled, dive-bombed and machine-gunned. They have also had to endure endless hours at their stations with little chance of respite. Future generations will admire the men for their bravery and the part they played in another great chapter in the history of the Isle of Man Steam Packet Company. But the price has been high.

OPERATION ARIEL

Of the ten Steam Packet ships commandeered for war service, two were unable to play their part in the evacuation of Dunkirk. The *Manx Maid*, with a Royal Navy

crew, and the *Viking* were both under repair at the time, the latter as a result of being bombed in the Thames Estuary. But both ships were to be involved in *Operation Ariel*, the evacuation of ports along the west coast of France. The *Manx Maid* embarked 3,000 French troops at Brest, nearly twice her normal passenger limit, and brought them to Southampton. Meanwhile, the *Viking* under Captain J. P. 'Ginger' Bridson, was present at the evacuation of both Le Havre and Cherbourg. She was sent later to Guernsey and evacuated over 3,000 islanders, including 1,800 children which was almost the entire child population. On her journey back to Weymouth the *Viking* was strafed by German fighters but the purser, Edgar Bishop, manned the anti-aircraft gun they had on board and helped keep the fighters at bay. The crew had been working non-stop for 18 hours and Captain Bridson dispensed what whisky was on board to fortify his men. Purser Edgar Bishop has been awarded the D.S.C. for the part he played in defending the ship.

Also taking part in the operation was the *Manxman*, with Captain Philip B. Cowley as master. Like other ships of the Steam Packet, the *Manxman* had operated as a 'personnel carrier' carrying troops to Le Havre and Cherbourg in the early months of the war. Now the process was in reverse. The *Manxman* was back again helping in the evacuation. On her final visit to Cherbourg she was fully laden at the pier when she came under fire from approaching tanks. A Royal Navy destroyer stood by to protect her as she made her escape, the last vessel to leave Cherbourg. On 16th June, the *Lady of Mann* joined in the operation and paid visits to Le Havre, Cherbourg and Brest. With 5,000 troops on board, and during an air attack, she was the last ship to leave Le Havre. Shortly afterwards, *Operation Ariel* was brought to a halt.

MEDALS FOR BRAVERY

In recognition of the tremendous courage and bravery shown by the Steam Packet crews, just a few have been chosen for awards. From the *Mona's Queen*, Captain R. Duggan and Radio Officer E. H. Ambler have both been awarded the Distinguished Service Cross, while the ship's bo'sun, Edgerton Watterson, receives the Distinguished Service Medal. Captain J. H. Whiteway of the *Tynwald* is awarded the D.S.C. together with his Chief Officer, A. Watterson and Radio Officer G. P. Mason, the latter of the Marconi Company. A/B Seaman T. Gribbin receives the D.S.M., and mentioned in despatches are purser W. E. Lister, carpenter J. Gawne and seaman A. J. Allen.

This dramatic photograph shows the 'Tynwald' flying the signal 'Full Speed' as she leaves Dunkirk with another load of troops. In the foreground can be seen the mast and funnel of the 'King Orry' which sank as the result of enemy air attacks. The 'Tynwald' had the distinction of rescuing nearly 3,000 soldiers, more than any other vessel taking part in the evacuation. Not so lucky was her sister ship 'Fenella' which was sunk by bombing during her first visit to Dunkirk. Sixteen of her crew perished.

(Photograph via Louis Bridson)

ISLAND ADJUSTS TO WARTIME SITUATION

The rationing of sugar in January (12oz) was followed in July by tea being limited to 2oz per person. This was followed in October by butter being rationed at 3oz per week, but this has since been reduced to 2oz. Apart from this there seem to be few shortages of other foods, though farmers are being subsidised to bring more land into cultivation, while a 'Dig for Victory' campaign is aimed at gardeners to make full use of allotments. Newspapers are now much slimmer and are only available to order. Imports of newsprint have had to be reduced because of Germany's U-boat blockade of Britain and the need to import more vitally important materials. Everyone is being encouraged to save waste paper to enable it to be recycled. Local authority workmen, scouts and guides are collecting bundles from home while children are playing their part in making school collections. One consequence is that very little paper is available in chip shops. People are collecting their meals in cooking basins wrapped in a cloth.

There is no petrol rationing as yet, but it is sure to come. One serious problem is that both petrol and fuel are being smuggled out of the Island, while private individuals or merchants have been caught trying to ship tea, sugar and other foodstuffs, presumably to sell on the black market. This is treated seriously and the authorities have warned offenders that they face imprisonment for breaking various emergency restrictions. The need for tighter controls has also been demonstrated by buyers from England buying up large quantities of fresh fish landed on the Island. People are being encouraged to stockpile at least one week's supply of food in their homes - in case there is an invasion. The authorities say they will try to keep deliveries of bread and milk going for 'as long as possible.' Provision has been made for the issuing of 'Iron Rations' for those unable to store a food reserve. They have been told to register their needs with the Food Executive Officer in their respective towns and villages. 'Iron Rations' will not be available in country districts, presumably because of problems of distribution.

THE BLACK-OUT

One of the effects of the black-out has been that many churches throughout the Island are holding Evensong in the afternoon this autumn. It means the churches will not have to finance black-out screens for their windows. The move also acknowledges that many people don't want to venture out in total darkness. There will be very little night time private motor traffic on Douglas promenade this winter, either. Speeds are being restricted to 10 m.p.h. and only side lights can be used. This is to to avoid light being seen out to sea from an area which has acquired considerable military significance. Public safety is also a logical reason for the restrictions, given the total absence of street lighting and the narrowness of the promenade now that barbed wire entanglements have been erected half way across the promenade to secure internment and military camps. The Government Order, applicable from half an hour after sunset or 7 p.m., whichever is the sooner, came into effect on 22nd October last. The masking of headlamps on all vehicles, whether private or on official duty, was made compulsory on 1st February.

FEAR OF PARACHUTISTS

Early in May, Mr Sargeaunt, the Government Secretary, received warning of the possibility of enemy parachutists landing on islands around the British coast and creating bases from which to attack the mainland. While nothing happened, local authorities and farmers responded to the Air Ministry request for obstructions to be placed on roadways and in large fields. This was to make it difficult for the landing of aircraft troop carriers. Port St Mary, for example, arranged to place lamp standards across roads. Motorists were warned to take extra care in the black-out. Fields were scattered with old farm machinery and oil drums.

To deny potential invaders knowledge of precisely where they are, the Highway Board removed all road signs including the historic ones dating back to the 1760s when the measuring of the Island's earthen roads began. Found throughout the Island, these ancient milestones, with details etched or cut into them, are made of limestone, sandstone or slate according to the locality in which they are found. About 50 were removed and it is doubtful if they will ever be returned. The more recent milestones with metal facings should be less of a problem.

AIR ALERTS

On moonlight nights the drone of German bombers can be heard overhead. There were alerts on the night of 26th October and on the nights of 20th and 21st December. On the latter nights the alerts lasted for five hours. Judging from the glare over the eastern horizon, and the vibration caused by the bombs and anti-aircraft fire, it was apparent that Liverpool was being heavily attacked. It has brought the horror of the Blitz a little nearer home and the chance of being bombed deliberately or accidentally cannot be ignored. Despite many demands there is still no properly organised A.R.P defence in place. There is plenty of advice to householders, such as covering windows with thin wire mesh or strips of sticky paper to prevent the hazard of splintered glass entering rooms. Meanwhile, many householders are building private air raid shelters in parts of their gardens.

Local authorities at last are providing public air raid shelters for those caught away from home which is still considered to be the safest place. Three large shelters have been built in the sunken gardens of Loch Promenade, roofed with concrete reinforced by railway lines. Other shelters in the town can now be found under the Villa Marina Colonnade, York Road bus depot, Shaw's Brow and next to Noble's Hall. Other designated shelters include hotel basements and the cellar of the Town Hall. Outside of Douglas, towns and villages are being provided with their own shelters. Peel now has five shelters capable of accommodating 900 people. Old tunnels under Castle Street, reputedly used by smugglers centuries ago, have been adapted for use. Probably the most exotic place of shelter of all is the old dungeons of Castle Rushen but they will not be available at night.

For the treatment of air raid casualties, 35 First Aid stations have been established throughout the Island by the St John Ambulance Association and the local branch of the British Red Cross Society. The stations are all equipped with beds for the injured and are manned by volunteer nurses whose uniforms now include trousers.

VOLUNTEERS FORM THE HOME GUARD

The Isle of Man has its own force of volunteers to fight any invader. In May the Secretary of State for War, Mr Anthony Eden, announced on the B.B.C. the Government's intention of raising an unpaid Local Defence Force as part of the defence of the United Kingdom. The raising of such a force in the Isle of Man was authorised immediately by the Lieutenant-Governor, its object being to prepare for any attempt by the enemy to land by parachute or any other means. The official notice from Government Office said that volunteers should be between the ages of 17 and 65, and of reasonable fitness. A total of 1,500 men responded and were asked to give details of their previous experience in weaponry and other military matters. The Island has been organised as a separate Zone under the control of Lieut.-Colonel G. S. Scott, O.B.E. of Western Command. Organised in groups covering the whole Island, the men first attended parades in civilian clothing and wearing arm bands bearing the letters L.D.V. Uniforms of the denim overall type arrived by the end of June. For arms training, use was made of any firearms available including rifles of pre-Great War vintage found in Douglas Police Station, along with 90,000 rounds of ammunition.

With the German invasion fleet massing in French ports across the English Channel, Prime Minister Winston Churchill announced on 28th July that the Local Defence Force was to be re-named the 'Home Guard' and brought to a higher degree of preparedness. On the Island the Zone groups were divided into two Battalions. The 1st Manx Batallion, based in Douglas with about 1,200 men, was divided into A and B Companies, the latter also containing men from Onchan, Braddan and Santon. Officer Commanding 1st Battalion is Deemster S. J. Kneale with Mr A. D. McEvoy as Second in Command. Company Officers are Messrs T. C. Greenfield, J. W. Royston, J. M. Cain, R. T. Wetherill and R. J. Wilkinson. The rest of the Island sectors make up the 2nd Manx Battalion which consists of five separate detachments, each with a Commanding Officer. These are: Ramsey Company i/c Major A. W. Dobbin, D.S.O.; Castletown Company i/c Mr P. D. Kissack; Peel Company i/c Mr G. W. Howie; Laxey Platoon i/c Mr E. Corteen, and Ballaugh-Michael Platoon i/c Mr W. Cain.

The Isle of Man Rifle Association has made its nine rifle ranges available together with rifles and equipment to provide further experience. Other outdoor ranges have been constructed and the Government range at Balnahow, Santon, has also been made available. By the middle of July the more modern Lee Enfield rifle and ammunition became available. Village halls are being put to good use for training sessions and lectures which members attend in their spare time. In addition, most men are required to do guard duty on one night out of eight, from one hour before dusk to one hour after dawn. Fifty-two observation posts have been established to give warning of the landing of parachutists. Improvised road blocks are also manned and patrols are set up to watch over vulnerable areas such as reservoirs, harbour installations and the new telephone radio station at Creg ny Baa. The men now have full uniform and have been issued with protective clothing and blankets for night duties. An Order issued by Government Office forbids the ringing of church bells at any time. They are only to be rung as a method of calling out the Home Guard in an emergency.

Throughout the Island, men have come forward to join the Local Defence Volunteers, later renamed the Home Guard. Here, men of Onchan line up near the Commissioners' Office. Standing in front is Mr George Shaw, history master at the Douglas High School for Boys. (Manx National Heritage)

ISLAND PROVIDES ACCOMMODATION FOR 14,000 ALIENS

Fourteen thousand enemy aliens have been interned on the Isle of Man. As the Germans swept into northern France at the beginning of May and occupied the Channel ports, a pressing need became apparent to ensure that anyone with German origins did not pose a threat to national security, especially should there be an invasion. The same applied to Italians when they became our enemies. There was little time to waste. Thousands of men and women, aged from 16 to 60, were summoned to appear before hastily convened tribunals. There they were classified roughly according to risk and then sent to make-shift transit camps. While many were shipped to Canada and Australia, the Isle of Man was selected as a secure place of internment within the British Isles. Under the Defence Regulations (Isle of Man) Act, Home Office officials, in co-operation with the Manx Government, created internment camps throughout the Island. Tynwald believed they would make an important contribution to the Manx economy while there was some consolation for boarding-house keepers who would be saved the deprivations of the last war. Nevertheless, there was considerable ill-feeling towards anyone seen to have German or Italian connections, even though they might be enemies of Nazism too. Another reason for hostility was the way Government officials commandeered properties without warning and required them to be vacated almost immediately.

An Internment Camp Division, headed by Government Secretary Mr Bertram Sargeaunt, was set up to administer the camps. Men, unlikely to be called up for military service, were employed as clerks and typists to deal with the mass of documents, forms and communications; others had the duty of arranging tenders with grocers, butchers and farmers for the supply of huge quantities of food. On 15th May, the Camp Division sent out the first batch of letters in buff envelopes marked 'On His Majesty's Service' to the occupiers of hotels and boarding houses along the Mooragh Promenade, Ramsey. The letters gave curt notification that occupiers were to vacate their premises by the end of the week. They had just five days in which to find alternative accommodation. They were permitted to take only the minimum amount of furniture, bedding and personal possessions. Everything else had to be left behind. Government valuers made lists of furniture, fixtures, bedding, cooking utensils and crockery etc. Those evicted were also informed that they would have the rents and rates of their properties paid, plus a small quarterly payment for the use of the household items according to the valuation.

That week the people of Ramsey became accustomed to the sound of pneumatic drills as hundreds of holes were made for the wooden posts which support the miles of barbed wire which now surrounds the MOORAGH CAMP. As the fever of activity came to an end, the *Rushen Castle* tied up at the Queen's Pier with 150 soldiers on board. They have been billeted in the town and guard the camp night and day. Everything was in position for the arrival of the first batch of 823 aliens on the evening of 27th May. They were brought by a Belgian steamer. Townsfolk turned out to watch them being marched from the pier, over the swing bridge and into the camp. The aliens appeared to be a strange mixture - young and old, rich and poor, each carrying from the transit camps what few possessions they were allowed to keep, packed in suitcases, parcels or bundles. That day the evacuation of Dunkirk was already under way.

Two days later the Belgian steamer arrived at Douglas for the first of three visits, each time packed with the first women aliens. They were entrained for open internment in what is being called RUSHEN CAMP. It includes the whole of Port Erin and Port St Mary. By November, the number of women internees rose to 4,000, thus nearly doubling the local population. Landladies are responsible for organising the accommodation of their new 'guests' for whom they receive £1 1s. a week, well below the normal rate for full board. An additional allowance is paid for extra staff, such as cooks.

While the Mooragh Camp was being prepared, two further camps were being created. Occupiers of 60 boarding houses in the Royal Avenue West area of Onchan were put under short notice to quit while about 34 properties on and behind the Central Promenade, Douglas, were being vacated. The *Rushen Castle*, assisted by the *Victoria,* were kept busy and by the middle of June, ONCHAN CAMP had received 1,200 German aliens and the CENTRAL CAMP nearly 1,000, a number which would be doubled by the end of the month. A non-stop stream of arrivals saw the opening of the PALACE CAMP made up of 28 large boarding houses above the sea front. This camp became the most crowded of all with nearly 3,000 accommodated by the end of June.

The entry of Italy into the war resulted in a further influx of internees. The well-practised machinery saw the METROPOLE CAMP on Queen's Promenade and HUTCHINSON CAMP being made ready by the middle of July. Metropole was used mainly for Italian internees while the first to arrive in Hutchinson were Germans and Austrians. GRANVILLE CAMP and REGENT CAMP on Loch Promenade were also made ready. By October there were 750 men in Granville though Regent remained empty. The small SEFTON CAMP was also occupied though the group of properties known as the FALCON CAMP had not yet been used. The PEVERIL CAMP on Peel promenade was filled with Italian aliens. This brought the number of occupied men's camps to nine. An estimated 10,000 male internees are now being held, in addition to the 4,000 females in the Rushen Camp.

While the net has been cast far and wide to round up those thought to be of the slightest risk to national security there has, nevertheless, been much heart-searching about the inhuman treatment meted out to many of those now classified as aliens. The most dangerous have been put in Category A, including suspected Fifth Columnists, and will be detained for the duration of the war. The vast majority, however, are Categories B and C and are thought by many to be completely harmless. Many of these are refugees, including Jews, who were welcomed to Britain as they escaped the clutches of the Nazis. Others are old and sick. In July, despite the desperate war situation, questions were raised in the House of Commons. Was it right to keep these people behind barbed wire when many could be employed to help the war effort? This led to the Home Office taking the first steps to investigate each individual case through tribunals. The process began in October and already there has been a marked fall in the number of men now detained. Women have also been released from the Rushen Camp. Slow progress, however, is causing a high degree of restlessness in the camps.

MANX REGIMENT IN ACTION

Early in May, 55 gunners were detached from the Regiment and joined the expedition to support Norway against the German invasion. They landed in the Namsos fjord and immediately came under attack by Stuka dive-bombers. After five days the expedition was withdrawn and returned to England, surviving heavy air attacks on the way. The gunners have since been posted to another regiment and replaced by strangers, much to the disappointment of Lieut.-Colonel MacClellan. By then, the rest of the Regiment had been deployed in the south and west of England, 41st Battery providing Troops for the defence of the radar station at Ventnor on the Isle of Wight. All three Batteries undertook intensive firing practice at St Agnes in Cornwall.

August saw what is now being called the 'Battle of Britain' at its height. R.A.F. fighters were locked in battle with the Luftwaffe flying from its newly-acquired bases in France. Troops from the Manx Regiment took up defensive positions stretching from Kent to Devon, including Southampton and Portsmouth. While the Hurricanes and Spitfires were in action, the Bofors guns remained silent but there was plenty of opportunity for the gunners to open up. On 12th August, 'Z' Troop of 41st Battery was officially credited with shooting down two enemy aircraft during an attack on the R.A.F. station at Warmwell in Dorset.

During the autumn many changes took place within the Regiment. Major W. S. Valentine took over command of the 42nd and his place as Adjutant of the Regiment was taken over by Captain J. B. Mylchreest. In October, the Regiment was ordered to move to Glasgow, in preparation for embarkation to the Middle East. The men were given three weeks' leave and were given a warm reception back on the Island. They were entertained by the Mayor and Corporation at a civic dinner in the Villa Marina. A farewell dance held in the Palais de Danse was attended by 800 people.

The men returned to Glasgow and on the 15th November the 129th, separated once again from the main part of the Regiment, embarked at Gouroch on the troopship *Strathaird* filled to capacity with boisterous Australian infantry. The following day saw the 41st and 42nd Batteries and Regimental Headquarters board the *Viceroy of India* still in its peacetime guise. The ships departed in convoy on a six-week voyage to Egypt via the Cape of Good Hope, stopping at Durban for four days' shore leave. Christmas was celebrated on board the ships as they entered the Gulf of Aden and the Red Sea. The Regiment was re-united at Beni Yusef in the shadow of the Great Pyramid.

The Ben my Chree made two trips to 'Hell's Alley' and is seen here arriving at Folkstone loaded with troops evacuated from Dunkirk.

(via Louis Bridson)

BUSY SCENE AT R.A.F. JURBY

Jurby has settled down to a regular routine in the training of aircrew in techniques of bombing and air gunnery. The bombing ranges off Jurby Head are in use every day and the early Bristol Blenheims have been joined by Handley Page Herefords. The accuracy of practice smoke bombs dropped on the targets are recorded from observation huts positioned along the coast. Whitleys and Wellingtons are frequent visitors to the station. They arrive from Operational Training Units in England. Their crews are in the final stages of training before being posted to a Bomber Command squadron. They 'attack' the targets night and day from high, low and medium heights, both in formation and alone.

Air to air gunnery practice also takes place out to sea. Obsolete aircraft such as Westland Wallaces, Hawker Henleys and Fairey Battles are used as target-towers. The targets take the form of a drogue let out on wire from the rear of the aircraft. The gunners operate Vickers machine guns from a manually operated turret with which the short-nosed Blenheim aircraft are equipped. Each trainee gunner fires rounds which have been dipped in paint of different colours. Hits on the drogue can then be identified with individual gunners. The towing aircraft has to release its drogue over the beach or designated area. This operation is particularly dangerous because the pilot has to come in low and reduce speed before releasing the drogue. The danger lies in stalling the aircraft. Already there have been some accidents as a result.

The accommodation at Jurby is already over-crowded so when Manx airmen arrive from initial training stations, and are waiting a posting to a squadron, S.W.O. Radcliffe has no hestitation in allowing them to live at home. Most cycle home to Douglas or Onchan but have to be back at Jurby by 8.00 a.m. each weekday. Many of the staff pilots are Poles who escaped to England. They are accommodated mostly in farm houses in the district and have been befriended by local families despite the language difficulties. The Poles are noted for their fearless flying, and they love to join in a game of football organised on the station. They play with great gusto and are difficult to beat, even when playing in bare feet!

To add to the congestion, Jurby is now host to a night fighter squadron which arrived in November and brought more Poles to the station. Under an English squadron leader, and with British groundcrew, the pilots and gunners formerly belonged to the Polish Forces. They have been assigned to fly Defiant aircraft which have a four-gun turret and are being pressed into service as night fighters. They are sent into action to help in the defence of the North-West, now that Manchester, Liverpool, Belfast and Glasgow are threatened by mass formations of German bombers. They have the duty also of undertaking daylight convoy patrols which arrive north of Ireland as a result of the German occupation of France. One of the Defiants has been lost in a crash, fortunately without loss of life.

People in the north of the Island are becoming used to the amount of flying taking place. Aircraft are in the air every day and they are joined by others from other training stations around the Irish Sea, especially those of Silloth and Millom in Cumberland. It is noticeable also that the number of flying accidents is increasing. They are usually the result of engine failure, pilot error or because of bad visibility which hides the perils of Snaefell and other areas of high ground. It has been esti-

Heavy snowfalls affected the whole Island at the end of January, bringing flying operations at Jurby to a week-long halt. Here can be seen a Fairey Battle (above) and a Bristol Blenheim Mk1 (below) caught in snow drifts. (Flt. Lt. Norman Radcliffe)

mated that crashes occur on average once a month. Some of those involved are lucky to escape unscathed. Those badly injured or burned are attended to in the sick quarters at Jurby, which is in liaison with the Ramsey Cottage Hospital. During the year five Jurby aircrew have lost their lives including a sergeant pilot of the Polish Forces.

FATAL AIR ACCIDENT REPORTS, 1940

1st January : Handley Page Hampden on training flight from Upper Heyford crashed on Snaefell in thick cloud. Three crew were killed and one survived with injuries.

11th January : An Airspeed Oxford from Jurby on night flying exercise stalled when climbing away from airfield. Pilot under training was killed.

24th August : An O.T.U. Wellington from Jurby crashed in sea at an unknown place with the loss of two lives. One body retrieved at Fleshwick.

1st October : Fairey Battle target tower from Jurby spun out of control and crashed at Greenhill's Estate, Andreas. Polish pilot and drogue operator killed.

17th December : Wallace aircraft from Ronaldsway on towing drogue duty ditched in rough sea 300 yards south-east of Langness Lighthouse. Both the pilot (Polish) and the drogue operator were drowned. The body of the latter was recovered from Jurby foreshore some time later.

HERE IS THE NEWS : **1941**
PEEL SHAKEN BY RIOT AT 'FASCIST CAMP'

Hundreds of British Fascists detained in the Peveril Camp at Peel have run amok in a week-end of rioting and violence. The situation has become so serious that the Home Office has ordered 50 experienced London policemen to move to Peel and stiffen the military guard. We have this report.

In May the Italian internees in the Peveril Camp were replaced by some 600 so-called Regulation 18b detainees who are mostly members of Sir Oswald Mosley's British Union of Fascists - the 'Blackshirts' - while others are convicted I.R.A. terrorists. When they arrived in Douglas harbour they were greeted by the jeers and catcalls of local people who regard them as traitors. The camp is regarded by many as a hot-bed of intrigue and on Saturday, 20th September, the situation erupted in violence. On the previous Wednesday evening three of the internees, who had been attending a concert in a hall just outside the camp, slipped their guards and disappeared into the night. It was not until the following morning that their absence was discovered and a thorough search began both on and around the Island by the military and local police. It was discovered that a small fishing boat had disappeared from its mooring in Castletown harbour. Its engine was without sparking plugs, according to regulations, but two pairs of oars had been stolen from a warehouse in School Lane. On Saturday afternoon the escapees were picked up by a naval patrol boat seven miles off the Calf of Man and they were then returned to Peel.

Earlier on Saturday the camp had been inspected by an Under Secretary from the Home Office, accompanied by the Camp Commandant. They had been given a rough time and many of the detainees hurled abuse and obscenities at them. It was in this atmosphere that the three escapees, heroes to many, returned to the camp and were locked in cells. This sparked the riot. A demolished stone hedge was used for 'ammunition' along with dust bin lids and even lavatory seats. The guards were targets but they were not permitted to fire back

into the camp. The Creg Malin Hotel, across Walpole Road, was an easy target and it took a battering. Many of its windows and slates were smashed and the whole area was littered with debris. As darkness fell the surrounding camp lights were switched on and the whole place was illuminated, making a dramatic and fearful sight for the hundreds of onlookers on the Promenade. It was not until midnight that things began to simmer down. The Home Office ordered an immediate inquiry, questions were asked in the House of Commons, national newspapers reported the 'scandalous affair' and the B.B.C. also reported the incident. The three 'heroes' were found guilty of the theft of the small fishing boat and sentenced to prison on the 'mainland.' A senior police officer from Scotland Yard visited Peel and it was announced that 50 London policemen, experienced in dealing with Mosley's Fascists, were to be drafted in to help the military guards keep control over what locals call the 'Fascists Camp.'

THE DETESTED WOMEN
Matters in Peel are made worse by the visits of women from Rushen Camp who, since May, have been permitted to visit their husbands on a regular basis. The women arrive by coach and are at liberty to shop in the town. Their display of arrogance is matched only by the amount of money they have to spend. Their buying up of large quantities of unrationed food is a sore point with the townsfolk. The women then congregate at the Creg Malin before being escorted into the camp. Hotelier Mr A. E. Ostick is so incensed by their behaviour that he has refused to serve them. Peel Town Commissioners are concerned about the large amounts of food being taken into the camp and it is noted that there seems to be no shortage of beer, judging by the number of deliveries being made to the camp. Another irksome feature is that locals are not permitted to be on the beach while the detainees are bathing. Following the riot, the women's visits have been suspended for a month and will be less frequent in future; also only one small parcel of food will be allowed each visit.

The Creg Malin has now been commandeered and will be used for stores and interview rooms. A wooden hut behind the hotel will serve as a waiting room for the women.

MORE TROUBLE IN PEEL
Barely a week after the riot in the Peveril Camp, an Army officer noticed, by chance, a loose sod in a narrow footpath opposite the top end of the camp and passing the guard house. Beneath the sod was a short ladder leading from what appeared to be a tunnel. The hard-pressed Manx police were called to investigate and a team led by Inspector Kneen made an amazing discovery in the front room of No 13, Peveril Road. Floor boards had been cut and below there was a ten foot shaft. With great precision an 18" tunnel had been dug out leading for 25 yards under the road and wire fencing to the pathway directly opposite. The tunnel, through sand and clay, was timbered at intervals and illuminated by an electric light wired to the mains of the house. Obviously there were many collaborators and 18 men who are considered to be the ring leaders are to be transferred to Walton Gaol, Liverpool. They will be escorted by the newly-arrived Metropolitan police. Peel is also to be subject to tighter security and it has been declared a Protected Area. Only residents and those on legitimate business can enter the town; spot checks will be made and identity cards must be shown.

CHANGES AT RUSHEN CAMP
The work of the Tribunals has seen a considerable reduction in the number of internees being held on the Island, including the Rushen Camp. Much of Port St Mary has been freed of the women held there, but the boarding houses along the promenade and the Ballaqueeney Hotel have been fenced off to form married quarters for the wives held in the Rushen Camp. They have been joined by their husbands from the men's camps. Up to now the wives have travelled on what locals call the 'love trains' to Douglas to meet their husbands in Derby Castle and its grounds. Commandant of the new camp, which opened in May, is Mr Cuthbert, a Divisional Inspector from Scotland Yard. The remaining women from Port St Mary have been

Women interned in Port St. Mary have been transferred to Port Erin, apart from those who have husbands interned in other camps on the Island. They are now confined to Ballaqueeney and neighbouring boarding houses which have been wired off to form married quarters.

(Manx National Heritage)

transferred to Port Erin. The changes were not to the liking of the formidable Dame Joanna Cruickshank so she has resigned as Rushen Camp Commandant and returned to London. A nurse by training, she ran a strict, though caring, regime for the women in her charge. She had little time for the Chief Constable who has the ultimate responsibility for the camp, and no doubt Major Young will welcome Mr Cuthbert as the new Camp Commandant.

H.M.S. VALKYRIE

The Granville and Regent Internment Camps on Loch Promenade, Douglas, have been taken over by the Admiralty and commissioned as *H.M.S. Valkyrie*. Here ratings are being accommodated as they train in the latest 'hush hush' technology of radio detection in what is called the Royal Navy's No 1 Radar Training School. Each morning ranks of the young sailors are marched up to Douglas Head where the school has classrooms in the Douglas Head Hotel, Collinson's cafe and even the ticket office of the incline railway. A three-storeyed concrete building is also being built to provide 18 additional classrooms. The Principal Training Officer is J. L. T. Jackson who was a former chief instructor in wireless telegraphy. After recovering from a bout of dysentery which he contracted in Malta, he was commissioned to equip and operate the school. It is estimated the school has cost £3 million to establish and already the whole area is bristling with masts and scanners. Those who complete the course will be posted to Royal Navy ships from battle ships to submarines. Every vessel will require numerous radar operators to use this vital equipment which can

locate enemy ships and aircraft beyond visual range.

AIR RAID VICTIMS

Many Manx homes have been bereaved by members of their families being killed by German air attacks on London and Merseyside. Some 14 are known to have lost their lives by the end of May. At the beginning of the month, babies from the bombed areas of Liverpool and Birkenhead were evacuated to the Island. About 90 under-fives are being looked after by members of the Manx Women's Guild either in private homes or hostels. It is estimated that nearly a thousand evacuated children from various parts of England and Scotland are now being cared for in Manx homes. Most of them have been found places in local schools. The Manx Women's Guild has been formed to provide knitted comforts and other articles for Manxmen serving in the fighting

forces and also for the relief of civilians affected by the war.

TWO GIRLS DROWNED

Two 12-year-old Douglas girls were drowned while swimming in the sea near Victoria Pier. They got into difficulties after going into the water off the Peveril jetty. Hundreds of people watched as officer cadets and Navy men went to their rescue. But they were both dead from drowning by the time they were brought ashore.

Two Douglas boys had a remarkable escape from death after falling down cliffs below the Marine Drive. Eleven-year-old Dennis Ekin and 15-year-old Colin Savage landed on a ledge eight feet from the high-water mark. Both were injured and spent the night on the ledge. The next day the older boy, despite his injuries, climbed 200 feet to the top of the cliff and alerted Coastguards who rescued his friend.

FIRE DAMAGE

Fire caused serious damage to part of the White City amusement resort on Onchan Head, where thousands of visitors used to have summertime fun before the war. It destroyed the attraction known as the River Caves and threatened the timber-built Onchan Pavilion theatre. In September a fire caused £5,000 worth of damage in the projection room of the Strand Cinema, Douglas, after it had closed for the night.

DARING ESCAPE FROM MOORAGH CAMP

On the night of Wednesday, 15th October, three Dutchmen, all pro-Nazi, made a bold escape from Mooragh Camp. Two officers in the

The Douglas Bay Hotel is now bristling with aerials which are used in the highly secret art of radio detection. Here operators posted to H.M.S. Valkyrie are trained in the Royal Navy's No 1 Radar Training School.

(Manx National Heritage)

Dutch mercantile marine and a civilian pilot had been planning the escape for some time with the help of a ladder to climb the barbed-wire fence, and a wooden plank to cross the two rows of fencing. The ladder had been discovered, however, so pliers were used to cut through the fencing. They had attended the six o'clock roll call and waited for dark before making a move. They headed for Ramsey Harbour where they had already noted the position of a small yacht when out on exercise walks. Its engine had been immobilised but they used a pole to get the yacht away and then raised its sails as they left the harbour. They met mountainous seas and had little hope of reaching Dublin where they planned to contact the German Consul. A strong south-westerly gale was blowing.

The absence of the three escapees was noted at roll call on Thursday morning and a massive search was carried out on the Island. Naval patrol vessels and aircraft from Jurby also joined in the search but were hampered by poor visibility. It was not until the next day, Friday, that the yacht was spotted from one of the aircraft. The Dutchmen were drifting helplessly towards St Bees Head where they scrambled ashore, exhausted and saturated. A military guard was waiting for them. They were given dry clothes and taken to Whitehaven police station. From there, Manx police escorted them back to Ramsey via Fleetwood. At their trial they were found guilty of stealing the yacht, valued at £300, and committed to Victoria Road Gaol for six months. After serving their sentence they are to be transferred to the Peveril Camp in Peel.

RATIONING BITES DEEPER

The U-boat blockade has started to hit everyone at their meal table. Towards the end of last year butter rationing was added to that of sugar, and the use of milk for the making of ice cream was banned. In January the making of synthetic cream was banned. Families now have to register with a grocer for their rations of preserves, syrup and treacle; sugar has been reduced to 4oz per person and cheese is also rationed at 2oz per person. The Island's food supplies are carefully regulated by the Food Control Office, bearing in mind that thousands of military personnel and internees have also to be fed. November saw the rationing of petrol begin with an allowance of six gallons per month per car. Motorcycles get two gallons. Many

View of the Mooragh Internment Camp, Ramsey. In October, three pro-Nazi Dutchmen made a daring escape but were re-captured two days later off the Cumberland coast.

(Manx National Heritage)

cars have been put away for 'the duration' and people are resorting to the steam railway for transport. The Government is also considering putting clothing on coupons. This follows the U.K. Board of Trade limiting the amount of clothing, cloth of all kinds and shoes. The announcement resulted in local shops being invaded, but Earl Granville put a stop to that by closing all relevant shops for three days. They had to report the exact amount of stock they held and must record all sales in future. Only those holding a Manx identity card can make purchases of reasonable quantities.

MANX GUNNER MEETS ROMMEL

Sergeant Ken Conibear of Douglas has met Field-Marshal Rommel. It happened in a hospital in Athens where Sgt. Conibear is recovering from serious wounds received during the evacuation of Crete. Rommel stopped at his bed and in perfect English enquired where he was from. The British doctor in attendance said he was a Manxman. Rommel seemed unsure what he meant. "Ah, Insel Man," he said when the doctor explained that Conibear was from the Isle of Man. Rommel then stood to attention and gave the Manxman the Nazi salute.

AIR RAID ALERTS

On the nights of 7th, 15th and 16th April enemy bombers were again over the Island. On the first occasion the sky was illuminated by flares and an incendiary bomb landed near Port Soderick. On the 15th an h.e. bomb caused slight damage to the Cronk Ruagh Sanatorium near Ramsey and the following night a bomb fell near the radio detection station at Scarlett in the south of the Island. Considerable alarm was caused on the night of 8/9th May when two bombs fell on the outskirts of Douglas. One fell at Ballaoates. A bungalow on the corner had its roof damaged and windows blown in. The second bomb exploded in a field above Willaston Corner. A lady was blown out of bed and windows were smashed along Ballanard Road and as far away as Norwood Drive and Park Avenue. The only casualty was a frog whose seared body was found near the crater. The end of the year saw further alerts as Liverpool and Belfast came under heavy attacks.

LATEST WAR CASUALTY FIGURES

During the year news has been received of the loss of a further 60 lives of men from the Island as a result of enemy action.

BRITISH ARMY   21 casualties , including nine who were killed in Crete and one who died in hospital later.
ROYAL AIR FORCE 13 killed on operations.
ROYAL NAVY   8 lost in ships sunk
MERCHANT NAVY 17, mostly lost at sea when ships have been torpedoed.

In addition 4 have died whilst in service and 14 Manx persons are known to have been killed during air raids on London and Merseyside.

Members of the Manx Regiment H.Q. staff photographed in the Suez Canal Zone. Seated in the centre is the Regiment's C.O., Lieutenant-Colonel G.P. MacClellan, now retired. On his right is Captain J. B. Mylchreest, and on his left, Captain Guy Pantin, the Regiment's medical officer. (Manx National Heritage)

One of the Bofors gun teams of 41st Battery which took part in the Eritrean Campaign in the early months of the year.

DISASTER FOR THE 129th BATTERY IN CRETE

Towards the end of May, news filtered through to the Island, mainly via German propaganda radio broadcasts, concerning the fate of the 129th Battery. It was not good. In January the Battery had been sent to Crete to help defend the base at Suda on the north coast of Crete. The base had been set up following the Italian invasion of Greece last year and the 129th encamped among the olive groves on the surrounding hills. While Mussolini's soldiers were making slow progress, the situation changed rapidly with the German Blitzkrieg of Yugoslavia, and then Greece. Athens fell in April and it was imperative to support the limited British and Commonwealth force sent to aid the Greeks. Suda was the main supply port and protection was given by Royal Navy ships, including *H.M.S. Warspite*. The 11 Bofors guns were mounted in concrete and, together with a lone Vickers Mk11 gun, were positioned at various points in the hills around Suda Bay. Visits by Italian aircraft were made at a high level and caused little trouble, but matters changed for the worse with the arrival of the Luftwaffe. Swarms of Ju88 bombers and Ju87 dive-bombers attacked the port relentlessly. Following the collapse of Greece, Heinkel and Dornier bombers together with ME 109 fighters joined in as German forces were massed to invade the island.

On the morning of 20th May the whole area was machine-gunned from the air. It was the prelude to the arrival of the German crack Airborne Division with hundreds of parachutists landing in the hills. They met stiff opposition from British and Commonwealth troops who were under orders to hold the island at all costs. But they were fighting against overwhelming odds and on the 26th the order was given to evacuate the island. The 129th had been in almost constant action for days and had succeeded in bringing down between 30 and 40 enemy aircraft. Orders were given to destroy the guns and to return to Suda Bay in darkness while hiding among rocks in the day. On the night of the 31st the men reached the beach. The wounded, 35 in all, were given priority and places for them were found on what turned out to be the last ship to leave Suda. The beaches were crowded with waiting troops, but they were strafed mercilessly by Me110s. Nine of the 129th were killed and more than 20 hospitalised with serious wounds. The remainder, some 110 including Major Cain and Captain Maley, were taken prisoner and sent to camps throughout Germany.

Meanwhile, the 41st Battery had been giving support to the 4th Indian Division. Together with the 5th Division, it had been sent to Abyssinia to halt the Italians adding to their East Africa Empire. The men had to endure desert conditions, snakes and scorpions and, the dreaded dysentery which claimed the life of one of the gunners. There was plenty of action against Italian aircraft and progress into Eritrea meant covering hundreds of miles of desert and mountain terrain. The Battery was present at the vital battle to take the town of Keren in March. Resistance began to crumble and the Italians surrendered at the beginning of June. Since then the 41st Battery has returned to Egypt and has joined the 42nd in the defence of the Suez Canal. Lieut.-Colonel MacClellan has been placed in charge of the defence of the Canal Zone.

1941 NEWS IN BRIEF

FEBRUARY
21 - No 440 (1st Manx) Squadron of the Air Training Corps formed. Flights to be based at Douglas High School, King William's College and Ramsey Grammar School.

MARCH
18 - Tynwald grant £500,000 as war contribution to British Exchequer.

MAY
12 - Fascists arrive for detention at Peel.

JUNE
1 - *H.M.S. Manxman* commissioned.
13 - First news of Battery of Manx Regiment operating in Crete trapped when evacuation took place.
17 - British women Fascists arrive in Port Erin
17 - Higher income tax and surtax approved.
30 - GERMAN FORCES INVADE RUSSIA.

AUGUST
29 - All-Island A.R.P. scheme announced.

SEPTEMBER
20 - Night of riots at Peel following arrest of escaped Fascists.
30 - Keys approve shorter licensing hours.

OCTOBER
1 - London police arrive to take over Fascist Camp.
18 - National Savings Campaign : 'Warship Week' opens, £640,000 subscribed.

NOVEMBER
14 - Bigger National Insurance benefits announced, and higher weekly payments.
14 - 'Aid for Russia' Fund launched.

DECEMBER
7 - PEARL HARBOUR ATTACKED. U.S. ENTERS WAR - Japanese, Rumanian and Hungarian internees arrive.
12 - Order in Council extending Military Service Act (1941) to Island.

THE HOME GUARD AND THE CIVIL DEFENCE

During the year considerable improvement has been made in the training and preparedness of the Home Guard. Every opportunity has been taken to co-operate with the regular units and training establishments in contests and exercises. All Home Guard members have been equipped with army battle dress and boots as worn by the regular army, while there has also been a good supply of other items of equipment. In April the War Office sanctioned the appointment of Officers and N.C.O.s throughout the echelons of command. Colonel Scott, O.B.E., remains Zone Commander with Major S. W. Corlett appointed his Staff Officer. Battalion Commanders have been made Lieutenant-Colonels, and Company Commanders either Majors or Captains.

On 5th July the Manx Home Guard was honoured by a visit from the Director-General of the Home Guard, Major-General Viscount Bridgeman, D.S.O.,M.C., who arrived with his Staff Officers to attend the Tynwald Ceremony. A Home Guard detachment from Peel and St John's provided part of the Guard of Honour for the ceremony and were complimented on their smart appearance. The following day Lord Bridgeman inspected the 1st Battalion at Tromode and the Ballasalla Platoon, Southern Company, 2nd Battalion.

The Tromode Drill Hall was designed originally for the Manx Territorial Regiment. Building had only just begun when war broke out. Work was stopped but, following approaches from the Manx Territorial Association, the War Office decided to complete the building. At the end of last year it was handed over to the 1st Battalion as a headquarters and training centre. The fine building has a large hall with social rooms, gymnasium, showers, Officers' and N.C.O.s' messes and canteen, with a parade ground and sports field alongside.

This summer a series of three week-end training camps under canvas were held at *H.M.S. St George* (Cunningham's Camp). Nearly 500 members took the opportunity of intensive training assisted by regular officers and sergeant instructors. The increased efficiency of the Home Guard enabled large scale exercises to be carried out. One Sunday morning in August, the whole of 1st Battalion was involved in an exercise in which 150 'parachutists' attempted to capture Douglas, but without success. In October, Major P. D. Kissack of the Castletown Company provided a cup and medals for a knock-out competition between fighting patrols. The final was held in December in the Baldrine area in atrocious conditions. The winners were the Bride Patrol.

CIVIL DEFENCE (A.R.P.)

During last winter the schoolroom of Victoria Street Church in Douglas was a busy scene as unemployed men assembled thousands of gas masks, enough to supply every man, woman and child not already in possession of one. In March over 36,000 gas masks were distributed throughout the Island by members of the Manx Women's Guild. While adults can use their discretion, school children must carry theirs when going to school. Younger

An architect's impression of the new Drill Hall at Tromode. It was due to be built for the Manx Territorial Regiment but was not completed until the end of last year. It is now the headquarters of 1st Battalion, Isle of Man Home Guard. *(Frank Cowin Library)*

children have been provided with gas masks with 'Mickey Mouse' faces. The supply of gas masks has been followed by the arrival of large amounts of first aid and fire-fighting equipment.

After months of waiting, the tentative arrangements already in place are to be put on a more efficient footing as a result of the Civil Defence Commission issuing plans for an all-Island scheme. An A.R.P. Executive, under the direction of the Chief Constable (Major J. W. Young, O.B.E.), will consist of a Staff Officer and Training Officer seconded from the Police Force. They will be responsible for directing Air Raid Precautions throughout the Island. 500 Wardens - men and women - are required for the Wardens' posts. Many of the Wardens are members of the Loyal Manx Association formed during the Great War for civil defence. They are the backbone of the scheme and will contact every household, noting the number of occupants, and checking that everyone has an appropriate gas mask. They will also train stirrup pump parties for every street. Buckets and sand will be provided. In the event of a bomb falling the Wardens will cordon off the area and summon the service of the Ambulance or Fire units. A special Corps of Messengers, aged between 16 and 18, is being formed to maintain communications should telephones be put out of action.

Hundreds of more volunteers are required for the Ambulance Section to become proficient in first aid and to act as stretcher bearers and ambulance staff. The Masonic Temple in Douglas has been equipped as an emergency hospital. Instruction is also given in dealing with a gas attack and decontamination centres are being established where victims can be hosed down. Volunteers are also required in the Fire Section to undertake nightly fire-watching at the various posts being set up in the towns. The fire tenders ordered for the Auxiliary Fire Service are expected to arrive early next year. A new A.R.P. Headquarters and an all-Island Control Room has been set up in a four-storeyed building in Woodbourne Road, Douglas. It is linked to various points on the Island by 25 telephone circuits.

NEW AIRFIELD UNDER CONSTRUCTION AT ANDREAS

A new airfield is taking shape at Andreas. It is being built for Fighter Command as part of the R.A.F.'s defences of the North-West. Notices were served on landowners at the end of last year and 500 acres of fine fertile farmland have been commandeered. Ballaghaue, farmed by Mr Crellin, and Braust, farmed by Mr Callow, provide 200 acres with smaller amounts stretching into neighbouring Bride. These are needed to complete the extremities of the airfield and for the construction of a new road to replace the Ballacottier road to Bride. Other areas around the village will be used for the accommodation compounds, messes, station hospital and N.A.A.F.I.

The main contractor is the English firm of Moss and Co., though much of the construction work is being undertaken by local building and haulage firms, together with the Highways, Water and Electricity Boards. Many local men are employed and hundreds of Irish navvies have been brought in to assist. The airfield is being built to the full specification of Fighter Command. All buildings are of brick construction with asbestos roofing. The airfield has three intersecting runways. The main NE/SW runway is 1,100 yards in length. 'Deads' from the Laxey and Foxdale mines have been used for the 12" hard-core base of the runways which have been topped by 3" of tarmacadam. A total of 24 blast pens have been built at dispersal points around the perimeter track and the whole airfield has been surrounded by high roller concertina barbed-wire. The main entrance is from the Ballacottier Road before Braust Farm is reached. Concrete roads connect the buildings and lead to three maintenance hangars and flying control.

The Rectory is to be used as officers' quarters. As soon as they are completed, communals are being occupied to relieve the overcrowding at Jurby. which continues to host fighter squadrons. The Polish squadron was followed by three others during the year, each squadron flying Hurricanes. At present there is an Australian squadron of Spitfires and in October its groundcrew and administrative staff began the move to Andreas. The Spitfires, too, have arrived though operations are still undertaken from Jurby. Andreas should be fully operational early next year. December saw an unfortunate accident when a Spitfire coming in to land hit a truck which was crossing the runway. The driver was killed. The Spitfire nosed in and overturned, but the pilot escaped with minor injuries.

Vicar and wardens of Kirk Andreas have been informed that the 120 feet tower and bell turret will have to be reduced by half. In line with the southern end of the main runway of the Andreas airfield, it is likely to be a hazard to aircraft taking off and landing.   (Manx National Heritage)

Another Andreas Spitfire crashed whilst on a training flight at Aust Farm, Lezayre. The Canadian pilot, Flt. Lt. Edy jumped by parachute from a low height but was killed on hitting the ground.

In July R.A.F. Jurby was renamed No 5 Air Observers School and navigation was added to bomb aiming and gunnery instruction. Lysanders have joined the target towing flight and ex-squadron Hampdens have replaced the Herefords. They are being used for navigation and bombing exercises. A visiting Hampden from an O.T.U. caused quite a stir in December. It was on a training flight and flown by Pilot Officer Turner Chrystal of the well-known Ramsey auctioneering family. The aircraft was fully loaded and armed. On the

Ex-operational Handley Page Hampdens are replacing the unreliable Herefords at Jurby. The Hampdens will be used for navigational and bomb aiming exercises.

(Left) Hawker Hurricanes of 312 (Czech) Squadron, which was based at Jurby during April and May for night fighter and convoy patrol duties. (Right) October 8th saw the tragic loss of four American volunteer pilots belonging to 133 (Eagle) Squadron who were caught in thick mist over the Maughold area. This particular Hurricane found its way into the upper Laxey valley before nosing into the hillside, a few yards from the former Snaefell Mine Captain's house. (Flt. Lt. Norman Radcliffe)

approach one of the engines developed trouble and a tricky landing resulted in the aircraft slewing into the boundary hedge near Ballavarran Farm. The crew managed to escape before the fuel tanks erupted in fire and destroyed the aircraft. Fortunately the bombs were blown clear and did not explode. A few days later Turner Chrystal and the crew were collected by another Hampden and returned to their Saltby base accompanied by some turkeys prepared for Christmas!

The beginning of the year saw Wing-Commander Alford take over as Commanding Officer. One of his first tasks was to improve the defences of the airfield. There were no rifles available so a huge quantity of steel pikes were ordered from Gelling's Foundry in Douglas. Now every man is armed with one and has to carry it wherever he goes on the station. There are night exercises with the men taking up positions ready for a mock landing by parachutists in the light of flares. Apparently, the pikes are a source of much amusement but no one dare appear without one. The Officers' Mess now boasts silver and glass ware and is decorated with palms. The C.O. has also provided two blister hangars which have been converted into the Jurby Ritz Theatre. Through the efforts of S.W.O. Radcliffe a camp orchestra has been formed from musicians on the station. 'The Aeronautics' are trained by Jack Hart, the famous conductor from the Savoy, London. Local dance band leader Harold Moorhouse has been transferred to Jurby to take charge of the camp entertainments.

The grim side of life has been the number of fatal flying accidents this year. The whole Island was saddened by the loss of four American flyers belonging to one of the Eagle Squadrons formed by volunteers. Five of them were on their way to Northern Ireland when they entered low cloud over the Maughold area. Completely lost, they circled and lost height to locate their position. The result was that four of them crashed with the loss of all four pilots. The aircraft were located at Ballaskeig Mooar, Corteen's Ballafayle, Cornaa above Corrany and in the Laxey valley below the Snaefell Mine Captain's house.

FATAL AIR ACCIDENT REPORTS, 1941

15th January. Lockheed Hudson aircraft from Silloth ditched in sea off Port Mooar. Only one crewman out of seven survived and only one body was recovered.

23rd February. Hawker Henley on target towing duty ditched in sea two miles south-east of Point of Ayre with engine on fire. Air Sea Rescue launch from Ramsey recovered the two drowned aircrew, including the Polish pilot.

27th March. Fully-laden Hampden on training flight from Cottesmore struck Mr J. R. Quilleash's farmhouse at Ballaragh, Lonan, with visibility down to 20 yards. Aircraft crashed in flames and Bomb Disposal Team from Jurby recovered six bombs and incendiaries. Three crewmen died as a result of the crash and one survived.

2nd May. Blackburn Botha from Squire's Gate, Blackpool, ditched in sea at north-east end of Carrick Point, Port St.Mary. The four crew died, two bodies being recovered by divers from sunken wreck.

10th June. Blenheim on gunnery practice from Jurby spun into field at Upper Geary Farm, Lezayre. Polish pilot and two trainee gunners killed.

9th September. Blenheim from Jurby on training flight was seen to spin into the ground with smoke coming from tail at Ballacregga, Bride. Pilot and three others killed.

9th September. Hudson from Silloth struck upper slopes of North Barrule in thick fog. Aircraft exploded on impact killing the four occupants.

8th October. Four Hurricanes out of a flight of five from American Eagle Squadron crashed in Maughold area with loss of the four pilots.

8th October. Wellington from Hawarden on flight to Aldergrove hit south-eastern flank of Snaefell. American ferry pilot killed.

18th November. Hampden on approach to Ronaldsway hit R.A.F. mail van on Balthane Road, killing one and injuring three. Aircraft recovered to land damaged.

1st December. Spitfire hit truck on runway when coming in to land at Andreas killing the driver. Pilot slightly injured after aircraft turned over.

5th December. Spitfire from Andreas during aerobatics nosed in from 2,500 feet at Vondy's Aust Farm, Lezayre. Canadian pilot killed when attempting parachute landing.

17th December. Avro Anson from Lichfield struck west flank of Snaefell and disintegrated. Three were killed with four survivors seriously injured.

HERE IS THE NEWS : **1942**
ROW OVER CONSCRIPTION: HOUSE OF KEYS IN REVOLT

As the Isle of Man enters the third year of the war, the question of extending conscription has led to a heated debate as to whether or not the Imperial Parliament's recent National Service Act (No.2) should be applied to the Island, as in 1939. The matter this time has been left to Tynwald and it has aroused an unseemly division between those in favour and those who believe the Island is already doing enough. We have this report.

Ever since conscription for National Service was applied to the Island in 1939, there have been consistent rumblings about those who have been exempted by the tribunals. Are they being too lenient? While some men in reserved occupations have been retained to carry out essential maintenance work, such as in connection with the many military establishments, others are being accused of escaping conscription for reasons which have nothing to do with the war effort. At a Home Guard dinner, the Lieutenant-Governor described such people as "the shirkers, the beastly rats" - a phrase that attracted instant, if not widespread, condemnation.

In January, His Excellency introduced in Tynwald the new Act which would make women between the ages of 20 and 30 liable for National Service, while the upper limit for men would be increased from 41 to 51. Immediate uproar ensued. To the Keys it seemed as if the Executive Government was determined to impose the new measures without regard to their opinions. They walked out and met separately to consider the matter. They decided on a number of amendments, one being that women should be excluded from the Act, and another that older men if called up should not be required to leave the Island. To many Manx people the arguments advanced by the Keys for their instransigence seemed insubstantial to say the least. Others, however, believe that the needs of the Island and its economy are unique; the removal of women will upset industry and deprive the Civil Defence organisations of essential numbers; in the U.K. women can undertake essen-tial war work in the factories without leaving home; calling up the older men would deplete the Home Guard, and already young Irishmen are being called upon because of the shortage of labour. It can also be argued that the Island already contributes a higher percentage of its population to the Forces, Auxiliary Forces or war work than any other part of the Empire.**

Nevertheless, the great majority take the view that it is imperative that the Island should be seen to be pulling its proper weight in the combined effort to defeat the scourge of Nazism. However, the Keys began to raise the standards of democracy and nationalism in the face of the dictatorial attitude of the Lieutenant-Governor and the Legislative Council. They remained adamant and would only accept the compulsory enrolment of unmarried women aged 20 to 30 provided that they could only be directed to war work in the Isle of Man. When the U.K. National Service Act was re-introduced at the March sitting of Tynwald, the Keys voted 18 to 3 against it being applied to the Island. They were supported by only one member of the Legislative Council. Many of the women in the age group are already involved in the Women's Services or in hospitals and factories. Those at home have the opportunity of joining the Woman's Land Army while others are now members of the 'Mannin Wrens' who undertake duties at H.M.S. Valkyrie. The whole affair may have been something of a storm in a tea cup, but perhaps the last word should be left to a local man serving with the Royal Army Service Corps. In a letter home he writes, somewhat cynically, that when the time for the victory celebrations at last arrives, the same 19 who voted against the Act will be in the forefront of the celebrations!

MORE SHORTAGES
Shortage of supplies is becoming increasingly difficult for traders and shopkeepers, especially with regard to paper, cigarettes and tobacco, chocolates and sweets. Beer is still plentiful but spirits are in limited supply and join other items 'under the counter' which are reserved for regular customers. Meat is also becoming less plentiful and 'beefless weeks' have been introduced when only mutton, lamb and pork can be bought. However, this is regarded as preferable to the strict rationing imposed in England where the habit of endless queues is now the custom. Nevertheless, it has been necessary for families to register with a butcher of their choice. He sees that his customers are treated fairly as regards meat and offal, including liver and sausages. The rabbit population of the Island is also the source of an alternative meat while the traditional 'spuds and herring' is coming back into fashion. In order to protect crops, those with shot guns are being issued with cartridges for the purpose of shooting rooks to lessen the number feeding on newly-sown seed. Food waste in the way of potato and vegetable peelings, and known as 'swill' is being scavenged by farmers for the feeding of pigs. One result of the shortages has been the considerable rise in prices for just about everything.

WOMEN'S LAND ARMY
As more and more men are being called up for the Armed Forces, women are being called upon to help on the farms. The Women's Land Army was formed in July last year to help hard-pressed farmers who are being pressured to bring more land into cultivation. Recruits receive six weeks' training at Knockaloe Experimental Farm. The training includes how to milk a cow, look after hens and chickens (including how to wring a chicken's neck) and generally attune themselves to undertake hard physical work on the land. This includes turnip-thinning, haymaking and mucking out. After training, the women are allocated to farms throughout the Island where some become 'livers-in' while others are 'mobiles' billeted at either Peel or Lezayre. From here they travel to work each day bringing packed lunches. Hours of work expected are 109 hours a fortnight, but often this is exceeded if a job is to be finished. Pay is 18 shillings a week plus meals for those staying on farms while mobiles receive 40 shillings. This year members of the Women's Land Army have been provided with two sets of clothes, one suitable for work-

ing in and a 'walking out' uniform which includes fawn riding breeches, shirt, green V-necked pullover, donkey brown great coat and brown shoes.

ARMY CADET FORCE FORMED

In January, sanction was given for the formation of the Isle of Man Cadet Force which is affiliated to the Isle of Man Territorial Association and units of the Home Guard. Commandant of the Cadet Force is Captain B. J. Pendlebury, M.A., Senior English Master at the Douglas High School for Boys. Recruitment began for boys between the ages of $14^{1}/_{2}$ and 17 and the ceiling of 400 was quickly realised. The boys undertake a military-style training which will stand them in good stead when they are called up for Army service.

Boys with an interest in the Navy are well catered for by units of the Sea Cadets which are found throughout the Island. Flights of 404 Squadron of the Air Training Corps founded last year have become so numerous that a further squadron has been formed. This is 506 Squadron and is made up of the original flights belonging to King William's College, the Boys High School and Ramsey Grammar School.

DOUGLAS SCHOOL HIT BY BOMB.

Children attending Tynwald Street School had a frightening experience on the morning of 11th March. An aircraft from Jurby on a training mission accidentally dropped an 11 lb smoke bomb when flying over Douglas. The bomb pierced the roof of the upper hall where a class of seven-year-olds was in the middle of a P.E. lesson. The bomb then penetrated the floor and smashed through the infant assembly hall floor and imbedded itself in the earth. Incredibly, no one was hurt, not even by flying glass when the windows were shattered. Some girls were shocked but that was the worst of it. There were 240 children in the school at the time and fortunately the bomb missed the classrooms. The pilot of the aircraft came to school next day to apologise to the children. One of them said later that the Headmistress gave him a good ticking off!

CIVIL DEFENCE ENFORCED

While the air raid sirens continue to give warning of German aircraft in the vicinity of the Island, Tynwald has taken steps to ensure that the air raid precautions organised by the Civil Defence Commission are brought to a high state of efficiency. As a result of a shortage of volunteers, men between 18 and 60, and not already involved in Home Guard or A.R.P. duties, now have to register for Civil defence purposes and Fire Sections. Many have been enrolled as wardens. Whilst there is still an air of complacency, every step should be taken to protect not only the local population, but also the many thousands of military personnel at present in the Island being trained to play a vital rôle in the war effort.

SILK FOR THE LADIES

Drogues used as targets for those under instruction at the R.A.F. Gunnery School at Ronaldsway are being salvaged for unauthorised use. They are made of silk which is unobtainable in the shops. The drogues are towed by aircraft off Langness and are fired at from the gun emplacements near the lighthouse. The drogues are then released at Knock-y-Vriew where two aircraftmen are stationed in a wooden hut to collect them. Despite £5 rewards being offered for those which drift away, local women regard them as being much more valuable and are putting the silk to good personal use. The galvanised wire is also of great value.

DOING THEIR BIT

The staff and management of Clucas' Laundry at Tromode are doing their bit to help the war effort. They are cleaning bedding and blankets for the military stationed on the Island free of charge. A similar service is being provided for the hospitals and maternity home. Staff undertake the work after their normal working hours and sometimes turn in on Saturday mornings. They are not paid as management has told them the company is not charging for the service

RECORD COMPANY PROFITS

The Isle of Man continues to profit economically from the war. This year's Budget revealed continuing record surpluses arising from increased Customs and Excise duties as a result of the presence of thousands of service personnel and enemy aliens on the Island. A Budget for £1 million was introduced. The Steam Packet, Douglas Gas and Railway Companies and the electricity undertakings have all announced record profits. Meanwhile, as casualties mount among Manx servicemen, there was bitter anger in the Island when a London Sunday newspaper described it as a "Shangri-La of luxury in a world at war."

Tynwald's contribution to the war costs is another £500,000 and over £1 million has been raised from Island savers through War Savings and defence bonds. The Government has also issued a £500,000 War Loan at 3% for local investment.

JUVENILE DELINQUENCY

The Isle of Man Magistrates' Association has called for tougher measures to deal with the rising tide of juvenile crime on the Island. It has proposed compulsory membership of youth organisations, an evening curfew on young people and an extension of the birching powers of the courts. The Association blamed the increasing delinquency on lack of discipline in the home and lack of parental responsibility.

Recent cases have seen a 13-year-old page boy in a Douglas hotel being given six strokes of the birch for stealing £3 from a guest's bedroom. The court also ruled that his father had not met his responsibilities, and fined him £3. In another case a boy of 13 was given four strokes of the birch for stealing two pears from trees in the gardens of The Nunnery.

STEAM PACKET LOSES ANOTHER VESSEL

After playing a heroic part in the Dunkirk evacuation the *Tynwald* was commandeered by the Admiralty and fitted out as an auxiliary anti-aircraft ship and commissioned in October

---

LATEST WAR CASUALTIES

The number of casualties as a result of enemy action notified during the year totals 68. They include those who have been killed in the Far East and indicate that Manxmen are in action in the many theatres of war.

BRITISH ARMY 21, including 11 in the Middle East and North Africa, some of whom were with the Manx Regiment.
ROYAL AIR FORCE 18, on flying operations.
ROYAL NAVY 16, including losses from the Prince of Wales and Repulse sunk by Japanese action
MERCHANT NAVY 13

In addition 21 Manx persons have died in service as a result of accidents or illness. This figure includes three in the Women's Services and one in a German prisoner of war camp.

Commissioned by the Royal Navy, 'H.M.S. Tynwald' took part in the North Africa landings but was sunk after being hit by a mine or a torpedo. She is the fourth Steam Packet vessel to be lost during the war. (Imperial War Museum)

1941 as *H.M.S. Tynwald*. Manned by Navy personnel, she served in Home Waters on convoy escort duties before being assigned to Operation Torch, the recent Allied landing in North Africa. On 8th November she was involved in the attack on Algiers and three days later was part of a task force, including infantry landing craft, sent to capture the airfield at Bougie, 100 miles to the east of Algiers. While the harbour was successfully taken, further landings were prevented by adverse sea conditions and the attacking force came under heavy air attacks. On 12th November *H.M.S. Tynwald* was hit by a mine or torpedo and sank in about seven fathoms of water. It is believed ten of her crew were lost. This is the fourth Steam Packet ship to have been lost. They include the three newest ships in the fleet.

News of other Steam Packet ships is that the *Viking*, after a short period on the Fleetwood service, was requisitioned again and is at present serving as a Fleet Air Arm target vessel based in Scotland, where she has been joined by the *Victoria* carrying out similar duties. The *Manxman* has been fitted out as a Radio Direction Finding vessel and commissioned as *H.M.S. Caduseus*. Based in Douglas for a short while, she has been on patrol in the Irish Sea and has been used in exercises with the radar station on Douglas Head. The *Lady of Mann* is fully occupied as a troop transport operating around the Scottish coast and helping in the ferrying of American troops and Air Force personnel arriving at Belfast on the *Queen Mary*. Also in Scottish waters, the *Ben my Chree* has been a frequent visitor to Iceland with its vital North Atlantic base.

SAMUEL NORRIS DEMANDS MORE HOME RULE

The crusading M.H.K. for North Douglas, Mr Samuel Norris, has asked the House of Keys to adopt a series of demands to the U.K. Government for more Home Rule. He proposed a drastic reduction in the powers of the Lieutenant-Governor and the handing of executive power to a form of Manx Cabinet. But after three hours of debate at the December meeting of the Keys, the House decided to send his proposals to a committee for consideration. Angrily, Mr Norris said this was "the funkhole of the faint-hearted." In October, Mr Norris resigned from the War Committee.

MORE AIR ALERTS

The year saw by far the greatest number of air raid warnings. The sirens were sounded on no less than 32 occasions. The great majority of these were caused by lone high-flying Ju 88s sent to reconnoitre the Irish Sea in order to report the movements of convoys entering and leaving Liverpool. They follow a route which takes them northwards over the coast of Ireland, then turning southwards to their base in northern France. It is noticeable that cities in the North-West are receiving fewer attacks from the Luftwaffe.

1942 NEWS IN BRIEF

FEBRUARY
14 - Two meatless days weekly introduced.

MARCH
18 - Fat Cattle subsidy increased and £4 wheat subsidy offered.
23 - Wheatmeal bread introduced.
31 - Keys throw out Military Service Act in Tynwald.

MAY
27 - Miss W. S. Naylor appointed headmistress of Douglas High School for Girls in succession to Miss G. D. Hasler, M.A.

JUNE
25 - Tynwald pays tribute to Lieut.-Colonel MacClellan who has been retired from his position as C.O. of the Manx Regiment.

JULY
5 - Home Secretary Mr Herbert Morrison attends Tynwald Ceremony during visit to inspect Internment Camps. Lieut.-Colonel MacClellan acts as Sword Bearer for the Ceremony.
7 - Keys refuse to discuss Death Duties.

AUGUST
28 - Duke of Kent killed when Sunderland flying boat crashes in Scotland. He was the youngest brother of the king and, as Prince George, paid a memorable visit to the Island in 1932.

OCTOBER
15 - Agricultural Wages Board recommend £3 minimum wage for farm labourers.
23 - Canon John Ralph Strickland Taylor appointed Lord Bishop of Sodor and Man to succeed Rt Rev. W. Stanton Jones who has resigned.

MORE STRANGERS IN OUR MIDST

The beginning of the year saw the arrival of nearly 600 internees whose countries had joined the Axis powers. Over half of them were merchant seamen from Finland, while others were from Hungary, Romania and Japan. The Palace Camp was emptied of the few remaining Italians, and the new arrivals were placed in different sections of the camp. The 90 Japanese were mostly smartly-dressed bankers and press correspondents from London, but more recent arrivals included a dozen expert chicken sexers. They were soon released so that their skill in identifying pullets for egg laying should not be wasted to the poultry industry!

Despite these new additions, the number of male internees held has continued to decline as more are released, many to be employed in munition factories. During last year, 2,000 were freed bringing the total still held to about 3,500, including 500 detainees in the Peveril Camp. The stream of releases has meant extra work for the Manx Police who are responsible for visiting the camps and checking each individual's documents and escorting them to the boat for departure. Whereas the men's camps have military guards, mainly from the Pioneer Corps, the Police have also the responsibility for the security of women internees in the south of the Island. As constables are choosing to join the Armed Services, the Chief Constable is having to rely more and more on 'specials.'

The number of women confined to the Rushen Camp has also dwindled. It is now down to about a thousand, a quarter of the original total. In August Commander Cuthbert decided to move the married camp from Port St Mary to Port Erin. The move was made smoothly in a day with everyone, including the landladies, assisting. Couples who are pro-Nazi have been accommodated in the Towers and separated by a wire fence from the Italians who are in the Waverley. Uncommitted couples are housed nearby. The move means that Port St Mary ceases to be a restricted area. The former married quarters has been taken over by the Royal Army Pay Corps O.C.T.U., with the Ballaqueeney as its headquarters.

The occupation of Vichy French-controlled Madagascar by the British resulted in, perhaps, the strangest arrivals of all. They were the French women whose husbands were serving in the French colony. They were transported to Scotland and held pending a decision about their future. In September, about 60 women and children arrived in Laxey and were billeted in ten houses in the care of Miss Banks who had been transferred from Rushen Camp. She can be found now in the offices of the Village Commissioners where she deals with queries and complaints. A recent one was that four of the houses were without baths! An interpreter is available at the post office. While the women are free to move about the village, a permit is required to go beyond the three-mile limit. As they are all Roman Catholics, Mass is celebrated in the Pavilion of Laxey Glen Gardens, the priest being Father McGrath of St Anthony's, Onchan. Because they have come from a hot climate, Miss Banks has instructed the landladies to ensure that good fires are provided for the women. However, the sojourn in Laxey of these forlorn, though friendly, women is not to be for long. Their menfolk have decided to join the Free French Forces under General de Gaulle. Arrangements are in hand to transfer the women and children early in the new year to the warmer climes of northern Africa.

B Company, 1st Battalion Home Guard at Knockaloe after winning the Governor's Cup for general use of weaponry. Next to Earl Granville on the left is Lieut. J. B. Ritchie, holding the cup. On the right is Capt. B. J. Pendlebury, Commandant of the Island's Cadet Force.   (Manx National Heritage)

CHANGES IN THE HOME GUARD

The legislation introducing compulsory enrolment for Civil Defence duties meant that Home Guard members were now committed to serve for the rest of the emergency period and would not be released without good cause. Attendance at parades and duties of up to 48 hours each month became obligatory. In February, the 2nd Battalion was organised on similar lines to 1st Battalion. Major G. W. Howie who, in civil life is the Island's Agricultural Organiser, and had commanded the Peel Company, was promoted to command the Battalion with the rank of Lieutenant-Colonel. At the same time, Major K. G. Groves of the Ramsey Company was made 2nd-in-command with the rank of Major. Following his retirement from the Manx Regiment, Lieut.-Colonel G. P. MacClellan, D.S.O., O.B.E., was appointed 2nd-in-command of the Isle of Man Home Guard in September.

The arrival of a number of Hotchkiss 6 pounder anti-tank weapons resulted in the formation of the Manx Troop Artillery under the command of Captain H. S. Cain of 1st Battalion. The unit made rapid progress and in April demonstrated their efficiency on Langness. Concerning medical matters, doctors were appointed to each Battalion under Lieut.-Colonel J. Wood and their first duties were to ensure that medical arrangements should be in force on all practical exercises. First Aid instruction and stretcher bearing are now included in the training manuals. Meanwhile, training on automatic weapons, field exercises, bayonet fighting, signalling and map reading is leading to higher degrees of proficiency.

On the Home Guard's second anniversary there were no ceremonial parades but, instead, the public were invited to attend training sessions and displays. The Colby Platoon put on an exhibition of weapons they first used two years ago. These included rusty old .22 rifles, billiard cues, hammers and sticks! July saw week-end training camps begin at Glen Wyllin which lasted throughout the summer with up to 100 men attending each camp. Also during the summer His Excellency the Lieutenant-Governor presented a cup for general efficiency in the use of weapons. Every Company entered and competitions were held on various ranges with the final taking place at Peel in August between 'B' Company, 1st Battalion and Ramsey Company, 2nd Battalion. The cup was presented by His Excellency in front of a large gathering to Captain J. B. Ritchie of 'B' Company which won by five events to three.

MANX REGIMENT JOINS THE DESERT RATS

The beginning of the year saw the two Batteries continuing their deployment in the Suez Canal Zone, the survivors of the 129th having joined the 42nd Battery under Major Valentine. The vital sea link, its ports and R.A.F. bases were subject to frequent air attacks, especially when convoys arrived with troops and supplies in the great build up of British and Commonwealth Forces. The Bofors fired thousands of rounds and their tally of aircraft shot down continued to grow. Changes within the Regiment saw Captain Henry Kelly leave to take over command, as Major, of the 1st LAA Battery. The 1st had carried out most of the early trials with the Bofors gun and already had a distinguished war record, having served in France and the Western Desert. It had been with the Eighth Army which had routed the Italians. But the situation was reversed with the arrival of Rommel and the Afrika Corps. The 1st was retained to protect the withdrawal of the Eighth Army and was heavily engaged in the seige of Tobruk from where it was evacuated to Alexandria. During its time in the Desert it had accounted for 87 aircraft but had lost 100 men. After taking over command, Major Kelly was delighted to be signalled that the 1st was to be assigned to the 15th LAA, thus replacing the 129th and maintaining its regimental status.

In February, the three Batteries and Regimental HQ left the Canal Zone and entered the Desert to take up positions on the Gazala line in Libya which was being established by the Eighth Army in an attempt to halt the advancing German-Italian army. 41st and 42nd Batteries were soon in action against Messerschmitt fighters while the 1st was sent 200 miles to the south to help protect the left flank. In April more Manxmen arrived to reinforce the Batteries and were soon in the thick of the action. Lieut.-Colonel MacClellan was placed on the Retired List because of his age and returned to the Isle of Man where the veteran was given a hero's reception. Lieut.-Colonel T. Eustace Smith took over as Commander of the Regiment. The 1st Battery returned and the 15th LAA now became part of the 7th Division, which has been nick-named the 'Desert Rats'.

Field Marshal Rommel launched his expected offensive at the end of May. The 7th Division bore the brunt of the heavy fighting and when the R.A.F. was forced to withdraw from its forward airfield, the order was given to withdraw all guns to the El Alamein defensive position, just 50 miles west of Alexandria. The Regiment and the R.A.F. fighters joined in combating the constant air attacks to assist in the withdrawal which was successfully completed without heavy losses. At this point Major Clifford Kniveton left 41st Battery to become second-in-command of the Regiment and Major Brian Mylchreest succeeded him as Battery commander. Major Valentine (later to become Lieutenant-Colonel) was transferred to a Staff appointment and Major H. S. Balls took over command of the 42nd Battery. At the end of July, the Regiment came under regular attacks by Stuka dive bombers and suffered casualties including two killed and a number of wounded by shrapnel. The wounded were swiftly attended to by the medical staff, but it was necessary for Major Mylchreest to be invalided home to make a full recovery from his wounds. On promotion, Major T. W. Cain took over command of the 41st.

As the Eighth Army steadily built up its resources to face the inevitable attack on the El Alamein line, Prime Minister Churchill visited the area to assess the situation and make important changes in command. General Auckinleck was succeeded by General Alexander as Commander-in-Chief, and Lieut.-General Montgomery was placed in command of the Eighth Army. Their orders were to repulse any assault on the El Alamein positions and prepare to go on the offensive. Rommel struck on the last day of August, his plan being to drive round the southern point of the line supported by hundreds of aircraft and then strike towards the coast. Montgomery pulled back units to prevent this and, despite a succession of all-out attacks, the German tanks were forced to a halt and turned tail. With the rest of the line holding, it was tempting to give pursuit but Montgomery called a halt in order to stabilise the situation. The three Batteries had played their part and scored many hits, though not without casualties. During the lull in the fighting, Lieut.-General Horrocks, commander of the X111th Corps, which included the 7th Armoured Division, ordered a First Aid Competition in which all units would be represented. The Regiment's M.O., Major Guy Pantin, hastily gathered a team together under the leadership of Bombardier Curwen Clague and prepared for the tests ahead. The competition went on for days and the 15th Regiment distinguished itself as not only being adjudged the best from 7th Armoured Division, but from all the 40 teams from the Corps!

The great barrage of the heavy guns, which was the prelude to the battle ahead, began on the night of 23/24th October as troops moved forward to clear passages through the minefields. The Regiment's job was to protect the 25 pounders from air attack and during the ensuing days fired 7,500 rounds, bagging more enemy aircraft. On the 31st the 7th Divison was taken out of the southern flank and moved northwards nearer to El Alamein ready for the planned breakthrough. The whole area was jammed with tanks, guns and supply vehicles and came under constant ground and air attack. Then on the morning of 4th November, came the great breakthrough with the Germans and Italians overwhelmed by the superior forces of the Eighth Army. By the 11th, advances of up to 300 miles had been made, 30,000 prisoners taken and hundreds of tanks, guns etc. captured. On the 13th November, 1st Battery reached Tobruk from where it had been evacuated over a year ago.

The beginning of December saw the 7th Armoured Division's progress come to a halt as they waited for reinforcements and supplies of ammunition and fuel. Time was also needed for the R.A.F. to move forward to bases within range of El Agheila where Rommel's forces had gathered. He was relying more and more on his aircraft to halt the advance and all Batteries were in constant action, meeting with considerable success but not without further casualties. Major-General Harding, the Divisional Commander, visited some of the gunsites and expressed his appreciation of the skill of the Batteries. By the middle of December the assault on the Agheila line had been successfully completed and the 15th's guns began the 300 mile trek to Tripoli. By the 23rd December the Batteries gathered in the Nofilia area where General Montgomery paid them a visit. He spent three hours touring the units and presenting medals. Christmas Day was a rest day and there was time to enjoy a full breakfast, beer and cigarettes supplied by the N.A.A.F.I., a celebration cocktail party, and an excellent Christmas dinner with roast pork, Christmas pudding and all the trimmings.

The three batteries of the 15th LAA (Isle of Man) Regiment have been playing a prominent part in the defence of the 7th Armoured Division ('The Desert Rats') as the Eighth Army pursues Rommel's forces following the decisive Battle of El Alamein in October. Here one of the Bofors gun teams digs in to meet further attacks by German and Italian aircraft. *(Manx National Heritage)*

R.A.F. ANDREAS BECOMES OPERATIONAL

The fighter station at Andreas became fully operational in March as a sector of 9 Group Fighter Command. Group Control was at Preston. When the first fighters arrived at Jurby towards the end of 1940, the newly-completed wing of Ramsey Grammar School was adapted as Sector Control. The windows were protected by blast walls while, inside, heavy partitions divided the building into compact units for offices and communication centres. The assembly hall made a splendid operations' centre. WAAF plotters use it to record the movement of aircraft. The Centre is linked to the radar stations at Dalby, Scarlett and Bride. Information is passed to Preston from where instructions are passed back to Ramsey and then to the operations room at Andreas.

The Spitfires of 457 Squadron were replaced by those of another Australian squadron, 452. Shipping patrols over the Irish Sea are maintained daily, while occasionally orders to scramble are received when hostile aircraft are detected, usually high-flying Ju88s searching for convoy movements. Much time is also spent over the air-to-ground firing range on the Ayres below Smeale. A large square is mounted on a rail and provides a moving target for practice. In May, two of the Spitfires, one with cine camera to take film of the other, collided head on, resulting in the attack plane diving into Farrant's Fort Farm, Close Lake, with its dead pilot. The other Spitfire was badly damaged and the pilot parachuted into a field at Andreas. June saw 452 leave Andreas. Villagers turned out to wave to the squadron as it made a final fly-past. It has since joined 457 and is on its way to Australia, now threatened by the Japanese.

The Australians were replaced by 93 squadron which was converting to Spitfires and using the facilities at Andreas to work up to operational efficiency. After a four months' stay the squadron left for Algiers in readiness for the North Africa landings. The crisis which led to the formation of 9 Group has largely passed and the Andreas personnel of over a thousand have been posted out. While the future of this fine airfield is being determined, Air Sea Rescue aircraft are still present together with a detachment from the Fleet Air Arm which provide 'targets' for the trainee radar operators of *H.M.S. Valkyrie* on Douglas Head.

Spitfires of 457 (R.A.A.F.) Squadron line up at Andreas which became fully operational as a fighter station in March.

In August, another tragic accident happened when Andreas lost its Commanding Officer. On a quiet Sunday afternoon a Whitley bomber arrived to refuel. Wing-Commander E. F. Knowles, D.F.C. had served with Bomber Command and decided to take the Whitley up for a short flight. He was joined by his lady friend and six others, including four corporals who acted as ballast in the rear of the aircraft. The Whitley took off on the main runway but failed to gain sufficient height to clear the Bride Hills where it crashed in flames. The four corporals escaped from the rear but one died later from his burns after being taken to the Military Hospital at Onchan's Majestic Hotel. He and the four who perished in the nose of the aircraft were buried in Andreas churchyard.

The training at Jurby continues apace and is closely linked to the requirements of Bomber Command which, under Air Vice-Marshal Harris, is mounting a great offensive against German industrial targets. Developments on the airfield have seen the completion of two runways and the provision of additional hangars and improved accommodation for the airmen, and the hundreds of WAAFS now stationed at Jurby. Nearby Ballamoar Castle, which had been used as a rest haven for Battle of Britain pilots, is now the WAAF Officers' quarters. Most of the supplies for the station, including coal, are shipped in through Ramsey while local suppliers provide huge quantities of farm produce, fish, meat and bakery items. Shell and Esso tankers provide a constant supply of petrol from their depots at Douglas.

AIR ACCIDENT REPORTS, 1942

12th February. Avro Anson left Jurby at 7.OO p.m. and crashed near summit of North Barrule. Two were killed while there were two survivors found next morning in freezing conditions

2nd March. Hampden on training flight stalled and crashed at Ballagarraghyn after missed landing at Jurby in bad visibility. Canadian pilot and two airmen killed.

8th March. Australian pilot from 457 Squadron lost when Spitfire from Andreas broke up after exploding and then disintegrating over Ramsey Bay.

12th March. Blackburn Botha on training flight from Squire's Gate hit Cronk ny Irrey Laa in bad visibility. All five on board were lost.

24th March. Wallace aircraft from Ronaldsway crashed at Quayle's Orchard, Malew after colliding with another Wallace, killing the pilot and a cadet from King William's College Flight of 506 Squadron, A.T.C.

8th May. Two Spitfires from 452 Squadron, Andreas, collided in mid-air resulting in the loss of one of the Australian pilots.

25th June. Two Blenheims from Jurby on early morning gunnery practice crashed at Knockaloe Farm after colliding, with the loss of all six airmen. Parts of the wreckage hit Patrick School damaging the roof. No childen were present at the time.

26th June. Anson from R.A.F. Bobbington on low flying exercise in vicinity of Douglas hit tree at Ballacreetch Farm and Ballanard Road junction and crashed at Scouts Glen, Castleward, Braddan. Aircraft went on fire and wreckage was widely spread. The five R.A.F. sergeants on board all perished in the accident.

29th June. Two Spitfires from Andreas on intercepting training at 25,000 feet became separated and one disappeared without trace. The body of the pilot was recovered eventually from the sea, two miles west of the Calf of Man.

10th July. Remains of German airman washed up on Peel side of Niarbyl Bay.

17th July. Anson from R.A.F. Cark struck North Barrule in thick cloud and driving rain. Pilot and two others were killed.

4th August. Bristol Beaufighter on fuel consumption test flight from R.A.F. Lynham, Wiltshire, to Jurby stalled on final approach and crashed at Ballacottier, Lezayre. Crew of two were killed.

23rd August. Whitley bomber flown by Wing Commander Knowles, C.O. Andreas, crashed at 400 feet into field of West Kimmeragh Farm, Bride. The Wing Commander and three others died in the impact. An R.A.F Corporal later died from burns.

21st September. Lockheed Hudson on morning training flight from Silloth crashed into Slieu Freoaghane, near Kirk Michael, killing all four occupants.

HERE IS THE NEWS : **1943**
ADMIRALTY TAKES OVER RONALDSWAY

Throughout the year one of the biggest projects ever witnessed on the Island has seen Ronaldsway Farm and its two neighbours being transformed into a Royal Navy Air Station. This will train thousands of air crew to fly the Barracuda aircraft now in production for the Fleet Air Arm. The project has seen a massive 850 acres of farmland being commandeered; over 500 men are employed on the site, many of whom are Gaelic-speaking Irish navvies. We have this report.

Acting under the U.K. Defence of the Realm Acts, extended to the Isle of Man by Order in Council, the Lieutenant-Governor, Vice-Admiral Earl Granville, served notices of compulsory purchase on all the land and property-owners involved. Ronaldsway Estate is by far the largest area. Its 17th century farm house, once the home of Illiam Dhone, together with six farm cottages and three fine houses in The Crescent have been demolished, being in line with the runways. Subject to a separate purchase is the Turkeyland limestone quarry operated by C. Kniveton Ltd. The second farm is Ballagilley adjoining King William's College. It belongs to the historic Barrow Trust. Thirdly, the Creggans Farm, which stretches from neighbouring Ronaldsway to the Silverburn river, has also been taken over. Additional land acquired includes 70 acres of Balthane Farm north of the Balthane Road which has been now closed to traffic wishing to reach Derbyhaven from where the civilian air services continue to operate. Nissen huts for the accommodation of 2,000 personnel have been provided within Ballasalla for squadron staff and at Janet's Corner for administrative staff.

The main contractors for the airfield and hundreds of brick-built buildings are the Carlisle firm of John Laing and Sons, whose key workers are billeted in Castletown. Their heavy machinery has removed all hedges and levelled the area. Local hauliers are having another field day providing sand and gravel from as far away as the Point of Ayre, where concrete bricks are also produced. A major part of the scheme is the

Another war victim. Ronaldsway House, once the home of the Manx patriot William Christian (Illiam Dhone) is to be demolished as part of the development of the airfield for the Admiralty.

construction of four runways. The main 27/09 runway is 1,400 yards in length. This is intersected by three shorter ones. Over 16,000 tons of hardcore have been quarried from Turkeyland which is then crushed to size at Ballahot. The drainage problem has been solved by laying concrete channels on either side of the runways. The final coating of the runways is provided by the Paenmaenmayr Trinidad Asphalt Company and is laid by Laing's Berber-Greene tarmac pavers, the first seen on the Island.

Overlooking the airfield is the three-storeyed Control Tower built to standard Admiralty design. Nearby is the Creggans farm house which is to become headquarters for the Admiralty's Works Department. Here are found the generators which supply the entire area, while across the Ballasalla-Castletown road is the administrative site and communications centre. The whole of the Balthane corner of the airfield is devoted to the maintenance section with stores, radio repair shop, and fuel dump. Still awaited are the prefabricated materials for 12 hangars of different types which are imported and will arrive early in the new year. Laing are extremely pleased with the progress made and are confident that the station will be ready for use at the beginning of next summer.

BATTLE RELICS UNEARTHED
Local historians will be interested to hear that when the footings for the eastern end of the main runway were being prepared, complete human skeletons, together with swords and shields, were unearthed. It was on this site that the Battle of Ronaldsway took place in 1275 when emissaries of Alexander 111 of Scotland came to claim the Isle of Man for his kingdom. The Manx, leaderless since the death of Magnus ten years before, had refused to submit to Scottish rule. But here they were heavily defeated by the Scots. According to ancient records, some 537 Manxmen were killed. In order that the skeletons should not be further disturbed, it was agreed to raise the level of the runway at this end, thus protecting much of the battle area.

WELL-KNOWN FARMERS IN GAOL
The farmers of Ronaldsway, Ballagilley and The Creggans each had all of their farm equipment and livestock valued by the Government Property Trustees prior to public auction, where they would be guaranteed the valuation prices as fair compensation. During the auction of stock at The Creggans it was discovered that 31 cattle had already been removed and sold privately, and had been replaced by inferior Irish stock only recently imported. The scandal shook

Inside the Mooragh Camp, Ramsey. It was on the pavement in the foreground that the Finn internee was found stabbed to death. *(Manx National Heritage)*

the farming community and the farmer, the highly-respected Mr Percy Kermode, together with two accomplices, were charged with conspiring to defraud the Manx Government. At a Court of General Gaol, George Percy Kermode, John Stanley Kermode and James Martin were given a nine months' gaol sentence with hard labour.

R.A.F. REGIMENT FORMED

When the R.A.F. Ground Defence Gunnery School at Ronaldsway was disbanded in March, most of its personnel moved to Douglas where accommodation was provided in the vacant Central Internment Camp. It is next to the Empress Hotel which, since 1940, has been the Headquarters of the Gunnery School. In 1942 the many hundreds of those trained in airfield defence became members of the R.A.F. Regiment, and the Empress Hotel is now the Headquarters of this new branch of the Royal Air Force. New intakes continue to arrive for training and Douglas Corporation has made available part of the Villa Marina grounds for the construction of a large concrete dome. Inside, instruction in the use of the Bofors gun is given, using simulated 'targets' projected on the roof of the dome. Instruction is also given by infantry instructors of the O.C.T.U. based at the Villiers

MURDER AT MOORAGH CAMP?

An incident which took place in the Mooragh Camp has led to one of the Finnish internees being charged with murder. The remaining Finns held at the Palace Camp were transferred to Ramsey at the end of last year. There are about 140 of them, all merchant seamen and are noted for their boisterous and noisy behaviour. The majority are pro-Nazi because of their hatred for the Russians, while a few are supporters of the Allied cause. Shortly after noon on 20th April, one of the Finns, carrying a bucket of dirty water, approached another sitting on the steps and threw the water in his face. Taken by surprise, the man stood up and approached the man with the bucket and lunged at him with a blow to the stomach. But hidden in his hand was a shortened table knife and the Finn staggered backwards and died in a pool of blood. This caused uproar and the guards were soon on the scene. The body was removed on a handcart and the attacker was taken into custody and ended up in Noble's Hospital with a broken nose after being badly beaten up in the camp.

The prisoner was charged with murder and the case came before Deemster Cowley in June. The Attorney-General, Mr Ramsey B. Moore, applied for the trial to be held in camera for security reasons. To

outsiders, the case seemed clear-cut, but defence advocate, Mr R. Kinley Eason persisted with the argument that the killing was a result of provocation and that the man feared for his life. After the hearing which lasted for five days, the jurors returned a verdict of Not Guilty. The result led to rumours that the British Government had brought pressure to bear on the result for political reasons, but such rumours are without foundation.

HOME SECRETARY RETURNS

Britain's Home Secretary, Mr Herbert Morrison made a second visit to the Island in August to inspect the internee camps for which the Home Office is responsible. He stayed at Government House and, accompanied by His Excellency and members of the War Committee, made a speech to a gathering in the grounds of the Villa Marina. He said the Island's war effort was second to none. The number of Manxmen registered for military service was higher per head of population than anywhere else in Britain, something which was also achieved in the 1914-1918 War. In fact, over 5,000 of the Island's fit men up to 40 years of age are now serving with His Majesty's Forces in many parts of the world. While the women have not been conscripted, thousands have joined the women's sections of the Armed Forces, or, in the case of those up to the age of 30, are involved in essential work either here or outside the Island.

ISLAND POPULATION SOARS

Despite so many Manx people being off the Island on war service, the Island's population has soared to a record 93,205. It is an unofficial, but well-informed, figure which suggests that, with the internees down to about 2,000, over 40,000 service personnel are at present based on the Island. They are, of course, playing their part in maintaining the Island's buoyant economy. The Steam Packet's *Rushen Castle* and *Snaefell* are filled to capacity carrying personnel to and from the Island.

HOME RULE BATTLE CONTINUES

The battle over Manx Home Rule, begun by Mr Samuel Norris, goes on. The House of Keys has backed recommendations that a Cabinet of seven members should be formed to take over the executive powers of the Lieutenant-Governor. At the same time the Keys are angry that the

1943

British Government has seen fit to appoint a new Government Secretary without consulting them. Mr J. N. Panes is to succeed Mr B. E. Sargeaunt, M.V.O., O.B.E. who retires at the end of the year after 33 years in the post. The Keys wanted the position to go to a member of the Manx Civil Service and, as a result, have passed a vote of no confidence in the Lieutenant-Governor, Vice-Admiral Earl Granville.

RAMSEY CHILDREN IN DEATH FALL

Two small children have died tragically after falling from the top floor bedroom window of a house on West Quay, Ramsey. Five-year-old Adrienne Smith and her three-year-old cousin Cornelius Corlett, were playing in the room. They are believed to have fallen while leaning out of the window after climbing on a table. Both landed on the pavement below and died later in the Ramsey Cottage Hospital.

TRAGEDY AT KIONSLIEU

Six cadets from the 166 O.C.T.U. have been killed during a night exercise at Kionslieu Dam, some way above the Eairy Dam, Foxdale. On the night of 2nd November cadets were attempting to cross the dam by dinghy under cover of fire. Live ammunition was being used, machine guns opened up, mortar bombs exploded and the night sky was lit by flares. Then something went badly wrong as one of the dinghies was blown sky high as a result of a box of Mills bombs being detonated. Six cadets, in the final stages of being commissioned, died in the tragedy. At the enquiry, the exact cause of the explosion could not be explained but one theory is that a parachute flare landed on the dinghy. Onchan men of 'B' Company, 1st Battalion Home Guard witnessed the accident when observing the exercise.

BOMBER CRASHES ON RUSHEN FARM

While most air accidents occur in remoter parts of the Island, the horrors of such a crash have been brought home to people in the south of the Island. Eye-witnesses have described how, on the afternoon of Saturday, 6th November, a four-engined Halifax bomber passed over Port St Mary with one of its engines on fire and trailing black smoke. The Halifax was then seen passing over the bottom of Fishers Hill before it corkscrewed into the ground close to the buildings of Cronkmooar Farm. Wreckage was spread over a wide area and set light to several haystacks. Farmer Mr Bertie Qualtrough was leading a horse and cart but the noise of the impact caused the horse to bolt over a nearby hedge. Port St Mary fire-tender was soon on the scene and prevented the fires spreading. It is believed the Halifax had requested to land at the new airfield at Ronaldsway, but as the latter had no facilities to deal with a fire it was diverted to Jurby. The aircraft was on a training mission from the O.T.U. at Topcliffe, Yorkshire and all but one of the seven crew were Canadians. On impact, the rear of the fuselage broke away and the rear gunner was found some distance away buried deeply in the ground with his parachute still unopened.

DECORATION AWARDS

During the year a large number of decorations for gallantry have been won by Manxmen serving in the Armed Services. Bombardier, now Acting Sergeant, Bill Watterson of Allan Street, Douglas, is the first member of the Manx Regiment to be decorated, winning the Military Medal for outstanding bravery when his anti-aircraft gun position was under heavy attack by German Stuka dive-bombers in North Africa. Also, Commander B. Bryant, D.S.C. of Ramsey, one of the Royal Navy's submarine aces, has been awarded the D.S.O.

VISIT OF LADY MONTGOMERY

Finally, a visitor to the Isle of Man has been Lady Montgomery, mother of General Sir Bernard Montgomery, commander of the Eighth Army. She stayed at Government House and visited the Manx Museum and King William's College. She also went to a dance at the Pool Ballroom, Ramsey, where she did the Lambeth Walk with a young R.A.F. officer from Jurby. When she left the Island she took a Manx kitten with her, and a Manx travelling rug for her famous son.

LATEST WAR CASUALTIES

During the year notification of 53 war casualties has been received from the War Office. Details are as follows.

BRITISH ARMY - 27, which includes 13 members of the Manx Regiment, one who died of malaria and one who died in a German P.O.W. Camp. Two others from the Army have died in Japanese P.O.W. Camps.
ROYAL AIR FORCE - 10, mostly on operations over enemy territory.
ROYAL NAVY - 6, including one in the Royal Marines and one in the Fleet Air Arm.
MERCHANT NAVY - 10.

In addition, four have died while on active service.

1943 NEWS IN BRIEF

FEBRUARY
2 - The new Lord Bishop, the Right Reverend J. R. Strickland Taylor, M.A., was enthroned in St George's Church, Douglas.

MARCH
3 - As a result of the first use of artificial insemination on the Island, a pedigree Friesian cow, owned by Mr R. G. Shimmin of Sulby Farm, Onchan, gave birth to a bull calf. The insemination was carried out by the Government Veterinary Officer, Mr Douglas Kerruish.

APRIL
4 - Jubilee of Main Road Wesleyan Church, Ballasalla.
16 - Keys challenge Governor on their right to consultation on Budget proposals.
18 - Lord Bridgman, Director of the Home Guard carries out inspection of all units. He expressed himself as being well pleased with what he had seen.

MAY
16 - Third Anniversary of formation of Home Guard. Celebrations took the form of Ceremonial Marches and Church Parades.

JUNE
6-13 'Wings for Victory' Savings Campaign raises £1,301,112 for war effort.
23 - Imperial Government decide to exercise right to purchase furniture in requisitioned boarding houses.
29 - Jubilee of Broadway Baptist Church.

AUGUST
6 - Mr J. R. Quayle appointed chairman of Isle of Man Bank Ltd. in succession to Mr T. Cubbon, J.P.
8 - St John's Battle Platoon, 2nd Battalion, beat Onchan Battle Platoon, 1st Battalion, in Final for Kissack Cup.

SEPTEMBER
19 - Governor's Cup for use of firearms won by Ramsey Company, 2nd Battalion after defeating 'E' Company, 1st Battalion by 5 wins to 3.

OCTOBER
26,27 Eight Manx prisoners of war, repatriated from Germany, given great reception on arriving on Island.

LIFE BEHIND
THE WIRE

The number of internees continues to fall. Many have been released to undertake war work in Britain, while a few have been repatriated to Germany in exchange for our own people. Nevertheless, there are still over 3,000 males interned. These are in the Hutchinson, Metropole, Onchan, Mooragh and Peveril Camps. To satisfy outsiders who find the internees a source of curiosity, it is now possible to give some idea of what life is like behind the barbed wire fences, with special reference to Hutchinson Camp which still has some 400 internees, about a third of the original total.

Hutchinson Camp in Douglas consists of the garden area of the Square on either side of which are two rows or terraces of boarding houses. Also included in the camp is the parallel row of houses facing Ballaquayle Road. The whole area is surrounded by a perimeter fence of barbed wire with the main gate into the camp found at the south-west corner by Ballaquayle Road. 42 houses are available for accommodation, all of which were built about 1890. The few properties overlooking the gardens at the top of the Square and facing seawards are wired off from the main camp, and form a separate compound which is used for administration and stores. A gap in the northernmost terrace has been used to provide showers and a laundry, and more recently a hall for recreation and indoor sports.

When the internees arrive they are allocated to one of the houses, but are free to rearrange themselves so they can be with relatives, friends or other interest groups. There are between 20 and 25 men in each house and each man is provided with a single bed, mattress, pillow and four blankets. Those in poor health can claim a fifth blanket. When the camp was first opened, only double beds were available. As married men were not used to sharing a bed even with their wives, sleeping with someone else, especially another man, caused considerable embarrassment and resentment. In the early days the top mattress was often dragged on to the floor for use by one of the room mates, while the other made do with the springs!

All the men are responsible for the cleanliness of their rooms and have to undertake other duties. Every house has two cooks and three cleaners who are paid 3/6d a week pocket-money which is credited to their account with the camp bank. These are the regular workers but everyone still has to take a share. Each house elects a House Captain who is responsible for the good-running of his house and the general good order of everyone within. Then, each of the three rows of houses select a Row Captain who keeps in touch with the House Captains and passes on to the Camp Captain and the Works Organiser any requests or complaints originating from the men. The Camp Captain liaises with the Camp Commander who gives his approval to those elected as Row and Camp Captains. The Works Organiser is responsible for all work carried out by camp members, whether inside or outside the camp. Camp workshops produce items for sale either within

or outside the camp, whilst outside work is in supervised groups on local farms. All work is paid for at nominal rates into the camp bank.

Each house cooks for itself with one of the daily tasks being to draw the house rations from the camp stores. The rations are issued according to a set scale and used at the discretion of the house cooks who are helped by the rota cooks. Soon after the camp opened, an internee chef and a doctor combined to publish a book of 100 recipes based on the camp rations. The book was soon circulated to other camps on the Island, and beyond!

The internees run their own canteen which is stocked with such necessities as soap, razor blades, writing paper, pencils, tobacco and some wine and beer. Additional foodstuffs are also available. The policy is to sell foodstuffs and essentials at little or no profit and to sell luxury items at an extra charge so that the overall enterprise makes a profit of just over 10%. A cafe is run separately and also makes a small profit which, with the profit from the canteen, provides pocket money and clothing for anyone who is destitute and unable to work.

Newspapers, both English and Manx, and periodicals are available by ordering through the camp post office. A camp newspaper has been produced on a regular basis since the camp first opened. Other camps also had their own publications, although many of these have now been lost since the closing of the camps. Some of the staff involved in producing these papers have joined *The Camp* as the Hutchinson Camp paper is called. Its No 1 issue is dated 21st September, 1940 and cost two pence. It carries an apology for the technical difficulties and admits the paper leaves a lot to be desired. While there is little mention of the daily life of the camp, a good deal of space is given to the hopes and dreams of the writers, and quite a lot about the cultural activities of the camp.

The day starts at 7.00 a.m. with roll call followed by

One of the guards on duty in the Hutchinson Camp.
(Manx National Heritage)

ablutions, house cleaning and breakfast. Work, physical exercise, cultural activities, walks out of the camp accompanied by guards, and the occasional visit to a local cinema fill the days which end with another roll call. Within the camp is a hospital for minor ailments in charge of a local doctor and an internee doctor. Serious cases are taken by ambulance to Noble's Hospital while those who require long-term treatment of a none too serious nature are taken to the special internee hospital at Falcon Cliff in Douglas. This serves all the camps, except Peel, and is staffed by the R.A.M.C., supplemented by both internees and civilians. Hutchinson has its own dental surgery run by an English dentist who visits daily and is assisted by an internee dentist.

The Cultural Committee has been an important influence in camp life since the start, and because of the constant arrivals and departures of internees, has changed frequently during its life. It arranges and encourages lectures on a variety of topics. In the early days lectures were given in the open in the central gardens, but the New Hall was available by Christmas, 1940. Lectures average attendances of 80 to 100, though one well-known historian attracted an audience of between 300 and 400. He left to go to America but was drowned when his ship was sunk in the Atlantic. The Debating Society meetings, musical performances and the Library are all organised by the Cultural Committee.

The New Hall is also used as a theatre. Already 40 performances have been staged. There is no admission charge. The actors have included professionals, while there are many helpers back stage. The plays have been mainly by English writers but there have also been Czechoslovakian and Russian works. The Library started with the gift of a few paperbacks, but has grown to 7,600 volumes on a wide range of topics. There is a well-appointed reading room and a loan ser-vice from Douglas Town Library and national organisations, including the Victoria and Albert Museum in London.

Music is also an important feature of camp life. With a large number of the internees being accomplished musicians, many being members of bands, concert parties, orchestras or soloists in their own right, it is not surprising that the standard is high and events frequent. The importance placed upon music can be seen, perhaps, from the incident when Captain Daniels, the Camp Commander, realised that the Austrian internee Marian Rawicz he had in his camp was one half of the pre-war piano partnership of Rawicz and Landauer. He traced the latter to another Island camp and arranged his transfer to Hutchinson. He then set about acquiring two grand pianos for them to play! Other well-known musicians include Charlie Kunz.

The camp roll also includes well-known names from the world of art and architecture. Within weeks of the camp opening, an art exhibition had been arranged and the first edition of *The Camp* reviews it. The report is dotted with names such as Kurt Schwitters, Markiowitz, Stern, Kahn and Uhlmann. Others with an equal or even greater claim to fame are recorded in later reviews here and in other camps. Some more simple work was even used to illustrate the various camp newspapers, perhaps most notably the now defunct *Onchan Pioneer*.

Meanwhile, life goes on in its regular routine behind the wire. Whatever interests are provided for the inmates, they all have the one abiding interest - freedom. While numbers continue to fall there is still no sign of the final release for all. They remain in a segregated community, and to schoolchildren passing by they are all prisoners of some kind about which fantastic tales are concocted. Perhaps now they will have a better idea of what really goes on!

OUR CAMP IN PICTURES No. 3 *Royal Avenue.*

Camp Picture No. 8.

Illustrations from
The Onchan Pioneer
(Frank Cowin Library)

The "well-heated" Cabin.

The C A M P C A F E is open from 10.30-12.45, 3.0-4.30 and 7.15-9.45.
Fridays closed from 3.0 to 4.30.

194

CRISIS OF FEEDING WARTIME POPULATION

The efforts to make the Island self-sufficient in the provision of basic food items for a population of over 90,000 are being intensified. Farmers are being forced to plough up meadowland and areas which have not been cultivated for many years. The scheme is being overseen by Agricultural Adviser, Mr George Howie who insists that every available acre is brought into cultivation for potato, corn and green crops. Douglas Corporation has been forced to give over seven acres of its prized golf course for cultivation. This urgency applies throughout the Island and farmers are desperate for tractors to supplement the hard-worked horses. Tractors and ploughs are supplied from the United States under the Lend-lease arrangements, but many have been lost in the Atlantic as convoys continue to suffer losses from U-boat attacks.

Farmers are being paid £2 an acre for bringing new land into cultivation, while the Board of Agriculture is paying an increasing amount of subsidies in order to expand production and to stabilise prices. For growing wheat, £4 an acre is paid to the farmer, and £10 an acre for potatoes which are in short supply, as evidenced by chip shops frequently displaying signs 'No frying tonight.' Consumption of milk and eggs is limited by the supplies available, but are not rationed. There are also subsidies for cattle, sheep and pigs; all imports of live-stock are prohibited, except under licence. Meat rationing at two shillings per person per week is now in force and is likely to be reduced even further, though not to the stringent levels in Britain.

Another side to the crisis is the shortage of manpower on the farms. While farmers and those employed full time in agriculture are exempt from military service, few casual workers are now available. An urgent appeal has been launched for more recruits to join the Women's Land Army. More and more internees, especially Italians, are being employed on farms. Groups of these with their guards are now a familiar sight in various parts of the Island. However, this valuable source of labour is diminishing as more of the internees are being released.

Posters asking us to 'Dig for Victory' have not gone unheeded. Spare land in the towns and villages has been given over to allotments which produce potatoes and vegetables to help with domestic supplies. Schools are closing for half-day holidays in September so that children can undertake blackberry picking. Thousands of pounds of berries are brought to school and then collected for taking to the jam factory at Rushen Abbey. Children are also being encouraged to collect cocksfoot grass seed for hay crops, now that supplies from Norway are no longer available.

WITH THE 15TH FROM TRIPOLI TO ITALY

The 15th LAA (Isle of Man) Regiment, as part of the 7th Armoured Division, continued to be in the vanguard of the victorious Eighth Army as it advanced across Libya. German and Italian aircraft were constantly doing their damnest to stave off the inevitable, providing plenty of action for the Bofors guns. On 23rd January the first troops entered a deserted Tripoli and early in February, the Prime Minister arrived to join in the celebrations and witness the Eighth Army's Victory Parade through the city. Lieut.-Colonel Eustace Smith, C.O. of the Manx Regiment, was presented to Mr Churchill.

The end of the month saw the Eighth Army take up positions for the advance into Tunisia. The fighting ahead was to be some of the hardest of the whole campaign, with the German and Italian armies desperately trying to survive as the American First Army advanced from the west. Rommel's counter-offensive inflicted heavy casualties, including gunners from the Regiment who were either killed or wounded. Then an attack on the German Mareth Line was repulsed and 1st Battery was forced to abandon its front positions. It was not until 20th March that a breakthrough was achieved and the Regiment passed through the Mareth Line. A link up with the First Army was made and time given for it to be reinforced. On the night of 30th April the final offensive was launched and Rommel's forces were overwhelmed after bitter fighting. On 7th May, Tunis was reached and the 1st Battery was the first to take up defensive positions to defend the port. Later they were joined by 41st and 42nd Batteries, but there was now little action following the surrender of the Germans and Italians.

In the ten months since August of last year, the Regiment had travelled 2,000 miles from Cairo to Tunis and its guns had been credited with 249 enemy aircraft destroyed, probably destroyed or damaged. The Regiment received many accolades for the part it had played, not least from G.O.C. Major-General Erskine of the 7th Armoured Division. In March, Sergeant W. H. Watterson was awarded the Military Medal for gallantry and later Sergeants R. Owen and L. C. Parry received similar awards.

Orders were then given to return to the Tripoli area for a rest period followed by intensive training, including landing craft exercises. By now, Major Clifford Kniveton had left the Regiment on being given command of the 34th LAA Regiment and was promoted Lieut.-Colonel. Major Henry Kelly took over command of 41st Battery and Major H. E. Hutton was given command of 1st Battery. Following the occupation of Sicily in August, the Regiment made ready to sail in support of 7th Division for the landing north of Salerno, near Naples. The first three days were critical as the Germans put up strong resistance, supported by ME 109s and FW 190s. Progress was made and the Batteries were operating together in the Vesuvius area when the vanguard of the Division entered Naples on 1st October. The Regiment continued to add to their score but not without further casualties. As the Allied advance continued, the Division was under orders to pull out and prepare for the sea journey back home. The Regiment left Naples on 20th December on its way to Gourock, Scotland. Earlier, in October, a group of 15 gunners and Captain J. J. Christian had left North Africa having been selected as 'battle experienced personnel' for home leave. They were given an emotional welcome as they landed on the pier at Douglas.

ANDREAS HOSTS No. 11 AIR GUNNERY SCHOOL

After the winter lull, R.A.F. Andreas is once again bustling with over a thousand R.A.F. and W.A.A.F. personnel billeted in the compounds. Everyone has a bicycle issued so that they can get to and from their place of work. In May all was in place to open as an Air Gunnery School and the first intake of volunteer pupils, most of them in their 'teens, arrived to undergo an intensive ten-week course. The training huts are equipped with the latest power-operated turrets which are vital to the defence of the Lancasters and Halifaxes now coming into service in greater numbers. All the instructors are experienced gunners, having completed a tour of operations.

Air experience is gained first on Ansons with Martinets towing the familiar drogues. These are released by the side of Braust Farm, after the Martinets have come in low across the new road from Andreas to Bride which is being called the 'Burma' road. As the course advances, the pupils move on to the turrets of the Wellingtons which have been retired from operations. They are in the air daily with Spitfires providing targets for the cine-guns of the turrets. Practice takes place in allotted zones, care being taken to avoid the bombing ranges used by Jurby. Those who complete the course satisfactorily are then posted to an O.T.U. before joining one of Bomber Command's squadrons which are mounting the great offensive in the night skies over Germany.

For those off duty the N.A.A.F.I. along Smeale Road provides a place of relaxation, as does the Y.M.C.A. on the Bride Road which is run by local ladies. Here dances are held with visits from Jack Hart's Jurby Band, although Andreas has formed its own. Clegg's stores and Rainer's cafe in the centre of the village do good trade in providing cups of tea and 'sticky' buns while the Grosvenor is well patronised making Mrs Breadner a busy hostess. At week-ends, front rooms of many a home in the parish welcome the airmen for ham and eggs, in return for which help is given with the harvest. Crennell's coaches are available for a night out at the Plaza and Corner Cinemas, while the Pool Ballroom is a popular Saturday night venue.

Jurby has now become No 5 Navigation and Bombing School and is equipped with up to 80 Ansons which provide 'flying classrooms' for the students. Those on the navigation course set off from Jurby on long cross-country flights taking in many points around Britain and Northern Ireland. Exercises are undertaken both day and night. Flights last up to $3^{1}/_{2}$ hours and each aircraft has a staff pilot, wireless operator and two trainees. For bomb aiming the Ansons are fitted with a perspex nose and the trainee bomb aimers take turns in a prone position over the ranges, using 22lb flash bombs. Results are recorded from observation huts positioned on the cliffs. The ranges in use are off Peel, Ballaugh, Jurby, Ballghennie and Cranstal. The Ansons have proved particularly reliable. Accidents are often the result of weather conditions or running out of fuel, especially when head winds are met on long navigation flights. There have been a number of accidents also involving aircraft from other stations.

One of the elderly Jurby Blenheims used for gunnery practice seen here with groundcrew

(Manx National Heritage)

Newly-qualified aircrew pose in front of one of the Hampdens at Jurby. Proudly wearing the Observer 'O' and half-wing, they will be posted to Operational Training Units of Bomber Command.

(Manx National Heritage)

AIR ACCIDENT REPORTS, 1943

18th April. Beaufighter on training flight from R.A.F. Ballyhalbert ditched in sea off south-west coast of Island. Crew of three were drowned.

28th April. Beaufighter from Crosby-on-Eden, Carlisle, crashed at Ellanbane Farm, Lezayre at 12.20 a.m. as a result of engine failure. Crew of two killed.

9th September. Wellington from R.A.F. Hixon on night flying exercise requested emergency landing at Jurby. Was seen from control tower but then disappeared. Caught wing tip on cliffs and crashed on Sartfield beach, north of Jurby Head. Exploded and burnt on impact with the loss of all five crew.

6th November. Halifax bomber crashed on Cronk Moar Farm, Rushen with engine on fire. Six Canadians and one R.A.F. crew lost.

14th December. Spitfire from R.A.F. Ballyhalbert hit the Rheast, near Kirk Michael, in bad weather. Polish pilot from 303 Squadron killed.

30th December. Anson from West Freugh, Wigtownshire, flew into cliff face above Horseleap Viaduct, Douglas Head Marine Drive at about 200 feet. Wreckage and remains fell back on to the railtrack below. All five Australians were lost.

On the morning of 6th June, the Headquarters of General Eisenhower, the Supreme Allied Commander, issued a terse announcement informing the world that the long-awaited invasion of Europe had at last begun: "Allied naval forces, supported by strong air forces, began landing Allied armies on the northern coast of France this morning." Of the thousands of Manx personnel in the Armed Services, many are involved in the biggest operation of its kind ever staged. We have this report.

After almost exactly four years to the day, ships of the Steam Packet Company returned to northern France and were involved in the initial landings of troops early on the morning of D-Day. This time the *Lady of Mann*, crewed by the Royal Navy, acted as headquarters for one of the Assault Flotillas responsible for getting the first troops ashore. The *Lady* had been converted to carry six landing craft which were hoisted into the water. On the initial wave she carried 490 infantry of the assault force responsible for establishing the Juno beach-head. Similarly equipped, the *Ben my Chree* arrived off the Omaha beach acting as headquarters for another Assault Flotilla and carried some of the first U.S. Rangers to land. A third Steam Packet vessel to take part was the *Victoria* which had Steam Packet officers on board under the command of Captain Keig. The *Victoria* landed troops at Arromanches where stiff opposition was met. A footing was secured and here one of the Mulberry artificial harbours was established.

Not far behind were the three Manx Batteries. Major Henry Kelly, second in command of the Regiment, went ashore on D + 1 with five other officers to make arrangements for the arrival of the Batteries. The first Troops landed on the Juno beach-head on D + 3 to be followed later by the rest of the Regiment. It is part of the British Second Army and once again the Regiment finds itself with the 7th Armoured Division. The weather has been most unseasonal and moving along the narrow farm lanes has not been easy.

Nevertheless, the troops have now been deployed to defend units of the Division whose immediate objectives are Bayeux and Caen.

HOME ON LEAVE
After leaving Italy at the end of last year, the Manx Regiment arrived at Gourock from where it had embarked over three years ago. Three weeks' home leave began on 10th January and members received a heroes' welcome from families and friends. An official welcome was given to them in the Villa Marina by Mayor of Douglas, Alderman S. A. Quirk. Special guest was Lieut.-Colonel MacClellan who received a great ovation. A special toast was given to 129 Battery which was represented by the wounded and repatriated Sgt. J. K. Conibear. In replying, he claimed that the 129th was the first Manx unit to enter Germany! Returning from leave, the Batteries began the work-up for the invasion - 'Operation Overlord'. On separate occasions the Regiment paraded with other units for inspection by General Sir Bernard Montgomery and H.M. King George V1. Captains K. C. Cowley and J. J. Christian, and Sergeant S. Cain have been Mentioned in Despatches.

FIVE PERISH
OFF DOUGLAS HEAD
On the night of 11th January an Anson on a night navigation exercise from Wigtown, flew into bad visibility and ditched in the sea 100 yards south of the Coastguard hut on Douglas Head. The crash was heard from the Admiralty Civil Police hut between Douglas Head Hotel and Marine Drive tollgate, and Air Sea Rescue, Douglas was informed. The wind was south-east Force 5 and voices could be heard calling in the darkness for nearly an hour. It was later revealed that the R.A.F. rescue launch was aground at the top of Douglas Harbour because of the weather conditions. The Douglas lifeboat was informed but not requested to launch for another half hour. When it reached the scene of the ditching all cries for help had ceased. Steps are being taken to ensure that a rescue craft will at all times be available in the outer harbour.

HIGHLY SECRET
While the general public is unaware of what is going on at the 'radio' station on Douglas Head, it is also mystified by the aerials which were erected last year across the bay on the Douglas Bay Hotel. A large wooden structure on a circular mounting was bolted to one of the hotel's towers. The structure supports tubular aerials which can be rotated to ensure the best reception. The transmissions received are coded messages sent from German and Italian bases, and even from the Japanese 'Singapore Sam.' These interceptions are part of the work of the Special Operations Training Establishment set up by the Royal Corps of Signals. Its main base is in the former Palace Internment Camp including the Hydro. Because of the secretive nature of their work, the trainees are restricted in their movements and have the use of the Derby Castle Ballroom as a gymnasium and for recreational purposes.

Young men and women of high intelligence are selected to receive instruction in the Morse code. Headphones are linked to their instructors' Morse keys or tape machines. Proficiency is achieved when they are able to take down Morse at the maximum sending speed of 24 words per minute. They then move to the Douglas Bay Hotel to practise taking down the coded German messages until they can deal with 150 letters a minute. They are then posted as 'Y' signallers who continue the interception of enemy coded messages. The intercepts are then translated at the headquarters of British Secret Intelligence.

H.M.S. SALAMANDER
Stories are circulating that six weeks after the D-Day landings, R.A.F. Typhoons attacked a number of ships belonging to the 1st Minesweeping Flotilla. The Flotilla was engaged in sweeping the English Channel between Portsmouth and Arromanches and, not having completed its task, was given permission to continue the operation. Shortly afterwards they were attacked by rockets and cannon fire from the Typhoons resulting in two ships being sunk and three damaged with loss of life said to be about 80, with another 150 wounded. One of the minesweepers, damaged beyond repair, is well

(Above) A pre-war view of the Douglas Bay Hotel whose appearance has been altered by the construction of a huge aerial on its tower. It is used for wireless interception for training special operators for the Royal Corps of Signals.
(R. and L. Kelly Collection)

(Below) Some of the 2,000 members of the A.T.S. special operators, photographed outside the Crescent Hotel. These well-educated and highly intelligent young women are trained to take down enemy morse messages which are then sent to British Intelligence for decoding.
(Manx National Heritage)

known in the Island. It is *H.M.S. Salamander* which before the war acted as a Fishery Protection Vessel and was a frequent visitor to Manx ports. It is also known she was present at Dunkirk and saved some Manx servicemen who would otherwise have been trapped.

INTERNEE FINED
A fine of £10 has been imposed on an Italian alien who built a secret still in his detention camp in Douglas. The Court of General Gaol heard that he distilled a 44% proof spirit from fermented potatoes, beetroot, fruit and sugar. He was originally fined £200 because of the 1867 Act of Tynwald under which the charge was brought. However, the sum was reduced after a memorial was presented to the Lieutenant-Governor.

HALIFAX CRASHES ON LONAN.
The horrors of flying accidents were brought home to the people of Laxey and Lonan on the afternoon of Friday, 14th July. A Canadian Halifax bomber from R.A.F. Leeming was on a cross-country training flight and entered low cloud which covered the Island. As it passed over Agneash and Laxey, the bomber was seen to be on fire and shedding fragments of wreckage, some of which landed amongst schoolchildren enjoying their sports day in Glen Road. Five of the seven crew jumped from the aircraft but there was no time for the parachutes to open. At 4.20 the Halifax finally broke up and crashed near Lonan Church, spreading wreckage over two miles. Two of the engines land-

ed near the vicarage and another in a field down Church Road where a farmer had just finished harrowing. Such was the violence of the impact, that the fourth engine, with part of the mainplane and undercarriage, crashed on Pinfold Hill, sending the wheel and undercarriage on to the rocks of Laxey beach. The engine hit 'Hokang' bungalow which went on fire, burning the three occupants who were taken to the Military Hospital in Onchan for treatment. A little boy, aged 3½, died from severe burns and shock. He had come from Newcastle with his mother for a holiday. The five aircrew who jumped from the stricken bomber have been buried at Andreas churchyard.

MORE DEMANDS FOR HOME RULE
The Manx Government has taken the unprecedented step of calling a Press conference in London to publicise its demands for Home Rule. It was given by Speaker of the House of Keys Mr J. D. Qualtrough and Middle M.H.K. Mr Eric Fargher, the well-known advocate. They received extensive coverage in the newspapers and on the B.B.C. The Government is to petition the Home Office for more control over the Island's domestic affairs.

FINANCIAL SUPPORT
The Manx Legislature this year voted another free grant of £250,000 to the British Government in support of the war effort. This makes a total grant of £1,250,000 in addition to the £750,000 already lent free of interest. These have been funded by increased taxes. The recent 'Salute to the Soldier' Week raised £1,204,405 in savings making a grand total of over £6,280,000 of Manx War Savings invested since the beginning of the war. The Island's buoyant economy is reflected in the high price for dwelling houses. Small houses with possession are fetching three times their pre-war cost.

NOT A 'DOODLE-BUG'!
The most sensational non-war event in the Island was the result of an 18-ton flywheel running out of control at the Douglas Power Station on the North Quay. Its rim, composed of six parts which were bolted together, disintegrated and parts were hurled through the roof up to a thousand feet before landing all over the centre of the town. One section of the wheel crashed through the roof

and floor of the stokers' mess room of the Douglas Gas Works and ended up near a boiler. A few feet more and there could have been an explosion and fire with serious consequences. Another piece hit the roof of the *Isle of Man Times* building in Athol Street, while a further piece hit a house and trapped two women in the debris. They were rescued by firemen and no-one was injured in the incident.

On duty at the power station was Roy Motion who had survived with an injured leg the sinking of the *Fenella* at Dunkirk. Subsequently, he served on a merchant ship which was torpedoed before he returned to the *safety* of the Island! The resulting power failure spread to the entire Island and lasted for up to 14 hours in places. Cinemas and places of entertainment had to be evacuated and closed for the night. The noise of the airborne wheel was likened to that of the Flying Bombs, otherwise known as 'Doodlebugs' which the Germans are deploying against London. At first, some people thought Douglas had been hit by one. Hence the flying wheel being nicknamed 'The Kelly Bug'!

INVASION PLANS!

According to military maps discovered recently in a former German barracks in Belgium, the Isle of Man may have been in the direct path of the invasion of Britain, had it gone ahead. The maps suggest that the Nazis planned to seize the Isle of Man from Ireland and use it as a bridge-head to northern industrial England. R.A.S.C. driver George Hinds from Kirk Michael returned to the Island with the map of the Isle Man in October. He says the map indicates sea depths around the Island. It was revised with the other maps up to 1943.

MANXMAN WINS V.C.

It has been announced that Major Robert Cain, a Shanghai-born Manxman, has been awarded the Victoria Cross after taking part in the audacious attempt to capture the bridge over the lower River Rhine at Arnhem in September. In the desperate defence mounted by British paratroops against overwhelming German forces, Major Cain destroyed a tank single-handedly with an anti-tank gun at close range. His citation says he showed gallantry, endurance and leadership throughout the battle. Educated at King William's College, Major Cain

---

LATEST WAR CASUALTIES

Up to the end of November next of kin have been informed of a further 71 casualties as being killed or missing on the war fronts.

BRITISH ARMY	- 40, including losses in Europe.
ROYAL AIR FORCE	- 18, mostly from Bomber Command.
ROYAL NAVY	- 1
MERCHANT NAVY	- 12
TOTAL	- 71

A total of 12 have also died on active service either by accident or illness, including two who are known to have died in Japanese P.O.W. camps.

---

worked for an oil company in the Far East before the war.

FIRST PRISONERS OF WAR ARRIVE

The first batch of 320 German prisoners of war arrived at the end of November. They were watched by crowds of curious local people as they arrived by sea at Douglas, looking sullen and very young. Accommodation for the prisoners was provided at the Metropole and Onchan Internment Camps which were adapted by the War Office as prison 'cages.' It meant that every item of furniture in the two camps was removed for storage at Derby Castle. It is the policy of the War Office to provide its own items of basic furniture. As the Allies advance towards Germany it is estimated that 5,000 prisoners will be brought to the Island.

Meanwhile, further repatriation of internees has taken place during the year. On 1st September more than 600 men, women and children (including babes in arms) departed from Port Erin, leaving fewer than 400 in the resort. At the same time 100 from the men's camps left leaving less than 2,000 men and women still held on the Island at Port Erin, Mooragh and Peveril. Hutchinson was emptied in March when its last 300 inmates were transferred to Peel. Hutchinson Camp was checked over by the military ready for returning to the peacetime owners and tenants. The houses and contents were found to be in a reasonable state, and improvements had been made by the camp authorities such as the provision of shower-bath units and cubicles. Another sign of normality is the fair number of visitors arriving this year despite the limited space available on the Steam Packet vessels which have to give priority to service personnel.

A section of the Metropole Camp which is now rapidly filling with German prisoners captured by the Allied armies advancing into Europe.

(Manx National Heritage)

WITH THE 15th LAA REGIMENT
INTO BELGIUM AND HOLLAND

By the middle of June the Manx Regiment was ready to play its part with the British Second Army in Normandy. The 1st Battery was in command of Major J. B. Mylchreest; the 41st was under Major T. W. Cain and the 42nd under Major H. S. Balls. The Second Army's task was to protect the left flank of the Normandy beaches at all costs against the XX1 Panzer Division counter attacks. Fighting was some of the fiercest of the invasion. The three Manx Batteries were constantly switched between units of the 7th Armoured Division. Initially there was not a great deal of enemy air activity, the Allied air forces having complete control. There was the constant threat, however, of low-flying ME 109s and FW 190s which kept everyone on their toes. There were the inevitable casualties as the score of aircraft shot down or damaged continued to rise. The month-long siege of Caen began on 18th June, the town being heavily shelled and bombed. The Division was in the centre of the final thrust, but on 10th August was pulled back and on the 17th joined the First Canadian Army to make the advance to the River Seine, some 65 miles away. On the last day of August the Regiment crossed the river south of Rouen in heavy rain. The task of 21st Army Group now was to clear the enemy from Northern France, destroy the Flying Bomb sites, capture the airfields in Belgium and take the port of Antwerp. Rapid progress was made until the Regiment was called to a halt as its supply vehicles were diverted to help other units. Six days later the Regiment was back with the Division as it approached Brussels. It received a rapturous welcome as each city was passed.

'Operation Market Garden' was to secure a footing in the Low Countries for a startline to attack the Ruhr. The Battle of Arnhem at the end of September was the focal point of the operation. The Airborne Division suffered disastrous losses and units of the Regiment were employed, not for the first time, in low-level shooting at enemy positions. Hundreds of rounds were being fired in a week. The Dutch people gave a warm welcome, but the onset of winter brought bitterly cold and damp conditions. Winter clothing was issued and this was supported by woollen garments arriving from the Island's Comforts Fund. By 28th November enemy gun positions overlooking Antwerp were neutralised and the port was opened to Allied convoys.

The Regiment moved across the River Maas into the Sittard area. A day later the Germans took the advantage of atrocious weather to launch its offensive in the Ardennes with bitter fighting lasting for a month and holding up 2nd Army's advance. The Regiment was soon called into action. It became the first Royal Artillery of the 7th Armoured Division to fire from German territory. The new ME 262 jet fighters put in their first appearance in large numbers. The Bofors continued the ground shoots. The 41st was particularly busy in the last week of December, some 3,500 rounds being pumped at the targets. There was little time for Christmas festivities but seasonal fare was available, and ENSA and cinema shows provided some welcome entertainment. More importantly, everyone is confident this will be the last Christmas of the war, at least in Europe.

1944 NEWS IN BRIEF

JANUARY

1 - New Year's Honours - Captain John Higgins, Supt. Isle of Man Air Services, M.B.E.; Sergt Walter L. Christian, Home Guard, B.E.M.; Wing Commander J. A. C. Karran, Air Force Cross.

21 - With an eye to the future, Steam Packet Company increases its holding in Isle of Man Air Services Ltd to 50%.

MAY

10 - Chief Constable Major Young is awarded £250 damages from the *Isle of Man Times* for libel. In an article the newspaper accused him of being a social climber and imposing a policing regime of 'unfairness and tyranny.'

12 - Douglas Corporation buys Willaston Estate (77 acres) for housing.

30 - Mr H. E. George, M.A., B.Sc., appointed headmaster of Ramsey Grammar School.

31 - Lieutenant-Governor's term of office is extended for one year.

JUNE

6 - D-DAY -ALLIED INVASION OF FRANCE.

20 - Decided to open Tynwald Court with prayer.

JULY

6 - Lady Louis Mountbatten visits Island

6 - Lady Baden-Powell opens new Scout and Guide headquarters (Cunningham House)

20 - Memorial to Miss Josephine Kermode ('Cushag') unveiled in Maughold churchyard.

SEPTEMBER

6 - Visit of Prince Olav, Crown Prince of Norway to meet Norwegians housed in the Onchan Camp who had escaped and were waiting to join their country's 'free' armed services.

17 - Blackout restrictions relaxed.

OCTOBER

2 - Ramsey Swing Bridge taken over by Harbour Commissioners.

26 - Four interned Manx soldiers who had escaped welcomed home.

30 - Government Commission's proposals for £250,000 Brine Spa at Ramsey outlined.

31 - Announced in Tynwald that agreement had been reached with Imperial Government for repurchase of requisitioned boardinghouse furniture.

NOVEMBER

3 - L.G.B. approve Douglas Corporation's application to borrow £25,000 to acquire Glen Falcon House and garden for widening of Broadway.

17 & Manx women prosecuted and fined for failing to obey
24 Lieutenant-Governor's directive that they should join the Women's Land Army.

18 - Braddan Commissioners decide to purchase Snugborough estate for housing.

DECEMBER

3 - Home Guard Farewell 'Stand Down' Parade.

BLACKOUT RESTRICTIONS LIFTED : HOME GUARD STANDS DOWN

After five years of restrictions, street lighting has been restored on the Island and blackout curtains have become redundant. The big switch-on happened on the evening of Sunday, 17th September. Not having been used for such a long time and lacking maintenance because of shortage of manpower, it was not possible for all the lights to be made operational immediately. In Douglas, only 300 of its 671 lights were switched on and just a few of its 174 powered by gas. Even so, to a community accustomed to stygian darkness the event seemed like a light spectacular, particularly on Douglas promenade where hundreds turned out to experience the sight. Conservation of fuel and resources, however, meant that the amount of illumination, compared with pre-war days, was very poor. Light standards on the promenade, for example, were each fitted with one 150 watt bulb compared with the normal loading of two 300 watt bulbs. The lights were screened also from the sea as the risk from enemy attack from the sea still remains. The removal of the light restriction follows the lifting some time ago of the compulsory requirement for children to carry their gas masks with them on schooldays.

During the year the Home Guard Battalions continued to maintain a high standard of training. This was put into practice at the annual competitions and summer weekend camps at Glen Wyllin. A feature of the camps this year were battle simulation courses at which men were given the experience of advancing against a position whilst being under live fire. The summer over and the Allied advance into Europe making steady progress, preparations were made for the possible Standing Down of the Home Guard. The compulsory drills and training introduced in 1942 were discontinued and all duties reverted to being voluntary. Attendance was little affected, but by the end of October arrangements for the Stand Down and withdrawal of arms and equipment were put into effect.

A grand Stand Down Parade was held in the Villa Marina on 3rd December. Over a thousand men from all parts of the Island belonging to the 1st and 2nd Battalions assembled in the Lord Street Car Park, wearing uniform for the last time. Led by the Band of the Royal Naval School of Music, based at the Howstrake Holiday Camp in Onchan, the men in Company formation marched along the Loch Promenade where His Excellency Earl Granville took the salute from the War Memorial. The Guard of Honour was made up of men representing all the Companies. Assembled in the Villa Marina, a short service was conducted by Archdeacon, the Ven. C. V. Stockwood. The singing of 'Guide me, O Thou great Jehovah' was most moving, especially the second verse which was sung unaccompanied. Earl Granville expressed the appreciation of all for the many hours the men had given to training and carrying out their duties, and paid tribute to the high standards that had been achieved since the L.D.V. was formed over four years ago. Then, armed with little more than 'patriotic spirit', the Home Guard had become a well-trained, well-armed and efficient military force.

The Maughold Platoon, 1944 winners of the Governor's Cup which is competed for by all sections of the Home Guard. Seated behind the cup is the Platoon Commander, Maughold farmer Lieutenant H. C. Kerruish.   *(Barry Quilliam)*

H.M.S. URLEY COMMISSIONED

The Royal Navy Air Station at Ronaldsway was commissioned on 21st June as *H.M.S. Urley*, taking its name from the Manx for 'eagle.' Its Commanding Officer is Captain W. P. Shirley-Rollinson, R.N. and over a thousand personnel are now resident in the accommodation huts at Ballasalla and Janet's Corner. The station is an Operational Training Unit for aircrew flying the Fairey Barracuda torpedo/bomber/reconnaissance aircraft now in service with the Fleet Air Arm. *H.M.S. Urley* is seen as an important part of the preparations for the expected long campaign in the Far East, leading to the eventual capitulation of Japan. Many of those under training at Ronaldsway are from Australia and New Zealand.

Badge of the newly-commissioned H.M.S. Urley. The badge is surmounted by a 'crown' of galleons and Viking ships and incorporates the Eagle and Child, ancient crest of the House of Stanley whose family once provided Kings and Lords of Man.

(The late Jack Callister)

The Barracuda is a complex aircraft which can be used either as a torpedo bomber or dive bomber. It is equipped also with air to surface radar and, with a weight of nearly eight tons, is powered by an up-rated Merlin engine which makes it particularly noisy, something the people of Castletown have learned to their chagrin. Three training squadrons, with a total of over a hundred Barracudas, are based at Ronaldsway. Each has a crew of three housed beneath a canopy over the wing, these being the pilot, observer/radar operator and the telegraphist/airgunner. The course lasts for 14 weeks during which each crew are in the air for about 90 hours. A third of this is at night, and either individually or in formation. Many hours are spent on navigation exercises around the Irish Sea. Torpedo dropping is practised on targets towed by motor launches off the coast. The most demanding part of the course is the intensive dive bombing at targets found off Perwick and Port Soderick, where observation huts record results. At night a flare is released to light up the target which just gives sufficient time for the aircraft to dive down to 200 feet before dropping the practice bomb.

At Jurby the training navigation and bombing schedules continue, though the pace slackened before D-Day as pilots were posted out to take up positions in support of the Normandy invasion. Many of them flew Ansons which had been converted as air ambulances. More specialised training at Jurby involved navigators acting as bomb-aimers in the twin-engined Bostons, Beaufighters and Mosquitoes. In the spring Wing-Commander Guy Gibson, V.C., of Dambuster fame paid a visit to all R.A.F. establishments, including Andreas and the radar stations. While Andreas continues to train airgunners, its former Control Centre at Ramsey Grammar School has been given a new role. The Operations Room now plots all aircraft movements over the Irish Sea and wireless contact with the aircraft can be made to pass on information and instructions.

When an aircraft is 'lost' the Coast Guard is informed and Rescue Sections are summoned to undertake 'search and rescue' in a given area. The year has seen a number of crashes involving aircraft from the United States Army Air Force as they cross the Island on flights between their bases in England and Northern Ireland.

AIR CRASH FATALITIES, 1944

11th January. Anson from Wigtown ditched at night off Douglas Head. Air Sea Rescue unable to assist and Douglas lifeboat was later requested to launch, but was unable to find the five aircrew.

5th April. Anson from R.A.F. Cark ditched in sea between Mull of Galloway and Burrow Head. Air Sea Rescue Walrus from Andreas made search and recovered one body of the five aircrew.

8th June. U.S.A.A.F Liberator struck east shoulder of Snaefell, 50 feet from summit. Crew of four were fatally injured.

13th June. Anson from Wigtown struck North Barrule at night and disintegrated on impact. Four crew were killed.

6th July. U.S.A.A.F. Liberator flew into thick fog and struck North Barrule 100 feet from summit. Impact followed by explosion and fire. Four crew lost.

14th July. U.S.A.A.F. Marauder flew into thick cloud and struck Cronk ny Arrey Laa. Aircraft completely destroyed but two of the eight on board were found alive in the widespread wreckage.

14th July. Halifax on cross-country training flight seen on fire over Agneash and Laxey before crashing near Lonan Church. Wreckage spread over wide area, an engine setting fire to a bungalow on Pinfold Hill. Small boy died from burns. The crew of eight, including seven Canadians, was lost.

8th August. Anson from Squire's Gate struck Beinn-y-Phott at 1,100 feet and broke up. Pilot and navigator survived but two others were killed.

13th August. Anson from Wigtown flew into north-west face of Cronk ny Arrey Laa at full power killing all five on board.

27th October. R.N.A.S. Hurricane based at Andreas on exercise with Radar School on Douglas Head crashed near the incline railway, killing the pilot.

21st December. Barracuda from *H.M.S. Urley* dived on target in Port Soderick Bay when wing fell off. Pilot and observer were killed.

22nd December. Wellington from R.A.F. Shawbury, Salop, flew into South Barrule in thick fog, killing all four crew.

31st December. A mid-air collision involving two Ansons from mainland stations occurred during the morning over the south of the Island. One of the Ansons was able to land in a large field and the crew survived. The other Anson was seen to go into a dive and crashed at Ballabeg, Arbory, killing all four crew.

HERE IS THE NEWS : 1945
BONFIRES LIGHT UP VICTORY CELEBRATIONS

The news of the surrender of German forces came late on the morning of Tuesday, 8th May. That afternoon everyone, at home or at work, was glued to a wireless set to hear Prime Minister Winston Churchill make his triumphal address to the nation. The Manx Music Festival, which had just started the previous day at the Gaiety Theatre, was interrupted to enable the audience to listen to the broadcast from the stage. Everyone then sang the National Anthem and the rest of the day the whole Island joined in the celebrations. We have this report:

Church bells, which for long had been silent, pealed and were joined by ships' sirens and hooters. Air raid sirens sounded the 'all clear' for five minutes. Streets were gaily decorated with flags and bunting, and street parties hastily organised. Elsewhere, people went to church for special Thanksgiving services. Service personnel and locals joined in the merriment with much singing and music. At Ramsey black-faced Minstrels roamed the flag-decorated streets, one of them beating an enamel dish like a drum. The general noise everywhere was something one had to experience to believe. At night, the Island was lit by bonfires in the towns and villages, and on the beaches. Shopkeepers produced boxes of fireworks and rockets which had been hidden away since 1939. Little work was done on VE Day and the following day which was classed as a general holiday. Workers were either given the time off or, if their services were needed paid extra. There was no mail for two days because there were no postmen on duty!

At midnight on Tuesday, 14th August, Britain's new Prime Minister, Clement Attlee announced that Japan had finally surrendered. This brought huge crowds on to the promenades at Douglas as the Royal Navy ships fired their guns and lit up the night skies with flares. The following day was celebrated as VJ Day and a general holiday was proclaimed. There were more street parties in many parts of the Island and at night pubs had to close when supplies ran out. Many came in from 'the country' to join the festivities and the Villa Marina and

Following VE Day, a Victory Parade was held on Sunday, 13th May, with over 2,000 taking part. The Guard of Honour was provided by a contingent from H.M.S. St. George seen here being inspected by the Island's wartime Governor, His Excellency Vice-Admiral The Earl Granville, K.C.V.O., C.B., D.S.O. Much better weather was enjoyed for the Victory Parade following VJ Day in August. *(Manx National Heritage)*

Palais de Danse were packed with dancers. Billy Ternent and his band appeared on the roof of the Colonnade and, lit up by naval searchlights, played for thousands of dancers on the promenade opposite. It was a perfect summer evening which was also enjoyed by visitors already on the Island. It is estimated that 100,000 have arrived this summer - a welcome sign for the future.

VICTORY PARADES

The VE celebrations culminated on the following Sunday with a great parade in Douglas in which 2,000 took part, headed by a band of 70 musicians from the Royal Naval School of Music. The parade left the Victoria Pier Arcade and His Excellency Earl Granville took the salute at the War Memorial. The Guard of Honour was provided by officers and sailors from *H.M.S. St George*, with the bugle band also in attendance. The parade consisted of detachments from *H.M.S. Valkyrie*, *H.M.S. St George* and *H.M.S. Urley* followed by the Wrens. Then came units from the O.C.T.U., Royal Corps of Signals, P.O.W. Camp guards, A.T.S., R.A.F. Jurby and R.A.F. Andreas, the R.A.F. Regiment with members of the Home Guard, Civil

Defence, Army and Sea Cadets and A.T.C. Cadets taking up the rear. Weather conditions were dismal for the assembly in the Villa Marina Gardens and the parade was concluded by a short service during which the Lord Bishop gave a short address.

Glorious summer weather prevailed for the Victory Parade held to celebrate VJ Day. The proceedings were similar to those for VE Day, with all organisations again represented. The O.C.T.U. provided the Guard of Honour and the music was by the Douglas Brass Band conducted by Mr Sam Brough. In many ways it was also a Farewell Parade with the imminent closing of many of the training establishments and camps on the Island.

ROYAL VISIT

Adding to the excitement of the summer was the visit of Their Majesties King George VI and Queen Elizabeth - the first Royal Visit they had been able to undertake outside Great Britain since the war began. It was a three-day visit beginning on 4th July when they arrived at Victoria Pier, Douglas. The first stop was at the Villa Marina where 4,000 schoolchildren had assembled to greet them with massed singing. The rest of the day was spent touring towns and villages throughout the Island, before retiring to Government House. Thursday was Tynwald Day where record crowds assembled to witness the historic occasion when, for the first time, a King and Queen took their places on Tynwald Hill. In the afternoon a visit was made to *H.M.S. St George,* which was followed next morning by a visit to *H.M.S. Valkyrie* where the ship's company of 1,800 were paraded, watched by a huge crowd. Time was also spent at the machine shops of the Dowty engineering works at Castle Hill, Douglas, where 250 employees are engaged in making hydraulic undercarriages for aircraft. Then it was northwards to R.A.F. Jurby where over a thousand airmen and WAAFs were inspected. A Dakota aircraft left at 3 p.m. to return Their Majesties to London.

(Top) His Majesty King George VI presides at a meeting of members of Tynwald in St. John's Church prior to the Tynwald Ceremony.　　*(R. and L. Kelly Collection)*
(Above) The historic occasion which saw, for the first time, a King and Queen take their places on Tynwald Hill. Their Majesties are seen accompanied by His Excellency Earl Granville and Lord Bishop Strickland Taylor, with Deemster R. D. Farrant, Clerk of the Rolls on the right.
　　(Douglas Town Hall Archives)
(Below) Last engagement of Their Majesties before leaving the Island was an inspection of personnel at R.A.F. Jurby. Queen Elizabeth is seen here inspecting the parade of W.A.A.F.s in front of Flying Control.
　　(via Laura Briggs)

FISHING TRAGEDY AT PEEL
In January, two members of the crew of the Peel fishing boat *Manx Lily* died in drowning accidents within four days of each other. First, her acting skipper, Thomas Walter Quilliam, was dragged into the sea as the scallop dredge fell back into the water as it was being hauled inboard. Then the vessel's skipper, David Craine, died when he fell overboard while taking her to Scotland for overhaul.

ISLAND'S WORST AIR DISASTER
On the morning of 23rd April, a Boeing B17 Flying Fortress set off from its base in Essex to Nutt's

Corner, Belfast. At 10.20 a.m. it was seen passing over Maughold at about 500 feet and entered low cloud which covered North Barrule. A moment later an explosion was heard as it crashed into the mountainside. Police and ambulance staff from R.A.F. Andreas were sent to the scene to recover the bodies. All 31 on board, including a dog, had perished, making it the most appalling aircraft accident on Manx soil. Every available space in the Fortress had been crammed with American airmen on their way for a rest period. The aircraft was found to be on automatic pilot while the mountainside was littered with playing cards and dollar bills.

Just nine days before, on 14th April, another Fortress on its way to Northern Ireland was seen flying very low in thick fog heading west over the Perwick Bay Hotel. The aircraft just cleared the trees beyond the swimming pool, banked left and crashed on Cronk ny Arrey, about half a mile from Glen Chass. All ten on board perished in the impact which was followed by an explosion.

NEW GOVERNOR SWORN IN

A great ceremonial occasion was staged at *H.M.S. Urley* when 2,000 of the ship's personnel paraded on 25th August. They were to witness the departure of the Island's wartime Lieutenant-Governor, Earl Granville and his wife, Lady Margaret Rose, sister to the Queen. Before they

LEST WE FORGET

While most of those held in German Prisoner of War Camps had returned to the Island before VE Day, including men of the 129th Battery, Manx Regiment, it was not until the end of the year that over 40 survivors from Japanese camps returned to their families. Throughout the year further details were received about those who had been killed, were missing presumed killed, or had died as a result of accidents or illness. It has been difficult to get information from the Far East. The latest numbers include those who have had to be presumed killed after a considerable lapse of time. According to the latest local records, a total of 451 service personnel from the Island, including five women, have been killed in action or have died whilst on active service. Official figures show that 5,455 men from the Island served with H.M. Forces and Merchant Navy

FINAL WAR CASUALTIES

BRITISH ARMY	-	22 (including 7 on Western Front, 2 in Italy and 4 in Burma and Malaysia)
ROYAL AIR FORCE	-	15 (on operations)
ROYAL NAVY	-	10
MERCHANT NAVY	-	5
TOTAL	-	52

In addition 13 have been killed in accidents or have died in hospitals. A further 16 have died in Prisoner of War Camps, 13 of whom were held by the Japanese.

departed for Northern Ireland they greeted the incoming Lieutenant-Governor, Air Vice Marshal Sir Geoffrey Bromet, who had served with Coastal Command during the war. He arrived in a Lockheed Electra and the Marine Band played as the two Lieutenant-Governors inspected the Guard of Honour. The departing Lieutenant-Governor flew off in the Electra while Sir Geoffrey was driven to Castle Rushen to be sworn in as the Island's new Lieutenant-Governor.

FIRE CHIEF GAOLED

After a sensational trial at the Court of General Gaol, Douglas fire chief Stephen Albert Caugherty was sentenced to 15 months hard labour and fined £700. He pleaded guilty to stealing hundreds of ration books stored in Douglas Town Hall and selling them on the Black Market. Deemster Cowley said Caugherty had been a traitor to his country. The Manchester businessman who bought the ration books was also gaoled.

(Top) View from the control tower of part of the parade of H.M.S. Urley personnel to mark the departure of the Lieutenant-Governor and the arrival of his replacement, Air Vice-Marshal Sir Geoffrey Bromet.
(Above) Commanding Officer of H.M.S. Urley, Captain Shirley-Rollinson R.N., inspecting W.R.N.s based on the station.
(Below) His Excellency Earl Granville making a final tour of inspection before greeting Air Vice-Marshal Sir Geoffrey Bromet and departing for his new appointment as Governor of Northern Ireland on 25th August. (Photographs: The late Jack Callister)

ROYAL VISIT

The Royal Visit began with a welcome from 4,000 schoolchildren from Douglas who assembled in the Villa Marina Gardens. Their Majesties are seen here accompanied by the Mayor of Douglas, Councillor Stephen Quirk.

A stop in Royal Avenue Onchan, gave local children and villagers a chance to greet Their Majesties. Sergeant Fred Faragher of the Isle of Man Constabulary keeps a watchful eye over the proceedings.

Thousands of people from the north assembled in Parliament Square, Ramsey, to make the most of the Royal Visit.

(Photographs from Douglas

IN PICTURES

An historic Tynwald Day. The Sword Bearer leads Their Majesties to Tynwald Hill upon which they became the first King and Queen to take part in the ancient ceremony.

Members of the Women's Land Army based at Knockaloe are honoured by a visit by Their Majesties seen with Organiser Miss E. Teare. The W.L.A. played a vital part during the war in helping food production.

Their Majesties, in company with Captain Poland, Officer Commanding H.M.S. St George, during an inspection of the entire ship's complement on the field adjoining Cunningham's Camp. Throughout the war, over 8,500 young sailors were taught at the Ballakermeen High Schools before being posted to ships of the Royal Navy.

(Town Hall Archives)

PROUD RECORD OF THE MANX REGIMENT

The new year saw the 15th LAA Batteries in constant action on the German border, firing thousands of rounds as enemy fighters and bombers attacked R.A.F. landing grounds nearby. Then the guns were used to attack ground targets as units of the 7th Armoured Division pressed on with their relentless advance against stubborn German resistance. At the end of January, Earl Granville, accompanied by Lieut.-Colonel MacClellan, paid a two-day visit to the Regiment to see members in action and to discuss post-war matters.

The next major obstacle for Field-Marshal Montgomery's 21st Army was the crossing of the Rhine and on 22nd March 41st Battery was positioned in support of the vanguard and made the crossing on the 25th, to be followed by the other two Batteries. They were met by a mass of surrendering enemy, but carried on changing positions almost daily to defend bridges over the Dortmund-Ems Canal. The beginning of April saw the 1st and 42nd helping to marshal captured men and displaced persons from the concentration camps. Elsewhere, 41st was involved in resisting counter attacks. The 7th Division then turned south-east towards Nienburg and during the last weeks of April, the Regiment were involved in some of the most intensive anti-aircraft gunnery since the invasion. The Luftwaffe's ME 109s and FW 190s regularly appeared in force at low level to harrass the advance, and the Batteries were frequently called upon to wipe out pockets of resistance as towns and villages were entered. 1st Battery had the experience of moving through Fallingbostel where 10,000 British POWs (including some of the 129th Battery) had been freed.

Further progress brought the Divison within range of Hamburg. The Regiment was now more than 200 miles from the Rhine, after 27 days on the move during which they had fired 10,000 rounds with 27 'hits' scored. At this point Major Henry Kelly was made Lieut.-Colonel and took over command of the Regiment. Major H. S. Balls became Second in Command, handing over 42nd Battery to Major D. D. Lay. By the end of April, German resistance was waning and on 1st May, 42nd Battery made the last anti-aircraft firings of the war by the Regiment's guns. Hamburg surrendered on the 3rd and news of Adolf Hitler's suicide was followed quickly by the German surrender on 7th May. The regiment has the proud record of accounting for over 350 enemy aircraft destroyed or damaged - a total unrivalled by any other L.A.A. Regiment. Eighty of the Regiment lost their lives.

129th BATTERY COMES HOME

Since that fateful day in Crete four years ago, the survivors of the 129th Battery endured the deprivations of German prison camps. Those who had been repatriated, and the three gunners who had escaped, told of the harsh treatment that had been meted out by their custodians who seemed to be unaware of the Geneva Convention. Red cross parcels brought welcome relief from the endless soup and black bread, while parcels from home helped to keep up morale.

The Americans were the first to reach the prison camps in Austria and by the end of April, groups were being welcomed home at the pier in Douglas. Among them was Major W. H. Cain, 129th Battery's Commander. A large number of the 129th were released in Bavaria on 17th April and were left to begin their trek southwards. They were picked up eventually by Americans and flown to an R.A.F. airfield adjoining Rheims. They were then allotted to one of the waiting Lancasters and made the flight back to England. The last of the 129th survivors landed in Douglas a week after VE Day.

1945 NEWS IN BRIEF

JANUARY
24 - Island in frost grip - 18 degrees of frost.
26 - Government announce financial assistance to local authorities and private enterprise for housing.

FEBRUARY
16 - Government to purchase Marine Drive, Douglas Head, for £14,000 from owners. It has been closed throughout the war and its electric railway fell into disuse.
23 - Agricultural Wages Board amended farm workers' wages to £3. 10s. per week.

MARCH
31 - Mr Ramsey Moore (Attorney-General) retired after 25 years' service. Succeeded by Mr Sydney Kneale, O.B.E.

APRIL
1 - Mr D. F. Barwell appointed manager of the Palace and Derby Castle Ltd.
27 - Cunningham's Camp, Britain's first holiday camp, sold by the Cunningham family for £400,000. A public company is to be floated to operate it.

MAY
4 - Castletown Brewery Company bought Clinch's Brewery, Douglas.
5 - VE-DAY - Germany capitulated.
10 - Proposed National Testimonial to Mr Noah Moore, Island's veteran conductor, on his retirement.

26 - Mr Herbert Morrison, Home Secretary, conferred with Tynwald deputation re Manx Constitution representations.

JUNE
1 - Basic petrol ration begins.
9 - Serious fire at Strand Cinema causing £7,000 of damage.
14 - His Honour Deemster Cowley awarded C.B.E. in King's Birthday honours.
19 - Earl Granville presented his last Budget showing surplus of £59,296 for the year. Reserves stand at a record £1,000,000, of which £700,000 is earmarked for post-war reconstruction.
22 - Okell's Brewery taken over by Heron and Brearley Ltd. at a cost of £250,000.
26 - Coal heavers' unofficial strike in Douglas regarding working practices. The strike was settled after a week when the Lieutenant-Governor ordered German PoWs to take over the men's work.

JULY
4 - KING AND QUEEN ARRIVE FOR THREE DAY VISIT.

AUGUST
14 - VJ-DAY - Japan capitulated. WORLD WAR ENDED.
24 - Palace and Derby Castle Company acquire Strand Cinema and Palais de Danse.

OCTOBER
27 - Thanksgiving Savings Week begins. £1,003,448 raised.

NOVEMBER
22 - *King Orry* launched at Birkenhead.

H.M.S. URLEY TO BE DE-COMMISSIONED

Although the hectic training programme for Barracuda aircrew continued unabated after the surrender of Japanese forces in August, it was only a matter of time before the training station would close down. In fact, the squadrons on the base were disbanded by the middle of December. It has been announced now that *H.M.S. Urley* is to be de-commissioned early in the new year. After 18 months of day and night activity, peace has returned to Ronaldsway. Gone is the growl of the Merlin engines which were called upon to power the eight-ton aircraft, and gone are the many complaints to local newspapers about sleepless nights endured by the people of Castletown. Because of wartime censorship, such complaints were never published.

Two of the Fairey Barracuda torpedo/dive bombers from H.M.S. Urley. Seated behind the pilot are the observer and the telegraphist/air gunner.

(R.A.F. Museum, Hendon)

Schoolboys, however, found a holiday pastime in observing the antics of the Barracuda pilots who were required to undertake hazardous manoeuvres at low level when dropping practice torpedoes or diving on the targets located off Perwick and Port Soderick. Pilot error and mechanical failure of one sort or another caused many a crash landing on land and sea. Port Soderick Bay was nicknamed 'Barracuda Bay' because of the number of aircraft lost in its waters. There was always a rescue vessel in attendance and, although many aircrew were saved, many were lost.

On the afternoon of Wednesday, 17th July, a tragic accident happened involving a civilian. At 16.55 a general signal was sent to all aircraft to return to Ronaldsway at once. It had been a fine afternoon, but suddenly the weather began to close in. Dozens of Barracudas queued up to land on runway 13, the approach being across the road just south of the Creggans administrative site. Caught in a down-current, one of the Barracudas crashed through the hedge on either side of the roadway and slid to a stop just short of the runway. It was some time later that a body of a young man was found half buried in a hay rick. He had been hit by the wing of the Barracuda and carried on to the grass. The young man of 16 was David Kelly, son of Castletown's Police Sergeant. David worked at the Creggans which he left at five o'clock to walk home.

At the end of May, R.A.F. Jurby was re-designated No 5 Air Navigation School though it made no difference to its training programme. The Ansons still on charge were joined by numerous Wellingtons. It can be revealed now that Jurby was rocked to its foundations when a Sunderland flying boat crash landed on the airfield. Belonging to a Canadian Squadron based at Lough Neagh, Northern Ireland, it had taken off, fully armed, in search of surrendering U-boats when it clipped the top of a mountain, causing severe damage to its hull. Over the sea it let down through the cloud and spotted Jurby where it made an emergency landing. The crew scrambled to safety as the flying boat caught fire. Then four 1,000 lb depth charges exploded causing extensive damage to parked aircraft and buildings. Many windows were blown out, including the east window of Jurby Church. Much quieter was the visit of Their Majesties in July. The whole station was subjected to much 'spit and polish.' While King George inspected the parade of airmen, Queen Elizabeth inspected the WAAFS.

The routine of training air gunners at R.A.F. Andreas shows no let up. Numbers under training have been maintained by the arrival of gunners already wearing the AG flash but had been shot down over enemy occupied territory. Released from prisoner of war camps, they returned to England for rehabilitation and leave. Those arriving at Andreas have opted to re-train on the latest marks of gun turrets with a view to continuing serving in the R.A.F., either with a squadron or as instructors.

FATAL AIR CRASHES, 1945

6th February. Royal Navy Hurricane based at Andreas for training exercises with *H.M.S. Valkyrie*, crashed in East Baldwin valley. Wreckage spread over a wide area and body of pilot found under parachute, though he had not baled out.

14th April. Boeing B17 Flying Fortress on flight to Northern Ireland crashed in fog on slopes of Cronk ny Arree near Glen Chass, Rushen. None of the ten on board survived.

23rd April. Boeing B17 Flying Fortress on way to Northern Ireland with 31 on board crashed into cloud-covered North Barrule at 500 feet. Violent explosion killed all on board, making it the worst air disaster on Manx soil.

24th May. Firefly from R.N.A.S. Burscough, Lancashire crashed through deck barriers while landing on *H.M.S. Puncher*, ten miles south-west of Chicken Rock. Both aircrew were drowned.

12th July. Civilian killed on Ballasalla/Castletown road after being hit by Barracuda aircraft coming in to land at *H.M.S. Urley*.

7th August. Barracuda on night anti-submarine exercise at Port Soderick failed to pull out of dive through possible airframe failure and plunged into sea. Two of the bodies of the three crew were recovered.

WARTIME MEMORIES

Officers and instructors of H.M.S. Valkyrie, the Royal Navy's No. 1 Radar Training School, which occupies the Granville Camp on Loch Promenade.

Ratings from H.M.S. Valkyrie marching to Douglas Head to undertake training as radar operatives, vital to all ships in the Royal Navy.

(Below) One of the many intakes of officer cadets of 166 O.C.T.U. based at Clarendon House, Loch Promenade. The cadets undertook a gruelling 17-week course in infantry tactics before being commissioned in one of the Army regiments.

(Photographs Manx National Heritage)

210

One of the Lysanders used at Jurby for target towing seen in company with groundcrew, 1943.

A Blenheim aircraft used for air-to-air gunnery practice at Jurby, 1943. Ballamoar Castle can be seen in the background.

Members of 54 Air Sea Rescue Unit seen at their base in North Shore Road, Ramsey. Launches are in constant readiness at the Queen's Pier and at Douglas and Peel.

Trainee air gunners in front of the rear turret of a Wellington at R.A.F. Andreas.

One of the Spitfires at Andreas used as 'targets' for cine-guns in the advanced stage of the gunnery course.

Bomb aiming instructors pose in front of one of the many Ansons based at R.A.F. Jurby.
(Flt. Lt. Ron Savage)

TYNWALD MATTERS :
THE AFTERMATH OF WAR

Early in the war, indeed in 1940, the Douglas Dilettante Debating Society, in an act of supreme confidence, chose as a subject for discussion the possible post-war needs and problems that might confront the Island. Well, now the time has come and actions, not words, are needed. One thing is imperative - the hardships endured by many people after the Great War must not be repeated. The major issues are readily identified - the de-requisitioning and restoration of hundreds of boarding houses; the rapid release of Steam Packet vessels; and the provision of work and financial assistance for the 5,500 returning ex-servicemen and women.

A hopeful start was made in June when Earl Granville, in presenting the last wartime Budget, claimed that the Island was in its strongest financial position ever, with over £1,000,000 in the Reserve Fund. Up to £700,000 was earmarked for reconstruction and housing, while £250,000 was noted as an interest-free loan to the Imperial Government. Wealth indeed, and while the contribution to the war expenses was far more speedy than the shameful procrastination of the 1920s, many would argue it was still insufficient. Another development, perhaps not totally unexpected, has been the apparently insatiable desire of war-weary people to celebrate the first summer of peace by taking a holiday. Despite travelling difficulties, accommodation problems and shortages of all kinds, something like 100,000 arrived in June and July alone. The visiting industry has clearly a very bright future indeed.

One of the most pressing problems concerns the boarding houses which have been freed of servicemen and women, while the internees, detainees and prisoners of war have departed. But many of the houses have been found to be in an absolutely deplorable condition and their restoration has become a major burden for the occupiers. Furniture and fittings have vanished in many cases, and inadequate records of their disposal and storage were kept. Wartime austerity means that replacements are hard to come by. The Imperial Government still, of course, remain in possession of great blocks of such houses. *H.M.S. Valkyrie* continues to hold sway on Douglas promenade, and elsewhere on the Island service establishments still maintain an active presence. Many voices are heard urging Tynwald to be more active in securing the release of accommodation and in pursuing the many claims for compensation.

A similar view is being taken over the release of Steam Packet vessels which provide the Island's life blood. Everyone has been delighted to see the early return of the *Viking* and *Mona's Isle*, still in their war paint, with the *Manx Maid* soon joining them. Better news came in November with the launch of the *King Orry*, one of two new passenger ships being built in Birkenhead for the Steam Packet Company as replacements for wartime losses. Some, however, are looking to an alternative system of travel, perhaps more important for the future. Civil aviation has great potential and, now that *H.M.S. Urley* is to be de-commissioned

Looking to the future, Lieutenant-Governor Air Vice-Marshal Sir Geoffrey Bromet, K.B.E., C.B., D.S.O., who will work with Tynwald to solve the Island's post-war problems.

(Manx National Heritage)

early in the new year, Ronaldsway could well play an increasingly important part in bringing visitors to our shores.

In human terms by far the major concern is still the absorbing of the returning ex-servicemen and women into the economy of the Island. The visiting industry, which is the major employer, is unlikely to be back to pre-war levels for some time. Already, Tynwald is being heavily criticised for what is seen as its lethargy, although it is difficult to see what can be done swiftly, apart from the much-maligned winter works schemes which seem to have become a permanent part of Manx life! Still, despite this year's Budget with its vast sum marked for reconstruction, few construction work plans have been announced as yet. Over three months after the war ended, a Resettlement Advisory Officer was appointed, but it was late and he was to be guided by Voluntary Advisory Committees that were to be formed later! By this time many of the unemployed had decided to take matters into their own hands. A Government Vigilance Committee was set up to press for immediate action, and they were not disappointed. Tynwald almost immediately provided funds for the completion of the promenade widening scheme at Derby Castle which had begun in 1938. It will find work for 100 men during the winter months - a short term measure it is true, but it is a start. Other important matters of state have already surfaced, as well. Constitutional reform is still uppermost in the minds of our leading politicians, while the innovative plans, introduced in 1938, to provide a new and exciting secondary system of education for all demands immediate attention. Many of the answers to our post-war problems will be addressed by the new House of Keys, which will be formed after the General Election to be held sometime in the new year.

HERE IS THE NEWS : 1946
ACCOMMODATION CRISIS: FOOD SHORTAGES CONTINUE

The first full year of peace has seen an encouraging revival of the Island's visiting industry, with more than 400,000 arrivals during the summer, nearly up to pre-war numbers. There were accommodation problems, however, as hotel and boarding house owners reoccupied their premises, used as PoW and alien detention camps. They found that extensive damage had been caused. With food shortages and rationing there were also long queues at cafés and shops. We have this report:

The aftermath of war left the visiting industry infrastructure in disarray. Hoteliers struggled hard to get ready for the summer in the face of a shortage of building materials and new furnishings. There were also food shortages in spite of efforts by the Manx Government to get increased quotas in order to feed its visitors. This led to complaints about quantity and quality of meals. But nearly all the main places of entertainment in Douglas were open again and June saw an all-time record arrival of nearly 90,000 visitors as war-weary Britons rushed to take holidays. The shortages included beer and spirits, and, in the absence of imported beer, the visitors eagerly drank the local brews of Okell's and Castletown Breweries which faced record demand. There was also a clear sign of thankfulness among visitors that the war was over. There were congregations of up to 16,000 people at the Sunday open-air services at Kirk Braddan.

EDUCATION REFORMS
The Education Authority has carried through the biggest ever reform of the Island's school system, to provide secondary education for all. A spokesman said this would eliminate "snobbery and class distinction." Up to now elementary school children had to pass a scholarship exam to get to secondary school - or pay fees which parents could not always afford. Under the new multilateral system all 11-year-olds will go into the new single system operated by Ballakermeen and the Douglas High Schools for Boys and Girls. Children in the north of the Island will attend

Lieutenant-Governor, Sir Geoffrey Bromet, attended his first Tynwald Ceremony this year. His Excellency is preceded by Sword Bearer, Lieutenant-Colonel A. H. Kissack, and is followed by his A.D.C., Major J. M. Cain. *(Frank Cowin Library)*

Ramsey Grammar School when the new wing is made ready.

LADY OF MANN RETURNS
On 9th March the *Lady of Mann*, pride of the Steam Packet fleet, returned to her home port after completing her war service. Bedecked in flags which contrasted with her drab camouflage the *Lady* was greeted by a large crowd and emotional singing of 'Ellan Vannin' and the Manx National Anthem. The fine vessel had gone to war in 1939 under the command of the Steam Packet's Commodore, Captain T. C. Woods who vowed to bring her back. Mayor of Douglas, Councillor Tom Cowin, greeted him and his officers at the pier and took them by bus to the Town Hall for a civic reception. Captain Woods was awarded the O.B.E. in the New Year's Honours List in recognition of his achievements throughout the war, including Dunkirk and the D-Day landings. Aged 66, Captain Woods is to retire and will be replaced by Captain J. W. Cubbon as fleet Commodore. After her brief visit, the *Lady* departed to be made ready for the coming season.

DANGER OF SEA MINES
Sea mines were swept ashore around the Manx coastline early this year. Several exploded but upwards of a dozen others were made safe by Royal Navy experts. The mines were

believed to have been swept by a storm from their moorings in a minefield to the south of the Calf of Man. Some reached as far as Kirk Michael. This led to agitation that the minefield should be cleared as quickly as possible.

CONSTITUTIONAL REFORM
Tynwald gave unanimous approval in April to a resolution seen as a big step forward to Manx Home Rule. Instead of absolute control of the Island's domestic affairs being vested in the Lieutenant-Governor, a Manx 'Cabinet' is to be introduced consisting of seven members of Tynwald. The Lieutenant-Governor, however, will still be in a strong position as chairman of the new Executive Council.

INCOME TAX REDUCED
The Island has finished the war in its strongest financial position for many years. As a result, income tax is to be reduced to 2 shillings in the pound. The first post-war Manx Budget showed revenues of more than £1 million. The presence in the Island of thousands of aliens, PoWs and British Service personnel doubled the amount of indirect taxation coming in from the Common Purse.

DOUBLE-DECKER BUSES
Isle of Man Road Services Ltd took delivery in August of its first double-

The "King Orry IV" which, along with "Mona's Queen IV", entered service with the Isle of Man Steam Packet Co this year, the first vessels to replace wartime losses. They are both of similar design and, with a tonnage of 2,485, are certified for 68 crew and 2,163 passengers. Speed capability is 21 knots. (R. and L. Kelly Collection)

decker bus - a Leyland Titan 56-seater. It is one of ten on order. The remainder are expected to arrive by passenger boat next year. The use of the first is being confined to the Douglas-Onchan route until the relative road traffic law is amended so that double-deckers can be used throughout the Island. As current law only permits the carrying of 34 passengers, the double-decker now in service operates with only eight seats on the upper deck. The rest are sealed off. The required amendments to the Island's Highways Acts are being opposed by some M.H.K.s on the grounds that the new buses will be too big for Manx road conditions. Nevertheless, it is confidently predicted that Royal Assent will be given to the amendments next year, so that Road Services Ltd. will be able to fully utilise the double-deckers. Douglas Corporation Transport introduced the first of six AEC double-deckers in 1933. Last year it acquired a further three, these being diesel-engined Daimlers with wartime utility finish including wooden slatted seats.

NEW STEAM PACKET VESSELS

Two new passenger ships, built by Cammell Laird, Birkenhead, and named *King Orry* and *Mona's Queen*, have joined the Steam Packet fleet. They are the first replacements for the four vessels lost during the war, and the *Snaefell* which has been scrapped. Each of the new ships, with a tonnage of 2,485, have twin-screw turbines and are certificated to carry 2,163 passengers. They join the *Lady of Mann, Ben my Chree, Viking, Mona's Isle, Manx Maid* and *Rushen Castle*, the latter due to be scrapped at the end of the year. The *Victoria* returns next year while the *Manxman* will remain on war commission as a personnel carrier. She is not likely to return.

T.T. TROPHIES SAFE

While the A-C.U. found it impossible to stage the T.T. Races this year, the trophies which went to Italy and Germany in 1939 have been found. The Lightweight Trophy, won by Benelli, was discovered at the end of last year. It had been taken to Italy by Giovanni Benelli and hidden in a garden away from potential looters. Appropriately, it was found by a former T.T. rider, E. A. Simcocks who discovered it under a hen coop. The Senior Trophy was discovered earlier this year by an officer stationed at Hochst, near Frankfurt. He was informed by a former senior B.M.W. executive that he had last seen the trophy in Vienna at a B.M.W. agency. At first the manager claimed it had been plundered by the Allies but after "a little gentle persuasion", he produced it.

Meanwhile, there is news about Georg Meier and the B.M.W.s which did so well in the 1939 T.T. All have survived. The racing machines were hidden to prevent them being lost in Germany's war effort. Meier hopes to return to the Island one day. The report that Meier had been killed in an air accident early in the war was mistaken.

H.M.S. Manxman was completed in 1940 and 'adopted' by the Isle of Man. Designed as a high speed minelayer of 2,650 tons, she is said to be the fastest ship in the Royal Navy, being capable of cruising at 44 knots. She paid an official visit to Douglas in December. (Frank Cowin Library)

MANX GRAND PRIX

The news that the Manx Motor Cycle Club was to stage the September races was greeted with immense enthusiasm. It had been made possible by the Manx Government overcoming petrol rationing by making sufficient low-octane 'pool' petrol available. Winner of the Junior race was Ken Bills who showed he had lost none of his pre-war touch. He was followed by Peter Aitchison and Denis Parkinson, all on Nortons. L.W. Parsons (Rudge) won the Lightweight class with Ben Drinkwater and R.S. Simpson, on Excelsiors coming second and third. The Senior M.G.P. was run in atrocious conditions - thick mist and heavy rain. The bravery and fantastic riding of Dubliner Ernie Lyons led to a Triumph-twin victory, but at the end of the race it was discovered that the down tube of the frame had been completely severed! Ken Bills had to be content with second place, while local rider Harold Rowell (brother of fellow-rider, Albert) was third. Over 7,000 race fans flocked to the Palace for the prize presentations, each rider receiving tumultuous applause. A sad note was the news that popular rider Peter Aitchison had died after crashing at the 33rd Milestone.

GENERAL ELECTION

The results of the General Election on 27th and 28th September brought to an end the Island's 'Long Parliament' which was elected in 1934. The elections were held in May but the results were delayed in order to account for the many absentee voters still on national service. There were 54 candidates, 18 representing the Manx Labour Party. The poll resulted in a massive defeat for Labour which won only two seats. The new member for Garff, Mr. Charles Kerruish, is by far the youngest M.H.K. Mr. J. D. Qualtrough (Castletown) was re-elected Speaker. Elections of Keys' members to the Legislative Council resulted in Mr. Samuel Norris, for long the champion of constitutional reform, being unseated.

DESPERATE HOUSING SHORTAGE

The severe post-war shortage of housing in the Island, especially for newly-married ex-Servicemen, has been relieved by the Government's purchase of former Nissen hut encampments at Janet's Corner, Castletown, and in Ballasalla. The huts at Ballasalla, arranged in avenues, have been converted into two-, three- and four-bedroomed habitations and will accommodate 92 families. Huts at Janet's Corner have been made ready for 120 families. The conversion was completed in the autumn. Each unit has an allotment as a garden. However, the accommodation is very basic and is reported to be rat-infested. Separate cooking and washing facilities have been provided after a petition against a communal system. A typical hut consists of a living room with a curtained-off kitchen and two small bedrooms at one end. Heating is provided by a round combustion stove with a pipe acting as a 'chimney' through the thin corrugated roof. On cold days everyone has to wear heavy clothing. Dampness is another problem about which there have been many complaints. Every hut has an outside toilet a short distance from their entrances, and blocks of lockable bathrooms, one per hut, are dotted about the estates. Hot water is available only on certain days.

LAXEY WHEEL PURCHASED

Finally, the man credited with saving the Laxey Wheel from dereliction, Laxey builder Mr. E. C. Kneale, has now become its owner. He first leased it in 1938 from a local family which had owned it since 1918 and allowed it to fall into decay and disrepair. Mr. Kneale restored it to showpiece condition - and now he has bought it outright. This summer the Wheel was visited by about 40,000 people.

1946 NEWS IN BRIEF

JANUARY
24 - Island in grip of 18 degrees of frost.
26 - Government announce financial assistance to local authorities and private enterprise for housing.
21 - Dr. C. Guy Pantin appointed first honorary pathologist at Noble's Hospital.

FEBRUARY
4 - Manx People's Political Association formed.
5 - Launch of *Mona's Queen* at Birkenhead.
13 - Mr. S. A. Perry appointed Entertainments Manager for Douglas Corporation.

MARCH
2 - Golden Jubilee of incorporation of Douglas as a borough celebrated at a civic luncheon in the Villa Marina.

APRIL
10 - Diocesan Conference approves Tithes Bill providing redemption of tithes in the Isle of Man.

MAY
16 - Lieutenant-Governor re-opened Douglas horse tram service.
17-23 House of Keys General Election.
28 - House of Keys Election Bill, introduced by Mr. Samuel Norris to effect re-distribution of seats, "shelved" for six months by Legislative Council
31 - Victory Ball held in Villa Marina.

JUNE
16 - Payment of Members Bill passed, giving members of the Legislature increase from £100 to £150 a year.
24 - Lieutenant-Governor laid inauguration stone of widening scheme at Victoria Pier.

JULY
2 - Anson from Jurby, involved in evening search for a missing R.A.F. aircraft off the south of the Island, struck and carried away the mizzen mast of *Boy Alex* which was in company with other herring boats out from Peel. The Anson ditched five miles off Chicken Rock; only two bodies of the five airmen on board were recovered.
5 - Air Vice Marshal Sir Geoffrey Bromet presided at Tynwald Ceremony for the first time as Lieutenant-Governor.
18 - Arrival of *Millie Walton*, new Douglas lifeboat, most up-to-date of its kind in British Isles.
28 - Bread rationing scheme introduced on the Island.

AUGUST
6 - Family Allowance scheme began.
21 - Douglas Corporation accept tender for £166,511 for erection of 110 houses at Spring Valley.
26-27 Manx General Election results announced.

OCTOBER
16 - Provisional Order constituting new Island Water Board approved by Tynwald. Mr. A. J. Teare, J.P., M.H.K., M.B.E., appointed chairman.
23 - First reunion celebration of 15th Light Anti-Aircraft (Isle of Man) Regiment, R.A., held with Earl Granville as special guest.
28 - Manx Hotels Ltd fined £50 for obtaining unauthorised supply of rationed preserves for Majestic Lido Hotel.

NOVEMBER
9 - Following Douglas municipal elections, first since 1938, Councillor T. C. Cowin, J.P., M.H.K. elected Mayor for second term.

DECEMBER
6 - *H.M.S. Manxman*, 'adopted' by the Isle of Man at the beginning of the war, anchored in Douglas Bay for official visit. Receptions and cocktail parties were held on board and at the Town Hall. Members of the crew were treated to coach trips, ending with a dance in the Villa Marina.

HOTELIERS BATTLE WITH SHORTAGES

Anger and frustration marked the re-birth of the Island's tourist industry this summer. It was a remarkable transformation: from a place of barbed wire fences, military, internment and prisoner of war camps, to a traditional seaside holiday resort. The rushed hand-over of commandeered hotels and boarding houses and the quest, not only to repair damaged furnishings and equipment, but to locate much of what had gone missing led to raised tempers. Hoteliers and boarding house keepers were furious with the military over the slow decommissioning of their properties - and when the latter were handed over they were found in many cases to be in a terrible condition: some altered beyond recognition. One hotelier found that his entire lift system had vanished! Assessors brought in by both the military and property owners disputed what compensation should be paid. The military offered only 50% of what was claimed.

Whilst that issue rumbled on, the rush to get what properties were available in a fit state for the season was not easy. Many windows were boarded up and glass was not readily available. Interiors needed repainting but before that could be done damaged walls needed repairing, and there was a shortage of basic materials like plaster. Plumbing and electrics had been changed to suit all-male establishments and the old equipment had been apparently discarded. In some cases furnishings used by internees or prisoners of war had been defaced with deep carvings of "Heil Hitler" or "Il Duce". Cupboard doors and drawers had been removed as raw material in the making of toys. Stores of linen and equipment, believed to have been securely locked away, had been plundered. One hotelier found a missing gas range eventually but all its jets had been removed. Iron bedsteads were badly damaged, caused, reputedly, by being thrown out of buildings during decommissioning.

Thousands of mattresses removed from requisitioned properties were found to be either verminous, moth-eaten or damaged by poor storage. Some were capable of re-use after disinfecting but many had to be replaced. Large quantities were made last winter and early summer this year at Derby Castle. The ballroom and theatre complex was established by Tynwald's Furniture Restoration Division as a clearing and main repair centre for furnishings and equipment. It was manned by a staff of 100, 30 of them joiners. Hoteliers were invited there to claim what they believed to be theirs. Some identified items but there were rival claims. Consequently, many items had to be auctioned. Indicative of the chaos was a mound of rusting, fat-caked frying pans which the Derby Castle team had to clean and disinfect for re-use.

Bureaucracy in England delayed the production of all the required mattresses and pillows. Earlier this year Tynwald sent a buyer to England to acquire the necessary ticking for a further 930 mattresses. Delays in official paper work prevented the seller sending the material on time. Other supplies did get through, however. These included 25,000 yards of curtaining material bought by Tynwald for re-sale, and large quantities of linoleum. Some blankets were made also at the Tynwald Mill, St. John's. Even so, there were insufficient floor coverings. Some hotels had to settle for the simple staining of bedroom floorboards. Combined with the absence of clothing coupons to provide hotel staff with proper clothing, hoteliers were worried about the impression this would make on tourists. The Hotel Alexandra

reported using cut-down pieces of old curtaining as aprons and its waitresses wore trousers. Tynwald managed to ease the situation further by buying war surplus stores and equipment from the Services as they vacated their bases on the Island and then re-selling them to hoteliers. When the latter did not want the items, they were offered to householders who had accommodated servicemen in their private homes during the war.

Planning for the summer season was preceded by a highly speculative property market. This was led by the floating of a new public company to operate the Douglas Holiday Camp. The scramble for shares in January led to a temporary suspension in dealing in the shares by the London Stock Exchange. The fact that Admiralty use of the camp had devastated its facilities and chalet accommodation for 1,000 campers had been destroyed, did not deter the speculators. A spirit of regeneration was in the air, typified by the arrival at the camp of 120 builders shortly before and during its decommissioning by the Admiralty in January.

Buyers of hotels and boarding houses, who anticipated a sudden post-war tourist boom in which quick fortunes could be made from tourists not too fussy about standards, were reported to have paid "fantastic prices" for holiday property, despite their poor condition and the chronic shortages of plaster, bricks, wood, glass and paint to repair them.

Among the hotels which changed hands were the Majestic in Onchan, which had been used as a military hospital between 1940 and January this year, and the Fort Anne on Douglas Head which had remained an hotel during the war. Both were bought by the London theatre manager, Archie Shenborn, who also leased the wooden Pavilion Theatre in Onchan's amusement park. Shenborn got the Majestic restored in time for opening on 1st July.

Food for holidaymakers was another problem. There was no crisis, claimed the Government, anxious to avoid a scare which would deter visitors from coming to the Island, but, equally, the Island was no "food paradise". In fact, the summer was dogged by every conceivable shortage, despite the importation of Irish cattle, 148 tons of potatoes from Belfast and other goods. Hence, perhaps, a surprise decision by Lieutenant-Governor Bromet to spend a night with the Peel fishing fleet to see how it was managing to land much-needed herring. He spent the night with Peel's M.H.K., George Moore, aboard the 50 foot fishing boat *Manx Fuchsia*, skippered by Stanley Gorry. Next morning, after attending the auction of the herring, he returned to Government House with some herring on a string!

At the height of the season, on 28th July, one week behind the U.K., even bread rationing had to be introduced. Bakers and hoteliers hoped that it could be delayed until the autumn but problems with national flour supplies meant it had to be imposed. The ration of nine ounces a day for the average consumer, 15 ounces for a male manual worker and between four and 12 ounces for children, depending on their age, was reckoned to be not much less than what an average person ate in a day - and there was provision for people to gain more bread in exchange for other ration coupons, such as cakes or sweets. It did not seem to offer the prospect of much hardship but it was another major headache for the tourist industry.

At least there were enough eggs for breakfast. Anticipating problems in respect of eggs, hoteliers started "putting down" all the unrationed Manx eggs they could get direct from Manx farmers last spring. "Putting down" involved preserving fresh eggs by placing them in metal barrels filled with a mixture of water and a substance known as 'Water Glass'. This forms a white sealant around egg shells.

Problems with food supplies meant that most hoteliers and boarding house keepers had to confine their services to tea, bed and breakfast. Visitors had to queue for their principal meals in cafes and restaurants which seemed to be able to get better supplies. Reports of food shortages were believed to have reduced August Bank Holiday arrivals. Despite the chaos, some normality crept back into Manx life this summer. The Palace Ballroom, which had been used as a naval dining room during the war and a training centre for D-Day visible signalling, throbbed to the sound of dance music again.

Now planning has begun, to get the tourist industry launched properly in 1947. It will not be easy. Some hoteliers and boarding house keepers are still waiting to gain possession of their properties from the military. This is notably so in respect of the £3 million radar instruction camp *H.M.S. Valkyrie I*. The camp is not due to be decommissioned until the end of December. A Royal Navy landing craft is expected in Douglas some time after that to collect the station's secret equipment. Even then it is estimated that some of the *H.M.S. Valkyrie I* properties on the promenade will not be avail-

able for civilian use until May, 1947. Douglas Head, meanwhile, which is still sealed off from public use and is littered with mysterious aerial systems, is not likely to be restored to tourist use until 1948.

To help equip hotels and boarding houses, three factories have been established for the local manufacture of basic short-life furniture like wardrobes and beds which is desperately needed. One is on Douglas Head, another at Kirk Michael and a third in the former Victorian paper mill in Glen Road, Laxey.

One of the holiday places which should be ready next year to take visitors is the former Howstrake Holiday Camp. It was decommissioned in August-September. Since July 1941 it had been used as the Royal Naval School of Music. Four hundred of Britain's most musically-talented youngsters aged between 14 and 18 were trained by 24 instructors for membership of the navy's top bands. From its very beginning the school provided a band for many functions, the Tynwald Ceremony and for morale-boosting summer afternoon concerts in the Villa Marina gardens. Now it is reported that many of those taught here, and who learned to swim in the nearby Groudle Bay, are likely to become the top players in Britain's dance hall bands.

During its occupation of the holiday camp, the school adapted the tennis courts for drill. A parade ground was added on and the chalets were adapted to serve as dormitories for groups of between 20 to 30 young men. This included the installation of central heating.

Howstrake Holiday Camp served as the Royal Naval School of Music and hundreds of young bandsmen were trained here for service in the Navy. Now decommissioned, preparations have begun to make the Camp ready for next season. (Frank Cowin Library)

TYNWALD MATTERS:
THE 1946 GENERAL ELECTION

Ayear ago the voters of the United Kingdom gave unequivocal backing to the British Labour Party and its programme for post-war reconstruction in one of the biggest election victories ever recorded. No doubt encouraged by this, our own Manx Labour Party has made its most determined effort yet. It would seem from its public statements that it was not content with aiming for, say, half a dozen seats to form a significant pressure group. Rather, its intention was to produce a House of Keys in which Labour members were so numerous and dominant

Mr J. D. Qualtrough, who has been re-elected Speaker of the House of Keys following this year's General Election.
(Frank Cowin Library)

that it would be able to form a party government. Its programme was the Socialist one: nationalisation of essential services, a comprehensive social and health system and so on. This message was trumpeted out at the many public meetings held all over the Island in April and May as the Island was gripped by election fever. In all, 18 Labour Party candidates took the field.

Needless to say, this bold and determined assault produced its counterblast. As early as February many citizens, especially those of the business class, were perturbed enough to embark on forming their own political party. A public meeting was held at the Villa Marina attended by over 200 people and presided over by the ex-Attorney-General, Mr. R. B. Moore. Out of it came a new political party representing, it may be fairly said, the more conservative sections of the community. Perhaps clumsily, it named itself the Manx People's Political Association but there was little doubt about its character. Candidates sponsored

by this new party were identified in the *Isle of Man Weekly Times* as "Anti-Socialist"! The election days in May, lasting from the 17th in Rushen to the 23rd in Garff, saw scenes of great excitement although this was tempered by the knowledge that because of the difficulties in gathering in the servicemen's votes the results would not be announced until September.

The issues were certainly no major considerations of principle. On the contrary, the Manx electorate seemed far more concerned with practical affairs: employment and the need for industries to complement the visiting industry; farming subsidies; rural housing. There are still 239 farms with no piped water. As far as public housing is concerned, no new house should be built without a bath; the boarding houses must be modernised and so on. Big political ideas seemed unwelcome and now, at the end of September with the results, exactly how unwelcome is clear. Of the 24 members returned it can reasonably be said that 22 are anti-socialist. Only 2 Labour candidates were returned out of 18 and those two were of such stature and worth that any label would have sufficed.

The new House is assembled. Half of its members are newcomers, and their overwhelming character is conservative. The problems facing the House are great, not least the constitutional developments which were announced secretly. However, the Island has just experienced a prosperous season and in this, at least for the foreseeable future, the prospects are excellent. Our new House must see that they are fulfilled.

THE MANX CABINET

For a considerable time voices have been raised in the Island demanding more participation in our Executive. The position of the Lieutenant-Governor and the Legislative Council and, indeed, the complete authority vested in them, have been under attack from many quarters. Indeed, in the recent election campaign one of the planks of the anti-Socialist campaign, even if not pressed too hard, was an extension of Home Rule.

Perhaps the return of a Labour Government in the United Kingdom provided a heaven-sent opportunity for those who advocated a reform of the old ways. The new Home Secretary, Mr Chuter Ede, no doubt acting upon comments from his predecessor, Mr. Herbert Morrison, has proved sympathetic to the demands for an extension of democratic control.

In April the Home Secretary expressed his interest in the establishment of an Executive Council to assist the Lieutenant-Governor in the performance of his duties *vis a vis* the government of the Island. Having considered his proposals, the Speaker of the House of Keys moved that they should be adopted and this was agreed unanimously. The essence of these proposals was that the Lieutenant-Governor should be guided

and assisted by seven members of Tynwald, five of whom should be the Chairmen of the main Boards of Agriculture and Fisheries, Highways and Transport, Social Services, Local Government and Education. Two other members would be recommended and appointed by resolution of Tynwald. An important condition was that the Lieutenant-Governor, Legislative Council and the Keys should be consulted prior to the appointments.

Now, following the first meeting of the new House of Keys after the General Election, history has been made. The Executive Council has been nominated and accepted, the one exception being that it was felt that the Speaker, although Chairman of the Board of Education, should not take a place. Another member of the Board has become a member instead. Some have carped that only three members of the Keys are on the Council. It is less than the democratic revolution anticipated, but the fact remains, the Island does have a "Cabinet", it is an important part of the Executive and nothing in Manx Government can ever be the same again.

Home Rule it may not be, but a sizeable stride towards it, it certainly is.

A REVOLUTION IN EDUCATION

Home Secretary, Mr. Chuter Ede, officially opened the new multilateral School at Ballakermeen in Douglas on 25th October. This has two wings - one for boys and another for girls. The opening marked a radical transformation in the entire educational system of the Island which has been welcomed and applauded across the entire spectrum of the Manx nation. It may be as well to remind ourselves of the system it replaced. At the age of 11 all pupils, boys and girls, sat for the "Scholarship" examination. Those clever enough to pass, a generous 25% or more, then went to the two High Schools in Douglas and the Grammar School in Ramsey. The remaining 75% or so, not being selected, were rejected and remained at their Elementary Schools. Thus was established an 'education snobbery and class distinction', and the futures of whole generations of pupils were decided irrevocably at the age of 11.

The Island was very fortunate indeed in that just before the outbreak of war two brand new buildings, one in Douglas, one in Ramsey, were constructed to form part of the revolutionary system, both doing valiant war service. Both could be fitted into the new system. In this every pupil, boy or girl aged 11 or over, are being transferred to a new multilateral or comprehensive High School. There, in classes that can be streamed according to ability, they will all complete their education. Ballakermeen will serve as a Junior High School in Douglas. After two years, girls will move on to Park Road High School and boys will go to St Ninian's.

The administrative problems in effecting the multilateral revolution were great. Not only had the pupils and their parents to be informed of events, but the teachers in the old elementary schools had to be redeployed now that their upper classes were going to Ballakermeen or Ramsey Grammar. Furthermore, some old schools, notably Hanover Street in Douglas, part and parcel of the fabric of their communities for more than half a century, are seen now to be superfluous to requirements and, one supposes, at some point must close. Still, these new schools are magnificent. They are superbly equipped, light and airy, ideally situated in their playing fields, a credit to the Island. On 16th September all roads led to them. Long crocodiles of youngsters, marshalled by their teachers marched, no doubt with some apprehension, to their futures. One lady living near Ballakermeen said that she stood at her window all morning watching, and no doubt hearing, hundreds of children flood the hitherto quiet streets and avenue. The dining room staff at Ballakermeen didn't have time to stand and stare. They started at 8 a.m. peeling hundreds of pounds of potatoes and carrots.

Like first days everywhere, there was a little confusion but the staffs in Douglas and Ramsey, by dint of exceptional care and devotion, ensured that not only was it kept to a minimum but that the vital element in any school, namely the teaching of the pupils, got under way with remarkable speed and efficiency.

The official opening ceremony at Ballakermeen was held in the Boys Hall. One hundred boys, 100 girls, 100 parents and 100 politicians, officials and guests heard Mr. Chuter Ede speak glowingly of the new school and the system it represented. "Few schools can more fittingly represent the spirit of modern education." The facilities, he remarked, were for everyone and, in conclusion, he made a formal request for a school holiday, a plea heard with delight by the 500 or so pupils in the Girls Hall. They may not have been able to see him, but hear him they certainly could, and favourable comments were heard on all sides about the behaviour and appearance of the children.

There can be little doubt that the term "educational revolution", so often misapplied, is now totally accurate. It is a revolution and dramatically different from the tripartite and divisive arrangement in operation in the United Kingdom. Is it the pattern for the future? It is too early to tell. Of one thing the Island *can* be sure, the progress and achievements of these Manx bi-laterals, or comprehensives as they are increasingly being called, will be scrutinised with eagle eyes. If they are successful it may be that the Island really has formed the pattern for the future.

Completed in 1939 and used throughout the war as part of the H.M.S. St George training ship, the Ballakermeen High School was officially opened in October and is now part of the Education Authority's policy of providing secondary education for all children of 11 and over.

(R. and L. Kelly Collection)

AIR SERVICES NATIONALISED

One of the most immediate effects on the Isle of Man as a result of the Labour Government's policy of nationalisation concerned the Island's air services. All airlines and airports came under the control of the Ministry of Civil Aviation. Isle of Man Air Services Ltd is a Manx registered company operating from an airport outside the United Kingdom, albeit controlled by the Ministry of Civil Aviation now that Ronaldsway has been vacated by the Admiralty. A Commission set up by Tynwald last year to make representations to the U.K. Government regarding the future ownership of Ronaldsway has made little progress, though it was made clear that the Ministry of Civil Aviation would continue to operate the airport for the foreseeable future. This involved the provision of safety factors including the installation of Standard Beam Approach (VHF D/F) on the main runway which makes Ronaldsway one of the best equipped in the British Isles. As regards the air services to and from the Isle of Man, it has been made clear these are to be taken over by British European Airways Corporation next year. For the present, Isle of Man Air Services Ltd will operate the routes established before the war as an associate of B.E.A. The local airline has three de Havilland Rapides available and on 15th July this year Captain John Higgins, M.B.E. flew the first post-war inaugural flight of Isle of Man Air Services on the Manchester route.

R.A.F. ANDREAS TO CLOSE

The one and only opportunity the general public had of visiting R.A.F. Andreas was on Battle of Britain Day this September. Already it had been announced that the station was to close and that the Gunnery School would transfer to Jurby after being vacated by the Air Navigation School. The Commanding Officer of Andreas, Group Captain Crawford, and his personnel made every effort to present the activities of the station and many had the opportunity of operating the gun turrets on display in the training huts. Low cloud and rain, however, put a dampener on the proceedings. The Y.M.C.A., run by local volunteers since the station was opened, dispensed welcome hot drinks, though the public was warned beforehand to bring their own food because of rationing difficulties. Much of the flying programme had to be abandoned but one of the station's Wellingtons and a Spitfire gave a brave demonstration in what was some of the last flying from the airfield. Until the lifting of wartime censorship, many Manx people in other parts of the Island were unaware of its existence!

By the end of September, the transfer to Jurby was completed and the gates of R.A.F. Andreas finally closed. Immediate steps were taken by the Local Government Board to acquire three of the communal sites near the village for conversion into badly needed family accommodation. Built of single brick, the huts are in some ways better than Nissen huts, but are still cold and damp in wintry conditions. Every effort is being made to convert the huts into attractive two- and three-bedroomed homes, with electrically heated living rooms and kitchens. Each will have a toilet but bathrooms have to be shared. In the new year it is expected that 81 families will be accommodated as a temporary measure until proper housing can be provided sometime in the future. The old gymnasium cum church on the Smeale Road is to become a useful Parish Hall.

DOG RESCUES AIRMAN

A Manx dog has won an award for saving a life. An Anson aircraft on a navigation exercise was returning to Jurby on the afternoon of Thursday, 3rd January. On board were the normal crew of four, plus two Avro technicians who had been picked up at Hooton Park, Wirral. The Anson was due to arrive at 4.50 p.m. but it failed to appear and, as darkness fell, search and rescue operations began without any indication of the whereabouts of the aircraft. Coastal fog covered the Bulgham area and low cloud hid Slieu Ruy, which rises steeply to 1,500 feet and is known locally as Red Mountain. The Anson struck the hillside 150 feet below the summit. The search was abandoned that night but continued the following day without success, hampered by fog and low cloud.

On the Saturday morning, Mr and Mrs Shooter, living at Fern Cottage, Agneash, were alerted by the whining and growling of their Alsatian, Peg-leg, so called because it had lost one of its feet when a puppy. When let out, it went straight to a little glen nearby, but Mrs Shooter could hear nothing above the noise of the stream and the wind in the trees. Back indoors, Peg-leg kept growling and eventually Mrs Shooter, keeping hold of her dog, was led a hundred yards up the hillside. It was then that she saw a hand reach out above a bush. The frightened Mrs Shooter discovered a cold, wet and terribly injured airman. He was the wireless operator, Warrant Officer Charles Jones, the sole survivor of the six on board. His right leg was shattered with bare bone exposed, but he had managed to cover a mile and half using a piece of wood to climb over a stone wall and barbed wire. The Shooters summoned help from neighbours who supplied brandy, tea and blankets. There being no telephone in this remote area, another ran down to Laxey to inform the police and Jurby. Transport arrived and the injured airman was stretchered down the hillside and taken to the Navy Hospital on Glencrutchery Road, Douglas. Wireless operator Jones was immediately operated on and, mercifully, his leg was saved.

Now that the war is over, it is possible to give further details about air accidents on and around the Isle of Man. Records indicate that over 200 military aircraft were involved in accidents up to the end of this year. Some of the airmen involved were fortunate to escape uninjured, while many survived their injuries. Nevertheless, a total of over 250 died, including British, Canadian, Australian, Polish, Dutch and American airmen. Overlooking Jurby airfield is the parish church of St. Patrick. The east window, replaced by R.A.F. Jurby, looks down upon three neat rows of white headstones marking the graves of 42 airmen. A further 24 are found at Kirk Andreas. All are in memory of the airmen who died on Manx soil.

Mrs Shooter of Agneash, with Peg-leg.   *(Manx National Heritage)*

HERE IS THE NEWS : 1947
MANX GOVERNMENT PURCHASES RONALDSWAY AIRPORT

The Isle of Man is ready for the expected post-war boom in civil aviation after the Government's purchase of the wartime Fleet Air Arm training station at Ronaldsway. The pre-war aerodrome, where aircraft used to land on the grass, has been turned into a fine modern airport with tarmacadamed runways and all necessary safety facilities. We have this report:

When His Excellency Air Vice-Marshal Sir Geoffrey Bromet was informed that the Ministry of Civil Aviation had changed its mind about ownership and administration of Ronaldsway, it left the way clear to reaching agreement over a purchase price. It was conditional that the Ministry of Civil Aviation would continue to provide and operate the technical services subject to a percentage of landing fees and a financial arrangement whereby the British taxpayer would be alleviated of any charges. Second Deemster Percy Cowley, was given the task of thrashing out a deal with the Admiralty. It was pointed out that the cost of construction had been £1 million, and that £105,000 had been spent on the purchase of the 825 acres of land. The Deemster's offer was £100,000. He said that the airfield was not to the design of the Manx Government and that maintenance costs would be heavy. Deemster Cowley returned with an agreed purchase price of £200,000 for the airport, land and buildings. That was put before Tynwald in July and accepted unanimously, the Deemster being showered with congratulations. This paves the way for the Island having its own national airport - and at a bargain price!

COLDEST WINTER

The Island endured its coldest winter for 70 years with heavy snowfalls which halted road and rail traffic. Passengers were trapped by drifts in a train near Ballasalla for three hours before being rescued. Temperatures remained below freezing for days on end, and February was the coldest since records began, recording a mean for the month of 31.6 degrees Fahrenheit. This was followed by March recording a record 7.84 inches of rain.

B.E.A. TAKE OVER

Isle of Man Air Services Ltd was taken over by British European Airways in January. The three partners, Olley Air Services, Railway Air Services and the Isle of Man Steam Packet Company, were reimbursed to the full share value of £75,000. The local airline had carried 137,000 passengers during its 13 year history, without loss of life and setting high standards of regularity and safety. In February, B.E.A. took over all scheduled passenger routes from Ronaldsway. These were to Blackpool, Liverpool, Carlisle, Newcastle, Glasgow and Belfast. Passengers for Manchester and London change at Liverpool. Mr R. L. Carter, who was originally with Olley Air Services, was appointed Isle of Man area manager. Aircraft being used are De Havilland Rapides. One was involved in an accident shortly after the summer schedules got under way. Fortunately, the five passengers and two crew were not seriously injured. Bad weather resulted in a diversion to Jurby and the aircraft crashed into the mist-covered slopes between Greeba and Slieau Ruy. One of the passengers was able to make his way down to Crosby where he summoned help from the post office. The police alerted the Jurby Rescue Party which made its way to the scene of the accident.

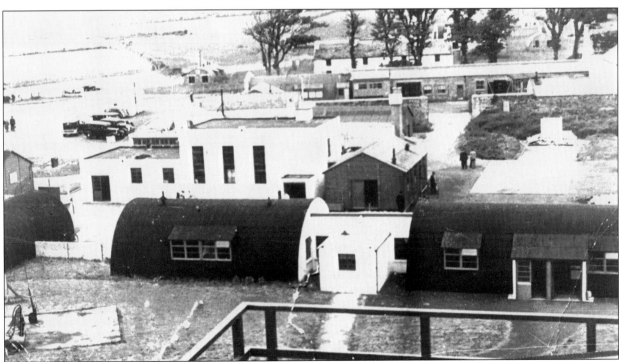

A view of the wartime buildings, taken from the Control Tower and looking towards the Creggans farm, which now serve as part of the airport terminal. The tall white building was formerly the parachute house which has been converted by British European Airways as offices and waiting hall.
(Terry Faragher Collection)

Though badly cut and bruised, the passengers were able to complete their study visit to the Marine Biological Station at Port Erin.

FAREWELL TO
H.M.S. VALKYRIE

Nearly two years after the end of the war, *H.M.S. Valkyrie* was decommissioned at the end of March. The Royal Navy's largest radar training school had provided thousands of operators for all ships of the Navy. Millions of pounds worth of equipment has been removed from Douglas Head and the boarding houses along Loch Promenade have been vacated. The closure of the station has opened Douglas Head for the first time since 1941. Many of the visitor attractions are being brought back into use although some, like the old incline railway, are in serious need of repair and renovation. The Marine Drive has also been re-opened but although the property of the Marine Drive Company has been purchased by the Manx Government, no attempt is to be made to resurrect the electric railway.

T.T. RACES RETURN

The first post-war Tourist Trophy Races were held in June. They attracted a total of 169 entries, of which 64 were for the newly inaugurated Clubman's T.T. The entries included many pre-war stars who were joined by a new generation of young men anxious to make their name on the world famous T.T. Course. Victory in the Junior Race went to Bob Foster (Velocette) and the Lightweight was won by

The bespectacled Harold Daniell who won this year's Senior T.T. He is sitting astride the Norton which has been little altered since he set up the record lap of 91 m.p.h. during his win in 1938.
(Keig Collection)

Manliff Barrington (Moto Guzzi). The Senior was dominated by Nortons though there was a strong challenge from the A.J.S. 'Porcupines', ridden by Les Graham and Jock West. The A.J.S. twins are so named because of their distinctive cooling fins. The race was won by Norton teamster Harold Daniell, holder of the 91 m.p.h record lap from 1938. Speeds were predictably slower than pre-war days because of the use of low-octane 'Pool' petrol. The fastest lap time of 84 m.p.h. was set up jointly by Artie Bell (Norton) and Peter Goodman (Velocette), who came second and third respectively.

RESTORATION
OF CATHEDRAL

The Archbishop of York, Dr. Cyril Garbett, called for the restoration of the ruined St. German's Cathedral on St. Patrick's Isle at Peel. He was on the Island for the 1,500th anniversary celebrations of the Manx Church. He told a big public meeting in Douglas that restoring the cathedral would be a wonderful expression of the noble heritage of the Manx diocese.

VICAR DEFROCKED

A Manx clergyman made national headlines when he was sentenced to 18 months hard labour at Wiltshire Assizes after admitting a charge of bigamy. The Revd. Harry Lamb, 36-year-old chaplain of St. John's, who was born at Santon, was alleged to have married a member of the W.A.A.F. at Salisbury when he was serving in the R.A.F. as a wartime chaplain in 1944. At the time, his wife, Dorothy, was living at home in the Island with their son. Lamb has been excluded from the Church by the Lord Bishop of Sodor and Man.

STATIONMASTER KILLED

The Isle of Man Railway's stationmaster at Union Mills, Mr. George Henry Hogg, was killed in July when he stumbled and fell under the wheels of a Douglas bound train passing through the station. The train was travelling at only 10 miles an hour as he went under the leading coach. Mr. Hogg had more than 60 years service with the railway com-

British European Airways' de Havilland Rapide which crashed in bad weather on the slopes between Greeba and Slieau Ruy. Miraculously, the crew of two and the five passengers escaped without serious injury.
(Terry Faragher Collection)

pany - and was the oldest station-master in Britain. In another tragedy two elderly sisters were burned to death in a fire at their home in Malew Street, Castletown.

SUCCESSFUL SUNNY SUMMER
As if to compensate for the bad winter, the Island enjoyed one of its best summers. August enjoyed a record 305 hours of sunshine, with just a trace of rain. This was a great help to the tourist industry as it got back to near normal, despite many difficulties. A total of 602,230 visitors arrived during the season, including 10,000 delegates to the conferences staged by Rotary International and the British Legion. The Douglas entertainments were in full swing with 'Two Ton' Tessie O'Shea starring in the Summer Show at the Palace Coliseum, while Joe Loss and his Orchestra proved a big attraction for dancers at the Villa Marina.

CAR RACING RETURNS
Car racing returned to the Isle of Man in August and an estimated 50,000 people turned out to see it. There were not many cars (33 starters in all spread between two races) and the available fuel was poor - just 72 octane - but excitement was intense nevertheless.

The two events were run over the 3.8 mile Willaston Circuit. One was the British Empire Trophy Race for cars up to 4.5 litres unsupercharged; the other, the Manx Cup Race for lighter weight cars with a maximum of two litres. The British Racing Drivers Club had organised the British Empire Trophy Race at Donington prior to the war. It switched its ninth race to the Isle of Man because of a lack of suitable circuits in post-war Britain.

Winner of the Empire Trophy race over 40 laps was Bob Gerard at the wheel of a supercharged 1,488 c.c. E.R.A. His average speed was 68.02 m.p.h. Earlier it had been speculated that the international favourite, Prince Bira of Siam, might achieve the double. In fact, he came fifth in the major race in a supercharged 1.5 litre Maserati then won the 12 lap Manx Cup race in a 1,100 c.c. Simca-Gordini, averaging 66.05 m.p.h.

VISIT OF de VALERA
The President of the Irish Republic, Eamon de Valera, paid an informal visit to the Island while on a holiday cruise round the North British Isles in an Irish Navy corvette. It was a low key visit which attracted little public attention, at Mr. de Valera's wish. He went to Peel Castle, Tynwald Hill and Cregneash - where he met Ned Maddrell, one of the Island's last surviving native speakers of Manx. The two men conversed in their respective Gaelics. As a result, Mr. de Valera arranged for the Irish Folklore Commission to come to the Island to record the voice of Mr. Maddrell and other Manx speakers.

T. E. BROWN ANNIVERSARY
The 50th anniversary of the death of our national poet, on 29th October, has not engendered celebrations of the sort seen in 1930 on the centenary of his birth. Indeed, the only noteworthy event has been the appearance of the book 'Two Men of Manxland', written by Samuel Norris and published by his printing firm, Norris Modern Press Limited.

Famous dance band leader Joe Loss, whose orchestra proved a big attraction to visitors and locals at the Villa Marina this year.
(Douglas Town Hall Archives)

(Above) Popular pre-war E.R.A. racing driver Prince Bira of Siam returned this year with a Maserati. He is seen here at Cronk ny Mona during the British Empire Trophy Race in which he finished 5th.

(Below) T. C. Harrison in his pre-war Riley cornering at the Manx Arms, Onchan, during the Manx Cup Race for smaller cars.

It will be remembered that Mr Norris, who is a reporter and politician, recorded the political turmoil of the early years of this century in his book 'Manx Memories and Movements'. His latest book deals separately with the lives of Hall Caine and T. E. Brown. Inevitable comparisons are drawn and Mr Norris is seen to clearly favour Brown. Great interest has been shown in the book and a second print is planned for next year.

R.A.F. JURBY TO CLOSE

The post-war contraction of the Royal Air Force has led to the closure of R.A.F. Jurby. The Gunnery School, which transferred from Andreas last year, is to be disbanded. The station will retain a care and maintenance staff while its future is being decided. Since 1939, R.A.F. Jurby has trained thousands of navigators, bomb aimers and gunners for Bomber Command. It has a proud record, and the station has played a prominent part in the life of the north of the Island. It is hoped that another role for the station will be found in the not too distant future.

It is sad to record that in March a Spitfire being flown to Jurby crashed into Maughold Head which was covered in low cloud. It struck the headland just below the lighthouse and was thrown against the gable end of the keepers' quarters, scattering debris over a wide area. A car inside the garage was set on fire and destroyed. With the telephone not working, help was summoned from the vicarage. Ramsey Fire Brigade soon had the fires under control, but Dr. Paton was unable to help the badly injured pilot. He was a highly respected pilot who lived in Ramsey with his wife.

Fortunately, the keepers' children were at school at the time and their wives were attending a sale of work in the church hall.

PURCHASE OF ANDREAS AIRFIELD

Negotiations with the Air Ministry have resulted in Tynwald agreeing to purchase Andreas airfield for £23,750, the original price paid to the landowners. No charge was made for the brick buildings, hangars and services laid on. The Air Ministry agreed to this as a gesture of appreciation for the co-operation shown during the early years of the war. Conditions are that the runways are to remain intact and no building should take place within the perimeter track. The majority of Tynwald agreed that they had got a bargain, though Mr. H. C. Kerruish lamented the loss of two prime farms whose fields would never be the same again.

When put up for auction by the Government, the airfield was purchased by Mr. Morrey for £33,000 who plans to revert to the original farms of Ballaghaue, to be farmed by the owner's son, and Braust to be farmed by a tenant. It is understood that some of the buildings are to be used as a Landrace pig farm.

It was always the intention of the Air Ministry to restore the upper part of the tower of Kirk Andreas church, which was removed as a hazard to flying. The keystones were carefully numbered to help in the restoration. However, the church wardens have agreed now to accept a sum of money instead, so that the fine old organ can be equipped with an electric blower.

1947 NEWS IN BRIEF

JANUARY
14 - Rotary Club of Ramsey inaugurated.

FEBRUARY
10 - Mr. T. C. Greenfield, Water Engineer to Douglas Corporation, appointed Engineer Manager to new Isle of Man Water Board.

MARCH
20 - Territorial Army presence in the Isle of Man to continue with the formation of the 515th (I.O.M.) Light Anti-Aircraft Regiment, R.A. Lieut.-Colonel J. B. Mylchreest appointed Commanding Officer.
25 - *Tynwald V* launched at Birkenhead.

MAY
7 - Mr. Robert Nicholl (tenor) won Cleveland Medal at Manx Music Festival for second time.
22 - Mr. W. A. Kirkpatrick won Manx Golf Championship for third successive time.
24-26 Revival of Manx Air Races at Ronaldsway. Veteran Major Tommy Rose won the Manx Air Derby in his Miles Hawk.

JUNE
19 - Record entry of 213 for International Bicycle T.T.

JULY
10 - New list of magistrates included for the first time the appointment of women justices on the Island.
19 - Retirement of His Honour Deemster R. D. Farrant, Clerk of the Rolls. Deemster W. P. Cowley is elevated to succeed him. High Bailiff Mr. R. G. Johnson, O.B.E., appointed Second Deemster and Mr. Howard D. Lay appointed new High Bailiff.

AUGUST
26 - Tynwald approve resolution to implement five-year plan for all-Island water supplies costing £200,000.

SEPTEMBER
9-11 Manx Grand Prix drew record entry of 284 for the three events. Lightweight race marred by death of B. B. Russell in crash at Ramsey when in the lead. The race was won by Austin Monks (Moto Guzzi) while Eric Briggs achieved the 'double' by winning the Junior and Senior races on Nortons.
11 - Title of 'Mona's Queen of Beauty' won by Miss Joyce Lewis of Douglas in final contest of successful season of competition organised by the June Effort and Season Extension Committee.
22 - Island milk exported to Liverpool to relieve mainland emergency. In all, 26,000 gallons were sent in 41 days.
27 - Manx farm workers receive new weekly wage of £5.0s.4d. for 56-hour week.

OCTOBER
9 - New multilateral school at Ramsey opened by His Excellency the Lieutenant-Governor.

NOVEMBER
1 - Potato price fixed at £12. 10s a ton, an increase of £4.3s.4d over 1946.
3 - By 21 votes to one, Douglas Corporation reject motion to abolish the horse tram service as a result of huge public support.
5 - Education Authority approve recommendation from Reorganisation Committee that Andreas School be transferred to former R.A.F. communal site, and that Bride and St. Jude's Schools should be closed.
11 - Potato rationing scheme, inaugurated in England, extended to the Island.
14 - Tynwald adopted main provisions of Imperial Government's interim budget increasing Purchase Tax on wines and spirits, estimated to produce £100,500 a year for the Island.
16 - For the first time in 26 years Island has snowfall in November.
18 - Lieutenant-Governor announces that basic petrol rationing is to be ended.
20 - Wedding of H.R.H. Princess Elizabeth and H.R.H. Prince Philip, Duke of Edinburgh. Island's wedding gifts are a carved oak chest, designed by Mr. W. T. Quayle, made at the Kirk Michael workshops of Messrs. Kelly Bros., and a supply of woollen rugs and blankets from Tynwald and Sulby Mills.

DECEMBER
10 - Plans to carry out £300,000 extensions to electricity power station and change distribution to alternating current, adopted by Douglas Corporation.
16 - Tynwald appointed committee to inquire into position regarding National Service after Keys rejected adoption of Imperial Government's National Service Act, 1947.

GETTING BACK TO NORMAL

Newly-weds, and others who are setting up home for the first time, are to be given the chance to buy Manx-made furniture tax free. As Purchase Tax accounts for 50 per cent of the price, it is a significant gesture by Tynwald. The concession includes a restriction on retail pricing to prevent the imposition of higher profit margins by shops. It is to be targeted at people who are furnishing a home or some rooms for the first time, have married since the outbreak of war in 1939, or are having to cater for the needs of a growing family.

The Manx plan is an up-graded version of a U.K. one which is encouraging the manufacture there of cheap, inferior 'utility' furniture but there will be no emphasis on low quality here. Tynwald members want something better. That is why there are going to be delays in implementing the Manx scheme. Initially, the plan was to introduce it this year but problems arose over getting advice from the U.K.'s Board of Trade on furniture specifications. Now supplies will not be available until about mid-1948. Those who want to take advantage of the concession will have to apply then to the Clothing Control Division of Government Office for a Buying Permit.

Foreign imports have started to arrive, of course, principally from Scandinavia, but prices are high. Hence the need to provide assistance for people setting up home. Hence, too, the protests by hoteliers in their negotiations for compensation for furnishings damaged or lost by the military during the commandeering of hotels during the war. One Douglas hotelier says he was offered £2 recently for a chair which had been valued at £1 at the outbreak of war. The offer sounded good until he realised that it would cost £4 now to replace it.

The local manufacture of furniture - mainly tables, chairs, wardrobes and beds - has been underway for some time. As yet, however, it has concentrated on satisfying the urgent needs of hoteliers and boarding house keepers. There are now 56 craftsmen and 34 women and apprentices involved in the work, using timber imported on their behalf by Tynwald to overcome chronic national shortages. The builders, Kelly Bros., at Kirk Michael are one of the main manufacturers. During World War I and the recent war they made strap-on wooden clogs because of the shortage of leather for shoes. The French polishing of its furniture is undertaken by specialists in Douglas.

SUPPORT FOR HOTELIERS

During the year outright grants totalling £10,000 were voted by Tynwald for hoteliers and boarding house keepers who missed all or part of last season and, perhaps, some of this season also, because of military occupation of their premises. Assessment of losses proved to be difficult because many hoteliers were unable to provide proper accounts to show the sort of business they had experienced prior to the war. Some said their books had been lost or destroyed. In investigating what grants should be given, a Tynwald team established that profits at hotels which were not requisitioned by the military are now 100 per cent up on their immediate pre-war level. Those hotels which managed to open last summer after overcoming repair and equipment difficulties, are experiencing a growth of 90 per cent in profits.

Complaints about the condition of properties continued this year with the decommissioning of hotels occupied by *H.M.S. Valkyrie* in Regent Street and Granville Street on Loch Promenade. There were protests about broken walls, panelless doors, sagging ceilings, cracked washbasins, and brown and grey paint daubing over wall coverings. This was particularly so in respect of the Mayfair Hotel. Other faults listed by its proprietor included the asphalting of some bedroom floors, so they could be used for showers and urinals, and the absence of door knobs. They had been replaced by bolts and padlocks.

The repair of hotels in the *H.M.S. Valkyrie* camp marked a significant advance in the Island's struggle to normality. Advances elsewhere included the re-opening of the Metropole Hotel, the recommissioning of Peel's swimming pool and the building of additional accommodation at Douglas Holiday Camp on the Falcon Cliff side. Niarbyl with its radar station, may remain sealed off by the military. Douglas Head Minstrel shows may still be impossible until a new stage and dressing room is built.

LOW STANDARDS

Weather-wise, the past summer was good, hence the crowded scenes on Douglas beach. Not everyone was pleased, though. It was too fine for indoor entertainments to thrive, it was reckoned. Still, such problems seemed small in comparison with the crises which marked the early days of the year. In February national fuel stocks were so low consumers were warned that unless they consumed less voluntarily there would be official cuts in gas, coal and electricity supplies. That meant the Island shivered. Public transport was so poor, meanwhile, that there was barely standing room at times on many buses. Residents at Foxdale even had to walk to and from the Eairy Dam to use a bus at all - a practice which looks like continuing for some time!

In this austere age, of course, people are having to tolerate lower standards. During the season's peak, some boarding house keepers split families so as to maximise bedroom use: so many men to one room and so many women to another. Queueing at cafes remained an accepted part of life. One had to queue for most things. The queues at local cinemas were sometimes hundreds of yards long.

During the August Bank Holiday rush when only about half as many people came here as in 1939, some people slept in charabancs on Douglas Promenade or under the Villa Marina colonnade. At 5 a.m., when early morning arrivals had nowhere to go, the Villa Marina café opened and cups of tea were served to visitors seated on deck chairs on the ballroom floor.

FRUSTRATIONS

Shortages continue to frustrate. Some people may have made a good profit in the re-born tourist industry but there is little for them to spend it on. The shortage of new clothing is such that the re-making and re-styling of old clothes is flourishing. Material taken from second-hand men's suits is being used in women's fashions. New cars cannot be bought. Almost all are being exported to save Britain from bankruptcy. A new model was announced recently by a British manufacturer but its Manx agent received just one token model for the year. Inevitably, second hand pre-war cars are commanding ridiculous prices and even they are a rarity.

Hoteliers face 1948 worried about feeding visitors. Demand for eggs was such this summer that they sold at six shillings a dozen compared with a subsidised two shillings in England. Whilst the situation in respect of meat may not have reached the stage that whale meat is evident in Manx shops as it is in England, hard pressed butchers are appealing for freshly-caught rabbits. Even the basic potato is in short supply. Amid bitter attacks on farmers for failing to grow enough and their protests that they are not being paid sufficiently to do so, shortages this autumn resulted in potatoes being rationed. Everyone is asking now: Will there be no end to the misery?

HOPEFUL SIGNS

In fact, perhaps one is in sight. The first post-war lemons from Sicily, grapefruits from Texas, oranges from South Africa and bananas arrived in shops this year. Because none were rationed and quantities were small, the Government appealed to shopkeepers to ensure a fair distribution. It meant only a small amount for everyone but at least their arrival provided a foretaste of better times. Manx people who managed to holiday in Dublin this autumn, meanwhile, found that shops there were well-stocked with 'luxury' goods - from fully fashioned

nylon stockings to mouth-watering tinned salmon. Some of the latter were smuggled back to the Island, which suggests that extensive smuggling could develop once regular steamer services are re-established with Dublin.

In anticipation of better times, Tynwald has adopted a plan to spend £100,000, about a tenth of its reserves, on a brine spa at Ramsey. Critics reckon that the costings are over-optimistic and the spa will never materialise. They are probably correct but at least Tynwald's apparent willingness to invest in the future suggests that there is one there in which one can have some confidence. Too many are beginning to fear that we could all disappear overnight in World War III. Ten years ago poison gas was the bogeyman. Now vaporisation by the atom bomb is the nightmare as the world polarises between the democratic west and the communist east.

Those who can imagine the after-effects of an atomic war in which the Island is not hit but is isolated in a devastated world and suffers from radioactive fall-out are persuading the authorities of the continued need for a Manx Home Guard and Civil Defence. Others are wondering: Would such a world be worth living in?

Seen at Douglas Railway Station are a few of the 1,312,780 passengers carried by the Isle of Man Steam Railway last year. With petrol rationing in force, the railway has enjoyed a post-war boom and passenger returns are the best since 1925! The Manx Electric Railway has seen figures return to normal and is now carrying over 750,000 passengers a year. But the steam railway is facing a crisis with the track, engines and rolling stock badly in need of repair. Materials are in short supply and costs are rising. The railway carried over a million passengers a year throughout the war and provided 14,000 'specials' to meet service requirements.

(I.M.R.)

NEW RAMSEY MULTILATERAL SCHOOL OPENED

The multilateral School in Ramsey was officially opened on 9th October by the Lieutenant-Governor Sir Geoffrey Bromet. The north of the Island was thus formally incorporated into the new comprehensive system of education that has been meeting with widespread approval, not only here but in the United Kingdom. A problem at Ramsey, as in Douglas of course, is that this new school will occupy two separate buildings, Fortunately they are only 100 yards or so apart. It will be remembered the new building was designed in 1937 and completed shortly before the outbreak of the war. It was commandeered immediately by the R.A.F. and remained under their control until recently. The conversion, it is believed, has cost some £44,000. Together with the existing Grammar School on Lezayre Road, it has been in existence for the past year catering for some 300 boys and girls with Mr. H. E. George M.A. as the Headmaster. The Lieutenant-Governor has praised this new concept in education as giving 'more opportunity' - as he put it - to the ordinary boy and girl. It was remarked also by some that as the school had had such an important association with the R.A.F. during the war, it might be seen as appropriate, especially as the school had been given no official name as yet, to commemorate this important part of its history in whatever name was finally chosen.

The new west wing of Ramsey Grammar School.
(R. and L. Kelly Collection)

1,500th ANNIVERSARY OF THE MANX CHURCH

May 11th to 18th was chosen as the period to celebrate the 1,500th Anniversary of the Manx Church. On the opening Sunday, all churches were encouraged to celebrate with an early Communion and then to join in special services during the day. The Archbishop of York preached at St. George's in the morning and at St. Mary's, Castletown in the evening, which was broadcast by the B.B.C. Home Service. At this service the Archbishop was joined by the Bishop of Sodor and Man who had earlier conducted a service at St. Thomas's in Douglas, this being broadcast for overseas listeners. The Bishop of Nidaros (Trondheim) preached at Peel in the morning and at St. Thomas's in the evening.

Coat of Arms of the Diocese of Sodor and Man.

Monday saw a Diocesan Conference and a public meeting at which the visiting Archbishop and Bishops took part. On the Thursday, a service was held at Peel, which was addressed by the Archbishop of Dublin. On the closing Sunday a series of services were addressed by the Archbishop of Dublin and the Bishop of Argyll and the Isles. The celebrations were based on the traditional date for the introduction of Christianity to the Isle of Man by Patrick of Ireland. However, the date calculated uses somewhat dubious evidence produced by James Ussher, Archbishop of Dublin, in the 17th century.

The programme published for the celebrations contained a short summary of the history of Christianity in the Isle of Man written specially by Canon E. H. Stenning, Vice-Principal of King William's College. In it he divided the 1,500 years into six periods beginning with the coming of Christianity from the Patrick Church of Ireland in the fifth century. This was followed by the suppression of the Celtic Church by the Norse Vikings beginning about the end of the seventh century and lasting until the tenth century. It was towards the end of that century that Christianity was reintroduced by the Norse Church. This was followed by the establishment of the Diocese of Sodor and Man and its progress from the eleventh century until the Reformation. This was followed by a difficult period until the revival in the nineteenth century, partly attributed to the preaching of John Wesley. This revival led to the re-building of many of today's parish churches.

Canon Stenning ended by stating: "One may look back over fifteen centuries of Christianity in Man and see therein a very interesting miniature survey of Christianity in the civilized world. There have been the ebbs and flows of the spirit, the same mistakes and misguided zeal of men, and the same over-ruling certainty of the power of God that one may see in the world at large."

The Conferment of the Honorary Freedom of the Borough of Douglas to Field Marshal the Viscount Montgomery of Alamein was a splendid occasion. The presentation took place in the Villa Marina Royal Hall, in May, before an invited audience from all parts of the Island. The Mayor, Councillor F. M. Corkill, J.P., was joined on stage by the Aldermen and Councillors of the Borough.

Field Marshal Montgomery received a warm welcome on his arrival at Victoria Pier.

In company with His Excellency The Lieutenant-Governor, Air Vice-Marshal Sir Geoffrey Bromet, Lord Montgomery inspects members of the Manx branch of the Royal British Legion outside the Villa Marina.

(Photographs from Douglas Town Hall Archives)

HERE IS THE NEWS : 1948
WORST YEAR FOR CIVILIAN AIR CRASHES

The Island has had its worst year ever for civilian air crashes. Seventeen people died in three plane crashes. The worst was in the River Mersey when a Mannin Airways' charter aircraft from Ronaldsway had to ditch in the sea. We have this report:

One of the seven who died in the Mersey crash was the pilot, 48-year-old Captain John Higgins, the best known of all Manx civil aviation pioneers. The others killed were the radio officer, Manxman Noel Clucas, Douglas jeweller Mr. Louis Jacobs; British Army Lieutenant Juan Kelly, son of the late High Bailiff Kelly; Mrs. Doris May Bridson and her daughter Alice Winifred Bridson, of Douglas; and Mrs. Joan Cannan whose 26-year-old husband Matt, of Belmont Hill, Douglas, was the only survivor. The aircraft, a de Havilland Rapide, was on a flight from Dublin to Ronaldsway on 11th November but bad visibility forced air traffic control to divert Captain Higgins to Speke Airport at Liverpool. Three miles short of Speke he ran out of fuel and came down in the Mersey near Garston Docks, quarter of a mile off the beach. The plane stayed afloat and its occupants got out and clung to it in the dark, cold November evening - until, after 25 minutes, it sank, leaving everyone in the sea. Mr Cannan tried to save his wife, unsuccessfully, and was the only person who managed to swim to shore, shocked and exhausted. It emerged that no one had been told to put on life jackets. The Ministry of Civil Aviation report on the accident said Captain Higgins had miscalculated the amount of fuel he had to get him safely to Speke. Another pint of petrol would have enabled him to reach Speke which was in view.

The other accidents happened on the Island. One involved a Rapide on charter for the Senior T.T. race. Early in the morning it overflew Ronaldsway and shortly afterwards crashed high on the slopes of Cronk ny Arrey Lhaa and burst into flames. Despite an all-night search it was not until the following day that the wreckage was discovered. The pilot, three lady passengers, a man and a six-year-old boy were all killed while two badly injured men survived. Also on Senior Race Day, an Avro XIX ditched in Port Erin Bay when out of fuel. The seven passengers, pilot and radio operator climbed out on to the wings and were saved by local lobster fisherman Mr. F. Watterson before the aircraft sank.

At the end of September, Cronk ny Arrey Lhaa claimed another victim when a converted Halifax bomber on the 'milk run' from Nutt's Corner to Liverpool crashed in thick fog. All four of the crew were killed. The Halifax was loaded with 1,100 gallons of milk and wreckage of the aircraft and milk churns were scattered over a wide area.

NINE LOST AT SEA
Early in January, nine men were lost when the 300 ton motor vessel *Teasel* of Cardiff, carrying cargo from Belfast to Manchester foundered in heavy seas off the Point of Ayre. She got into difficulties when her cargo shifted. The Ramsey lifeboat *Thomas Corbett* went to the scene and Coxswain E. Starkey had a lucky escape after being washed overboard. In July, the ketch *Sarah Latham* foundered in rough seas off Langness Point. The five on board were rescued by Port St. Mary lifeboat *Civil Service No. 5*.

FIRST WITH RADAR
Douglas harbour has become the first in the world to be equipped with radar. A 60 foot high steel mast was erected on Victoria Pier with a scanning range of three miles. It will enable vessels to leave and enter port safely in bad visibility. One of the guests at its inauguration was Sir Robert Watson Watt, one of the pioneers of the development of radar as a secret weapon in the Second World War.

HONOUR FOR MONTGOMERY
Field Marshal Lord Montgomery of Alamein was made a Freeman of the Borough of Douglas at a special meeting of the Town Council held in the Villa Marina. Britain's most successful wartime general was mobbed by admirers when he got off the boat in Douglas. The Manx Regiment served under him in the Eighth Army and in his speech he said Manxmen were descended from Vikings and had inherited the qualities that go into the making of good soldiers.

ROBBED OF VICTORY
Racing star Reg Parnell was robbed of victory in the British Empire Trophy Race held in May. He was comfortably in the lead when his Maserati ran out of fuel at Parkfield Corner on the last lap. Geoffrey Ansell in an E.R.A. swept past to win the race. Winner of the Manx Cup Race was George Nixon in a Riley Special. The Castletown Cup, a new race for pre-war cars, went to Kenneth Bear in a Bugatti.

NATIONAL HEALTH SERVICE
Britain's Welfare State, introduced by the U.K.'s Labour Government this year, is to be followed in the Island. Though the service started unofficially in July, delays in passing the necessary legislation meant that the service was not legally operational until 16th November. The Health Service

Most fortunate were the five passengers and crew of this Anson XIX which ditched off Port Erin after running out of petrol. They were rescued by local fisherman, Mr F. Watterson, a Dunkirk veteran. The passengers went off to watch the Senior T.T. race and one of them had this dramatic photograph published later on the front page of the Daily Express.

Members and Executive Officers of the newly-formed Isle of Man Airports Board. Seated, centre, is its chairman, Mr T. C. Cowin, M.H.K.

offers free medical treatment by doctors, dentists and opticians, while there will be no charge for prescriptions. This means that the many Friendly Societies that abound on the Island, such as the Rechabites and Oddfellows, are likely to fade away. Also, Manx hospitals will not have to rely any longer on charity as their Management Committees will be financed by grants from the National Health Service. It will be possible also to eliminate deficiencies at Noble's Hospital which has only two specialist surgeons and one specialist medical man to satisfy hospital requirements. The hospital only has one ambulance which is not manned all the time.

DISASTROUS FIRES
Four people died in a fire at a lodging house at 2, Mona Terrace, Douglas, in August. The dead were an Irish labourer and three women. There were 11 people in the house when the fire started on the ground floor at 5 a.m. The dead were trapped on the upper floors. Eight days later fire devastated the Douglas Head Hotel in the early hours of the morning. No one was hurt but the only part of the premises to escape destruction was the concert hall.

NEW AIRPORTS BOARD
The new Isle of Man Airports Board, nominated by the Lieutenant-Governor, held its first meeting in August. Under the chairmanship of Mr. T. C. Cowin, M.H.K., it is entrusted with the development of Ronaldsway Airport and air services from the Island. Mr. Gwynn Griffiths

is confirmed as Airport Manager and Commandant. He arrived at Ronaldsway with I.O.M. Air Services in pre-war days and his services were

retained by the Admiralty during the war.

The monopoly of B.E.A. has done little to dampen the enthusiasm of the independents to operate charter services for passengers and freight on routes which the national airline regards as unprofitable. Last year Manx Air Charter Experts Ltd was formed by Mr. George Drummond and his agent, Mr. Leslie Vondy. It was soon found that there were many deficiencies in the B.E.A. service and the company was expanded and renamed Manx Air Charters Ltd. Mr. G. S. Hankinson was appointed managing director and plenty of work has been provided for the four Rapides which were named after Manx glens.

Earlier this year a second charter company was formed. Mannin Airways Ltd was formed by the redoubtable Captain John Higgins, the pre-war pioneer. Three Rapides were acquired and the company was granted a licence to fly a scheduled service to Newcastle via Carlisle this summer. However, the future of Mannin Airways is uncertain following the loss of Captain Higgins at the end of the year.

BUS CREWS ON STRIKE
Douglas bus crews staged a four day strike in protest at the sacking of eight men by the Corporation Transport Department. They went back to work after a court of inquiry set up by the Lieutenant-Governor upheld their grievance and ordered the sackings to be withdrawn. However, it added that in going on strike the men had shown a lack of concern for the travelling public.

DIVORCED VICAR
Mrs. Dorothy Lamb, wife of the disgraced former chaplain of St. John's, the Reverend Harry Lamb, who was gaoled for 18 months at Wiltshire Assizes last year for bigamy, has divorced him. The Douglas Divorce Court was told that she is living now at Barrow-in-Furness with their son. She left the Island after her husband

On the left is aviation pioneer Captain John Higgins who, earlier in the year, formed Mannin Airways Limited. Standing next to him is comedian Norman Evans who plays to packed audiences at the Palace Coliseum. On the right is Airport Manager Gwynn Griffiths. Later in the year, Captain Higgins was drowned following a tragic accident in the River Mersey.

lost his living at St. John's. He admitted bigamously marrying a WAAF while he was an R.A.F. padre during the war.

MANX SPEAKERS RECORDED

Last year's proposal by Eamon de Valera, Taoiseach of Ireland, during his brief holiday visit to the Isle of Man, that the Irish Folklore Commission should undertake to record the voices of the last native Manx Gaelic speakers had unexpected results. It was discovered that the Irish Folklore Commission did not possess the necessary mobile equipment and this had to be rectified by the special provision of a van and battery-operated recording equipment. The van was craned aboard a cattle ship and stowed in the hold. Unfortunately, the cattle were housed at a higher level and by the time the van arrived on the Island it was well camouflaged! When Mr. Basil Megaw, director of the Manx Museum, saw it arrive he ordered the crew to stay in the van while it was hosed down. The visit has resulted in the first good sound recordings of Manx speakers, including the voices of John Kneen (95), Ned Maddrell, Harry Boyde and John Tom Kaighin. Assisting in the recordings were the present few 'custodians' of the language who are keen to preserve Manx Gaelic for posterity.

NEAR-RECORD SEASON

The huge post-war rush of holiday-

Recording the voices of Manx language speakers John Kneen (95) and Harry Boyde (78). Making the recordings are enthusiasts Bill Radcliffe and Mark Braide with the help of the Irish Folklore Commission's van. *(Manx National Heritage)*

makers to the Island continued during the past season. The 1948 summer arrival figure was 624,737 which included 36,000 arriving by air. The overall total was more than last year, but was 10,000 short of the all-time record of the 634,512 figure established in 1913. One of the highlights of the season was 18-year-old Joyce Lewis winning the Miss Isle of Man Bathing Beauty Competition for the second year in succession.

SUCCESS AT BLACKPOOL

Over 400 Manx competitors took part in the Blackpool Music Festival in November. They returned with a long list of successes, including: Miss Barbara Taggart, open pianoforte solo winner; Messrs. J. Miles and N. Kaighin, duet winners; Messrs. A. W. Quirk and R. R. Nicholl, winners of bass and tenor lieder classes respectively; Miss Mavis Kelly, winner sight reading, singing; Mr. Bert Gray, second in tenor class; Miss S. Corlett, third in girls' solo; Miss Eileen Peters, winner, soprano class, and third in Rose Bowl contest; Lhon Dhoo choir, conductor Douglas Buxton, third in male voice choir class, and Mr. C. Jones, second in baritone lieder.

1948 NEWS IN BRIEF

JANUARY
20 - Tynwald rejected resolution to introduce universal suffrage for all local elections.
20 - Constitution for Whitley Council for civil servants approved by Tynwald.

FEBRUARY
3 - Keys pass third reading of the Rent Restrictions Bill after record session of eight hours.
11 - Mr. Maurice Holmes, M.A., (41) appointed Headmaster of Douglas High School for Boys to succeed Mr. A. H. Sykes, B.Sc., upon his retirement in March after being head for 27 years.
23 - Rev. R. H. Reid, M.A., elected chairman of the Manx Motor Cycle Club in succession to Alderman Robt. Cowell, chairman of the club for 25 years.

MARCH
30 - W. H. Kelly, of Onchan, won the North of England 26½-mile marathon championship.

MAY
4 - House of Keys adopt amendment to the Education Bill depriving school teachers of representation on the Education Authority, and carry amendment that universal suffrage apply to Authority elections in place of restricted voting by ratepayers.
5 - Mr. A. W. Quirk wins Cleveland Medal at the Manx Music Festival.
17 - Football history made when Sheffield United and Sheffield Wednesday played a match at King George V Park.

JUNE
8 - Memorial seat, erected on Quarterbridge Road at junction with Alexander Drive, in honour of the late W. L. Handley, famous racing motorcyclist, unveiled by Mr. Graham Walker.
12 - Death of 'Noel' Christmas from injuries received the previous day at Michael in the Senior T.T. The race was won by Artie

Bell (Norton) and the fastest lap at 88 m.p.h. was set by O. Tenni (Moto Guzzi).
15 - During Cycling Week Reg Harris, amateur sprint cycling champion of the world, took part in grass track meeting at King George V Park.
23 - Important decision by Deemster Johnson at General Gaol in ruling that Manx law did not give legal power to the police to hold a man for being found drunk and incapable.

JULY
5 - Earl of Derby among the distinguished visitors to the Tynwald Ceremony, and later a guest at the World Manx Association gathering.
19 - *Snaefell V*, latest addition to the Steam Packet's fleet, arrived in Douglas for the first time. *Mona's Isle* is to be sold after 28 years' service.

SEPTEMBER
8 - Miss Doris Oakley (17), of Douglas, swam Douglas Bay from Port Jack to Port Skillion in 63 mins 48 secs.
12-16 Centenary celebrations of the Douglas Town and Seamen's Mission (The Bethel).

OCTOBER
1 - Standard 44-hour week for general workers came into force.
7 - Commission recommends that a new Electricity Authority be set up for the Island to take over the assets of the Douglas Corporation and the Electricity Board.
18 - Mr. Jack Nivison (Labour) elected to the House of Keys in Middle Sheading bye-election caused by the resignation of Col. Clifford Kniveton, M.C..

NOVEMBER
16 - Tynwald adopted recommendations to amend income tax law, including introduction of a standard rate of 4 shillings in the pound.

TYNWALD MATTERS:
THE MANX NATIONAL HEALTH SERVICE

In little more than six months this year one of the most momentous and far reaching pieces of social legislation made its way through the various stages of Tynwald. Although the Royal Assent to the legislation is not expected until November, the medical community has started to implement its terms already. The establishment of the Manx National Health Service will surely be seen in years to come as one of the great achievements of a civilised society.

Initial stages occurred in April when a Bill detailing the establishment of a comprehensive Health Service in the Isle of Man was circulated. While it was true to argue, as some did, that it merely represented an extension of the Health Insurance Scheme of the 1920s, it was also true that its real genesis lay in the National Health Service introduced in the U.K. Here on the Island, however, our Bill differed in some respects from the English scheme. Voluntary hospitals, for example, were permitted to continue as independent charity-funded organisations, if they wished, though none has done so. The various professional societies, such as the Medical Society, will have representatives on the administering committees.

The Health Services Board of Tynwald is to be assisted by an Advisory Council which, it is proposed, will consist of the Medical Officer for Health, the Medical Superintendent of Ballamona and nine other members -three doctors, one consultant, one dentist, one chemist, and a midwife, an experienced manager and an official of a government department.

It is probably true to say that it was the composition of this Advisory Council that occasioned the greatest unease and, in some cases, fairly vitriolic criticism. Claims that this would give the doctors more or less complete executive control of the scheme were widely expressed and there were fears, unlikely though they may be, that the doctors would operate a closed shop. Indeed, some argued that the Manx Bill had been acceptable to the medical profession only because all the points to which the doctors in Britain objected were deleted from it! Any objective view of the situation would suggest that many of the worries were unfounded. Apart from a general consensus that professionals are the best people to oversee the working of the new scheme, it seems inconceivable that highly respected and regarded doctors would act in an irresponsible manner.

There were other concerns, too, not least the fate of the various charitable endowments that exist throughout the Island for the relief of distress. These are being transferred to the Health Services Board 'free of any trust' but that has not allayed the doubts of the several groups of trustees. The Corrin Endowment in Peel was directed towards the establishment of a Peel and District Cottage Hospital. Agreement has been reached now that a clinic or home for the elderly will be provided.

Another problem was the reluctance by Manx doctors to have their private practices nationalised. Initially, the Manx legislation omitted this U.K. plan, but in mid-May, when the Bill was in the middle of its parliamentary stages the doctors said they now wanted the same provisions. The reason for this change of mind was that in the United Kingdom certain alterations had been made to the British Scheme largely to do with the acquisition, sale or not of medical practices and other conditions of service which were more acceptable to the medical profession here than had hitherto been the case, particularly with regard to the compensation to be paid when practices were acquired. Despite the upset that this caused, the Legislative Council accepted the doctors' amendments and in early June gave the third reading to the Bill.

Matters progressed swiftly from that point. On Tuesday, 29th June the Bill was given its second reading in the Keys and passed by 15 votes to 8. There was a hard core of opposition in the House but it is probably fair to say that such opponents directed their fire not at the principles of the Bill, but at the financial consequences of its introduction. There were predictions that income tax could soar to 10 shillings or 17s 6d in the pound. It did not stop the opponents being described as eight 'Canutes' standing in the way of progress, however. During this debate doctors, dentists, opticians and chemists were well represented in the public area and they had already made it known that if the second reading was passed they were prepared to start the scheme the following Monday without waiting for the third reading.

This generous spirit on the part of the medical professionals was very well received by the population at large and from all over the Island reports were received that many doctors were already treating patients under the new system. There was some confusion as people were urged to register now with a chosen doctor but when, on 13th July, the Bill received its third reading and passed without a division, the message that came across was to get on with it. A new government form, HS1, for people to register with a doctor, appeared on the Island. By 30th July the Legislative Council had accepted the Bill.

There will be growing pains. Such a gigantic scheme will certainly produce immense organisational and administrative problems and the professional officers of the Health Services Board will be working long hours and at full stretch to find solutions. But already, in September, it is clear that the basic structure has not only been put in place but is working with remarkable smoothness and efficiency. Already over 35,000 people, some 65% of our population, have chosen their doctors, and each doctor has approximately 2,000 patients on his list. Concurrent with the launch of the new Health Service, a new Social Security system for the payment of benefits during times of hardship has also been introduced, partly financed from the Island's Income Tax fund. Employers and employees will have to pay higher contributions, but this is not begrudged because now the Social Security and Health Service will care for everyone 'from cradle to the grave'. These represent the most beneficent measures ever introduced by the Manx Legislature.

NATIONAL SERVICE TO CONTINUE

Young, fit Manxmen will be legally obliged to give 18 months National Service in one of Britain's armed services - but only after considerable hesitation by the House of Keys. It will be recalled that last November, when the proposed extension of the U.K's 1947 National Service Act to the Isle of Man came up for discussion, a resolution extending it to the Island was passed in the Legislative Council but fell in the House of Keys. The reasons for this apparent disarray were varied. For a few, a very few, the fact that the United Kingdom was not at war seems to have had some weight. But for the majority the complications arose when the Imperial Government amalgamated all its previous legislation dealing with National Service but left the Island under the jurisdiction of the existing National Service Act. This suggested that Manxmen could be called up and asked to serve under conditions more onerous in some respects than those called up in the United Kingdom.

As the reality of the situation dawned upon Tynwald members, this, coupled with increasingly forthright demands that the Island should follow the 'path of duty', led to the setting up of a Commission to enquire into the position regarding the extension of National Service to the Isle of Man. The views of the Committee became available recently and in October, Tynwald Court was asked once again to give 'most careful and favourable consideration' to a resolution asking His Majesty to extend to the Isle of Man by Order in Council the National Service Act 1947. When the matter was debated in Tynwald, the majority of the members were fully aware of all the implications of their decision. An impassioned speech by a new Labour member may well have swung the doubters - 'I appeal to you as a conscript, and as a young man likely to go again, to adopt the resolution'. The resolution was adopted and young Manx men, like their peers in the United Kingdom, will now find that their careers and aspirations will be put on hold, as it were, while they serve King and Country all over the world.

BLINDED OFFICER ADMITTED TO MANX BAR

One man's triumph over adversity should be an inspiration to other war-wounded. Despite being blinded, 28-year-old Howard Simcocks of Rushen Abbey, Ballasalla has qualified as an advocate. He did it through his indomitable courage and with the support of his family and friends. Before the war he was studying to be an accountant, then joined the Manx Regiment and served with it in Egypt until being commissioned and being transferred to another Light A.A. regiment. It was during the battle for Monte Casino, after the Salerno landings, that the jeep in which he was travelling was blown up by a mine. Lieutenant Simcocks was badly wounded in the head, rushed to hospital in Naples and, from there, to St. Dunstan's. He was told that he would never see again.

Whilst at St. Dunstan's, Mr. Simcocks learned to type and read Braille. This was particularly difficult for he was left handed, and his left hand had been damaged so badly he could not use his fingers for such delicate work. It was now that he began to develop what is now regarded as an amazing memory. Accountancy was out of the question, so he decided to embark on a career as an advocate. He sought the help of former Attorney- General, Mr. Ramsey Moore, who was more than willing to accept the challenge. He undertook to provide daily lectures in Manx law and Lieut-Colonel Henry Kelly, the Commanding Officer of the Manx Regiment, agreed to accept Mr. Simcocks as an arti-

cled student in his law firm of Kelly, Moore and Kelly. Mr Simcocks was able to make some notes from Mr. Moore's lectures and each night these were read to him at Rushen Abbey. He was then able to transcribe them into Braille on thick brown paper using a machine supplied to him by St. Dunstan's.

Despite many frustrations, Mr. Simcocks passed his intermediate examination after eight months. He then attended courts and sat in on interviews with clients. Law was read to him by advocates Arthur Luft and Stanley Allen. Mr. Simcocks noted some points, others he simply memorised. His prodigious memory enabled him to walk about home and office so long as no furniture was moved. Now it enabled him to memorise the whole of the prospectus for his final six hour examination. In the Rolls Office the questions were read to him and his answers were taken down in shorthand and transcribed. Mr. Simcocks passed, and was sworn in as a member of the Manx Bar in August by Deemster Cowley.

It is understood that Mr. Simcocks now aspires to be a member of Malew Parish Commissioners and the House of Keys, too. Given his determination, no one doubts he will succeed. Before the war Mr. Simcocks was a keen motorcyclist. Now he rides pillion when his secretary, 18-year-old Helen Kinvig, takes him to his office in Castletown. Occasionally they visit clients and sometimes travel as far as Douglas. Truly, he is a remarkable man and an example to us all.

THE ISLAND BACK IN ITS HOLIDAY STRIDE

Enjoying the sun on Douglas sands.

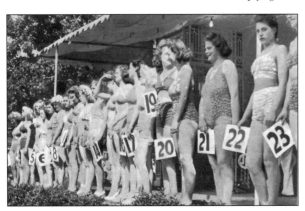

The popular bathing beauty competitions.

Mooragh Park, Ramsey.

Relaxing in the Villa Marina Gardens.

The Swimming Pool, Ramsey

BOOM TIME FOR RESORTS AND ENTERTAINMENTS

Peel Sands and Castle.

Chapel Bay, Port St. Mary.

Information Bureau, Victoria Pier, Douglas.

Port Erin Sands   *(Illustrations from Publicity Board Guide, Frank Cowin Library)*

HERE IS THE NEWS : 1949
ISLAND TO RECEIVE TELEVISION?

People in the Isle of Man could soon be watching television for the first time. A new high-powered transmitter is under construction in the Midlands and will start beaming the television transmissions from Alexandra Palace in London next year. Its range will come close to reaching the Island. We have this report:

Britain's first television service was started by the BBC in 1936. It could be seen only in the London area, and only a few thousand people could afford a television receiving set. During the 1939 to 1945 war years the service was suspended, but now it is expanding rapidly. The new transmitter at Sutton Coldfield will have a range conservatively estimated to be a hundred miles - and the Isle of Man is only 150 miles away. Local radio dealers, notably Harold Colebourn, Ernie Dickinson and Russell Fox, plan to test local levels of reception and provide public demonstrations. Mr. Fox, who came to the Island during the war to work in the radar installations on Douglas Head, worked in television in London before the war. He says he believes the new developments in

television technology are bringing the Island close to being able to receive reasonably good television pictures. That means something that is rather sparkly, shadowy and inclined to fade. Screens will be no bigger than nine inches. Even so, he believes television will be highly popular in the Island, especially when major sports events are screened. In the meantime, the BBC's Controller of Television, Mr. Norman Collins, has said his long-term intention, backed by a £12 million development programme, is that television will reach out across the whole of the British Isles. The problem is that the emphasis at first will be on providing good reception in areas of high population. Because of post-war shortages it could be years before transmitters are provided to give better reception in the peripheral areas.

STRIKE AVERTED
Last minute intervention by the Government saved the Island from a potentially disastrous general strike at the start of the visiting season. After six months of negotiation between employers and unions had failed to

reach a settlement on improved pay and conditions, a deputation of M.H.K.s brought the two sides together at the eleventh hour. The strike was called off when the employers conceded the main demand of an increase in basic pay for the Island's 5,000 general workers.

INDEPENDENT AIRLINES TO THE RESCUE
In February, the Lieutenant-Governor, reported the results of a meeting with the Minister of Civil Aviation following the announcement that B.E.A. was to make drastic cuts in the summer services to the Island because of heavy losses. Only Liverpool and Belfast would be served, with a week-end service to London. His Excellency said these cuts had to be accepted, but to compensate for what could have been a calamitous situation, independent airlines would be permitted to provide services to the Island on other routes. Many willing and eager private companies responded. One of the first was North West Airlines (Isle of Man) Ltd. It was formed out of Mannin Airways, now without Captain Higgins, combining with

An aerial view of Ronaldsway Airport showing a multitude of aircraft parked near the terminal buildings. Many of the aircraft are operated by independent airlines which have been permitted to fly on routes which are not the preserve of British European Airways. Connections with many parts of the British Isles have boosted the number of passengers handled at Ronaldsway over the 100,000 mark for the first time. (Aerofilms Limited)

With local farmers unable to meet the huge demand for milk this summer, supplies have had to be ferried in from Northern Ireland. Here, one of the Miles Aerovans being employed in the operation is being loaded with the car of a local resident intent on holidaying in Ireland.

During the year Isle of Man Road Services Limited added a further 18 56-seater Leyland double-decker buses to their fleet, bringing the total to 28 of this type. The new buses arrived together as 'cargo' for a large tank-landing craft employed in the D-Day landings. Here, four of them can be seen after being craned on to the King Edward Pier.

(Frank Cowin Library)

Ulster Aviation. Immediate steps were taken to add two Dakotas to their fleet of smaller aircraft and licences were granted to provide services from Manchester, Blackpool, Carlisle and Prestwick. Other independents appeared and services were provided from Leeds, Birmingham and Newcastle. It was these independents that boosted the number of passengers handled at Ronaldsway over the 100,000 mark for the first time.

ACQUITTED OF MANSLAUGHTER

Applause and cheering broke out in Douglas Court House when the jury returned a verdict of 'Not Guilty' at the trial of William Henry Wattleworth, a 22-year-old painter from Liverpool who also boxes professionally under the name of Bill Watts. He was involved in a violent brawl in Strand Street, Douglas, involving nine men. One of them, 29-year-old Henry Yates, of Wellington Square, Douglas, died of head injuries after being punched to the ground by Wattleworth. The latter entered a plea of self defence, saying he had been provoked by Yates.

PRISONER ESCAPES, TWICE!

A London criminal, 20-year-old Raymond Henry Spicer, escaped from the Island's prison in Victoria Road, Douglas - not once, but twice in two months. He was on remand on a burglary charge when he made his first escape. He was recaptured by the police after 54 hours on the run as he tried to get away from the Island in a stolen motor boat. His second break for freedom lasted 42 hours until he was recaptured in a hay loft near Castletown. He is serving two years imprisonment with hard labour.

WARDEN QUITS CALF OF MAN

The man who has been the English National Trust warden on the Calf of Man for the last 10 years is giving up. Forty-nine-year-old Robert Mitchell and his wife Norah said it had been the loneliest job in Britain, suitable only for a Robinson Crusoe. They farmed on the Calf but found it a hard life with bad weather cutting them off for up to five weeks at a time. A Manx National Trust is now being formed and this is to take over a long lease on the Calf.

DROWNED IN CALF SOUND

A Scots holidaymaker drowned while trying to swim across the tidal race in the Calf Sound. Twenty-seven-year-old Andrew Young had swum across to Kitterland but got into difficulties when he tried to make the return trip. His body was washed up later at Port Erin. A plucky but unsuccessful attempt at rescue was made by Port St. Mary art student Edward Cannell who was among scores of people who witnessed the tragedy.

In another sea tragedy a young man, Michael Walker from Blackpool, lost his life following the capsizing of a small yacht in which he and his uncle James Norris were fishing in Ramsey Bay. Mr. Norris, practically a non-swimmer, was picked up after clinging to the upturned boat for over two hours. Michael, a powerful swimmer, lost his life when trying to swim ashore for assistance.

NEW RACING STARS

Two bright new British sports stars emerged in the Island during this year. Geoff Duke, a 26-year-old motor-cyclist from St. Helens, won the Senior Manx Grand Prix at record speed and set up a new lap record of 87.5 m.p.h. Second was Cromie McCandless who beat Duke in the Junior Race after a terrific battle. Duke first appeared in June this year when he won the Senior Clubman's T.T.

In the Manx Cup Race on the Willaston Circuit, 18-year-old Stirling Moss attracted much attention for his spectacular driving in a Cooper J.A.P. He was well in the lead until forced out with magneto problems. He recorded the fastest lap in the race which was won by John Heath driving an H.W. Alta. In the main race, Bob Gerard won the British Empire Trophy in an E.R.A. for the second time.

In June, Senior Race Day was honoured by a visit from H.R.H. The Duke of Edinburgh, Patron of the A-C.U. He witnessed the massed start of the Lightweight Race which was won again by Manliff Barrington riding for Moto Guzzi. The Duke flagged off Artie Bell to start the Senior Race which had a dramatic finish. Les Graham, on one of the A.J.S. 'Porcupines', started the last lap with a comfortable lead but had to stop at Hillberry with magneto failure. Les managed to push the heavy machine to the finish where the ex-fighter pilot received a standing ovation from the crowded grandstand. He finished tenth. His misfortune allowed Harold Daniell to notch up another win for Norton.

This year the Isle of Man T.T. was

(Above) Newcomer Geoff Duke relaxes after winning the Senior Clubman's T.T. in June. A few weeks later he returned and took the Manx Grand Prix by storm, coming second in the Junior and winning the Senior. It could be that a T.T. star of the future has been born. *(Keig Collection)*

(Below) H.R.H. The Duke of Edinburgh, Patron of the A-C.U., chats with Harold Daniell before the start of the Senior T.T. The Norton rider went on to win his third Senior race.

(Manx National Heritage)

the first round of the new World Motor-Cycling Championships being held in various European countries. Enthusiasts followed the fortunes of British riders and it is good to report that two T.T. favourites have become World Champions. Freddie Frith, this year's Junior T.T. winner, is the first World Champion in the 350 c.c. class while Les Graham is the first 500 c.c. World Champion.

DOUGLAS ILLUMINATIONS RETURN

The attractive feature of the illumina-

tions along Douglas promenade made a welcome return this year. They had not been seen since 1939. The steam ferries across Douglas harbour which take thousands of visitors to the attractions of Douglas Head, also made a welcome return as did the incline railway towards the end of the season. The steam ferry owners are objecting strongly to the proposed bus service to Douglas Head which the Corporation plan to introduce next year. The number of visitors to the Island this year once again topped the 600,000 mark but

was slightly down on last year's figure. The season was marked by a shortage of milk. Extra supplies had to be ferried in from Northern Ireland.

ISLAND'S CONTRIBUTION TO WESTMINSTER SETTLED

After a political row lasting six months, Tynwald has settled at last the basis on which a contribution to the cost of Imperial Defence, diplomatic and other common services should be paid. In May it was decided unanimously that five members of the Finance and Consultative committee should accompany His Excellency the Lieutenant-Governor to London to discuss the matter with His Majesty's Government, and to agree on the amount of the annual payment with a further reduction in the National Debt arising from the cost of the war. In June the deputation's report on the Defence Contribution recommended that the Island should pay the British Exchequer a sum based on a percentage of our Common Purse receipts. The suggested rate was $6^1/2\%$. At present, that would have amounted to £100,000. The proposal was that as these receipts rose or fell the contribution would vary with a minimum limit of £50,000. It was recommended also that the sum of £500,000, the balance of money loaned to the U.K. Government during the war, should be converted into a gift. The report was considered by Tynwald twice during June, but a decision was deferred until October.

The October meeting of Tynwald resulted in stalemate when Keys and Council failed to agree on the final details of the contribution. This led to a series of private meetings, and in November a compromise solution to the controversy was agreed without a division in Tynwald. The decision means that the Isle of Man will make an annual payment to the Imperial Government of a sum equal to 5% of the Common Purse receipts, currently approximately £80,000. This may be decreased or increased in any year by resolution of Tynwald. It was agreed also that the £500,000 on loan to the U.K. Government free of interest should not be converted to a gift at this stage. In response, the U.K. Government said it would accept the offer but only reluctantly because the offer did not truly reflect the services the Island received at the expense of U.K. taxpayers.

BLESSED ARE THE PEACEMAKERS

Last minute intervention by the House of Keys saved the Island from being paralysed by a major strike in late June. It was in the Spring that what had been vague flickers of discontent amongst the Island's workers, particularly those in the T.G.W.U. and the Electrical Trades Union, seemed ready to burst into a serious conflagration. Union demands for both wage increases, some 3 shillings a week for general workers, and zonal upgradings in conjunction with other requirements, had produced a head-on clash with the Employers' Federation. General workers, municipal passenger and transport workers, Gas Company and Steam Packet Company employees, laundry and quay workers - all the wide spectrum of T.G.W.U. members - meant that should the issue fail to be resolved then the subsequent strike would to all intents and purposes shut down the entire Island.

From March, despite the Lieutenant-Governor's proposal for arbitration, which was accepted by the unions but not by the employers, continuous talks had got nowhere. The main sticking point seemed to be that the employers wanted the case of the General Workers dealt with first, before moving on to the rest, while the unions wanted the whole package to be considered. Negotiations ended in acrimony in May with the employers finally accepting arbitration but the unions rejecting the notion. On 10th June the unions issued a formal notice of strike action. This would expire at midnight on Sunday, 19th June and a general stoppage would be implemented.

The effect of such a stoppage would have been cat-astrophic. This undoubtedly played a great part in the decision of the House of Keys to depute three of their members - Messrs. A. J. Teare, H. K. Corlett and J. C. Nivison - to make one final attempt to bring the parties together. On Wednesday morning, 15th June, they met representatives of the unions involved, and by early evening they had discussed matters with those of the Employers' Federation. At 8 p.m. a joint meeting was held in a Tynwald Committee room. This continued until midnight. On the following morning the meeting was resumed and at 2 p.m. the unions withdrew their notice of strike action.

The outcome was that the general workers would receive their rise, from 97 to 100 shillings a week, but not their upgrading. Other workers received modest increases, all retrospective to 1st March. Most people believe that this result could, and should have been achieved without the months of tension, and perhaps some good will come out of it. Certainly, some form of machinery should exist before they threaten the economy. There is a reasonable case for setting up a cost of living index for everyone's guidance. It might end the uninformed comparisons that always seem to add fuel to whatever fire is burning - although human nature being what it is, even that seems 'pie in the sky'!

In October, His Excellency the Lieutenant-Governor announced to Tynwald his intention to make an Order giving the necessary powers to safeguard public interests in connections with trades disputes. The Order came into effect on 14th November.

1949 NEWS IN BRIEF

JANUARY

1 - Manxman Sir Ralph Stevenson, British Ambassador to China, awarded the Grand Cross of St. Michael and St. George.

FEBRUARY

16 - After having been on Government service for over nine years, the steamer *Manxman* docked in Barrow. She is to be sold for breaking-up purposes.

MARCH

1 - Tynwald agrees to appropriate money to support industries which promise to provide employment. The Court also autho-rised the Electricity Board to set up its own generating station at an estimated cost of £212,000.

8 - Legislative Council rejected by five votes to four, a Bill designed to give women the right to serve on juries.

22 - Fiftieth anniversary of the founding of Yn Cheshaght Ghailckagh, the Manx Language Society.

22 - Manx Operatic Society founded.

APRIL

22 - Mr. Bryan Kneale, a student at the Royal Academy Schools, awarded the 1949 Rome Scholarship in Mural Painting.

MAY

4 - Mr. Lewis Gale (baritone) scored a notable 'double' by winning the Cleveland Medal and the new 'F. M. Cubbon' silver rose bowl in the final of the Lieder classes.

22 - Centenary of St. John's Church commemorated by special ser-vices.

28 - Visit of Lord Rowallan, Chief Scout of the British Empire, and the Hon. Lady Cochrane, Chief Guide Commissioner for England.

JUNE

9 - Speaker of the House of Keys, Mr. J. D. Qualtrough, awarded the C.B.E. in the King's Birthday Honours List. Superintendent Alfred Kelly, Deputy Chief Constable, awarded the King's Police Medal.

JULY

13 - Douglas Town Council adopt plan for the lay-out of King George V Park to provide a stadium and football pitch, and run-ning and cycle tracks.

14 - Ramsey's new lifeboat, the *Thomas Corbett*, named by Lady Bromet.

AUGUST

16 - John James Foster (46), living at Ballaghaue Housing Estate, Andreas, lost his life by a fall of sand when working at the Kimmeragh sand-pit.

SEPTEMBER

14 - Mr. William Teare (66), of Ballaghennie Farm, Bride, acciden-tally killed when duck-shooting near the farm.

16-19 Douglas bus services stopped by unofficial strike of drivers and conductors following the suspension of driver Thomas Gale for failing to observe the compulsory stop on Prospect Hill. He was reported by Councillor T. C. Cowin, chairman of the Tramways Committee. The strike ended when the Tramways Committee, acting on a legal opinion in respect of Councillor Cowin's occu-pancy of the chair when Driver Gale appeared before them, rescinded the suspension of the driver.

OCTOBER

31 - Francis Thomas Cubbon (aged 2) died in a fire which destroyed Glen View Cottage, West Baldwin.

NOVEMBER

7-12 Many successes by Manx competitors at Blackpool Music Festival.

12 - Mr. William Hughes of Peel killed when thrown into crankpit of Ramsey Steamship Co's vessel *Ben Jee*, during severe gale in Preston Bay.

16 - By 13 votes to 5 in the Keys, a resolution asking for approval to a proposal that the Airports Board provide licensed catering facilities at Ronaldsway Airport rejected in Tynwald.

NEW SECONDARY SCHOOL FOR THE SOUTH

The new secondary school for children in the south of the Island was formally opened on Friday, 6th May by British Home Secretary, Mr. Chuter Ede. He referred to the Island's bilateral (or comprehensive) educational system as 'one of the great educational ventures of our time'. The Manx system is the brainchild of our Director of Education, Mr. H. L. Fletcher, O.B.E., M.A., who envisaged in pre-war days all children of secondary school age being educated together, rather than being separated by passing, or failing, a scholarship examination. As a symbol of stability and security, the new school has been named Castle Rushen High School. It is unique in that it makes use of wartime single-brick buildings of Admiralty design, built to accommodate personnel of the highly secret Air Radar School. Here thousands of personnel were trained in the intricacies of radar. The school operated in conjunction with the radar stations at Scarlett and Dalby.

The task of converting the site into a school was given to the firm of Davidson, Marsh and Co., architects and surveyors. All the main classrooms were linked by a long corridor. Three other corridors which linked the offices, dining room, staff room, music room, art room and handicraft workshop and additional classrooms, formed a garden quadrangle for use as a rural science centre. Other rooms were fitted out for general science and domestic science. Another unique feature of the school was that all rooms were linked by a tannoy system, enabling the headmaster to communicate with the whole school. A new assembly hall/gymnasium was completed this spring. It was here that the formal opening took place. Mr. Chuter Ede was joined by His Excellency the Lieutenant-Governor, the Ven. Archdeacon C. V. Stockwood (chairman of the Education Authority) and Mr. J. D. Qualtrough, S.H.K. (Member for Castletown and chairman of the Board of Education).

The school actually received its first pupils last September when those already attending the lower two forms at the Douglas High Schools were joined by those of eleven years and over attending the elementary schools in the south of the Island. Children living outside Castletown are 'bussed' from Port Erin, Port St. Mary, Colby, Ballabeg, Foxdale and Santon. The school,

Pupils line up in the main corridor which links the former buildings now used as class rooms and specialist rooms.

opened with 147 boys and 116 girls who met in the dining hall for the first assembly under the school's headmaster, Mr. Godfrey Cretney, B.A. He held up a blank piece of paper and emphasised that everyone was making a fresh start. 'This school has great potentialities,' said Mr. Cretney, 'but it needs prestige, and that is what I want to give it.' The pupils have been streamed in mixed forms according to suggested ability, but flexibility will allow transfers to be made as pupils progress through the school.

The establishment of this school in the south fulfils the aspirations of those who had argued long ago that such a school was essential not only to counterbalance the preponderance of Douglas interests, but also to put the south on a parity with the north of the Island. It is seen as the last stone in implementing the revolutionary concept of secondary education pioneered on the Island. But perhaps it is not quite the last stone. People living in the west of the Island will dispute that! How long will they have to wait? Ten years? Fifty years? Surely not half a century!

The first members of staff of Castle Rushen High School. Standing centre is Headmaster Mr Godfrey Cretney, B.A.

1949

Plan of the wartime Admiralty buildings built to accommodate trainee radar operators.

Plan of the school showing the ingenious use of corridors to link the buildings now converted into classrooms and specialised rooms.

(Photographs by kind permission of Mr W. C. Callister)

THE 20th CENTURY

School entrance.

Nissen huts used for metalwork, and the groundsman's hut.

The quadrangle forming the school garden.

Building being used as the chemistry lab.
(Below) The domestic science room.

The Isle of Man's fledgling National Health Service, launched in July, 1948, was brought close to collapse this year because of the cost to the taxpayer of dental treatment and prescriptions. When the Government introduced tough new regulations under which patients would have to pay a charge of sixpence for prescriptions, the Island's chemists rebelled and withdrew from the N.H.S. Only crisis talks with the Health Services Board saved the situation. We have this report:

At a secret session of Tynwald in April, members were shocked to discover that the cost of the all-free N.H.S. had soared to an estimated £800,000 a year, well beyond expectations. It was decided that there would have to be cutbacks, and the public would have to contribute to the cost. The charges, announced by Mr. T. C. Cowin, chairman of the Health Services Board, came into effect on 1st October. They provide for a charge of sixpence for each form of prescription; a charge for medicine or drug containers; the payment of 10% of the excess over £1 of the cost of dental treatment, and that all children under school leaving age should receive free treatment only by the School Dental Officers. The moves were opposed strongly by the Island's doctors, dentists and chemists, but only the Manx Chemists Association stood out against the Government. With over 40 members, all but seven decided to pull out of the N.H.S., as they felt the collection of the charges would be unworkable. It amounted to a strike and led to the Isle of Man Medical Society issuing a statement that the N.H.S. was in chaos and on the brink of collapse. The situation forced the Health Services Board to bring in the police. It was arranged that patients' prescriptions would be collected at police stations and brought to Douglas to be dispensed, Atkinson's Pharmacy in Granville Street and Boots the Chemists in Victoria Street not having joined the boycott. The dispensed articles were then returned to the various police stations for collection by or on behalf

of the patients. The situation persisted for 18 days during which 150 prescriptions a day were processed. The deadlock was broken after talks between the Chemists Association and the Government although no official details of the agreement have been made public.

TRAWLER LOST ON ROCKS
A Lowestoft trawler, the *Mary Heeley*, was lost when she went aground in fog on the rocks north of Onchan Harbour in April. Her crew of 10 were rescued by the Douglas lifeboat, the *Millie Walton*. She was making her first service call in charge of coxswain Mr. Robert Lee. It happened at midnight and the trawler's S.O.S. was picked up by a radio ham in Douglas who raised the alarm. The Island was hit by the worst storms for years in September with 80 mile an hour winds and torrential rain. Steam Packet sailings were delayed, but not halted.

DAMAGES AWARD REVERSED
A schoolboy has been awarded £760 damages in the High Court at Douglas for the loss of the sight in one eye during a game of conkers on a school train. Fourteen-year-old John Donald Bridson, of Glen Maye, was hit by a conker wielded by another boy while the train was travelling from Peel to Douglas. The Education Authority was held responsible for failing to exercise proper supervision on the train. However, the Court's decision was reversed on appeal.

STREET PARKING PROHIBITED
A major clamp-down on all-day car parking in Douglas has been launched by the Town Council. Restrictions have been imposed on all the town's main roads and streets under which cars will not be allowed to park longer than it takes to drop off or pick up passengers and goods. Works Committee chairman Alderman J. C. Fargher told the Council: "Streets were never made for the parking of motor cars".

LICENCE FOR SPIRITS REFUSED
The Douglas Licensing Bench has refused to allow boarding houses to

serve their guests spirits in addition to wine and beer. The Bench refused to accept the argument of 91 applicants that drinking habits had changed and spirits were more in demand. The Manx Temperance Federation opposed the applications. It is questionable that the decision will have much impact on the majority of guesthouses. They are unlicensed but are selling drinks to their guests even so, under a dubious scheme that argues that the drinks have been bought in on behalf of the guests and are, therefore, the property of the guests. Meanwhile, the Island's Appeal Court has upheld a decision by the High-Bailiff that publicans who instal juke boxes in their pubs must have a music licence.

T.T. RECORDS SMASHED
All pre-war records were smashed in this year's T.T. Races. Irishman Artie Bell set up new race and lap records in the Junior T.T., raising Stanley Wood's 1938 lap of 85.3 m.p.h. to 87.3 m.p.h. in a time of 25 mins 56 secs. The new Lightweight records were set up by Dario Ambrosini on a Benelli. Kluge's 1938 lap record of 80.35 m.p.h. was lifted to 80.9 m.p.h. by the Italian rider. But it was the brilliant riding of newcomer Geoff Duke which caught everyone's attention on Senior Race Day. He won last year's Senior Clubman's T.T. and Senior M.G.P., and had been enlisted into the Norton works team along with Artie Bell, Harold Daniell and Johnny Lockett. They were riding the new 'Featherbed' Nortons, so called because of the suspension of the revolutionary frame designed by Cromie and Rex McCandless. Duke astonished the crowd by being the first to lap at under 25 minutes and, in the process, breaking team-mate Harold Daniell's lap record of 91 m.p.h. which had stood since 1938. On the fifth of the seven laps, Duke sped round at 93.33 m.p.h., altering the record books with a time of 24 mins. 16 secs. Geoff Duke was the main topic at teatime in the boarding houses that day. It is confidently predicted that he is a World Champion in the making.

CONTRABAND FROM IRELAND
Customs officers who boarded an

Harold Daniell's 1938 Senior T.T. lap record was finally eclipsed this year by rising star Geoff Duke of the Norton team. Here he is flat out on the new 'featherbed' Norton at the bottom of Bray Hill during the Senior race when he set up a new lap record of 93.33 m.p.h., in a time of 25 mins 56 secs.
(Island Photographics)

After escaping a dramatic three-car pile up involving Prince Bira's Maserati at Parkfield Corner, Bob Gerard went on to complete a hat-trick of wins in the British Empire Trophy series. Here he is seen cornering at Parkfield in his 1,488 c.c. supercharged E.R.A.
(Doug Baird)

Irish cargo ship when she called into Douglas while on passage from Dublin to Silloth in Scotland found thousands of pounds worth of contraband on board. A hundred thousand cigarettes and a thousand pairs of nylons were seized. The ship was detained in Douglas for six days. Her owners denied all knowledge of the contraband and the ship was released after they paid £2,500 demanded by H.M.Customs.

COUPLE FOUND SHOT
A Douglas inquest has decided that a retired Army officer murdered his wife by shooting her and then turned his Service revolver on himself. The bodies of 54-year-old Captain Ernest Thompson and his 48-year-old wife Margaret were found at their flat in Finch Road. Captain

Thompson was posted to the Island during the Second World War and stayed on afterwards. He was said to have had business worries and concerns about his wife's health. In another tragic case of suicide, Mr. and Mrs. William Kelly, formerly of Ballachrink, Bride, were found gassed in their home 'Millway', Lezayre Road, Ramsey. Verdicts of suicide through financial worries were recorded.

OBJECTIONS TO HOTEL INSPECTIONS
The Island's hoteliers and boarding house keepers have rejected proposals that their premises should be subject to Government inspection and registration in future. They say they know the requirements of visitors best and they do not need any

kind of Government interference. It was in the House of Keys that Mr. Spencer Kelly (Ramsey) sought to bring about the registration of visitor accommodation by an amendment to the Publicity Bill. He withdrew the amendment later, but intends to introduce a separate Bill to deal with the matter.

GRAMMAR SCHOOL SAVED
The Island's oldest building has been saved from demolition. Castletown Grammar School has been given to the Manx Museum by the Town Commissioners. It had been intended to demolish the school in a clearance scheme to create car parking. Preservers of the Island's past will be relieved to hear of the change of mind as this ancient building dates back to the middle of

The trawler 'Mary Heeley' which was wrecked after going aground in fog on the rocks to the north of Onchan Harbour. The Douglas lifeboat rescued all ten of the crew.
(Frank Cowin Library)

It has come as a relief to many that the ancient Castletown Grammar School (left foreground) is to be placed in the charge of the Manx Museum. Some of the nearby buildings have already disappeared, while the rest await demolition to provide a car park for the town.
(Frank Cowin Library)

the 13th century when it was built as St. Mary's Chapel by the monks of Rushen Abbey. In 1698 it became the Academic School for the training of clergy and is the forerunner of King William's College. The Grammar School continued in use until 1930.

DRASTIC ATTEMPT TO ERADICATE TUBERCULOSIS

The most determined bid yet to eradicate tuberculosis - one of the most feared diseases this century - is underway. It involves the wholesale slaughter of Manx dairy cattle. Better housing and improvements in hygiene have helped to reduce the incidence of T.B. but contaminated milk supplies continue to perpetuate the disease.

It has been known for most of this century that milk is one of the main causes of spreading the disease, hence repeated attempts to eliminate bovine T.B. These have failed, however, as evidenced by the fact that at least a third of the Island's cattle population and between 60 and 100 per cent of dairy herds have been tested as carriers. Now it has been decided that the only way to eradicate the disease is to slaughter systematically, parish by parish, all cattle which test positive. It is expected to take between seven and eight years.

This will be a costly exercise for Tynwald, which is to provide compensation for farmers, and for the farmers too, for they say the compensation is not enough to

cover the purchase of replacement stock which must be T.B. free and is, therefore, quite rare and expensive.

One benefit for the Island, of course, is that there should be more beef than usual available for summer tourists at a time when food shortages are still a problem. There is concern about milk supplies, however. In the last two years milk has had to be imported from Northern Ireland during the height of the summer. This led to suggestions that local ice cream production should be curbed to release Manx milk for drinking purposes. Such a proposal, however, would have encouraged the importation of ice cream for tourists and that would have helped destroy the local industry.

1950 NEWS IN BRIEF

JANUARY
1 - Retirement, after 37 years incumbency of Kirk Braddan Parish, of Rev. Canon W. A. Rushworth, M.A. He is to be succeeded by Rev. Bertram Kelly, formerly Chief Electrical Engineer to the Borough of Douglas.
12 - Completion of a year's work by the British Mission Micro-Film Unit in micro-filming of Manx archives totalling 350,000 facsimiles of separate scripts.
24 - Rev. F. M. Cubbon inaugurates start of work on the Thomas Cubbon Wing at Noble's Hospital made possible by the £20,000 bequest of the late Thomas Cubbon, J.P., and a similar amount by himself.
25 - Appointment of Mr. Emrys Griffiths as headmaster of Murray's Road School in succession to Mr. T. C. Corris who retired.
31 - House of Keys pass Fire Services Bill providing for the appointment of a Chief Fire Officer for the Island.

FEBRUARY
3 - Mr. Nigel Kneale, of Douglas, and brother of Bryan, awarded the Somerset Maugham Award for his book of short stories, "Tomato Cain", which has a strong Manx connection.
12 - Report of Local Government Commission recommends abolition of village and parish commissioners by amalgamation of local districts on a sheading basis for administration by rural district authorities.

MARCH
1 - Tynwald approves £29,585 scheme for undergrounding by Electricity Board of electric cables in the out-town districts.
29 - Dr. A. K. Soutar, School Medical Officer for 27 years, resigned. He is to be succeeded by Dr. S. V. Cullen, M.B., Ch.B.

APRIL
6 - Resignation from Legislative Council of Mr. J. H. L. Cowin, chairman of the Board of Agriculture since July, 1944.
28 - Mr. J. R. Bregazzi, chief reporter of the *Isle of Man Times*, completed 60 years in Manx journalism.

MAY
2 - Opening of new Castletown Sports Stadium by the Lieutenant-Governor with a match between South Liverpool F.C. and an Island XI selected by ballot of *Green Final* readers.
3 - Cleveland Medal at the Manx Music Festival won by Eileen Peters of Douglas, first lady to win the award for 16 years.
6 - John Edward Moore (64) of Braddan electrocuted and died when an overhead cable carrying 33,000 volts was touched by tipping gear on a lorry he was working at Pulrose.
18 - W. A. Kirkpatrick won the Manx Golf Championship for the fourth time.
20 - Bob Gerard achieved his hat-trick of wins in the Manx series of the British Empire Trophy Races.

JUNE
1 - The Mayor of Douglas (Councillor T. Radcliffe, J.P.) speaking at the Junior T.T. presentation of awards, vigorously attacked the Lord Bishop (Dr. J. R. Strickland Taylor) for his remarks on the organisation for T.T. practising as expressed in an interview

with the representative of a national newspaper. Two riders were killed during the practices.
14 - For the second time, Douglas Town Council rejected a recommendation from the Estates Committee that refrigerators be made available for tenants in Council houses.
20 - For the first time in 30 years Budget proposals submitted by the Lieutenant-Governor came under criticism. Tynwald retired until the next day and the proposed increase of a shilling in the pound income tax was reduced to sixpence. The Court agreed to raise the duty on Manx brewed beer by 2d a pint.
25 - Well Road Methodist Church, Douglas, closed after being used for 113 years, the last sermon being preached by Mr. J. J. Kerruish of Laxey.

JULY
14 - Local Government report reveals that 1,449 families have been housed since the war. Permanent houses completed totalled 1,148, erected by private enterprise and local authorities.
19 - First excursion sailing to Dublin since 1939.
20-21 Visit to R.A.F. Station, Jurby, of the Rt. Hon. Arthur Henderson, Secretary of State for Air. The station was partially re-activated in November last year for ground combat training and this year became the base for No. 1 Initial Training School for pre-flying training of pilots and navigators.

AUGUST
17 - First two houses on the Willaston Estate occupied by selected tenants.

SEPTEMBER
19 - With seven members of the House of Keys opposing, Tynwald carried a resolution extending the period of National Service by six months to two years.
27 - Peel Commissioners protested against rejection by Public Works Commission of a project to construct a new pier at a cost of £200,000.

OCTOBER
12 - Launch of the *Mona's Isle V* at Cammell Laird's shipyard, Birkenhead. Due to be launched later this year is the new cargo vessel to be named *Fenella III*. She is the company's first motor ship and is being built by the Ailsa Shipbuilding Company at Troon. The *Manx Maid* is to be sold for breaking up.
20 - Announcement made that a Nurses' Home, costing £160,000, is to be built on land opposite Noble's Hospital.
24 - Onchan Village Commissioners abandoned a proposal to seek town status for the area under their control.

NOVEMBER
6-11 Among further successes by Manx competitors at the Blackpool Music Festival, Mr. Arthur Quirk (bass) won the Rose Bowl, the premier award.

DECEMBER
5 - House of Keys pass final stages of National Assistance Bill which abolishes Poor Law Guardians and the poor rate, and passes administration to the Board of Social Services.

CHORAL UNION SURVIVES . . . AND CELEBRATES!

Douglas Choral Union, the Island's longest established amateur operatic society, has been saved from closure after a dispute over auditions led to the formation of a rival Manx Operatic Society. The central issue which tore the D.C.U. apart was a tendency by the "old guard" to operate a "closed shop" in respect of principal parts. They expected to be given the parts, almost as a right, because of their proven record with the Society. This meant that new blood was unwelcome unless needed for a specific part.

Recently the music teacher and choir conductor, Douglas Buxton, son of Fred Buxton, the former operator of pierrot shows in Douglas, was appointed as Musical Director. He accepted the post, however, only on the condition that he could institute auditions for the principal parts and thereby open the way for new blood. This was accepted begrudgingly - until the D.C.U. started to plan for this year's golden jubilee celebrations. Inevitably, all the veteran members wanted to play significant roles.

Trouble erupted early last year at the annual general meeting of the Choral Union in the Savoy Restaurant in Victoria Street, Douglas. One faction, representing veterans who had refused to submit to auditions and, therefore, had ceased to be given principal parts, proposed that the society should get rid of the recently introduced "audition nonsense". Douglas Buxton said this would not happen as long as he was Musical Director. When the proposition carried, therefore, he left the meeting vowing that he would have no more to do with the Choral Union. Others followed.

Supporters of Mr. Buxton resigned their membership and, almost overnight, formed a rival Manx Operatic Society, with a target of February this year for their first show. The disaffected included the D.C.U.'s chairman, Stephen Quirk, former London dance school operator, Eira Elma, Rene Gibson (a talented producer) and Dan Minay, brother of the dynamic veteran star of so many D.C.U. productions and, more recently, its producer, Margaret Minay. There was such a movement of younger talent to the Manx Operatic Society that there were fears that the D.C.U. might collapse. Indeed, it is estimated now that the Operatic Society is 75 per cent ex-D.C.U.

The D.C.U. owes its survival principally to the efforts of Margaret Minay - one of the veterans who had refused to submit to auditions. An emergency meeting of the society filled all the committee posts such as chairman, treasurer, librarian, which had been vacated, then, undeterred by the loss of membership, the mem-

'PISH-TUSH' DOUG. COOLE
'THE MIKADO' FRANK BULL
THE MIKADO
'YUM-YUM' MARIE DAWSON
'KATISHA'
'KO-KO'
WILL COWLEY
'NANKI-POO' 'BOBBY' NICHOLL
'MARSIE' WHITE
'PEEP-BO' MRS FRANK BULL
'PITTI-SING' THEA. CRAINE
D.C.U'S GOLDEN JUBILEE PRODUCTION 1950
DUSTY
'POOH-BAH' ARTHUR QUIRK

bers committed themselves to the production for the society's jubilee of Gilbert and Sullivan's *The Mikado*. Frank Bull was given the title role. Three of the society's founder members, who played principal roles in *The Mikado* when it was staged by the D.C.U. in 1901, were invited to the show as special guests. They were Winifred Adams, Fred Minay and Willy Craine.

Young singers who had never appeared on stage before were recruited at the Manx Music Festival and from elsewhere, then coached at Margaret Minay's home before appearing for an obligatory voice test which precedes confirmation of D.C.U. membership. Recruits included a number of potential stars for the future. Among them were Onchan butcher Jack Hampson, Marie Dawson, Fran Quirk, Thea Craine, Marion Hampton, Harry Butterworth, Cranston Laidlaw, Marsie White and Shirley Currie.

The 79-year-old former bandmaster and Musical Director, "J. T." Wood, came out of retirement to act as Musical Director. Despite his age, he stood "as straight as a die" at the Gaiety Theatre every night of the show

- and afterwards he walked unaided up the steep Crellin's Hill to his home in central Douglas! He must have felt well satisfied. On the opening night, the show received a standing ovation.

The Choral Union has thus been re-born and the Island has gained two thriving amateur choral societies, each striving to better the other. Typical of this rivalry was a pre-show promotional stunt undertaken by D.C.U. secretary, Jack Cretney, and Tom Humphrey. They used a rickshaw which had been brought to the Island as a stage prop to give each other rides through Douglas. The stunt worked well as an attention-grabber until three days before the show when the rickshaw lost one of its wheels after hitting a kerb.

This sort of new spirit will raise standards, says Mr. Buxton. Although the division has been painful, he believes the result to have been beneficial. The noted singer and music teacher, Gladys Skillicorn, says that the Choral Union had become too big anyway. Sometimes there had been so many on stage that anyone with lines to say had to squeeze past others.

PRICE FOURPENCE

MANX OPERATIC SOCIETY
(Amateur Operatic & Dramatic Society)

Under the distinguished patronage of His Excellency the Lieut.-Governor, Sir Geoffrey Bromet, K.B.E., C.B., D.S.O., and Lady Bromet, His Worship the Mayor of Douglas (Councillor T. Radcliffe, Esq., J.P.) and Mrs Radcliffe, and members and officials of the Insular Legislature, Town Council and other public bodies.

Present their First Production—for 6 Performances Only

"The Vagabond King"
(By arrangement with Samuel French Ltd.)

A Musical Play founded upon Justin Huntly McCarthy's Romance:
"IF I WERE KING."
Book and Lyrics by Brian Hooker and W. H. Post.   Music by Rudolph Friml.

GAIETY THEATRE : : DOUGLAS
FEBRUARY 6th, 7th, 8th, 9th, 10th and 11th, 1950
Overture 7-10 p.m. : Curtain 7-15 p.m. prompt : Final Curtain approx. 10-30 p.m.

COACH AND PRODUCER
Rene Gibson

CHORUS MASTER AND MUSICAL DIRECTOR
F. D. Buxton

HON. LIBRARIAN
Margaret Killip

DANCING MISTRESS
Eira Elma

STAGE MANAGER AND CHAIRMAN
Dan Minay

HON. SECRETARY
S. G. Quirk

HON. TREASURER
J. H. Cowin

ACCOMPANIST
Ethel Barrow

TAKING A BREAK: MYSTERY TOUR

The Manx Experience

ACKNOWLEDGEMENTS

On behalf of the team involved in the preparation of this volume, the Editor expresses his gratitude for the assistance of Mr Roger Sims, Archivist and Librarian to the Manx Museum, and all his staff in making available newspapers and relevant documents. Thanks are also due to Mr Sims for providing copies of photographs which add greatly to the text. We should also like to thank the many others who have assisted through their own recollections and photographic material. In addition to his editorial contributions, Robert Kelly, helped by his wife Linda, has provided invaluable service in the scrutiny of initial page proofs. Finally, a special word of appreciation to Mr Peter Hulme for his meticulous help in checking the final proofs.